VERGIL'S AENEID

Selections from Books 1, 2, 4, 6, 10, and 12

2nd Edition

Barbara Weiden Boyd

Bolchazy-Carducci Publishers, Inc.
Mundelein, Illinois USA

General Editor
Laurie Haight Keenan

Contributing Editor
D. Scott Van Horn

Cover Illustration
"Into the Darkened City"
by Thom Kapheim

Cover and Page Design
Cameron Marshall

Typography
Charlene M. Hernandez
GREEN TREE DESIGN

Cartography by
Margaret W. Pearce

Vergil's *Aeneid*: Selections from Books 1, 2, 4, 6, 10, and 12, 2nd Edition
The selections and notes from Books 1, 2, 4, and 6
are revised from *Vergil's Aeneid, Books I–VI,*
by Clyde Pharr (Bolchazy-Carducci Publishers, 1998).
The General Directions, Grammatical Appendix and its Index, and Word Lists
are reprinted from Pharr's edition.

The Latin text is from *P. Vergili Maronis Opera*
(Oxford, 1969; repr. with corrections, 1972)
R. A. B. Mynors, ed., by permission of Oxford University Press.

Bolchazy-Carducci Publishers, Inc.
1570 Baskin Road
Mundelein, IL 60060 USA
www.bolchazy.com

Printed in the United States of America
2009
by United Graphics

Paperback:
978-0-86516-584-7

Hardbound:
978-0-86516-583-0

Library of Congress Cataloging-in-Publication Data

Virgil.
[Aeneis. Selections]
Vergil's Aeneid : selections from books 1, 2, 4, 6, 10, and 12 / [edited by] Barbara Weiden
Boyd.-- 2nd ed.
    p. cm.
Text in Latin, with introd., notes, and vocabulary in English.
Includes bibliographical references and index.
ISBN 0-86516-584-X (pbk.) -- ISBN 0-86516-583-1 (hardbound)
1. Aeneas (Legendary character)--Poetry. 2. Latin language--Readers. 3. Epic poetry, Latin. I.
Boyd, Barbara Weiden, 1952- II. Title.

PA6802.A1B65 2004
873'.01--dc22

2004010649

CONTENTS

Preface to the AP* Edition and Introductory Notes v

Preface (Clyde Pharr) xi

Preface to the Revised Edition (Clyde Pharr) xv

Introduction xvii

Life of Vergil...xvii; Works of Vergil...xviii;
First Century BCE and the Principate of Augustus...xxii;
The *Aeneid*...xxii; Vergil's Influence...xxviii;
Timeline...xxix; Bibliography...xxxii

General Directions (Clyde Pharr) xxxv

Signs and Abbreviations xxxvii

Map, "Wanderings of Aeneas" xxxviii

The Aeneid

Book 1, lines 1–519 1
Book 2, lines 1–56, 199–297, 469–566, and 735–804 69
Book 4, lines 1–449, 642–705 109
Book 6, lines 1–211, 450–476, and 847–901 163
Book 10, lines 420–509... 201
Book 12, lines 791–842 and 887–952 215

A Selected Bibliography...................................... 235

APPENDICES

Grammatical Appendix (Clyde Pharr)........................ 241

Vergil's Meter: The Dactylic Hexameter...................... 314

Glossary of Rhetorical Terms, Figures of Speech,
and Metrical Devices Mentioned in the Notes.............. 316

Index to the Grammatical Appendix 321

Frequency Lists for Vocabulary Drill,
Aeneid 1–6 (Clyde Pharr) 337

General Word List (Clyde Pharr)............................ 347

Vocabulary 353

LIST OF ILLUSTRATIONS

"Showed herself a goddess" by Thom Kapheim.................... 1

Neptune and his chariot 25

"Into the darkened city" by Thom Kapheim 69

Laocoon and his sons 77

Aeneas flees Troy, carrying Anchises 103

"And free you from your body" by Thom Kapheim 109

Knidian Aphrodite 120

"Was I the cause?" by Thom Kapheim........................... 163

Sibyl's cave 170

Cape of Misenum.. 189

Mausoleum of Augustus 199

Theater of Marcellus 199

"Every man's last day is fixed" by Thom Kapheim 201

"It is the gods I fear" by Thom Kapheim 215

Column of Jupiter 219

Aeneas performing a sacrifice
     upon his arrival in Italy................................ 222

Ceres (or Venus?) promoting
     the peaceful fertility of Italy.......................... 224

A PREFACE TO THE AP* EDITION
AND
INTRODUCTORY NOTES

This edition of selections from Books 1, 2, 4, 6, 10, and 12 of Vergil's *Aeneid* is aimed primarily at two audiences: high school students preparing for the Vergil Advanced Placement* Latin examination; and college students reading selections from the *Aeneid* for the first time in a fourth through sixth semester of college Latin. High school students not preparing for the Advanced Placement* examination but prepared to read Vergil should also find this textbook accessible and helpful. The widespread popularity of Clyde Pharr's school edition of the first six books of the *Aeneid* in their entirety (*Vergil's Aeneid Books 1–6* [Lexington, MA: D.C. Heath, 1930; repr. 1964]; now available from Bolchazy-Carducci) in Latin courses at both of these levels has in recent years been qualified at least a little by the implicit definition of Pharr's ideal reader as someone with little need—or taste—for literary subtlety *per se* in the notes. At the same time, its user-friendly layout, with text, vocabulary, and notes neatly arranged on the same page, has made it seem sensible to me to emulate the format and particular virtues of Pharr's edition in the preparation of this revision of the AP* selections. I shall indicate more precisely under the separate headings below those features of Pharr's textbook I have adapted for use here, as well as those places where I diverge.

Pharr's text has survived and thrived among several generations of American readers at least in part because, whatever its particular format and technical characteristics, the original editor's devotion to his poet is patent in the book's laborious—and useful—details. I have aimed to emulate this devotion myself, not so much out of a desire to keep the spirit of Pharr alive (although I confess to some residual fondness for the book, remembering as I do my own first acquaintance with it in high school), but because of the gift I have been given in being taught, enabled, and empowered to read, many times over now, Vergil's great poem. I wish for my readers as rewarding an introduction to the *Aeneid* as I myself once experienced.

While it is inevitable that in a book of this sort undetected misprints and occasional opaque comments will survive even the most alert reader's eye, clarity and accuracy remain desirable goals. The preparation of a second edition gives me the opportunity to extend my thanks to the many readers who have contacted me with their suggestions, observations, and corrections. I offer my gratitude in particular to Darryl Phillips, Ronnie Ancona, and Charles Fornara, Jr., *primi inter pares*, for their attentiveness and scholarly *amicitia*. They have helped to make this a better book

Barbara Weiden Boyd
Bowdoin College

Introduction

With this edition, I have provided an entirely new Introduction to Vergil and the *Aeneid*, to replace Pharr's venerable but dated contribution. Writing with the aim of serving the needs of modern teachers and students, I have drawn on many years of teaching and reading Vergil myself. The focus of this essay is primarily literary, locating Vergil and his work in the intellectual and historical matrices of the late Republic and early Principate. The Introduction's narrative is complemented by a timeline of political and literary events and monumental constructions marking significant occasions in Vergil's lifetime, and by a brief bibliography of recent general works on the period and our poet.

Text

The text used here is that printed in R. A. B. Mynors' 1969 edition of the Oxford Classical Text of Vergil. I have made a few cosmetic alterations to make this text more congenial to the intermediate or AP* Latin student: the initial letters of words beginning a new sentence are printed in the upper case; and third-declension accusative plural nouns ending in -**is** are here printed as ending in -**es.**

Orthography

In keeping with contemporary usage (as well as with the format followed by Pharr), I have printed consonantal **u** as **v**. Consonantal **i**, however, remains **i** throughout the text and notes. Thus, the Latin names of the king and queen of the gods appear as **Iuppiter** and **Iuno.**

---

*AP is a registered trademark of the College Entrance Examination Board, which was not involved in the production of, and does not endorse, this product.

Vocabulary Lists

An alphabetical list of all vocabulary glossed appears at the end of the text. In determining what vocabulary is to be glossed, I have used Pharr's general Word List as a guide and have not glossed the words on this list. In addition, for the selections from Books 10 and 12 I have incorporated into my expectation of students' working vocabulary those words which Pharr includes in his list of words found 12–23 times in *Aeneid* 1–6. Thus, teachers can raise their expectations of their students' working vocabulary as they turn to the selections ocurring later in their reading of the *Aeneid*, and add the words on this list to their regular vocabulary drills. Like Pharr, I have distinguished between glossed and unglossed vocabulary in the text by printing all glossed vocabulary in Roman font, and all unglossed vocabulary in italic.

Macrons

The Latin text in the selections from Books 1, 2, 4, and 6 and relevant running vocabulary lists and notes is printed with macrons to indicate long syllables; the selections from the later books, however, along with their running vocabulary lists and notes, appear without macrons. Again, I hope thus to encourage students and teachers alike to grow gradually more comfortable with a macron-less text. Students should be encouraged to realize that the Romans did not write with macrons (nor do ancient manuscripts generally feature word division, punctuation, or a distinction between upper- and lower-case letters!). They should also be encouraged to practice scansion on a text without macrons. Macrons are included in the alphabetical vocabulary listing at the end of the book, and so provide to teachers and students alike a point of reference.

Grammatical Appendix

I have not changed Pharr's grammatical appendix, although some readers may find a few of his explanations somewhat dated; other good Latin grammars are available to remedy this situation. I have, however, altered the two concluding sections of Pharr's appendix as follows:

Dactylic Hexameter

In providing a brief description and discussion of Vergilian hexameter, I have updated Pharr's discussion to make it more accessible to contemporary students and teachers. I have also tried to suggest that Vergilian hexameter is not an "add-on" to the plot, but an essential component in the rich texture of the poetry of the *Aeneid*.

Rhetorical Terms, Figures of Speech, and Metrical Devices

I have included immediately before the vocabulary a glossary of the rhetorical terms, figures of speech, and metrical devices mentioned in the notes. In most cases, I have adapted Pharr's original definitions to examples chosen from the selections in this textbook; some terms, however, are new additions, and a few have been redefined. I have also attempted to suggest that many metrical features of the poem are poetic devices in their own right.

Abbreviations

I have kept abbreviations in the vocabulary and notes to a minimum, and have tempted to avoid any source of confusion. Thus, "nom.," "gen.," "dat.," "acc.," and "abl.," as well as other familiar abbreviations, are used here; but wherever confusion might result, e.g., between "subj." ("subject") and "subj." ("subjunctive"), I have not abbreviated the terminology used.

In the vocabulary lists, I have usually abbreviated only the second principal part of verbs (first conjugation verbs are indicated by a (1) in place of a full listing of principal parts). The genitive forms of third-declension nouns, when abbreviated, are intended to show students the root of a given word.

Grammatical and Syntactical Terminology

In the teaching of Latin in the schools, a wide variety of terminology for grammatical and syntactical constructions is current. Thus, for example, the subject-accusative + infinitive construction with verbs of knowing, saying, thinking, etc., is more commonly learned in American schools as "indirect discourse" or "indirect statement" (and also, albeit much less frequently, as "oratio obliqua"). In choosing to call this construction "indirect statement" in the notes, I am not endorsing a particular method or otherwise attempting to offer a value judgment on the available terminology; rather, I am attempting to represent to the best of my ability, based on many years of college teaching and nine years with the Advanced Placement* Latin Test Development Committee, the terminology most likely to be familiar to students reading at this level. The real test of a commentary of this sort is the degree to which it allows students to read Latin independently; I hope that my commentary can make this possible in as unobtrusive a manner as possible.

Teachers and students should also note that I frequently offer two possible interpretations for a given construction (e.g., on 10.490, I comment on the lemma **super**, "either adv., or prep. with **quem**"). My purpose in offering these alternatives is not to cause confusion, but to suggest to students that

---

*AP is a registered trademark of the College Entrance Examination Board, which was not involved in the production of, and does not endorse, this product.

their instincts are often right when they are puzzled by the ambiguity of a particular construction. This occasion also offers teachers an opportunity to remind their students that terms such as "abl. of cause" and "dat. of agent" are artificial constructs—no Roman reader would have needed, or understood, these categories.

Interpretive Comments

While I have not engaged in lengthy discussions of the interpretation of a given passage or subsection, I have on occasion permitted myself to comment on features of Vergil's style that repay close examination. I have attempted to make these comments in an "open," that is, suggestive, manner, rather than as "closed" and definitive statements of Vergil's purpose. I hope that these comments will offer to teachers and students the opportunity for rewarding discussion of the complexities of Vergil's poem.

PREFACE
BY CLYDE PHARR

This book is intended to introduce high school and college students to the *Aeneid* and to enable them to read this great masterpiece with interest and appreciation.

The present edition is based on the cumulative results of the past centuries of Vergilian scholarship and pedagogical method, and the author is indebted to his many predecessors, ancient and modern, American and foreign, who have worked in this field. The author would make grateful acknowledgment to all those who have contributed in any way to a better understanding of the *Aeneid,* but it is manifestly impossible to enumerate the countless sources from which the present work has been drawn.

In preparing the present text an attempt has been made to profit by the contributions furnished by the printer's art in the differentiation of vocalic and consonantal **i** (**i, j**) as well as in the differentiation of vocalic and consonantal **u** (**u, v**). For what seems to be adequate pedagogical reasons such forms as **dējiciō, subjiciō,** and **conjiciō** are given in the printed text instead of the **dēiciō, subiciō, and coniciō** of the inscriptions and manuscripts. For the use of **j** and **v** the author feels that no more apology is needed than for the use of lower case letters in general instead of the square capitals of the inscriptions and early manuscripts. The employment of such forms as **dējicio, subjiciō,** and **conjiciō** is abundantly justified by their simplicity as well as by the ease with which they are understood in connection with the rest of their conjugational systems.

The text is that of Hirtzel, Oxford University Press, 1900, and the author here gratefully acknowledges the kind permission granted by the Syndics of this Press to reproduce their text. Only a few changes have been made from the Oxford text, such as the use of capitals in this book at the beginning of each new sentence instead of merely at the beginning of each new paragraph, the use of **j** in this text to represent consonantal **i,** and the spellings **relligio, relligiosus, relliquiae,** to represent more accurately the pronunciation of these words in Vergil's day.

In the definitions of the Latin words given in the page vocabularies the author has not sought to secure a mechanical uniformity, but has attempted merely to preserve such a general consistency that the student may from the definitions recognize any later occurrence of a word and associate it with its earlier appearances. In the number of meanings given for each Latin word, the author has tried to preserve some mean between a poverty which is barren and a wealth which is confusing to the student who is trying at the same time both to read Vergil and to learn Latin.

The chief distinction of this book is its visible vocabulary system. The acquisition of a vocabulary is generally recognized as one of the most important as well as one of the most troublesome problems in learning either to read or speak a foreign language. No important advance has been made in this field for thousands of years, and the present antiquated methods are wasteful of much valuable time and effort, especially in the case of the more difficult languages, such as Latin and Greek.

This book attempts to attack the problem from another angle and prints adjacent to any given passage the whole of its vocabulary, making it unnecessary ever to turn a page for the purpose of learning the meaning of any word.

The use of the special word list, printed on the extensible sheet at the back of the book, adds certain features of considerable value educationally. This list contains the most common words in the work being studied. Each word which occurs in this list is indicated in the text by being printed in italics. This use of italics serves several distinct purposes. First, it indicates to the student where he must look for the meaning of these words, whether in the special list or in one of the vocabularies at the foot of the page. In the second place, the difference in type assists in impressing these more important words on the memory without as much conscious effort as has ordinarily been needed and hence, perhaps, removes an element of discouragement from the task. The word list also furnishes convenient material for the use of teachers who still prefer to require their students to memorize the most important words in their text. In addition to this word list, two word lists for vocabulary drill may be found at the back of the book.

The author is convinced that this new method is an advance over the old both pedagogically and psychologically. The old system involves not merely a great waste of time, but it necessitates continual interruption in the continuity of attention of the student, hindering or even preventing concentration upon the work at hand and thus making for bad mental habits.

This plan has been tried in a number of secondary schools and in every case it has met with a most enthusiastic response on the part of both teachers and students. After an extensive series of experiments, it is agreed that the following are some of the manifest advantages of this method :

1. Students are able to read intelligently a great deal more in a given period of time than has heretofore been possible.

2. Reading of the great classical authors can be begun at a much earlier stage than was formerly practicable. With a modicum of grammar one can

begin reading the great classics and can read them rapidly enough to enjoy them as literature.

3. Since the vocabulary for any given passage is comparatively small, the possibility of error is much less and the student seldom selects the wrong word or the wrong meaning from the vocabulary.

4. With the elimination or great lessening of vocabulary difficulties, the student has a much better opportunity of gaining a thorough foundation in the essentials of grammar, reinforced continually by more copious reading than has hitherto been possible.

5. The student learns his vocabulary without much conscious effort at memorizing, in the easiest and most natural way possible, by meeting the words constantly in his reading, with their meanings always before him. Similarly he learns the forms of his words, by constantly seeing the indications of their structure, as denoted in the vocabulary by the principal parts of the verbs, the nominative and genitive singular of the nouns, together with an indication of their gender, and other information presented in the vocabularies.

6. Printing this vocabulary in sight of the passage not only conserves the time of the student commonly spent in mechanically looking up words, but allows him to concentrate his attention on the problems involved in translation, in the development of thought, in the literary, historical, and other problems of his author, and in various other features of the text.

There is no pedagogical value attached to the mechanical labor involved in looking up words according to the old system which, moreover, entails an enormous waste of time. According to the arrangement employed in this book, the student has constantly before him the same information which he formerly was compelled to seek elsewhere at the cost of so much labor.

This visible vocabulary system is far better than a parallel translation, since this method does not solve the problems for the student, but merely places in his hands, in the most readily accessible form, all the requisite data for making his own solutions. By thus ridding him of drudgery and by making this feature of his work lighter and more interesting, this vocabulary system helps to eliminate the improper use of translations by the student, for he now finds that he can prepare his lesson quite as quickly and much more intelligently without a translation than he formerly could with its help.

The vocabularies of the ordinary school editions, arranged according to the old system, must give the general meaning of each word and then exhaust all the special meanings found in the whole text, and this to most students is a source of considerable confusion and loss of time. In this text the student will always have the general meaning of each word as well as the special meaning necessary for each passage. This enables him to fix the general meaning and to build up his knowledge of the special meanings as he meets them in his reading.

In the notes of this book a great many constructions are explained, partly as a key to the proper understanding of the Latin text and partly as a device to make it unnecessary for the teacher to spend valuable time in requiring the class to analyze constructions. It is believed that this feature will enable the ordinary student to proceed more securely and expeditiously with the work of translation and comprehension of his text and will make it possible for him to solve for himself the difficulties of many passages where the perplexities are so great that many editors have felt it necessary to do the work of translation for the student. A generous use is made in this text of the Grammatical Appendix and the student is constantly referred to it for additional information. If, for example, the student knows the meaning of such terms as ablative absolute or subjunctive of result, he spends no time in consulting the grammatical reference. If he does not know the meaning of these terms or if he shows by his translation that he has a wrong conception, it is very easy for the teacher to correct his fault at once by requiring him to consult the Grammatical Appendix.

A number of circumstances have combined to delay the appearance of this book. By a happy coincidence it is now issued on the two thousandth anniversary of Vergil's birth, and the author is much pleased to offer this little volume in homage to the spirit of the bard of Mantua at a time when all the world is uniting to pay him tribute.

The author wishes to express his special gratitude to the late Dr. Dix Harwood, Assistant Editor of D. C. Heath and Company, for selecting the illustrations in this book, and to Professor W. L. Carr, of Columbia University, whose advice and assistance have been invaluable.

Clyde Pharr

PREFACE TO THE REVISED EDITION
BY CLYDE PHARR

In addition to the General Word List already appearing in the end papers, two new word lists have been inserted after the Index in this revision. It will be recalled that the General Word List contains all the words that occur 24 or more times in Books I–VI of the *Aeneid*. The new lists contain those words that occur 12–23 times and 6–11 times, respectively, in Books I–VI. They will provide the same type of vocabulary drill that has made the General Word List useful and popular.

A few misprints and oversights throughout the text have been corrected, affecting mostly the notes and the visible vocabulary, though one or two small corrections have been introduced into the text itself.

It is hoped that these innovations and changes will find favor with the Latin teachers who for years have been faithful friends of this edition of the *Aeneid*.

INTRODUCTION
BY BARBARA WEIDEN BOYD

a. The Life of Vergil

Vergil's literary pre-eminence since antiquity has made not only his work but also his life the subjects of intense study for two millennia. Reliable information about Vergil's life, however, can be gleaned from our ancient sources only with difficulty or not at all. Contemporary (or nearly so) evidence is limited to a few passing references in other writers (e.g., an allusion by the contemporary elegist Propertius, at 2.34.65–66, to the forthcoming *Aeneid*) which tend to tell us something about the work rather than the person. Allusions to Vergil's friendships with e.g. Varius Rufus (see Quintilian 10.3.8) and Horace (*Odes* 1.3.6, 1.24.10, and perhaps 4.12.13) do little more than confirm what we would be able to surmise without them, i.e., that he was part of a generation of writers who frequented the highest social and intellectual circles. The most reliable tidbit of information is also the most recent to come to light: that is the mention of Vergil among four poets named by the Greek philosopher-poet Philodemus in one of the newly accessible Herculaneum papyri. Vergil's poems themselves contain numerous mentions of historical characters, places, and events, all of which have been used repeatedly by scholars in attempts to reconstruct a biography of Vergil; but their presence in works not of historical data-collecting but of reflective imagination and intertextual richness compromises, to say the least, their reliability as evidence for anything other than Vergil's poetic genius.

Both as a result and perpetuating cause of Vergil's almost overnight inclusion in the Roman school curriculum and speedy ascension to "classic" status in Roman literary tradition, posthumous stories about *Vergilius noster* quickly accumulated and were transmitted, and elaborated upon, through the centuries. The popular historian and celebrity biographer **Suetonius** (c. 70–130 CE) included much of this material in his (now fragmentary) *De poetis*; this in turn provided the basis for the *Vita Donati*, attributed to the fourth-century Vergilian commentator **Aelius Donatus**. Donatus was the teacher of both **Servius**, the Vergilian commentator whose surviving work is one of our greatest repositories of both valuable fact and wildly unreliable (dis)information about Vergil's world, and **St. Jerome**, who collected and translated sources on ancient chronology. Donatus' *Vita Vergilii* is the source of most of the "facts" we think we know about Vergil's life, from his shy and retiring nature and sexual preferences, to the loss of his family's lands during the confiscations after Philippi in 41 BCE, the effect of his recitation of *Aeneid* 6 on Marcellus' mother Octavia, and his deathbed wish that the not-yet-perfect *Aeneid* be burned. In fact, these anecdotes and others are far more likely to be based on (mis)readings of Vergil's works than on any historical reality, and bear witness to the velocity with which Vergil became a secular "saint" long before his "Christianization" in late antiquity and the early middle ages.

What we are left with, then, is little more than a skeleton of fact—itself not provable by any scientific means, but agreed upon by most scholars as offering a reliable framework upon which to hang Vergil's work and experience. He was born on October 15, 70 BCE, in or near Mantua (modern Mantova) in what was then Cisalpine Gaul. He traveled through the northern Italian cities of Cremona and Milan before coming to Rome; he spent time in and around the Bay of Naples as well. He died on September 21, 19 BCE, at Brundisium, and was buried in Naples.

b. The Works of Vergil

Three separate poems or collections of poems are ascribed to Vergil, all composed in dactylic hexameter: the *Eclogues*, a collection of ten primarily bucolic poems; the *Georgics*, a didactic poem in four books; and the *Aeneid*, an epic poem in twelve books. A fourth collection, the so-called *Appendix Vergiliana*, consisting of a wide variety of poems, has been ascribed to Vergil since antiquity, but most scholars now agree that the works in this compendium are by and large the efforts of Vergilian imitators, rather than authentic juvenilia from the poet's hand. Ranging from epigrams and Catullan-style short lyrics to the mock-epic epyllia (the term "epyllion," meaning "little epic," is a modern convenience, not an ancient category) *Culex* and *Moretum*, the poems in the *Appendix* open a window onto the poetic aspirations of numerous now-anonymous poets working in Vergil's shadow; they also serve as ample evidence of the degree to which the works of Vergil, especially but not exclusively the *Aeneid*, served as a central component in the "core curriculum" offered to elite youth in the centuries following Vergil's death. Like the Vergilian anecdotes transmitted by Suetonius and Donatus, these poems are evidence not so much of Vergil's career as of the power of the myth of Vergil.

The *Eclogues*, on the other hand, provide valuable insight into the formative influences shaping the young Vergil's literary aspirations. Attributed to the years immediately following the redistribution of land following the battle of Philippi—an event for which the *Eclogues* are in fact major "evidence" (see above)—these poems bear powerful witness to the political and social turbulence of the late 40s and early 30s BCE. Their formal model is the collection of *Idyls* by **Theocritus**, one of the great Alexandrian court poets of the third century BCE. Together with **Callimachus** and **Apollonius** (see below), Theocritus articulated a new attitude towards poetry as a mode of communication: unlike the writers of earlier centuries, these men composed in a self-consciously literary, and literate, fashion for a self-consciously literary, and literate, audience. Their readers were by and large elite men, with both the education and the leisure time to enjoy learned texts. It is certainly possible that some at least of this poetry could be performed as well as read—certainly some of the *Idyls*, as well as e.g. Callimachus' *Hymns*, lend themselves to performance. Nonetheless, enjoyment of this kind of poetry was clearly, and intentionally, most accessible to those who could recognize and be entertained by learned allusion: Apollonius' clever deployment of an Homeric *hapax legomenon* in a novel context, or Theocritus' "prequel" to the Homeric Cyclops in his romantic portrayal of Polyphemus. The *Eclogues* too appeal to the reader first and foremost—especially the reader already familiar with the Hellenistic poets, as well as the work of the "new" poets in Rome, like Catullus, Cinna, Varro Atacinus, and Calvus. Aside from Theocritus himself, however, the single greatest influence upon the shape taken by the *Eclogues* is likely to have been exerted by **Gaius Cornelius Gallus**, a contemporary of Vergil whose elegiac *Amores* (and perhaps other works) are known to us not directly (a bare ten lines survive), but through Vergil himself, who makes a fictionalized Gallus the central character in *Eclogue* 10 and whose learning and elegant style are likely to be reflected in the so-called Aristaeus epyllion of *Georgics* 4 (see below).

The dominant themes of the *Eclogues* combine escapist fantasy and nostalgia on the one hand with realistic Italian landscape on the other. Many scholars—this one included—have been tempted to see in the *Eclogues* a desperate, even self-delusive, attempt to replace the harsh realities of the 30s BCE with a better, simpler, and more promising picture of Italy and its inhabitants. *Eclogue* 4 in particular has attracted attention because of its self-fulfilling prophecy of the Golden Age renewed; like the contemporaneous *Epode* 16 of Horace, this *Eclogue* locates at an impossible distance the very escape from the here and now that it imagines. Some readers have found Vergil's love for Italy to be the dominant thematic key to the *Eclogues*, while others have argued that this love itself is compromised by the harsh reality that occasionally intrudes. Whatever the prevailing interpretation of the *Eclogues*, however, one thing remains clear: though these may well be the first formally published work of a young poet (Vergil was 35 in 35 BCE), they reveal a writer already at the top of his form, capable of a delicacy and vividness of expression and a sensitivity to language and rhythm rarely matched in his day—or any other.

To the modern reader, the *Georgics* may well seem an odd second project—a versified handbook of agricultural lore and advice seems hardly the best means to assert one's claim to major literary status. The tradition of didactic poetry is indeed one which has not translated well into the twentieth- and twenty-first century literary vernacular; for us, didacticism is the stuff of tedious textbooks, while the intimate expression of the self we associate with poetry presumes a density of an entirely different sort. For us, the language of poetry and the language of instruction rarely intersect; mnemonic dog-gerel (e.g., "Thirty days hath September, …"; "After *si, nisi, num*, and *ne*, …") is the only modern approximation, i.e., it is no equivalent at all. The ancient world, however, provides a very different context for didactic poetry: second only to the Homeric poems in both temporal roots and cultural impact are the compositions of **Hesiod** (fl. 700 BCE), in particular, the *Works and Days*, combining farming advice, seasonal and meteorological lore, and popular morality in a hexameter poem that challenges the boundaries of genre even as it invents didactic. Hesiod's work, and in particular the richness of his didactic voice, were rediscovered in the Hellenistic era, when the scholarly revolu-tion enabled poets to combine the inspiration of the Muses with their own abstruse researches. The impact of Hesiod is visible everywhere in Hellenistic poetry; only the most obvious index of this is the didactic fashion that gave us everything from the *Phaenomena* of **Aratus** (c. 315–240 BCE), a hexameter poem on the constellations and heavens, to the appropriation of the teacher's role by **Nicander** (fl. 130 BCE). His extant poems the *Theriaca* (on poisonous insects and snakes, and remedies for their toxins) and the *Alexipharmaca* (on antidotes found in nature to various toxins) suggest simply by their titles the extremes to which this tradition was prone. We know, furthermore, of many other no-longer-extant poems that trod similar ground, collecting arcane lore of one sort or another; and scholars have now amply demonstrated the role played by all of these influences in Vergil's poetic instruction.

Vergil looks to a native form of didacticism in shaping his didactic voice in the *Georgics*, too. Prose handbooks of agricultural instruction, written primarily for those elite readers who would eventually end up managing vast estates of their own, synthesized centuries of agricultural knowledge and tradition, covering everything from the proper clothing for slaves to the limits of intra-species grafting. Two of these handbooks survive, in whole or in part: **Cato the Elder's** *De agri cultura* (usually dated to 160 BCE) and **Varro's** *De re rustica* (usually dated to 37 BCE). Especially the latter of these, written in Vergil's own lifetime, exerted a great influence on Vergil; scholars have drawn increasing attention in recent years to the way in which Vergil transforms technical prose into Vergilian hexameters.

What is Vergil's own gift, however, is the ability he demonstrates in the *Georgics* (probably completed in 29 BCE) to transform even the most mundane details of a farmer's life into a powerful poetic lesson about the nature of life, especially human life, itself. The hierarchical organization of the poem, with its four books treating crops and vines, trees and shrubs, domestic animals, and bees, respectively, has long been understood to represent the gradual and continuing process by which man brings order to nature, and in the process creates a place for himself within it. Does the *Georgics* present us with a depiction of human interaction with the natural world as a happy cooperation enabled in the first place by the arts of civilization, or as a constant struggle for survival in a hostile universe? This is the fundamental question that has been asked by the poem's readers over the centuries; and this question is further complicated when we look at the world in which Vergil wrote this poem, a world marked by both the supreme accomplishments of human civilization and the chaos of war.

Similar concerns preoccupy both Vergil and his readers when we turn to the *Aeneid*. In undertaking an epic, Vergil appropriates not only the style and subject-matter of the genre established by Homer but also its concern with empire and its symbols. The story Vergil tells—of how Aeneas, escaped from Troy, struggles to bring his people and traditions from Troy to a new home in Italy and there to create a new life for himself and them among the native (at least relatively speaking) peoples of Italy—deals with themes of both national and individual identity, of both personal responsibility and fate, of both the power of desire and the destructiveness of passion. I shall describe more fully below some of the central features of the poem as well as the many literary traditions that informed its creation; here I note simply that there is some evidence to suggest that, having begun the *Aeneid* in 29 BCE, Vergil died ten years later with it not quite complete. The numerous half-lines found throughout the poem (but not found in the *Eclogues* and *Georgics*) are the most frequently cited indication of the poem's incompleteness; it may be noted, therefore, that at least some of these incomplete hexameters occur at moments of high intensity in the poem, and they can therefore at least be argued to serve the poet's intention in their current state. More subtle indications of the lack of final authorial revision have been detected in studies focusing closely on the technicalities of Vergil's diction and meter. For the purposes of this discussion and throughout my notes, however, I shall speak of the *Aeneid* as a complete poem, bearing ample evidence of its maker's careful fashioning. Perhaps most important from a practical point of view, furthermore, I shall use the poem's allegedly unfinished state only as a last resort to explain away difficulties in the text.

c. The First Century BCE and the Principate of Augustus

The social, intellectual, and political turmoil and its consequences that came increasingly to dominate life in the Roman world after the third Punic War are at the heart of a story both too complex and too familiar to allow full discussion here. Readers are encouraged, therefore, to consult any of a number of up-to-date histories of the late Republic and early Principate; I provide a list of suggested titles at the end of this Introduction, noting as I do so the increasing, and therefore increasingly valuable, appearance of studies that synthesize various aspects of life in this period rather than focusing only on, e.g., Rome's great military leaders or battle outcomes. It is possible, to be sure, to read the *Aeneid* in a cultural vacuum, equipped with little more than a cast of characters and a list of ablative constructions. Such a reading, however, necessarily entails treating the poem as a fiction rather than as both beneficiary and shaper of the defining issues of its day and indeed of Roman culture generally. In order to help my readers make at least a beginning at seeing the *Aeneid* as part of a larger cultural matrix, I have also located at the end of this Introduction a timeline that is meant to illustrate the relative chronology of several landmarks—physical, intellectual, and/or historical— during Vergil's lifetime.

d. The *Aeneid*

i) Models

The epic ancestors of the *Aeneid* have been known since antiquity, yet they continue to provide rich new insights into both the methods and the meanings of Vergil's work. The twelve-book design of the poem, clearly divided into two halves (the Wandering and the War), both acknowledges and inverts the narrative sequence of the **Homeric epics**. This structural principle is echoed on countless occasions in the smallest details of the poem, beginning with the opening two words, *arma virumque*, evoking the central concerns of the *Iliad* (*arma*) and the *Odyssey* (*virum*). The movement back and forth between divine and human perspectives—as well as the occasional confluence or clash of the two—is also a central feature of Homeric narrative. Other Homeric features of Vergil's work will be observed in my notes on the poem.

A second prominent model for Vergil's epic is the ***Argonautica* of Apollonius of Rhodes** (third century BCE), a dactylic-hexameter poem in four books describing the gathering of Jason's companions; their voyage eastward to Colchis; their arrival there and involvement with the ruling family of Aeetes, especially his daughter, Medea; Jason's acquisition of the golden fleece; and the homeward journey of the Argonauts accompanied by the young princess.

While the eventual outcome of Jason and Medea's love affair remains in the future from the perspective of Apollonius' narrator, his ancient audience already knew the full story in all its sorrowful detail from earlier literary treatments, especially Euripides' *Medea*. Apollonius' depiction of Medea's infatuation with Jason, therefore, pregnant as it is with foreshadowed doom, had a powerful influence on Vergil's depiction of Dido. New studies of Apollonius have shown, however, that his influence upon Vergil is hardly limited to the Medea/Dido parallel, but rather in its pervasiveness challenges the Homeric poems themselves.

The role of **tragedy**, both Greek and Roman, in the shaping of the *Aeneid* is also clear, although until recently it has generally received less attention from scholars than have epic influences. Indeed, the points of contact are too numerous to list here; instead, therefore, I simply note a few prominent instances worthy of further exploration. **Euripides'** *Medea* has already been alluded to; this play's reworking by **Ennius** (239–169 BCE), of which only fragments now remain, is likely to have been of equal importance. The fall of Troy so vividly depicted in Aeneas' narrative of Book 2 looks back to numerous plays on the Trojan theme, including, e.g., the Euripidean and Ennian *Andromaches*, Euripides' *Trojan Women*, and Ennius' *Alexander*; the "invasion" of Turnus by Allecto in Book 7 draws on Euripides' *Hercules Furens*; and the final combat between Turnus and Aeneas in Book 12 follows in many details the description of Hercules' engagement with Achelous, competing for Deanira, in **Sophocles'** *Trachiniae*.

The **great Roman poets of earlier generations** must have played a formative role in Vergil's early education; unfortunately, most of their work survives to us only in fragments. First and foremost was undoubtedly **Ennius'** *Annales*, an epic in 15 books following the history of Rome from its foundations down to Ennius' own time. In its early articulation of the dactylic hexameter we find the origins of Vergil's beautifully balanced lines. In the early books of this poem, furthermore, Aeneas was a central character, and his struggle to achieve a Trojan foothold in Italy a central theme. The *Bellum Punicum* of **Naevius** (late third century BCE), too, was important, both in its treatment of the foundation of Rome in the early books and in its focus on the conflict between the two great peoples of the Mediterranean, the Romans and the Carthaginians. Other writers and their works, about whom we know even less, are too numerous to mention here; but whenever we are inclined to question the meaning or purpose of a particular genealogical or topographical detail in Vergil's poem, it is worth remembering how many of the texts that shaped his intellectual world are lost to us.

The interrelationship of all of Vergil's poetry with the *De rerum natura* of **Lucretius** (c. 94–55 BCE) is also evident, although exactly how this relationship should be described is a matter of some debate. Lucretius' hexameter didactic poem on the physics and metaphysics of Epicurean philosophy is a daring and powerful work, and Vergil's redeployment of Lucretian material—everything from particular words and phrases to images and even whole scenes—is undisputed. Whether Vergil's admiration of Lucretian didactic extended to his philosophy as well, however, is far less clear. On a purely technical level, a juxtaposition of Lucretian and Vergilian hexameter techniques indicates just how singular was Vergil's mastery of his poetic equipment.

Perhaps the single most important model, at least notionally, in fact, is the **Hellenistic poet** renowned for his rejection of epic—at least post-Homeric epic—and his espousal of a learned, self-conscious, and modernist poetics: I mean **Callimachus** (first half of the third century BCE), the author of numerous scholarly and literary works, most of which survive only as a list of titles but an important few of which we have at least in significant fragments. His *Aetia*, a four-book poem in elegiac couplets, was a virtuoso display of different subjects and narrative techniques, comprising a series of otherwise unrelated stories about the origins of various rituals, cults, places, and names. We also have six of his *Hymns*, modeled in some ways on the archaic *Homeric Hymns* but displaying as well the innovative style and intellectual detachment of the *Aetia*, and a large number of his *Epigrams*, again highly polished works that by their very brevity instantiate a rejection of epic values.

Because of Callimachus' evident distaste for post-Homeric epic (though not for Homer himself), scholars have long puzzled over how Vergil was able to find some compromise between the apparent polar opposites of epic and Alexandrianism, and how that compromise is articulated in the *Aeneid*. A more thoughtful appreciation of Vergil's accomplishment is made possible nonetheless—and suggests that no compromise was in fact needed—when one realizes that Callimachus' stance was not against epic *per se*, but against epic in the degraded and tedious form it often took in the centuries following the recording of the Homeric poems. In fact, Vergil's other great Hellenistic model, very much a complement to the poetry of Callimachus, is the epic *Argonautica* of Apollonius (see above)—a new epic, composed with a new sort of literary self-consciousness and in its learnedness very much suited to modern tastes.

Indeed, the depth and range of learning that was first possible in the Hellenistic world so profoundly informed Vergil's poetics that a comprehensive listing of important intellectual influences on his thought and works would be excessively long for the present purposes (if not simply impossible). In this discussion, therefore, I have chosen to focus on the most exemplary models rather than to provide a real catalogue; my readers are encouraged to make new connections on their own, using this short introduction as just that—an entry into a fascinating subject, and nothing more. But even this introduction would not be complete without the inclusion of three other names, each of whom played a direct and virtually unmediated role in the development of Vergil's poetic consciousness: Parthenius, Gallus, and Catullus. **Parthenius** of Nicaea, taken as a captive during the third Macedonian War and brought to Italy in 73 BCE, remained after being freed and became a teacher in Naples. Tradition has it that he single-handedly introduced educated elite Roman youth to the poetry of Callimachus and the other Alexandrians, and imbued his pupils with a new poetic aesthetic. While the remains of Latin poetry predating Parthenius demonstrate, scant as they are, that this is both an overstatement and oversimplification of the facts, there can be little doubt that he played a central role in the new cultural and intellectual awareness that characterized almost every aspect of life in the first half of the first century BCE. A precious indication of this is the one work of Parthenius of which we have a substantial portion, his *Erotica Pathemata* (Tales of Tormented Lovers), a textbook of sorts addressed to his pupil C. Cornelius Gallus and consisting of brief summaries of mythical love stories, for the most part obscure and for the most part concluding in tragic fashion. This document suggests *in parvo* not only how Hellenistic learning was transmitted to Roman boys but also how Hellenistic literary tastes shaped Roman ones—the stories included by Parthenius are, *mutatis mutandis*, obvious prototypes for, among other things, the story of Dido and Aeneas.

Parthenius' student **Gallus** (c. 69–26 BCE) is an equally important figure, though again we have little to go on from his own hand. The author of (at least) a collection of elegies called the *Amores*, Gallus is best known to modern readers not for the surviving ten lines of elegiac couplets attached to his name but as a figure of inspiration in Vergil's *Eclogues* 6 and 10 and as an elusive shadow behind the so-called Aristaeus epyllion with which the fourth book of the *Georgics* culminates. Whether this episode is inspired by Gallus in its subject, style, and narrative treatment, or whether Vergil composed it to replace an earlier conclusion in which Gallus himself featured, remains a matter of scholarly debate; but the episode clearly illustrates a fashion for which we also have compelling evidence from **Catullus** (c. 85–55 BCE), whose "new poetry" is likely to have made a strong impression on the adolescent Vergil. Catullus' poem 64, an epyllion on the marriage of Peleus and Thetis containing the inset narrative of Ariadne's betrayal by Theseus, has long been recognized to be a pervasive intertextual presence in Vergil's Dido and Aeneas episode; what is now becoming more apparent is that this is only the most obvious indication of Catullus' profound impact not only on Vergil's poetic sensibilities but also on his mode of expression.

Finally, I note—but can hardly do justice to here—Vergil's contemporaries, including particularly the poets **Horace** (65–8 BCE), **Propertius** (c. 54–16 BCE), and **Tibullus** (c. 55–19 BCE). Side-by-side reading of their poetry and Vergil's can only begin to suggest how these poets interacted, socially, politically, and intellectually; it offers a vivid picture nonetheless of the life-shattering turmoil which each, in his own way, survived and in which each found the inspiration to serve as spokesperson for a generation. The resulting portrait—or perhaps collage would be a better metaphor—renders the Augustan age a period for which there are few comparisons, in terms of both historical significance and creative richness.

ii) Characters and Plot

Aeneas is a relatively minor Homeric character, best known for escaping from duels with both Diomedes and Achilles through divine intervention (*Iliad* Books 5 and 20, respectively). He also figures, at least as a name, in the *Homeric Hymn to Aphrodite*, where the goddess' seduction of the unknowing Anchises is promised to result in the birth of a son. He is likely to have appeared in lesser or greater roles elsewhere as well in the ancient literary record, but we know of no real starring roles before the Roman poets take him up. I have already referred to his place in the poems of Ennius and Naevius; he also was a standard figure in the lists of names of ancestors with which the annalistic historians of Rome legitimized their work. The *Aeneid*, however, is effectively the first poem in which Aeneas is the central character throughout the work.

Much has been made since antiquity of the perceived similarities between the Vergilian Aeneas and the new *princeps*, Augustus, who brought peace to the Roman state after decades of civil strife; and indeed much contemporary evidence extraneous to the *Aeneid* indicates that this analogy was the seemingly natural outcome of a larger program of renewed emphasis on divine and heroic origins and lineage carried out through much of the first century BCE by the *gens Iulia*. Scholars are almost unanimous in their agreement, however, that an allegorical reading of the *Aeneid* (i.e., Aeneas "equals" Augustus) is not only a rash oversimplification of the facts but also ignores the complexities of Vergil's creative genius. The idea that the *Aeneid* is Augustan "propaganda" is both provocative and reductive, better used as the starting-point for a critical reading of the poem than as its conclusion.

Dido makes her first appearance in late fourth-century BCE Hellenistic history, as the expansion of Carthage and other developments in the western Mediterranean give new prominence to the cultural and political reach of the Phoenicians. The encounter of Aeneas and Dido probably appeared in Naevius' *Bellum Punicum*, but at least according to Varro it was Dido's sister Anna, rather than Dido herself, who fell in love with the Trojan leader and committed suicide. The Vergilian version of the cultural confrontation represented by Dido's encounter with Aeneas and her subsequent demise is therefore likely to have been read as an innovation upon the traditional story, and is clearly informed by both contemporary political discourse about foreign, especially Eastern, peoples (of whom the Egyptian ruler Cleopatra is typecast as representative) and the status of women in the Roman world. Insofar as the conflict between Dido and Aeneas has been read as analogous to that between Carthage and Rome, furthermore, Dido has been interpreted as a stand-in of sorts for Hannibal. As with Aeneas, however, the temptation to allegorize is best avoided, at least in its simplest form; for it is clear that the historical models for Dido must share the limelight with her literary forerunners, like Ariadne, Medea, and Deianira.

Turnus, chief of the Rutulians and leader of the anti-Trojan opposition in Italy, is first and foremost the Virgilian equivalent of Homer's Hector, although the fact that Turnus is not Trojan but rather Troy's sworn enemy is only one of many ironies in his depiction. Scholars have also seen Turnus as an analogue for either Antony, or the assassins of Julius Caesar, or both; and while these figures certainly offer some suggestive parallels, they tell us little about Turnus as Vergilian character. Very little is heard of Turnus before his appearance in the *Aeneid*; his name appears linked with Aeneas' as early as the second century BCE, but Vergil clearly turned first to both Homer and tragedy to help shape his creation of a fit match for Aeneas. Whether Turnus is better seen as a hotheaded outlaw promoting both a lost and an unjust cause or the true tragic hero of the poem, destroyed by forces beyond his control, remains one of the great questions in Vergilian studies. Equally important, however, are the questions raised by the figure of Turnus about Italian identity and the place of Rome in the history and destiny of the Italian peninsula, questions constantly renewed by our increasing ability to understand the cultural and social politics of the era in which Vergil wrote.

Aside from these three—i.e., Aeneas and his two adversaries—there are **numerous other characters** in the *Aeneid* who play roles of some significance, both Trojans (e.g., Anchises, Ascanius, Priam, Laocoon, Helenus, Palinurus, Achates, Creusa, Nisus, Euryalus) and the ethnically diverse inhabitants of Italy (e.g., Latinus, Lavinia, Evander, Pallas, Camilla, Iuturna, Mezentius, Lausus); the Greeks too are central to the narrative, although their roles are more often described by others than directly depicted (e.g., Odysseus [Ulysses], Achilles, Patroclus, Neoptolemus [Pyrrhus], Helen). All of these characters bear comparison with their Homeric and tragic prototypes; in these notes I shall attempt to indicate at least how to begin such comparative examination.

Arguably, however, **the gods**—or at least a few of them—are even more important than the humans in Vergil's epic narrative: Juno, Venus, Apollo, and Jupiter—as well as traditionally "minor" figures like Aeolus, Iris, and Mercury—are not only constant observers of human action in the poem but also play a central role in shaping human action. It has often been asked with some skepticism whether Vergil or his first audience, the sophisticated elite of the early principate, would have taken these gods seriously, i.e., whether these gods would have been believed in and believable, both because of their obviously literary origins and because of the apparent absence of religious sentiment, at least in the modern sense, from Roman life in the first century BCE. Yet if we ignore the gods in the *Aeneid*, or see them simply as some sort of epic window-dressing, we risk writing off almost half of the poem, including moreover numerous scenes whose fundamental purpose seems to be to show the crucial part played by forces outside ourselves in human affairs: indeed, it is possible to read the *Aeneid* as evidence for the deep religiosity of the Augustan era, a religiosity that is best understood not in terms of belief or morality but in terms of cultural identity. The gods are as central to this identity as is Aeneas himself.

e. Vergil's Influence

The history of Vergil's reception as "the classic of all Europe," as T.S. Eliot called him, and indeed of all the West, can only be given in rough outline here; readers who wish to proceed further into this terrain are therefore advised to look at one or more of the many new treatments of Vergilian reception, and indeed of reception of Roman poetry as a whole, that have emerged in recent years. A few moments from Vergil's rich afterlife can nonetheless be noted here.

First witness to the Vergilian achievement is **Ovid**, who grew up reading Vergil's poetry and was undoubtedly deeply influenced by its language, its cadences, and its central themes. Ovid returns repeatedly in his poetry to Vergilian themes and characters, from the love-letter written by the abandoned Dido to Aeneas (*Heroides* 7) to a rewriting of the *Aeneid*, from a new and sometimes subversive perspective, in the last books of the *Metamorphoses*. Ovid even exploits the Vergilian model from his place of exile, Tomis, imagining his departure from Rome in terms that are clearly modeled on Aeneas' escape from Troy (*Tristia* 1.3).

Three centuries after Ovid, the emperor **Constantine** (in a sermon dated to the early 320s CE) would read the fourth *Eclogue* as a prophecy of the birth of Jesus and thus of Christianity, and see Vergil therefore as a proto-Christian; and **Augustine** (354–430 CE) too would look to Vergil's characters as models for understanding human behavior and emotions, even as he rejected the pagan world-view of Vergil's work.

With Christian hegemony in Europe came an increasing tendency to read Vergil in Christian terms; the culmination of this trend appears in **Dante**, whose first-person narrator throughout the *Divine Comedy* (composed during the first quarter of the fourteenth century) is escorted, at least in the earliest stages of the poem's journey, by the soul of Vergil, "l'altissimo poeta." Indeed,

Dante's relationship to Vergil has been seen by modern scholars as a metaphor of sorts for the way in which great works of art are kept alive, allowed—or even compelled—to transcend the boundaries of their own historical roots.

The resulting tension proved to be fertile ground for the poets of Europe throughout the ensuing centuries, particularly those engaged in the project of viewing epic through the lens of empire, and vice versa. This tradition saw its culmination, at least in some ways, in the work of **John Milton**, whose great poem *Paradise Lost* (1667) is richly Vergilian in its intertextuality even as it equates the empire-building burden of epic with the aspirations of Satan.

I leave for others, some of who are included in the bibliographical list below, to continue this story, never-ending as it is; I mention here only two of the greatest poets of the late twentieth century, **Joseph Brodsky** and **Seamus Heaney**, each of whom has not only paid homage to Vergil but renewed Vergil in his own work. The very fact that you are reading this, before engaging in the interpretive act of translating the *Aeneid*, offers a paradigm for Vergil's vitality: with each (re-)reading the poem is renewed and transformed, as are its readers.

f. Timeline

Augustan Rome - a timetable - *Barbara Weiden Boyd*			
Year(s)	Historical and Political Events	Monuments and Building Projects	Significant Texts/ Literary Events
79 BCE	Pompey's first triumph		
71	Pompey's second triumph		
70			Birth of Virgil
68	Julius Caesar's funeral oration for aunt Julia in Forum Romanum		
65			Birth of Horace
63	C. Octavius born September 23		
60	First Triumvirate formed		
59	Pompey marries Julius Caesar's daughter Julia		
55		Theater of Pompey and Temple of Venus Victrix (first use of *opus reticulatum*)	Deaths of Lucretius and Catullus

54	Julius Caesar's daughter Julia dies	Cicero purchases land for Julius Caesar's Forum (Forum Iulium)	Birth of Propertius (or 47?)
53	Battle of Carrhae – Crassus loses Roman standards to Parthians		
52	Pompey elected sole consul	Curia Hostilia and Basilica Porcia in Forum Romanum burn down	
49	Julius Caesar crosses the Rubicon		
48	Battle of Pharsalus – Julius Caesar defeats Pompey		
46	Julius Caesar's triumph in Rome	Dedication of Temple of Venus Genetrix in Forum Iulium	
44	Assassination of Julius Caesar; Antony's funeral oration for Julius Caesar in Roman forum; adoption of Octavian	Altar and column erected in Forum Romanum with inscription PARENTI PATRIAE	
43	Octavian becomes consul; formation of second Triumvirate		Birth of Ovid
42	Battle of Philippi; deification of Julius Caesar; division of empire	Building of temple of Divus Iulius in Forum Romanum decreed; Octavian vows temple to Mars Ultor	
41	Land confiscations		Virgil begins *Eclogues*
40	Antony marries Octavia		
38	Octavian marries Livia		
36	Octavian defeats Sextus Pompey at Naulochus; Lepidus removed from triumvirate		
34	Donations of Alexandria		
32	Octavian reads Antony's will; Antony divorces Octavia		
31	Battle of Actium		
30	Suicides of Antony and Cleopatra	Octavian's campsite memorial built at Actium	Horace publishes *Epodes*

29	Octavian's triple triumph	Curia Iulia in Forum Romanum finished by Octavian; temple of Divus Iulius in Forum Romanum completed	Virgil completes *Georgics*, begins *Aeneid*
28		Forum Iulium and Basilica Iulia finished by Octavian; dedication of the Temple of Apollo on the Palatine; Octavian's Mausoleum begun	
27	January 13 – *res publica restituta*; Octavian becomes Augustus		
25	Marriage of Julia and Marcellus		
23	Augustus receives tribunician powers for life; death of Marcellus; Agrippa heads to East	(approx.) Theater of Marcellus begun	Horace publishes *Odes* Books 1-3
21	Marriage of Agrippa and Julia		
20s	Lex Iulia theatralis		
20	Recovery of Roman standards from Parthia; birth of Gaius Caesar	Dedication of small Temple of Mars Ultor on Capitoline?	
19		Arch of Augustus (Parthian Arch) erected in Forum Romanum	Publication of *Aeneid*; deaths of Virgil and Tibullus
18	*Lex Iulia de maritandis ordinibus* and *Lex Iulia de adulteriis coercendis*		
17	Birth of Lucius Caesar; Augustus adopts Gaius and Lucius; *Ludi Saeculares*		Horace's *Carmen Saeculare* commissioned
16			Publication of Horace's *Odes* Book 4; death of Propertius
13	Augustus returns from Spain and Gaul	Ara Pacis Augustae vowed by Senate	
12	Death of Lepidus (or late 13?); Augustus is made Pontifex Maximus; Agrippa dies in late March		

11	Tiberius divorces Vipsania, marries Julia; Drusus marries Antonia Minor		
9	Death of Drusus	Dedication of Ara Pacis Augustae	
8			Death of Horace
2	Julia daughter of Augustus is relegated	Dedication of Forum of Augustus, including Temple of Mars Ultor; Augustus receives title PATER PATRIAE	
2 CE	Death of Lucius Caesar		
2–8 CE			Ovid works on *Fasti* and *Metamorphoses*
4 CE	Death of Gaius Caesar; adoption of Tiberius by Augustus; adoption of Germanicus son of Drusus by Tiberius		
7 CE	Julia granddaughter of Augustus is relegated; Agrippa Postumus is exiled		
8 CE			Ovid is relegated to Tomis, where he writes *Tristia* and *Epistulae ex Ponto*
9 CE	*Lex Papia Poppaea* modifies earlier social legislation		
14 CE	Death of Augustus		Augustus' *Res Gestae* read in the Senate by the Vestal Virgins

BIBLIOGRAPHY

Collections of Essays on Vergil's Life and Work

Anderson, W. S. and L. Quartarone, eds. *Approaches to Teaching Vergil's Aeneid.* New York: Modern Language Association of America, 2002.

Harrison, S. J., ed. *Oxford Readings in Vergil's Aeneid.* Oxford and New York: Oxford University Press, 1990.

Horsfall, N. *A Companion to the Study of Virgil.* Leiden: E.J. Brill Publishers, 1995.

Martindale, C., ed. *The Cambridge Companion to Virgil.* Cambridge: Cambridge University Press, 1997.

Perkell, C., ed. *Reading Vergil's Aeneid: An Interpretive Guide.* Norman, OK: University of Oklahoma Press, 1999.

Quinn, S., ed. *Why Vergil? A Collection of Interpretations.* Wauconda, IL: Bolchazy-Carducci Publishers, Inc., 2000.

Stahl, H.-P., ed. *Vergil's Aeneid: Augustan Epic and Political Context.* London: Duckworth/The Classical Press of Wales, 1998.

The First Century BCE and the Augustan Principate

Galinsky, K. *Augustan Culture: An Interpretive Introduction.* Princeton: Princeton University Press, 1996.

Gurval, R. A. *Actium and Augustus: The Politics and Emotions of Civil War.* Ann Arbor: University of Michigan Press, 1995.

Raaflaub, K. A. and M. Toher, eds. *Between Republic and Empire: Interpretations of Augustus and His Principate.* Berkeley and Los Angeles: University of California Press, 1990.

Zanker, P. *The Power of Images in the Age of Augustus.* Translated by A. Shapiro. Ann Arbor: University of Michigan Press, 1988.

The *Aeneid*: Literary Traditions

Anderson, R. J., P. J. Parsons, and R. G. M. Nisbet. "Elegiacs by Gallus from Qasr Ibrim." *Journal of Roman Studies* 69 (1979) 125–55.

Clausen, W., ed. *Virgil: Eclogues.* Oxford: Clarendon Press, 1994.

Feeney, D. *The Gods in Epic.* Oxford: Clarendon Press, 1991.

Gale, M. *Virgil on the Nature of Things: The Georgics, Lucretius and the Didactic Tradition.* Cambridge: Cambridge University Press, 2000.

Gigante, M. *Philodemus in Italy: The Books from Herculaneum.* Translated by D. Obbink. Ann Arbor: University of Michigan Press, 1995.

Goldberg, S. M. *Epic in Republican Rome.* Oxford and New York: Oxford University Press, 1995.

Nelis, D. *Vergil's Aeneid and the Argonautica of Apollonius Rhodius.* Leeds: Francis Cairns Ltd., 2001.

Pease, A. S., ed. *Virgil, Aeneid IV.* Cambridge, MA: Harvard University Press, 1935.

Ross, D. O. *Backgrounds to Augustan Poetry: Gallus, Elegy and Rome*. Cambridge: Cambridge University Press, 1975.

Skutsch, O., ed. *The Annals of Quintus Ennius*. Oxford: Clarendon Press, 1985.

Thomas, R. F., ed. *Virgil: Georgics*. 2 vols. Cambridge: Cambridge University Press, 1988.

The Influence of Vergil

Gransden, K. W., ed. *Virgil in English*. London and New York: Penguin Books, 1996.

Jacoff, R. and J. T. Schnapp, eds. *The Poetry of Allusion: Virgil and Ovid in Dante's Commedia*. Stanford, CA: Stanford University Press, 1991.

Martindale, C. *John Milton and the Transformation of Classical Epic*. 2d edition. London: Bristol Classical Press, 2002.

McDonough, C. M., R. E. Prior, and M. Stansbury. *Servius' Commentary on Book Four of Virgil's Aeneid: An Annotated Translation*. Wauconda, IL: Bolchazy-Carducci Publishers, Inc., 2004.

Thomas, R. F. *Virgil and the Augustan Reception*. Cambridge: Cambridge University Press, 2001.

See also the valuable chapters on Vergil's reception in the *Companions* edited by Martindale and Horsfall (listed under *Collections of Essays* above).

GENERAL DIRECTIONS

This book, with its visible vocabulary system, is so arranged that the complete vocabulary of any given passage is constantly before the reader.

In beginning the work of a given lesson, the student should open the book at the passage to be studied, and unfold the extensible sheet at the back of the book.

The reader will find two varieties of type employed in the Latin text, roman (ordinary light-faced) and italics. Words printed in roman type in the text are to be found in the vocabulary at the foot of a given page. Those printed in italics in the text will be found on the extensible sheet at the back of the book. The list of the italicized words of the text, which represent the most common words in the author, should be mastered as early as possible.

Teachers who wish to give special vocabulary drills will find in the lists at the back of the book perhaps the most valuable and the least wasteful of any material which may be available for their purpose.

This book may be employed with good results in a variety of ways, a few of which are here suggested as possibilities:

(1) It may be used as any other Latin text is commonly studied; that is, the teacher may assign a definite amount of work at each recitation, and the students may prepare this assignment and recite on it at the next meeting of the class. This is probably the least desirable method of studying any language.

(2) A much better method is to spend at least half of the recitation period in sight reading. The students should begin by quickly looking over the words in the vocabulary at the bottom of each page, and then be prepared to read. The teacher should never translate for them, but should give them an occasional hint or a question with respect to a form or a construction, and should make very brief comments on points that may appear obscure. In this way the students should usually cover the advanced lesson in class, so that their additional preparation would primarily consist in a review or elaboration of the work already done in class under the direction of the teacher.

(3) A still more satisfactory method is, however, to arrange for twice as much time for class meeting as has been customary. The whole of this time should be spent working on the text under the direct supervision of the teacher, and should be devoted primarily to sight reading. The work of the students outside the class meeting should consist in a limited amount

of supplementary reading and in a continual review of the grammar, both forms and syntax, as found in the grammatical appendix of this book. Since little or no outside preparation would be required, such a course should have no more credit than the ordinary type which meets the customary number of hours a week. Schools which can arrange their schedule on this basis will find their students making much more satisfactory progress and developing much more enthusiasm for their work.

All Latin students in high school and college work should make a thorough review of Latin grammar at the beginning of each school year. Even though it may be done rapidly this review should be comprehensive and should include all forms and syntax previously studied. Some attention should be paid to any additional features which are to be used during the new year. This new matter, together with the review, may be briefly summarized in the first three or four meetings of the class. When the reading of poetry is begun a careful study should be made of the elementary principles of versification. All principles learned or reviewed should be continually applied as the class proceeds. The material for this work will be found in the Grammatical Appendix of this book, distributed as follows:

Pronunciation and Inflection	1–235
Syntax	236–390
Versification	391–410
Figures of Syntax and Rhetoric	411–477

The Index to the Appendix will be found useful in locating material which may otherwise be difficult to find. It is important to remember that no one can ever read intelligently any language without a practical working knowledge of the grammar. In general it will be found that a careful and systematic study of the grammar, with a constant application of its principles and with frequent reviews, will mean a great saving of time and a great increase in the power of the students to comprehend the language which is being studied.

NOTE TO THE STUDENT: For the meaning of the signs and abbreviations see page xxxvii.

SIGNS AND ABBREVIATIONS

abl. = ablative
abs. = absolute
acc. = accusative
act. = active
adj. = adjective
adv. = adverb, adverbial
advers. = adversative
App. = the Grammatical Appendix in this book
appos. = apposition, appositive
asynd. = asyndeton
cf. = Latin cōnfer, i.e. *compare*
char. = characteristic
coll. = collective
compar. = comparative
condit. = condition, conditional
conj. = conjunction
constr. = construction
dat. = dative
dem. = demonstrative
dep. = deponent
dim. = diminutive
e.g. = Latin exemplī grātiā, i.e. *for example*
esp. = especial, especially
f., fem. = feminine
fig. = figurative, figuratively
freq. = frequentative
fut. = future
gen. = genitive
hist. = historical
i.e. = Latin id est, *that is*
imp. = imperative
imperf. = imperfect
impers. = impersonal, impersonally
indecl. = indeclinable
indef. = indefinite
indic. = indicative
indir. = indirect
inf. = infinitive

instr. = instrumental
interj. = interjection
interrog. = interrogative
intr. = intransitive
Introd. = the Introduction of this book
l. = line; *ll.* = lines
lit. = literal, literally
loc. = locative
m., masc. = masculine
n., neut. = neuter
neg. = negative
nom. = nominative
num. = numeral
obj. = object, objective
opt. = optative
part. = participle, partitive
pass. = passive
perf. = perfect
pers. = personal
pl. = plural
pluperf. = pluperfect
poss. = possessive
pred. = predicate
prep. = preposition
pres. = present
pron. = pronoun
ref. = reference
reflex. = reflexive
rel. = relative
sc. = Latin scīlicet, i.e. *supply, understand*
sing. = singular
spec. = specification
subst. = substantive
sup. = superlative
temp. = temporal
tr. = transitive, transitively
soc. = vocative
vol. = volitive

(1), this numeral after a Latin word in the vocabulary indicates that the word is a verb of the first conjugation and is to be inflected as **amō, āre, āvī, ātus,** *love, cherish.*

All Latin words in the notes and vocabularies are in bold face type. All definitions in the vocabularies are in italics. All translations in the notes are in italics.

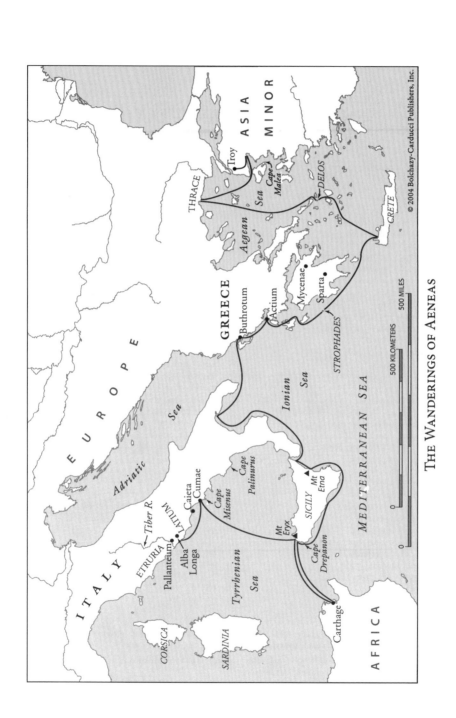

THE WANDERINGS OF AENEAS

SELECTIONS FROM
BOOK 1

...patuit dea (1.405)

Illustration for Book 1
"Showed herself a goddess" by Thom Kapheim

SELECTIONS FROM
VERGIL'S *AENEID*

BOOK 1.1–519

ARMA virumque canō, *Troiae quī prīmus ab ōrīs*
Ītaliam fātō profugus Lāvīnia*que vēnit*
lītora, multum ille et terrīs iactātus *et* altō   3

---

altum, ī *n.* the deep (sea)
canō, ere, cecinī, cantus sing (of), chant,
  proclaim

iactō (1) toss, buffet
Lāvīn(i)us, a, um Lavinian, of Lavinium
profugus, a, um exiled, fugitive

1–7. The theme of the poem,
namely, the wanderings and wars of
Aeneas, who after many struggles
established the foundation for the
greatness of future Rome, in
accordance with the decrees of fate.

From the more extended
introduction to the poem (lines 1–33)
we learn: (1) the plan of the poet to
describe the adventures of his hero,
as is done in the *Odyssey*, and to
depict wars and battles, as in the *Iliad*;
(2) the importance of the gods, ruling
over all mortal affairs, in the design
of the poem; and (3) the story's
relevance to Roman history, focusing
as it does on the human trials that
made possible the birth of Rome.

1. Arma virumque: the theme of the
Aeneid; **arma** stands by METONYMY for *deeds
of arms, wars*, referring to the wars in which
Aeneas engaged, both in Troy and in Italy;
virum refers to Aeneas, so well known that
he is not mentioned by name until 92.
Troiae: with the first syllable long by

position; App. 6, *b*. **quī prīmus ab ōrīs
Troiae (ad) Ītaliam vēnit.** Aeneas was the
first of the Trojans to come to Italy after his
native city Troy had been captured, sacked,
and destroyed by the Greeks in the Trojan
War. Strictly speaking, the Trojan Antenor
had preceded him, but Antenor's arrival,
mentioned below at 242–49, is part of a
narrative tradition different from that
followed by Vergil here, and is not
associated with the foundation of Rome
proper.

2–3. (ad or **in) Ītaliam, (ad** or **in)
lītora:** acc. of place to which; the omission
of prepositions here is typical of Latin
poetry, and you will see this often in the
Aeneid; App. 315. **fātō:** abl. of means or
cause; App. 331, 332; "through the will
of heaven." **Lāvīn(i)a:** *of Lavinium*, an
ancient city on the western coast of Italy,
near the spot where Rome was later
founded. Lavinium was said by many
historians in antiquity to have been the
first Trojan settlement in Italy and to have
been named for Lavinia, the Italian
princess whom Aeneas eventually married.
Lavinia was the daughter of Latinus, king
of the Latins. Lavinia herself first appears

vī superum, saevae memorem *Iūnōnis* ob īram,
5   *multa* quoque et *bellō* passus, *dum* conderet *urbem*
īnferret*que* deōs Latiō; *genus* unde Latīnum
Albānī*que* patrēs atque altae moenia Rōmae.

Albānus, a, um Alban, of Alba Longa in central Italy, mother city of Rome
condō, ere, didī, ditus found, establish
īnferō, ferre, tulī, lātus bring (into)
Latīnus, a, um Latin, of Latium
Latium, (i)ī *n.* district of central Italy around Rome

memor, oris mindful, remembering, unforgetting
ob on account of (+ *acc.*)
patior, ī, passus suffer, endure
quoque also
Rōma, ae *f.* Rome, a city and empire
saevus, a, um cruel, stern, fierce
unde whence, from which source

---

in the *Aeneid* in Book 7 (although a reference to her is made earlier by Anchises, at 6.764). Some of the oldest manuscripts of the *Aeneid* we have, dating from the 4th and 5th centuries A.D., have the alternate spelling **Lāvīna**, because Vergil's earliest readers recognized that he was doing something unusual with the scansion of this line. The epithet **Lāvīn(i)a** must be scanned as two long syllables followed by one short syllable, and so the usual second -i- in the word must either drop out (i.e., **Lāvīna**) or be treated as a semi-consonant (i.e., **Lāvīnia**, with the second -i- sounding more like -y-, as in the English word "yoyo").

3. multum: adverbial, modifying **iactātus. ille:** Aeneas, the **virum** of 1. **et (in) terrīs, et (in) altō:** abl. of place where; App. 319. **iactātus (est).**

4. vī: abl. of cause or means; App. 331, 332. **superum = superōrum**, gen. pl., *of the gods above.* **memorem:** an example of ENALLAGE (or transferred epithet), logically describing **Iūnōnis,** but poetically applied to **īram. saevae memorem Iūnōnis ob īram:** an example of SYNCHESIS (or interlocked order), **saevae** modifying **Iūnōnis,** and **memorem** modifying **īram.** This pattern is often found in Latin poetry. **Iūnōnis ob īram:** the reasons for Juno's hatred of Aeneas and the Trojans are given by Vergil at 12–28.

5–6. conderet, īnferret: subjunctives in a purpose clause introduced by **dum,** expressing anticipated rather than completed action; App. 374.

5. urbem: Lavinium. **passus (est Aenēās). (in) bellō:** abl. of place; App. 319; referring to the enemies whom he had to conquer after landing in Italy. **multa:** obj. of the participle **passus;** App. 307, 313.

6. īnferret deōs: App. 374; when travelling to found a new settlement, the migrating peoples of the ancient Greek and Roman world regularly carried with them their gods, either as images or other sacred symbols; see 68 and 378. **Latiō:** dat. of motion towards = **ad (in) Latium;** App. 306. **unde genus Latīnum (est):** Roman legends traced the origin of the Latin people, the kingdom of Alba Longa (forerunner of Rome), and the founding of Rome back to the coming of the Trojans under Aeneas to Italy.

7. (unde) Albānī patrēs (sunt): many of the noble senatorial families of Rome took much pride in tracing their families back to the early inhabitants of Alba Longa. **patrēs:** with the first syllable short; App. 17. **altae:** ENALLAGE (transferred epithet). Since it more accurately describes the walls, the transferred epithet suggests both the position, *situated on the (seven) high hills,* and the power and prestige of *lofty (mighty) Rome.*

Mūsa, *mihī* causās memorā, *quō nūmine* laesō
quidve dolēns *rēgīna deum* tot *volvere cāsūs*
īnsignem pietāte *virum*, tot adīre *labōrēs*
impulerit. *Tantaene animīs* caelestibus *īrae?*

[handwritten: So great soul anger of the heavens]

10

---

adeō, īre, iī (īvī), itus approach,
  encounter
causa, ae *f.* reason, cause
caelestis, e divine, heavenly
doleō, ēre, uī, itus suffer, grieve (at), be
  angry (at, with), resent
impellō, ere, pulī,·pulsus strike
  (against), drive, force

īnsignis, e distinguished, marked, splendid
laedō, ere, sī, sus strike, hurt, offend,
  thwart
memorō (1) (re)call, recount, relate
Mūsa, ae *f.* Muse, patron goddess of the
  liberal arts
pietās, ātis *f.* loyalty, devotion, sense of
  duty
tot so many

> 8–11. Invocation of the Muse.

8. Mūsa: Jupiter and Mnemosyne
("Memory") were the parents of nine
daughters, the Muses. From Homer
onwards, it is the custom of epic poets to
invoke one or all of the Muses for
inspiration and to assign to their divine
influence the gift of being able to
compose poetry. **mihī:** this word in
poetry may have the final **i** either long or
short. The same is true of **tibi, sibi, ubi,**
and **ibi. quō nūmine (Iūnōnis) laesō:** abl.
abs. or abl. of cause; App. 332, 343.
9. quidve dolēns: *or vexed at what;*
quid is the direct obj. of **dolēns. rēgīna
de(ōr)um:** Juno as Jupiter's wife was
queen of the gods. **cāsūs:** direct object of
the infinitive **volvere,** *to undergo, pass
through.*

10. virum = Aenēān, subject of
volvere, which depends upon **impulerit.
pietāte:** abl. of quality (sometimes called
abl. of specification), explaining in what
feature Aeneas was especially outstanding
(**īnsignem**); App. 330. Aeneas' **pietās,**
loyalty or *devotion to duty,* is an
important motif in the poem.
11. impulerit: perf. subj. in indir.
question; App. 349, 350. **Tantaene =
suntne tantae īrae caelestibus animīs?
animīs:** dat. of possession; App. 299.
īrae: poetic plural, often employed in
Latin where English would ordinarily use
the singular. Vergil's use of **īrae** as the
concluding word of his introduction to
the poem and invocation of the Muse
echoes the appearance of "wrath" (**mēnis**)
as the first word of Homer's *Iliad.* There
is an important difference, however:
Homer's theme was the wrath of his hero,
Achilles; in Vergil's poem, wrath
originates with the gods.

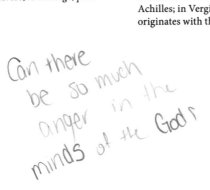

[handwritten: Can there be so much anger in the minds of the Gods?]

Urbs antīqua fuit (Tyriī tenuēre colōnī) Phoenicia
Karthāgō, Ītaliam contrā Tiberīna*que* longē
ōstia, dīves opum studiīs*que* asperrima *bellī,*
15 *quam Iūnō fertur terrīs* magis *omnibus ūnam*
posthabitā coluisse Samō. *hīc illius arma,*

---

asper, era, erum harsh, rough, fierce
colō, ere, uī, cultus cultivate, dwell
  (in), honor, cherish
colōnus, ī *m.* colonist, settler
contrā opposite, facing (+ *acc.*)
dī(ve)s, dī(vi)tis rich, wealthy (+ *gen.*)
Karthāgō, inis *f.* Carthage, great
  commercial city in North Africa,
  rival of Rome
longē *adv.* far (off), at a distance

magis *adv.* more, rather
ops, opis *f.* help, resources, power, wealth
ōstium, (i)ī *n.* mouth, entrance
posthabeō, ēre, uī, itus place after,
  esteem less
Samos, ī *f.* island of the Aegean, center of
  the worship of Juno
studium, (i)ī *n.* zeal, desire, pursuit
Tiberīnus, a, um of the Tiber, an Italian
  river on which Rome is situated

> 12–33. Reasons for the wrath of
> Juno against Aeneas and the Trojans.

12. Urbs antīqua fuit: it is curious that Vergil here refers to Carthage as "ancient," since Carthage was in fact founded some four hundred years later than the traditional date of the fall of Troy, 1184 B.C. Vergil is introducing the perspective of his readers into the poem—to the Romans of the first century B.C., as to us, Carthage was a very ancient city indeed, and had in fact been razed to the ground by P. Cornelius Scipio Aemilianus (henceforth, Africanus) in 146 B.C., at the end of the Third Punic War. **Tyriī:** *from Tyre,* a city of Phoenicia, whence Carthage was said to have been settled. The Phoenicians were the great traders of their time, and Carthage, on the northern shore of Africa and on the Mediterranean, occupied a strategic position for controlling the commerce of these regions. **tenuēre:** shorter (syncopated) form for **tenuērunt;** App. 204, 4.

13. longē: modifying **contrā,** which governs both **Ītaliam** and **Tiberīna ōstia.**

14. ōstia: see note on **īrae,** 11. The general expression **Ītaliam** is followed by the more specific **Tiberīna ōstia** for the

sake of greater clearness and vividness. **opum:** gen. of respect (also called gen. of specification), with **dīves,** *rich in resources;* App. 294, or gen. with special adj., App. 287. **studiīs:** abl. of respect, depends on **asperrima;** App. 325. This phrase would remind the Romans of their bitter struggles with Carthage in the Punic Wars.

15. quam: refers to **urbs,** 12, and is direct object of **coluisse. fertur:** *is said,* a common meaning for this verb in poetry. **terrīs omnibus = terrīs aliīs; terrīs** is abl. with comparative **magis;** App. 327. **ūnam = sōlam,** as often.

16. posthabitā Samō: abl. abs.; App. 343. Juno greatly loved Samos, an island off the western coast of Asia Minor. According to the myth, the goddess had been reared in Samos, had married Jupiter there, and one of her temples, among the most famous in the world, was situated there. Vergil's point here is probably that Juno prefers Carthage even to her beloved Samos (although some scholars still consider this abl. abs. difficult to interpret). **Samō:** the final vowel is not elided, although the following word begins with an h. This failure to elide is called HIATUS. **illius (Iūnōnis):** the -i of the genitive ending of the nine pronouns and

hīc currus *fuit; hoc rēgnum dea gentibus esse,*
sī quā *fāta* sinant, *iam tum tenditque* fovet*que.*
Prōgeniem *sed enim* Troiānō *ā sanguine dūcī*
audierat Tyriās ōlim *quae* verteret *arcēs;*
hinc populum lātē *rēgem bellōque* superbum
ventūrum excidiō Libyae; *sīc volvere* Parcās.
Id metuēns veteris*que* memor Sāturnia *bellī,*

20

Fearing this and
Changing the Trojan
War

---

currus, ūs *m.* chariot, car
enim for, indeed, in truth
excidium, (i)ī *n.* destruction, overthrow
foveō, ēre, fōvī, fōtus cherish, fondle
lātē *adv.* widely, far and wide
Libya, ae *f.* region of North Africa
memor, oris remembering, mindful,
　unforgetting (+ *gen.*)
metuō, ere, uī fear, dread
ōlim *adv.* (at) some time, once
Parcae, ārum *f.* the Fates

populus, ī *m.* people, nation
prōgeniēs, ēī *f.* offspring, race
quā *adv.* in any (some) way, where
Sāturnia, ae *f.* Juno, daughter of Saturn,
　father of the gods
sinō, ere, sīvī, situs permit, allow
superbus, a, um proud, haughty
Troiānus, a, um Trojan, of Troy
vertō, ere, ī, rsus (over)turn, change
vetus, eris old, former, ancient

---

adjectives ending in **-ius** is usually long,
but often short in poetry as here. **arma**
(fuērunt): doubtless refers to ancient
arms, chariot, and other relics preserved
in Juno's temple at Samos.

16–17. hīc, hīc, hoc: repeated for
emphasis; this repetition is called ANAPHORA.
hoc: refers to **urbs** 12, but is attracted to
the gender of the predicate noun **rēgnum,**
the ruling power. **Iūno dea iam tum**
tenditque fovetque hanc urbem
(Karthāginem) esse rēgnum omnibus
gentibus, sed fāta voluērunt Rōmam esse
hoc rēgnum. gentibus: dat. of reference;
App. 301.

18. quā (viā): abl. of manner; **quā** is an
indef. pron. (= **aliquā**, but **ali-** is dropped
after **sī**). **fāta:** the power of the fates was
greater even than that of the gods.

19. Prōgeniem: the Romans. **dūcī:** *was*
being derived, pres. pass. inf. used in
indir. disc.; App. 390; depends on
audi(v)erat (20), of which Juno is the
understood subject.

20. Tyriās arcēs = Karthāginem. ōlim
looks to the future, i.e., to the Punic Wars.
verteret: subj. of characteristic; App. 389,
or rel. clause of purpose; App. 388.

21. hinc: ā Troiānō sanguine, or **ab**
hāc prōgeniē. populum: subj. of
ventūrum (esse) (22), an inf. in indir.
disc., depending on **audierat**; App. 390.
rēgem: used like a participle (**rēgnantem**)
here, and modified by **lātē. bellō:** abl.
of respect, depending on **superbum**; App.
325.

22. excidiō: dat. of purpose; App. 303;
for the destruction; used with **Libyae** in
the so-called double dative construction.
Libyae: for **Āfricae,** meaning especially
Karthāginī. Parcās = fāta: subject of
volvere. The Parcae were represented as
three sisters, Clotho (*Spinner*), who spun
the thread of life for each mortal; Lachesis
(*Measurer*), who measured the thread;
and Atropos (*Inevitable*), who cut the
thread when a human had reached his or
her own allotted day. **volvere** probably
describes the unrolling of the thread. **sīc**
(Iūnō audîverat) Parcās volvere.

23. Id: the destined supremacy of
Rome and overthrow of Carthage (19–22).
metuēns: modifies **Sāturnia (Iūnō)** and
has **Id** as object. **Sāturnia:** *Saturn's*
daughter, subject of **arcēbat. veteris**
bellī: the Trojan War.

prīma quod ad Troiam prō cārīs gesserat Argīs—
25   *necdum etiam causae īrārum saevīque dolōrēs*
    exciderant animō; manet altā mente repostum
    iūdicium Paridis sprētaeque iniūria formae
    et genus invīsum et raptī Ganymēdis honōrēs:
    hīs accēnsa super iactātōs aequore tōtō

---

accendō, ere, ī, ēnsus inflame, enrage
Argī, ōrum *m.* Argos, a city in Greece, center of the worship of Juno; Greece
cārus, a, um dear, fond, beloved
causa, ae *f.* reason, cause
dolor, ōris *m.* pain, grief, anger, passion
etiam *adv.* besides, also, even
excidō, ere, ī fall from, perish
forma, ae *f.* beauty, shape, form
Ganymēdēs, is *m.* son of Laōmedon, king of Troy; carried off by Jupiter's eagle and made cupbearer to the gods
gerō, ere, gessī, gestus carry (on), wage
iactō (1) toss, buffet

iniūria, ae *f.* wrong, insult, injustice
invīsus, a, um hated, hateful, odious
iūdicium, (i)ī *n.* decision, judgment
necdum *adv.* not yet, nor yet
Paris, idis *m.* Trojan prince, son of Priam, took Helen from her husband Menelaus and thus caused the Trojan War
prō before, for, on behalf of (+ *abl.*)
rapiō, ere, uī, ptus snatch (up), plunder
repōnō, ere, posuī, pos(i)tus put (back, away), store up
saevus, a, um cruel, stern, fierce
spernō, ere, sprēvi, sprētus despise, reject

---

24. prīma: *(as) chief, leader, foremost,* modifies **ea** (understood), which refers to Juno. The goddess had taken a leading part in assisting the Greeks against the Trojans. The reasons for her hatred of the Trojans are given in 27–28. See also Introd. 10. **cārīs Argīs:** Argos, a noted center of the worship of Juno, stands here for all Greece and the Greeks.

25. īrārum: poetic plural; see note on **īrae** (11), and *cf.* App. 243.

26. (ex) animō: abl. of separation; App. 340. **(in) altā mente:** abl. of place where, *in her deep mind,* i.e., *deep in her mind;* App. 319. **repos(i)tum:** the longer form, with its three successive short syllables, could not be used in hexameter verse.

27. iūdicium Paridis: refers to the famous Judgment of Paris. See Introd. 10 for the story. **sprētae formae:** appositional gen. with **iniūria;** App. 281; *the insult to her slighted beauty,* shown by the adverse decision of Paris.

28. genus invīsum: Juno hated the Trojan people, partly because of Paris,

but also because Dardanus, the founder of the Trojans, was the son of Electra and Jupiter, and so a constant reminder of Jupiter's betrayal. **Ganymēdis:** a royal Trojan youth, brother of Priam, was snatched up (**raptī**) by an eagle into heaven; there he was beloved by Jupiter, who made him his cupbearer, instead of giving the task to Juno's daughter, Hebe. Ganymede's story is told in more detail at 5.252–57. Alternatively, **raptī** may be taken as nom., modifying **honōrēs**—the "stolen honors" of Ganymede, i.e., stolen indirectly from Juno, who believes they are owed to her by Jupiter.

29. hīs: abl. of means or cause (App. 331, 332), or abl. with **super;** the first option treats **hīs** as dependent on **accēnsa,** and referring to the three chief causes of Juno's hatred which had just been mentioned in 26–28; **super** thus functions as an adverb, meaning *also, in addition* (i.e., in addition to her fears for Carthage). The second option would mean *angered over these things.* The placement of a preposition after the noun it introduces is

Trōas, reliquiās *Danaum atque* immītis Achillī,   30
arcēbat longē Latiō, *multōsque per* annōs
errābant āctī fātīs maria omnia circum.
Tantae mōlis *erat* Rōmānam condere *gentem.*

Achillēs, is (ī) *m.* Greek leader before Troy
annus, ī *m.* year
arceō, ēre, uī keep off, defend, restrain
condō, ere, didī, ditus found, establish
immītis, e fierce, cruel
Latium, (i)ī *n.* district of central Italy
  around Rome

longē *adv.* far (off), afar
mōlēs, is *f.* mass, burden, difficulty
re(l)liquiae, ārum *f.* rest, remnant(s),
  leaving(s)
Rōmānus, a, um of Rome, Roman
Trōs, Trōis *m.* Trojan

---

called ANASTROPHE. **accēnsa (Iūnō). (in)
aequore tōtō:** abl. of place where; App.
319.

30. Trōās: a Greek form; acc. pl. of
Trōs. rēliquiās: sometimes written with
-ll-, to show that the first syllable is long
and the word is thus able to be used in
hexameter verse. **Dana(ōr)um, Achillī:**
subjective genitives, *the leavings
(remnants) of the Greeks and of Achilles,*
i.e., those Trojans whom the Greeks and
Achilles had allowed to escape.

31. arcēbat: the imperfect of continued
action; App. 351, 2. **(ā) Latiō:** separation;
App. 340. **longē Latiō:** note the repetition
of the letter **l**; such a repetition is called
ALLITERATION. Alliteration, or the recurrence
of the same sounds, usually consonantal, in
successive syllables or words, is found in
all languages, and is a characteristic feature
of early Latin poetry and prose. Vergil's
use of alliteration can sometimes be

explained as a conscious attempt on his
part to recall the style of archaic Latin
verse, especially early Latin epic (although
alliteration by itself should never be over-
interpreted by modern readers; the point is
mainly that it makes the words memorable). It is also a special characteristic of
early Germanic poetry, nearly all Old
English verse being alliterative.

32. (Trōes) errābant. fātīs: abl. of
means. **āctī:** participle of **agō,** modifies the
understood subject **Trōes. maria omnia
circum:** another example of ANASTROPHE; see
above on 29.

33. Tantae mōlis: gen. of quality in
the predicate; App. 285, *a.*; *of so great
effort was it.* This line, summarizing the
preceding lines, forms a powerful and
effective close to this first section of the
Aeneid and serves as a general introduction
to the whole poem.

> *Vix ē* cōnspectū Siculae *tellūris in* altum
> 35   *vēla dabant laetī et* spūmās salis aere *ruēbant,*
> *cum Iūnō* aeternum *servāns sub pectore* vulnus
> *haec sēcum: "Mēne* inceptō dēsistere *victam*
> *nec posse Ītaliā Teucrōrum* āvertere *rēgem!*
> Quippe vetor *fātīs.* Pallasne exūrere *classem*
> 40   Argīvum *atque ipsōs potuit* summergere pontō

Teucrose
I>tkin of Trojans

---

aes, aeris *n.* bronze
aeternus, a, um eternal, everlasting
altum, ī *n.* the deep (sea)
Argīvus, a, um Argive, Greek
āvertō, ere, ī, rsus keep off, turn aside
cōnspectus, ūs *m.* sight, view
dēsistō, ere, stitī, stitus cease (from), desist
exūrō, ere, ussī, ustus burn (up)
inceptum, ī *n.* beginning, undertaking, purpose

Pallas, adis *f.* Minerva, goddess of wisdom and the arts
pontus, ī *m.* sea
quippe truly, indeed, surely, forsooth
sal, salis *n.* (or *m.*) salt (water), sea
Siculus, a, um Sicilian, of Sicily, a large island south of Italy
summergō (subm-), ere, rsī, rsus sink, drown
spūma, ae *f.* foam, froth, spray
vetō, āre, uī, itus forbid, prevent
vulnus, eris *n.* wound, blow

> 34-49. Aeneas and the Trojans set sail from Sicily for Italy, as they hope, happy at the prospect of the end of their wanderings. Juno gives a bitter soliloquy, chafing at the apparent failure of her plans to keep Aeneas and the Trojans from reaching Italy.

34. The reader is now plunged **in mediās rēs:** "into the midst of the action," and is abruptly introduced to Aeneas and his followers sailing away from the coast of Sicily. They have now been wandering for seven years since the destruction of Troy, their native city. These earlier events (the fall of Troy and their seven years of wandering) are later on narrated by Aeneas to Dido (Books 2 and 3).
35. laetī (Trōes): subject of **dabant.**
spūmās salis aere ruēbant: note the ALLITERATION. **salis:** METONYMY for the salt water of the sea. **aere:** the prows of the ships were sheathed with bronze; this too is a METONYMY, for the prows or even the ships themselves.

36-37. Iūnō . . . haec sēcum (dīxit).
36. aeternum vulnus: the causes of this anger have been given above: her fear for Carthage, the Judgment of Paris, her love for the Greeks and hatred of the Trojans. **sub pectore:** *deep in her heart.*
37. sēcum = **cum sē;** App. 321, *a;* **mē:** subject of **dēsistere** and **nec posse. Mēne:** **-ne** is the interrogative particle appended to the pronoun **mē.**
37-38. dēsistere . . . nec posse: infinitives in an exclamatory question: *Am I, beaten, to desist from my undertaking and not to be able?*, etc.; App. 262. **(ab) inceptō:** abl. of separation; App. 340. **victam:** from **vincō;** it modifies **mē.**
38. (ab) Ītaliā: abl. of separation; App. 340. **Teucrōrum:** the Trojans are often referred to as **Teucrī,** a name derived from Teucer, one of the founders of the Trojan people.
39. Quippe vetor: ironical. **fātīs:** abl. of means; App. 331. **-ne = nōnne. Pallas (Athēna):** Minerva.
40. Argīvum: = **Argīvōrum;** App. 37, *d.* **ipsōs:** *(the masters) themselves,* i.e., the

ūnius ob noxam *et* furiās **Aiācis** Oīleī?
Ipsa Iovis rapidum iaculāta *ē* nūbibus *ignem*
disiēcit*que* ratēs ēvertit*que aequora ventīs,*
illum exspīrantem trānsfīxō *pectore flammās*
turbine corripuit scopulō*que* īnfīxit acūtō;   45
ast ego, quae dīvum incēdō *rēgīna Iovisque*
et soror *et coniūnx, ūnā cum gente* tot annōs

---

acūtus, a, um sharp, pointed
Aiāx, ācis *m.* Greek leader, who in the
    sack of Troy had taken Priam's
    daughter, Cassandra, by force from
    the sanctuary of Minerva
annus, ī *m.* year
corripiō, ere, uī, reptus snatch (up)
disiciō, ere, iēcī, iectus scatter, disperse
ēvertō, ere, ī, rsus (over)turn
exspīrō (1) breathe out, exhale
furiae, ārum *f.* madness, rage
iaculor, ārī, ātus hurl, throw
incēdō, ere, cessī, cessus walk (proudly),
    stride

īnfīgō, ere, xī, xus fasten on, impale
noxa, ae *f.* crime, fault, hurt, harm
nūbēs, is *f.* cloud, mist, fog
ob on account of (+ *acc.*)
Oīleus, eī *m.* Greek king, father of Ajax
rapidus, a, um swift, whirling, consum-
    ing
ratis, is *f.* raft, ship
scopulus, ī *m.* rock, cliff, crag
soror, ōris *f.* sister
tot so many
trānsfīgō, ere, xī, xus pierce, transfix
turbō, inis *m.* whirl(wind, pool), storm

Argives, as contrasted with **classem. Ipse**
often means *the master,* the one of most
importance in a situation, as contrasted
with persons or things of less importance.
pontō: abl. of place where; App. 319, or
abl. of means; App. 331.
    41. ūnius Aiācis Oīleī: a whole fleet was
destroyed on account of one man. For the
short -i- in **ūnius** see the note on **illius** (16).
ob noxam et furiās: Ajax, son of Oīleus,
had desecrated the temple of Minerva during
the sack of Troy, when before the very altar
of the sanctuary he had seized Cassandra,
daughter of Priam and priestess of Minerva.
Enraged at such rash irreverence, Minerva
later sank the ship of Ajax and destroyed
him with lightning. **Aiācis Oīleī:** *of Ajax
(son) of Oīleus.* The first letter of **Oīleī** is
a single short syllable; the following -ī- is
a long syllable; and the ending -eī is here
read as one syllable by SYNIZESIS. This Ajax
was less renowned than another Greek hero
of the same name, Ajax, son of Telamon.
    42. Ipsa: *(The goddess, Minerva) in
person.* She was the only divinity, except

Jupiter, who could hurl Jupiter's lightning;
Juno did not have this ability. **Iovis
ignem:** *lightning.*
    43. -que . . . -que: *both . . . and;* POLY-
SYNDETON. **ventīs:** abl. of means.
    44. illum (Aiācem): with emphatic first
position, which contrasts it with the ships
and the sea previously mentioned. **(ex)
pectore:** abl. of separation; App. 340.
    45. turbine: abl. of means; App. 331.
(Pallas) corripuit. scopulō: dat. with
compound verb **īnfīxit,** or abl. of place
where, as **īnfīgō** may take either
construction; App. 298, 319.
    46. ego: with proud self-consciousness
and in contrast with Minerva; **ego** is
usually not expressed unless emphatic.
dīv(ōr)um: App. 37, *d.*
    47. tot annōs: acc. of extent (duration)
of time; App. 314; ten years around Troy,
and now seven more years while the Trojans
wander. **ūnā cum gente = cum Teucrīs.**
Note the pattern adj.+prep.+noun in this
phrase, a pattern very frequent in Vergil
and in Latin poetry generally.

bella gerō. *Et* quisquam *nūmen Iūnōnis* adōrat
49   praetereā *aut* supplex *ārīs* impōnet *honōrem?*" ‖

---

adōrō (1) worship, adore, honor
gerō, ere, gessī, gestus carry (on), wage
impōnō, ere, posuī, positus place on (+
    dat.)

praetereā *adv.* besides, hereafter
quisquam, quaequam, quicquam
    any(one), any(thing)
supplex, icis suppliant, humble

---

48. gerō: of past action continued into
the present; App. 351, 1, *b.* **Et quisquam:**
Juno thinks to herself, "Can any one
hereafter respect me, if I show myself
such a weakling?" Her use of the pronoun
quisquam implies that the answer, if
expressed, would be "no." This figure is
called a RHETORICAL QUESTION; Juno does not
really expect an answer. **Iūnōnis = meum:**
Juno is speaking, but the use of her own
name is more picturesque and effective
than the use of the possessive adjective.

49. supplex: *(as a) suppliant.* **ārīs:** dat.
with compound verb; App. 298.
honōrem: *honor,* i.e., an *offering* which
would honor Juno.

Tālia flammātō *sēcum dea* corde volūtāns   50
nimbōrum *in* patriam, *loca* fēta *furentibus* Austrīs,
Aeoliam *venit. hīc vastō rēx* Aeolus antrō
luctantēs *ventōs* tempestātēs*que* sonōrās
imperiō premit *ac* vinclīs *et* carcere frēnat.
Illī indignantēs *magnō cum* murmure *montis*   55
circum claustra fremunt; celsā sedet Aeolus *arce*
scēptra *tenēns* mollit*que animōs et* temperat *īrās.*

Aeolia, ae *f.* one of the Liparian Islands
near Sicily
Aeolus, ī *m.* god of the winds
antrum, ī *n.* cave, cavern
Auster, trī *m.* (south) wind
carcer, eris *m.* prison, inclosure
celsus, a, um lofty, high, towering
claustrum, ī *n.* bar(rier), bolt
cor, cordis *n.* heart, spirit, feelings
fētus, a, um teeming, prgnant
flammō (1) inflame, kindle
fremō, ere, uī, itus murmur, roar
frēnō (1) curb, check, restrain
indignor, ārī, ātus be angry, chafe

luctor, ārī, ātus wrestle, struggle
molliō, īre, īvī (iī), ītus soothe, tame
murmur, uris *n.* murmur, roar, rumble
nimbus, ī *m.* storm cloud, rainstorm
patria, ae *f.* homeland, country
premō, ere, pressī, pressus (re)press,
control
scēptrum, ī *n.* staff, scepter, power
sedeō, ēre, sēdī, sessus sit
sonōrus, a, um roaring, howling
temperō (1) control, calm, refrain
tempestās, ātis *f.* tempest, storm
vinc(u)lum, ī *n.* bond, chain
volūtō (1) roll, revolve, ponder

50–80. Juno persuades Aeolus,
god of the winds, to send forth a
storm to prevent Aeneas and the
Trojans from reaching Italy.

50. Tālia: used substantively, as object
of **volūtāns;** *such things,* i.e., *such
thoughts.* **(in) flammātō corde:** abl. of
place where; App. 319. **sēcum = cum sē,**
as in 37; App. 321, *a.*
51. patriam; with the first syllable short;
App. 17. **Austrīs:** abl. with **fēta,** literally,
south winds, but often meaning *winds* in
general; App. 433. **fēta furentibus:** note the
ALLITERATION.
51–52. loca . . . Aeoliam: both nouns
in apposition with **patriam. Hīc:** adverb,
here. **(in) vastō antrō:** abl. of place
where; App. 319.

54. vinclīs: the syncopated form of
vinculīs, which because of its central
short syllable can not be used in
hexameter. **imperiō, vinc(u)līs, carcere:**
ablatives of means; App. 331. The two
nouns may be understood as a true pair,
or may be translated as an example of
HENDIADYS: "by means of the restraints of
their prison"; App. 425. **frēnat:** a picture
drawn from managing spirited horses, as
in 63, **premere et dare laxās habēnās.**
55. magnō cum murmure montis:
ALLITERATION **(m)** and ONOMATOPOEIA;
murmure is abl. of manner; App. 328.
56. (in) celsā arce: abl. of place,
apparently a lofty seat within the cave or
just outside on a mountain top.
57. scēptra: for the use of the poetic
plural see the note on **īrae (11). animōs
(ventōrum) et īrās (ventōrum).**

nī *faciat, maria ac terrās caelumque* profundum
quippe *ferant* rapidi *sēcum* verrant*que per aurās;*
60   *sed pater* omnipotēns spēluncīs abdidit *ātrīs*
hoc metuēns mōlem*que et montēs* īnsuper *altōs*
imposuit, *rēgemque dedit quī* foedere certō
et premere *et* laxās scīret *dare iussus* habēnās. *Cult, name*
Ad quem tum Iūnō supplex *hīs vōcibus* ūsa est:
65   "Aeole (*namque tibī dīvum pater atque* hominum *rēx*
et mulcēre *dedit flūctūs et tollere ventō),*

---

abdō, ere, didī, ditus put away, hide
Aeolus, ī *m.* god of the winds
certus, a, um fixed, sure
foedus, eris *n.* agreement, condition, treaty
habēna, ae *f.* rein
homō, inis *m. (f.)* man, mortal, human
impōnō, ere, posuī, positus place upon
īnsuper *adv.* above, besides
laxus, a, um loose, free, lax
metuō, ere, uī fear, dread
mōlēs, is *f.* mass, burden, structure
mulceō, ēre, lsī, lsus calm, soothe
nī, nisi if not, unless

omnipotēns, entis almighty, all-powerful
premō, ere, pressī, pressus (re)press,
   control
profundus, a, um deep, high, vast
quippe indeed, surely, forsooth
rapidus, a, um swift, whirling, consuming
sciō, īre, īvī (iī), ītus know (how),
   understand
spēlunca, ae *f.* cave, cavern
supplex, icis suppliant, humble
ūtor, ī, ūsus use, employ (+ *abl.*)
verrō, ere, ī, versus sweep

**58. nī (Aeolus id) faciat = nī
molliat (eōrum); faciat** is pres.
subjunctive in a pres. contrary-to-fact
condition (as opposed to the more usual
impf. subjunctive); the result is a far more
vivid scene; App. 382, c.
   59. (ventī) rapidī: *the winds in their
madness.* **sēcum = cum sē;** App. 321, *a.*
**ferant, verrant (maria ac terrās
caelumque profundum).** Both pres.
subjunctives continue the condition
begun in 58, **ni faciat.**
   **60. pater omnipotēns: Iuppiter. (in)
spēluncīs ātrīs = antrō** (52), abl. of place
where; App. 319. **abdidit (illōs ventōs).**
   61. hoc: obj. of **metuēns. mōlem et
montēs:** ALLITERATION. This is an example
of HENDIADYS (a pair of nouns translated as
a single idea).

**62. rēgem (Aeolum) dedit (ventīs).
foedere certō:** abl. of manner or of
means; App. 328, 331.
   63. premere: object of **scīret,** *would
know (how) to grasp tightly,* so as to draw
in the reins. For the figure of horsemanship
see the note on **frēnat** (54). **scīret,** rel.
clause of purpose or characteristic; App.
388, 389. **dare:** also obj. of **scīret. iussus**
(ā Iove): *(when) ordered (by Jupiter).*
   64. hīs vōcibus: abl. with **ūtor;** App.
342.
   65. Aeole: voc. **dīv(ōr)um pater
atque hominum rēx: Iuppiter. tibī:** for
the length of the final -i, see the note on
mihi (8).
   66. mulcēre, tollere (flūctūs):
infinitives used as objects of **dedit,** *has
granted.* **ventō:** abl. of means; App. 331.

*Juno, acting like a beggar,
uses those words to him*

gēns inimīca *mihī* Tyrrhēnum nāvigat *aequor*
Īlium *in Ītaliam* portāns *victōsque* penātēs:
incute *vim ventīs* submersās*que* obrue *puppēs,*
aut age dīversōs *et* dissice *corpora* pontō.   70
Sunt mihi bis septem praestantī *corpore* Nymphae,
quārum quae formā pulcherrima Dēiopēa,

---

bis twice
Dēiopēa, ae *f.* a nymph
dis(s)iciō, ere, iēcī, iectus scatter,
    disperse
dīversus, a, um scattered, diverse
forma, ae *f.* beauty, shape, form
Īlium, (i)ī *n.* Ilium, Troy, a city of Asia
    Minor
incutiō, ere, cussī, cussus strike (into)
    (+ *dat.*)
inimīcus, a, um hostile, unfriendly
nāvigō (1) sail, navigate
Nympha, ae *f.* nymph, one of the minor
    divinities of nature represented as

beautiful maidens dwelling in the
    forests, streams, meadows, mountains,
    etc.
obruō, ere, uī, utus overwhelm, crush
penātēs, ium *m.* household gods
pontus, ī *m.* sea
portō (1) carry, bear, bring
praestāns, antis surpassing, excellent
septem seven
summergō (subm-), ere, rsī, rsus sink
Tyrrhēnus, a, um Tyrrhenian, of Etruria,
    a district of northwestern Italy

---

67. gēns inimīca mihī: i.e., *Teucrī.*
Tyrrhēnum aequor: that part of the
Mediterranean west of Italy, east of
Corsica and Sardinia, and north of Sicily.
**68. Īlium . . . portāns victōsque
penātēs:** see note on **īnferret deōs (6).**
They were *bearing Ilium* in their plan to
found a new city, which was to continue
the people and the customs of the Īlium
(Troy) which had been destroyed. The
worship of the penates, household gods at
Rome, was an essential part of Roman
daily life, and was seen as a link to the
Romans' Trojan past. **victōs:** *defeated* by
the Greeks in the Trojan War.
69. incute: imp. **vim ventīs:** ALLITERA-
TION; App. 411. **ventīs:** dat. with a
compound; App. 298. **summersās obrue
puppēs:** *overwhelm the sunken ships,* i.e.,
sink and overwhelm the ships, a good
example of the figure known as PROLEPSIS,
or *anticipation.*

70. age: imp. **dīversōs (Teucrōs):** i.e.,
drive the Trojans in different directions and
scatter their corpses over the sea; another
example of PROLEPSIS. **dissice:** usually written
with one -s-; the doubled consonant here
gives Juno's words an extra hissing sound,
perhaps not coincidentally. **pontō:** abl. of
place where; App. 319.
71. mihi: dat. of possession; App. 299.
bis septem: *twice seven;* more poetic than
to say simply *fourteen.* **praestantī
corpore:** abl. of quality; App. 330.
72. formā: abl. of respect; App. 325;
dependent on **pulcherrima. Dēiopēa:**
nom. by attraction into the case of the
relative pronoun, **quae;** the accusative
would be expected, as object of **iungam;**
App. 242, *a.* **quārum:** use the English
demonstrative in translation, and read
accordingly: **Dēiopēam, quae (est)
eārum (nymphārum) pulcherrima
formā, iungam (tibi) stabilī cōnūbīo et
(eam) dicābō (tuam) propriam.**

cōnūbiō iungam stabilī propriam*que* dicābō,
omnēs ut tēcum meritīs prō *tālibus* annōs
75   exigat *et* pulchrā *faciat tē* prōle *parentem.*"
Aeolus *haec* contrā: "*Tuus, Ō rēgīna, quid* optēs
explōrāre *labor; mihi* iussa capessere fās *est.*
Tū mihi quodcumque *hoc rēgnī, tū* scēptra *Iovemque*
conciliās, *tū dās* epulīs accumbere *dīvum*
80   nimbōrum*que facis* tempestātum*que* potentem."

---

accumbō, ere, cubuī, cubitus recline (at) (+ *dat.*)
Aeolus, ī *m.* god of the winds
annus, ī *m.* year
capessō, ere, īvī, ītus (under)take, perform
conciliō (1) win over, unite
contra opposite, against, in reply (+ *acc.*)
cōnūbium, (i)ī *n.* marriage, wedlock
dicō (1) consecrate, dedicate
epulae, ārum *f.* banquet, feast
exigō, ere, ēgī, āctus complete, pass
explōrō (1) examine, search out
fās *n. indecl.* right, divine law, duty
iungō, ere, iūnxī, iūnctus join, yoke, unite

iussum, ī *n.* command, order
meritum, ī *n.* desert, merit
nimbus, ī *m.* storm cloud, rainstorm
optō (1) desire, choose, hope (for)
potēns, entis powerful, ruling (+ *gen.*)
prō before, for (+ *abl.*)
prōlēs, is *f.* offspring, progeny
proprius, a, um one's own, permanent
pulcher, chra, chrum beautiful, handsome, illustrious
quīcumque, quaecumque, quodcumque whoever, whatever
scēptrum, ī *n.* staff, scepter, power
stabilis, e firm, lasting, stable
tempestās, ātis *f.* tempest, storm; time

---

73. cōnūbiō: *in wedlock,* abl. of place where or means; App. 319, 331. **cōnūbiō** is either trisyllabic by SYNIZESIS, and pronounced as though written cōnūbyō (i.e., consonantal -i-), or quadrisyllabic, with the variable syllable -nub- scanned as short. **iungam (tibi) dicābō (eam) propriam:** *I shall dedicate her (Deiopea) to you (as) your very own.* Juno was goddess of marriage. **propriam:** with the first syllable short; App. 17.

74. tēcum = cum tē; App. 321, *a.*

75. prōle: abl. of quality; App. 330, or means; App. 331. **pulchrā prōle parentem:** ALLITERATION. **exigat, faciat:** subjunctives of result or purpose; App. 364, 388. **parentem** = patrem.

76. haec (dīxit). optēs: indir. quest.; App. 349. **Tuus (est) labor:** *yours (is) the task.* Aeolus thus absolves himself from responsibility, if his obedience to Juno gets him into trouble.

77. mihi: dat. of reference; App. 301. **iussa (tua).**

78. quodcumque hoc (est) rēgnī: *whatever this is (in the way) of a kingdom,* an expression of modesty. **rēgnī:** part. gen. with **quodcumque**; App. 286. **Tū:** always emphatic, and an example of ANAPHORA, the repetition of a single word at the beginning of successive clauses or phrases.

79. conciliās: this one verb should be translated twice, first with its obj. **quodcumque hoc regni** ("win for") and then with its objects **sceptra Iovemque** ("win over"). **epulīs:** dat. with compound; App. 298. The ancient Romans regularly reclined at meals. **dīv(ōr)um:** App. 37, *d.* **accumbere:** infinitive used as object of **dās,** *you grant (me) the privilege of reclining.* As one of the lesser gods, Aeolus was dependent upon the favor of the more powerful divinities.

80. facis (mē) potentem nimbōrum tempestātumque.

Haec ubi dicta, cavum conversā cuspide *montem*
impulit *in* latus; *ac ventī* velut *agmine factō,*
quā *data* porta, *ruunt et terrās* turbine perflant.
Incubuēre *marī tōtumque ā sēdibus īmīs*
ūnā Eurus*que* Notus*que ruunt* crēber*que* procellīs   85
Āfricus, *et vastōs volvunt ad lītora flūctūs.*
Īnsequitur *clāmorque virum* strīdor*que* rudentum;
ēripiunt subitō nūbēs *caelumque diemque*

Āfricus, ī *m.* (southwest) wind
cavus, a, um hollow, vaulted
convertō, ere, ī, rsus turn (around),
    reverse
crēber, bra, brum frequent, crowded
cuspis, idis *f.* point, spear
Eurus, ī *m.* (east) wind
impellō, ere, pulī, pulsus drive, strike
    (against)
incumbō, ere, cubuī, cubitus lie upon,
    brood over (+ *dat.*)
īnsequor, ī, secūtus follow, pursue
latus, eris *n.* side, flank

Notus, ī *m.* (south) wind
nūbēs, is *f.* cloud, fog, mist
perflō (1) blow (over, through)
porta, ae *f.* gate, door, opening
procella, ae *f.* blast, gust
quā *adv.* where, in any way
rudēns, entis *m.* rope, cable
strīdor, ōris *m.* creaking, grating,
    whirring
subitō *adv.* suddenly
turbō, inis *m.* whirl(wind, pool), storm
ūnā *adv.* together, at the same time
velut(ī) (even) as, just as

81–123. A storm wrecks some of
the Trojan ships and scatters the rest.
The entire scene is indebted to the
description of a storm at sea given
by Homer in *Odyssey* 5.

81. ubi haec dicta (sunt ab Aeolō).
cavum conversa cuspide: observe the
ALLITERATION.
82. impulit: Aeolus thus opens the
barriers and lets out the winds. **agmine**
factō: abl. abs.; App. 343; a SIMILE (**velut**)
drawn from the imagery of military life.
83. Observe the ALLITERATION: every
word but one in this line contains a **t**.
data (est). turbine: abl. of manner; App.
328; or means.

84. Incubuēre = incubuērunt, from
incumbō. The perfect, after a series of
presents, denotes rapid or instantaneous
action; *they have fallen upon the sea.*
marī: dat. with compound; App. 298.
tōtum (mare): obj. of **ruunt,** 85.
85. ruunt: *overturn.* **Eurus, Notus,**
Āfricus: all the winds blow at once, and
in their struggles produce a mighty storm.
procellīs: abl. of respect or means with
crēber; App. 325, 331. **-que, -que, -que:**
POLYSYNDETON; App. 439.
86. vastōs volvunt: ALLITERATION,
employed very effectively here to evoke
the noise of the storm.
87. vir(ōr)um: Aeneas and the other
Trojans. **-que, -que:** POLYSYNDETON.
88. diem = lūcem diēī; alternatively,
caelumque diemque may be construed as
an instance of HENDIADYS, = **caelum diei.**
-que, -que: POLYSYNDETON.

Teucrōrum ex oculīs; pontō *nox* incubat *ātra;*
90   intonuēre polī *et* crēbrīs micat *ignibus* aethēr
   praesentem*que virīs* intentant *omnia mortem.*
   Extemplō *Aenēae* solvuntur frigore membra;
   ingemit *et* duplicēs *tendēns ad sīdera* palmās
   tālia vōce refert: "Ō ter*que* quater*que* beātī,
95   *quīs ante ōra patrum Troiae sub moenibus altīs*
   contigit oppetere! Ō *Danaum* fortissime *gentis*
   Tȳdīdē! *Mēne* Īliacis occumbere *campīs*

---

aethēr, eris *m.* upper air, sky, ether
beātus, a, um happy, blessed
contingō, ere, tigī, tāctus touch, befall
crēber, bra, brum frequent, crowded
duplex, icis double, both
extemplō *adv.* immediately, straightaway
fortis, e strong, brave, valiant
frīgus, oris *n.* cold, chill
Īliacus, a, um of Ilium, Trojan
incubō, āre, uī (āvī), itus (ātus) lie
   upon, brood over (+ *dat.*)
ingemō, ere, uī groan
intentō (1) threaten, aim
intonō, āre, uī thunder, roar
membrum, ī *n.* limb, member, part
micō, āre, uī quiver, flash

occumbō, ere, cubuī, cubitus fall (in
   death)
oppetō, ere, īvī (iī), ītus encounter, meet
   (death)
palma, ae *f.* palm, hand
polus, ī *m.* pole, sky, heaven
pontus, ī *m.* sea
praesēns, entis present, instant
quater four times
solvō, ere, ī, solūtus relax, loose(n)
ter thrice, three times
Tȳdīdēs, ae *m.* son of Tydeus, Diomedes,
   who fought against Aeneas in single
   combat before Troy and would have
   killed him had Venus not spirited her
   son away

---

89. pontō: dat. with compound; App. 298.

90. Intonuēre = intonuērunt; App. 204, 4. **ignibus (Iovis):** *lightning,* abl. of means or manner; App. 328, 331.

91. virīs = Teucrīs; dat. of reference; App. 301. **omnia:** used substantively, *all things,* as subj. of **intentant.** The terror that comes over the Trojans is all-encompassing.

92. frīgore: *chilly fear;* the ancient heroes were not ashamed to display their emotions, and often gave way to terror or grief, weeping copiously on occasion.

93. duplicēs palmās: In prayer the ancient Greeks and Romans extended their hands with the palms upward, ready to accept the gods' blessing.

94. tālia (dicta). beātī (vōs): voc.

95. quīs ante ōra patrum (vestrum) sub moenia Troiae contigit oppetere

(mortem). **quīs = quibus;** App. 109, *c*; observe the quantity of the -i-; dat. with **contigit;** App. 298. **ante ōra:** where their kinsmen and friends might witness their glorious deeds and death and would bury their bodies, thus giving rest to their souls; for the souls of the unburied must wander restlessly after death.

96. oppetere (mortem): subject of **contigit. Dana(ōr)um:** App. 37, *d.*

97. Mē: subj. of **potuisse. Mēne potuisse:** *could I not,* etc. inf. in an exclamatory question; App. 262. The construction, opening as it does with **Mēne,** recalls Juno's rhetorical question at 37. **Tȳdīde:** Greek voc.: the final **-e** is long. Aeneas engaged in a disastrous duel at Troy with Diomedes and barely escaped with his life, being rescued by his mother, the goddess Venus. **(in) campīs:**

nōn potuisse tuāque animam hanc effundere *dextrā,*
saevus *ubi* Aeacidae *tēlō* iacet Hector, *ubi ingēns*
Sarpēdōn, *ubi* tot Simoīs correpta *sub undīs*   100
scūta *virum* galeās*que et* fortia *corpora volvit!"*
    Tālia iactantī strīdēns Aquilōne procella
vēlum adversa ferit, *flūctūsque ad sīdera tollit.*
Franguntur *rēmī, tum* prōra āvertit *et undīs*
dat latus, īnsequitur cumulō praeruptus aquae *mōns.*   105
Hī summō in flūctū pendent; *hīs unda* dehīscēns

---

adversus, a, um opposite, in front
Aeacidēs, ae *m.* descendant of Aeacus,
    Achilles, Greek chieftain
aqua, ae *f.* water
Aquilō, ōnis *m.* (north) wind
āvertō, ere, ī, rsus turn away, avert
corripiō, ere, uī, reptus snatch (up)
cumulus, ī *m.* heap, mass
dehīscō, ere, hīvī gape, split, open
effundō, ere, fūdī, fūsus pour out
feriō, īre strike, beat
fortis, e strong, brave, valiant
frangō, ere, frēgī, frāctus break, shatter
galea, ae *f.* helmet
Hector, oris *m.* leader of the Trojans

īnsequor, ī, secūtus follow, pursue
iaceō, ēre, uī, itus lie (low, outspread)
iactō (1) toss, buffet; utter
latus, eris *n.* side, flank
pendeō, ēre, pependī hang
praeruptus, a, um steep, towering
procella, ae *f.* blast, gale
prōra, ae *f.* prow
saevus, a, um fierce, cruel, stern
Sarpēdōn, onis *m.* king of Lydia, ally of
    the Trojans
scūtum, ī *n.* shield
Simoīs, entis *m.* river near Troy
strīd(e)ō, ēre, dī creak, rustle, roar
tot so many

---

abl. of place where; App. 319.
occumbere (mortī): complementary
infin. with **potuisse**, as is also **effundere**
in 98.
    **98. hanc = meam. (tuā) dextrā
(manū):** abl. of means; App. 331.
    99. tēlō: construe as if with **ictus** *(slain
by the spear)* as abl. of means, or with
iacet *(lies dead because of the spear)* as
abl. of cause; App. 331, 332. Observe the
emphasis obtained by ANAPHORA of **ubi**;
App. 413.
    100. Sarpēdōn (iacet): an ally of the
Trojans, and son of Jupiter. Cf. the
reference to his death made in conversation between Hercules and Jupiter at
10.470–71. **Simoīs . . . volvit.**
    101. vir(ōr)um. correpta sub undīs:
goes with **scūta** and **galeās** as well as with
corpora and refers to the corpses and

armor of slain warriors swept along by
(under) the water.
    102. (Aenēae) iactantī: dat. of
reference; App. 301. **Tālia (dicta):** obj.
of **iactantī. Aquilōne:** abl. of means;
App. 331.
    103. ferit: from **feriō;** not to be
confused with the verb **ferō. adversa
(procella). ad sīdera:** such exaggerated
language is called HYPERBOLE.
    104. rēmī: the ancient ship used both
oars and sails. **prōra (sē) āvertit et undīs
dat latus (nāvis).**
    105. cumulō: abl. of manner; App.
328. **mōns:** more HYPERBOLE; note the
smashing effect of the monosyllable at the
end of the line.
    106. Hī (virī). hīs (virīs): dat. of
reference; App. 301. **hī . . . hīs:** *these . . .
for those; some . . . for others,* referring to
the crews of different ships; ANAPHORA.

terram inter flūctūs aperit, furit aestus harēnīs.
Trēs Notus abreptās *in saxa* latentia torquet
(*saxa vocant* Italī *mediīs quae in flūctibus* Ārās,
110   dorsum *immāne marī summō*), trēs Eurus *ab* altō
in brevia *et* syrtēs urget, miserābile *vīsū*,
inlīdit*que* vadīs *atque* aggere cingit harēnae.
Ūnam, quae Lyciōs fīdum*que* vehēbat Orontēn,
ipsius ante oculōs ingēns ā vertice pontus

---

abripiō, ere, uī, reptus carry off,
    snatch away
aestus, ūs *m.* boiling (surge), tide
agger, eris *m.* mound, wall, bank
altum, ī *n.* the deep (sea)
aperiō, īre, uī, ertus open, disclose
Ārae, ārum *f.* the Altars, a ledge of rocks
    between Sicily and Africa
brevis, e short, shallow
cingō, ere, cīnxī, cīnctus gird(le),
    encircle
dorsum, ī *n.* back, ridge, reef
Eurus, ī *m.* (east) wind
fīdus, a, um faithful, trustworthy
harēna, ae *f.* sand, beach
inlīdō, ere, sī, sus dash against (into)
    (+ *dat.*)

Italus, a, um Italian
lateō, ēre, ūi lie hid, hide, lurk
Lycius, a, um Lycian, of Lycia, a
    country of Asia Minor
miserābilis, e pitiable, wretched
Notus, ī *m.* (south) wind
Orontēs, is (ī) *m.* comrade of Aeneas
pontus, ī *m.* sea
syrtis, is *f.* sand bar, reef
torqueō, ēre, rsī, rtus turn, twist, whirl
trēs, tria three
urgeō, ēre, ursī drive, force, press
vadum, ī *n.* shallow, shoal, depth(s)
vehō, ere, vēxī, vectus carry, convey
vertex, icis *m.* peak, summit, head, top;
    whirlpool

---

107. terram: *the bottom* (of the sea);
the HYPERBOLE is continued. **harēnīs:** *with
the sands*, abl. of means; App. 331.

108–9. Trēs (nāvēs) abreptās: obj. of
torquet. saxa . . . saxa: ANAPHORA. **mediīs
in flūctibus:** *in the middle (of the) waves*;
App. 246. **quae saxa Italī vocant Ārās:**
quae is a rel. adj. agreeing with **saxa;
saxa** is obj. of **vocant,** and **Ārās** is
predicate acc. **Ārās:** *the Altars*, the
Roman name for a ledge of rocks off the
African coast, just outside the harbor of
ancient Carthage.

110. (in) marī summō: *at the surface
of the sea*; abl. of place where; App. 319,
246. **dorsum:** apposition with **saxa. trēs
(nāvēs):** obj. of **urget.**

111. miserābile vīsū: *piteous to
behold;* **miserābile** is a neuter adj.
modifying the idea expressed in the
preceding sentence, while **vīsū** is the
supine of **video** and an abl. of respect;
App. 325.

112. vadīs = in vada, understand
either as dat. of direction, sometimes used
instead of the acc. of place to which; App.
306, or as dat. with a compound verb;
App. 298.

113. Ūnam (nāvem). Orontēn: acc., a
Greek form.

114. ipsius (Aeneāe): *of the master*, a
common use of **ipse.** Compare **ipsa (42)**
and **ipsōs (40).** Note the shortening of -i-
in the -ius gen. ending of this adj., and
see the note on **illius (16). ā vertice:** *from
high above.* **ferit:** from **feriō.**

in puppim ferit: excutitur prōnus*que* magister   115
volvitur in caput, ast illam ter *flūctus* ibīdem
torquet *agēns circum et* rapidus vorat *aequore* vertex.
Appārent rārī nantēs *in* gurgite *vastō*,
arma virum tabulae*que et* Trōia gaza *per undās.*
Iam validam Īlioneī *nāvem, iam* fortis Achātae,   120
et quā vectus Abās, *et quā* grandaevus Alētēs,
vīcit hiems; laxīs laterum compāgibus *omnēs*
accipiunt inimīcum imbrem rīmīs*que* fatīscunt.

Abās, antis *m.* Trojan leader
Achātēs, ae *m.* faithful comrade of
     Aeneas
Alētēs, ae *m.* Trojan leader
appāreō, ēre, uī, itus appear
compāgēs, is *f.* joint, seam, fastening
excutiō, ere, cussī, cussus cast out, shake
     off
fatīscō, ere split, open, gape
feriō, īre strike, beat
fortis, e brave, strong, valiant
gaza, ae *f.* treasure, wealth
grandaevus, a, um aged, old
gurges, itis *m.* abyss, gulf, whirlpool
hiems, emis *f.* winter, storm
ibīdem *adv.* in the same place
Īlioneus, eī *m.* Trojan leader
imber, bris *m.* rain, flood, water
inimīcus, a, um hostile, unfriendly

latus, eris *n.* side, flank
laxus, a, um loose, open, lax
magister, trī *m.* master, pilot
nō (1) swim, float
prōnus, a, um leaning forward, headlong
rapidus, a, um swift, whirling,
     consuming
rārus, a, um scattered, far apart
rīma, ae *f.* crack, fissure
tabula, ae *f.* plank, board
ter three times, thrice
torqueō, ēre, rsī, rtus turn, twist, whirl
Trōius, a, um Trojan, of Troy
validus, a, um strong, stout, mighty
vehō, ere, vēxī, vectus carry, convey
vertex, icis *m.* top, summit; whirlpool
vorō (1) swallow (up)

---

115. in: *upon.* **excutitur (ē nāvī).**
116. in caput: *headlong.* **illam
(nāvem):** contrasted with the helmsman
(magister).
117. (in) aequore: abl. of place where;
App. 319.
118. nantēs: pres. part. of **nō,**
modifying **rārī (virī), arma, tabulae,**
and **gaza,** but agreeing with the nearest
word, **rārī (virī),** *men here and there;*
App. 238.
119. vir(ōr)um. arma: such as
wooden shields and leather helmets made

of light and buoyant material. **gaza:** the
first syllable is long by position; App. 15.
120. Īlioneī: gen., with the final **eī**
pronounced as one syllable by SYNIZESIS.
(nāvem) fortis Achātae. Iam . . . iam:
ANAPHORA.
**121. et (nāvem) quā vectus (est)
Abās, et (nāvem) quā (vectus est)
Alētēs. et quā . . . et quā:** ANAPHORA.
122. laxīs compāgibus: abl. of means
or instrument, or abl. abs. **omnēs (nāvēs).**
123. rīmīs: abl. of means or manner;
App. 328, 331. Cf. 83, 105. **imbrem =
aquam maris.**

Intereā *magnō* miscērī murmure pontum
125   ēmissam*que* hiemem sēnsit Neptūnus *et īmīs*
stāgna refūsa vadīs, graviter commōtus, *et* altō
prōspiciēns *summā* placidum *caput* extulit *undā*.
Disiectam *Aenēae tōtō videt aequore classem,*
flūctibus oppressōs Trōas *caelīque* ruīnā;
130   *Nec* latuēre dolī frātrem Iūnōnis *et īrae.*
Eurum *ad sē* Zephyrum*que vocat*, dehinc *tālia fātur:*
"*Tantane vōs generis tenuit* fīdūcia vestrī?
Iam caelum terramque meō sine *nūmine, ventī,*

---

altum, ī *n.* the deep (sea)
commoveō, ēre, mōvī, mōtus move,
    disturb
dehinc *adv.* then, thereupon
disiciō, ere, iēcī, iectus scatter, disperse
dolus, ī *m.* deceit, wiles, trick, fraud
efferō, ferre, extulī, ēlātus raise, lift
    (up)
ēmittō, ere, mīsī, missus send forth
fīdūcia, ae *f.* confidence, trust
frāter, tris *m.* brother
graviter *adv.* heavily, violently, greatly
hiems, hiemis, *f.* winter, storm
intereā *adv.* meanwhile, meantime
lateō, ēre, uī lie hid, escape the notice (of)
misceō, ēre, uī, mixtus mix, confuse, stir
murmur, uris *n.* murmur, roar, rumble

Neptūnus, ī *m.* Neptune, god of the sea
opprimō, ere, pressī, pressus overwhelm,
    crush
placidus, a, um calm, quiet, peaceful
pontus, ī, *m.* sea
prōspiciō, ere, spexī, spectus look out (on),
    see
refundō, ere, fūdī, fūsus pour back
ruīna, ae *f.* downfall, ruin
sentiō, īre, sēnsī, sēnsus feel, perceive
sine without (+ *abl.*)
stāgnum, ī *n.* still waters, depth
Trōs, Trōis *m.* Trojan
vadum, ī *n.* shallow, shoal, depth(s)
vester, tra, trum your(s), your own
Zephyrus, ī *m.* (west) wind

124–56. Neptune, god of the sea,
intervenes; he rebukes the winds and
calms the sea.

124. magnō miscērī murmure:
ALLITERATION (**m**) and ONOMATOPOEIA.
murmure: abl. of attendant circumstance
or manner; App. 329, 328.
    125. ēmissam (esse).
    126. refūsa (esse). vadīs: either abl. of
separation; App. 340, or dat. of direction;
App. 306. The ambiguity of construction
may well be meant to reflect the confused
movement of the water back and forth. (in)
altō: *over the sea*; abl. of place where; App.
319. commōtus (animō): although disturbed
in spirit as a god he maintains an outward
calm (**placidum caput** of 127).

127. (ex) undā: abl. of separation;
App. 340; *from the crest of the wave;*
App. 246.
    128. (in) tōtō aequore: abl. of place
where; App. 319.
    129. Trōas: acc. pl., a Greek form. (et
videt) Trōas oppressōs (esse). caelī
ruīnā: HYPERBOLE.
    130. latuēre = latuērunt; App. 204, 4.
frātrem: Neptune was Juno's brother,
and he knew her tricky nature (**dolī**) and
her ugly temper (**īrae**).
    131. dehinc: one syllable by SYNIZESIS.
tālia (dicta).
    132. generis fīdūcia vestrī: this verse
is sarcastic; the winds were of divine
origin, being descended from Aurora,
goddess of the dawn, and from Astraeus,
a Titan rival of the gods. **caelum
terramque:** HYPERBOLE.

miscēre *et tantās* audētis *tollere* mōlēs?

Quōs ego–sed mōtōs praestat compōnere *fluctūs.*   135

Post *mihi nōn similī poenā* commissa *luētis.*

Mātūrāte *fugam rēgīque haec dīcite* vestrō:

nōn illī imperium pelagī saevum*que* tridentem,

sed mihi sorte *datum. Tenet ille immānia saxa,*

vestrās, Eure, *domōs; illā sē* iactet *in* aulā   140

Aeolus *et* clausō *ventōrum* carcere rēgnet."

Sīc ait, et dictō citius tumida *aequora* plācat

collēctās*que* fugat nūbēs sōlem*que* redūcit.

Aeolus, ī *m.* god of the winds
audeō, ēre, ausus sum dare, venture
aula, ae *f.* court, hall
carcer, eris *m.* prison, inclosure
citō *adv.* quickly, soon
claudō, ere, sī, sus (en)close, hem in
colligō, ere, lēgī, lēctus collect, gather
commissum, ī *n.* fault, crime
compōnō, ere, posuī, pos(i)tus compose,
    construct, calm, quiet
fugō (1) put to flight, rout
iactō (1) toss, buffet, vaunt
luō, ere, ī atone for
mātūrō (1) hasten, speed; ripen
misceō, ēre, uī, mixtus mix, confuse, stir (up)
mōlēs, is *f.* mass, burden, heap

nūbēs, is *f.* cloud, mist, fog
plācō (1) calm, quiet
post *adv.* afterward; *prep. + acc.* after,
    behind
praestō, āre, stitī, stitus surpass, be better
redūcō, ere, dūxī, ductus lead back,
    bring back
rēgnō (1) rule, reign
saevus, a, um fierce, cruel, stern
similis, e like similar
sōl, sōlis *m.* sun, day
sors, rtis *f.* lot, fate, destiny
tridēns, entis *m.* trident, symbol of
    Neptune as god of the sea
tumidus, a, um swelling, swollen
vester, tra, trum your(s), your own

---

134. miscēre, tollere: depend on
audētis, as complementary inf.; App. 259.

135. Quōs = Vōs. Quōs ego—: a good
and famous example of APOSIOPESIS; i.e.,
instead of completing his sentence, the
speaker breaks off abruptly and leaves to
the imagination, as being beyond the power
of adequate expression in words, just what
sort of dire punishment he may inflict upon
the guilty winds; **Quōs** is thus the object
and **ego** the subject of the unexpressed verb.

136. nōn similī poenā: abl. of means;
App. 331; *by no similar punishment,* i.e.,
by a much greater one; this figure of
speech is called LITOTES.

137. rēgī vestrō = Aeolō.

138. illī: dat. of indir. obj. in emphatic
position contrasted with **mihi** in the same

position in the following line. **tridentem:**
subject of **datum (esse),** an inf. in indir.
disc., dependent on **dīcite,** in 137.

139. sorte: when Saturn was over-
thrown, the three gods, Jupiter, Neptune,
and Pluto, divided his dominion among
them by lot, Jupiter receiving the dominion
of heaven, Neptune of the sea, and Pluto of
the realm of the dead in the lower world.

140. vestrās: referring to all the winds,
although Neptune is directly addressing
Eurus only.

140–41. illā, clausō: emphatic by
position. **iactet, rēgnet:** volitive or jussive
subjunctives; App. 254. **(in) clausō
carcere:** abl. of place where; App. 319.

142. ait: third sing. of aiō. **dictō:** abl.
with comp.; App. 327.

Cȳmothoē *simul et* Tritōn adnixus acūtō
145 dētrūdunt *nāvēs* scopulō; levat *ipse* tridentī
et vastās aperit syrtēs *et* temperat *aequor*
atque rotīs *summās* levibus perlābitur *undās.*
Ac velutī *magnō in* populō *cum* saepe coörta *est*
sēditiō saevit*que animīs* ignōbile vulgus
150 *iamque* facēs *et saxa* volant, furor *arma* ministrat;
tum, pietāte gravem *ac* meritīs *sī forte virum quem*
cōnspexēre, silent arrēctīs*que* auribus astant;

[handwritten: Next; fying saw of stars men and]

---

acūtus, a, um sharp, pointed, keen
adnītor, ī, sus (nixus) strive, lean against
aperiō, īre, uī, ertus open, disclose
arrigō, ere, rēxī, rēctus raise, prick up
a(d)stō, āre, stitī stand (near, by)
auris, is *f.* ear
cōnspiciō, ere, spexī, spectus see, behold
coörior, īrī, ortus (a)rise
Cȳmothoē, ēs *f.* a sea nymph
dētrūdō, ere, sī, sus push off, dislodge
fax, facis *f.* firebrand, torch
furor, ōris *m.* madness, frenzy, rage
gravis, e heavy, weighty; venerable
ignōbilis, e inglorious, common
levis, e light, swift
levō (1) lift, raise
meritum, ī *n.* desert, service, merit
ministrō (1) tend, serve, supply

perlābor, ī, lāpsus glide over *[handwritten: because]*
pietās, ātis *f.* loyalty, devotion, duty *[handwritten: of hi]*
populus, ī *m.* people, nation, crowd
rota, ae *f.* wheel; chariot *[handwritten: service]*
saepe *adv.* often
saeviō, īre, īvī (iī), ītus rage, be fierce *[handwritten: of an]*
scopulus, ī *m.* rock, cliff, crag
sēditiō, ōnis *f.* riot, strife *[handwritten: they are]*
sileō, ēre, uī be silent, be still *[handwritten: silently]*
syrtis, i *f.* sand bar, reef
temperō (1) calm, control *[handwritten: listen]*
tridēns, entis *m.* trident, symbol of *[handwritten: intently]*
  Neptune
Trītōn, onis *m.* Triton, a minor sea-god *[handwritten: with]*
velut(ī) as, just as
volō (1) fly, speed *[handwritten: their ears]*
vulgus, ī *n. (m.)* crowd, throng, herd *[handwritten: erect]*

---

144. **Cȳmothoē:** nom.; a Greek form.

145. **ipse:** *the master* (Neptune). See note on **ipsōs (40).** (**dē**) **scopulō:** abl. of separation; App. 340. **levat:** with the trident as a lever. **tridentī:** abl. of an *i*-stem.

147. **rotīs levibus:** abl. of manner; App. 328, or of means.

148. **velutī saepe cum:** *just as often (happens) when;* this phrase introduces one of Vergil's most famous SIMILES, the first to appear in the *Aeneid.*

149. **animīs:** abl. of place where or manner; App. 319, 328.

150. **facēs:** very dangerous in a city with so many wooden buildings as there were in ancient Rome. **furor arma ministrat:** *Madness provides weapons,* i.e., in the people's fury any object serves as a weapon.

151. **quem:** *some,* the indefinite pronoun. **pietāte, meritīs:** abl. of cause or respect with **gravem;** App. 325, 332.

152. **arrēctīs auribus:** abl. abs. or abl. of manner; App. 343, 328. **arrēctīs auribus astant:** ALLITERATION. **cōnspexēre** = **cōnspexērunt;** App. 204, 4. **silent, astant:** plurals, because of the collective idea in **vulgus** and **populō;** App. 236, *a.*

ille rēgit *dictīs animōs et pectora* mulcet:
sīc cūnctus pelagī cecidit fragor, *aequora* postquam
prōspiciēns *genitor caelōque* invectus apertō   155
flectit *equōs* currū*que* volāns *dat* lōra secundō.

---

apertus, a, um open, clear
cadō, ere, cedidī, cāsus fall, subside
currus, ūs *m.* chariot, car
flectō, ere, exī, exus bend, turn, guide
fragor, ōris *m.* crash, uproar
invehō, ere, ēxī, ectus carry in, convey
lōrum, ī *n.* rein, thong

mulceō, ēre, lsī, lsus soothe, calm
postquam after (that), when
prōspiciō, ere, spexī, spectus look out on
secundus, a, um following, favorable,
    obedient
regō, ere, rēxī, rēctus rule, control
volō (1) fly, speed

154–5. sic: correlative with velutī in 148. postquam genitor . . . flectit et . . . dat. aequora: obj. of prōspiciēns.

155. (in) caelō apertō: abl. of place where; App. 319. genitor: Neptune. invectus (currū): *riding in his car.*

156. flectit . . . dat: historical present; App. 351,1, *a.* currū: dat. of indir. obj.; App. 295.

𝒩eptune in his sea-chariot, 𝔅aths of 𝒩eptune at 𝒪stia.
Photograph by Raymond V. Schoder, S.J.

Dēfessī Aeneadae *quae* proxima *lītora cursū*
contendunt *petere, et* Libyae vertuntur *ad ōrās.*
Est in sēcessū *longō locus:* īnsula *portum*
160   efficit obiectū laterum, *quibus omnis ab* altō
frangitur *inque* sinūs scindit *sēsē unda* reductōs.
Hinc atque hinc vastae rūpēs *geminīque* minantur
in caelum scopulī, *quōrum sub* vertice lātē
aequora tūta silent; *tum silvīs* scaena coruscīs
165   dēsuper, horrentī*que ātrum* nemus imminet *umbrā.*

Aeneadae, (ār)um *m.* descendants
   (followers) of Aeneas
altum, ī *n.* the deep (sea); heaven
contendō, ere, ī, ntus strive; hasten
coruscus, a, um waving, quivering,
   flashing
dēfessus, a, um weary, tired, worn
dēsuper *adv.* from above
efficiō, ere, fēcī, fectus make, form
frangō, ere, frēgī, frāctus break, shatter
horreō, ēre, uī bristle, shudder, tremble
immineō, ēre hang over, threaten
īnsula, ae *f.* island
lātē *adv.* widely, far and wide
latus, eris *n.* side, flank
Libya, ae *f.* region of North Africa

minor, ārī, ātus threaten, tower
nemus, oris *n.* (sacred) grove, forest
obiectus, ūs *m.* projection, overhang
proximus, a, um nearest
redūcō, ere, dūxī, ductus bring back,
   lead back
rūpēs, is *f.* crag, cliff
scaena, ae *f.* background, stage
scindō, ere, scidī, scissus split, divide
scopulus, ī *m.* rock, cliff
sēcessus, ūs *m.* inlet, recess
sileō, ēre, uī be silent, be still
sinus, ūs *m.* fold, gulf, bay
tūtus, a, um safe, protected, secure
vertex, icis *m.* summit, top
vertō, ere, ī, rsus (over)turn,
   (ex)change

157-207. Aeneas, with seven out
of twenty ships, lands on the coast
of North Africa near Carthage. He
kills seven fine stags, which he
divides among his comrades, whom
he tries to console and encourage.

**157-8. Aeneadae lītora, quae (sunt)
proxima, cursū petere contendunt.** The
word **cursū** has two implications, both of
which are probably relevant here: the
men are moving with speed, i.e.,
"running"; and they travel on their "course."

159. The opening words **est . . . locus**
mark this passage as an ECPHRASIS, the
detailed and vivid description of a place
or work of art.

**159-60. īnsula efficit (hunc locum)
portum. portum:** predicate acc. **in
sēcessū longō:** the inlet extends deep
into the land.

160. quibus: abl. of means; App. 331;
the antecedent is **laterum.**

**160-61. omnis unda (veniēns) ab altō
frangitur et sē in sinūs reductōs scindit.
sēsē = sē.** Observe the ALLITERATION.

162. Hinc atque hinc: *on (from) this
side and that,* i.e., on both sides. **rūpēs
(sunt).**

164. scaena: the place resembles a
stage with its scenery. **silvīs coruscīs:** abl.
of quality; App. 330.

165. horrentī umbrā: abl. of cause if
taken with **ātrum,** or of manner if taken
with **imminet;** App. 332, 328. It is
curious that Vergil uses here a verb the

Fronte *sub* adversā scopulīs pendentibus antrum;
intus aquae dulcēs vīvō*que* sedīlia *saxō*,
Nymphārum *domus. hīc fessās nōn* vincula *nāvēs*
ūlla tenent, uncō *nōn* alligat ancora morsū.
Hūc septem *Aenēās* collēctīs *nāvibus omnī*   170
ex numerō *subit, ac magnō tellūris amōre*
ēgressī optātā potiuntur Trōes harēnā
et sale tābentēs artūs *in lītore pōnunt.*

---

adversus, a, um opposite, facing
alligō (1) bind, hold (to)
ancora, ae *f.* anchor
antrum, ī *n.* cave, cavern
aqua, ae *f.* water
artus, ūs *m.* joint, limb
colligō, ere, lēgī, lēctus collect, gather
dulcis, e sweet, dear, fresh
ēgredior, ī, gressus go out, disembark
frōns, ontis *f.* front, face, brow
harēna, ae *f.* sand, beach
intus *adv.* within
morsus, ūs *m.* bite, bit
numerus, ī *m.* number, multitude

Nympha, ae *f.* nymph, a minor divinity
of nature, represented as a beautiful
maiden
optō (1) choose, desire, hope (for)
pendeō, ēre, pependi hang
potior, īrī, ītus gain, win (+ *abl.*)
sal, salis *n. (m.)* salt (water), sea
scopulus, ī *m.* rock, cliff
sedīle, is *n.* seat, bench
septem seven
tābeō, ēre drip, soak, melt, waste
Trōs, Trōis *m.* Trojan
uncus, a, um curved, bent, hooked
vinc(u)lum, ī *n.* chain, bent, hooked
vīvus, a, um living, natural, alive

---

literal meaning of which, "threatens" (cf.
minantur, 162), is at odds with the
apparent peacefulness of the scene. This
is meant to be a safe harbor for Aeneas
and his men; yet twice its features are
characterized in a less than entirely
benign manner. **horrentī:** abl. of an *i*-
stem; this word is probably used here to
suggest the shade of bristling evergreens,
such as cedars, firs, or pines.
166. fronte sub adversā: i.e., the cave
is at the innermost end of the bay, facing
the island. **scopulīs pendentibus:** abl. of
quality or material; App. 330, 324.
167. vīvō saxō: denotes natural, not
artificial, seats.
168. domus: in apposition with **antrum,**
the cave just described; nymphs were
supposed to frequent remote spots with

beautiful natural scenery. **Hīc:** adverb,
here; observe that the -i- is long in the
adverb but short in the pronoun. **fessās
nāvēs:** PERSONIFICATION; or possibly a
transferred epithet, since it is actually the
Trojans who were tired; App. 446.
169. ancora: anachronistic; hooked
anchors were not used in the Bronze Age.
alligat (nāvēs). uncō morsū: abl. of
means; App. 331.
170. collēctīs nāvibus: abl. abs.; App.
343. **omnī ex numerō:** we see from 393
that Aeneas had set out with twenty ships.
For this pattern of words, see the note on 47.
171. magnō amōre: abl. of manner;
App. 328.
172. Trōes: nom. pl., a Greek form.
173. sale: abl. of means with **tābentēs.**

Ac prīmum silicī scintillam excūdit Achātēs
175   suscēpit*que ignem* foliīs *atque* ārida *circum*
nūtrīmenta *dedit* rapuit*que in* fōmite *flammam.*
Tum Cererem corruptam *undīs* Cereālia*que arma*
expediunt *fessī rērum,* frūgēs*que* receptās
et torrēre *parant flammīs et* frangere *saxō.*
180   *Aenēās* scopulum intereā cōnscendit, *et omnem*
prōspectum lātē *pelagō petit,* Anthea *sī quem*
iactātum *ventō videat* Phrygiās*que* birēmēs
aut Capyn *aut* celsīs *in puppibus arma* Caīcī.

Achātēs, ae *m.* faithful comrade of
    Aeneas
Antheus, eī, *acc.* **ea,** *m.* comrade of
    Aeneas
āridus, a, um dry
birēmis, is *f.* bireme, galley (with two
    banks of oars)
Caīcus, ī *m.* comrade of Aeneas
Capys, yos, *acc.* **yn** *m.* comrade of
    Aeneas
celsus, a, um high, lofty, towering
Cereālis, e of Ceres, (goddess of) grain
Cerēs, eris *f.* (goddess of) grain
cōnscendō, ere, ī, ēnsus climb, mount
corrumpō, ere, rūpī, ruptus spoil, ruin
excūdō, ere, dī, sus strike out
expediō, īre, īvī (iī), ītus bring out,
    prepare
folium, (i)ī *n* leaf

fōmes, itis *m.* tinder, fuel, shaving
frangō, ere, frēgī, frāctus break, crush
frūx, frūgis *f.* fruit, grain
iactō (1) toss, buffet
intereā *adv.* meanwhile, meantime
lātē *adv.* widely, far and wide
nūtrīmentum, ī *n.* food, fuel, nourishment
Phrygius, a, um Phrygian, Trojan
prōspectus, ūs *m.* view
rapiō, ere, uī, ptus snatch (up), whirl
recipiō, ere, cēpī, ceptus take back,
    recover
scintilla, ae *f.* spark
scopulus, ī *m.* rock, cliff, crag
silix, icis *m. (f.)* flint
suscipiō, ere, cēpī, ceptus catch (up),
    receive
torreō, ēre, uī, tostus parch, roast

---

174. silicī: dat. of separation; App. 305.
    175. foliīs: abl. of means; App. 331.
circum: adv. modifying **dedit:** *he places*
fuel around; or else understand **circum**
(ignem).
    177. Cererem: *the goddess of grain.*
The use of her name here to signify the
gift she gives to humans, grain, is an
example of METONYMY. **Cereālia arma:**
the utensils of Ceres, i.e., utensils or tools for
grinding and for cooking grain.
    178. expediunt (ex nāvibus). rērum:
gen. with the adj. **fessī;** App. 287, *weary*
of their misfortunes. **receptās (ex marī).**
    179. torrēre: to make it easier to grind.

frangere: to make coarse meal. **flammīs**
. . . saxō: abl. of means; App. 331.
    181. pelagō: dat. of direction = **in**
pelagus; App. 306, or else = **in pelagō,**
abl. of place where; App. 319. **quem:**
indef. *any,* modifying **Anthea,** Greek
acc., *if he can see any Antheus;* in English
we should say *if he can see anything of*
Antheus.
    182. videat: subjunctive in an indir.
quest.; App. 349.
    183. Capyn: acc., a Greek form.
puppibus: poetic plural. **arma:** especially
shields fastened on the ship and conspicu-
ous at a great distance.

Nāvem in cōnspectū *nūllam*, trēs *lītore* cervōs
prōspicit *errantēs; hōs tōta* armenta *sequuntur*   185
ā tergō *et longum per* vallēs pascitur *agmen.*
Cōnstitit *hīc* arcum*que manū* celerēs*que* sagittās
corripuit fīdus *quae tēla* gerēbat Achātēs,
ductorēs*que ipsōs prīmum capita alta ferentēs*
cornibus arboreīs sternit, *tum* vulgus *et omnem*   190
miscet *agēns tēlīs* nemora *inter* frondea turbam;
nec prius absistit quam septem *ingentia victor*
corpora fundat humi *et* numerum *cum nāvibus* aequet;

---

absistō, ere, stitī cease, stop
Achātēs, ae *m.* faithful comrade of
   Aeneas
aequō (1) (make) equal
arboreus, a, um branching, tree-like
arcus, ūs *m.* bow
armentum, ī *n.* herd, drove
celer, eris, ere swift
cervus, ī *m.* stag, deer
cōnsistō, ere, stitī, stitus stop, settle
cōnspectus, ūs *m.* sight, view
cornū, ūs *n.* horn
corripiō, ere, uī, reptus snatch (up)
ductor, ōris *m.* leader
fīdus, a, um faithful, trusty
frondeus, a, um leafy
gerō, ere, gessī, gestus carry (on)
humus, ī *f.* ground, soil, earth

misceō, ēre, uī, mixtus confuse, mix,
   mingle
nemus, oris *n.* (sacred) grove, forest
numerus, ī *m.* number, multitude
pascor, ī, pāstus feed, graze
prius *adv.* first, sooner
prōspiciō, ere, spexī, spectus look out
   on, see
quam how, than, as
sagitta, ae *f.* arrow
septem seven
sternō, ere, strāvī, strātus lay low,
   spread, strew
tergum, ī *n.* back, hide, rear
trēs, tria three
turba, ae *f.* mob, crowd
vallis, is *f.* valley
vulgus, ī *n. (m.)* crowd, throng, herd

---

184. Nāvem (prōspicit). (in) lītore:
abl. of place where; App. 319. **Nāvem
nūllam, trēs cervōs:** CHIASMUS and
ASYNDETON.
   185. hōs (cervōs): the three stags are at
the head of the feeding herd.
   186. vallēs: pl., but probably referring
to a single valley; see the note on **īrae**
(11), and *cf.* App. 243.
   187. Cōnstitit (Aenēās). hīc: adverb,
here; distinguish from the pronoun,
which has a short -**i**-.
   188. tēla: attracted into the rel. clause,
it refers back to **arcum** and **sagittās**,
objects of **corripuit.**
   189–91. ductōrēs: the three stags
(184). tum vulgus (sternit) et omnem

turbam miscet, agēns (eōs = cervōs)
tēlīs inter frondea nemora.
   190. cornibus arboreīs: abl. of
quality; App. 330. **tum vulgus (sternit).**
vulgus: acc., *the herd,* as opposed to the
leaders, **ductōrēs.**
   191. nemora: poetic plural. **turbam:**
the **vulgus** has now become a panic-
stricken and tumultuous **turba,** *a mob.*
   192. victor: *(as) victor;* apposition
with **Aenēās,** the understood subject.
   193. humī: loc.; App. 37, *c.* **numerum**
(cervōrum). cum nāvibus = cum numerō
nāvium. aequet: temporal or anticipatory
subjunctive with **priusquam;** App. 376, *a.*

hinc portum petit et sociōs partitur *in omnēs.*

195   Vina bonus *quae* deinde cadīs onerārat *Acestēs*
lītore Trīnacriō *dederatque* abeuntibus hērōs
dīvidit, *et dictīs* maerentia *pectora* mulcet:
"Ō *sociī (neque* enim ignārī *sumus ante* malōrum),
Ō passī graviōra, *dabit deus hīs* quoque *fīnem.*

200   *Vōs et* Scyllaeam rabiem penitus*que* sonantēs
accestis scopulōs, *vōs et* Cyclōpia *saxa*
expertī: revocāte *animōs* maestum*que* timōrem

---

abeō, īre, iī (īvī), itus depart
accēdō, ere, cessī, cessus approach
bonus, a, um good, kind(ly), useful
cadus, ī *m.* jar, urn
Cyclōpius, a, um Cyclopean, of the
    Cyclopes, huge one-eyed giants of
    Sicily
deinde *adv.* then, thereupon, next
dīvidō, ere, vīsī, vīsus divide, distribute
enim *adv.* for, indeed, surely
experior, īrī, pertus try, experience
gravis, e heavy, grievous, serious
hērōs, ōis *m.* hero, mighty warrior
ignārus, a, um ignorant, inexperienced
maereō, ēre mourn, grieve (for)
malum, ī *n.* evil, misfortune, trouble
maestus, a, um sad, mournful, gloomy
mulceō, ēre, lsī, lsus soothe, calm
onerō (1) load, burden

partior, īrī, ītus distribute, divide
patior, ī, passus suffer, endure
penitus *adv.* within, deep(ly), wholly
quoque also
rabiēs, ēī *f.* rage, madness, fury
revocō (1) recall, restore
scopulus, ī *m.* rock, cliff, crag
Scyllaeus, a, um of Scylla, a ravenous
    sea-monster, part woman and part
    sea creature, girdled with fierce dogs
    and destructive to mariners who
    attempted to sail past her cave
    situated on a narrow strait opposite
    the great whirlpool Charybdis
sonō, āre, uī, itus (re)sound, roar
timor, ōris *m.* fear, dread, anxiety
Trīnacrius, a, um Trinacrian, Sicilian
vīnum, ī *n.* wine

---

194. et partītur (cervōs) in (*among*)
omnēs sociōs (suōs).

195–97. Deinde vīna, quae bonus
Acestēs onerā(ve)rat (in) cadīs (in)
Trīnacriō lītore et quae (ille) hērōs
dederat (illīs = Teucrīs) abeuntibus,
dīvidit (Aenēās). deinde: two syllables by
SYNIZESIS. **onerā(ve)rat:** App. 204. **cadīs:**
dat. of direction; App. 306; or else = **in**
cadīs, abl. of place where; App. 319. **Vīna**
. . . dīvidit (Aenēās).

196. hērōs (Acestēs): nom. sing., Gk.
form. Acestes had entertained Aeneas and
his comrades during the preceding winter
and had funished them with supplies for
the rest of their journey. **abeuntibus**

(Teucrīs): indir. obj. of **dederat.**

197. pectora (suōrum sociōrum).

199. Ō (vōs) passī graviōra (mala).
hīs (malīs): indir. obj. of **dabit;** App.
295.

201. acces(sis)tis: syncopated perfect;
App. 204. **vōs et:** correlative with **vōs et**
in 200; ANAPHORA; App. 413. **Cyclōpia:** *of*
the Cyclopes, huge one-eyed giants, one
of whom, Polyphemus, had killed and
eaten several of the comrades of Odysseus
while they were shut up in his cave.
Odysseus and his men finally succeeded
in blinding Polyphemus and escaping.
For the story, see 3.613–38, and the Book
9 of Homer's *Odyssey.*

202. expertī (estis).

mittite; forsan *et haec* ōlim meminisse iuvābit.
Per variōs *cāsūs, per* tot discrīmina *rērum*
tendimus in Latium, *sēdēs ubi fāta* quiētās   205
ostendunt; illīc fās *rēgna* resurgere *Troiae.*
Dūrāte, *et vōsmet rēbus servāte* secundis."

---

discrīmen, inis *n.* crisis, danger
dūrō (1) harden, endure
fās *n. indecl.* divine will, right, duty
fors(it)an *adv.* perhaps, perchance,
    possibly
illīc *adv.* there
iuvō, āre, iūvī, iūtus help, please
Latium, (i)ī *n.* district of central Italy
    around Rome

meminī, isse remember, recall
ōlim *adv.* once, at some time
ostendō, ere, ī, ntus show, promise
quiētus, a, um calm, peaceful
resurgō, ere, surrēxī, surrēctus rise
    again
secundus, a, um following, favorable
tot so many
varius, a, um varied, different

---

203. mittite: *dismiss.* **et** = **etiam,**
even. **haec:** obj. of **meminisse. forsan
et haec,** etc.: *perhaps at some time we
shall be glad to remember even these
things.* A famous verse, often quoted.
iuvābit (nōs): *it will please (us),* with
meminisse as subject.

205. tendimus (cursum) in Latium:
it is curious that here Aeneas mentions
Latium, since previously he has not
known the name of their destination.
    206. fās (est), etc.: *it is divine will that
the realms of Troy rise there again.*
rēgna: poetic plural; App. 243.
    207. vōsmet: an emphatic form of **vōs.**

Tālia vōce refert cūrīsque ingentibus aeger
spem vultū simulat, premit *altum* corde dolōrem.
Illī sē praedae accingunt dapibus*que futūrīs:*   210
tergora dīripiunt costīs *et* vīscera nūdant;
pars in frusta secant veribus*que* trementia fīgunt,
lītore aēna locant *aliī flammāsque* ministrant.
Tum vīctū revocant *vīrēs, fūsīque per* herbam

---

accingō, ere, īnxī, īnctus gird
aeger, gra, grum sick, weary
aēnum, ī *n.* bronze (vessel, kettle)
cor, cordis *n.* heart, spirit, feelings
costa, ae *f.* rib, side
daps, dapis *f.* feast, banquet
dīripiō, ere, uī, reptus tear from
dolor, ōris *m.* grief, pain, suffering
fīgō, ere, fīxī, fīxus pierce, fasten
frustum, ī *n.* piece, part
herba, ae *f.* grass, herb(age)
locō (1) place, locate, establish
ministrō (1) tend, serve, supply
nūdō (1) (lay) bare, strip

praeda, ae *f.* booty, prey
premō, ere, pressī, pressus (re)press, control
revocō (1) recall, restore
secō, āre, uī, sectus cut, divide
simulō (1) imitate, pretend, feign
spēs, eī *f.* hope, expectation
tergus, oris *n.* back, hide
tremō, ere, uī tremble, quiver
verū, ūs *n.* spit, spike
vīctus, ūs *m.* living, food, victuals
vīscus, eris *n.* vitals, flesh
vultus, ūs *m.* countenance, face

> 208–22. The Trojans first feast
> and then lament their lost comrades.

208. Tālia (dicta). vōce: contrasted with **corde,** 209. **refert (Aenēās). cūrīs ingentibus:** abl. of cause with **aeger;** App. 332. **aeger:** concessive, i.e., *(although) sick at heart.*

209. (in) vultū: abl. of place where or (less likely) means, sharply contrasted with **corde. corde:** abl. of place where or (less likely) means. **spem:** contrasted with **dolōrem. altum corde:** *deep in his heart.* **spem simulat, premit dolōrem:** this figure is known as CHIASMUS. The contrast is here emphasized by placing the two pairs of words in inverse (reverse) order; that is, **spem** begins the first clause and is contrasted with **dolōrem,** which ends the second, while **simulat** ends the first clause and is thus contrasted with **premit,** which

begins the second; App. 420; see the note on 184. Note also the ASYNDETON (lack of connective) between the two clauses, making the CHIASMUS all the more emphatic.

210. Illī: Teucrī. praedae, dapibus: dat. of purpose; App. 303; i.e., they prepare themselves for the venison and the banquet. **dapibus:** poetic plural.

211. costīs: abl. of separation; App. 320, 340.

212. pars (sociōrum) secant (vīscera) in frusta: the use of the pl. verb with a sing. (collective) subject is common in many languages, including English; App. 236, *a.* **trementia (frusta):** the flesh of the recently slain animals is still quivering. **veribus:** abl. of means, App. 331.

213. (in) lītore: abl. of place where; App. 319.

214. vīrēs: acc. pl. of **vīs;** observe the quantity of the first syllable, do not confuse with the acc. pl. of **vir,** *man.*

implentur veteris Bacchī pinguis*que* ferīnae.   215
Postquam exēmpta famēs epulīs mēnsae*que* remōtae,
āmissōs *longō sociōs* sermōne requīrunt,
spem*que* metum*que* *inter* dubiī, seu vīvere crēdant
sīve extrēma patī *nec iam* exaudīre *vocātōs*.
Praecipuē *pius Aenēās nunc* ācris Orontī,   220

ācer, cris, cre sharp, spirited
āmittō, ere, mīsī, missus lose, let go
Bacchus, ī *m.* (god of) wine
crēdō, ere, didī, ditus believe, trust
dubius, a, um doubtful, wavering
epulae, ārum *f.* banquet, feast
exaudiō, īre, īvī (iī), ītus hear, hearken
eximō, ere, ēmī, ēmptus take away, remove
extrēma, ōrum *n.* final fate, death
famēs, is *f.* hunger
ferīna, ae *f.* game, venison
impleō, ēre, ēvī, ētus fill (with) (+ *gen.*)
mēnsa, ae *f.* table

metus, ūs *m.* fear, dread, anxiety
Orontēs, is (ī, ae) *m.* Trojan leader
patior, ī, passus endure, suffer
pinguis, e fat, rich, fertile
postquam after (that), when
praecipuē especially
removeō, ēre, mōvī, mōtus remove
requīrō, ere, quīsīvī (siī), quīsītus seek again, deplore
sermō, ōnis *m.* conversation, speech
seu, sīve whether, or (if)
spēs, eī *f.* hope, expectation
vetus, eris old, former, ancient
vīvō, ere, vīxī, vīctus live

---

215. implentur: a (Greek) middle voice or reflexive use; *they fill themselves;* App. 115, 2, *a*; 309. **Bacchī, ferīnae:** gen. with special verb, **impleō**, closely related to the partitive gen.; App. 286, 287. **Bacchus:** *god of wine,* by METONYMY *wine.*

216. exēmpta (est). mēnsae remōtae (sunt): in Vergil's day the tables were removed at the end of the banquet; so this phrase came to mean simply the end of the feasting. Vergil uses it here in that general sense, as Aeneas and his companion presumably had no tables.

218. inter spemque metumque dubiī: ANASTROPHE. **seu (sociōs suōs) vīvere crēdant:** deliberative indir. quest.; App. 348, 349; the clause is dependent on **dubiī,** which modifies **Teucrī** understood

as subject of **requīrunt. vīvere** is an inf. in ind. statement following **crēdant.**

219. extrēma = mortem: EUPHEMISM. **patī, exaudīre:** inf. in ind. statement after **crēdant;** Vergil's use of the present tense in **patī** suggests that the lost men are suffering even as their friends enjoy a feast, although in fact he might also have used a perf. inf., since their death is likely to have preceded. **vocātōs (sociōs):** this may refer to the Roman custom (**conclāmātiō**) of loudly calling the name of the dead three times as a part of the funeral ceremony; or may simply suggest that their names have been called out in vain by their friends.

220. Praecipuē: modifying **gemit,** not **pius. pius:** not *pious,* but *devoted, loyal, noble;* see note on **pietāte (10). Aenēās ācris Orontī (cāsum gemit).**

nunc Amycī *cāsum* gemit *et* crūdēlia *sēcum*
222   *fāta* Lycī fortem*que* Gyān fortem*que* Cloanthum.

Amycus, ī *m.* a Trojan
Cloanthus, ī *m.* a Trojan
crūdēlis, e cruel, bitter, bloody
fortis, e brave, strong, valiant

gemō, ere, uī, itus groan (for), lament
Gyās, ae, *acc.* **ān** *m.* a Trojan
Lycus, ī *m.* a Trojan

---

221. sēcum = cum sē; i.e., silently; for the thought compare 208–209.

222. fāta, Gyān, Cloanthum (gemit Aenēās). fortem, fortem: pathetic repetition. **Gyān:** acc., a Greek form.

Et iam finis erat, cum Iuppiter aethere *summō*
despiciēns *mare* vēlivolum *terrāsque* iacentēs
lītoraque et lātōs populōs, *sīc* vertice *caelī*   225
cōnstitit *et* Libyae dēfixit *lūmina rēgnīs.*
Atque illum tālēs iactantem *pectore cūrās*
trīstior et lacrimīs oculōs suffūsa nitentēs
adloquitur Venus: *"Ō quī rēs* hominum*que deum*que
aeternīs rēgis *imperiīs et* fulmine terrēs,   230
quid meus Aenēās in tē committere *tantum,*

---

adloquor, ī, locūtus address, accost
aeternus, a, um eternal, everlasting
aethēr, eris *m.* upper air, sky, ether
committō, ere, mīsī, missus commit
cōnsistō, ere, stitī, stitus stand (fast), rest
dēfīgō, ere, fīxī, fīxus fix, fasten
despiciō, ere, spexī, spectus see, discern, descry
fulmen, inis *n.* thunderbolt, lightning
homō, inis *m. (f.)* man, mortal, human
iaceō, ēre, uī, itus lie (outspread, low)

iactō (1) toss, buffet, ponder
lātus, a, um broad, wide, spacious
Libya, ae *f.* district of North Africa
nitēns, entis bright, shining
populus, ī *m.* people, nation
regō, ere, rēxī, rēctus rule, direct
suffundō, ere, fūdī, fūsus fill, suffuse
terreō, ēre, uī, itus frighten, terrify
vēlivolus, a, um winged with sails
Venus, eris *f.* goddess of love and beauty
vertex, icis *m.* summit, head, top

> 223–96. Venus complains to Jupiter of the hard lot of the Trojans and of her son Aeneas. Jupiter consoles her with the promise of universal empire for the Trojans through their descendants, the Roman people.

223. fīnis (epulārum et dictōrum). There is a change of scene from earth to heaven. **(dē) aethere summō:** abl. of separation with **despiciēns;** App. 340.

224. vēlivolum: a TRANSFERRED EPITHET, as it refers to the ships on the sea, instead of the sea itself.

225. (in) vertice: abl. of place where.

226. lūmina = oculōs. rēgnīs: dat. of direction or abl. of place where; App. 306, 319.

227–29. tālēs cūrās: *such cares,* i.e., as were natural for the father of gods and

king of men, with the government of the universe resting on his shoulders. **(in) pectore:** abl. of place where; App. 319. **illum adloquitur Venus. trīstior (quam solita):** *sadder (than was her wont);* Venus, as goddess of love and beauty, is usually seen smiling, even laughing. **lacrimīs:** abl. of means; App. 331. **nitentēs oculōs:** acc. of respect with **suffūsa,** or else object of **suffūsa** used as a reflexive verb (in either case, the construction is also known as the Greek acc.); App. 115, 2, *a*; 309.

229–30. Ō (tū) quī rēs regis et terrēs. regis: from **regō,** not from **rēx. -que . . . -que:** *both . . . and.* **de(ōr)um.**

231. quid meus Aenēās tantum committere (potuit)? = *What (so) great offense, etc.* **quid . . quid:** ANAPHORA. Here, as often, ANAPHORA is combined with ASYNDETON and ELLIPSIS.

quid Trões *potuēre, quibus* tot fūnera passīs
cūnctus ob *Ītaliam terrārum* clauditur orbis?
Certē *hinc* Rōmānōs ōlim *volventibus* annīs,
235   *hinc fore* ductōrēs, revocātō ā sanguine Teucrī,
quī mare, quī terrās omnēs diciōne *tenērent,*
pollicitus—*quae tē, genitor,* sententia vertit?
Hōc equidem occāsum *Troiae trīstēsque* ruīnās
sōlābar *fātīs* contrāria *fāta* rependēns;
240   *nunc eadem fortūna virōs* tot *cāsibus āctōs*
īnsequitur. *Quem dās fīnem, rēx magne, labōrum?*

---

annus, ī *m.* year
certē *adv.* certainly, surely
claudō, ere, sī, sus close, shut
contrārius, a, um opposite, opposing
diciō, ōnis *f.* power, rule, sway
ductor, ōris *m.* leader, chief
equidem *adv.* indeed, surely
fūnus, eris *n.* funeral, death, disaster
īnsequor, ī, secūtus follow, pursue
ob on account of (+ *acc.*)
occāsus, ūs *m.* fall, destruction
ōlim *adv.* once, at some time
orbis, is *m.* circle, orb, earth
patior, ī, passus endure, suffer

polliceor, ērī, itus promise, offer
rependō, ere, ī, ēnsus balance,
     compensate
revocō (1) recall, restore
Rōmānus, a, um Roman
ruīna, ae *f.* downfall, ruin
sententia, ae *f.* opinion, purpose
sōlor, ārī, ātus console, find consolation
     for
Teucer (crus), crī *m.* early king of Troy
tot so many
Trōs, Trōis *m.* Trojan
vertō, ere, ī, rsus turn, change, rout

---

232. potuēre = potuērunt
(committere). **quibus:** dat. of reference
or of interest; App. 301. **fūnera:** obj. of
passīs which modifies **quibus;** the
Trojans had suffered many disasters
(**fūnera**) in the destruction of their city
and during the seven years thereafter,
while they wandered as homeless exiles.
     233. cūnctus orbis terrārum: *the
whole world,* an emotional exaggeration
or HYPERBOLE. **ob Ītaliam:** *on account of
Italy,* which was destined to be the seat of
a great new world-power hostile to Juno's
cherished plans.
     **234–37. Certē pollicitus (es) hinc
Rōmānōs (futūrōs esse), hinc ductōrēs
fore** (= futūrōs esse) **ā revocātō sanguine
Teucrī. hinc** = ex Aeneā et aliīs Teucrī.
volventibus annīs: *as the years roll (by);*
abl. abs.; App. 343. **hinc . . . hinc:** ANAPHORA.
quī . . . quī: ANAPHORA.

     235. fore = futūrōs esse, inf. in indir.
disc., dependent on **pollicitus (es)** in
237; App. 263, 390. **ā revocātō
sanguine:** explaining **hinc.**
     236. quī . . tenērent: rel. clause of
purpose or characteristic; App. 388, 389.
     237. Quae tē sententia vertit: *what
idea turns you (from your earlier plan)?*
An idea may change a person as well as a
person may change an opinion.
     238. Hōc: neut., abl. of cause or
means, *with this (hope).* **occāsum
sōlābar:** *I tried to console myself for the
fall;* a conative imperfect, denoting
attempted action; App. 351, 2, *a.*
     239. fātīs: abl. of means or dat. with
contraria; App. 331, 304.
     240. Observe the ASYNDETON. **cāsibus:**
abl. of means; App. 331.

Antēnor *potuit mediīs* ēlāpsus Achīvīs
Illyricōs penetrāre sinūs *atque* intima tūtus
rēgna Liburnōrum *et* fontem superāre Timāvī,
unde *per ōra* novem *vastō cum* murmure *montis*   245
it mare prōruptum *et pelagō* premit *arva* sonantī.
Hīc tamen *ille urbem* Patavī *sēdēsque* locāvit
Teucrōrum et gentī nōmen dedit armaque fīxit
Trōia, *nunc* placidā compostus pāce quiēscit:

Achīvus, a, um Achaean, Greek
Antēnor, ōris *m.* Trojan leader, fled after
the fall of Troy and settled in northern
Italy at Patavium, modern Padua
compōnō, ere, posuī, pos(i)tus compose,
construct, settle
ēlābor, ī, lāpsus slip out, escape
fīgō, ere, fīxī, fīxus fasten, fix
fōns, fontis *m.* fountain, source
Illyricus, a, um Illyrian, Dalmatian, of
Illyria, a region east of the Adriatic
intimus, a, um inmost
Liburni, orum *m.* Liburnians, Illyrians
locō (1) place, locate, establish
murmur, uris *n.* murmur, rumble, roar
novem *indecl. adj.* nine
Patavium, (i)ī *n.* city of northern Italy,
modern Padua, about twenty miles
west of Venice

pāx, pācis *f.* peace, quiet, rest
penetrō (1) enter, penetrate
placidus, a, um peaceful, calm, quiet
premō, ere, pressī, pressus (re)press,
overwhelm
prōruptus, a, um dashing, furious
quiēscō, ere, ēvī, ētus rest, repose
sinus, ūs *m.* fold, gulf, bay
sonō, āre, uī, itus (re)sound, roar
superō (1) surpass, pass beyond
tamen *adv.* nevertheless, however
Timāvus, ī *m.* river of northern Italy, runs
underground about twenty-five
miles and emerges near the upper
end of the Adriatic Sea into which it
flows with a strong current
Trōius, a, um Trojan
tūtus, a, um safe, protected, secure
unde whence, from which; from whom

---

242. mediīs Achīvīs: *from the midst of the Greeks (fighting around Troy).*

243. Illyricōs sinūs: the Adriatic was proverbial for its dangers to navigation. **Liburnōrum:** a wild and savage people, warlike and hostile to strangers. **tūtus:** in emphatic position, contrasting his present safety with the dangers previously indicated.

245. unde = ex quō fonte (Timāvī). Observe the ALLITERATION.

246. (Timāvus) it mare prōrumptum: *(the Timavus) goes (as) a dashing sea*, to indicate the great volume, roar, and strong current of the river. **pelagō:** *with its flood (sea).* The ALLITERATION is perhaps

meant to suggest the choppy sound of the rushing water.

247. Hīc: adverb, *here*; observe the quantity. **Patavī:** appositional gen.; App. 281.

248. arma fīxit: dedicated his arms to a divinity, by hanging them up in the temple as a sign that he was at peace with the world and would need them no more.

249. nunc: ASYNDETON. **compos(i)tus:** shortened for metrical reasons; this is called SYNCOPE or SYNCOPATION. Observe the ALLITERATION. **quiescit:** this does not mean that Antenor has died; Venus simply wishes to draw a vivid contrast between the dangers Antenor experienced earlier and the peaceful existence he enjoys now.

250   *nōs, tua* prōgeniēs, *caelī quibus* adnuis *arcem,*
      nāvibus (īnfandum!) āmissīs *ūnīus* ob *īram*
      prōdimur *atque* Italīs longē disiungimur *ōrīs.*
      Hic pietātis *honōs? Sīc nōs in* scēptra repōnis?"
          Ollī subrīdēns hominum sator *atque deōrum*
255   vultū, *quō caelum* tempestātēs*que* serēnat,
      ōscula lībāvit nātae, dehinc *tālia fātur:*
      "Parce metū, Cytherēa, *manent* immōta *tuōrum*
      fāta tibī; cernēs urbem et prōmissa Lavīnī
      moenia, sublīmem*que ferēs ad sīdera caelī*

---

adnuō, ere, uī, ūtus nod assent, promise
āmittō, ere, mīsī, missus lose, let go
Cytherēa, ae *f.* Venus, goddess of
   Cythera, a Greek island where Venus
   was born from the foam of the sea
dehinc *adv.* thence, thereafter
disiungō, ere, iūnxī, iūnctus separate,
   disconnect
homō, inis *m. (f.)* man, mortal, human
immōtus, a, um unmoved, unshaken
īnfandus, a, um unspeakable, accursed
Ītalus, a, um Italian
Lavīnium, (i)ī *n.* city in central Italy
lībō (1) taste, touch; pour
longē *adv.* far (from), afar
metus, ūs *m.* fear, dread, anxiety
nāta, ae *f.* daughter

ob on account of (+ *acc.*)
ōsculum, ī *n.* dainty lip, kiss
parcō, ere, pepercī (parsī), parsus
   spare (+ *dat.*)
pietās, ātis *f.* devotion, loyalty, duty
prōdō, ere, didī, ditus hand over, betray
prōgeniēs, ēī *f.* offspring, progeny
prōmittō, ere, mīsī, missus promise
repōnō, ere, posuī, pos(i)tus replace,
   restore
sator, ōris *m.* sower; begetter, father
scēptrum, ī *n.* staff, scepter, power
serēnō (1) calm, clear
sublīmis, e on high, aloft, uplifted
subrīdeō, ēre, rīsī smile (at)
tempestās, ātis *f.* tempest, storm
vultus, ūs *m.* countenance, face

**250. nōs: ego (Venus) et Aenēās et
aliī Teucrī.** Observe the emphatic tone
obtained by ASYNDETON. **tua prōgeniēs:** in
apposition with **nōs.** Venus was daughter
of Jupiter; Aeneas was her son. **caelī
arcem:** Venus reminds Jupiter (and us)
that Aeneas will become a god; for only
gods lived in heaven, while ordinary
mortals went to Hades after death. **adnuis:**
referring to the solemn nod of assent with
which Jupiter ratified his promises.
    251. nāvibus āmissīs: abl. abs.; App.
343. **ūnīus = Iūnōnis.**
    253. (estne) hic: for **hoc;** attracted to
the masc. of the predicate noun **honōs;**
App. 240, *a.*

    254. Ollī = illī: an archaic spelling;
dat. with compound; App. 298.
    255. vultū: abl. of means (App. 331),
to be understood with either **subridens,**
254, or **libavit,** 256; the latter is preferable.
    256. tālia (dicta). nātae: emphasizes
the fact that the kiss is due to the tender
affection of a father for his daughter.
dehinc: one syllable by SYNIZESIS.
    257. metū = metuī: dat. with special
verb; App. 297.
    258. tibī: dat. of reference or ethical
dat.; App. 301, 300.
    259. sublīmem: Aeneas shall become a
god in heaven; an answer to Venus's
complaint in 250.

magnanimum *Aenēān; neque mē* sententia vertit.   260
Hic tibi (fābor enim, quandō *haec tē cūra* remordet,
longius *et volvēns fātōrum* arcāna *movēbō)*
bellum ingēns geret *Ītaliā* populōs*que* ferōcēs
contundet mōrēs*que* virīs et moenia pōnet,
tertia *dum* Latiō rēgnantem *vīderit* aestās,   265
terna*que* trānsierint Rutulīs hīberna subāctis.
At *puer* Ascanius, *cui nunc* cognōmen Iūlō
additur (Īlus *erat, dum rēs stetit* Īlia *rēgnō),*

---

addō, ere, didī, ditus add
aestās, ātis *f.* summer
arcānum, ī *n.* secret, mystery
Ascanius, (i)ī *m.* son of Aeneas
cognōmen, inis *n.* (sur)name, cognomen
contundō, ere, tudī, tū(n)sus bruise,
  crush
enim *adv.* for, indeed, truly
ferōx, ōcis fierce, savage, wild
gerō, ere, gessī, gestus carry (on), wage
hīberna, ōrum *n.* winter (quarters)
Īlius, a, um Ilian, Trojan
Īlus, ī *m.* Ascanius, son of Aeneas
Iūlus, ī *m.* Ascanius, son of Aeneas
Latium, (i)ī *n.* district of central Italy

longē *adv.* far (from), afar
magnanimus, a, um great-souled
mōs, mōris *m.* custom, manner, law
populus, ī *m.* people, race, nation
quandō when, since
rēgnō (1) rule, reign
remordeō, ēre, dī, rsus gnaw, trouble
Rutulus, a, um Rutulian, of the Rutulians, a
  tribe of central Italy
sententia, ae *f.* opinion, purpose
subigō, ere, ēgī, āctus subdue
ternī, ae, a three (each), by threes
tertius, a, um third
trānseō, īre, iī (īvī), itus pass (by)
vertō, ere, ī, rsus turn, change, rout

---

260. neque mē sententia vertit: an answer
to the reproachful question of Venus in
237. **Aenēān:** acc., a Greek form; App. 66.
  261. Hic (Aenēās): subject of **geret,** 263.
tibi: dat. of reference or ethical dat.;
App. 301, 300.
  262. longius: modifies **fābor. fātōrum
arcāna:** dir. obj. of both **volvēns** and
movēbō, i.e., *Unrolling the [books
containing the] secrets of the fates, I shall put
them into motion.* **volvēns:** alludes to the fact
that ancient books took the form of scrolls;
thus, rather than turning pages to read, one
would unroll a scroll.
  263. (Aenēās) bellum ingēns geret:
referring to the war with Turnus in Italy,
described in the last six books of the
Aeneid. **(in) Ītaliā:** abl. of place where;
App. 319.
  264. mōrēs, moenia: emphatic
ALLITERATION. **virīs (suīs).**

  265. dum vīderit, trānsierint: future
perf. with **dum;** App. 373. **(Aenēān)
rēgnantem.**
  266. Rutulīs subāctīs: abl. abs. or dat.
of reference; App. 343, 301. The Rutuli
were a native Italian tribe hostile to
Aeneas, but whom he finally subdued.
terna: *three;* the distributive is often
employed instead of the cardinal with
words used only in the plural. **hīberna,**
winter quarters, hence *winters, years.*
  267. Iūlō: dat. attracted to the case of
cui; App. 242, *b.* This rather odd (to us)
naming construction is not infrequent in
Latin. The cognomen is meant as a
reminder that the family of Julius Caesar,
including Augustus, was descended from
Aeneas, throught Ascanius (Iulus). **Īlus
erat (cognōmen). rēs Īlia:** *the Ilian
(Trojan) state.*
  268. rēgnō: abl. of respect; App. 325.
dum stetit: App. 371.

270   trīgintā *magnōs volvendīs* mēnsibus orbēs
      imperiō explēbit, *rēgnumque ab sēde* Lavīnī
      trānsferet, *et* Longam *multā vī* mūniet Albam.
      Hīc iam ter centum *tōtōs* rēgnābitur annōs
      gente sub Hectoreā, dōnec *rēgīna* sacerdōs
      Mārte gravis *geminam* partū *dabit* Īlia prōlem.
275   Inde lupae fulvō nūtrīcis tegmine *laetus*

Alba, ae *f.* Alba Longa, city of central
    Italy
annus, ī *m.* year
centum hundred
dōnec until, while, as long as
expleō, ēre, ēvī, ētus fill (out), fulfil
fulvus, a, um tawny, yellow
gravis, e heavy, grievous, pregnant
Hectoreus, a, um Hectorean, of Hector,
    leader of the Trojans
Īlius, a, um Ilian, Trojan
inde *adv.* thence, afterward
Lavīnium, (i)ī *n.* city of central Italy
Longa, ae *f.* Alba Longa, a city in central
    Italy, mother city of Rome

lupa, ae *f.* she-wolf
Mārs, Mārtis *m.* god of war
mēnsis, is *m.* month
mūniō, īre, īvī (iī), ītus fortify
nūtrīx, īcis *f.* nurse
orbis, is *m.* circle, orb, revolution
partus, ūs m. birth, offspring
prōlēs, is *f.* offspring, progeny
rēgnō (1) rule, reign
sacerdōs, ōtis *m.* (*f.*) priest(ess)
teg(i)men, inis *n.* covering, skin
ter thrice, three times
trānsferō, ferre, tulī, lātus transfer
trīgintā thirty

---

269. orbēs (annōrum): *circles of years;* poetic for *years.* **volvendīs mēnsibus:** *with their swift passing months;* abl. of quality or means, App. 330, 331.

270. Lavīnī: appositional gen.; App. 281. Aeneas founded Lavinium, Ascanius founded Alba Longa.

271. Longam Albam: *Alba Longa;* according to tradition, Rome was founded from Alba Longa, a city whose name was believed to provide an etymological explanation for its location on a long (**Longa**) white (**Alba**) mountain ridge. **multā vī mūniet:** emphatic ALLITERATION.

272. Hīc: in Alba Longa. **rēgnābitur:** impersonal, *royal power shall be exercised.* **annōs:** acc. of duration of time; App. 314.

273–74. Hectoreā = Troiānā, since Hector was the crown prince and the

greatest of the Trojans. **rēgīna sacerdōs:** *a princess priestess (of Vesta);* she was the daughter of King Numitor, and in other sources she is named Rhea Silvia. **dōnec Īlia rēgīna sacerdōs gravis Mārte dabit prōlem geminam partū:** Īlia: another name for Rhea Silvia, used here to indicate her connection with Īlus (268) and with Īlium (Troy). **Mārte gravis:** *pregnant by Mars,* the god of war. **geminam prōlem:** Romulus and Remus. **partū dabit:** *shall give by birth, shall bear.*

275. Inde: temporal, *then.* **lupae fulvō nūtrīcis tegmine:** interlocked order; App. 442. **lupae nūtrīcis:** refers to the tradition that Romulus and Remus were suckled by a she-wolf. **fulvō tegmine:** abl. of cause with the adj. laetus; App. 332. As a mark of honor to his foster mother Romulus wore a wolfskin.

Rōmulus excipiet *gentem et* Māvortia condet
moenia Rōmānōs*que suō dē nōmine dīcet.*
Hīs ego nec mētās *rērum nec tempora pōnō:*
imperium sine *fīne dedī.* Quīn aspera Iūnō,
quae mare nunc terrāsque metū *caelumque* fatīgat,   280
cōnsilia *in* melius *referet, mēcumque* fovēbit
Rōmānōs, *rērum* dominōs *gentemque* togātam.
Sīc placitum. *Veniet* lūstrīs *lābentibus* aetās
cum domus Assaracī Phthīam clārās*que* Mycēnās

---

aetās, ātis *f.* age, time
asper, era, erum harsh, rough, fierce
Assaracus, ī *m.* early king of Troy
clārus, a, um clear, bright, illustrious
condō, ere, didī, ditus found, establish
cōnsilium, (i)ī *n.* plan, advice
dominus, ī *m.* lord, master
excipiō, ere, cēpī, ceptus take (up), inherit
fatīgō (1) weary, tire (out)
foveō, ēre, fōvī, fōtus cherish, fondle
lūstrum, ī *n.* space of five years, sacred season
Māvortius, a, um Martian, of Mars, god
    of war
melior, ius better, superior
mēta, ae *f.* goal, limit, bound

metus, ūs *m.* fear, dread, anxiety
Mycēnae, ārum *f.* city of central Greece,
    home of Agamemnon, leader of the
    Greek expedition against Troy
Phthīa, ae *f.* city and district of northern
    Greece, home of Achilles, a Greek
    chieftain against Troy
placeō, ēre, uī, itus please (+ *dat.*)
quīn nay (even), (but) that
Rōmānus, a, um Roman
Rōmulus, ī *m.* legendary founder of Rome,
    son of Mars and Rhea Silvia, a Vestal
    virgin
sine without (+ *abl.*)
togātus, a, um toga-clad

---

276. Māvortia: Romulus, the founder
of Rome, was the son of Mars (**Māvors,**
an alternate, archaic spelling of **Mars**),
the patron deity of Rome.

277. dīcet (= **vocābit**) **(gentem)
Rōmānōs:** the name "Romans" being thus
fancifully derived from the name of Romulus.

278. Hīs (Rōmānīs): dat. of reference;
App. 301. **tempora = mētās temporum.
imperium sine fīne (Rōmānīs) dedī:** a
magnificent climax; Aeneas is to rule *three*
years after his victory over the Italian
tribes (265–66), Ascanius for *thirty* years
(269), while Rome is to have dominion
world without end. To preserve the
symmetry, Vergil represents Alba Longa
as ruling *three hundred* years.

279. Quīn: *yes, even;* introducing an
almost unbelievable statement.

280. metū: abl. of means; App. 331;
refers either to her own fear for Carthage,
as represented in 19 ff. (cf. **id metuēns**
in 23), or the fear she instills in the

Trojans by presenting them with danger
wherever they turn.

281. in melius: *for the better.*

282. rērum: *of the world.* **-que:** links
two phrases, **rērum dominōs** and **gentem
togātam.** The reference to the characteristic
dress of the Romans in the last word
balances the emphatic **Rōmānōs** at the
beginning of the line. **togātam:** the toga was
the characteristic Roman dress.

283. Sīc placitum (est): impersonal use
of the perf.; literally, *Thus has it pleased* (i.e.,
the gods *or* fate). Jupiter uses understatement
to characterize Rome's destiny, with **sīc
placitum** echoing the language of decrees of
the Roman senate. **lūstrīs lābentibus:** abl.
abs.; *as the years go gliding by;* note the
ALLITERATION; App. 411.

284. domus Assaracī: *the house of
Assaracus,* a Trojan prince; Phthia refers
obliquely to Achilles, the greatest of
Greek warriors, for this was his home, and
Mycenae to Agamemnon, the general

285   servitiō premet *ac victīs* dominābitur Argīs.
Nāscētur pulchrā Troiānus orīgine Caesar,
imperium Ōceanō, *fāmam quī* terminet astrīs,
Iūlius, *ā magnō* dēmissum *nōmen* Iūlō.
Hunc tū ōlim *caelō* spoliīs Orientis onustum
290   *accipiēs* secūra; *vocābitur hic* quoque vōtīs.

Argī, ōrum *m.* Argos, city of southern
Greece, home of Diomedes, a Greek
chieftain against Troy
astrum, ī *n.* star, constellation
Caesar, aris *m.* (1) Julius Caesar; (2)
Augustus Caesar
dēmittō, ere, mīsī, missus send down,
drop, lower, derive
dominor, ārī, ātus rule (over) (+ *dat.*)
Iūlius, (i)ī *m.* (1) Julius Caesar; (2)
Augustus Caesar
Iūlus, ī *m.* Ascanius, son of Aeneas
nāscor, ī, nātus be born, arise
Ōceanus, ī *m.* ocean
ōlim *adv.* once, at some time

onustus, a, um laden, burdened
Oriēns, entis *m.* Orient, the East
orīgō, inis *f.* origin, beginning, source
premō, ere, pressī, pressus (re)press,
subject
pulcher, chra, chrum beautiful,
handsome, illustrious
quoque *adv.* also
secūrus, a, um free from care, un-
troubled
servitium, (i)ī *n.* slavery, bondage
spolium, (i)ī *n.* spoils, booty, plunder
terminō (1) bound, limit
Troiānus, a, um Trojan
vōtum, ī *n.* prayer, vow

---

who led the Greeks to Troy; i.e., the
Romans, descendants of the Trojans, shall
some day conquer and rule Greece. Jupiter
is in fact looking forward (from the
perspective of the time immediately after
the Trojan War) to 146 B.C., when Greece
was reduced to a Roman province.

285. victīs Argīs: dat. with special
verb or abl. of place where; App. 297,
319.

**286. pulchrā Troiānus orīgine
Caesar:** interlocked order; App. 442.
pulchrā orīgine: abl. of quality; App.
330. **Troiānus Caesar:** the controversial
reference here is either to Augustus, who
traced his ancestry back to Aeneas, or to
Julius Caesar, adoptive father of Augustus
and the immediate precursor of the
beginning of empire.

**287. (quī) imperium Ōceanō
(terminet).** quī terminet: rel. clause of
purpose; App. 388. Ōceanō: abl. of
means. The ancients thought that Oceanus
was a great river which flowed around the
earth.

288. Iūlius: in apposition with **Caesar**
(in 286), and referring either to Augustus
Caesar who as the adopted son of Julius
Caesar took this name, or to Julius Caesar
himself; see above, on 286. The name
Julius was fancifully derived from Iulus,
and the latter from Ilus, thus connecting
the word with Ilus, one of the early kings
of Ilium (Troy). Cf. note on 267.

289. (in) caelō: refers to the deifica-
tion of Augustus, who was worshipped as
a god and as the son of a god, Julius
Caesar, even during his lifetime. **Hunc
spoliīs Orientis onustum:** refers to
Augustus Caesar's conquests in the Orient,
especially to his recovery from the
Parthians of the Roman standards they
had captured from Crassus in 53 B.C., and
to his victory over Antony and Cleopatra at
Actium in 31 B.C.

290. secūra: adjective modifying **tū**
which is subject of **accipiēs. hic (Caesar)
quoque:** *he also*, as well as Aeneas, will
be worshipped (**vocābitur**) as a god; see
259-60.

Aspera *tum positīs* mītēscent saecula *bellīs;*
cāna Fidēs *et* Vesta, Remō *cum* frātre Quirīnus
iūra *dabunt;* dīrae *ferrō et* compāgibus artīs
claudentur *Bellī* portae; Furor impius intus
saeva sedēns *super arma et* centum vīnctus aēnīs   295
post tergum nōdīs fremet horridus *ōre* cruentō."

---

aēnus, a, um (of) bronze, brazen
artus, a, um close (fitting)
asper, era, erum harsh, rough, fierce
cānus, a, um white, gray, hoary
centum hundred
claudō, ere, sī, sus (en)close, fasten
compāgēs, is *f.* joint, seam, fastening
cruentus, a, um bloody, cruel
dīrus, a, um dire, awful
Fidēs, eī *f.* Faith, Honor (personified)
frāter, tris *m.* brother
fremō, ere, uī, itus rage, roar
Furor, ōris *m.* Madness, Rage, Frenzy
    (personified)
horridus, a, um horrible, bristling
impius, a, um unholy, impious, disloyal

intus *adv.* within
iūs, iūris *n.* justice, law, right
mītēscō, ere become mild
nōdus, ī *m.* knot
porta, ae *f.* door, gate, opening
post *adv.* afterward; *prep. + acc.* after,
    behind
Quirīnus, ī *m.* Romulus, legendary
    founder of Rome
Remus, ī *m.* twin brother of Romulus
saeculum, ī *n.* age, generation
saevus, a, um cruel, fierce, stern
sedeō, ēre, sēdī, sessus sit
tergum, ī *n.* back, hide, rear
Vesta, ae *f.* goddess of the hearth
vinciō, īre, vīnxī, vīnctus bind, tie

---

291. positīs bellīs: abl. abs.; App. 343.
A prophecy of the golden age of peace,
when all wars shall cease. **Aspera positīs
saecula bellīs:** interlocked order; App.
442. This and the following lines (292–96)
refer to the expected return of the Golden
Age, whch was ardently hoped for and
often prophesied in antiquity, when all the
world would be good and happy; faith and
honor and peace and love would prevail;
and crime and wickedness, suffering and
sorrow, would be no more.

292. cāna Fidēs: one of the earliest
shrines at Rome was dedicated to the
goddess Fides. This line is usually
interpreted symbolically: Fides and Vesta
represent the honor and sanctity of the old
Roman home, while the reconciliation of
Romulus and Remus (interestingly, without
any mention of their earlier feud and its
consequences) symbolizes the reconciliation
of differing political factions at Rome, long
engaged in deadly civil war.

293. ferrō et compāgibus artīs: abl.

of means with **claudentur** (294) or abl. of
respect with **dirae**; App. 325. The ambiguity
is pointed.

294. claudentur Bellī portae: apparently
referring to the temple of Janus, the doors of
which were opened in time of war and closed
in time of peace. Augustus closed the temple
in 29 B.C., after it had remained continuously
opened for more than two centuries. It had
been closed only twice before since the
foundation of Rome. **impius:** referring to the
unholy spirit of civil war.

295. saeva sedēns super: ALLITERATION
makes this image quite vivid. Vergil's
imagined description presages a famous
painting of *Furor impius* which Augustus,
several decades after Vergil's death, had
placed in the forum which bears his name.

295–96. vīnctus post tergum: (his
hands) *bound behind his back.* **ōre:** abl.
of means or cause, with **fremet;** App.
331, 332. **fremet:** from rage at not being
able to indulge in his favorite activity,
encouraging fratricidal strife.

> *Haec ait et* Maiā genitum dēmittit *ab* altō,
> *ut terrae utque novae* pateant Karthāginis *arcēs*
> hospitiō *Teucrīs, nē fātī* nescia *Dīdō*
> 300 *fīnibus* arcēret. Volat *ille per* āera *magnum*
> rēmigiō ālārum *ac* Libyae citus astitit *ōrīs.*
> *Et iam* iussa *facit, pōnuntque* ferōcia Poenī
> corda *volente deō; in prīmīs rēgīna* quiētum
> *accipit in Teucrōs animum mentemque* benignam.

āēr, āeris, *acc.* **āera** *m.* air, mist, fog
āla, ae *f.* wing
altum, ī *n.* the deep (sea); heaven
arceō, ēre, uī keep off, defend
a(d)stō, āre, stitī stand (on, at) (+ *dat.*)
benignus, a, um kind(ly), benign
citus, a, um quick, swift
cor, cordis *n.* heart, spirit, feelings
dēmittō, ere, mīsī, missus send down, drop
ferōx, ōcis fierce, savage, wild
gignō, ere, genuī, genitus bear, beget
hospitium, (i)ī *n.* hospitality, welcome

iussum, ī *n.* command, order
Karthāgō, inis *f.* great commercial city of North Africa, rival of Rome
Libya, ae *f.* district of North Africa
Maia, ae *f.* daughter of Atlas and mother of Mercury, messenger of the gods
nescius, a, um ignorant, unaware
pateō, ēre, uī lie open, extend
Poenus, a, um Phoenician, Carthaginian
quiētus, a, um calm, peaceful
rēmigium, (i)ī *n.* oarage, rowing
volō (1) fly, speed

297–304. Mercury is sent to Dido, at Carthage, to prepare the way for Aeneas and the Trojans.

297. ait: third sing. of **aiō. Maiā:** abl. of source or origin; thus, **Maiā genitum:** *the son of Maia.*
298–300. pateant, arcēret: subjunctives expressing purpose; App. 359; observe the difference in tense, made possible by the fact that the principle verb, **dēmittit,** as a historical present may be considered either primary or secondary; App. 353, *a*; 351, 1, *a.*
299. hospitiō Teucrīs: two datives; App. 301, 303; or **hospitiō** may be abl. of manner; App. 328. **fātī nescia Dīdō:** the description attached to this first naming of Dido in the poem is strikingly ambiguous; i.e.(construing **fātī** as referring to the

Trojans), Dido might not know that the Trojans were fated to settle in Italy and might repel them from her land as possible invaders; or (construing **fātī** as referring to Dido herself) the queen is naturally unaware of the destiny—and death—which await her because of her love for Aeneas.
300. (ā) fīnibus. (Teucrōs) arcēret: negative purpose; App. 359. **āera:** acc. sing. from **āēr,** a Greek form; App. 68.
301. rēmigiō: abl. of means; App. 331; this unusually vivid metaphor from seafaring will appear again at 6.19. **astitit:** perfect, to denote instantaneous action, after the historical present, **volat. (in) ōrīs.**
303. deō volente: abl. abs.; App. 343. **in prīmīs:** *among the first, especially.* **rēgīna:** Dido.
304. in: *toward.*

At pius Aenēās per noctem plūrima volvēns,   305
ut prīmum lūx alma data est, exīre *locōsque*
explōrāre *novōs, quās ventō* accesserit *ōrās,*
quī teneant (nam inculta *videt),* hominēsne feraene,
quaerere cōnstituit *sociīsque* exācta *referre.*
Classem in convexō nemorum *sub* rūpe cavātā   310
arboribus clausam *circum atque* horrentibus *umbrīs*
occulit; *ipse ūnō* graditur comitātus Achātē

---

accēdō, ere, cessī, cessus approach,
 reach
Achātēs, ae *m.* faithful comrade of
 Aeneas
almus, a, um nurturing, kind(ly)
arbōs (or), oris *f.* tree
cavō (1) hollow (out)
claudō, ere, sī, sus (en)close, hem in
comitō (1) accompany, attend
cōnstituō, ere, uī, ūtus establish, resolve
convexum, ī *n.* hollow, valley, sky
exeō, īre, iī (īvī), itus go out

exigō, ere, ēgī, āctus drive out;
 determine, discover
explōrō (1) explore, search (out)
fera, ae *f.* wild beast, animal
gradior, ī, gressus march, go, proceed
homō, inis *m.* (*f.*) man, mortal, human
horreō, ēre, uī bristle, shudder, tremble
incultus, a, um untilled, wild
nemus, oris *n.* (sacred) grove, forest
occulō, ere, uī, ltus hide, conceal
rūpēs, is *f.* cliff, crag, rock

305-417. Aeneas sets out to explore
the unknown region, and meets his
mother Venus disguised as a huntress.
The goddess tells him that he is near
Carthage, relates the history of Dido,
announces the safety of his remaining
ships, resumes her form as a divinity,
and disappears.

305. plūrima (mente) volvēns.
306-9. ut prīmum: *when first, as soon
as.* **exīre, explōrāre, quaerere, referre:**
depend on **cōnstituit** in 309. **Aenēās
cōnstituit exīre locōsque novōs
explōrāre, quaerere quās ōrās accesserit
ventō (et quaerere) quī teneant (illōs
locōs) referreque exācta sociīs (suīs).**
**307. quās (ōrās) accesserit, quī (eās)
teneant:** indir. questions dependent on
quaerere; App. 349. **ventō:** abl. of means
or cause; App. 331, 332.

308. (ea esse) inculta: inculta,
modifying an understood **ea,** is n. pl. and
refers to both **locōs** and **ōrās,** one a masc.
and the other a fem. noun; for its gender
see App. 239, *b.* **videt:** the final syllable
is long before a strong pause. **hominēsne
feraene (sint).** **-ne, -ne:** *whether, or.*
309. sociōs: indir. obj., **exācta:**
substantively, *the things determined,
learned.*
**311. horrentibus umbrīs: a TRANSFERRED
EPITHET; horrentibus** belongs logically to
the trees **(arboribus)** but is transferred to
their shadows **(umbrīs).** Cf. **horrentī
umbrā** (165) and note. **circum:** adverb,
round about.
312. ipse (Aenēās): *the master;* see
note on **ipsius** (114). **ūnō = sōlō,** a
common meaning. **ūnō Achātē:** abl. of
accompaniment without the preposition,
or abl. of means.

bīna *manū* lātō crispāns hastīlia *ferrō.*

Cui māter mediā sēsē tulit obvia *silvā*

315   virginis *ōs* habitum*que* gerēns *et* virginis *arma*

Spartānae, *vel* quālis *equōs* Thrēissa fatīgat

Harpalycē volucrem*que fugā* praevertitur Hebrum.

Namque umerīs dē mōre habilem suspenderat arcum

vēnātrīx *dederatque* comam diffundere *ventīs,*

320   nūda genū nōdō*que* sinūs collēcta fluentēs.

Ac prior "Heus," inquit, "iuvenēs, mōnstrāte, *meārum*

---

arcus, ūs *m.* bow
bīnī, ae, a two (each), by twos
colligō, ere, lēgī, lēctus gather, collect
coma, ae *f.* hair
crispō, āre, ātus brandish, wave
diffundō, ere, fūdī, fūsus scatter
fatīgō (1) weary, tire (out)
fluō, ere, flūxī, flūxus flow
heus ho! hello!
inquam, is, it say
genū, ūs *n.* knee
gerō, ere, gessī, gestus carry (on), wear
habilis, e easily handled, handy
habitus, ūs *m.* appearance, garb
Harpalycē, ēs *f.* Thracian princess and
     huntress, renowned for her speed
hastīle, is *n.* spear(-shaft), lance
Hebrus, ī *m.* slow Thracian river which
     Vergil thought fast

iuvenis, is *m. (f.)* youth, young (man,
     woman)
lātus, a, um broad, wide, spacious
mōnstrō (1) show, point out
mōs, mōris *m.* custom, manner, law
nōdus, ī *m.* knot
nūdus, a, um nude, bare
obvius, a, um in the way, to meet (+ *dat.*)
praevertor, ī, rsus outstrip, surpass
prior, ius former, first
quālis, e of what kind, such (as)
sinus, ūs *m.* fold, hollow, bay
Spartānus, a, um Spartan, of Sparta, in
     southern Greece
suspendō, ere, ī, ēnsus suspend, hang
Thrēissa, ae *f.* Thracian, of Thrace, a
     district northeast of Greece
vēnātrīx, īcis *f.* huntress
virgō, inis *f.* girl, maid(en)
volucer, cris, cre swift, winged

---

313. bīna: this distributive numeral is often used instead of the cardinal **duo** with objects that go in pairs. **manū:** abl. of place or means. **lātō ferrō:** *with broad iron (point);* abl. of quality; App. 330.

314. Cui: = **eī**, i.e., Aeneas, dat. with **obvia** which modifies **māter. (in) mediā silvā.**

316. vel (tālis virginis) quālis . . . fatīgat Harpalycē: *or (of) such a girl as the Thracian Harpalyce (when she) tires the horses* (by outstripping them in a race).

317. Harpalycē: nom., a Greek form. **fugā:** *in her swift course.* abl. of means; App. 331.

318. (dē) umerīs.

319. vēnātrīx: *(as a) huntress.* **diffundere:** inf. of purpose, a poetic use; App. 261.

320. genū: acc. of respect; App. 311. **sinūs:** obj. of the participle **collecta** *(having gathered),* treated here as a Greek middle participle capable of having a dir. obj.; alternatively, **sinūs** is a so-called Greek acc., i.e., acc. of respect *(having been gathered with respect to her robes);* App. 309, *a.*

321. prior: *first,* before Aeneas could speak.

vīdistis sī quam hīc errantem forte sorōrum
succīnctam pharetrā *et* maculōsae tegmine lyncis,
aut spūmantis aprī *cursum clāmōre* prementem."

    Sīc Venus *et* Veneris contrā *sīc* fīlius orsus: 325
"*Nūlla tuārum audīta mihī neque vīsa* sorōrum,
Ō quam tē memorem, virgō? *Namque haud tibi* vultus
mortālis, *nec vōx* hominem sonat; *Ō, dea* certē
(an Phoebī soror? An Nymphārum *sanguinis ūna?*),
sīs fēlīx *nostrumque* levēs, quaecumque, *labōrem*   330
et quō sub caelō tandem, quibus orbis *in ōrīs*

---

an *interrog.* or, whether
aper, prī *m.* wild boar
certē *adv.* certainly, surely
contrā *adv.* opposite, in turn
fēlīx, īcis happy, blessed; propitious
fīlius, (i)ī *m.* son
homō, inis *m.* *(f.)* man, mortal, human
levō (1) lift, lighten
lȳnx, lyncis *m.* *(f.)* lynx, wild cat
maculōsus, a, um spotted
memorō (1) recount, (re)call, relate
mortālis, e mortal, human
Nympha, ae *f.* numph, a minor divinity,
    appearing to humans as a beautiful
    maiden
orbis, is *m.* circle, orb, world
ordior, īrī, orsus begin, undertake

pharetra, ae *f.* quiver
Phoebus, ī *m.* Apollo, god of light,
    music, and prophecy, brother of
    Diana, goddess of the chase
premō, ere, pressī, pressus (re)press,
    control, pursue
quīcumque, quaecumque, quodcumque
    whoever, whichever, whatever
sonō, āre, uī, itus (re)sound, roar
soror, ōris *f.* sister, comrade
spūmō (1) foam, froth, spray
succingō, ere, cīnxī, cīnctus gird (up)
teg(i)men, inis *n.* cover(ing), skin
Venus, eris *f.* goddess of love and beauty
virgō, inis *f.* girl, maid(en)
vultus, ūs *m.* countenance, face

---

322. quam: indef., *any (one).* **sī**
quam meārum sorōrum hīc errantem
vīdistis, mōnstrāte (eam mihi).
    325. Sīc Venus (dīxit). Venus, Veneris
fīlius: brought together in the sentence,
emphasizing ironically that Venus and
Aeneas do not here meet as mother and
son. **orsus (est).**
    326. Nūlla (soror). audīta (est) mihī.
mihī: dat. of agent; App. 302; for the length
of the final -**i**, see the note on **mihi**, 8.
    327. quam tē (esse) memorem: *whom*
(what) shall I call you? **memorem** is
deliberative subj.; App. 348. **tibi:** dat. of
possession. **vultus (est) mortālis.**
    328. nec vōx hominem sonat: *nor*
does your voice sound human; **hom-**
inem is cognate acc., App. 313.

    329. an Phoebī soror (es)? Phoebī
soror: i.e., Phoebe, Diana, famed as the
goddess of the hunt. **sanguinis =**
generis: part. gen. with **ūna.**
    330. sīs, levēs: volitive or optative
subjunctive expressing Aeneas' wish;
App. 253, 254. **quaecumque (es).**
    331–32. et (mē) doceās sub quō caelō
tandem (iactēmur), in quibus ōrīs orbis
(terrārum) iactēmur. quō sub caelō . . .
iactēmur: indir. quest.; App. 349.
doceās: volitive or optative subjunctive;
App. 253, 254. -**que:** with the final -**e**
elided before the initial vowel of the next
verse. Such a verse is called HYPERMETRIC.
This unusual metrical effect, together with
the unusual elision of the long final
syllable of **ignārī** with the short opening

iactēmur doceās: ignārī hominum*que locōrumque*
errāmus ventō hūc vastīs et flūctibus āctī:
multa tibi ante ārās nostrā cadet hostia *dextrā.*"

335   *Tum* Venus: "*Haud* equidem *tālī mē* dignor *honōre;*
virginibus *Tyriīs* mōs *est* gestāre pharetram
purpureō*que* altē sūrās vincīre coturnō.
Pūnica *rēgna vidēs, Tyriōs et* Agēnoris *urbem;*
sed fīnēs Libycī, *genus* intractābile *bellō.*

340   *Imperium Dīdō Tyriā* rēgit *urbe* profecta,
germānum *fugiēns. Longa est* iniūria, *longae*
ambāgēs; *sed summa sequar* fastīgia *rērum.*

Agēnor, oris *m.* king of Phoenicia
altē *adv.* on high, high up
ambāgēs, is *f.* turning, devious tale
cadō, ere, cedidī, cāsus fall, sink, die
cot(h)urnus, ī *m.* high boot, buskin
dignor, ārī, ātus deem worthy (+ *abl.*)
doceō, ēre, uī, ctus teach, tell
equidem *adv.* indeed, surely
fastīgium, (i)ī *n.* summit, top, point
germānus, ī *m.* brother
gestō (1) bear, wear, carry
homō, inis *m.* (*f.*) man, mortal, human
hostia, ae *f.* victim, sacrifice
ignārus, a, um ignorant, unaware
iniūria, ae *f.* wrong, insult, injustice

intractābilis, e unmanageable, intractable
iactō (1) toss, buffet
Libycus, a, um Libyan, of Libya, a
district of North Africa
mōs, mōris *m.* custom, manner, law
pharetra, ae *f.* quiver
proficīscor, ī, fectus set out, depart
Pūnicus, a, um Phoenician, Punic,
Carthaginian
purpureus, a, um purple, crimson
regō, ere, rēxī, rēctus rule, direct
sūra, ae *f.* (calf of) leg
Venus, eris *f.* goddess of love and beauty
vinciō, īre, vīnxī, vīnctus bind, tie
virgō, inis *f.* girl, maid(en)

---

syllable of **hominum,** may be meant to
hint at a momentary lack of emotional
control in Aeneas as he speaks.
    333. ventō, flūctibus: abl. of means;
App. 331. **vastīs:** modifies **flūctibus.**
    **334. multa hostia cadet tibi nostrā
dextrā (manū) ante ārās (tuās):** Aeneas
promises a generous sacrifice to this
unknown goddess, if she will grant his
prayer. He wishes to make a good
bargain, typified by the formulaic **dō ut
dēs** of Roman religion. **nostrā** (= **meā**)
dextrā (manū): abl. of means.
    335–36. Tum Venus (dīxit). honōre:
abl. with **dignor:** App. 337, *a.*
virginibus: dat. of possession or
reference; App. 299, 301. **Tyriīs:**
Carthage was settled from Tyre; cf. **Tyriī
tenuēre colōnī** (12).

336–37. Venus tries to pass herself off
as a typical Tyrian girl, devoted to hunting.
    337 purpureō: Tyrian "purple" (really
scarlet) was a famous textile dye, derived
from the murex and marketed throughout
the Mediterranean by the Phoenicians.
    338. Pūnica: a Latin word equivalent
to *Phoenician.* **Agēnoris:** as a Phoenician
settlement, Carthage could be called the
city of Agenor, founder of the Phoenician
people.
    339. fīnēs (sunt) Libycī. genus: in
apposition with Libyans, implied in **Libycī.**
    340. (ex) Tyriā urbe profecta: *having
come from Tyre.*
    **341. Longa est iniūria = longum est
dīcere (nārrāre) iniūriam:** *the story of
her wrongs is a long one.* **longae (sunt).**

Huic coniūnx Sȳchaeus *erat,* dītissimus aurī
Phoenīcum, *et magnō miserae* dilēctus *amōre,*
cui pater intāctam *dederat prīmīsque* iugārat   345
ōminibus. *Sed rēgna* Tyrī germānus *habēbat*
Pygmaliōn, scelere *ante aliōs immānior omnēs.*
Quōs inter medius vēnit furor. *Ille* Sychaeum
impius *ante ārās atque aurī* caecus *amōre*
clam *ferrō* incautum superat, sēcūrus *amōrum*   350
germānae; factum*que* diū cēlāvit *et* aegram

---

aeger, gra, grum sick (at heart), weary
caecus, a, um blind, hidden, dark
cēlō (1) hide, conceal
clam *adv.* secretly
dīligō, ere, lēxī, lēctus love, cherish
diū *adv.* a long time, long
dī(ve)s, dī(vi)tis rich, wealthy (+ *gen.*)
factum, ī *n.* deed, undertaking, exploit
furor, ōris *m.* madness, frenzy, rage
germāna, ae *f.* sister
germānus, ī *m.* brother
impius, a, um unholy, unnatural, disloyal
incautus, a, um unsuspecting, careless

intāctus, a, um untouched, virgin
iungō (1) join, unite, yoke together
ōmen, inis *n.* omen, auspices
Phoenīx, īcis *m.* Phoenician
Pygmaliōn, ōnis *m.* wicked brother of
Dido
scelus, eris *n.* crime, villainy, sin
sēcūrus, a, um free from care, careless,
heedless (+ *gen.*)
superō (1) overcome, surpass; kill
Sȳchaeus, ī *m.* deceased husband of Dido
Tyrus, ī *f.* famous city of Phoenicia

---

343. Huic (Dīdōnī): dat. of possession; App. 299. **Sȳchaeus:** the first
syllable of this name is treated as either
long or short by Vergil: long in this line,
but short below in 348. **aurī:** gen. with
adj. **dītissimus:** App. 287; *richest in
gold.* Some texts of the *Aeneid* print **agrī**
here rather than **aurī**, since in fact **agrī**
appears in all the earliest surviving
manuscripts. However, given the
important role played by gold in the
following scene, this emendation (a technical
term for a change in the transmitted text)
is accepted by many modern scholars.
   344. (Dīdōnī) miserae: dat. of agent;
App. 302.
   **345. pater = Bēlus. (eam = Dīdōnem)
intāctam. iugā(ve)rat. ōminibus:** abl. of
means; App. 331; by METONYMY for
marriage, since the omens were always
consulted for weddings.

   347. scelere: abl. of respect with
immānior; App. 325.
   **348–51. inter quōs = inter
Pygmaliōnem et Sychaeum;** ANASTROPHE.
**Ille (= Pygmaliōn) impius atque caecus
amōre aurī, sēcūrus amōrum germānae
(suae), clam ferrō superat Sychaeum
incautum ante ārās.** Observe how
strongly the speaker (Venus in disguise)
portrays the wicked character of
Pygmalion and his disregard for all
human or divine considerations.
   349. amōre: abl. of cause; App. 332.
   350. amōrum: obj. gen. with adj.
sēcūrus; App. 284; *heedless of his sister's
love* (for her husband).
   351. aegram: modifies **amantem**,
which is used substantively, *lover, loving
wife.*

multa malus simulāns vānā spē lūsit amantem.
Ipsa sed in somnīs inhumātī *vēnit* imāgō
coniugis ōra modīs attollēns pallida mīrīs;
355   crūdēlēs *ārās* trāiecta*que pectora ferrō*
nūdāvit, caecum*que domūs* scelus *omne* retēxit.
Tum celerāre *fugam* patriā*que* excēdere suādet
auxilium*que viae* veterēs *tellūre* reclūdit
thēsaurōs, ignōtum argentī pondus *et aurī.*
360   *Hīs* commōta *fugam Dīdō sociōsque parābat.*
Conveniunt *quibus aut* odium crūdēle tyrannī
aut metus ācer *erat; nāvēs, quae forte parātae,*

ācer, cris, cre sharp, fierce, spirited
amāns, antis *m.* (*f.*) lover
argentum, ī *n.* silver
attollō, ere lift, raise
auxilium, (i)ī *n.* help, aid, assistance
caecus, a, um blind, hidden, dark
celerō (1) hasten, hurry, speed
commoveō, ēre, mōvī, mōtus move, arouse
conveniō, īre, vēnī, ventus come together, assemble
crūdēlis, e cruel, bloody, fierce
excēdō, ere, cessī, cessus withdraw, depart
ignōtus, a, um unknown, strange
imāgō, inis *f.* image, likeness, ghost
inhumātus, a, um unburied
lūdō, ere, sī, sus play with, deceive, mock
malus, a, um bad, evil, wicked
metus, ūs *m.* fear, dread, anxiety

mīrus, a, um wonderful, marvelous
modus, ī *m.* manner, measure
nūdō (1) bare, expose
odium, (i)ī *n.* hate, hatred, enmity
pallidus, a, um pale
patria, ae *f.* homeland, country
pondus, eris *n.* weight, burden
reclūdō, ere, sī, sus disclose, reveal
retegō, ere, tēxī, tēctus uncover, disclose
scelus, eris *n.* crime, villainy, sin
simulō (1) imitate, pretend, feign
spēs, eī *f.* hope, expectation
suādeō, ēre, āsī, āsus advise, urge
thēsaurus, ī *m.* treasure-house, treasure
tyrannus, ī *m.* tyrant, usurper, ruler
trāiciō, ere, iēcī, iectus pierce
vānus, a, um empty, idle, false
vetus, eris old, ancient, former

---

352. multa simulāns: to account for the absence of Sychaeus. **lūsit vānā spē** (Dīdōnem) aegram amantem; sed ipsa imāgō inhumātī coniugis (Sychaeī) vēnit in somnīs (ad eam = Dīdōnem).

353. inhumātī: the ancients believed that unless the corpse were properly buried, the ghost of the dead would wander restlessly about.

354. modīs mīrīs: ALLITERATION; abl. of manner, with **pallida**; App. 328.

355. ārās, pectora: poetic plural. **ferrō:** abl. of means.

356. domūs: gen.

357. suādet: the ghost urges Dido to flee. **celerāre, excēdere:** infinitives with **suādet;** ordinary prose would employ ut with the subjunctive.

358. auxilium viae: *(as) an aid* for her flight; **auxilium** is in apposition with **thēsaurōs. veterēs:** and so unknown to Pygmalion.

360. Hīs (dictīs Sychaeī).

361. (illī) conveniunt. tyrannī: of Pygmalion; obj. gen. with **odium** and **metus;** App. 284.

362. parātae (sunt).

corripiunt onerant*que auro*. Portantur avārī
Pygmaliōnis opēs *pelagō;* dux fēmina factī.
Dēvēnēre *locōs ubi nunc ingentia cernēs*   365
moenia surgentemque novae Karthāginis *arcem,*
mercātī*que* solum, factī *dē nōmine* Byrsam,
taurīnō quantum *possent* circumdare tergō.
Sed vōs quī tandem? Quibus aut vēnistis ab ōrīs?
Quōve tenētis iter?" *Quaerentī tālibus ille*   370
suspīrāns *īmōque trahēns ā pectore vōcem:*
    "*Ō dea, sī prīmā* repetēns *ab* orīgine pergam
et vacet annālēs *nostrōrum audīre labōrum,*

---

annālis, is *m.* story, record, annals
avārus, a, um covetous, greedy
Byrsa, ae *f.* citadel of Carthage
circumdō, āre, dedī, datus surround
corripiō, ere, uī, reptus snatch (up),
    seize
dēveniō, īre, vēnī, ventus arrive (at)
dux, ducis *m. (f.)* leader, guide, chieftain
factum, ī *n.* deed, undertaking, exploit
fēmina, ae *f.* woman
iter, itineris *n.* way, road, journey
Karthāgō, inis *f.* great commercial city of
    North Africa, rival of Rome
mercor, ārī, ātus buy, purchase
onerō (1) load, burden

ops, opis *f.* help, resources, wealth, power
orīgō, inis *f.* origin, beginning, source
pergō, ere, perrēxī, perrēctus proceed
portō (1) carry (off), bear, bring
Pygmaliōn, ōnis *m.* wicked brother of
    Dido
quantus, a, um how great, how much,
    how many, as much (as)
repetō, ere, īvī (iī), ītus seek again,
    repeat, retrace
solum, ī *n.* soil, ground, earth
suspīrō (1) draw a deep breath, sigh
taurīnus, a, um of a bull
tergum, ī *n.* back, hide
vacō (1) be free (from), be at leisure

---

364. pelagō: abl. of route; App. 338.
opēs: the Roman historian Tacitus (*Annals,*
16.1) tells us that the Emperor Nero sent a
commission to Carthage to find the gold
which Dido had brought and presumably
buried there. **fēmina (erat) dux factī.**
    365. Dēvēnēre = dēvēnērunt; App.
204, 4. **(ad or in) locōs;** acc. of place
toward which; App. 315.
    **367-68. mercātī (sunt). (tantum)
solum (vocātum) Byrsam:** *(as much)
ground* or *land (called) Byrsa.* **Byrsam:** a
Greek word meaning *bull's hide,* later
confused with the Carthaginian (Punic)
word *bosra,* meaning *citadel;* hence the
story that the Libyan natives agreed to sell
to the Phoenicians as much land as could
be covered with a bull's hide and that the

Carthaginians cut the hide into long strips,
thus securing a considerable area.
    369. Sed quī (estis) vōs? It is Aeneas'
turn to speak.
    **370. (Venerī) quaerentī tālibus
(vōcibus) ille (Aenēās dīxit).**
    372. Ō dea: Aeneas insists upon his
contention that he is addressing a
goddess, in spite of Venus' denial (335–
37); or does he subconsciously sense her
true identity? **Sī pergam (dīcere annālēs
nostrōrum labōrum):** the protasis of a
future less vivid condition; App. 381.
    372-73. et (sī) vacet (tibi): a second
protasis; *and if you should have the leisure;*
vacet is used impersonally. **audīre:** inf. of
purpose, sometimes used in poetry in place
of a subordinate purpose clause; App. 261.

ante diem clausō compōnet Vesper Olympō.
375 *Nōs Troiā antīquā, sī* vestrās *forte per* aurēs
Troiae nōmen iit, dīversa per aequora vectōs
forte suā Libycīs tempestās appulit *ōrīs.*
Sum pius Aenēās, raptōs *quī ex* hoste penātēs
classe vehō *mēcum, fāmā super* aethera nōtus;
380 *Ītaliam quaerō* patriam, *et genus ab Iove summō.*
Bis dēnīs Phrygium cōnscendī *nāvibus aequor,*

---

aethēr, eris, *acc.* **era,** *m.* upper air, sky, ether
appellō, ere, pulī, pulsus drive to (+ *dat.*)
auris, is *f.* ear
bis twice
claudō, ere, sī, sus (en)close, fasten
compōnō, ere, posuī, positus compose, construct, settle
cōnscendō, ere, ī, ēnsus ascend, embark
dēnī, ae, a ten (each), by tens
dīversus, a, um scattered, various
hostis, is *m.* (*f.*) stranger, enemy, foe
Libycus, a, um Libyan, of Libya, a district of North Africa

nōtus, a, um (well) known, familiar
Olympus, ī *m.* Greek mountain, home of the gods, heaven
patria, ae *f.* homeland, country
penātēs, ium *m.* household gods
Phrygius, a, um Phrygian, Trojan
rapiō, ere, uī, ptus snatch (up), rob
tempestās, ātis *f.* tempest, storm; time
vehō, ere, vēxī, vectus bear, convey
Vesper, eris (erī) *m.* (god of the) evening (star)
vester, tra, trum your(s), your own

---

374. ante: *sooner,* that is, than my story would be told. **compōnet:** future indicative is used in the apodosis of this mixed condition (although some manuscripts read **compōnat,** presumably as the result of an attempt by a scribe to regularize the two halves of the condition). **clausō Olympō:** abl. abs.; when Phoebus, the sun god, returned to Olympus at the end of the day, the doors of heaven were closed for the night.

375-77. tempestās suā forte appulit nōs vectōs (ab) antīquā Troiā—sī forte nōmen Troiae iit per aurēs vestrās—per dīversa aequora Libycīs ōrīs (= ad Libycās ōrās). Nōs: acc., obj. of **appulit,** in 377. **Troiā antīquā (vectōs):** abl. of place from which without a preposition; App. 320, *a.*

377. forte suā: abl. of means; App. 331. The storm was driven by a destiny

opposite to that of Aeneas. **ōrīs:** dat. with a compound verb; App. 298.

378. pius: see the note on **pietāte (10)** and on **pius (220).**

379. classe: abl. of means; App. 331, 332. **fāmā:** abl. of cause or means; App. 331, 332. Aeneas' naïve sense of self-importance will be ironically fulfilled later in Book 1. **aethera:** acc., a Greek form; App. 68.

380. (quaerō) Ītaliam patriam et genus (patrium) ab Iove: refers to the legend that Dardanus, the son of Jupiter and Electra, and founder of the Trojan people, had formerly lived in Italy.

381. Bis dēnīs: *twice ten;* more poetic than simply *twenty.* With adverbs of multiplication, like **bis,** etc., the distributive numerals are commonly employed instead of the cardinals. **Phrygium aequor:** *the sea near Troy.* **nāvibus:** abl. of means; App. 331.

mātre deā mōnstrante *viam data fāta secūtus;*
vix septem convulsae *undīs* Eurōque supersunt.
Ipse ignōtus, egēns, Libyae dēserta peragrō,
Eurōpā *atque* Asiā pulsus." *Nec plūra* querentem   385
passa Venus *mediō sīc* interfāta dolōre *est:*
     "Quisquis *es, haud,* crēdō, invīsus caelestibus *aurās*
vītālēs carpis, *Tyriam quī* advēneris *urbem*;
perge modo *atque hinc tē rēgīnae ad līmina* perfer.
Namque tibī reducēs *sociōs classemque relātam*   390
nuntiō *et in* tūtum versīs Aquilōnibus *āctam,*

---

adveniō, īre, vēnī, ventus arrive, reach
Aquilō, ōnis *m.* (north) wind
Asia, ae *f.* Asia (Minor)
caelestēs, ium (um) *m. (f.)* divinities, gods
carpō, ere, psī, ptus pluck, take, consume
convellō, ere, ī, vulsus tear, shatter
crēdō, ere, didī, ditus believe, trust
dolor, ōris *m.* pain, grief, anger, passion
egeō, ēre, uī be needy, lack
Eurōpa, ae *f.* Europe
Eurus, ī *m.* (east) wind
ignōtus, a, um unknown, strange
interfor, fārī, fātus interrupt
invīsus, a, um hateful, hated, odious
Libya, ae *f.* district of North Africa
modo *adv.* only, (just) now

mōnstrō (1) show, point out
nuntiō (1) announce
patior, ī, passus suffer, endure, allow
pellō, ere, pepulī, pulsus drive, force
peragrō (1) wander through
perferō, ferre, tulī, lātus bear, betake
pergō, ere, perrēxī, perrēctus proceed
queror, ī, questus complain, lament
quisquis, quicquid whoever, whatever
redux, ucis led back, restored
septem seven
supersum, esse, fuī survive, remain
tūtus, a, um safe, protected, secure
Venus, eris *f.* goddess of love and beauty
vertō, ere, ī, rsus turn, change, rout
vītālis, e of life, vital

---

382. (meā) mātre deā mōnstrante: abl. abs.; App. 343. Another irony: Aeneas mentions his mother's helpfulness in a speech to his mother, who in her refusal to identify herself to her son during this exchange is at least temporarily unhelpful!

384. (ego) ipse ignōtus: the adj., taken in a passive sense, means that Aeneas is unknown at present here, even though his fame is widespread (379); in an active sense, it suggests that Aeneas is unaware of how his destiny will be affected by his stop here in Carthage.

385. (ex) Eurōpā, (ex) Asiā: abl. of separation. **Eurōpā** = **Ītaliā:** because of Juno's interference; compare 251–52. **Asiā** = **Troiā:** because of the destruction of Troy. **Plūra (Aenēān) querentem. Venus nōn passa (eum = Aenēān) querentem plūra (= querī plūra) sīc interfāta (est in)**

mediō dolōre. plūra: obj. of **querentem; Aenēān** is understood as obj. of **passa.**

387–88. haud invīsus: this figure of speech is called LITOTES. **caelestibus:** dat. with **invīsus. aurās vītālēs carpis:** *you breathe, live.* **quī advēneris:** subjunctive in a rel. clause of characteristic, with additional idea of cause; App. 389. **advēneris:** either future perf. indicative, or subjunctive in a rel. clause of characteristic; App. 389. **(ad) urbem.**

389. perfer: imperative of **perferō;** App. 202.

390–91. classem: his twelve lost ships. **nam tibi nuntiō sociōs (tuōs esse) reducēs classemque (tuam esse) relātam et āctam in tūtum versīs Aquilōnibus.**

391. in tūtum (portum). versīs Aquilōnibus: abl. abs.; App. 343, or abl. of means, App. 331. **āctam:** from **agō;** modifies **classem.**

nī frūstrā augurium vānī docuēre *parentēs.*
Aspice bis sēnōs laetantēs *agmine* cycnōs,
aetheriā *quōs lāpsa* plagā *Iovis* āles apertō
turbābat *caelō; nunc terrās* ordine *longō*
aut capere aut captās iam dēspectāre *videntur:*
ut reducēs *illī* lūdunt strīdentibus ālīs
et coetū cīnxēre polum cantūs*que dedēre,*

395

---

aetherius, a, um of the upper air, ethereal
āles, itis *m. (f.)* bird, fowl
a(d)spiciō, ere, spexī, spectus see, look at
apertus, a, um open(ed), clear
augurium, (i)ī *n.* augury, prophecy
bis twice
cantus, ūs *m.* song, melody, music
cingō, ere, īnxī, cīnctus encircle, gird
coetus, ūs *m.* company, band, flock
cycnus, ī *m.* swan
dēspectō (1) look down (on)

doceō, ēre, uī, ctus teach, tell, inform
frūstrā *adv.* in vain, uselessly
laetor, ārī, ātus rejoice, exult
lūdō, ere, sī, sus sport, mock
nī, nisi if not, unless, except
ordō, inis *m.* order, line, array
plaga, ae *f.* region, tract
polus, ī *m.* pole, sky, heaven
redux, ucis led back, restored
sēnī, ae, a six (each), by sixes
strīd(e)ō, ēre, dī creak, rustle, whir
turbō (1) throw into confusion, agitate
vānus, a, um empty, idle, false

---

392. docuēre = docuērunt (mē). The omission of the personal pronoun and adj. (i.e., **parentēs meī mē docuēre**) makes her wording interestingly ambiguous, since Venus herself is a **falsa parens,** *deceptive parent,* in this scene; and she is likewise the one who explains to Aeneas the meaning of the omen they see.

393. sēnōs: see note on **dēnīs (381).** The two groups of swans, which had been separated through flight and had reunited after the danger was past, correspond to the two groups of the twelve ships under Ilioneus, which will reunite after a short separation. Thus **sociōs reducēs** of 390 corresponds to **ut reducēs illī** of 397. **agmine:** abl. of manner; App. 328; the swans had just been put to flight and scattered by the eagle. It is probably no coincidence that the omen interpreted here involves swans, birds sacred to Venus.

394. quōs āles Iovis lāpsa aetheriā

plagā turbābat (in) apertō caelō. Iovis āles: the eagle was the bird of Jove and bore his thunderbolt. **(dē) aetheriā plagā:** *from the height of heaven...*

395-96. terrās capere: *to alight.* **caelō:** abl. of place where or of route; App. 319, 338. **nunc videntur:** now, after the eagle has disappeared, the swans are seen in two groups. One group, in a long row, returns to its feeding place on the land; the other group flies above and gazes down at the places occupied (**terrās captās**) by their comrades.

396. captās (terrās) dēspectāre: *to look down upon the places* (**terrās**) *already occupied.*

397. illī = cycnī.

398. coetū: abl. of manner; App. 328. **cīnxēre, dedēre = cīnxērunt, dedērunt;** App. 204, 4. The perfect tenses are used here to suggest single actions, as opposed to **lūdunt,** describing more general and continuous activity. **cantūs:** acc. plural.

haud aliter *puppēsque tuae* pūbēs*que tuōrum*
aut portum tenet aut plēnō *subit* ōstia vēlō.   400
Perge modo *et*, quā *tē dūcit via*, dērige gressum."
    Dīxit et āvertēns roseā cervīce refulsit,
ambrosiae*que* comae dīvīnum vertice odōrem
spīrāvēre; *pedēs* vestis dēflūxit *ad īmōs*,
et vēra incessū patuit *dea. Ille ubi mātrem*   405
agnōvit *tālī fugientem est vōce secūtus:*
"*Quid nātum* totiēns, crūdēlis *tū* quoque, falsīs
lūdis imāginibus? Cūr *dextrae* iungere *dextram*

---

agnōscō, ere, nōvī, nitus recognize
āla, ae *f.* wing
aliter *adv.* otherwise
ambrosius, a, um ambrosial, immortal
āvertō, ere, ī, rusus turn (aside), avert
cervīx, īcis *f.* neck
coma, ae *f.* hair
crūdēlis, e cruel, harsh, bloody
cūr why?
dēfluō, ere, flūxī, flūxus flow down
dērigō, ere, rēxī, rēctus direct, guide
dīvīnus, a, um divine, holy
falsus, a, um false, deceitful, pretended
gressus, ūs *m.* step, walk, gait
imāgō, inis *f.* image, shape, ghost
incessus, ūs *m.* walk, gait, stride
lūdō, ere, sī, sus sport, mock

iungō, ere, iūnxī, iūnctus join, yoke
modo *adv.* only, (just) now
odor, ōris *m.* odor, fragrance
ōstium, (i)ī *n.* mouth, harbor, entrance
pateō, ēre, uī lie open, be evident
pergō, ere, perrēxī, perrēctus proceed
plēnus, a, um full, complete, swelling
pūbēs, is *f.* youth, young men
quā *adv.* where(by), in any way
quoque *adv.* also
refulgeō, ēre, lsī shine, gleam
roseus, a, um rosy, pink
spīrō (1) breathe (forth), exhale
totiēns so often, so many times
vertex, icis *m.* top, summit, head
vērus, a, um true, real, honest
vestis, is *f.* cloth(ing), robe

---

399. haud aliter: LITOTES. The main point of the comparison is in the happy return to safety of both swans and Trojans after their disaster. **-que . . . -que:** POLYSYNDETON.

400. tenet, subit: the subjects are **puppēs** and **pūbēs**, but the verbs agree in number with **pūbēs**, the nearest; App. 236, *b.*

402. Dīxit (Venus) et (sē) āvertēns. cervīce: abl. of means (*with her neck*) or souce (*from her neck*).

403. (ā) vertice: abl. of separation. **dīvīnum odōrem:** a special fragrance is often the sign of the presence of a god.

404. spīravēre = spīrāvērunt. vestis dēflūxit: with the exception of Diana, all

the goddesses normally wore flowing robes.

405. Ille: Aeneas. The HIATUS (lack of elision) between **dea** and **Ille** is justified by the pause in thought after **dea**; cf. **Samō: hīc,** 16.

406. (eam) fugientem.

407. Quid tū quoque crūdēlis totiēns lūdis (mē) nātum (tuum) falsīs imāginibus? quid: adverbial, *why?* **nātum (tuum):** emphatic by position. **tū quoque:** "*even you,* as well as others who might be expected to deceive me."

408. dextrae (manuī): dat. with **iungere;** App. 297.

nōn datur ac vērās *audīre et* reddere *vōcēs?"*
410   *Tālibus* incūsat gressum*que ad moenia tendit.*
At Venus obscūrō gradientēs āere saepsit,
et multō nebulae *circum dea fūdit* amictū,
cernere nē quis eōs neu *quis* contingere *posset*
mōlīrī*ve* moram *aut veniendī* poscere causās.
415   *Ipsa* Paphum sublīmis abit *sēdēsque* revīsit
laeta suās, ubi templum *illī,* centum*que* Sabaeō
tūre calent *ārae* sertīs*que* recentibus hālant.

---

abeō, īre, iī (īvī), itus depart
āēr, āeris, *acc.* āera, *m.* air, mist, fog
amictus, ūs *m.* wrap, robe
caleō, ēre, uī be hot, burn
causa, ae *f.* cause, reason
centum hundred
contingō, ere, tigī, tāctus touch, befall
gradior, ī, gressus step, go, proceed
gressus, ūs *m.* step, walk, gait
hālō (1) breathe (forth), be fragrant
incūsō (1) reproach, chide, blame
mōlior, īrī, ītus work, effect, make
mora, ae *f.* delay, hindrance, hestation
nebula, ae *f.* cloud, mist, fog
neu, nēve and (that) not, and lest
obscūrus, a, um dark

Paphus (os), ī *f.* city of Cyprus, famous
    center of the worship of Venus
poscō, ere, poposcī demand, seek
recēns, entis fresh, recent
reddō, ere, didī, ditus return, reply
revīsō, ere revisit
Sabaeus, a, um Sabaean, of Saba in
    southern Arabia, famous for its
    incense
saepiō, īre, psī, ptus hedge in, enclose
sertum, ī *n.* wreath, garland
sublīmis, e on high, aloft, uplifted
templum, ī *n.* temple, shrine, sanctuary
tūs, tūris *n.* incense, unguent
Venus, eris *f.* goddess of love and beauty

---

409. vērās vōcēs: contrasted with
falsīs imāginibus of 407.
    410. Tālibus (dictīs Aenēās) incūsat
(mātrem suam). moenia (Karthāginis).
    411. obscūrō āere: such a concealing
cloud or mist is a device very common in
epic tradition and in folk tales. **(Aenēān
Achātēnque) gradientēs.**
    412. circum (eōs) fūdit: *surrounded
(them).* The separation of **circum** and **fudit,**
actually one word (**circumfudit**), is called
TMESIS ("cutting" or "split" in Greek). The
splitting of the verb into two parts is
repeated in the pattern of the line, in which
amictū and its adj. **multō** are separated
from each other and placed at the two ends
of the line, while the goddess who is

responsible for this is at the center. **dea:** *(as)
a goddess,* i.e., by her supernatural power.
    413. quis: indef. pronoun after **ne,**
used in place of **aliquis. cernere (eōs). ne
. . . neu . . . posset:** negative purpose;
App. 359.
    414. mōlīrī moram: ALLITERATION.
veniendī: a gerund in the gen. with
causās.
    415. Ipsa: Venus; see the note on **ipsa**
(42) and on **ipsius** (114). **Paphum:** acc.
of place to which; App. 315, *a.*
    416. laeta: contrasted with **trīstior** (l.
228). **templum (est) illī. illī:** Venerī, dat.
of possession; App. 299.

Corripuēre *viam* intereā, quā sēmita mōnstrat.
Iamque ascendēbant collem, *quī plūrimus urbī*
imminet adversāsque aspectat dēsuper *arcēs.*   420
Mīrātur mōlem *Aenēās,* māgalia *quondam,*
mīrātur portās strepitumque *et* strāta *viārum.*
Īnstant *ardentēs Tyriī: pars dūcere* mūrōs
mōlīrīque *arcem et manibus* subvolvere *saxa,*
pars optāre *locum tēctō et* conclūdere sulcō;   425
iūra magistrātūsque legunt sānctumque senātum.
Hīc portūs aliī effodiunt; *hīc alta* theātrīs
fundāmenta locant *aliī, immānēsque* columnās

---

adversus, a, um opposite, facing
ascendō, ere, ī, ēnsus ascend, mount
a(d)spectō (1) look at, see, face
collis, is *m.* hill
columna, ae *f.* column, pillar
conclūdō, ere, sī, sus (en)close
corripiō, ere, uī, reptus snatch (up),
 hasten on
dēsuper *adv.* from above
effodiō, ere, fōdī, fossus dig out,
 excavate
fundāmentum, ī *n.* foundation
immineō, ēre hang over, menace (+ *dat.*)
īnstō, āre, stitī urge on, press on (+ *dat.*)
intereā *adv.* meanwhile, meantime
iūs, iūris *n.* law, justice, decree
legō, ere, lēgī, lēctus choose, gather
locō (1) place, locate, establish

māgālia, ium *n.* huts, hovels
magistrātus, ūs *m.* magistrate, officer
mīror, ārī, ātus wonder (at), admire
mōlēs, is *f.* mass, burden, structure
mōlior, īrī, ītus work, effect, make
mōnstrō (1) show, point out
mūrus, ī *m.* (city) wall, rampart
optō (1) choose, desire, hope (for)
porta, ae *f.* gate, door, opening
quā *adv.* where(by), in any way
sānctus, a, um sacred, holy, revered
sēmita, ae *f.* path
senātus, ūs *m.* senate, council of elders
strātum, ī *n.* pavement; bed
strepitus, ūs *m.* noise, uproar
subvolvō, ere, ī, volūtus roll up
sulcus, ī *m.* furrow, trench, ditch
theātrum, ī *n.* theater

> 418–40. Aeneas and Achates,
> rendered invisible by Venus, proceed
> to Carthage and admire the rising city.

**418. (Aenēās Achātēsque)
corripuērunt viam:** *they hurried along
their way.* **sēmita (sē) mōnstrat.**
 419. plūrimus: *with imposing size.*
urbī: dat. with compound; App. 298.
 421. mōlem (urbis). quondam: before
the building of the city. **Mīrātur . . .**

mīrātur: ANAPHORA, here—as often—
combined with ASYNDETON.
 423. dūcere: *extend*; this and the
following infinitives either depend on
Īnstant; App. 259, or are to be construed
as historical inf. App. 257.
 423–25. pars, pars: in partitive
apposition with **Tyriī.**
 425. tēctō: *for a house*: dat. of
purpose; App. 303. **conclūdere (locum
tēctī) sulcō:** for the foundation.
 426. magistrātūs: acc. plural.
 427–28. aliī . . . aliī: *some . . . others.*

pars...
saxe

part of them want to ~~fot~~ touch extend their walls
hands and a part of them want to
make a forres parts of them
want to oll up the rakes w/ their
hand

rūpibus excīdunt, scaenīs decora *alta futūrīs.*
430 Quālis apēs aestāte *novā per* flōrea rūra
exercet *sub* sōle *labor, cum gentis* adultōs
ēdūcunt fētūs, *aut cum* līquentia mella
stīpant *et* dulcī distendunt nectare cellās,
aut onera *accipiunt venientum, aut agmine factō*
435 ignāvum fūcōs pecus *ā* praesēpibus arcent;
fervet opus redolent*que* thymō fraglantia mella.
"Ō fortunātī, *quōrum iam moenia surgunt!"*
Aenēās ait et fastīgia suspicit *urbis.*

---

adultus, a, um grown, adult
aestās, ātis *f.* summer
apis, is *f.* bee
arceō, ēre, uī keep off, defend
cella, ae *f.* cell, storeroom
decus, oris *n.* ornament, beauty, dignity
distendō, ere, ī, ntus distend, stretch
dulcis, e sweet, dear, fresh
ēdūcō, ere, dūxī, ductus lead forth
excīdō, ere, ī, sus cut out, destroy
exerceō, ēre, uī, itus be busy, train
fastīgium, (i)ī *n.* summit, top, height
ferv(e)ō, ēre, (ferbu)ī glow, boil
fētus, ūs *m.* offspring, brood, swarm
flōreus, a, um flowery
fortūnātus, a, um fortunate, blessed
fraglāns, antis fragrant, sweet-smelling
fūcus, ī *n.* drone

ignāvus, a, um lazy, idle
līquēns, entis liquid, flowing
mel, mellis *n.* honey
nectar, aris *n.* nectar
onus, eris *n.* burden, load
opus, eris *n.* work, deed, toil
pecus, oris *n.* flock, herd, swarm
praesēpe, is *n.* stall, hive
quālis, e such (as), of what sort, as
redoleō, ēre, uī be fragrant, smell (of)
rūpēs, is *f.* rock, cliff, crag
rūs, rūris *n.* country (district)
scaena, ae *f.* stage, background
sōl, sōlis *m.* sun; day
stīpō (1) stuff, crowd, stow
suspiciō, ere, spexī, spectus look up (at)
thymum, ī *n.* thyme, a flowering plant

---

429. (ex) rūpibus: the typical open-air theater of classical Greece (less frequently, Rome) was commonly excavated from a hillside. **scaenīs:** dat. **decora:** apposition with **columnās.**

430–31. (tālis est labor illīs) quālis (labor) exercet apēs: the SIMILE is famous. **aestāte novā:** abl. of time; App. 322.

434. venient(i)um (apium).

435. fūcōs: *the drones;* apposition with **ignāvum pecus.**

436. fraglantia: this unusual form, which appears as **flagrantia** in some of

the earliest manuscripts of Vergil's works, is cognate with the English *fragrant;* but in Latin words, one of two similar consonantal sounds (here, **l** and **r**) sometimes changes so as to become more pronounceable (the process is called "dissimilation" by linguists).

437. Ō fortūnātī: substantively, *O fortunate ones!* **iam moenia surgunt:** Aeneas was impatiently looking forward to the time when the walls of his own city would rise.

438. ait: third sing. of **aiō.**

Īnfert *sē* saeptus nebulā (mīrābile *dictū*)
per mediōs, miscet*que virīs neque cernitur ūllī.*   440

īnferō, ferre, tulī, lātus bear (in, into)
mīrābilis, e wonderful, marvelous
misceō, ēre, uī, mixtus mix, mingle

nebula, ae *f.* cloud, mist, fog
saepiō, īre, psī, ptus hedge in, inclose

---

439. dictū: supine, abl. of respect with **mīrābile;** App. 271, 325.

440. per mediōs (virōs): *through the midst (of) the men;* App. 246. **(sē) miscet virīs: virīs** is dat. with **miscet;** App. 297. **ūllī:** dat. of agent; App. 302.

either the hive accepts the burden of the coming bees
or when the battle lines has been made defend c¹⁴²⁹shorn, the drones, defend from hive

Lūcus *in urbe fuit mediā, laetissimus umbrae,*
quō prīmum iactātī *undīs et* turbine Poenī
effōdēre *locō* signum, *quod* rēgia Iūnō
mōnstrārat, *caput* ācris *equī; sīc nam fore bellō*
445   ēgrēgiam *et* facilem victū *per* saecula *gentem.*
Hīc templum *Iūnōnī ingēns* Sīdōnia *Dīdō*
condēbat, *dōnīs* opulentum *et nūmine dīvae,*
aerea *cui* gradibus *surgēbant* līmina nexae*que*

ācer, cris, cre sharp, keen, spirited
aereus, a, um (of) bronze, brazen
condō, ere, didī, ditus found, build
effodiō, ere, fōdī, fossus dig out, excavate
ēgregius, a, um remarkable, distinguished
facilis, e easy
gradus, ūs *m.* step, stride, gait
iactō (1) toss, buffet
lūcus, ī *m.* (sacred) grove, wood
mōnstrō (1) show, point out

nectō, ere, x(u)ī, xus bind, fasten
opulentus, a, um rich, wealthy
Poenus, a, um Phoenician, Carthaginian
rēgius, a, um royal, regal, kingly
saeculum, ī *n.* generation, age
Sīdōnius, a, um Sidonian, Phoenician
signum, ī *n.* sign, token, signal
templum, ī *n.* temple, shrine, sanctuary
turbō, inis *m.* whirl(wind, pool), storm
vīvō, ere, vīxī, vīctus live, be alive

441–93. Aeneas visits the temple of Juno where he sees depicted the leading incidents of the Trojan War.

441. laetissimus: the basic meaning of the adj. **laetus** is "fertile," "productive," and from this it comes to mean "happy." **umbrae:** gen. with adj.; App. 287.

442. (in) quō . . . locō = ubi. iactātī: on the stormy voyage from Tyre; Vergil momentarily suggests that the Carthaginians and Trojans have much in common. **prīmum:** immediately after landing.

443. effōdēre = effōdērunt.

444. mōnstrā(ve)rat: App. 204, 1. **caput equī:** a common symbol on Carthaginian coins. **fore = futūram esse:** ind. statement depending on a verb of speaking implied in **mōnstrā(ve)rat;** App. 263. **bellō:** abl. of specification or respect.

445. vīctū: supine from **vīvō, vīvere,** abl. of specification or respect with **facilem;** App. 271, 325, *easy to live, to sustain,* referring to the great commercial success of Carthage. **gentem (Pūnicam).**

446. Sīdōnia: *Phoenician;* Tyre and Sidon, each a famous Phoenician city, came to be synonymous with Phoenicia.

447. dōnīs, nūmine: abl. of respect depending on **opulentum;** App. 325.

448-49. cui surgēbant gradibus aerea līmina trabēsque nexae aere, (et) cardō strīdēbat foribus aēnīs. aerea, aere, aēnīs: the lavish use of costly bronze helps to indicate the magnificence of the temple. **cui gradibus:** *on the steps of which;* **cui** is dat. of reference, closely related to dat. of possession; App. 301. **nexae (erant). -que:** the elision of the final -e before the initial diphthong of the first word of the next line forms a HYPERMETRIC verse; cf. 332. This unusual elision also reflects the meaning of the words thus joined.

aere trabēs, foribus cardō strīdēbat aēnīs.

Hōc prīmum in lūcō *nova rēs* oblāta timōrem   450
lēniit, *hīc prīmum Aenēās* spērāre salūtem
ausus *et* adflīctīs melius cōnfīdere *rēbus.*
Namque sub ingentī lūstrat *dum* singula templō
rēgīnam opperiēns, *dum quae fortūna sit urbī*
artificum*que manūs intēr sē* operum*que labōrem*   455
mīrātur, *videt* Īliacās *ex* ordine pugnās
bellaque iam fāmā tōtum vulgāta *per* orbem,
Atrīdās *Priamumque et* saevum ambōbus Achillem.

Achillēs, is (ī) *m.* Greek chieftain
adflīgō, ere, xī, ctus strike down, shatter
aēnus, a, um (of) bronze, brazen
aes, aeris *n.* bronze
ambō, ae, ō both
artifex, icis *m.* artist, artisan
Atrīdēs, ae *m.* son of Atreus, (1) Agamemnon, (2) Menelaus; leaders of the Greeks against Troy
audeō, ēre, ausus sum dare, venture
cardō, inis *m.* hinge, pivot, socket
cōnfīdō, ere, sus sum trust (in) (+ *dat.*)
foris, is *f.* door, gate, entrance
Īliacus, a, um Ilian, Trojan
lēniō, īre, īvī (iī), itus soothe, soften
lūcus, ī *m.* (sacred) grove, wood
lūstrō (1) purify, survey, traverse

melior, ius better, superior
mīror, ārī, ātus wonder (at), admire
offerō, ferre, obtulī, oblātus present
opperior, īrī, per(i)tus await, wait for
opus, eris *n.* work, deed, toil
orbis, is *m.* circle, orb, earth
ordō, inis *m.* order, line, array
pugna, ae *f.* battle, fight
saevus, a, um fierce, harsh, stern
salūs, ūtis *f.* safety, security, health
singulī, ae, a separate, single
spērō (1) hope (for), expect
strīd(e)ō, ere (or ēre), dī grate, creak, whir
timor, ōris *m.* fear, anxiety, dread
trabs (trabēs), trabis *f.* beam, timber
vulgō (1) publish, make known

---

449. aere: abl. of means. **foribus aēnīs:** abl. of place where or origin, or dat. of reference; App. 319, 301.

450. timōrem (Aenēae).

452. ausus (est). rēbus: abl. or dat. with special verb, **cōnfīdere;** App. 319, 297.

453. sub ingentī templō: Aeneas is standing so close to the temple that it seems to be looming above him. **singula:** i.e., each and every individual detail of the temple's design.

454. sit: subjunctive in an indir. quest.; App. 349. **urbī:** dat. of possession; App. 299.

455. artificum manūs intēr sē: *the rival deeds of skill of the artists,* referring to the temple and its decoration.

456. ex ordine: *in order.* **fāmā:** abl. of means. **tōtum orbem (terrārum):** *the whole world.*

458. ambōbus (Atrīdīs Priamōque): Achilles was fighting against the Trojans, and of course was hostile to Priam, the Trojan king; furthermore, a bitter feud arose near the end of the war between Achilles and the sons of Atreus, Agamemnon and Menelaüs, because Agamemnon had forcibly deprived Achilles of one of his war prizes, the captive girl Brisēïs. This feud was the occasion of the "Wrath of Achilles," the theme of Homer's *Iliad.*

Cōnstitit *et* lacrimāns "*Quis iam locus,*" inquit, "Achātē,
460   *quae* rēgiō *in terrīs nostrī nōn* plēna *labōris?*
       Ēn Priamus. *Sunt hīc* etiam *sua* praemia laudī,
       sunt lacrimae rērum et mentem mortālia tangunt.
       Solve metūs; *feret haec* aliquam *tibi fāma* salūtem."
       Sīc ait atque animum pictūrā pascit inānī
465   *multa* gemēns, largō*que* ūmectat flūmine vultum.
       Namque vidēbat utī bellantēs Pergama *circum*
       hāc *fugerent* Graī, premeret Troiāna iuventūs;

Achātēs, ae *m.* faithful comrade of
    Aeneas
aliquī, qua, quod some, any
bellō (1) wage war, battle
cōnsistō, ere, stitī, stitus stand fast, halt
ēn see! look! behold!
etiam *adv.* also, even
flūmen, inis *n.* river, stream
gemō, ere, uī, itus groan (for), lament
Graius, a, um Greek
inānis, e empty, idle, vain
inquam, is, it say
iuventūs, ūtis *f.* youth, (group of) young
    men
largus, a, um copious, plentiful
laus, laudis *f.* praise, glory, merit

metus, ūs *m.* fear, dread, anxiety
mortālis, e mortal, human
pascō, ere, pāvī, pāstus feed (on), graze
Pergama, ōrum *n.* (citadel of) Troy
pictūra, ae *f.* picture, painting
plēnus, a, um full, complete, swelling
praemium, (i)ī *n.* reward, prize
premō, ere, pressī, pressus (re)press,
    urge
regiō, ōnis *f.* region, district
salūs, ūtis *f.* safety, security, health
solvō, ere, ī, solūtus loosen, dismiss
tangō, ere, tetigī, tāctus touch
Troiānus, a, um Trojan
ūmectō (1) wet, moisten
vultus, ūs *m.* countenance, face

---

459. lacrimāns: see the note on
frīgore (92). **Achātē:** vocative.
    460. nōn (est) plēna.
    461. hīc etiam: *here also,* i.e., even in
this place so distant from Troy, as well as
elsewhere. **laudī:** dat. of possession; App.
299.
    462. lacrimae rērum: *compassion for
suffering.* **mentem mortālia:** ALLITERATION,
heightening the pathos. **mortālia:** neut.
pl. adj. used substantively, *human (woes).*
    463. metūs: acc. pl. **haec fāma**
(**Teucrōrum**).
    464. ait: third sing. of aiō. **inānī:**
etymologically connected to **anima,** with
the negative prefix **in-;** thus, the word

essentially means "lifeless." **pictūrā:** with
this word Vergil introduces one of the
most memorable ECPHRASES (in the sing.,
ECPHRASIS) in the poem. The description is
elaborate, yet the exact location of the
images on the temple remains elusive.
    **466–67. utī hāc Graī bellantēs
circum Pergama fugerent. utī:** *how;*
introduces three indirect questions. **Graī:**
pl. of **Graius** and pronounced as though
spelled **Graiī,** making the first syllable
long by position; App. 6, *b.*
    467–68. fugerent, premeret, īnstāret:
impf. subjunctives in indir. quest.; App.
349. **hāc . . . hāc:** *here . . . there,* in the
series of images being described.

hāc Phryges, īnstāret currū cristātus Achillēs.

Nec procul hinc Rhēsī niveīs tentōria *vēlīs*
agnōscit lacrimāns, *prīmō quae* prōdita *somnō*   470
Tȳdīdēs *multā* vastābat caede cruentus,
ardentēsque āvertit *equōs in* castra prius quam
pābula gustāssent *Troiae* Xanthum*que* bibissent.
Parte aliā fugiēns āmissīs Trōilus *armīs*,
īnfēlīx puer atque impār congressus Achillī,   475

Achillēs, is (ī) *m.* Greek chieftain,
  central character in the *Iliad*
agnōscō, ere, nōvī, nitus recognize
āmittō, ere, mīsī, missus let go, lose
āvertō, ere, ī, rsus turn away, avert
bibō, ere, ī drink (of, in)
caedēs, is *f.* slaughter
castra, ōrum *n.* camp, encampment
congredior, ī, gressus meet, fight with (+
  dat.)
cristātus, a, um plumed, crested
cruentus, a, um bloody, cruel
currus, ūs *m.* chariot, car
gustō (1) taste, eat
hāc *adv.* here, there
impār, aris unequal, ill-matched
īnstō, āre, stitī press on, urge (on)

lacrimō (1) weep, shed tears, lament
niveus, a, um snowy, white
pābulus, ī *n.* fodder, pasture
Phryx, Phrygis Phrygian, Trojan
prius *adv.* former, sooner, first
prōdō, ere, didī, ditus hand over, betray
quam how, than, as
Rhēsus, ī *m.* Thracian prince, ally of the
  Trojans, slain on the first night after
  his arrival at Troy
tentōrium, (i)ī *n.* tent
Trōilus, ī *m.* youngest son of Priam
Tȳdīdēs, ae *m.* son of Tydeus, Diomedes,
  famous Greek chieftain
vastō (1) ravage, devastate, (lay) waste
Xanthus, ī *m.* river near Troy

---

468. Phryges (fugerent). cristātus:
the Homeric warrior wore a helmet with
waving plumes.

469. Nec procul hinc: in another
scene. **Rhēsī:** an ally of the Trojans. An
oracle had proclaimed that Troy could
not be captured if Rhesus' horses ever
drank of the waters of the Xanthus or
grazed on the Trojan meadows. Odysseus
and Diomedes surprised Rhesus on the
night of his arrival, killed him, and drove
off his horses before they had partaken of
the fateful water and grass. Homer had
included the story in *Iliad* Book 10.

470. prīmō prōdita: ALLITERATION.
prīmō somnō: abl. of time when or
means; App. 322, 331.

471. vastābat: action represented as
taking place in the picture. **caede
cruentus:** ALLITERATION. **multā caede:** abl.
of manner; App. 328.

472. in castra: i.e., to the Greek camp.

473. gustā(vi)ssent, bibissent:
descriptive or anticipatory subjunctives;
App. 376, *a*.

474. (in) Parte aliā: in a fourth scene.
āmissīs armīs: abl. abs., referring to only
a part of his arms, such as his shield, for
he still holds his spear. **Trōilus:** slain by
Achilles (but not featured in the *Iliad*).

475. impār congressus Achillī:
unequal to Achilles in battle.

fertur equīs currū*que* haeret resupīnus inānī,
lōra *tenēns* tamen; *huic* cervīx*que* comae*que trahuntur*
per terram, et versā pulvis īnscrībitur hastā.
Intereā *ad* templum *nōn* aequae Palladis *ībant*
crīnibus Īliades passīs peplum*que ferēbant*
suppliciter, *trīstēs et* tūnsae *pectora* palmīs;
dīva solō fixōs *oculōs* āversa *tenēbat.*
Ter *circum* Īliacōs raptāverat Hectora mūrōs

480

---

aequus, a, um equal, even, impartial
āvertō, ere, ī, rsus turn away, avert
cervīx, īcis *f.* neck
coma, ae *f.* hair
crīnis, is *m.* locks, hair
currus, ūs *m.* chariot, car
fīgō, ere, fīxī, fīxus fix, fasten
hasta, ae *f.* spear
haereō, ēre, haesī, haesus hang, cling to (+ *dat.*)
Hector, oris, *acc.* **ora,** *m.* Trojan leader
Īliacus, a, um Ilian, Trojan
Īlias, adis *f.* Trojan woman
inānis, e empty, idle, vain
īnscrībō, ere, psī, ptus mark
intereā *adv.* meanwhile, meantime
lōrum, ī *n.* thong, rein

mūrus, ī *m.* (city) wall, rampart
Pallas, adis *f.* Minerva, goddess of wisdom and the arts
palma, ae *f.* palm, hand
pandō, ere, ī, passus spread, dishevel
peplus (um), ī *m.* *(n.)* robe, gown
pulvis, eris *m.* dust
raptō (1) snatch, drag
resupīnus, a, um supine, on the back
solum, ī *n.* soil, ground, earth
suppliciter *adv.* beseechingly, humbly
tamen *adv.* nevertheless, however
templum, ī *n.* temple, shrine
ter thrice, three times
tundō, ere, tutudī, tū(n)sus beat
vertō, ere, ī, rsus turn, change, rout

---

476. His foot seems to have caught in the chariot as he fell backward. **currū inānī:** currū is either dat. (= **curruī**) or abl. with **haeret.**

477. huic: dat. of reference, closely connected to dat. of possession.

478. versā hastā: *with trailing* (lit. *turned) spear.* **pulvis:** with the last syllable irregularly long, here probably for emotional emphasis.

479. nōn aequae: *hostile,* because of Minerva's resentment toward Troy after the adverse judgment of Paris.

480. crīnibus passīs: abl. of quality or description; App. 330. **passīs:** from **pandō;** dishevelled hair was a sign of mourning for women. **peplum:** in the worship of many of the female Greek divinities, a finely woven, and often elaborately decorated, robe was presented to the statue of the goddess by a procession

of women and girls. Hecuba and the other Trojan women offer a finely crafted *peplos* to Athena in *Iliad* Book 6, in vain.

481. pectora: obj. of the participle **tūnsae** *(having beaten),* treated here as a Greek middle participle capable of having a dir. obj.; alternatively, **pectora** is a so-called Greek acc., i.e., acc. of respect *(having been beaten with respect to their breasts);* App. 309, *a.*

482. dīva (Pallas). solō: dat. of direction; App. 306; her eyes were directed to the ground, as a sign of sullen displeasure.

483. Hectora: acc., a Greek form; App. 68. This sixth scene represents the ransom of Hector's body from Achilles, who had dragged it three times around the walls of Troy. The ransoming of Hector is the major concluding episode of the *Iliad.*

exanimum*que aurō corpus* vendēbat Achillēs.

Tum vērō *ingentem* gemitum *dat pectore ab īmō,*   485
ut spolia, *ut* currūs, *utque ipsum corpus* amīcī
tendentemque manūs Priamum cōnspexit inermēs.
Sē quoque principibus permixtum agnōvit Achīvīs,
Ēōās*que* aciēs *et* nigrī Memnonis *arma.*
Dūcit Amāzonidum lūnātīs *agmina* peltīs   490
Penthesilēa *furēns mediīsque in* mīlibus *ardet,*
aurea subnectēns exsertae cingula mammae
bellātrīx, audet*que virīs* concurrere virgō.

Achillēs, is (ī) *m.* Greek chieftain
Achīvus, a, um Achaean, Greek
aciēs, ēī *f.* edge, battle line, army
agnōscō, ere, nōvī, nitus recognize
Amāzonis, idis *f.* Amazon, female warrior
amīcus, ī *m.* friend
audeō, ēre, ausus sum dare, venture
aureus, a, um gold(en), of gold
bellātrīx, īcis *f.* warrior
cingulum, ī *n.* belt, girdle
concurrō, ere, (cu)currī, cursus run
     together, fight with (+ *dat.*)
cōnspiciō, ere, spexī, spectus see, behold
currus, ūs *m.* chariot, car
Ēōus, a, um of the dawn, eastern
exanimus, a, um breathless, lifeless
exserō, ere, uī, rtus thrust out, expose
gemitus, ūs *m.* groan, lament
inermis, e unarmed

lūnātus, a, um crescent, moon-shaped
mamma, ae *f.* breast
Memnōn, onis *m.* Ethiopian king, son of
     Aurora and ally of the Trojans, slain
     by Achilles
mīlle; *pl.* mīlia, ium *n.* thousand
niger, gra, grum black, dusky
pelta, ae *f.* light shield
Penthesilēa, ae *f.* queen of the Amazons,
     ally of the Trojans, slain by Achilles
permisceō, ēre, uī, mixtus mix, mingle
princeps, cipis *m.* (*f.*) chief, leader
quoque *adv.* also
spolium, (i)ī *n.* spoil(s), booty, plunder
subnectō, ere, x(u)ī, xus fasten beneath
vendō, ere, didī, ditus sell
vērō *adv.* truly, indeed, but
virgō, inis *f.* girl, maid(en)

---

484. aurō: abl. of price; App. 336.
corpus vendēbat Achillēs (Priamō).
     485. (Aenēās) dat.
     486. currūs: poetic plural; the chariot
with which Achilles dragged Hector
around Troy. **ut, ut, ut:** ANAPHORA, here as
often combined with ASYNDETON.
     487. spolia: taken by Achilles from
Hector. **manūs inermēs:** as a suppliant.
     488. Sē: seeing himself depicted in the
decoration of this temple reminds Aeneas
of his own losses in the Trojan war.
principibus: dat. or abl. with
permixtum.

     489. Ēōāsque aciēs (agnōvit):
Trojan allies from Ethiopia led by
Memnon. The epithet **Ēōās** is based on
the name of Memnon's mother, Eos
(Aurora in Latin). The roles of the
Ethiopians and Amazons in the Trojan
war were the subject of another epic
poem, the *Aethiopis,* of which only
fragments now remain.
     490. lūnātīs peltīs: abl. of quality;
App. 330; crescent shields were characteristic of the Amazons.
     493. virīs: dat. with the special verb,
concurrere. virgō: (although) *a girl;*
contrasted with **virīs.**

Haec dum Dardaniō *Aenēae* mīranda *videntur,*
495 *dum* stupet obtūtū*que* haeret dēfīxus *in ūnō,*
rēgīna *ad* templum, formā pulcherrima *Dīdō,*
incessit *magnā* iuvenum stīpante catervā.
Quālis *in* Eurōtae rīpīs *aut per* iuga Cynthī
exercet Dīāna chorōs, *quam* mīlle *secūtae*
500 *hinc atque hinc* glomerantur Orēades; *illa* pharetram
fert umerō gradiēns*que deās* superēminet *omnēs*
(Lātōnae tacitum pertemptant gaudia *pectus*):
tālis erat Dīdō, tālem sē laeta ferēbat
per mediōs īnstāns operī *rēgnīsque futūrīs.*

---

caterva, ae *f.* band, troop, crowd
chorus, ī *m.* chorus, dance, band
Cynthus, ī *m.* mountain in Delos, birthplace of Apollo and Diana
Dardanius, a, um Dardanian, Trojan
Dīāna, ae *f.* goddess of the hunt and of the mountains
dēfīgō, ere, fīxī, fīxus fix, fasten
Eurōtās, ae *m.* river of Sparta, center of the worship of Diana
exerceō, ēre, uī, itus busy, train
forma, ae *f.* form, beauty, shape
gaudium, (i)ī *n.* joy, rejoicing
glomerō (1) gather, roll together
gradior, ī, gressus step, go, proceed
haereō, ēre, haesī, haesus hang, cling (to)
incēdō, ere, cessī, cessus march, go (majestically)
īnstō, āre, stitī press on, urge (+ *dat.*)

iugum, ī *n.* yoke, (mountain) ridge
iuvenis, is *m.* (*f.*) youth, young (man or woman)
Lātōna, ae *f.* mother of Apollo and Diana
mīlle; *pl.* **mīlia, ium** *n.* thousand
mīrandus, a, um wonderful, marvelous
obtūtus, ūs *m.* gaze, view
opus, eris *n.* work, deed, toil
Orēas, adis *f.* Oread, a mountain nymph
pertemptō (1) try; master, possess
pharetra, ae *f.* quiver
pulcher, chra, chrum beautiful, handsome, illustrious
quālis, e such (as), of what sort
rīpa, ae *f.* bank, shore
stīpō (1) stuff, crowd, throng, stow
stupeō, ēre, uī stand agape, be dazed
superēmineō, ēre tower above
tacitus, a, um silent, speechless, still
templum, ī *n.* temple, shrine, sanctuary

> 494–519. Dido visits the temple and welcomes the newly arrived Trojans.

494. Dardaniō: *Trojan;* reminding us why these scenes had so much meaning for Aeneas.

496. formā: abl. of respect with **pulcherrima:** App. 325.

497. stīpante catervā: abl. abs.; App. 343.

498. Quālis: correlative with **tālis** (503). This SIMILE was inspired by Homer, who described the Phaeacian princess Nausicaa in similar terms when she was first seen by Odysseus (*Odyssey* Book 6).

499. Dīāna: with long -i-; elsewhere with short -i-.

500. illa: Dīāna. hinc atque hinc: *on this side and on that; on both sides.*

501. (in) umerō. deās (Orēadas).

502. tacitum pectus: indicating joy too deep for words.

504. per mediōs (virōs).

Tum foribus *dīvae, mediā* testūdine templī,   505
saepta *armīs* soliō*que* altē subnixa resēdit.
Iūra *dabat* lēgēs*que virīs,* operum*que labōrem*
partibus aequābat iūstīs *aut* sorte *trahēbat:*
cum subitō *Aenēās* concursū accēdere *magnō*
Anthea Sergestum*que videt* fortem*que* Cloanthum   510
Teucrōrumque aliōs, āter quōs aequore turbō
dispulerat penitus*que aliās* āvēxerat *ōrās.*
Obstipuit *simul ipse, simul* percussus Achātēs
laetitiā*que* metū*que;* avidī coniungere *dextrās*
ardēbant, sed rēs animōs incognita turbat.   515

---

accēdō, ere, cessī, cessus approach
Achātēs, ae *m.* faithful comrade of Aeneas
aequō (1) equal(ize)
altē *adv.* on high, loftily
Antheus, eī, *acc.* **ea,** *m.* Trojan leader
āvehō, ere, vēxī, vectus bear away
avidus, a, um eager, greedy
Cloanthus, ī *m.* Trojan leader
concursus, ūs *m.* throng, crowd
coniungō, ere, iūnxī, iūnctus join
dispellō, ere, pulī, pulsus drive apart, disperse, scatter
foris, is *f.* door, gate, entrance
fortis, e strong, brave, valiant
incognitus, a, um unknown
iūs, iūris *n.* law, justice, right
iūstus, a, um just, fair, right(eous)
laetitia, eae *f.* joy, gladness, delight

lēx, lēgis *f.* law, regulation, decree
metus, ūs *m.* fear, anxiety, dread
obstipēscō, ere, stipuī stand agape
opus, eris *n.* work, deed, toil
penitus *adv.* deep within, deeply, wholly
percutiō, ere, cussī, cussus strike, astound
resīdō, ere, sēdī sit down
saepiō, īre, psī, ptus hedge in, enclose
Sergestus, ī *m.* Trojan leader
solium, (i)ī *n.* throne, seat
sors, rtis *f.* lot, fate, destiny
subitō *adv.* suddenly
subnixus, a, um resting on (+ *abl.*)
templum, ī *n.* temple, shrine, sanctuary
testūdō, inis *f.* tortoise, vault, dome
turbō (1) confuse, disturb, perplex
turbō, inis *m.* whirl(wind, pool), storm

---

505. dīvae: *of the shrine* (lit. *of the goddess*).

505–6. (in) foribus, (in) testūdine, (in) soliō.

507. virīs (Tyriīs): her subjects. The use of temples for the transaction of public business was very common in ancient Rome; hence Vergil assigned a similar custom to the Carthaginians.

508. sorte trahēbat: *assigned the work by lot.*

509–12. cum Aenēās subitō videt accēdere Anthea (acc.) **Sergestumque fortemque Clanthum aliōsque Teucrōrum, quōs āter turbō dispulerat (in) aequore. concursū magnō:** abl. of manner; App. 328. **(ad) aliās ōrās.**

513. ipse: Aeneas; see the note on 114. **simul . . . simul = et . . . et. percussus (est).**

515. rēs incognita: the uncertainty of the situation keeps them silent.

Dissimulant *et* nūbe cavā speculantur amictī
quae fortūna virīs, classem quō lītore linquant,
quid veniant; cūnctīs nam lēctī *nāvibus ībant*
519   ōrantēs veniam *et* templum *clāmōre petēbant.*

---

amiciō, īre, uī (ixī), ictus enfold, wrap
cavus, a, um hollow
dissimulō (1) hide, disguise
legō, ere, lēgī, lēctus choose, gather
linquō, ere, līquī, lictus leave, desert

nūbēs, is *f.* cloud, mist, fog
ōrō (1) pray (for), entreat, beseech
speculor, ārī, ātus spy out, watch
templum, ī *n.* temple, shrine, sanctuary
venia, ae *f.* favor, grace, pardon

---

516. Dissimulant (animōs).
517. quae (sit) fortūna: indir. quest.
App. 349. **virīs:** dat. of possession. **(in)
quō lītore.**

517–18. linquant, veniant: subjunctives in indir. quest.; App. 349.
518. quid = cūr, *why?* **(virī) lēctī.
(ex) cūnctīs nāvibus.**
519. clāmōre: abl. of manner; App. 328.

SELECTIONS FROM
BOOK 2

Invadunt urbem somno vinoque sepultam (2.265)

Illustration for Book 2
"Into the darkened city" by Thom Kapheim

BOOK 2.1–56

CONTICUĒRE *omnēs* intentī*que ōra tenēbant*;
inde torō *pater Aenēās sīc* orsus *ab altō:*
"Īnfandum, *rēgīna, iubēs* renovāre dolōrem,
Troiānās *ut* opēs *et* lāmentābile *rēgnum*
ēruerint *Danaī, quaeque ipse miserrima vīdī*   5
et quōrum pars magna fuī. Quis tālia fandō

---

conticēscō, ere, ticuī become silent,
  hush
dolor, ōris *m.* grief, anger, pain, passion
ēruō, ere, uī, utus overthrow, tear up
inde *adv.* thence, afterward, thereupon
īnfandus, a, um unspeakable, accursed
intentus, a, um intent, eager, strained

lāmentābilis, e lamentable, pitiable, sad
ops, opis *f.* help, resources, power, wealth
ordior, īrī, orsus begin, undertake
renovō (1) renew, revive
torus, ī *m.* (banqueting) couch, cushion
Troiānus, a, um Trojan, of Troy

1–39. Granting Dido's request,
Aeneas agrees to describe the fall of
Troy, in spite of the sorrow renewed
by such memories. He begins with
the story of the wooden horse, left
behind by the Greeks when they
feigned their departure from Troy.

  1. conticuēre (= **conticuērunt**),
tenēbant: observe the difference in tense,
the perfect denoting instantaneous,
complete result, *they grew silent;* the
imperf. denotes continued action, *they
continued to hold;* App. 351, 2 and 4.
ōra (in or **ad Aenēān) tenēbant.**
  2. pater: a title of honor and venera-
tion, regularly used in Rome to describe a
member of the senatorial aristocracy. Here,
it suggests the paternal care Aeneas will
show throughout Book 2 for his fellow
Trojans. **torō ab altō:** on which he was
reclining at the banquet. The word order is

unusual: when placing the preposition
between the adj. and noun, Vergil usually
places the noun after its preposition, and
the adj. modifying it before the preposition. **orsus (est):** from **ordior.**
  3. Īnfandum: emphatic by position.
The noun it modifies, **dolorem,** balances
this epithet through its positioning at the
end of the line. **iubēs (mē) renovāre.**
  **4. ut Danaī ēruerint Troiānās opēs et
lāmentābile rēgnum (ea)que miserrima
quae (ego) ipse vīdī. ut:** *how,* introduces
an indir. question implied in the verb
renovare; i.e., Aeneas will renew his grief
by telling about how the Greeks took the
city of Troy.
  5. ēruerint: perf. subj. in an indir.
quest.; App. 349. **miserrima:** substantively: *the heart-breaking events;* dir. obj.
of **renovare.**
  6. tālia: substantively, obj. of **fandō.**
fandō: gerund of **for;** abl. of attendant
circumstance or of means; App. 329.

Myrmidonum Dolopum*ve aut* dūrī mīles Ulixī
temperet *ā lacrimīs? Et iam nox* ūmida *caelō*
praecipitat suādent*que* cadentia *sīdera somnōs.*

10 *Sed sī tantus amor cāsūs* cognōscere *nostrōs*
et breviter *Troiae suprēmum audīre labōrem,*
quamquam *animus* meminisse horret luctu*que* refūgit
incipiam. Frāctī *bellō fātīsque* repulsī
ductōrēs *Danaum* tot *iam lābentibus* annīs

15 īnstar *montis equum* dīvīnā Palladis arte

---

annus, ī *m.* year, season
ars, artis *f.* art(istry), skill, artifice
breviter *adv.* shortly, briefly, concisely
cadō, ere, cecidī, cāsus fall, sink, die
cognōscō, ere, nōvī, nitus learn; know
dīvīnus, a, um divine, celestial, holy
Dolopes, um *m.* Greeks of Thessaly
ductor, ōris *m.* leader, chieftain, guide
dūrus, a, um hard(y), harsh, stern
frangō, ere, frēgī, frāctus break, shatter
horreō, ēre, uī bristle, shudder, tremble
incipiō, ere, cēpī, ceptus begin, undertake
īnstar *n. indecl.* likeness, image (+ *gen.*)
lūctus, ūs *m.* grief, mourning, sorrow
meminī, isse remember, recall
mīles, itis *m.* soldier(y), warrior(s)

Myrmidones, um *m.* Greeks of
    Thessaly, subjects of Achilles
Pallas, adis *f.* Minerva, goddess of
    wisdom and the arts
praecipitō (1) throw (headlong), fall
quamquam although; however, but
refugiō, ere, fūgī flee, retreat, recoil
repellō, ere, reppulī, repulsus drive
    back, repel
suādeō, ēre, āsī, āsus advise, urge
temperō (1) control, restrain, refrain
tot so many, as many
Ulixēs, is (eī, ī) *m.* Odysseus, the wily
    Greek leader who is the central
    character in Homer's *Odyssey* (his
    name in Latin is **Ulixes,** or Ulysses)
ūmidus, a, um moist, dewy, damp

**7. (quis) mīles. Myrmidonum
Dolopumve:** partitive gen., depending on
quis; App. 286.

8. temperet: deliberative subjunctive;
App. 348. **(dē) caelō:** the night is
PERSONIFIED; after passing the zenith at
midnight in her chariot, she is now
rushing down into the western wave; it is
thus after midnight.

9. praecipitat (in mare).

**10. sī amor (est tibi) cognōscere = sī
vīs** (from **volō**) **cognōscere;** App. 264.

11. suprēmum labōrem: *the final
agony.*

12. lūctū: abl. of cause; App. 332. **refūgit:**
perfect; note the long -**u**-.

13. incipiam: the placement of this
verb at the beginning of a line, though
logically and syntactically connected to
what has preceded, isolates it and gives it

increased emphasis; this device, known
from Homer onwards, is called
ENJAMBMENT. Aeneas' decision to fulfill
Dido's request comes only after he
acknowledges the traumatic nature of the
memory; but he is determined to speak.
bellō, fātīs: abl. of means; App. 331.

14. ductōrēs = ducēs. Dana(ōr)um:
App. 37, *d.* **lābentibus annīs:** abl. abs.,
denoting cause or attendant circumstance;
App. 343; cf. 329, 332. The siege of
Troy was now in its tenth and final year.

15. īnstar montis equum: "big as a
mountain," HYPERBOLE. **Palladis arte:** as
goddess of wisdom and the arts, Minerva
had inspired the Greeks with the idea and
with the skill necessary for its execution.
Throughout their war with the Trojans,
Minerva stands with the Greeks.

aedificant, sectā*que* intexunt abiete costās;
vōtum prō reditū simulant; *ea fāma* vagātur.
Hūc dēlēcta *virum* sortītī *corpora* fūrtim
inclūdunt caecō laterī penitus*que* cavernās
ingentēs uterum*que* armātō mīlite complent.   20
  Est in cōnspectū Tenedos, nōtissima *fāma*
īnsula, dīves opum *Priamī dum rēgna manēbant,*
nunc tantum sinus *et* statiō male fīda carīnīs:
hūc sē prōvectī dēsertō *in lītore* condunt;

---

abiēs, etis *f.* fir, pine
aedificō (1) build, construct, erect
armō (1) arm, equip, furnish
caecus, a, um blind, dark, hidden
carīna, ae *f.* keep, ship
caverna, ae *f.* hollow, cavity, cavern
compleō, ēre, ēvī, ētus fill, complete
condō, ere, didī, ditus establish; hide
cōnspectus, ūs *m.* sight, view
costa, ae *f.* rib, side
dēligō, ere, lēgī, lēctus choose, select
dēserō, ere, uī, rtus desert, forsake
dī(ve)s, dī(vi)tis rich, wealthy (+ *gen.*)
fīdus, a, um faithful, trustworthy, safe
fūrtim *adv.* stealthily, secretly, furtively
inclūdo, ere, sī, sus enclose, confine
īnsula, ae *f.* island
intexō, ere, xuī, xtus weave (in), cover
latus, eris *n.* side, flank

male *adv.* badly, not
mīles, itis *m.* soldier(y), warrior(s)
nōtus, a, um (well) known, familiar
ops, opis *f.* help, resources, power, wealth
penitus *adv.* deep(ly), within, completely
prō before, for, on behalf of (+ *abl.*)
prōvehō, ere, vēxī, vectus carry, convey
reditus, ūs *m.* return (home)
secō, āre, uī, sectus cut, slice, cleave
simulō (1) pretend, imitate, feign
sinus, ūs *m.* fold, hollow, bosom, bay
statiō, ōnis *f.* station, anchorage
sortior, īrī, ītus draw (by) lot, allot
tantum *adv.* so much, so great, only
Tenedos, ī *f.* small island near Troy
uterus, ī *m.* belly, womb
vagor, ārī, ātus wander, spread abroad
vōtum, ī *n.* vow, prayer, (votive) offering
voveō, ēre, vōvī, vōtus vow, consecrate

---

16. ābiete: pronounce -i- consonantally here (i.e., as **ābyete**), making the first syllable long by position. **intexunt:** properly used of weaving, the verb is metaphorical here, and a reminder that Minerva is the patron of weaving as well as of war.

17. (Danaī) **simulant** (equum esse) **vōtum prō** (suō) **reditū:** *for their (safe) return (home).*

18. dēlēcta vir(ōr)um corpora = virōs dēlēctōs. **Hūc** (= in hunc equum) **caecō laterī fūrtim inclūdunt dēlēcta corpora vir(ōr)um, sortītī** (ea).

19. caecō laterī = in caecum latus, dat. of direction or with compound; App. 306, 298.

20. uterum: the metaphor is vivid—the horse is a monster pregnant with trouble for Troy.

21. Est: *there is*; so begins an ECPHRASIS. **in cōnspectū (Troiae). fāmā:** abl. of respect; App. 325.

22. opum: gen. of respect with the adj. dīves; App. 294. **Priamī rēgna:** poetic plural; App. 243.

23. nunc (īnsula est) **tantum sinus. male fīda** = īnfīda: *unsafe, treacherous;* LITOTES. **carīnīs** = nāvibus: dat. with īnfīda; App. 304, 443.

24. hūc = ad hanc īnsulam. (Danaī) **prōvectī** (per pelagus).

25   *nōs* abiisse ratī *et ventō petiisse* Mycēnās.

      Ergō *omnis longō* solvit *sē* Teucria lūctū;
      panduntur portae, iuvat *īre et* Dōrica castra
      dēsertōs*que vidēre locōs lītusque relictum:*
      hīc Dolopum *manus, hīc* saevus *tendēbat* Achillēs;

30   *classibus hīc locus, hīc* aciē certāre solēbant.

      Pars stupet innūptae *dōnum* exitiāle Minervae
      et mōlem mīrantur *equī; prīmusque* Thymoetēs
      dūcī intrā mūrōs hortātur *et arce* locārī,

---

abeō, īre, iī (īvī), itus depart, go (away)
Achillēs, is (ī) *m.* Greek leader
aciēs, ēī *f.* battle line, army
castra, ōrum *n.* camp, encampment
certō (1) strive, rival, fight, vie
dēserō, ere, uī, rtus desert, forsake
Dolopes, um *m.* Greeks of Thessaly
Dōricus, a, um Doric, Spartan, Greek
ergō *adv.* therefore, then, consequently
exitiālis, e fatal, destructive, deadly
hortor, ārī, ātus exhort, urge, incite
innūptus, a, um unwed, virgin
intrā within, inside, in(to) (+ *acc.*)
iuvō, āre, iūvī, iūtus help, please
locō (1) place, locate, establish
lūctus, ūs *m.* grief, mourning, sorrow

Minerva, ae *f.* goddess of wisdom and the arts
mīror, ārī, ātus wonder (at), admire
mōlēs, is *f.* (huge) mass, structure, burden
mūrus, ī *m.* (city) wall, rampart
Mycēnae, ārum *f.* Greek city; Greece
pandō, ere, ī, passus spread, open, loosen
porta, ae *f.* gate, entrance, exit, portal
reor, rērī, ratus suppose, think, reckon
saevus, a, um stern, fierce, raging
soleō, ēre, itus sum be accustomed
solvō, ere, ī, solūtus loose(n), free, pay
stupeō, ēre, uī be dazed, stand agape (at)
Teucria, ae *f.* Troy (the land of Teucer)
Thymoetēs, ae *m.* Trojan leader

---

25. Nōs: contrasted with the treacherous Greeks; App. 247. **Nōs ratī (sumus Danaōs) abiisse. ventō:** abl. of means; App. 331. **Mycēnās:** the name of this famous Greek city is used in SYNECDOCHE for all of Greece.

26. lūctū: abl. of separation; App. 340. **omnis longō Teucria lūctū:** interlocked order; App. 442.

27. iuvat (nōs) īre (ex urbe): impersonal, *it pleases (us), we delight.*

29–30. hīc manus (tendēbat). tendēbat: the verb has at least two prominent meanings here: this is where Aeneas lived and worked for ten years; this is also where he and his men pitched their tents (**tentōria**). **hīc . . . hīc . . . hīc:** the Trojans point out these places to one another. The ANAPHORA adds to the vividness—Aeneas himself must have

taken part in this expedition. **hīc (erat) locus classibus (Danaōrum):** refers to the place where the Greek vessels had been drawn up on shore. **classibus = nāvibus:** dat. of reference; App. 301. **aciē:** abl. of manner; App. 328, **hīc (Danaī) aciē certāre solēbant.**

31. stupet = mīrātur: its obj. is **dōnum. exitiāle:** *fatal* (for Troy), as will be seen in the sequel. **Minervae:** obj. gen.; App. 284.

32. mīrantur: pl. with a collective noun, **pars,** although the preceding verb, **stupet,** is singular; App. 236, *a.*

33. hortātur (equum) dūcī et (in) arce locārī = hortātur ut equus dūcātur et locētur in arce (Troiae): ind. statement with **hortor,** rather than ind. command usual in prose; App. 360.

sīve dolō seu *iam Troiae sīc fāta ferēbant.*

At Capys, *et quōrum* melior sententia *mentī,*   35
aut pelagō Danaum īnsidiās suspecta*que dōna*
praecipitāre *iubent* subiectīs*que* ūrere *flammīs,*
aut terebrāre cavās uterī *et* temptāre latebrās.
Scinditur incertum studia *in* contrāria vulgus.

Capys, yos *m.* Trojan leader
cavus, a, um hollow, vaulted
contrārius, a, um opposite, opposing
dolus, ī *m.* deceit, wiles, trick, fraud
incertus, a, um uncertain, wavering
īnsidiae, ārum *f.* snare, ambush, treachery
latebra, ae *f.* hiding place, cavern, lair
melior, ius better, superior, nobler
praecipitō (1) throw (headlong), fall
scindō, ere, scidī, scissus split, divide

sententia, ae *f.* opinion, purpose, view
sīve, seu or (if), whether, either
studium, (i)ī *n.* zeal, desire, pursuit
subiciō, ere, iēcī, iectus place under
suspiciō, ere, spexī, spectus suspect
temptō (1) try, test, examine, explore
terebrō (1) bore into, pierce
ūrō, ere, ussī, ustus burn, consume
uterus, ī *m.* belly, womb
vulgus, ī *n. (m.)* rabble, crowd, herd

---

34. dolō: abl. of cause; App. 332. **fāta (sē) ferēbant:** *fates were tending;* an oracle had foretold that a child born on a certain day would cause the destruction of Troy. The fourth-century A.D. commentator on Vergil, Servius, reports that a child was born to Thymoetes and Paris was born to Priam on the same day; consequently, Priam put to death the son and wife of Thymoetes, hoping thereby to avert ruin for the state.

35. et (eī) quōrum sententia melior (erat) mentī: *and those whose mind had*

a better counsel. **mentī:** dat. of possession; App. 299.

36. pelagō: dat. of direction; App. 306. **Dana(ōr)um īnsidiās suspectaque dōna =** equum.

37. -que = -ve; some advise the destruction of the horse in the sea or by fire; others want to examine its contents. **(nōs) iubent. ūrere (equum) subiectīs flammīs:** abl. of means; App. 331.

38. cavās latebrās: obj. of both terebrāre and temptāre.

40   Prīmus ibi *ante omnēs magnā* comitante catervā
            Lāocoön *ardēns summā* dēcurrit *ab arce,*
            et procul 'Ō miserī, quae tanta īnsānia, cīvēs?
            Crēditis āvectōs hostēs? *Aut ūlla* putātis
            dōna carēre dolīs *Danaum? Sīc* nōtus Ulixēs?
45   *Aut hōc* inclūsī lignō occultantur Achīvī,
            aut haec in nostrōs fabricāta *est* māchina mūrōs,
            īnspectūra *domōs ventūraque* dēsuper *urbī,*
            aut aliquis latet error; *equō nē* crēdite, *Teucrī.*
            Quidquid *id est,* timeō *Danaōs et dōna ferentēs.'*

Achīvus, a, um Achaean, Greek
aliquis (quī), qua, quid (quod)
    some(one), any(one)
āvehō, ere, vēxī, vectus carry, convey
    (away)
careō, ēre, uī, itus be free from, lack (+
    abl.)
caterva, ae *f.* crowd, band, troop
cīvis, is *m.* *(f.)* citizen, compatriot
comitō (1) accompany, attend, escort,
    follow
crēdō, ere, didī, ditus believe, trust (+ *dat.*)
dēcurrō, ere, (cu)currī, cursus run down
dēsuper *adv.* from above
dolus, ī *m.* deceit, wiles, trick, fraud
error, ōris *m.* error, deceit, trick
fabricō (1) fashion, make
hostis, is *m.* *(f.)* enemy, foe, stranger
ibi *adv.* there, then

inclūdō, ere, sī, sus (en)close, confine
īnsānia, ae *f.* madness, frenzy, folly
īnspiciō, ere, spexī, spectus look into
Lāocoön, ontis *m.* Trojan priest of
    Neptune
lateō, ēre, uī lie hidden, hide, lurk
lignum, ī *n.* wood, timber
māchina, ae *f.* machine, engine, device
mūrus, ī *m.* (city) wall, rampart
nōtus, a, um (well) known, familiar
occultō (1) hide, conceal, secrete
putō (1) suppose, think, consider
quisquis, quidquid whoever, whatever
timeō, ēre, uī fear, dread, be anxious
Ulixēs, is (eī, ī) *m.* Odysseus, the wily
    Greek leader who is the central
    character in Homer's *Odyssey* (his
    name in Latin is **Ulixes,** or Ulysses)

40-56. Laocoön, priest of
Neptune, tries to avert disaster by
taking the lead and striking the side
of the horse with his spear.

40. comitante catervā: abl. abs.; App.
343.
**42. et procul (clāmat). īnsānia (est
ista).**
43. āvectōs (esse).
44. dolīs: abl. of separation with
carēre; App. 340. **dōna Dana(ōr)um.**
nōtus (est vōbīs) Ulixēs: Odysseus (Latin,
Ulixes or Ulysses), Greek instigator of

cunning, craft, and treachery. Here, his
name is symbolic of the Greeks as a whole.
**45. (in) hōc lignō = in hōc equō, quī
est dē lignō factus:** METONYMY.
46. māchina (bellī).
47. īnspectūra, ventūra: the fut.
participles denote purpose; App. 274. **urbī:**
dat. of direction = **in urbem;** App. 306.
48. nē crēdite: nē with the imperative
is a poetic use, = **nōlīte crēdere;** App.
256, *a.* **equō:** dat. with **crēdō;** App. 297.
49. timeō Danaōs et (*even*) **dōna
ferentēs:** a proverbial line. The Greeks
are so treacherous that they are not to be
trusted even when making gifts (sacrific-
ing, as in this case) to their gods.

Sīc fātus validīs *ingentem vīribus* hastam   50
in latus *inque* ferī curvam compāgibus alvum
contorsit. *Stetit illa* tremēns, uterō*que* recussō
īnsonuēre cavae gemitum*que dedēre* cavernae.
Et, sī fāta deum, sī mēns nōn laeva *fuisset,*
impulerat *ferrō* Argolicās foedāre latebrās,   55
Troiaque nunc stāret, Priamīque arx alta manērēs.

---

alvus, ī *f.* belly, body
Argolicus, a, um Argive, Greek
caverna, ae *f.* hollow, cavity, cave
cavus, a, um hollow, vaulted
compāgēs, is *f.* joint, seam, fastening
contorqueō, ēre, rsī, rtus hurl, twirl
curvus, a, um *f.* curved, crooked
ferus, ī *m.* beast, monster, horse
foedō (1) befoul, defile; mar, mangle
gemitus, ūs *m.* groan, roar, moan
hasta, ae *f.* spear, lance, dart

impellō, ere, pulī, pulsus impel, drive
īnsonō, āre, uī (re)sound, roar, echo
laevus, a, um left, foolish, unlucky
latebra, ae *f.* hiding place, cavern, lair
latus, eris *n.* side, flank
recutiō, ere, cussī, cussus strike (back), shake
tremō, ere, uī tremble, quiver, shake
uterus, ī *m.* belly, womb
validus, a, um strong, stout, mighty

---

50. validīs ingentem vīribus hastam:
interlocked order; App. 442. **vīribus:** abl.
of manner; App. 328; from **vīs,** not **vir,**
as may be seen from the quantity of the
-i- as well as from its third-decl. ending.
   51. ferī = equī. compāgibus: with **curvam,** abl. of manner or means; App. 328, 331.
   52. illa = hasta. uterō recussō: abl.
abs. with causal force; App. 343, *a.*
   **53. īnsonuēre, dedēre = īnsonuērunt,
dedērunt:** App. 204, 4. **gemitum:** the
hollow sound is described ominously, and
almost as if the wooden horse were alive.

54–56. fuisset, stāret, manērēs: contrary
to fact condition, with indicative (**impulerat**)
instead of the standard subjunctive (**impulisset**)
in the apodosis; App. 382, *d.* **sī fāta deum,
sī mēns nōn laeva fuisset:** the combination
of ANAPHORA and ASYNDETON links the two
subjects closely, and suggests that the verb
and predicate adj. are to be understood with
each. **laeva:** here, not just passively *unlucky,*
but downright *hostile.*
   55. (Lāocoön nōs) impulerat.
   56. manērēs: observe the change to
the second person; PERSONIFICATION and
APOSTROPHE add to the pathos.

Laocoon and his sons, Vatican.

Photograph by
Raymond V. Schoder, S.J.

BOOK 2.199-297

Hīc aliud maius miserīs multōque tremendum
200   obicitur magis atque imprōvida pectora turbat.
Lāocoōn, ductus Neptūnō sorte sacerdōs,
sollemnēs taurum ingentem mactābat ad ārās.
Ecce autem geminī ā Tenedō tranquilla per alta
(horrēscō referēns) immēnsīs orbibus anguēs
205   incumbunt pelagō pariterque ad lītora tendunt;

---

altum, ī n. the deep (sea); heaven
anguis, is m. (f.) snake, serpent
autem adv. moreover, but, however
ecce see! look! behold!
horrēscō, ere, horruī shudder, tremble
immēnsus, a, um immense, immeasurable
imprōvidus, a, um unforeseeing, heedless
incumbō, ere, cubuī, cubitus lean upon,
    hang over, lower (over) (+ dat.)
Lāocoōn, ontis m. Trojan priest of
    Neptune
mactō (1) sacrifice, slaughter; honor
magis adv. more, rather

Neptūnus, ī m. Neptune, god of the sea
obiciō, ere, iēcī, iectus present, place
    before
orbis, is m. circle, fold, coil; earth
pariter adv. equally, side by side
sacerdōs, dōtis m. (f.) priest(ess)
sollemnis, e annual, customary, solemn
sors, rtis f. lot, fate, destiny, oracle
taurus, ī m. bull, bullock, ox
Tenedos, ī f. small island near Troy
tranquillus, a, um tranquil, calm
tremendus, a, um terrible, dreadful
turbō (1) confuse, agitate, disturb

199–227. As a punishment for
Laocoōn, who had struck the wooden
horse with his spear, two serpents come
from Tenedos and destroy him and his
two little sons.

199–200. **Hīc aliud** (another omen)
**maius multōque magis tremendum
obicitur** (nōbīs) **miserīs.** Throughout this
passage, Aeneas speaks of the awful
events witnessed by the Trojans,
including himself; yet his very limited use
of personal pronouns and adjs. (**nōs,
noster**) makes it easy for us to forget this
perspective from time to time when
translating the passage into English. Other

features of Aeneas' description, however,
are remarkably vivid, and are mentioned
in the notes below.
    201. **Neptūnō:** dat. of reference; App.
301. **ductus sorte:** drawn (chosen) by lot.
    203–4. **autem ecce geminī anguēs
immēnsibus orbibus—horrēscō** (haec
dicta) **referēns—**(venientēs) **ā Tenedō:**
symbolizing the later coming of the Greek
ships from Tenedos, bringing destruction
with them. **horrēscō referēns:** Aeneas was
indeed an eyewitness, and his use of the
present tense through much of this passage
makes the recollection vivid for his
listeners. **immēnsibus orbibus:** abl. of
quality or manner; App. 330, 328.
    205. **pelagō:** dat. with compound
incumbunt; App. 298.

pectora quōrum inter fl̄uctūs arrēcta iubae*que*
sanguineae superant *undās, pars* cētera pontum
pōne legit sinuat*que* immēnsa volūmine terga.
Fit sonitus spūmante salō; *iamque arva* tenēbant
ardentēs*que oculōs* suffectī *sanguine et ignī*   210
sībila lambēbant linguīs vibrantibus *ōra*.
Diffugimus vīsū exsanguēs. *Illī agmine* certō
Lāocoōnta *petunt; et prīmum* parva duōrum
corpora nātōrum serpēns amplexus uterque
implicat *et miserōs* morsū dēpascitur artūs;   215
post *ipsum* auxiliō *subeuntem ac tēla ferentem*

---

amplector, ī, plexus embrace, enfold
arrigō, ere, rēxī, rēctus raise, rear
artus, ūs *m.* joint, limb, body
auxilium, (i)ī *n.* help, aid, assistance
certus, a, um sure, fixed, certain, reliable
cēterus, a, um rest, remaining, other
dēpascor, ī, pāstus feed on, devour
diffugiō, ere, fūgī flee apart, scatter
duo, ae, o two
exsanguis, e bloodless, lifeless, pale
fīō, fierī, factus become, arise
immēnsus, a, um immense, immeasurable
implicō, āre, āvī (uī), ātus (itus)
   entwine
iuba, ae *f.* mane, crest
Lāocoōn, ontis *m.* Trojan priest of
   Neptune
lambō, ere lick, lap
legō, ere, lēgī, lēctus choose; skim
lingua, ae *f.* tongue, language

morsus, ūs *m.* bite, biting, jaws, fangs
parvus, a, um small, little
pōne *adv.* behind, after
pontus, ī *m.* sea, waves
post *adv.* afterward; *prep. + acc.* after,
   behind
salum, ī *n.* (lit., salt) sea, brine
sanguineus, a, um bloody, blood-red
serpēns, entis *m. (f.)* serpent, snake
sībilus, a, um hissing, whirring
sinuō (1) fold, curve, twist, wind
sonitus, ūs *m.* sound, roar, noise, crash
spūmō (1) foam, froth, spray
sufficiō, ere, fēcī, fectus supply, suffuse
superō (1) surmount, overcome, survive
tergum, ī *n.* back, body, rear
uterque, utraque, utrumque each, both
vibrō (1) quiver, vibrate, dart
vīsus, ūs *m.* sight, view, vision, aspect
volūmen, inis *n.* fold, coil, roll

---

206. pectora arrēcta: the snakes seem
almost to stand on the water.
   208. volūmine: abl. of manner or
respect; App. 328, 325.
   209. spūmante salō: abl. abs.; App.
343.
   210. oculōs: obj. of the participle
suffectī, treated here as a Greek middle
participle capable of having a dir. obj.;
alternatively, **oculōs** is a so-called Greek
acc., i.e., acc. of respect (*suffused with
respect to their eyes*); App. 309, *a*.

   212. Diffugimus: Aeneas inserts
himself and his companions again into the
scene. **vīsū:** either abl. of cause with
exsanguēs, or abl. of separation with
diffugimus; App. 332.
   213. Lāocoōnta: acc., a Greek form;
App. 68.
   **213–14. parva duōrum / corpora
nātōrum:** the interlocked word order is a
verbal approximation of the sight described.
   216. ipsum (Lāocoōnta). auxiliō: dat.
of purpose; App. 303.

corripiunt spīrīs*que* ligant *ingentibus; et iam*
bis *medium* amplexī, bis collō squāmea *circum*
terga *datī* superant *capite et* cervīcibus *altīs.*

220   *Ille simul manibus tendit* dīvellere nōdos
perfūsus saniē vittās *ātrōque* venēnō,
clāmōrēs simul horrendōs *ad sīdera tollit:*
quālis mūgītus, *fūgit cum* saucius *āram*
taurus *et* incertam excussit cervīce secūrim.

225   *At geminī* lāpsū dēlūbra *ad summa* dracōnēs

---

amplector, ī, plexus embrace, enfold
bis twice
cervīx, īcis *f.* neck
collum, ī *n.* neck
corripiō, ere, uī, reptus seize, snatch up
dēlūbrum, ī *n.* shrine, temple
dīvellō, ere, ī (or vulsī), vulsus tear apart
dracō, ōnis *m.* dragon, serpent
excutiō, ere, cussī, cussus shake off
horrendus, a, um horrible, horrifying
incertus, a, um uncertain, ill-aimed
lāpsus, ūs *m.* gliding, rolling, sinking
ligō (1) bind, tie, fasten

mūgītus, ūs *m.* bellow(ing), roar
nōdus, ī *m.* knot; fold, coil
perfundō, ere, fūdī, fūsus soak, drench
quālis, e (such) as, of what sort
saniēs, ēī *f.* blood, gore
saucius, a, um wounded, stricken
secūris, is *f.* ax
spīra, ae *f.* fold, coil, spire
squāmeus, a, um scaly
superō (1) surmount, overcome, survive
taurus, ī *m.* bull, bullock, ox
tergum, ī *n.* back, body, rear
venēnum, ī *n.* poison, venom, drug
vitta, ae *f.* fillet, garland, band

---

218. circum: with **datī** = **circumdatī,** *placed around;* the separation into two separate words of the parts of a compound is called TMESIS ("cutting"). **medium (illum = Lāocoönta). collō:** dat. with the compound **circumdatī;** App. 298.

219. terga: obj. of the participle **circumdatī** (*having placed*), treated here as a Greek middle participle capable of having a dir. obj.; alternatively, **terga** is a so-called Greek acc., i.e., acc. of respect (*having been placed around with respect to their bodies);* App. 309, *a.* **superant (illum = Lāocoönta). capite:** for **capitibus,** which could not be used in dactylic verse because of its three successive short syllables; abl. of means or degree of difference; App. 331, 335.

220. Ille: Lāocoön. **manibus:** abl. of means.

221. saniē ātrōque venēnō: abl. of means. **vittās:** acc. obj. of the participle **perfūsus,** treated here as a Greek middle participle capable of having a dir. obj.; alternatively, **vittās** is a so-called Greek acc., i.e., acc. of respect (*soaked with respect to his headbands);* App. 309, *a,* 311.

223. (tālis est mūgītus Lāocoöntis) quālis (est) mūgītus (taurī): a SIMILE; App. 441.

224. (ā) cervīce.

225. lāpsū: *with a gliding (movement):* abl. of manner; App. 328. Note how with this word Aeneas passes over in silence the death of Laocoon. **dēlubra summa = dēlūbra arcis Troiae,** where the temple of Minerva stood, 226.

effugiunt saevae*que petunt* Trītōnidis *arcem,*
   sub pedibusque deae clipeī*que sub* orbe teguntur.   227

---

clipeus, ī *m.* shield, buckler
effugiō, ere, fūgī flee, escape
orbis, is *m.* circle, fold, coil; earth

saevus, a, um fierce, cruel, stern
tegō, ere, tēxī, tēctus cover, hide
Trītōnis, idis *f.* Minerva, goddess of
   wisdom and the arts

---

226. saevae: *angry, hostile (to the Trojans).*
   227. deae = here, the statue of the goddess. **teguntur:** = **sē tegunt**, as if a Greek verb in the middle voice; App. 309.

The serpents return to the goddess who, at least indirectly (i.e., by her staunch patronage of the Greeks in general and Odysseus in particular), is responsible for their appearance.

Tum vērō tremefacta *novus per pectora cūnctīs*
īnsinuat pavor, *et* scelus expendisse merentem
230   Lāocoōnta *ferunt, sacrum quī* cuspide rōbur
laeserit *et* tergō scelerātam intorserit hastam.
Dūcendum ad sēdēs simulācrum ōranda*que dīvae*
nūmina conclāmant.
Dīvidimus mūrōs et *moenia* pandimus *urbis.*
235   Accingunt *omnēs* operī *pedibusque* rotārum
subiciunt lāpsūs, *et* stuppea vincula collō

---

accingō, ere, cīnxī, cīnctus gird (on),
    equip
collum, ī *n.* neck
conclāmō (1) cry, shout, exclaim
cuspis, pidis *f.* point, spear, lance
dīvidō, ere, vīsī, vīsus divide, separate
expendō, ere, ī, pēnsus expiate, pay (for)
hasta, ae *f.* spear, dart, lance
īnsinuō (1) wind, creep, coil
intorqueō, ēre, rsī, rtus hurl (against) (+
    dat.)
laedō, ere, ī, sus strike, hurt, offend
Lāocoōn, ontis *m.* Trojan priest of
    Neptune
lāpsus, ūs *m.* gliding, rolling, sinking
mereō, ēre, uī, itus deserve, merit, earn
mūrus, ī *m.* wall, rampart
opus, eris *n.* work, task, deed, labor

ōrō (1) entreat, pray (for), beseech
pandō, ere, ī, passus spread, open,
    loosen
pavor, ōris *m.* terror, shuddering, alarm
rōbur, oris *n.* oak; strength
rota, ae *f.* wheel
scelerātus, a, um criminal, wicked
scelus, eris *n.* crime, impiety, sin
simulācrum, ī *n.* image, statue, likeness
stuppeus, a, um (of) flax or hemp (used
    in the production of rope)
subiciō, ere, iēcī, iectus place under
    (+ *dat.*)
tergum, ī *n.* back, body, rear
tremefaciō, ere, fēcī, factus make
    tremble, appall, alarm
vērō *adv.* truly, indeed, but
vinc(u)lum, ī *n.* chain, bond, cable

228–67. The Trojans make a
breach in the walls of the city, drag
the horse inside, and celebrate in
thanksgiving to the gods for the
preservation of their city. When they
fall asleep, the hidden Greeks emerge
from the horse and, admitting their
comrades into the city, proceed to lay
waste to Troy.

228. cūnctīs (nōbis): dat. of reference;
App. 301.
229–30. īnsinuat (sē). expendisse:
indir. statement with ferunt, *say*; App. 263.
231. laeserit, intorserit: causal relative
clause, or characteristic clause with causal

force; App. 389. tergō: dat. with
compound intorserit; App. 298.
232. Dūcendum (esse), ōranda (esse):
infinitives in ind. statement with conclāmant.
ad sēdēs (deōrum) = ad dēlūbra summa,
225 = arcem. dīvae (Minervae).
233. This is one of the half-lines in the
Aeneid. Most scholars think the presence
of these lines indicates that Vergil had not
yet completed the *Aeneid* when he died.
235. omnēs (sē) accingunt operī.
operī: dat. of purpose; App. 303. rotārum
lāpsūs: *rollings (glidings) of wheels* =
rolling wheels; App. 425. pedibus (equī):
dat. with compound subiciunt.
236. (ā) collō: abl. of separation; App.
340; or dat. with compound intendunt;
App. 298.

intendunt: scandit fātālis māchina mūrōs
fēta *armīs. Puerī circum* innūptae*que* puellae
sacra canunt fūnem*que manū* contingere gaudent;
illa subit mediaeque mināns inlābitur *urbī.*   240
Ō patria, Ō *dīvum domus* Īlium *et* incluta *bellō*
moenia Dardanidum! quater *ipsō in līmine* portae
substitit *atque* uterō sonitum quater *arma dedēre;*
īnstāmus tamen immemorēs caecī*que* furōre
et mōnstrum *īnfēlīx* sacrātā sistimus *arce.*   245
Tunc etiam *fātīs* aperit Cassandra *futūrīs*
ōra deī iussū *nōn* umquam crēdita *Teucrīs.*

---

aperiō, īre, uī, rtus open, disclose
caecus, a, um blind, hidden, dark
canō, ere, cecinī, cantus sing (of), chant
Cassandra, ae *f.* Trojan prophetess,
    punished by Apollo and so never
    believed
contingō, ere, tigī, tāctus touch, befall
crēdō, ere, didī, ditus believe, trust (+ *dat.*)
Dardanidēs, ae *m.* Dardanian, Trojan
etiam *adv.* also, even, besides, yet, still
fātālis, e fatal, deadly, fated, fateful
fētus, a, um teeming, pregnant, filled
fūnis, is *m.* rope, cable
furor, ōris *m.* madness, frenzy, fury
gaudeō, ēre, gāvisus sum rejoice, exult
Īlium, (i)ī *n.* Ilium, Troy
immemor, oris unmindful, heedless
inclutus, a, um famous, renowned
inlābor, ī, lāpsus glide in(to) (+ *dat.*)
īnstō, āre, stitī press on, pursue

intendō, ere, ī, ntus stretch, extend
innūptus, a, um unmarried, virgin
iussus, ūs *m.* command, order, behest
māchina, ae *f.* machine, engine, device
minor, ārī, ātus tower (over); threaten
    (+ *dat.*)
mōnstrum, ī *n.* omen, portent, monster
mūrus, ī *m.* (city) wall, rampart
patria, ae *f.* fatherland, country
porta, ae *f.* gate, entrance, exit, portal
puella, ae *f.* girl
quater four times
sacrō (1) dedicate, consecrate, hallow
scandō, ere, ī, scānsus mount, climb
sistō, ere, stetī, status stand, stop, stay
sonitus, ūs *m.* sound, roar, crash, noise
subsistō, ere, stitī stop, halt, resist
tamen *adv.* nevertheless, however, but
umquam *adv.* ever, at any time
uterus, ī *m.* belly, womb

---

238. armīs: abl. with **fēta;** App. 337.
circum (equum).
    239. sacra (carmina): *sacred songs.*
    240. illa (māchina) = **equus. mediae
urbī:** dat. with compound **inlābitur;** App.
298.
    241. dīv(ōr)um domus: in apposition
with **Īlium.** Note the APOSTROPHE and
PERSONIFICATION, often used together in epic
at moments of great pathos.
    242. Dardanid(ār)um: App. 34, *b.* **in
līmine:** to stop or stumble on the

threshold was considered by the Romans
a bad omen and sure to bring misfortune.
    243. (ab) uterō: abl. of source or
separation; App. 323, 340. **dedēre** =
dedērunt: App. 204, 4.
    245. (in) sacrātā arce: since it
contained the temple and statues of the
gods; abl. of place where; App. 319, *b.*
    246. fātīs futūrīs: abl. of means or
dat. of purpose; App. 331, 303.
    247. deī: Apollo. **nōn crēdita:**
Cassandra had been beloved of Apollo,
who had granted her the gift of prophecy.

Nōs dēlūbra *deum miserī, quibus* ultimus *esset
ille diēs,* fēstā vēlāmus fronde *per urbem.*

250   Vertitur intereā *caelum et ruit* Ōceanō *nox*
involvēns *umbrā magnā terramque* polum*que*
Myrmidonum*que* dolōs; *fūsī per moenia Teucrī*
conticuēre; sopor *fessōs* complectitur artūs.

Et iam Argīva phalānx īnstrūctīs *nāvibus ībat*

255   *ā* Tenedō tacitae *per* amīca silentia lūnae
lītora nōta *petēns, flammās cum* rēgia *puppis*

---

amicus, a, um friendly, kind(ly)
Argīvus, a, um Argive, Greek
artus, ūs *m.* joint, limb, body
complector, ī, plexus embrace, enfold
conticēscō, ere, ticuī become silent,
    hush
dēlūbrum, ī *n.* shrine, temple
dolus, ī *m.* deceit, treachery, fraud
fēstus, a, um festal, festive
frōns, frondis *f.* branch, foliage
īnstruō, ere, strūxī, strūctus equip,
    array, build; instruct
intereā *adv.* meanwhile, (in the)
    meantime
involvō, ere, ī, volūtus wrap, envelop

lūna, ae *f.* moon, moonlight
Myrmidones, um *m.* Greeks of Thessaly,
    subjects of Achilles
nōtus, a, um (well) known, familiar
Ōceanus, ī *m.* ocean
phalānx, angis *f.* phalanx, troop
polus, ī *m.* pole; heavens, sky
rēgius, a, um royal, regal, kingly
silentium, (i)ī *n.* silence, quiet, stillness
sopor, ōris *m.* sleep, slumber
tacitus, a, um silent, still, quiet
Tenedos, ī *f.* small island near Troy
ultimus, a, um last, final, farthest
vēlō (1) veil, cover, deck, clothe
vertō, ere, ī, rsus turn, revolve, change

Because she reneged on her promise to be his in return for this gift, Apollo turned the gift into a curse, placing upon her the necessity of forever prophesying and of never being believed. Even today a person who predicts a future event rightly yet is not believed at the time is called a *Cassandra*. **Teucris:** dat. of agent; App. 302.

248. quibus esset: rel. clause of characteristic with accessory notion of cause; App. 388, 389.

248-49. Nōs: emphatic; App. 247. **Nōs miserī, quibus ille diēs esset ultimus, vēlāmus dēlūbra de(ōr)um.**

250. Vertitur caelum: The ancients believed that the earth remained stationary, while the heavens, including sun, moon, and stars, revolved around it. **Vertitur:** the Latin passive voice is here equivalent to the Greek middle. **(ex)**

Ōceanō: night was conceived as "rising" from the ocean as the sun sank into it.

252. Myrmidonum dolōs: as the third dir. obj. of **involvēns** (after **terram** and **polum**), this phrase reinforces the idea that Greek treachery is a natural phenomenon. **fūsī per moenia:** thus scattered in drunken sleep, the Trojans were later unable to oppose the attacking Greeks.

253. conticuēre = conticuērunt.

254. phalānx īnstrūctīs nāvibus: the fleet in battle order; abl. of quality or abl. abs.; App. 330.

255. amīca: *friendly*; again, night itself seems to be taking the side of the Greeks. **tacitae lūnae:** the adj. virtually personifies the moon.

256. flammās: as a signal for the other ships, but especially for Sinon, so that he may know when to open the horse and let out the Greeks. **rēgia puppis:** the flagship

extulerat, *fātīsque deum* dēfēnsus inīquīs
inclūsōs uterō *Danaōs et* pīnea fūrtim
laxat claustra Sinōn. *Illōs* patefactus *ad aurās*
reddit *equus laetīque* cavō *sē* rōbore prōmunt   260
Thessandrus Sthenelus*que* ducēs *et* dīrus Ulixēs,
dēmissum *lāpsī per* fūnem, Acamās*que* Thoās*que*
Pēlīdēs*que* Neoptolemus *prīmusque* Machāōn
et Menelāus *et ipse* dolī fabricātor Epēos.

Acamās, antis *m.* Greek leader
cavus, a, um hollow, vaulted
claustra, ōrum *n.* barrier, bar, bolt
dēfendō, ere, ī, fēnsus ward off, protect
dēmittō, ere, mīsī, missus let down, drop
dīrus, a, um dire, fearful, dreadful
dolus, ī *m.* deceit, treachery, trick, fraud
dux, ducis *m.* *(f.)* leader, guide, chief
efferō, ferre, extulī, ēlātus lift, carry off
Epēos, ī *m.* Greek leader, maker of the wooden horse
fabricātor, ōris *m.* constructor, maker
fūnis, is *m.* rope, cable
fūrtim *adv.* stealthily, furtively, secretly
inclūdō, ere, sī, sus (en)close, confine
inīquus, a, um unfair, unjust, hostile
laxō (1) loosen, free, open, release
Machāōn, onis *m.* Greek leader and surgeon

Menelāus, ī *m.* Greek leader, Helen's husband
Neoptolemus, ī *m.* Greek leader, son of Achilles
patefaciō, ere, fēcī, factus lay open
Pēlīdēs, ae *m.* descendant of Peleus
pīneus, a, um of pine
prōmō, ere, mpsī, mptus bring forth
reddō, ere, didī, ditus return, give back, render
rōbur, oris *n.* oak, strength
Sinōn, ōnis *m.* a lying Greek
Sthenelus, ī *m.* Greek leader
Thessandrus, ī *m.* Greek leader
Thoās, antis *m.* Greek leader
Ulixēs, is (eī, ī) *m.* Odysseus, the wily Greek leader who is the central character in Homer's *Odyssey* (his name in Latin is **Ulixes,** or Ulysses)
uterus, ī *m.* womb, belly

---

of the commander-in-chief, Agamemnon. **nōta:** since they had encamped there for ten years.

257. de(ōr)um. inīquīs: *unfriendly,* i.e., to the Trojans, especially in comparison to the friendliness of everything around them to the Greeks (see above on 255).

258. (in) uterō (equī): abl. of place where; App. 319, *b.* **pīnea:** in 16 the horse is of fir, in 112 of maple, in 186 of oak, here of pine; while some scholars have thought that Vergil was simply not attentive to such details, everything else about this poem suggests quite the opposite. It is far more likely that, with

each variant, Vergil refers to a different prior version of the story of the Trojan horse, and so recognizes the contributions of his predecessors to the poetic tradition.

258–59. Danaōs et claustra laxat: for the HYSTERON PROTERON, see 353; for the ZEUGMA see 1.356 and 2.54. **ad aurās:** *to the open air.*

260. (ex) rōbore.

262. lāpsī: *having descended,* deponent participle.

263. prīmus: *noble;* Machaon was probably not the first to climb down, nor was he their leader.

264. dolī fabricātor = equī fabricātor here.

265 Invādunt *urbem somnō* vīnō*que* sepultam;
caeduntur vigilēs, portīs*que* patentibus *omnēs*
accipiunt sociōs atque agmina cōnscia iungunt.

---

caedō, ere, cecīdī, caesus cut (down),
kill
cōnscius, a, um conscious; confederate
invādō, ere sī, sus attack, invade
iungō, ere, iūnxī, iūnctus join, unite

pateō, ēre, uī lie open, be evident
porta, ae *f.* door, gate, entrance, exit
sepeliō, īre, īvī (iī), pultus bury
vigil, īlis *m. (f.)* guard, watchman, sentinel
vīnum, ī *n.* wine

---

266. portīs patentibus: abl. of route, a
version of the abl. of means; 338, 331; or
abl. abs.

267. sociōs: i.e., the men who have
returned on the ships from Tenedos.

Tempus erat quō prīma quiēs mortālibus aegrīs
incipit *et dōnō dīvum* grātissima serpit.
In somnīs, ecce, ante oculōs maestissimus Hector   270
vīsus adesse mihī largōs*que* effundere flētūs,
raptātus bīgīs *ut quondam, āterque* cruentō
pulvere *perque pedēs* trāiectus lōra tumentēs.
Ei *mihi,* quālis *erat,* quantum mūtātus *ab illō*
Hectore *quī* redit exuviās indūtus Achillī   275
vel Danaum Phrygiōs iaculātus *puppibus ignēs;*

Achillēs, ī (is, eī) *m.* Greek leader who
   is the central character in Homer's *Iliad*
aeger, gra, grum sick, weary, wretched
bīgae, ārum *f.* two-horse chariot
cruentus, a, um bloody, cruel
ecce look! behold!
effundō, ere, fūdī, fūsus pour out
ei alas! ah!
exuviae, ārum *f.* spoils, booty
flētus, ūs *m.* weeping, tears, lament
grātus, a, um welcome, pleasing, grateful
Hector, oris *m.* Trojan leader
iaculor, ārī, ātus hurl, throw, fling
incipiō, ere, cēpī, ceptus begin, undertake
induō, ere, uī, ūtus don, clothe, put on
largus, a, um abundant, copious

lōrum, ī *n.* thong, leather strap, rein
maestus, a, um sad, mournful, gloomy
mortālis, is *m.* mortal, man, human
mūtō (1) (ex)change, transform, alter
Phrygius, a, um Phrygian, Trojan
pulvis, pulveris *m.* dust
quālis, e (such) as, of what sort
quantus, a, um how great, how much,
   how many, as
quiēs, ētis *f.* quiet, rest, sleep, peace
raptō (1) snatch, drag, carry off
redeō, īre, iī (īvī), itus return
serpō, ere, psī creep (on), crawl
trāiciō, ere, iēcī, iectus throw across,
   pierce
tumeō, ēre, uī swell, be swollen

268-97. The ghost of Hector
appears to Aeneas in a dream and
urges him to flee from the doomed
city and to rescue the paternal gods
from destruction.

268. quō: abl. of time when; App. 322.
With this scene, Aeneas directs the focus
of the story onto himself; at the same
time, the action of the story is suspended,
and the tension is allowed to build.

269. dīv(ōr)um. serpit: the description
of sleep, apparently so good to mortals,
ends on an ominous note, reminding us
of the snakes which came across the sea to
kill Laocoön and his sons.

270. (meōs) oculōs.

271. vīsus (est) adesse: *seemed to
appear.* In Latin poetry (as in Greek),

dreams are conventionally introduced this
way: persons "seem" or "appear to"
manifest themselves and speak.

272. raptātus bīgīs (Achillis): for the
story, cf. 1.483-84 and the note.

273. pedēs trāiectus lōra: *his feet
pierced with thongs;* **pedēs** is obj. of the
preposition **per** and **lōra** is obj. of the
participle **trāiectus** used as a Greek
middle participle, i.e., Greek acc.; App.
309, *a.*

274. mihi: dat. of reference or interest
with the interjection **ei;** App. 301.

275. exuviās: acc. obj. of **indūtus,**
used as a Greek middle participle, i.e.,
Greek acc.; App. 309, *a.* Hector had slain
and despoiled Patroclus, who was wearing
the armor of his friend Achilles.

276. Dana(ōr)um puppibus: dat. of
direction or reference; App. 306, 301.
Vergil refers to the battle around the

squālentem barbam *et* concrētōs *sanguine* crīnēs
vulnera*que illa* gerēns, *quae circum plūrima* mūrōs
accēpit patriōs. Ultrō flēns *ipse vidēbar*
280   compellāre *virum et* maestās exprōmere *vōcēs:*
'Ō *lūx* Dardaniae, spēs Ō fidissima *Teucrum,*
quae tantae tenuēre morae? *Quibus* Hector *ab ōrīs*
exspectāte *venīs? Ut tē* post *multa tuōrum*
fūnera, post variōs hominum*que urbisque labōrēs*
285   dēfessī aspicimus! *Quae* causa indigna serēnōs
foedāvit vultūs? *Aut* cūr *haec* vulnera *cernō?'*
Ille nihil, *nec mē quaerentem* vāna morātur,
sed graviter gemitūs *īmō dē* pectore *dūcēns,*
'Heu fuge, nāte deā, tēque his' ait 'ēripe flammīs.
290   Hostis *habet* mūrōs; *ruit altō ā* culmine *Troia.*

---

a(d)spiciō, ere, spexī, spectus see,
  look (at)
barba, ae *f.* beard, whiskers
causa, ae *f.* cause, reason, occasion
compellō (1) address, accost, speak to
concrētus, a, um grown together,
  hardened, matted
crīnis, is *m.* hair, locks, tresses
culmen, inis *n.* top, summit, peak, roof
cūr why? for what reason?
Dardania, ae *f.* city of Dardanus, Troy
dēfessus, a, um weary, tired, worn
exprōmō, ere, mpsī, mptus express,
  bring forth
exspectō (1) await (eagerly), expect
fīdus, a, um faithful, trustworthy, safe
fleō, ēre, ēvī, ētus weep, lament
foedō (1) defile, befoul, mar, mangle
fūnus, eris *n.* funeral, death, disaster
gemitus, ūs *m.* groan, lament, roar

gerō, ere, gessī, gestus bear, carry (on)
Hector, oris *m.* Trojan leader
homō, inis *m.* (*f.*) man, mortal, human
hostis, is *m.* (*f.*) enemy, foe, stranger
indignus, a, um undeserved, unworthy
maestus, a, um sad, mournful, gloomy
mora, ae *f.* delay, hesitation, hindrance
moror, ārī, ātus delay, tarry, heed
mūrus, ī *m.* (city) wall, rampart
nihil, nīl nothing, not at all
post *adv.* afterward; *prep.* + *acc.* after,
  behind
serēnus, a, um serene, calm, fair, clear
spēs, speī *f.* hope, expectation
squāleō, ēre, uī be rough, be filthy
ultrō *adv.* voluntarily, further
vānus, a, um vain, idle, useless, false
varius, a, um various, manifold, diverse
vulnus, eris *n.* wound, deadly blow
vultus, ūs *m.* countenance, face, aspect

Greek ships described in *Iliad* 15, when
the Trojans under Hector almost captured
the Greek camp and set fire to several of the
ships.
  278. quae plurima: acc. **circum
mūrōs.**
    281. Teucr(ōr)um.
    282. tenuēre = (tē) tenuērunt.
    282-83. Hector exspectāte: voc. (tū)
venīs.

  283. Ut: *how (gladly)*—although the
implication that Aeneas feels pleasure at the
sight of Hector in his gruesome post-mortem
condition is ironic, to say the least.
  **285-86. serēnōs vultūs (tuōs), haec
vulnera (tua).**
  287. Ille (dīcit) nihil.
  289. nāte: voc. **deā:** abl. of separation.
nāte deā: *goddess-born;* literally, *born
from a goddess.*

Sat patriae *Priamōque datum: sī* Pergama *dextrā*
dēfendi *possent,* etiam *hāc* dēfēnsa *fuissent.*
Sacra suōsque tibī commendat *Troia* penātēs;
hōs cape fātōrum comitēs, hīs moenia quaere
magna, pererrātō statuēs *quae* dēnique ponto.'   295
Sīc ait *et* manibus vittās Vestam*que* potentem
aeternum*que* adytīs effert penetrālibus ignem.

---

adytum, ī *n.* inner shrine, sanctuary
aeternus, a, um eternal, undying
commendō (1) entrust, commit
dēfendō, ere, ī, fēnsus defend, protect
dēnique *adv.* finally, at last
efferō, ferre, extulī, ēlatus carry forth,
 lift
etiam *adv.* also, even, besides, yet, still
patria, ae *f.* homeland, country
penātēs, ium *m.* household gods

penetrālis, e inmost, interior
pererrō (1) wander through, traverse
Pergama, ōrum *n.* (citadel of) Troy
potēns, entis powerful, mighty
pontus, ī *m.* sea, waves
sat(is) *adv.* enough, sufficient(ly)
statuō, ere, uī, ūtus set up, establish
vitta, ae *f.* fillet, garland, band

**291-92. Sat . . . datum (est ā tē). sī
(quā) dextrā dēfendī possent, hāc
(dextrā meā) dēfēnsa fuissent.** The
combination of impf. and plpf. subjunctives
here creates what is called a mixed condition;
each clause should be translated in accordance
with the English approximation appropriate
in each case, i.e., "were to" with the impf.
subj., "would have" with the plpf. subj.
 293. (sua) sacra: objects used in the
performance of rituals, statues, etc. **comitēs:**
(as) comrades, in apposition with **hōs.**

294. moenia = urbem, as often. **hīs
(penātibus):** dat. of reference; App. 301.
 295. pererrātō pontō: abl. abs.; App.
343. **quae (moenia magna) dēnique
statuēs.**
 297. aeternum ignem: the sacred fire
of Vesta was never allowed to go out, and
from it was always kindled the fire which
was given to each colony sent out from
Rome. The Romans believed that the
eternal burning of Vesta's flame ensured
the permanence of Rome.

BOOK 2.469-566

Vestibulum *ante ipsum prīmōque in līmine* Pyrrhus
470 exsultat *tēlīs et lūce* coruscus aēnā:
quālis *ubi in lūcem* coluber mala grāmina pāstus,
frīgida *sub terrā* tumidum *quem* brūma tegēbat,
nunc, positīs novus exuviīs nitidus*que* iuventā,
lūbrica convolvit *sublātō pectore* terga
475 arduus *ad* sōlem, *et* linguīs micat *ōre* trisulcīs.

---

aēnus, a, um bronze, brazen
arduus, a, um high, steep, lofty
brūma, ae *f.* midwinter
coluber, brī *m.* snake, serpent
convolvō, ere, ī, volūtus roll, coil
coruscus, a, um flashing, bright, waving
exsultō (1) leap forth, dance, surge, exult
exuviae, ārum *f.* spoils; skin, slough
frīgidus, a, um cold, frosty, chill
grāmen, inis *n.* grass, herb, plant
iuventa, ae *f.* youth, young manhood
lingua, ae *f.* tongue, language
lūbricus, a, um slippery, slimy

malus, a, um bad, evil, wicked, baneful
micō, āre, uī flash, quiver, dart
nitidus, a, um shining, bright, sleek
pascor, ī, pāstus feed (on), graze, eat
quālis, e such (as), of what sort
sōl, sōlis *m.* sun; day
tegō, ere, tēxī, tēctus cover, protect
tergum, ī *n.* back, body, rear
trisulcus, a, um threefold, tripartite, forked
tumidus, a, um swollen, swelling
vestibulum, ī *n.* entry, vestibule

469-525. A band of Greeks led by Achilles' son Pyrrhus (Neoptolemus) bursts into the palace of Priam, where Hecuba and Priam are taking refuge at the household altar.

469. Pyrrhus: Achilles' young son who has just come to Troy.
470. tēlīs et lūce aēnā coruscus = *flashing and gleaming in his bronze armor.* For a further description of his weapons and armor see 3.467-68.
471-75. The convoluted wording of the SIMILE suggests the movement of the snake.
471. quālis ubi: introduces the SIMILE.

in lūcem: the suddenness of Pyrrhus' appearance and his brilliance (**coruscus,** 470) play upon the meaning of his name (from the Greek word for *fire*) and foreshadow his destructiveness. **mala grāmina pāstus**: the poisonous herbs the snake eats suggest by association the poisonous effect the snake's bite can have on its victims.
472. frīgida: modifies **brūma**, the subject of the rel. clause introduced by **quem**.
tumidum: modifies **quem** (whose antecedent is **coluber,** 471).
473. positīs exuviīs: abl. abs.: *its skin having been shed.* **iuventā**: abl. of respect with **nitidus.**
475. linguīs trisulcīs: abl. of means; App. 331.

Ūnā *ingēns* Periphās *et equōrum* agitātor Achillis,
armiger Automedōn, ūnā *omnis* Scȳria pūbēs
succēdunt *tēctō et flammās ad* culmina iactant.
Ipse inter prīmōs correptā dūra bipennī
līmina perrumpit postēs*que ā* cardine vellit   480
aerātōs; *iamque* excīsā trabe firma cavāvit
rōbora *et ingentem* lātō *dedit ōre* fenestram.
Appāret *domus* intus *et* ātria *longa* patēscunt;
appārent *Priamī et* veterum penetrālia *rēgum*,
armātōs*que vident stantēs in līmine prīmō.*   485
At domus interior gemitū *miserōque* tumultū

Achillēs, is (ī, eī) *m.* Greek leader
aerātus, a, um bronze, brazen
agitātor, ōris *m.* driver, charioteer
appāreō, ēre, uī, itus appear
armiger, erī *m.* armorbearer, squire
armō (1) arm, equip, furnish
ātrium, (i)ī *n.* great hall, atrium
Automedōn, ontis *m.* Greek leader
bipennis, is *f.* double ax
cardō, inis *m.* hinge, pivot, socket
cavō (1) hollow out
corripiō, ere, uī, reptus snatch (up)
culmen, inis *n.* top, summit, peak, roof
dūrus, a, um hard(y), harsh, stern
excīdō, ere, ī, sus cut out; destroy
fenestra, ae *f.* window, opening, breach
firmus, a, um firm, strong, solid
gemitus, ūs *m.* groan, roar, lament
iactō (1) hurl, toss, buffet; utter
interior, ius inner, interior

intus *adv.* within, inside
lātus, a, um broad, wide, spacious
patēscō, ere, uī open up, be revealed
penetrālia, ium *n.* chamber, sanctuary,
   inner room
Periphās, antis *m.* Greek leader
perrumpō, ere, rūpī, ruptus break through
postis, is *m.* post, door, gate
pūbēs, is *f.* youth, young men
rōbur, oris *n.* oak, strength
Scȳrius, a, um Scyrian, of Scyros, an island
   in the Aegean sea where Neoptolemus
   (Pyrrhus) was born
succēdō, ere, cessī, cessus approach
   (+ *dat.*)
trabs (trabēs), is *f.* beam, timber
tumultus, ūs *m.* uproar, tumult, hubbub
ūnā *adv.* together, at the same time
vellō, ere, vulsī, vulsus tear (up)
vetus, eris old, aged, ancient, former

---

478. **tēctō (Priamī):** dat. with compound verb; App. 298.

479. **Ipse (Pyrrhus):** see the note on ipsius, 1.114. **correptā dūra bipennī līmina:** interlocked order; App. 442. **līmina:** *the doors.*

482. **lātō ōre:** *wide-mouthed*; abl. of quality; App. 330.

483. **ātria:** the atrium is a feature of a Roman rather than of a Greek or Trojan house; but Vergil recalls here the description of Priam's palace in *Iliad* 6, with its many bedrooms arranged around a central courtyard.

483–84. **appāret, appārent:** ANAPHORA and ASYNDETON.

485. **armātōs:** probably describing the Trojans protecting Priam and his family (**Teucrōs**): mentioned earlier in 449–50. **vident:** the implied subj. is probably **Danaī**. Note, however, that some readers have read this differently, and think that the "armed men" are the Greeks, standing on the threshold with Pyrrhus.

486. **domus interior:** *the inner house = the interior of the house*; App. 246; contrasted with the scene at the entrance (**in līmine prīmō**).

miscētur, penitus*que* cavae plangōribus aedēs
fēmineīs ululant; ferit aurea *sīdera clāmor.*
Tum pavidae *tēctīs mātrēs ingentibus errant*
490   amplexae*que tenent* postēs *atque* ōscula figunt.
Īnstat *vī patriā* Pyrrhus; *nec* claustra *nec ipsī*
custōdēs sufferre valent; labat ariete crēbrō
iānua, *et* ēmōtī prōcumbunt cardine postēs.
Fit *via vī;* rumpunt aditūs *prīmōsque* trucīdant
495   immissī *Danaī et* lātē *loca* mīlite complent.

---

aditus, ūs *m.* approach, entrance
aedēs, ium *f.* house, home
amplector, ī, exus embrace, encompass
ariēs, etis *m.* (battering) ram
aureus, a, um golden, (of) gold
cardō, inis *m.* hinge, pivot, socket
cavus, a, um hollow, vaulted
claustrum, ī *n.* bolt, fastening, barrier
compleō, ēre, ēvī, ētus fill, complete
crēber, bra, brum frequent, repeated
custōs, ōdis *m.* (*f.*) guard(ian), sentinel
ēmoveō, ēre, mōvī, mōtus move from
fēmineus, a, um feminine, women's
feriō, īre strike, smite, beat, kill
fīgō, ere, xī, xus fix, fasten, print
fīō, fierī, factus become, be made
iānua, ae *f.* door, gate, entrance
immittō, ere, mīsī, missus let in
īnstō, āre, stitī press on, urge on
labō (1) totter, waver, vacillate

lātē *adv.* widely, far and wide
mīles, itis *m.* soldier(y), warrior(s)
misceō, ēre, uī, mixtus mix, mingle
ōsculum, ī *n.* dainty lips; kiss
pavidus, a, um fearful, frightened
penitus *adv.* (deep) within, inside, completely
plangor, ōris *m.* clamor, wailing, beating (of the breast), shriek
postis, is *m.* post, door, gate
prōcumbō, ere, cubuī, cubitus fall, sink
Pyrrhus, ī *m.* Neoptolemus, son of Achilles
rumpō, ere, rūpī, ruptus break, burst (forth)
sufferō, ferre, sustulī, sublātus withstand, endure
trucīdō (1) slay, slaughter, butcher
ululō (1) howl, shriek, wail
valeō, ēre, uī be strong, avail, be able

---

488. ferit sīdera clāmor: HYPERBOLE.
489. (in) tēctīs. errant: Vergil suggests that, in their grief, the women are no longer aware of their surroundings.
490. ōscula: of farewell.
491. vī patriā: *with his father's might.* **patriā = patris =** Achillis.
492. sufferre (Pyrrhum). ariete crēbrō: abl. of means; App. 331; *with the frequent (battering) ram, with the repeated blows of the battering ram.*
ariete: -i- is treated as a consonant in this

word, making the first syllable long (**āryete**).
493. cardine: abl. of separation with ēmōtī; App. 340.
494. via vī: the combination of ALLITERATION and extreme brevity of expression suggests the swiftness with which Neoptolemus and his followers succeed. **aditūs:** acc. of effect; App. 307; cf. "he broke a hole in the ice." **prīmōs (virōs):** mentioned above in 485.

Nōn sīc, aggeribus ruptīs *cum* spūmeus amnis
exiit oppositās*que* ēvīcit gurgite mōlēs,
fertur īn arva furēns cumulō *campōsque per omnēs*
cum stabulīs armenta *trahit. Vīdī ipse furentem*
caede Neoptolemum *geminōsque in līmine* Atrīdās,   500
vīdī Hecubam centum*que* nurūs *Priamumque per ārās*
sanguine foedantem *quōs ipse* sacrāverat *ignēs*.
Quīnquāgintā *illī* thalamī, spēs tanta nepōtum,
barbaricō postēs *aurō* spoliīs*que* superbī
procubuēre; *tenent Danaī* quā dēficit *ignis*.   505

---

agger, eris *m.* mound, heap, dike, dam
amnis, is *m.* river, stream, torrent
armentum, ī *n.* herd, flock, drove, cattle
Atrīdēs, ae *m.* son of Atreus: (1)
   Agamemnon, (2) Menelaüs
barbaricus, a, um barbaric, foreign
caedēs, is *f.* slaughter, murder, massacre
centum hundred
cumulus, ī *m.* heap, mass, pile
dēficiō, ere, fēcī, fectus fail, be lacking
ēvincō, ere, vīcī, victus overcome,
   surmount
exeō, īre, iī (īvī), itus go forth, depart
foedō (1) defile, pollute, disfigure
gurges, itis *m.* whirlpool, abyss, gulf
Hecuba, ae *f.* wife of Priam
mōlēs, is *f.* (huge) mass, structure, dike
Neoptolemus, ī *m.* Pyrrhus, son of
   Achilles

nepōs, ōtis *m.* grandson; descendant
nurus, ūs *f.* daughter(-in-law)
oppōnō, ere, posuī, positus oppose,
   place against
postis, is *m.* post, door, gate
prōcumbō, ere, cubuī, cubitus fall
   (forward), sink
quā *adv.* where(by), in any (some) way
quīnquāgintā fifty
rumpō, ere, rūpī, ruptus break, burst
   (forth)
sacrō (1) hallow, consecrate, dedicate
spēs, eī *f.* hope, expectation
spolium, (i)ī *n.* spoils, booty, plunder
spūmeus, a, um foamy, frothy
stabulum, ī *n.* stable, stall, abode
superbus, a, um proud, haughty
thalamus, ī *m.* marriage chamber,
   bedroom

496–98. nōn sīc spūmeus amnis fertur
not so (furiously) does a foaming river
rush onward; LITOTES and a SIMILE,
suggesting that the Greeks' invasion of
Priam's palace is more violent than the
forces of nature. **exiit:** from its channel.
fertur furēns, cumulō campōs: double
ALLITERATION. **cumulō:** abl. of manner; App.
328; as in 1.105.
   499–501. Vīdī . . . vīdī: Aeneas
reminds Dido (and us) that he observed
all this in person.
   500. caede: abl. of manner or
specification with **furentem**; App. 328, *a.*

501. nurūs: daughters and daughters-
in-law; Priam and Hecuba had fifty of
each.
   502. foedantem ignēs.
   503. illī: *those famous*, as often.
thalamī: of Priam's fifty sons and their
wives.
   504. aurō spoliīsque: abl. of means,
cause, or description limiting **superbī**;
App. 331, 332. **barbaricō:** from a
Roman or Greek point of view; *foreign*.
   505. prōcubuēre = prōcubuērunt;
App. 204, 4.

Forsitan *et Priamī fuerint quae fāta* requīrās.
Urbis utī captae cāsum convulsa*que vīdit*
līmina tectōrum et medium in penetrālibus hostem,
arma diū senior dēsuēta trementibus aevō
510   circumdat nēquīquam *umerīs et* inūtile *ferrum*
cingitur, *ac* dēnsōs *fertur* moritūrus *in* hostēs.
Aedibus *in mediīs* nūdō*que sub* aetheris axe
ingēns āra fuit iuxtā*que* veterrima laurus
incumbēns *ārae atque umbrā* complexa penātēs.
515   *Hīc* Hecuba *et* nātae nēquīquam altāria *circum,*

---

aedēs, ium *f.* house, home
aethēr, eris *m.* upper air, sky, ether
aevum, ī *n.* age, life, time, eternity
altāria, ium *n.* altar
amplus, a, um ample, full, spacious, wide
axis, is *m.* axle, axis; height
cingō, ere, cīnxī, cīnctus gird, encircle
circumdō, dāre, dedī, datus surround,
    place around (+ *dat.*)
complector, ī, plexus embrace, enfold
convellō, ere, ī, vulsus tear up, shatter
dēnsus, a, um thick, crowded, dense
dēsuētus, a, um unaccustomed, unused
diū *adv.* a long time, long
fors(it)an *adv.* perhaps, possibly,
    perchance
Hecuba, ae *f.* wife of Priam

hostis, is *m. (f.)* enemy, foe, stranger
incumbō, ere, cubuī, cubitus lean (on,
    over) (+ *dat.*)
inūtilis, e useless, futile, valueless
iuxtā *adv.* next, close at hand
laurus, ī (ūs) *f.* laurel (tree)
morior, ī, mortuus die, perish
nāta, ae *f.* daughter
nēquīquam *adv.* in vain, uselessly, idly
nūdus, a, um naked, bare, nude, open
penātēs, ium *m.* household gods
penetrālia, ium *n.* chamber, sanctuary,
    inner room
requīrō, ere, sīvī, sītus ask, seek
senior, ōris *m.* old (aged) man, sire
tremō, ere, uī tremble, quiver, shake
vetus, eris ancient, old, aged, former

---

506. quae fuerint Priamī fāta: indir.
quest.; App. 349. **requīrās:** potential
subjunctive; or it may be taken as a
subjunctive in an indir. question
introduced by **an** and dependent upon
fors sit (in **forsitan**); **sit** would then be a
potential subjunctive.
    509–10. arma dēsuēta: acc. **diū:** modifies
dēsuēta. senior: i.e., Priam. The comparative
is intensifying: (*although*) *a very old man.*
trementibus umerīs: dat. with compound
verb **circumdat;** App. 298. **aevō:** abl. of
respect with **trementibus.**

    510–511. ferrum: acc. obj. of **cingitur,**
he girds on his sword. The verb, normally
transitive, is used in passive form here to
suggest the Greek middle voice, i.e., *he is
girded with respect to his sword;* App. 309.
    512. aedibus in mediīs: *in the inner
court of the palace,* open to the sky; App.
246. We are reminded again of the
palace's design, many rooms arranged
around an open-air courtyard.
    514. ārae: dat. with compound verb
incumbēns; App. 298.
    515. altāria circum = circum altāria:
ANASTROPHE.

praecipitēs *ātrā* ceu tempestāte columbae,
condēnsae *et dīvum* amplexae simulācra sedēbant.
Ipsum autem sūmptīs *Priamum* iuvenālibus *armīs*
ut vīdit, 'Quae mēns tam dīra, *miserrime coniūnx,*
impulit *hīs* cingī *tēlīs? Aut quō ruis?'* inquit.   520
'Nōn tālī auxiliō *nec* dēfēnsōribus istīs
tempus eget; *nōn, sī ipse meus nunc* adforet Hector.
Hūc tandem concēde; *haec āra* tuēbitur *omnēs,*
aut moriēre *simul.' Sīc ōre* effāta recēpit
ad sēsē et sacrā longaevum *in sēde* locāvit.   525

---

amplector, ī, plexus embrace, enfold
autem *adv.* but, however, moreover
auxilium, (i)ī *n.* aid, help, assistance
ceu (just) as, as if
cingō, ere, cīnxī, cīnctus gird, encircle
columba, ae *f.* dove, pigeon
concēdō, ere, cessī, cessus yield, come
condēnsus, a, um crowded, thick, dense
dēfēnsor, ōris *m.* defender, protector
dīrus, a, um dire, awful, dreadful
effor, ārī, ātus speak, utter, say
egeō, ēre, uī need, lack, require (+ *abl.*)
Hector, oris *m.* Trojan leader, son of
  Priam and Hecuba
impellō, ere, pulī, pulsus urge, drive

inquam, is, it say
iste, ta, tud that (of yours)
iuvenālis, e youthful, of a young man
locō (1) place, establish, locate
longaevus, a, um aged, very old
morior, ī, mortuus die, perish
praeceps, cipitis headlong, precipitate
recipiō, ere, cēpī, ceptus receive, accept
sedeō, ēre, sēdī, sessus sit
simulācrum, ī *n.* image, statue, likeness
sūmō, ere, mpsī, mptus take, assume
tam *adv.* so (much), such
tempestās, ātis *f.* tempest, storm; season
tueor, ērī, itus (tūtus) protect, watch

---

516. ātrā tempestāte: abl. of means
with the verbal idea implied in
praecipitēs (from **praecipiō**, *carry/take
headlong*).
  517. dīv(ōr)um.
  518. sūmptīs iuvenālibus armīs: abl.
abs.; App. 343.
  520. (tē) impulit. cingī: passive inf.,
here used as equivalent to Greek middle,
to gird oneself (see above on 2.510);
App. 309.
  521. auxiliō, dēfēnsōribus: abl. with
eget; App. 340. Hecuba is suggesting that

neither Priam himself nor his bodyguards
are of any use any longer; the situation is
beyond such remedies.
  522. adforet = adesset: contrary to
fact condition; App. 382.
  523. hūc concēde: imp.; *come here.*
(nōs) omnēs.
  524. moriēre = moriēris, fut. 2nd
sing.; App. 204, 4. **simul (cum nōbīs).**
ōre: picturesque PLEONASM, common with
expressions describing speech. **recēpit
(longaevum Priamum).**
  525. sacrā in sēde = in ārā.

Ecce autem ēlāpsus Pyrrhī *dē* caede Polītēs,
ūnus nātōrum Priamī, per tēla, per hostēs
porticibus *longīs fugit et* vacua ātria lūstrat
saucius. *Illum ardēns* īnfēstō vulnere Pyrrhus
530 īnsequitur, *iam iamque manū tenet et* premit hastā.
Ut tandem ante oculōs ēvāsit *et ōra parentum,*
concidit *ac multō vītam cum sanguine fūdit.*
Hīc Priamus, quamquam *in mediā iam morte tenētur,*
nōn tamen abstinuit *nec vōcī īraeque* pepercit:
535 'At tibi prō scelere,' exclāmat, 'prō *tālibus* ausīs
dī, si qua est caelō pietās *quae tālia* cūret,

---

abstineō, ēre, uī, tentus refrain, restrain
ātrium, (i)ī *n.* great hall, atrium
ausum, ī *n.* daring deed, daring
autem *adv.* but, however, moreover
caedēs, is *f.* slaughter, murder, massacre
concidō, ere, ī fall (in a heap)
cūrō (1) regard, care (for), heed
ecce see! look! behold!
ēlābor, ī, lāpsus slip out, escape
ēvādō, ere, sī, sus escape, come forth
exclāmō (1) cry (out), shout, exclaim
hasta, ae *f.* spear, lance, dart
hostis, is *m. (f.)* enemy, foe, stranger
īnfēstus, a, um hostile, threatening
īnsequor, ī, secūtus follow, pursue
lūstrō (1) traverse; survey; purify
parcō, ere, pepercī (parsī), parsus spare
  (+ *dat.*)

pietās, ātis *f.* loyalty, righteousness,
  justice, sense of duty, nobility
Polītēs, ae *m.* son of Priam, slain by
  Neoptolemus (Pyrrhus)
porticus, ūs *f.* colonnade, corridor, portico
premō, ere, pressī, pressus (re)press,
  pierce
prō for, on behalf of, before (+ *abl.*)
Pyrrhus, ī *m.* Neoptolemus, son of
  Achilles
quamquam *adv.* although, however, but
saucius, a, um wounded, hurt
scelus, eris *n.* crime, villainy, sin
tamen *adv.* however, nevertheless, but
vacuus, a, um empty, vacant, free
vulnus, eris *n.* wound, deadly blow

526-66. The deaths of Priam's son
Polites and Priam himself make
Aeneas think of his own dear father
and family.

526. Pyrrhī: subjective gen. with
caede; App. 284.
528. porticibus: around the inner court
of the palace; abl. of the route; App. 338.
529. illum: Polītēn. **īnfēstō vulnere:**
the expression is PROLEPTIC, i.e., it

anticipates Pyrrhus' intention to inflict a
hostile wound.
530. (illum) tenet et (illum) premit.
iam iam: rhetorical repetition to portray
the excited anticipation of Pyrrhus and
the frenzied fear of Polites; App. 413.
531. ante oculōs et ōra parentum.
534. vōcī īraeque: dat. with **parcō;**
App. 297.
535-37. at dī tibi persolvant grātēs
(= **grātiās**) **dignās. (in) caelō. quae**
cūret: rel. clause of characteristic; App.
389. **persolvant, reddant:** subjunctive
used to express a wish; App. 253.

persolvant grātēs dignās *et* praemia reddant
dēbita, *quī nātī* cōram *mē cernere* lētum
fēcisti et patriōs foedāstī fūnere vultūs.
At nōn ille, satum *quō tē* mentīris, Achillēs   540
tālis in hoste *fuit Priamō; sed* iūra fidem*que*
supplicis ērubuit *corpusque* exsangue sepulcrō
reddidit Hectoreum *mēque in mea rēgna* remisit.'
Sīc fātus senior *tēlumque* imbelle sine ictū
coniēcit, raucō *quod* prōtinus aere repulsum,   545
et summō clipeī nēquīquam umbōne pependit.

Achillēs, is (ī, eī) *m.* Greek leader
aes, aeris *n.* bronze
clipeus, ī *m.* shield, buckler
coniciō, ere, iēcī, iectus hurl, shoot
cōram *adv.* before the face, face to face, openly
dēbitus, a, um due, owed, destined
dignus, a, um worthy, suitable, fit(ting)
ērubescō, ere, ērubuī reverence, blush (before)
exsanguis, e bloodless, lifeless, pale
fidēs, eī *f.* faith, fidelity, reliance
foedō (1) defile, pollute, disfigure
fūnus, eris *n.* death, funeral, disaster
grātēs, ium *f.* thanks, requital, reward
Hectoreus, a, um of Hector, Trojan leader, son of Priam
hostis, is *m. (f.)* enemy, foe, stranger
ictus, ūs *m.* stroke, blow, wound
imbellis, e unwarlike, harmless

iūs, iūris *n.* law, right, justice
lētum, ī *n.* death, destruction, ruin
mentior, īrī, ītus lie, deceive, pretend
nēquīquam *adv.* in vain, uselessly, idly
pendeō, ēre, pependī hang
persolvō, ere, ī, solūtus pay fully
praemium, (i)ī *n.* reward, prize
prōtinus *adv.* immediately, forthwith
raucus, a, um hoarse, sounding, clanging
reddō, ere, didī, ditus return, render
remittō, ere, mīsī, missus send back
repellō, ere, reppulī, repulsus drive back, repel
senior, ōris *m.* old (aged) man, sire
sepulcrum, ī *n.* tomb, burial
serō, ere, sēvī, satus sow, beget
sine without (+ *abl.*)
supplex, icis *m. (f.)* suppliant
umbō, ōnis *m.* boss, knob, shield
vultus, ūs *m.* face, countenance, gaze

---

537. grātēs: *reward, requital.*
538. (tibī) quī. mē cernere = ut cernerem: depends on **fēcistī.**
539. foedā(vi)stī. fūnere (nātī).
540. ille: *that famous,* as often. **(ex) quō mentīris tē (esse) satum. mentīris:** *you falsely say.* **quō:** abl. of source; App. 323.
541. After the death of Hector, Priam had ransomed his corpse from Achilles; the scene of the return of Hector's body to Troy is the moving conclusion to the *Iliad.* Cf. 1.483–84. **in hoste Priamō:** *in*

the case of, *toward his enemy Priam;* Priam's use of his own name adds a touch of pathos.
542. sepulcrō: dat. of purpose; App. 303.
543. Hectoreum = Hectoris: an adj. for a gen. is a common usage.
544. Sīc fātus (est) senior.
545. repulsum (est).
546. (dē) summō umbōne: App. 246; Priam's spear stuck in the top of the boss of Pyrrhus' shield and now hangs there harmless.

Cui Pyrrhus: '*Referēs* ergō *haec et* nuntius *ībis*
Pēlīdae *genitorī. Illī mea trīstia* facta
dēgenerem*que* Neoptolemum nārrāre mementō.
550   *Nunc* morere.' *Hoc dīcēns* altāria *ad ipsa* trementem
trāxit et in multō lāpsantem *sanguine nātī,*
implicuit*que* comam laevā, *dextrāque* coruscum
extulit *ac* laterī capulō tenus abdidit ēnsem.
Haec fīnis Priamī fātōrum, hic exitus *illum*
555   sorte *tulit Troiam* incēnsam *et* prōlāpsa *videntem*
Pergama, tot *quondam* populīs *terrīsque* superbum

---

abdō, ere, didī, ditus hide, bury
altāria, ium *n.* altar
capulus, ī *m.* hilt, handle, head
coma, ae *f.* hair, locks, tresses
coruscus, a, um flashing, bright, waving
dēgener, eris degenerate, ignoble, base
efferō, ferre, extulī, ēlatus raise, lift
ēnsis, is *m.* sword, knife
ergō *adv.* therefore, then, consequently
exitus, ūs *m.* exit, issue, end
factum, ī *n.* deed, exploit, undertaking
implicō, āre, āvī (uī), ātus (itus) entwine
incendō, ere, ī, ēnsus burn, fire
laeva, ae *f.* left hand
lāpsō, āre slip, stumble, totter, fall
latus, eris *n.* side, flank
meminī, isse remember, recall

morior, ī, mortuus die, perish
nārrō (1) relate, recount, report, narrate
Neoptolemus, ī *m.* Pyrrhus, son of
   Achilles
nuntius, (i)ī *m.* messenger, message
Pēlīdēs, ae *m.* descendant of Peleus,
   Achilles
Pergama, ōrum *n.* (citadel of) Troy
populus, ī *m.* people, nation
prōlābor, ī, lāpsus slide, fall, perish
Pyrrhus, ī *m.* Neoptolemus, son of
   Achilles
sors, rtis *f.* lot, fate, destiny; oracle
superbus, a, um proud, haughty
tenus to, up to, as far as (+ *abl.*)
tot so many
tremō, ere, uī tremble, shake, quiver

---

547. Pyrrhus (dīxit). referēs et ībis:
HYSTERON PROTERON; the futures are here
used with the force of imperatives, *go and
tell*; App. 351, 3, *a.* **nuntius:** *(as) a messenger.*
   548. (meō) genitōrī = Achillī.
   **548–49. mea trīstia facta
dēgeneremque Neoptolemum:** ironical
and mocking: Neoptolemus' deeds have
caused sadness, not for himself but for
Priam and his family.
   549. mementō: imperative.
   550. morere: imperative. **altāria ad
ipsa:** Vergil mentions this detail to
emphasize the impiety of Neoptolemus'
deed. **trementem (Priamum):** probably
less from fear than from old age and
anger.

   551. lāpsantem sanguine nātī: again,
the added detail increases the vividness of
the terrible scene, as it evokes our pathos
for Priam.
   **552–53. coruscum (ēnsem). laterī = in
latus:** dat. of direction; App. 306. **capulō
tenus:** this prep. normally follows the abl.
it governs.
   554. haec (fuit) fīnis: haec is attracted
to the gender of the predicate, **fīnis,**
which is here fem., though ordinarily
masc. **hic:** -i- is lengthened here, perhaps
as a reminiscence of the word's earlier
spelling, **hicc(e). exitus (vītae).**
   556. populīs terrīsque: ablatives of
cause with **superbum;** App. 332.

rēgnātōrem Asiae. Iacet *ingēns lītore* truncus,
āvulsum*que umerīs caput et* sine *nōmine corpus.*
At mē tum prīmum saevus circumstetit horror.
Obstipuī; *subiit cārī genitōris* imāgō,   560
ut rēgem aequaevum crūdēlī vulnere *vīdī*
vītam exhālantem, *subiit* dēserta Creūsa
et dīrepta *domus et* parvī *cāsus* Iūlī.
Respiciō *et quae sit mē circum* cōpia lūstrō.
Dēseruēre *omnēs* dēfessī, *et corpora* saltū   565
ad terram mīsēre aut ignibus aegra *dedēre.*

---

aeger, gra, grum sick, weary, wretched
aequaevus, a, um of equal age
Asia, ae *f.* Asia (Minor)
āvellō, ere, āvellī or **āvulsī, āvulsus** tear from
cārus, a, um dear, beloved, fond
circumstō, āre, stetī surround, stand around
cōpia, ae *f.* abundance, plenty, forces
Creūsa, ae *f.* wife of Aeneas, lost during the sack of Troy
crūdēlis, e cruel, bloody, bitter
dēfessus, a, um tired, weary, worn
dēserō, ere, uī, rtus desert, forsake
dīripiō, ere, uī, reptus plunder, ravage
exhālō (1) breathe out, exhale

horror, ōris *m.* shudder(ing), horror, alarm
iaceō, ēre, uī, itus lie (low, outspread)
imāgō, inis *f.* image, picture, likeness
Iūlus, ī *m.* Ascanius, son of Aeneas
lūstrō (1) survey; traverse; purify
obstipēscō, ere, stipuī be dazed, stand agape
parvus, a, um small, little
respiciō, ere, spexī, spectus look back
rēgnātor, ōris *m.* ruler, sovereign, lord
saevus, a, um cruel, stern, fierce
saltus, ūs *m.* leap, bound, dancing
sine without (+ *abl.*)
truncus, ī *m.* trunk, body, torso
vulnus, eris *n.* wound, deadly blow

---

557. Asiae: objective gen. with rēgnātōrem; App. 284. **(in) lītore:** his headless corpse is thrown out on the beach for the dogs and birds to devour. In his fourth century A.D. commentary on the *Aeneid*, Servius believes that Vergil here has in mind the fate of Pompey, once one of the world's most powerful men; he was defeated in battle, lost his power, and was finally beheaded in Egypt, where his body was cast out and allowed to lie on the beach.

560. subiit: understand **meam mentem** as implied dir. obj., or take intransitively (*arose*).

561. aequaevum: Anchises was of about the same age as Priam.

563. dīrepta: i.e., in Aeneas' imagination. **domus:** nom. sing. with the final syllable long before the caesura; App. 394, *a.* The unusual metrical effect emphasizes Aeneas' sense of loss.

564. respiciō: Aeneas on the roof of the palace had been so transfixed in looking down on the murder of Priam that he had forgotten everything else. He now looks around for his followers and finds them gone. **quae sit...cōpia (virōrum):** indir. question; App. 349. **mē circum = circum mē:** ANASTROPHE.

565. saltū: abl. of means or manner.

565–66. dēseruēre, mīsēre, dedēre = dēseruērunt, mīsērunt, dedērunt.

566. aegra (corpora): *wearied and wounded (bodies).*

Book 2.735-805

735   *Hīc mihi* nescio *quod* trepidō male *nūmen* amīcum
cōnfūsam *ēripuit mentem. Namque* āvia *cursū*
dum sequor et nōtā excēdō regiōne *viārum,*
heu miserō coniūnx fātōne ērepta Creūsa
substitit, *errāvitne viā* seu *lapsa* resēdit,
740   incertum; *nec* post *oculīs est* reddita *nostrīs.*
Nec prius āmissam respexī *animumve* reflexī

---

amīcus, a, um friendly, kind(ly)
āmittō, ere, mīsī, missus let go, lose
āvius, a, um pathless, remote
cōnfundō, ere, fūdī, fūsus confuse
Creūsa, ae *f.* wife of Aeneas, left behind
    at the sack of Troy
excēdō, ere, cessī, cessus depart
incertus, a, um uncertain, doubtful
male *adv.* badly, poorly, not
nesciō, īre, īvī (iī) not know, know not
nōtus, a, um (well) known, familiar
post *adv.* afterward; *prep. + acc.* after,
    behind

prius *adv.* sooner, before, formerly
reddō, ere, didī, ditus return, give back,
    render
reflectō, ere flexī, flexus turn back
regiō, ōnis *f.* region, district
resīdō, ere, sēdī sit down
respiciō, ere, spexī, spectus look back
    (at, for)
sīve, seu of (if), whether
subsistō, ere, stitī halt, stop, withstand
trepidus, a, um agitated, alarmed

735-67. In the survivors'
panicked escape from the burning
city, Aeneas loses track of Creusa,
his wife; when he returns to the city
to seek her, he finds only the Greek
invaders, now in possession of all.

735. mihi trepidō: dat. of separation;
App. 305. **nesciō:** with the final -o
irregularly short; **nescio quod nūmen:** *I*
don't know what divinity = some divinity
or other. **male amīcum = inimīcum:**
unfriendly, hostile; LITOTES.
    736. āvia (loca): *out-of-the-way*
section. **cursū:** abl. of means.

738-40. heu, coniūnxne Creūsa, ērepta
miserō fātō, substitit, errāvitne (ex) viā,
seu lapsa resēdit, (est) incertum: *it is*
uncertain whether . . snatched away, alas!
by an unhappy fate, my wife Creüsa halted,
or . . . , etc. **(mihi) miserō:** dat. of separation;
App. 305. **-ne . . . -ne, seu:** *whether . . . or,*
or; the three clauses depend loosely on
incertum (est). Virgil's use of the indicative
rather than the subjunctive here makes
Aeneas' indirect questions more vivid,
and illustrates his panicked thinking.
    739. lapsa: some editors prefer to read
lassa *(tired, weary)* here, since it is both more
colloquial and more old-fashioned, and thus
more effectively evokes pathos for Creusa.
    741. Nec (eam = Creūsam) āmissam
respexī animumve reflexī: *nor did I look*

quam tumulum *antīquae* Cereris *sēdemque* sacrātam
vēnimus: hīc demum collēctīs *omnibus ūna*
dēfuit, *et comitēs nātumque virumque* fefellit.
Quem nōn incūsāvī āmēns hominum*que deōrumque,*   745
aut quid in ēversā *vīdī* crūdēlius *urbe?*
Ascanium *Anchīsēnque patrem Teucrōsque* penātēs
commendō *sociīs et* curvā valle recondō;
ipse urbem repetō *et* cingor fulgentibus *armīs.*
Stat cāsūs renovāre *omnēs omnemque* revertī   750
per Troiam et rūrsus *caput* obiectāre perīclīs.
Principiō mūrōs obscūra*que līmina* portae,

āmēns, entis mad, insane, distracted
Ascanius, (i)ī *m.* son of Aeneas
Cerēs, eris *f.* (goddess of) grain
cingō, ere, cīnxī, cīnctus gird, encircle
colligō, ere, lēgī, lēctus collect, gather
commendō (1) entrust, commit
crūdēlis, e cruel, harsh, bloody
curvus, a, um curved, winding, bent
dēmum *adv.* at length, finally
dēsum, esse, fuī be absent, lack
ēvertō, ere, ī, rsus overturn, destroy
fallō, ere, fefellī, falsus deceive, baffle,
   elude, escape the notice of
fulg(e)ō, ēre, lsī gleam, flash, glitter
homō, inis *m. (f.)* man, mortal, human
incūsō (1) accuse, blame, chide

mūrus, ī *m.* (city) wall, rampart
obiectō (1) throw to, expose
obscūrus, a, um dark, obscure, gloomy
penātēs, ium *m.* household gods
perīc(u)lum, ī *n.* danger, peril, risk
porta, ae *f.* gate, entrance, exit, portal
principiō *adv.* first, at first
quam *adv.* than, how, as
recondō, ere, didī, ditus establish; hide
renovō (1) renew, revive
repetō, ere, īvi (iī), ītus seek again
revertor, ī, rsus return, turn back
rūrsus, um *adv.* again, anew, back(ward)
sacrō (1) consecrate, dedicate, hallow
tumulus, ī *m.* hill, mound
vallis, is *f.* valley, vale, dale

---

*back for her lost as she was or cast a
thought behind.* In the excitement and
confusion, Aeneas forgets to look back
for his wife or even to think of her.
  742. (ad) tumulum, (ad) sēdem.
  743. collēctīs omnibus: abl. abs.
  745. Quem hominumque deōrumque:
partitive gen.; App. 286. **deōrumque:** the
final **-e** is elided before the initial
diphthong of the next verse, making 2.745
HYPERMETRIC; App. 402. This feature,
combined with the elision of **incūsāvī**
āmēns, captures Aeneas' near loss of
emotional control as he remembers this
moment.
  747. In this single verse, Aeneas names
the three entities to whom his sense of

pietas is absolute. The image of Aeneas
guiding them out of Troy was famous
even in antiquity—it appeared on coins,
and featured in an important sculptural
group in the forum of Augustus.
  748. (in) curvā valle.
  749. urbem repetō et cingor armīs:
for the HYSTERON PROTERON, see the note on
353. **cingor:** like the Gk. middle = **mē**
cingō; App. 309.
  750. Stat (mihi sententia): *I am*
determined.
  751. (meum) caput = vītam.
  752. Principiō: correlative with **inde** in
756.

q"ua gressum extuleram, repetō *et* vestīgia retrō
observāta *sequor per noctem et* lūmine lūstrō:

755   horror ubīque *animō, simul ipsa* silentia terrent.
  Inde *domum, sī forte pedem, sī forte tulisset,*
  mē referō: inruerant *Danaī et tēctum omne tenēbant.*
  Īlicet *ignis* edāx *summa ad* fastīgia *ventō*
  volvitur; exsuperant *flammae, furit* aestus *ad aurās.*

760   Prōcēdō *et Priamī sēdēs arcemque* revīsō:
  et iam porticibus vacuīs *Iūnōnis* asȳlō
  custōdēs lēctī Phoenīx *et* dīrus Ulixēs
  praedam adservābant. *Hūc* undique Trōia gaza
  incēnsīs *ērepta* adytīs, mēnsae*que deōrum*

---

adservō (1) guard, watch
adytum, ī *n.* inner shrine, sanctuary
aestus, ūs *m.* flood, tide, surge; heat
asȳlum, ī *n.* refuge, sanctuary
custōs, ōdis *m.* (*f.*) guard(ian), keeper
dīrus, a, um dire, terrible, cursed
edāx, ācis devouring, eating, consuming
efferō, ferre, extulī, ēlātus carry forth,
  raise, lift
exsuperō (1) surmount, mount (high)
fastīgium, (i)ī *n.* top, roof, summit
gaza, ae *f.* wealth, treasure
gressus, ūs *m.* step, course, gait
horror, ōris *m.* horror, terror, shudder(ing)
īlicet *adv.* immediately, at once
incendō, ere, ī, ēnsus burn, kindle
inde *adv.* thence, thereupon
inruō, ere, uī rush in
legō, ere, lēgī, lēctus choose, collect
lūstrō (1) survey; traverse; purify

mēnsa, ae *f.* table
observō (1) observe, watch, note
Phoenīx, īcis *m.* Greek leader
porticus, ūs *f.* colonnade, portico
praeda, ae *f.* booty, spoils, prey
prōcēdō, ere, cessī, cessus advance
quā *adv.* where(by), in any (some) way
repetō, ere, īvī (iī), ītus seek again
retrō *adv.* back(ward), again
revīsō, ere see again, revisit
silentium, (i)ī *n.* silence, stillness, quiet
terreō, ēre, uī, itus frighten, terrify
Trōius, a, um Trojan
ubīque *adv.* everywhere, anywhere
Ulixēs, is (eī, ī) *m.* Odysseus, a wily
  Greek leader
undique *adv.* everywhere, from all sides
vacuus, a, um empty, vacant, free
vestīgium, (i)ī *n.* step, track, trace

---

754. lūmine = oculō: this use of **lumen**
is more common in pl.

755. horror (est meō) animō.

756. sī forte, sī forte: rhetorical
repetition, representing the repeated
thought and desperate hope in the mind
of Aeneas; App. 413. **sī tulisset:** implied
indir. statement; App. 390.

759. ad aurās = ad caelum.

761. (in) porticibus: ablative of place
where. **asȳlō:** in apposition with
porticibus; the use of this Greek word,
meaning *a place not to be plundered,* or
a place of refuge, emphasizes the impiety
of the Greeks in thus descrating the holy
sanctuary of Juno's temple, and the irony
of holding Trojans as prisoners there.

764. adytīs: dat. of separation; App.
305. **mēnsae:** *tables* on which food and
other offerings were placed for the gods.

crātēres*que aurō* solidī, captīva*que* vestis   765
congeritur. *Puerī et* pavidae *longō* ordine *mātrēs*
stant circum.

---

captīvus, a, um captive, captured
congerō, ere, gessī, gestus heap up
crātēr, ēris *m.* mixing bowl
ordō, inis *m.* order, array, row

pavidus, a, um terrified, fearful
solidus, a, um solid, firm, massive
vestis, is *f.* garment, cloth(ing), robe

---

765. aurō: abl. of material; App. 324.
766. congeritur: agreeing in number with the nearest subject; App. 236, *b.*

Puerī, mātrēs (= fēminae): Trojan captives, to be carried off into slavery.

Aeneas flees Troy, carrying Anchises.
Attic black-figure oinochoe, c. 510-500 B.C.
Photograph by Raymond V. Schoder, S.J.

Ausus quīn etiam *vōcēs* iactāre *per umbram*
implēvī *clāmōre viās*, maestus*que* Creūsam
770   nēquīquam ingemināns iterum*que* iterum*que vocāvī.*
Quaerentī et tēctīs urbis sine fīne ruentī
īnfēlīx simulācrum *atque ipsius umbra* Creūsae
vīsa mihi ante oculōs et nōtā *maior* imāgō.
Obstipuī, *steteruntque* comae *et vōx* faucibus haesit.
775   *Tum sīc* adfārī *et cūrās hīs* dēmere *dictīs:*
'*Quid tantum* īnsānō iuvat indulgēre dolōrī,

---

adfor, fārī, fātus address, accost
audeō, ēre, ausus sum dare, venture
coma, ae *f.* hair, locks, tresses
Creūsa, ae *f.* wife of Aeneas, left behind
    during the sack of Troy
dēmō, ere, mpsī, mptus remove, take
    away
dolor, ōris *m.* grief, anger, pain, passion
etiam *adv.* even, also, besides, yet, still
faucēs, ium *f.* jaws, throat; pass, entrance
haereō, ēre, haesī, haesus stick, cling
    (to)
iactō (1) hurl, toss, fling; utter
imāgō, inis *f.* image, phantom, likeness
impleō, ēre, ēvī, ētus fill, satisfy

indulgeō, ēre, lsī, ltus indulge in, yield
    to (+ *dat.*)
ingeminō (1) redouble, repeat, increase
īnsānus, a, um mad, frantic, insane
iterum *adv.* again, anew, a second time
iuvō, āre, iūvī, iūtus help, please
maestus, a, um sad, mournful, gloomy
nēquīquam *adv.* in vain, uselessly, idly
nōtus, a, um (well) known, familiar
obstipēscō, ere, stipuī be dazed, stand
    agape
quīn in fact
simulācrum, ī *n.* image, phantom,
    likeness
sine without (+ *abl.*)

768–804. Aeneas is met by
Creusa's ghost, who informs him
of her death and urges him to leave
Troy for Hesperia. Aeneas returns to
his followers, and they leave Troy.

768. Ausus quīn: *in fact, I even dared.*
770. nēquīquam: understand with
either **ingemināns** or **vocāvī. iterumque
iterumque:** rhetorical repetition; App.
413. Placed immediately after
ingemināns, the two adverbs illustrate the
meaning of the participle.
771. (in) tēctīs.
**771–73. mihi quaerentī et ruentī
simulācrum et umbra Creūsae vīsa (est).
īnfēlix:** in one sense, a transferred epithet,
since the appearance of Creusa's shade makes

Aeneas unhappy. But the epithet **īnfēlīx** is
often used in other contexts to describe the
dead, since its root meaning (from **fe-**)
connects it with fertility and productiveness.
Thus, a tree that bears no fruit might also be
called **īnfēlīx,** as would an unpromising
omen. **ipsius:** for the short penult, see the
note on **illius,** 1.16. **vīsa (est):** agrees with
umbra, its nearest subject. **(imāgine mihi)
nōtā:** abl. with comparative; App. 327. The
shades of the dead, as well as the gods,
regularly appeared as larger than human
beings.
774. steterunt: with short penult.
775. (Creūsa) adfārī et dēmere:
construe with **vīsa (est)** in 2.773; or
historical inf.; App. 257.
776. Quid = cūr: *why?* **(tē) iuvat.
dolōrī:** dat. with compound verb
indulgēre; App. 297.

Ō dulcis *coniūnx? Nōn haec* sine *nūmine dīvum*
ēveniunt; *nec tē comitem hinc* portāre Creūsam
fās, *aut ille* sinit *superī* rēgnātor Olympī.
Longa tibi exsilia *et vastum maris aequor* arandum,   780
et terram Hesperiam *veniēs, ubi* Lȳdius *arva*
inter opīma *virum* lēnī fluit *agmine* Thybris.
Illīc *rēs laetae rēgnumque et* rēgia *coniūnx*
parta *tibī; lacrimās* dīlēctae pelle Creūsae.
Nōn ego Myrmidonum *sēdēs* Dolopum*ve* superbās   785

---

arō (1) plow, furrow, till
Creūsa, ae *f.* wife of Aeneas, lost during
  the sack of Troy
dīligō, ere, lēxī, lēctus love, cherish
Dolopes, um *m.* Greeks of Thessaly
dulcis, e sweet, dear, fond
ēveniō, īre, vēnī, ventus come out,
  happen
exsilium, (i)ī *n.* exile, place of exile
fās *n. indecl.* right, justice, divine will
fluō, ere, flūxī, flūxus flow, ebb, stream
Hesperius, a, um Hesperian, western,
  Italian
illīc *adv.* there, at that place
lēnis, e gentle, soft, mild
Lȳdius, a, um Lydian, of Lydia, a
  country of Asia Minor, said to be the

original home of the Etruscans who
  settled in Italy
Myrmidones, um *m.* Greeks of Thessaly
Olympus, ī *m.* a Greek mountain, home
  of the gods, heaven
opīmus, a, um rich, fertile, sumptuous
pariō, ere, peperī, partus acquire, win,
  produce
pellō, ere, pepulī, pulsus drive (away),
  dismiss
portō (1) carry
rēgius, a, um royal, regal, kingly
rēgnātor, ōris *m.* ruler, sovereign, lord
sine without (+ *abl.*)
sinō, ere, sīvī, situs permit, allow
superbus, a, um proud, haughty
Thybris, (id)is *m.* Tiber, a river of Italy

---

777. Nōn sine nūmine: LITOTES.
dīv(ōr)um.
   778. comitem: in apposition with
Creūsam.
   779. fās (est). aut = nec. rēgnātor:
Jupiter.
   780. exsilia tibi (ferenda sunt).
arandum (est tuīs nāvibus).
   781. (ad) terram. Hesperiam: this is
the first time Aeneas hears the name of
the place to which he is destined to travel.
   781–82. Lȳdius arva inter opīma
Thybris: the river Tiber flows south
through Etruria, the ancient home of the
Etruscans; here, Vergil alludes to a
tradition that the Etruscans had come to

Italy from Lydia, in the ancient near east.
And Lydian wealth and prosperity were
famous—King Croesus of Lydia (6th
century B.C.) was reputed to be the
wealthiest man in the world.
   782. vir(ōr)um: gen. with opīma;
App. 287.
   783. rēgia coniūnx: Lavinia, daughter
of King Latinus, was married to Aeneas
shortly after his arrival in Italy.
   784. parta (est or erit): agrees with
the nearest subject; App. 236, *b.*
Creūsae: obj. gen., *tears of (for) Creusa;*
App. 284.
   785. ego: emphatic, as always when
expressed; App. 247.

aspiciam *aut* Graīs servītum *mātribus ībō*,
Dardanis *et dīvae* Veneris nurus;
sed mē magna deum genetrīx *hīs* dētinet *ōrīs.*
Iamque valē *et nātī servā* commūnis *amōrem.*'
790   *Haec ubi dicta dedit*, lacrimantem *et multa volentem*
   dīcere dēseruit, tenuēs*que* recessit *in aurās.*
   Ter cōnātus ibī collō *dare* bracchia *circum*;
   ter frūstrā comprēnsa *manūs* effūgit imāgō,
   pār levibus *ventīs* volucrī*que* simillima *somnō.*
795   *Sīc* dēmum *sociōs* cōnsūmptā *nocte* revīsō.
      Atque hīc ingentem comitum adflūxisse *novōrum*
   inveniō admīrāns numerum, *mātrēsque virōsque,*

---

adfluō, ere, flūxī, flūxus flow together
admīror, ārī, ātus wonder (at), admire
a(d)spiciō, ere, spexī, spectus see, look (at)
bracchium, (i)ī *n.* (fore)arm
collum, ī *n.* neck
commūnis, e common, mutual, general
compre(he)ndō, ere, ī, ēnsus grasp
cōnor, ārī, ātus attempt, try, endeavor
cōnsūmō, ere, mpsī, mptus consume, waste
Dardanis, idis *f.* Trojan woman
dēmum *adv.* at length, finally
dēserō, ere, uī, rtus desert, forsake
dētineō, ēre, uī, tentus detain, hold back
effugiō, ere, fūgī escape, flee from
frūstrā *adv.* in vain, uselessly, ineffectually
genetrīx, īcis *f.* mother
Graius, a, um Greek

ibi *adv.* there, then
imāgō, inis *f.* image, likeness, phantom
inveniō, īre, vēnī, ventus find, come upon
lacrimō (1) weep, shed tears, lament
levis, e light, unsubstantial, slight
numerus, ī *m.* number, multitude
nurus, ūs *f.* daughter-in-law
pār, paris equal, like, similar (+ *dat.*)
recēdō, ere, cessī, cessus depart, retire
revīsō, ere revisit, see again
serviō, īre, īvī (iī), ītus be a slave, serve (+ *dat.*)
similis, e like, similar (+ *dat.*)
tenuis, e slight, thin, fine
ter thrice, three times
valeō, ēre, uī be strong, fare well, be able
Venus, eris *f.* goddess of love and beauty
volucer, cris, cre winged, swift

---

786. **servītum:** acc. supine in **-um** after a verb of motion, to express purpose; App. 270.

788. **de(ōr)um genetrīx:** Cybele, the Great Mother of the Gods, whose worship originated in the area around Troy. (**in**) **ōrīs.**

790. (**mē**) **lacrimantem.**

792. **cōnātus (sum). collō dare bracchia circum:** *to place my arms around her neck*; **circum** is here an adverb.

794. **ventīs:** dat. with the adj. **pār**; **somnō:** dat. with the adj. **simillima,** App. 304.

795. **cōnsūmptā nocte:** the night and Aeneas' recounting of it end together, at the end of the book.

collēctam exsiliō pūbem, miserābile vulgus.
Undique convēnēre *animīs* opibus*que parātī*
in quāscum*que velim pelagō* dēdūcere *terrās.*   800
Iamque iugīs *summae surgēbat* Lūcifer Îdae
dūcēbatque diem, Danaīque obsessa tenēbant
līmina portārum, *nec* spēs opis *ūlla dabātur.*
Cessī *et sublātō montēs genitōre petīvī.*

---

cēdō, ere, cessī, cessus yield, depart
colligō, ere, lēgī, lēctus collect, gather
conveniō, īre, vēnī, ventus come
  together, assemble
dēdūcō, ere, dūxī, ductus lead forth,
  launch
exsilium, (i)ī *n.* exile, place of exile
Īda, ae *f.* mountain near Troy
iugum, ī *n.* yoke, (mountain) ridge
Lūcifer, erī *m.* morning star, light-bringer

miserābilis, e miserable, wretched
obsideō, ēre, sēdī, sessus besiege, beset
ops, opis *f.* help, resources, power, wealth
porta, ae *f.* gate, entrance, exit, portal
pūbēs, is *f.* youth, young men
quīcumque, quaecumque, quodcumque
  whoever, whatever
spēs, speī *f.* hope, expectation
undique *adv.* everywhere, from all sides
vulgus, ī *n. (m.)* crowd, rabble, herd

---

798. exsiliō: dat. of purpose; App. 303.
  799. convēnēre = convēnērunt.
animīs, opibus: abl. of respect; App. 325.
parātī (īre mēcum).
  800. velim: subjunctive in implied
indir. statement; App. 390. **dēducere:** the
technical word among the Romans for
leading out a colony or for launching a ship.

801. (in) iugīs: abl. of place where or
abl. of separation.
  803. spēs opis: hope of helping Troy
or of receiving help from Troy.
  804. montēs: Mt. Ida, near Troy, thus
following the trail blazed out by the
meteor seen earlier in Book 2: 692–98.

SELECTIONS FROM
BOOK 4

teque isto corpore solvo (4.703)

Illustration for Book 4
" *And free you from your body*" by Thom Kapheim

BOOK 4.1–449

At rēgīna gravī iamdūdum saucia *cūrā*
vulnus alit vēnīs *et* caecō carpitur *ignī.*
Multa virī virtūs *animō multusque* recursat
gentis honōs; haerent īnfīxī *pectore* vultūs
verba*que nec* placidam membrīs *dat cūra* quiētem.   5
Postera Phoebēā lūstrābat lampade *terrās*

---

alō, ere, uī, (i)tus nourish, cherish
caecus, a, um blind, hidden, dark
carpō, ere, psī, ptus pluck, consume,
   waste
gravis, e heavy, grievous, serious
haereō, ēre, haesī, haesus stick (to),
   cling (to) (+ *dat.*)
iamdūdum *adv.* long since, for some time
īnfīgō, ere, xī, xus fix (in, on), fasten
lampas, adis *f.* torch, lamp, light
lūstrō (1) traverse; survey; purify
membrum, ī *n.* member, limb, body

Phoebēus, a, um of Phoebus (Apollo),
   god of light, music, and prophecy
placidus, a, um calm, kindly, quiet
posterus, a, um following, later, next
quiēs, ētis *f.* quiet, sleep, rest
recursō (1) run back, come back, recur
saucius, a, um wounded, hurt
vēna, ae *f.* vein
verbum, ī *n.* word, speech, talk
virtūs, ūtis *f.* manliness, virtue, valor
vulnus, eris *n.* wound, deadly blow
vultus, ūs *m.* countenance, face, aspect

> 1–53. Dido discloses her feelings
> about Aeneas to her sister Anna; Anna
> urges Dido to think of marrying Aeneas.

1. At: denotes the return of the poet to
his own narrative after the conclusion of
Aeneas' story and marks a strong contrast
between the restlessness of Dido and the
calm (**quiēvit**) indicated by the last line of
Book 3, **Conticuit tandem factōque hīc
fīne quiēvit. rēgīna:** Dido. **Gravī cūrā:**
passionate love.
   2. vēnīs: abl. of place where or of
means. **ignī:** abl. of means.

3. Multa, multus: the repetition
intentionally strengthens and makes more
vivid the idea of frequency and repetition:
many a virtue . . . many an honor . . . ;
App. 413. **virī = Aenēae. animō:** abl. of
place where or = **ad animum:** dat. of
direction.
   4. gentis honōs: his noble birth, since
he is both a member of the royal family
and descended from Jupiter and Venus.
(in) pectore.
   5. verba: the four causes mentioned as
arousing the love of the queen for Aeneas
are: his courage (**virtūs**), his noble birth
(**gentis honōs**), his handsome appearance
(**vultūs**), and his fine words (**verba**).
   6–7. Postera Aurōra lūstrābat.
Phoebēā lampade = *with the sun's rays.*

ūmentem*que* Aurōra polō dīmōverat *umbram*,
cum sīc ūnanimam adloquitur male sāna sorōrem:
"Anna soror, *quae mē* suspēnsam īnsomnia terrent!
10   *Quis novus hic nostrīs* successit *sēdibus* hospes,
quem sēsē ōre ferēns, quam fortī *pectore et armīs!*
Crēdō equidem, *nec* vāna fidēs, *genus esse deōrum.*
Dēgenerēs *animōs* timor arguit. *Heu, quibus ille*
iactātus *fātīs! Quae bella* exhausta canēbat!

---

adloquor, ī, locūtus address, accost
Anna, ae *f.* sister of Dido
arguō, ere, uī, ūtus prove, make clear
Aurōra, ae *f.* (goddess of) dawn
canō, ere, cecinī, cantus sing (of), chant,
     prophesy, recount
crēdō, ere, didī, ditus believe, trust
     (+ *dat.*)
dēgener, eris degenerate, base, ignoble
dīmoveō, ēre, ōvī, ōtus divide, remove
equidem *adv.* indeed, truly
exhauriō, īre, hausī, haustus drain,
     exhaust; bear
fidēs, eī *f.* faith, belief, trust(worthiness)
fortis, e brave, strong, valiant, stout
hospes, itis *m.* (*f.*) guest, host, stranger

iactō (1) toss, buffet, hurl, fling
īnsomnium, (i)ī *n.* dream, vision in sleep
male *adv.* badly, ill, scarcely, not
polus, ī *m.* pole, sky, heaven
quam *adv.* how, than, as
sānus, a, um sane, sound, rational
soror, ōris *f.* sister
succēdō, ere, cessī, cessus approach
     (+ *dat.*)
suspēnsus, a, um suspended, agitated
terreō, ēre, uī, itus terrify, frighten
timor, ōris *m.* fear, dread, cowardice
ūmēns, entis moist, dewy, wet
ūnanimus, a, um one-minded, sympathiz-
     ing
vānus, a, um vain, empty, idle, groundless

---

7. This is a verbatim echo of 3.589.

8. **male sāna = nōn sāna = īnsāna:** cf.
male fīda = īnfīda, 2.23; LITOTES.

10. **Quis (est) hic novus hospes, (quī)
nostrīs sēdibus successit:** *what a
marvelous stranger this is, who has come
to our house!*

11. **quem sēsē ōre ferēns:** *how noble
in appearance;* lit. *carrying himself* (as)
what (sort of) *person with respect to
appearance.* Some editors print **quam**
instead of **quem,** since even the earliest
surviving manuscripts of Vergil's work
(fourth-fifth centuries A.D.) are confused
on this point. It is most likely, however,
that Vergil's original **quem** was changed
to **quam** by a copyist at some point in the
history of the poem, either inadvertently

(i.e., as a result of a simple spelling
mistake or lapse in attention) or because it
would then parallel the adv. **quam** which
appears later in this line. **quam fortī
pectore et (fortibus) armīs:** ablatives of
quality; App. 330. **armīs:** some editors
have suggested that Dido is admiring his
(physical) arms (from **armus, i** *m.*) rather
than his weapons, although as leader of
her people she might just as easily be
attracted to the evidence he displays of his
military exploits.

12. **(illum) esse genus deōrum:** ind.
statement. **nec (mea) fidēs (est) vāna.**

13. **Dēgenerēs:** in other words, she
knows that Aeneas' soul is not **dēgener,**
as he has always been so fearless.

14. **iactātus (est).**

Sī mihi nōn animō fixum immōtum*que* sedēret   15
nē cui mē vinclō *vellem* sociāre iugālī,
postquam *prīmus amor* dēceptam *morte* fefellit;
sī *nōn* pertaesum thalamī taedae*que fuisset*,
huic ūnī forsan *potuī* succumbere culpae.
Anna (fatēbor enim) *miserī* post *fāta* Sychaeī   20
coniugis et sparsōs frāternā caede penātēs
sōlus hic īnflexit sēnsūs *animumque* labantem
impulit. Agnōscō veteris vestīgia *flammae*.

---

agnōscō, ere, nōvī, nitus recognize
Anna, ae *f.* sister of Dido
caedēs, is *f.* slaughter, murder, massacre
culpa, ae *f.* fault, blame, weakness, sin
dēcipiō, ere, cēpī, ceptus deceive
enim *adv.* for, indeed, truly
fallō, ere, fefellī, falsus deceive, cheat, mock
fateor, ērī, fassus confess, agree
fīgō, ere, xī, xus fix, fasten, imprint
fors(it)an *adv.* perhaps, perchance
frāternus, a, um fraternal, of a brother
immōtus, a, um unmoved, immovable
impellō, ere, pulī, pulsus strike, drive on
īnflectō, ere, flexī, flexus bend, turn
iugālis, e of wedlock, matrimonial
labō (1) totter, waver, vacillate
penātēs, ium *m.* household gods

pertaedet, ēre, taesum it wearies
  (+ *gen.*)
post *adv.* afterward; *prep.* + *acc.* after, behind
postquam. after (that), when
sedeō, ēre, sēdī, sessus sit, settle
sēnsus, ūs *m.* feeling, perception, sense
sociō (1) unite, ally, share (as partner)
spargō, ere, rsī, rsus scatter, sprinkle
succumbō, ere, cubuī, cubitus yield (to)
  (+ *dat.*)
Sychaeus, ī *m.* deceased husband of Dido
taeda, ae *f.* torch, pine
thalamus, ī *m.* (bridal) chamber, wedlock
vestīgium, (i)ī *n.* step, track, trace
vetus, eris old, aged, ancient, former
vinc(u)lum, ī *n.* chain, bond, cable

**15. (in) animō. sī . . . nōn . . .
sedēret:** present contrary-to-fact condition; App. 382.

16. nē vellem: *not to be willing*, substantive clause, subject of **sedēret**; App. 360. **cui:** indefinite, *any one*.
vinc(u)lō iugālī: *in bonds of wedlock*.

17. (mē) dēceptam fefellit = mē dēcēpit et fefellit.

18. sī nōn (mē) pertaesum fuisset: past contrary-to-fact condition; App. 382.
thalamī, taedae: gen. with the impersonal verb **pertaedet**; App. 290. **taedae:** *the (marriage) torch*, by METONYMY for *marriage*. Torches were carried by attendants in the wedding procession.

19. potuī: the ind. instead of the more usual subjunctive expresses the conclusion of the condition in a more positive way, as though it were practically realized; App. 382, *d*. **huic ūnī culpae:** dat. with coumpound; Dido refers to the weakness (**culpa**) of loving Aeneas after having sworn eternal fidelity to her former husband, Sychaeus.

21. frāternā: equivalent to subjective gen. **fratris** with **caede**; *the murder of Sychaeus by my brother*. Cf. 1.343–56.

22–23. sōlus hic (Aenēās). hic: with a short syllable here instead of the more usual long; App. 107, 3, *c*. **(meum) animum labantem impulit** = meum animum sīc impulit ut labāret.

     Sed mihi vel tellūs optem prius *īma* dehīscat
25   *vel pater* omnipotēns adigat *mē* fulmine *ad umbrās,*
     pallentēs *umbrās* Erebō *noctemque* profundam,
     ante, pudor, quam *tē* violō *aut tua* iūra resolvō.
     Ille meōs, prīmus quī mē sibi iūnxit, *amōrēs*
     abstulit; *ille habeat sēcum servetque* sepulcrō."
30   *Sīc* effāta sinum *lacrimīs* implēvit obortīs.
     Anna *refert:* "*Ō lūce* magis dīlēcta sorōrī,
     sōlane perpetuā maerēns carpēre iuventā
     nec dulcēs *nātōs* Veneris *nec* praemia nōris?

---

adigō, ere, ēgī, āctus drive (away), force
Anna, ae *f.* sister of Dido
auferō, erre, abstulī, ablātus take away, carry off
carpō, ere, psī, ptus pluck, consume, waste
dehīscō, ere yawn, gape, open (up)
dīligō, ere, lēxī, lēctus love, cherish
dulcis, e sweet, dear, fond
effor, ārī, ātus speak out, say
Erebus, ī *m.* underworld, Hades
fulmen, inis *n.* thunderbolt, lightning
impleō, ēre, ēvī, ētus fill
iungō, ere, iūnxī, iūnctus join, yoke
iūs, iūris *n.* right, law, decree, justice
iuventa, ae *f.* youth, young manhood, young womanhood
maereō, ēre mourn, grieve, pine (for)
magis *adv.* more, rather

nōscō, ere, nōvī, nōtus learn; *perf.* know
oborior, īrī, ortus (a)rise, spring up
omnipotēns, entis almighty, omnipotent
optō (1) desire, choose, hope (for, to)
pallēns, entis pale, pallid, wan
perpetuus, a, um continual, lasting
praemium, (i)ī *n.* reward, prize
prius *adv.* sooner, before
profundus, a, um deep, profound, vast
pudor, ōris *m.* shame, modesty, honor
quam *adv.* how, than, as
resolvō, ere, ī, solūtus loose(n), relax
sepulcrum, ī *n.* tomb, grave, burial
sinus, ūs *m.* fold, bosom, bay, hollow
soror, ōris *f.* sister
Venus, eris *f.* goddess of love and beauty, love
violō (1) outrage, violate, defile

24–25. tellūs īma: *the lowest (depths of the) earth;* App. 246. **prius:** with **quam,** 27, but repeated as **ante** in 27 because of the intervening clauses. **optem:** potential subjunctive; App. 252; *I wish that ...* **(ut) dehīscat, (ut) abigat:** substantive clauses expressing the content of Dido's wish (**optem**); the construction resembles an indirect command, with the subjunctive used to express the desired result; App. 360. **pater omnipotēns = Jupiter. ad umbrās = ad mortem,** defined by the next verse.

27. ante: repeating **prius,** 24. **pudor:** although many women (and men) in Vergil's day remarried after the death or divorce of a spouse, a woman who was **univira** (i.e., had had only one husband) was considered worthy of unusual respect.

28. Ille: Sychaeus.

29. habeat (meōs amōrēs) servetque (eōs in) sepulcrō: jussive subjunctives; App. 254.

30. lacrimīs: an indication of the strength of the feeling she is trying to suppress.

31. magis dīlēcta: *more beloved = dearer.* **lūce** (= **vītā**): abl. with comparative; App. 327. **sorōrī = mihi:** dat. of agent; App. 302.

32. iuventā: abl. of time, practically equivalent to an acc. of duration; App. 322, 314. **carpēre = carpēris;** App. 204, 4.

33. Veneris nec praemia: *the joys of love.* Note the postposition of **nec. nō(ve)ris:** fut. perf.; with force of a fut.

Id cinerem *aut* mānēs crēdis cūrāre sepultōs?

Estō: aegram *nūllī quondam* flexēre marītī,   35
nōn Libyae, *nōn ante* Tyrō; dēspectus Iarbās
ductōrēs*que aliī, quōs* Āfrica *terra* triumphīs
dīves alit: placitō*ne* etiam pugnābis *amōrī?*
Nec venit in mentem quōrum cōnsēderis *arvīs?*
Hinc Gaetūlae *urbēs, genus* īnsuperābile *bellō,*   40
et Numidae īnfrēnī cingunt *et* inhospita Syrtis;
hinc dēserta sitī rēgiō lātē*que furentēs*

---

aeger, gra, grum sick, weary, wretched
Āfricus, a, um African, of Africa
alō, ere, uī, (i)tus nourish, rear
cingō, ere, cīnxī, cīnctus surround, gird(le)
cinis, eris *m.* ashes (of the dead), embers
cōnsīdō, ere, sēdī, sessus sit (down), settle
crēdō, ere, didī, ditus believe, trust (+ *dat.*)
cūrō (1) care (for, to), heed, regard
dēserō, ere, uī, rtus desert, forsake
dēspiciō, ere, spexī, spectus look down on, scorn, despise, disdain
dī(ve)s, dī(vi)tis rich, wealthy
ductor, ōris *m.* leader, chieftain, guide
etiam *adv.* also, even, besides, yet, still
flectō, ere, flexī, flexus bend, move
Gaetūlus, a, um of the Gaetuli, a tribe of North Africa

Iarbās, ae *m.* African chieftain, one of Dido's suitors
īnfrēnus, a, um unbridled, without bridles
inhospitus, a, um inhospitable, wild
īnsuperābilis, e unconquerable
lātē *adv.* widely, far and wide
Libya, ae *f.* country of North Africa
mānēs, ium *m.* (souls of) the dead, Hades
marītus, ī *m.* (prospective) husband, suitor
Numidae, ārum *m.* tribe of North Africa
placeō, ēre, uī, itus please (+ *dat.*)
pugnō (1) fight, oppose, resist (+ *dat.*)
regiō, ōnis *f.* region, district, quarter
sepeliō, īre, īvī (ii), pultus bury, inter
sitis, is *f.* thirst, drought
Syrtis, is *f.* region of quicksand on the northern coast of Africa
triumphus, ī *m.* triumph, victory
Tyrus, ī *f.* famous city of Phoenicia, birthplace of Dido

---

34. Id: i.e., whether you remarry or not. **cinerem aut mānēs (Sychaeī),** subjects of **cūrāre.** Anna's answer to Dido's statement in 28-29 is that her actions cannot possibly disturb the ashes and shade of Sychaeus.

35. Estō: imp. 3d sing. of **sum;** *(so) be it, granted that.* **(tē) aegram:** sick, i.e., with grief; *while you mourned for your husband* (i.e., during the time immediately following his death).

36. Libyae: loc.; App. 345. **(in) Tyrō:** loc. abl. **dēspectus (est tibi).**

37-38. Āfrica terra triumphīs dīves: this is anachronistic, since Vergil is thinking of the many triumphs later

celebrated by Roman generals for their victories in Africa. **triumphīs:** abl. of respect with **dīves;** App. 325. **placitō:** with active force, *agreeable, pleasing (to you).* **pugnābis = resistēs. amōrī:** dat. with special verb; App. 297.

39. Nec venit in (tuam) mentem: *does it not occur to you?* **quōrum cōnsēderis (in) arvīs:** indir. quest.; App. 349; subject of **venit;** *what sort of people* (i.e., how fierce and hostile) *they are in whose territory you have settled.*

40-42. Hinc . . . hinc: *from this side . . . from that side.* **īnfrēnī:** unbridled; involving a play on words, since the Libyans rode their horses without bridles

Barcaeī. *Quid bella* Tyrō *surgentia dīcam*
germānī*que* minās?

45   *Dīs* equidem auspicibus reor *et Iūnōne secundā*
hunc cursum Īliacās *ventō tenuisse* carīnās.
Quam tū urbem, soror, *hanc cernēs, quae surgere rēgna*
coniugiō *tālī! Teucrum* comitantibus *armīs*
Pūnica *sē* quantīs attollet glōria *rēbus!*

50   *Tū* modo posce *deōs* veniam, *sacrīsque* litātīs
indulgē hospitiō causās*que* innecte morandī,
dum pelagō dēsaevit hiems *et* aquōsus Orīōn,
quassātae*que* ratēs, *dum nōn* tractābile *caelum.*"

---

aquōsus, a, um watery, rainy
attollō, ere lift, rear, raise
auspex, icis *m.* protector, guide; seer
Barcaeī, ōrum *m.* tribe of North Africa
carīna, ae *f.* keel; ship, boat
causa, ae *f.* cause, reason, pretext
comitor, ārī, ātus accompany, escort,
    attend, follow
coniugium, (i)ī *n.* wedlock; husband, wife
dēsaeviō, īre, īvī (iī), ītus rage (furiously)
equidem *adv.* indeed, surely, truly
germānus, ī *m.* brother
glōria, ae *f.* renown, glory, fame, pride
hiems, emis *f.* winter, storm
hospitium, (i)ī *n.* hospitality, welcome
Īliacus, a, um Trojan, Ilian
indulgeō, ēre, lsī, ltus indulge, favor (+
    dat.)
innectō, ere, x(u)ī, xus weave, connect
minae, ārum *f.* threat, menace, peril

litō (1) sacrifice (favorably), appease
modo *adv.* only, (just) now
moror, ārī, ātus delay, tarry, hinder
Orīōn, ōnis *m.* the storm-bringing
    constellation, named for a famous
    hunter transported to heaven
poscō, ere, poposcī demand, seek, ask
Pūnicus, a, um Punic, Carthaginian
quantus, a, um how great, how much,
    how many
quassō (1) shake, shatter, toss
ratis, is *f.* raft, ship, boat
reor, rērī, ratus think, suppose, resist (+
    dat.)
secundus, a, um second, favorable
soror, ōris *f.* sister
tractābilis, e manageable, favorable
Tyrus, ī *f.* famous city of Phoenicia,
    birthplace of Dido
venia, ae *f.* favor, pardon, grace

---

and were a wild, fierce, unrestrained
(unbridled) tribe. **cingunt (tē). sitī:** abl.
of cause with **dēserta.**

43. Barcaeī (sunt). Tyrō: abl. of place
from which; App. 320, *a.*

44. germānī: Pygmalion. See 1.346-64,
563-64.

45. Dīs auspicibus, Iūnōne secundā:
abl. abs. **Iūnōne:** both as goddess of
marriage and as guardian of Carthage.

46. hunc cursum: *their course to this*
place.

47. Quam, quae: *how great! what (a)!*
quam urbem hanc cernēs (surgere),
quae rēgna (cernēs) surgere.

48. coniugiō tālī: abl. of cause.
Teucr(ōr)um.

49. quantīs rēbus: *to what heights of*
achievement!

50. deōs veniam: two accusatives with
a verb of asking; App. 316.

52. Orīōn: a constellation rising at the
rainy and stormy season.

53. quassātae (sunt) ratēs, nōn
tractābile (est) caelum.

Hīs dictīs impēnsō *animum* flammāvit *amōre*
spem*que dedit* dubiae *mentī* solvit*que* pudōrem.　　55
Prīncipiō dēlūbra adeunt pācem*que per ārās*
exquīrunt; mactant lēctās *dē* mōre bidentēs
lēgiferae Cererī Phoebō*que patrīque* Lyaeō,
Iūnōnī ante omnēs, cui vincla iugālia *cūrae.*
Ipsa tenēns dextrā pateram pulcherrima *Dīdō*　　60
candentis vaccae *media inter* cornua *fundit,*
aut ante ōra deum pinguēs spatiātur *ad ārās,*
īnstaurat*que diem dōnīs,* pecudum*que* reclūsīs

---

adeō, īre, iī (īvī), itus approach
bidēns, entis *f.* with two teeth, two-year-
　old (sheep)
candēns, entis white, shining, sleek
Cerēs, eris *f.* (goddess of) grain
cornū, ūs *n.* horn, tip, end
dēlūbrum, ī *n.* shrine, temple, sanctuary
dubius, a, um doubtful, wavering
exquīrō, ere, quīsīvī, quīsītus seek (out)
flammō (1) inflame, burn, fire
impēnsus, a, um vast, vehement
īnstaurō (1) renew, refresh, repeat
iugālis, e of wedlock, matrimonial
lēgifer, era, erum law-bringing
legō, ere, lēgī, lēctus choose, collect
Lyaeus, ī *m.* Bacchus, (god of) wine
mactō (1) sacrifice, slaughter, kill; honor
mōs, mōris *m.* custom, ritual, manner

patera, ae *f.* (libation) bowl
pāx, pācis *f.* peace, favor, grace, repose
pecus, udis *f.* animal (of the flock)
Phoebus, ī *m.* Apollo, god of light,
　music, and prophecy
pinguis, e fat, rich, fertile
prīncipiō *adv.* at first, in the first place
pudor, ōris *m.* shame, modesty, honor
pulcher, chra, chrum beautiful, noble,
　splendid, handsome, illustrious
reclūdō, ere, sī, sus open, disclose
solvō, ere, ī, solūtus loose(n), release,
　break down, free, pay
spatior, ārī, ātus walk, stride
spēs, eī *f.* hope, expectation
vacca, ae *f.* heifer, young cow
vinc(u)lum, ī *n.* chain, bond, cable

```
┌─────────────────────────────────────┐
│  54–89. Love drives Dido to frenzy.  │
└─────────────────────────────────────┘
```

54. (iam) impēnsō.
56. (Dīdō Annaque) adeunt. dēlūbra
(urbis), ārās (urbis). pācem (deōrum), or
pācem (deōs). As we shall see below,
Dido is unable to rest; her prayers are not
answered.
57. bidentēs: literally *two-toothed,*
because of the two prominent teeth sheep
have when about two years old. In
Roman religious ritual, the sacrifice of
animals at this age was considered
particularly desirable.

58. lēgiferae: *law-giving,* because of
the civilizing influence of agriculture on
early man.
59. Iūnōnī: as presiding over
marriage. **ante omnēs** (aliōs deōs). **cui**
vinc(u)la (sunt) cūrae: cui and cūrae are
double datives, App. 303, *a.*
61. fundit (vīnum, *wine*): it was
customary to pour an offering of wine
between the horns of the victim as part of
the sacrificial cermeony.
62. ante ōra de(ōr)um: i.e., before
their images. **pinguēs:** modifying **ārās.**
The altars were fat (rich) with offerings.
63. dōnīs: *gifts* (to the gods), *sacrifices.*

pectoribus inhiāns spīrantia cōnsulit exta.

65   *Heu, vātum* ignārae *mentēs! Quid* vōta *furentem,*
     quid dēlubra iuvant? Ēst mollēs *flamma* medullās
     intereā *et* tacitum vīvit *sub pectore* vulnus.
     Ūritur *īnfēlīx Dīdō tōtāque* vagātur
     urbe furēns, quālis coniectā cerva sagittā,

70   *quam procul* incautam nemora *inter* Crēsia fīxit
     pāstor *agēns tēlīs* līquit*que* volātile *ferrum*
     nescius: *illa fugā silvās* saltūs*que* peragrat
     Dictaeōs; haeret laterī lētālis harundō.
     Nunc media Aenēān sēcum per moenia dūcit

---

cerva, ae *f.* deer, doe
coniciō, ere, iēcī, iectus hurl, shoot
cōnsulō, ere, uī, ltus consult, consider
Crēsius, a, um of Crete, Cretan
dēlūbrum, ī *n.* shrine, temple, sanctuary
Dictaeus, a, um of Dicte, a mountain in
   Crete; Cretan
edō, ere (ēsse), ēdī, ēsus eat, consume
exta, ōrum *n.* entrails, vitals
fīgō, ere, xī, xus fix, pierce, imprint
haereō, ēre, haesī, haesus cling to, stick
   to (+ *dat.*)
harundō, inis *f.* reed, arrow
ignārus, a, um ignorant, unaware
incautus, a, um unaware, unsuspecting
inhiō (1) yawn, gape
intereā *adv.* meanwhile, (in the)
   meantime
iuvō, āre, iūvī, iūtus help, please
latus, eris *n.* side, flank

lētālis, e deadly, mortal, lethal, fatal
linquō, ere, līquī, lictus leave, desert
medulla, ae *f.* marrow
mollis, e soft, yielding, tender
nemus, oris *n.* (sacred) grove, wood
nescius, a, um ignorant, unaware
pāstor, ōris *m.* shepherd, herdsman
peragrō (1) wander through, scour
quālis, e of what sort, (such) as
sagitta, ae *f.* arrow
saltus, ūs *m.* forest, glade, pasture
spīrō (1) breathe (forth), blow, quiver
   (i.e., with signs of life)
tacitus, a, um silent, noiseless, secret
ūrō, ere, ussī, ustus burn, consume
vagor, ārī, ātus wander, roam
vīvō, ere, vīxī, vīctus live, be alive
volātilis, e flying, winged, swift
vōtum, ī *n.* vow, prayer, (votive) offering
vulnus, eris *n.* wound, deadly blow

---

64. pectoribūs inhiāns: the unusual
lengthening of the last syllable of **pectoribūs**
may be meant to reflect a feature of early
Latin, where such lengthening could be used
to mark a pause. There is no pause in sense
here; but the metrical strangeness of the
line (note the metrically striking **inhiāns,**
with its short first syllable) may be meant to
complement Dido's increasingly unbalanced
behavior in this scene.

65. Notice how Vergil himself comments
here, and so suggests his sympathy for Dido.
vātum: the seers who interpret the omens
apparently encourage Dido in her hopeless
love, not realizing (**mentēs ignārae**) that
she is past praying for. **quid vōta (iuvant)**

furentem (amōre): *how can sacrifices help
one crazed (with love)?*

66. Ēst: from **edō;** the long vowel
distinguishes this form from the third person
pres. sing. ind. of the verb **sum, esse.**

**69–71. (in) urbe. furēns (amōre).
quālis cerva (vagātur), sagittā coniectā**
(abl. abs.), **quam incautam inter Crēsia
nemora pāstor agēns tēlīs procul fīxit.**
In this SIMILE, the chance shot of a
shepherd has taken effect without his
knowing it. **quam:** refers to the *deer*
(*cerva*).

72. nescius: i.e., of the success of his
shot, which has thus been in vain. **fugā:**
abl. of manner.

Sīdoniāsque ostentat opēs *urbemque parātam,*   75
incipit effārī *mediāque in vōce* resistit;
nunc eadem lābente diē convīvia *quaerit,*
Īliacōsque iterum dēmēns *audīre labōrēs*
exposcit pendetque iterum nārrantis *ab ōre.*
Post *ubi* dīgressī, lūmenque obscūra vicissim   80
lūna premit suādentque cadentia *sīdera somnōs,*
sōla domō maeret vacuā strātīsque *relictīs*
incubat. *Illum* absēns absentem *auditque videtque,*
aut gremiō Ascanium *genitōris* imāgine *capta*

---

absēns, entis absent, separated, distant
Ascanius, (i)ī *m.* son of Aeneas
cadō, ere, cedidī, cāsus fall, sink, set
convīvium, (i)ī *n.* feast, banquet
dēmēns, entis crazy, mad, distracted
dīgredior, ī, gressus (de)part, separate
effor, ārī, ātus speak (out), say
exposcō, ere, poposcī demand, entreat
gremium, (i)ī *n.* bosom, lap, embrace
Īliacus, a um Trojan, Ilian
imāgō, inis *f.* likeness, form, phantom
incipiō, ere, cēpī, ceptus begin, undertake
incubō, āre, uī, itus recline (upon) (+ *dat.*)
iterum *adv.* again, anew, a second time
lūna, ae *f.* moon, moonlight
maereō, ēre mourn, grieve, pine (for)

nārrō (1) narrate, tell, recount
obscūrus, a, um dark, obscure, gloomy
ops, opis *f.* help, resources, wealth, power
ostentō (1) show (off), display, exhibit,
   parade
pendeō, ēre, pependī hang, depend
post *adv.* afterward; *prep.* + *acc.* after,
   behind
premō, ere, pressī, pressus (re)press
resistō, ere, stitī stop, resist (+ *dat.*)
Sīdonius, a, um of Sidon, a famous city
   of Phoenicia
strātum, ī *n.* bed, couch; pavement
suādō, ēre, āsī, āsus persuade, advise
vacuus, a, um empty, free, vacant
vicissim *adv.* in turn, by turns

75-76. Sīdoniās: the names of Tyre
and Sidon, the two great cities of
Phoenicia, are used interchangeably by
Vergil. Cf. 1.338. **opēs urbemque:** subtle
temptations to the needy Aeneas and his
followers (**omnium egēnōs,** 1.599), who
were so eager to found a city where they
might end their wanderings. **mediā:** App.
246.
   77. eadem . . . convīvia: Dido repeats
the first day's banquet as if trying to
make Aeneas' time in Carthage never
end. **lābente diē:** *as the day wanes,* the
usual time for the chief meal.
   78. dēmēns: Aeneas' presence does
not relieve Dido's symptoms of love—it
only aggravates them.
   79. pendet ab ōre (Aenēae) nārrantis:
hangs on his words.

   80. Post: adv. **ubi (omnēs) dīgressī
(sunt). lūmen (suum).**
   **81. premit = reprimit. suadentque
cadentia sidera somnos:** = 2.9;
ONOMATOPOIEA.
   82. strātīs relictīs (ab Aenēā): in the
banqueting hall, after the guests have
departed, she throws herself on the couch
which Aeneas had occupied, to appease
her sense of desolation felt in the absence
of one secretly loved.
   83. absēns absentem: the repetition of
the same word in two different cases, like
the repetition of **iterum** in 78-79,
reinforces the depiction of Dido's
overpowering fixation on Aeneas.
   84-85. aut . . . detinet: i.e., in her
memory. **Ascanium:** is Ascanius present
in person, or does he appear to her in her

85   dētinet, īnfandum *sī* fallere *possit amōrem.*
      Nōn coeptae adsurgunt turrēs, *nōn arma* iuventūs
      exercet *portūsve aut* prōpugnācula *bellō*
      tūta *parant:* pendent opera interrupta minae*que*
      mūrōrum *ingentēs* aequāta*que* māchina *caelō.*

---

adsurgō, ere, surrēxī, surrēctus rise
aequō (1) (make) equal, match, level,
    even
coepī, isse, ptus begin, commence
dētineō, ēre, uī, tentus retain, hold back
exerceō, ēre, uī, itus drive, exercise
fallō, ere, fefellī, falsus deceive, cheat,
    mock, beguile
īnfandus, a, um unspeakable, unutterable

interrumpō, ere, rūpī, ruptus interrupt
iuventūs, ūtis *f.* youth, young men
māchina, ae *f.* machine, engine, device
minae, ārum *f.* threat, menace; pinnacle
mūrus, ī *m.* (city) wall, battlement
opus, eris *n.* work, labor, deed, task
pendeō, ēre, pependī hang, depend
prōpugnāculum, ī *n.* rampart, battlement
turris, is *f.* tower, turret
tūtus, a, um protected, safe, secure

---

mind? Scholars have long argued the
strengths and weaknesses of each
 interpretation; the literal sense does indeed
seem to be that she is holding Ascanius in
her lap. But given the otherwise total
silence and isolation in which the queen
finds herself during the night, we are
probably meant to imagine what Dido is
imagining; her emotions are so over-
whelming that fantasy and reality become

indistinguishable from each other.
genitōris imāgine: i.e., his resemblance to
his father.
    85. sī possit: implied indir. quest.;
App. 349.
    87. bellō: dat. of purpose.
    88-89. minae mūrōrum: *threatenings
of walls = threatening walls.* Cf. 2.235,
rotārum lāpsūs, *glidings of wheels =
gliding wheels.*

Knidian Aphrodite, Praxiteles.

Photograph by
Raymond V. Schoder, S.J.

Quam simul ac tālī persēnsit peste tenērī　　　90
cāra Iovis coniūnx nec fāmam obstāre furōrī,
tālibus adgreditur Venerem Sāturnia dictīs:
"Ēgrēgiam vērō laudem et spolia ampla refertis
tūque puerque tuus (magnum et memorābile nūmen),
ūna dolō dīvum sī fēmina victa duōrum est.　　　95
Nec mē adeō fallit veritam tē moenia nostra
suspectās habuisse domōs Karthāginis altae.
Sed quis erit modus, aut quō nunc certāmine tantō?
Quīn potius pācem aeternam pactōsque hymenaeōs

---

adeō *adv.* to such an extent, so (much)
adgredior, ī, gressus attack, address, approach
aeternus, a, um everlasting, eternal
amplus, a, um large, grand, ample, wide
cārus, a, um dear, beloved, fond
certāmen, inis *n.* contest, rivalry, strife
dolus, ī *m.* deceit, stratagem, fraud
duo, ae, a two
ēgregius, a, um remarkable, noble
fallō, ere, fefellī, falsus deceive, cheat, mock, escape the notice (of)
fēmina, ae *f.* woman, female
furor, ōris *m.* madness, frenzy, passion
hymenaeus, ī *m.* wedding (hymn), so-called after Hymen, god of marriage
Karthāgō, inis *f.* Carthage, a city of North Africa
laus, laudis *f.* praise, glory, merit
memorābilis, e memorable, glorious

modus, ī *m.* manner, measure, limit
obstō, āre, stitī, status oppose, resist (+ *dat.*)
pacīscor, ī, pactus stipulate, bargain, fix
pāx, pācis *f.* peace, favor, grace, repose
persentiō, īre, sēnsī, sēnsus feel deeply, perceive (thoroughly)
pestis, is *f.* plague, destruction. scourge
potius *adv.* rather, preferably
quīn that not, but that, why not, even in fact
Sāturnia, ae *f.* daughter of Saturn, Juno
spolium, (i)ī *n.* booty, spoils, plunder
suspiciō, ere, spexī, spectus look from beneath, suspect
Venus, eris *f.* goddess of love and beauty; love
vereor, ērī, itus fear, dread, revere
vērō *adv.* truly, indeed, but

90–128. Hoping to turn Aeneas aside from Italy, Juno favors the marriage, and so agrees to help Venus consummate the affair by means of a ruse.

90. Quam: Dido; subject of **tenērī,** inf. in ind. statement after **persensit,** *that she was held.* **peste** = **amōre;** or = **peste amōris.** The imagery of disease is often used in Latin literature to describe love.

91. fāmam: (concern for) *her reputation, good name.* **Iovis coniūnx:** Juno.

93. Ēgregiam: spoken with scornful sarcasm, and emphasized by its placement at the beginning of the speech and verse. **refertis:** a technical term for carrying off the spoils won in battle.

94. puer tuus: Cupid. **(est) nūmen (vestrum).**

96–97. adeō: *to such an extent* (as you think). **tē habuisse:** subj. of **fallit. moenia nostra:** dir. obj. of **veritam tē.**

98. modus (certāminis), aut quō (tenditis) certāmine tantō. quō: *whither, how far.*

99. Quīn = **cūr nōn. hymenaeōs (Dīdōnis Aenēaeque).**

100   exercēmus? *Habēs tōtā quod mente petīstī:*
ardet amāns Dīdō trāxit*que* per ossa furōrem.
Commūnem *hunc* ergō populum paribus*que* rēgāmus
auspiciīs; liceat Phrygiō servīre marītō
dōtālēs*que tuae Tyriōs* permittere *dextrae.*"
105   *Ollī* (sēnsit enim simulātā *mente* locūtam,
quō rēgnum Ītaliae Libycās āverteret *ōrās*)
sīc contrā *est* ingressa Venus: "*Quis tālia* dēmēns
abnuat *aut tēcum* mālit contendere *bellō?*
Sī modo *quod* memorās factum *fortūna sequātur.*

---

abnuō, ere, uī, ūtus nod, dissent, refuse
amō (1) love, like, cherish
auspicium, (i)ī *n.* auspices, power
āvertō, ere, ī, rsus turn aside, avert
commūnis, e (in) common, joint, mutual
contendō, ere, ī, ntus strive, contend
contrā *adv.* opposite, facing, in reply
dēmēns, entis crazy, mad, distracted
dōtālis, e of a dowry, as a dowry
enim *adv.* for, indeed, truly
ergō *adv.* therefore, then, consequently
exerceō, ēre, uī, itus drive, exercise, perform
factum, ī *n.* deed, act, exploit
furor, ōris *m.* madness, frenzy, passion
ingredior, ī, gressus enter, proceed
Libycus, a, um of Libya, a country of North Africa

licet, ēre, uit, itum it is permitted
loquor, ī, locūtus speak, say, tell, talk
mālō, mālle, māluī prefer, wish (in preference)
marītus, ī *m.* husband
memorō (1) recall, recount, relate, say
modo *adv.* only, (just) now
os, ossis *n.* bone
pār, paris equal, like, similar
permittō, ere, mīsī, missus entrust, allow
Phrygius, a, um Phrygian, Trojan
populus, ī *m.* people, nation
regō, ere, rēxī, rēctus rule, direct
sentiō, īre, sēnsī, sēnsus feel, perceive
serviō, īre, īvī (iī), ītus serve (+ *dat.*)
simulō (1) simulate, counterfeit, pretend
Venus, eris *f.* goddess of love and beauty; love

---

101. ardet amāns Dīdō = ardet amōre Dīdō.

102–3. paribus auspiciīs: only the highest Roman magistrates had the right to take the auspices. Juno proposes that she and Venus shall preside over the united peoples (Trojans and Carthaginians) with equal authority.

103. liceat (Dīdōnī): jussive subjunctive; App. 254. **marītō** = Aeneas: dat. with special verb, **servīre**; App. 297.

104. dōtālēs: predicatively, *as a dowry.*

105. Ollī (Iūnōnī): an archaic form of **illī**; it depends on **ingressa est (dīcere)** in

107. sēnsit (Iūnōnem) locūtam (esse).

106. quō (= ut) āverteret: purpose; App. 388. **rēgnum Ītaliae:** *the (destined) kingdom of Italy.* **(ad) ōrās.**

107. Quis dēmēns abnuat aut mālit: deliberative subjunctive; App. 348.

109. sī modo (= utinam) factum fortūna sequātur: *may fortune attend the deed* (of uniting the two peoples); subjunctive used to express a wish, like the Gk. optative; App. 253. Venus implies, but does not definitely promise, that she would consent to Juno's proposal under certain vaguely suggested conditions.

Sed fātīs incerta *feror, sī Iuppiter ūnam*   110
esse velit Tyriīs urbem Troiāque profectīs,
miscērī*ve* probet populōs *aut* foedera iungī.
Tū coniūnx, tibi fās *animum* temptāre precandō.
Perge, *sequar.*" *Tum sīc* excēpit rēgia *Iūnō:*
"*Mēcum erit* iste *labor. Nunc quā* ratiōne *quod* īnstat   115
cōnfierī *possit,* paucīs (adverte) docēbō.
Vēnātum *Aenēās* ūnā*que miserrima Dīdō*
in nemus *īre parant, ubi prīmōs* crāstinus ortūs
extulerit Tītān radiīs*que* retēxerit orbem.
Hīs ego nigrantem commixtā grandine nimbum,   120

---

advertō, ere, ī, rsus turn to, heed
commisceō, ēre, uī, mixtus mix, mingle
cōnfīō, fierī, fectus be done, be finished
crāstinus, a, um tomorrow's, of
    tommorrow
doceō, ēre, uī, ctus teach, tell, inform
efferō, ferre, extulī, ēlātus carry (out),
    raise
excipiō, ere, cēpī, ceptus take up, rejoin
fās *n.* right, justice, decree, law
foedus, eris *n.* treaty, pact, alliance
grandō, inis *f.* hail(storm, stones)
incertus, a, um uncertain, doubtful
īnstō, āre, stitī press on, desire, urge
iste, ta, tud that (of yours)
iungō, ere, iūnxī, iūnctus join, yoke
misceō, ēre, uī, mixtus mix, mingle
nemus, oris *n.* (sacred) grove, wood
nigrāns, antis black, dusky, dark

nimbus, ī *m.* (storm) cloud, rainstorm
orbis, is *m.* circle, orb(it), earth
ortus, ūs *m.* rising, source
paucus, a, um little, few, light, scanty
pergō, ere, perrēxī, rēctus proceed
populus, ī *m.* people, nation
precor, ārī, ātus pray, entreat, invoke
probō (1) test, prove, approve
proficīscor, ī, fectus set out, go
radius, (i)ī *m.* rod, spoke, ray
ratiō, ōnis *f.* manner, purpose, reason
rēgius, a, um royal, regal, kingly
retegō, ere, tēxī, tēctus uncover,
    recover
temptō (1) try, test, seek, examine
Tītān, ānis *m.* a divine ancestor of the
    Olympian gods, identified with the sun
ūnā *adv.* at the same time, together
vēnor, ārī, ātus hunt, go hunting

110–12. sī . . . velit . . . probet: indir.
quest.; App. 349. **Troiā:** abl. of separation; App. 340. **(illīs) profectīs:** dat. of
possession; equivalent to **Teucrīs.**
    112. miscērī, iungī: inf. with **probet,**
approve that.
    113. Tū (es) coniūnx (Iovis), tibi (est).
    115–16. mēcum = cum mē; App. 321,
a; here equivalent to **meus. quod īnstat:**
the business in hand; subject of **possit.**
quā ratiōne . . . possit: indir. quest.; App.
349. **paucīs (dictīs).**

    117. Vēnātum: acc. supine of **vēnor,**
after a verb of motion, to express
purpose; App. 270.
    119. extulerit, retēxerit: fut. perf.
ind., used to express the time in the future
by which something will happen.
    120. Hīs: i.e., Dido and Aeneas; dat.
indir. obj. of **dēsuper īnfundam** (122).
nigrantem commixtā grandine nimbum:
CHIASMUS parallels the effect of the cloud
surrounding them.

dum trepidant ālae saltūs*que* indāgine cingunt,
dēsuper īnfundam *et* tonitrū *caelum omne* ciēbō.
Diffugient *comitēs et nocte* tegentur opācā:
spēluncam *Dīdō* dux *et* Troiānus *eandem*

125   dēvenient. *Aderō et, tua sī mihi* certa voluntās,
cōnūbiō iungam stabilī propriam*que* dicābō.
Hic hymenaeus *erit.*" *Nōn* adversāta *petentī*
adnuit *atque* dolīs rīsit Cytherēa repertīs.

---

adnuō, ere, uī, ūtus nod assent, promise
adversor, ārī, ātus oppose, resist (+ *dat.*)
āla, ae *f.* wing, (group of) hunters
certus, a, um fixed, sure, certain,
    reliable
cieō, ēre, cīvī, citus stir up, arouse
cingō, ere, cīnxī, cīnctus surround,
    gird(le)
cōnūbium, (i)ī *n.* wedlock, matrimony
Cytherēa, ae *f.* Venus, born at Cythera
dēsuper *adv.* from above
dēveniō, īre, vēnī, ventus come down,
    arrive (at)
dicō (1) consecrate, assign, proclaim
diffugiō, ere, fūgī flee apart, scatter
dolus, ī *m.* deceit, stratagem, fraud
dux, ducis *m. (f.)* leader, guide, chief

hymenaeus, ī *m.* wedding (hymn), so-
    called after Hymen, god of marriage
indāgō, inis *f.* (circle of) nets, snares
īnfundō, ere, fūdī, fūsus pour (into,
    upon)
iungō, ere, iūnxī, iūnctus join, yoke
opācus, a, um dark, gloomy, dusky
proprius, a, um one's own, permanent
reperiō, īre, repperī, repertus find (out)
rīdeō, ēre, rīsī, rīsus smile, laugh (at)
saltus, ūs *m.* forest, glade, pasture
spelunca, ae *f.* cave, cavern, grotto
stabilis, e firm, stable, lasting
tegō, ere, tēxī, tēctus cover, protect
tonitrus, ūs *m.* thunder
trepidō (1) tremble; scurry; quiver
Troiānus, a, um Trojan, of Troy
voluntās, ātis *f.* will, wish, consent

---

121. **ālae:** troops of hunters, who beat the bushes to frighten the game and to drive them past the hunters.

122. **tonitrū:** ordinarily the prerogative of Jove, but here wielded by Juno, as by Pallas (Minerva) at 1.42.

124. **(in) spēluncam. Dīdō dux et Troiānus:** = Dīdō et Troiānus dux. The postposition of **et** creates the momentary suggestion that Dido is to be the leader in this union. Vergil describes Dido as **dux** (leader of the people who founded Carthage) at 1.364.

125. **Aderō:** in her capacity as goddess of marriage (**Iūnō Prōnuba**). **voluntās (est).**

126. **cōnūbiō:** pronounced here as though the -i- were a consonant (i.e., **cōnūbyō**), for the sake of the meter.

127. **Hic:** attracted into the gender of the predicate; App. 240, *a*; pronounce **hicc** (from the earlier spelling of the word, **hicce**), making a long syllable; App. 107, 3, *c.* **Nōn adversāta (Iūnōnī) petentī;** *not opposing her request.*

128. **dolīs (Iūnōnis) repertīs;** abl. abs.

Ōceanum intereā *surgēns* Aurōra *relīquit.*

It portīs iubare exortō dēlēcta iuventūs,   130
rētia rāra, plagae, lātō vēnābula *ferrō,*
Massȳlī*que ruunt* equitēs *et* odōra canum *vīs.*
Rēgīnam thalamō cūnctantem *ad līmina prīmī*
Poenōrum exspectant, ostrō*que* īnsignis *et aurō*
stat sonipēs *ac* frēna ferōx spūmantia mandit.   135
Tandem prōgreditur *magnā* stīpante catervā
Sīdoniam pictō chlamydem circumdata limbō;

Aurōra, ae *f.* (goddess of) dawn
canis, is *m. (f.)* dog, hound
caterva, ae *f.* band, troop, crowd
chlamys, ydis *f.* cloak, mantle, cape
circumdō, dāre, dedī, datus surround, encircle
cūnctor, ārī, ātus delay, linger, wait
dēligō, ere, lēgī, lēctus choose, select
eques, itis *m.* horseman, knight
exorior, īrī, ortus (a)rise, spring up
ex(s)pectō (1) expect, (a)wait, linger
ferōx, ōcis fierce, spirited, fiery, wild
frēnum, ī *n.* bridle, bit, curb
īnsignis, e marked, notable, splendid
intereā *adv.* meanwhile, (in the) meantime
iubar, aris *n.* ray of light, sunshine
iuventūs, ūtis *f.* youth, young men
lātus, a, um broad, wide, spacious
limbus, ī *m.* border, fringe, hem

mandō, ere, ī, mānsus champ, chew
Massȳlus, a, um of the Massyli, a people of North Africa
Ōceanus, ī *m.* Ocean
odōrus, a, um smelling, keen-scented
ostrum, ī *n.* purple, scarlet, crimson
pingō, ere, pīnxī, pictus paint, embroider
plaga, ae *f.* net, snare, toils
Poenus, ī *m.* Carthaginian, Phoenician
porta, ae *f.* gate, entrance, exit, portal
prōgredior, ī, gressus advance, proceed
rārus, a, um scattered, wide-meshed
rēte, is *n.* net, snare, toils
Sīdonius, a, um of Sidon, Sidonian
sonipēs, pedis *m.* prancing steed (lit., of resounding hoof)
spūmō (1) foam, froth, spray
stīpō (1) stuff, stow, crowd, throng
thalamus, ī *m.* (bridal) chamber, wedlock
vēnābulum, ī *n.* hunting spear

129–72. Aeneas and Dido go hunting with their attendants. A sudden storm drives the two of them into a cave.

130. portīs: abl. of the route or of separation. **iubare (sōlis) exortō:** abl. abs. **iuventūs,** collective noun = **Tyriī et Teucrī.**

131. The lack of verb allows for several interpretations: understand something like either **eīs sunt,** or

videntur, or use **ruunt** from the next line, in a sort of ZEUGMA meaning *are rushed forth* (i.e., by their masters).

132. odōra canum vīs: *keen-scented pack of hounds,* **odōra** being a transferred epithet; App. 411.

135. Note the ALLITERATION suggesting the stamping and snorting of the horse.

136. prōgreditur (Dīdō).

137. chlamydem: Gk. acc. with **circumdata,** a perf. pass. participle used as a middle; App. 309, *a.*

cui pharetra *ex aurō*, crīnēs nōdantur *in aurum,*
aurea purpuream subnectit fībula vestem.
140   *Nec nōn et* Phrygiī *comitēs et laetus* Iūlus
incēdunt. *Ipse ante aliōs* pulcherrimus *omnēs*
īnfert *sē socium Aenēās atque agmina* iungit.
Quālis *ubi* hībernam Lyciam Xanthī*que* fluenta
dēserit *ac* Dēlum māternam invīsit Apollō
145   īnstaurat*que* chorōs, mixtī*que* altāria *circum*
Crētes*que* Dryopes*que* fremunt pictī*que* Agathyrsī;
ipse iugīs Cynthī graditur mollī*que* fluentem

Agathyrsī, ōrum *m.* people of Scythia in southeastern Europe
altāria, ium *n.* altar
Apollō, inis *m.* god of light, music, and prophecy
aureus, a, um gold(en), of gold
chorus, ī *m.* song, dance, choral band
Crētes, ium *m.* Cretans, inhabitants of Crete
crīnis, is *m.* hair, tresses, locks
Cynthus, ī *m.* mountain of Delos
Dēlos, ī *f.* island of the Aegean, birthplace of Apollo
dēserō, ere, uī, rtus desert, forsake
Dryopes, um *m.* a people of northern Greece
fībula, ae *f.* brooch, buckle, clasp
fluentum, ī *n.* stream, flood
fluō, ere, flūxī, flūxus flow, stream, ebb
fremō, ere, uī, itus roar, shout, groan
gradior, ī, gressus walk, stride, march, go
hībernus, a, um wintry, of the winter, stormy
incēdō, ere, cessī, cessus go (proudly)

īnferō, ferre, tulī, lātus bring (to), present
īnstaurō (1) renew, refresh, repeat
invīsō, ere, ī, sus visit, look on, view
iugum, ī *n.* yoke, (mountain) ridge
Iūlus, ī *m.* Ascanius, son of Aeneas
iungō, ere, iūnxī, iūnctus join, yoke
Lycia, ae *f.* country of Asia Minor
māternus, a, um maternal, of one's mother
misceō, ēre, uī, mixtus mix, mingle
mollis, e soft, yielding, tender
nōdō (1) (tie in a) knot, bind, fasten
pharetra, ae *f.* quiver
Phrygius, a, um Phrygian, Trojan
pingō, ere, pīnxī, pictus paint, embroider, tattoo
pulcher, chra, chrum beautiful, handsome, splendid, illustrious
purpureus, a, um purple, crimson
quālis, e of what sort, (such) as
subnectō, ere, nex(u)ī, nexus tie (beneath), fasten
vestis, is *f.* cloth(ing), garment, robe
Xanthus, ī *m.* river near Troy

---

138. cui pharetra (est): dat. of possession. **crīnes nōdantur in aurum:** *her hair is tied into a knot with gold,* i.e., with a golden cord or clasp of some sort.

140. Nec nōn: *likewise;* LITOTES.

142. Aenēās agmina (sua) iungit (agminibus Dīdōnis).

143. Quālis: Aeneas is here likened to Apollo, as Dido was likened to Diana at 1.498–502. **hībernam Lyciam:** *his winter*

quarters in Lycia; Apollo had a shrine here, where he was worshipped in the winter.

146. Crētesque: the final syllable is long before the pause and before the following **Dr-**. See metrical appendix. **Crētes, Dryopes, Agathyrsī:** the worshippers of Apollo come to Delos from remote regions on the edges of the known world.

147. ipse: Apollo.

fronde premit crīnem fingēns *atque* implicat *aurō,*
tēla sonant *umerīs: haud illō* sēgnior *ībat*
Aenēās, tantum ēgregiō decus ēnitet *ōre.*   150
Postquam *altōs ventum in montēs atque* invia lūstra,
ecce ferae *saxī* dēiectae vertice caprae
dēcurrēre iugīs; *aliā dē parte* patentēs
trānsmittunt *cursū campōs atque agmina* cervī
pulverulenta *fugā* glomerant *montēsque relinquunt.*   155
At puer Ascanius *mediīs in* vallibus ācrī
gaudet *equō iamque hōs cursū, iam* praeterit *illōs,*
spūmantem*que darī* pecora *inter* inertia vōtīs

ācer, cris, cre sharp, spirited, fiery
Ascanius, (i)ī *m.* son of Aeneas
capra, ae *f.* she-goat
cervus, ī *m.* deer, stag
crīnis, is *m.* hair, tresses, locks
dēcurrō, ere, (cu)currī, cursus run (down), hasten
decus, oris *n.* ornament, glory, dignity
dēiciō, ere, iēcī, iectus throw (down), dislodge
ecce see! look! behold!
ēgregius, a, um remarkable, noble
ēniteō, ēre, uī shine forth, gleam, glitter
ferus, a, um wild, savage, fierce, cruel
fingō, ere, fīnxī, fictus form, fashion, mold
frōns, frondis *f.* leaf, foliage, garland
gaudeō, ēre, gāvīsus sum rejoice, exult
glomerō (1) roll together, gather, collect
implicō, āre, āvī (uī), ātus (itus) entwine

iners, rtis lazy, spiritless, tame, idle
invius, a, um pathless, trackless
iugum, ī *n.* yoke, (mountain) ridge
lūstrum, ī *n.* marsh, bog, lair
pateō, ēre, uī lie open, extend
pecus, oris *n.* flock, herd
postquam after (that), when
praetereō, īre, iī (īvī), itus surpass, pass (by)
premō, ere, pressī, pressus (re)press, cover, confine
pulverulentus, a, um dusty
sēgnis, e slow, slothful, inactive
spūmō (1) foam, froth, spray
sonō, āre, uī, itus (re)sound, roar
trānsmittō, ere, mīsī, missus cross, send across
vallis, is *f.* valley, vale, dale
vertex, icis *m.* peak, summit, head, top
vōtum, ī *n.* vow, prayer, desire

---

148. fronde: of the laurel, sacred to Apollo.

149. tēla sonant umerīs: Apollo was the archer god. A reader of Homer, *Iliad* 1.43-52, will recognize this as an ominous detail. **illō:** abl. with comparative; App. 327.

150. tantum (quantum Apollinis).

151. ventum (est illīs): impersonal perf. passive, *they came,* with the emphasis on the action rather than on the actors.

152. dēiectae: by the hunters composing the **ālae** of 121.

154. (sē) trānsmittunt cursū campōs: campōs is object of the preposition **trāns** in composition, while cursū is abl. of manner; App. 308, 328.

157. equō: abl. of cause or of specification.

158. pecora inertia: referring to **ferae caprae** and **cervī**, which Ascanius disdainfully considers *tame herds.* **inter:** note the position, reflecting the meaning. **vōtīs:** (in answer) *to his prayers;* indir. obj. with **darī**.

optat aprum, *aut* fulvum dēscendere *monte* leōnem.

160   Intereā *magnō* miscērī murmure *caelum*
incipit, īnsequitur commixtā grandine nimbus,
et *Tyriī comitēs* passim *et* Troiāna iuventūs
Dardanius*que* nepōs Veneris dīversa *per* agrōs
tēcta metū *petiēre; ruunt dē montibus* amnēs.

165   Spēluncam *Dīdō* dux *et* Troiānus *eandem*
dēveniunt. *Prīma et Tellūs et* prōnuba *Iūnō*
dant signum; fulsēre *ignēs et* cōnscius aethēr
cōnūbiīs *summōque* ululārunt vertice Nymphae.

---

aethēr, eris *m.* upper air, heaven, ether
ager, grī *m.* field, territory, land
amnis, is *m.* river, stream
aper, prī *m.* wild boar
commisceō, ēre, uī, mixtus mix, mingle
Dardanius, a, um Dardanian, Trojan
dēscendō, ere, ī, ēnsus descend
dēveniō, īre, vēnī, ventus come (down), arrive (at)
dīversus, a, um separated, different
dux, ducis *m. (f.)* leader, guide, chief
fulg(e)ō, ēre (or ere), lsī shine, flash, gleam
fulvus, a, um tawny, yellow, blond
grandō, inis *f.* hail(storm, stones)
incipiō, ere, cēpī, ceptus begin, undertake
īnsequor, ī, secūtus follow
intereā *adv.* meanwhile, (in the) meantime
iuventūs, ūtis *f.* youth, young men
leō, ōnis *m.* lion

metus, ūs *m.* fear, fright, anxiety
misceō, ēre, uī, mixtus mix, mingle, confuse
murmur, uris *n.* murmur, roar, rumble
nepōs, ōtis *m.* grandson; descendant
nimbus, ī *m.* rainstorm, (storm)cloud
Nympha, ae *f.* nymph, minor female divinity of the forests, waters, etc.
optō (1) choose, desire, hope (for, to)
passim *adv.* everywhere, all about
prōnuba, ae *f.* matron of honor, bride's attendant
signum, ī *n.* sign, signal, token, mark
spēlunca, ae *f.* cave, cavern, grotto
Troiānus, a, um Trojan, of Troy
ululō (1) howl, wail, shout, shriek
Venus, eris *f.* goddess of love and beauty; love
vertex, icis *m.* peak, summit, head, top

---

163. nepōs Veneris = Ascanius.

165. The close repetition of line 124 shows how effective Juno's plans have been.

166–68. Vergil here indicates the various features in a Roman wedding and represents Nature herself as performing these ceremonies. Earth and Heaven, parents of the universe, take the part of human parents in bringing the couple together; lightning (**ignēs**) represents the wedding torches (**taedae**); Juno performs the duty of the matron of honor (**prōnuba**), and the cries of the mountain nymphs take the place of the wedding song and festal cries. **Prīma Tellūs:** Earth

was called **prīma** as the oldest of the gods; as Mother Earth, the producer and nurse of life, she presided over marriage. **prōnuba:** the matron whose function it was to join the hand of the bride to that of the groom at the wedding.

167. dant signum: i.e., for the wedding. **ignes** (*lightning*): instead of the marriage torches ordinarily employed at weddings. **cōnscius:** *witness* (to the marriage).

168. cōnūbiīs: *to the marriage*; poetic plural; the first -i- is pronounced as a consonant (i.e., as -y-), for the sake of the meter. **ululā(vē)runt:** instead of the marriage songs ordinarily sung at

Ille diēs prīmus lētī *prīmusque* malōrum
causa *fuit; neque* enim speciē *fāmāve movētur*   170
nec iam fūrtīvum *Dīdō* meditātur *amōrem:*
coniugium *vocat, hōc* praetexit *nōmine* culpam.

---

causa, ae *f.* cause, reason, occasion
coniugium, (i)ī *n.* wedlock, marriage
culpa, ae *f.* fault, offense, guilt, blame
enim *adv.* for, indeed, truly
fūrtīvus, a, um secret, stolen

lētum, ī *n.* death, destruction, ruin
malum, ī *n.* evil, misfortune, trouble
meditor, ārī, ātus meditate, design
praetexō, ere, uī, xtus fringe, cloak
speciēs, ēī *f.* appearance, sight, aspect

---

weddings, the Nymphs make an eerie and ominous sound. **(in) vertice (montis).**
   170–71. speciē fāmāve: *by* (regard for) *appearances or* (for) *her reputation.*

neque movētur nec Dīdō meditātur: the subject of the two verbs is closer to the second of them.
   172. hōc nōmine: abl. of means.

Extemplō Libyae *magnās it Fāma per urbēs,*
Fāma, malum *quā nōn aliud* vēlōcius *ūllum:*
175   mōbilitāte viget *vīrēsque* adquīrit *eundō,*
parva metū prīmō, mox *sēsē* attollit *in aurās*
ingreditur*que* solō *et caput inter* nūbila condit.
Illam Terra parēns īrā inrītāta *deōrum*
extrēmam, *ut* perhibent, Coeō Enceladō*que* sorōrem
180   prōgenuit *pedibus* celerem *et* pernīcibus ālīs,
mōnstrum horrendum, *ingēns, cui* quot *sunt corpore* plūmae,

---

adquīrō, ere, quīsīvī, sītus acquire, gain
āla, ae *f.* wing
attollō, ēre lift, rear, raise
celer, eris, ere swift, speedy, quick
Coeus, ī *m.* one of the Titans, a giant, son of Earth
condō, ere, didī, ditus establish, hide
Enceladus, ī *m.* one of the Titans, a giant, son of Earth
extemplō *adv.* immediately, at once, suddenly
extrēmus, a, um final, last, furthest
horrendus, a, um awful, terrible, dire
ingredior, ī, gressus enter, proceed
inrītō (1) vex, enrage, provoke
Libya, ae *f.* country of North Africa
malum, ī *n.* evil, misfortune, trouble

metus, ūs *m.* fear, fright, anxiety
mōbilitās, ātis *f.* activity, motion, speed
mōnstrum, ī *n.* prodigy, portent, monster
mox *adv.* soon, presently
nūbila, ōrum *n.* clouds, cloudiness
parvus, a, um small, little
perhibeō, ēre, uī, itus present, say
pernīx, īcis active, nimble, swift
plūma, ae *f.* feather, plume
prīmō *adv.* at first, in the beginning
prōgignō, ere, genuī, genitus bring forth, bear
quot as many as
solum, ī *n.* ground, soil, earth
soror, ōris *f.* sister
vēlōx, ōcis swift, quick, rapid, fleet
vigeō, ēre, uī flourish, be strong, thrive

173-218. Rumor, a terrifying divinity, spreads gossip about the love affair, and finally carries the news to Iarbas, an African chieftain whose marriage proposal had been rejected by Dido. Iarbas reproaches his father, Jupiter Ammon, for not helping him.

174. quā: abl. with compar.; App. 327. **nōn (est).**

174-75. Fama . . . Fama: the repetition for emphasis of the same word in two contiguous lines is called EPANALEPSIS.

175. eundō: abl. of means, from the gerund of eō; App. 269.

176. metū: abl. of cause.

177. (in) solō = (in) terrā.

178. deōrum: objective gen. with īrā, abl. of means; App. 284. In anger at the Olympian gods for slaying her children, the Titans, Earth bore the giants, Rumor being one of them.

179. ut perhibent: Vergil often uses phrases like this to signal to his readers that he is alluding to an earlier work. In this case, he is recalling the cosmic myths of Hesiod's *Theogony,* where the battle of the Olympians and Titans is described.

181. cui: dat. of possession. **corpore:** abl. of specification.

181-83. Rumor is covered with feathers; and beneath each feather is an eye, a tongue, a mouth, and an ear.

tot vigilēs *oculī* subter (mīrābile *dictū*),
tot linguae, totidem *ōra* sonant, tot subrigit aurēs.
Nocte volat *caelī* mediō *terraeque per umbram*
strīdēns, *nec* dulcī dēclīnat *lūmina somnō;*   185
lūce sedet custōs *aut summī* culmine *tēctī*
turribus *aut altīs, et magnās* territat *urbēs,*
tam fictī prāvī*que* tenāx quam nuntia vērī.
Haec tum multiplicī populōs sermōne replēbat
gaudēns, *et* pariter facta *atque* īnfecta canēbat: 190
vēnisse Aenēān Troiānō *sanguine* crētum,
cui sē pulchra *virō* dignētur iungere *Dīdō;*

---

auris, is *f.* ear
canō, ere, cecinī, cantus sing (of),
   chant, tell, proclaim, prophesy
crētus, a, um grown, sprung
culmen, inis *n.* roof, summit, top, peak
custōs, ōdis *m. (f.)* guard(ian), sentinel
dēclīnō (1) turn aside, bend down, droop
dignor, ārī, ātus deem worthy, deign
   (+ *abl.*)
dulcis, e sweet, dear, fond
factum, ī *n.* deed, act, exploit
fictum, ī *n.* falsehood, fiction
gaudeō, ērē, gāvīsus sum rejoice, exult
īnfectus, a, um not done, false
iungō, ere, iūnxī, iūnctus join, yoke
lingua, ae *f.* tongue, language
medium, (i)ī *n.* middle, center
mīrābilis, e wonderful, marvelous
multiplex, icis manifold, multiple
nuntia, ae *f.* messenger
pariter *adv.* equally, alike

populus, ī *m.* people, nation
prāvum, ī *n.* wrong, perverse act
pulcher, chra, chrum beautiful,
   handsome, splendid, illustrious, noble
quam *adv.* how, than, as
repleō, ēre, ēvī, ētus fill, stuff
sedeō, ēre, sēdī, sessus sit (down), settle
sermō, ōnis *m.* conversation, gossip
sonō, āre, uī, itus (re)sound, roar
strīd(e)ō, ēre (or ere), ī hiss, whir, rustle
subrigō, ere, surrēxī, rēctus raise, rise
subter *adv.; prep + acc.* beneath, below
tam *adv.* so, as, such
tenāx, ācis tenacious, holding (to)
territō (1) frighten, terrify, alarm
tot so many, as many
totidem the same number, so many
Troiānus, a, um Trojan, of Troy
turris, is *f.* tower, turret
vērum, ī *n.* truth, right, reality
vigil, ilis wakeful, watchful, sleepless
volō (1) fly, flit, move with speed

---

182. oculī (sunt) subter (plūmās).
183. (Fāma) subrigit tot aurēs:
Rumor raises as many listening ears.
184. caelī mediō terraeque: *between
heaven and earth.* Note how the Latin
word order imitates the meaning of the
phrase.
185. strīdēns: with her wings as she
flies, referring to the buzz of gossip.
lūmina (sua) = **oculōs,** as often.
186–87. lūce: *by day,* abl. of time;
App. 322. **(in) culmine aut (in) turribus.**

188. fictī prāvīque . . . vērī: gen. with
tenāx; App. 287.
189. Haec = Fāma.
190. facta atque īnfecta: "fact and
fiction." Literally, *things done and not
done.* **canēbat:** followed by indir.
statement.
191. Troiānō sanguine: abl. of
separation/origin with **crētum.**
192. virō = coniugī. iungere:
complementary inf.; App. 259.

nunc hiemem *inter sē* luxū, quam *longa,* fovēre
rēgnōrum immemorēs turpī*que* cupīdine *captōs.*
195   *Haec* passim *dea* foeda *virum* diffundit *in ōra.*
Prōtinus *ad rēgem cursūs* dētorquet Iarbān
incendit*que animum dictīs atque* aggerat īrās.
     Hic Hammōne satus raptā Garamantide nymphā
templa *Iovī* centum lātīs *immānia rēgnīs,*
200   centum *ārās posuit* vigilem*que* sacrāverat *ignem,*
excubiās *dīvum* aeternās, pecudum*que* cruōre
pingue solum *et* variīs flōrentia *līmina* sertīs.

---

aeternus, a, um eternal, everlasting
aggerō (1) heap up, pile up, increase
centum hundred
cruor, ōris *m.* blood, gore
cupīdō, inis *f.* love, desire, longing
dētorqueō, ēre, rsī, rtus turn (away)
diffundō, ere, fūdī, fūsus scatter, spread
excubiae, ārum *f.* watch(fire), sentinel
flōreō, ēre, uī bloom, flourish, blossom
foedus, a, um foul, loathsome, filthy
foveō, ēre, fōvī, fōtus cherish, fondle
Garamantis, idis of the Garamantes, an
     African tribe
Hammōn, ōnis *m.* Hammon (or Ammon),
     god of North Africa, famous for his oracle
     and identified by the Romans with Jupiter
hiems, emis *f.* winter, storm
Iarbās, ae *m.* African chieftain, one of
     Dido's unsuccessful suitors
immemor, oris unmindful, forgetful

incendō, ere, ī, ēnsus kindle, burn, inflame
lātus, a, um wide, broad, spacious
luxus, ūs *m.* luxury, splendor, excess
nympha, ae *f.* nymph, minor female
     divinity of the forests, waters, etc.
passim *adv.* everywhere, all about
pecus, udis *f.* animal (of the flock)
pinguis, e fat, rich, fertile
prōtinus *adv.* continuously, immediately
quam *adv.* how, than, as
rapiō, ere, uī, ptus snatch (away), seize,
     ravish
sacrō (1) consecrate, hallow, dedicate
serō, ere, sēvī, satus sow, beget
sertum, ī *n.* wreath, garland
solum, ī *n.* ground, soil, earth
templum, ī *n.* temple, shrine, sanctuary
turpis, e shameful, disgraceful
varius, a, um varied, different, diverse
vigil, ilis watchful, wakeful, sleepless

---

193. (Dīdōnem et Aenēān) inter sē
fovēre hiemem quam longa (ea hiems
sit). inter sē fovēre: *were caressing one
another.* hiemem: *the whole long winter;*
either acc. of duration of time or dir.
object of fovēre, i.e., *they keep the winter
warm.* inter sē is commonly employed to
denote reciprocal action. quam longa
(sit): *however long it may be.*
     194. rēgnōrum: Carthage and Italy.
     195. vīr(ōr)um.
     198. Hic: pronounce hicc (as if from
the earlier spelling of the word, hicce).

199-200. templa centum (posuit),
centum ārās posuit: Latin commonly
expresses the verb with only the second
of two such clauses, English with the first.
Compare the note on 170-71.
     201. excubiās: in apposition with
ignem; the never-dying fire stands sentry
in honor of the gods, like the sacred fire
of Vesta at Rome.
     202. pingue: from the blood and the
animal-fat of many sacrifices. solum,
līmina: take either as obj. of sacrāverat
(202), like ignem, or supply erant.

Isque āmēns *animī et* rūmōre accēnsus amārō
dīcitur ante ārās media inter nūmina dīvum
multa Iovem manibus supplex ōrāsse supīnīs: 205
"*Iuppiter* omnipotēns, *cui nunc* Maurūsia pictīs
gēns epulāta torīs Lēnaeum lībat *honōrem,*
aspicis *haec?* An *tē, genitor, cum* fulmina torquēs
nēquīquam horrēmus, caecī*que in* nūbibus *ignēs*
terrificant *animōs et* inānia murmura miscent?   210
Fēmina, *quae nostrīs errāns in fīnibus urbem*
exiguam pretiō *posuit, cui lītus* arandum

---

an whether, or
accendō, ere, ī, ēnsus kindle, inflame
amārus, a, um bitter, unpleasant
āmēns, entis mad, crazy, frenzied
arō (1) plow, till, furrow
a(d)spiciō, ere, spexī, spectus see, behold
caecus, a, um blind, hidden, dark
epulor, ārī, ātus feast, banquet (+ *abl.*)
exiguus, a, um small, scanty, petty
fēmina, ae *f.* woman, female
fulmen, inis *n.* thunderbolt, lightning
horreō, ēre, uī shudder (at), quake
inānis, e empty, useless, vain, idle
Lēnaeus, a, um Lenaean, Bacchic, of Bacchus, god of wine
lēx, lēgis *f.* law, jurisdiction, term

lībō (1) pour (as a libation), offer
Maurūsius, a, um Moorish
misceō, ēre, uī, mixtus mix, mingle
murmur, uris *n.* murmur, roar, rumble
nēquīquam *adv.* in vain, uselessly, idly
nūbēs, is *f.* cloud, fog, mist
omnipotēns, entis almighty, omnipotent
ōrō (1) pray (for), beseech, entreat
pingō, ere, pīnxī, pictus paint, embroider
pretium, (i)ī *n.* price, reward, value
rūmor, ōris *m.* rumor, report, gossip
supīnus, a, um flat, upturned
supplex, icis suppliant, humble
terrificō (1) frighten, terrify, alarm
torqueō, ēre, rsī, rtus twist, sway, hurl
torus, ī *m.* (banqueting) couch, bed

---

203. Is: Iarbas. **animī:** gen. of reference (a rare usage) with **āmēns**, or loc.; App. 287, 37, *c.*
204. media inter nūmina: *amid the divine presences.* **dīv(ōr)um:** modifying either **ārās** or **nūmina.**
205. multa Iovem: double acc. with **ōrāsse.**
206-7. Maurūsia gēns: the people of Iarbas.
207. Lēnaeum honōrem: i.e., wine (associated with Bacchus Lenaeus) poured in libation as a sign of honor.
208-10. Iarbas challenges Jupiter with the suggestion that all the god's thunder and lightning are just empty threats.

211. Fēmina: Dido; emphatic by position. **errāns:** Vergil is incorporating a clever multilingual etymological wordplay into this line. An ancient dictionary tells us that the name **Dīdō** is a Punic word equivalent to the Greek word **planēs** or **planētis**, meaning *wandering* or *wanderer*; thus, the phrase **fēmina errāns** is an explanation in Latin of Dido's Punic name. (Note that the English word *planet* comes from the same Greek word.)
212. pretiō: abl. of price; App. 336. She had not taken the place by force, but had been compelled to buy it, a confession of weakness from Iarbas' perspective.

cuique locī lēgēs *dedimus,* cōnūbia *nostra*
reppulit *ac* dominum *Aenēān in rēgna* recēpit.

215　*Et nunc ille* Paris *cum* sēmivirō comitātū,
Maeoniā mentum mitrā crīnem*que* madentem
subnexus, raptō potitur: *nos mūnera* templīs
quippe *tuīs ferimus fāmamque* fovēmus inānem."

---

comitātus, ūs *m.* retinue, train,
　company
cōnūbium, (i)ī *n.* wedlock, marriage
crīnis, is *m.* long hair, locks, tresses
dominus, ī *m.* master, lord, ruler
foveō, ēre, fōvī, fōtus cherish, fondle
inānis, e empty, useless, vain, idle
lēx, lēgis *f.* law, jurisdiction, term
madeō, ēre, uī drip, be wet, reek
Maeonius, a, um Maeonian, Lydian,
　Asiatic
mentum, ī *n.* chin, beard

mitra, ae *f.* mitre, cap, turban
Paris, idis *m.* Trojan prince, eloped with
　Helen and thus caused the Trojan War
potior, īrī, ītus possess, gain (+ *abl.*)
quippe *adv.* to be sure, surely, indeed
raptum, ī *n.* plunder, prey, booty
recipiō, ere, cēpī, ceptus receive, recover
repellō, ere, reppulī, repulsus reject,
　repel
sēmivir, virī half-man, effeminate
subnectō, ere, nex(u)ī, nexus tie (under)
templum, ī *n.* temple, shrine, sanctuary

212-13. For the ELLIPSIS of **dedimus** in
the first clause, see the note on 199-200.

214. dominum: in apposition; said with
bitter disdain.

215. Paris: In stealing the woman
Iarbas was planning to marry, Aeneas is
like Paris, who stole Menelaus' wife
Helen and so provoked the Trojan War.
sēmivirō: the African chieftain despises
the Trojans and so challenges their
masculinity. This insult reflects an ancient
bias against the peoples of the Near East,
whose luxurious life was believed by the
Greeks and Romans to be conducive to
effeminate behavior. Iarbas may also be

thinking of the castrated priests of
Cybele, whose cult was based in Asia
Minor, near Troy, and suggesting that
Aeneas and the Trojans are similar.

216-17. mentum, crīnem: Gk. acc. of
respect with **subnexus,** here used as a Gk.
middle participle; App. 309, *a.*
madentem: *dripping* (with perfume),
another mark of effeminacy. **raptō:** abl.
with **potior;** App. 342. **potitur:** with -i-
irregularly short.

218. quippe: sarcastic. **fāmam
fovēmus inānem:** *we keep alive a
baseless belief* in your power and justice.

Tālibus ōrantem *dictīs ārāsque tenentem*
audiit Omnipotēns, *oculōsque ad moenia* torsit   220
rēgia *et* oblitōs *fāmae* meliōris amantēs.
Tum sīc Mercurium adloquitur *ac tālia* mandat:
"Vāde *age, nāte, vocā* Zephyrōs *et lābere* pennīs
Dardanium*que* ducem, *Tyriā* Karthāgine *quī nunc*
exspectat *fātīsque datās nōn* respicit *urbēs,*   225
adloquere *et* celerēs dēfer *mea dicta per aurās.*
Nōn illum nōbīs genetrīx pulcherrima *tālem*
prōmīsit Graium*que* ideō bis vindicat *armīs;*

---

adloquor, ī, locūtus address, accost
amāns, antis *m. (f.)* lover
bis twice
celer, eris, ere swift, speedy, quick
Dardanius, a, um Dardanian, Trojan
dēferō, ferre, tulī, lātus carry (down), report
dux, ducis *m. (f.)* leader, guide, chief
ex(s)pectō (1) (a)wait, expect, linger, tarry, dally
genetrīx, trīcis *f.* mother
Graius, a, um Greek
ideō *adv.* therefore, for this reason
Karthāgō, inis *f.* Carthage, a city of North Africa
mandō (1) command, intrust, enjoin
melior, ius better, superior, preferable

Mercurius, (i)ī *m.* messenger of the gods, god of commerce, and escort of departed souls to Hades
oblīvīscor, ī, litus forget (+ *gen.*)
omnipotēns, entis almighty, omnipotent
oblīvīscor, ī, litus forget (+ *gen.*)
ōrō (1) pray (for), plead, entreat
penna, ae *f.* wing, feather
prōmittō, ere, mīsī, missus promise
pulcher, chra, chrum beautiful, noble, splendid, handsome, illustrious
rēgius, a, um royal, regal, kingly
respiciō, ere, spexī, spectus look (back) at, regard
torqueō, ēre, rsī, rtus twist, sway, hurl
vādō, ere go, proceed, advance
vindicō (1) vindicate, claim (as free), rescue
Zephyrus, ī *m.* (west) wind

219–95. Moved by the prayer of Iarbas, Jupiter sends Mercury to Aeneas to remind him of his high destiny and of his duty to his son Ascanius. Mercury finds Aeneas in Carthage, delivers his message, and disappears. Aeneas is unsure how to inform Dido of his imminent departure.

219. (Iarbān) ōrantem: obj. of **audiit.**
220–21. moenia rēgia: of Carthage. **fāmae:** gen. with **oblītōs;** App. 288.
222. adloquitur: with final syllable irregularly long before a strong caesura; App. 394, *a.*

223. Zephyrōs, pennīs: Mercury's travel companions and equipment are all suited to his speed. **lābere** imp. **pennīs:** attached to his sandals.
224. ducem: object of the imp. **adloquere,** 226.
226. dēfer: imp.; App. 202.
227. tālem (virum).
228. ideō: *for this purpose;* that he might indulge in a love affair and the comfort of Carthage. **bis vindicat:** *rescued;* once from Diomedes (1.96–98, and notes), and again at the fall of Troy (2.620 ff.). **vindicat:** present for perf., to make the description of Venus' protectiveness more vivid. **armīs:** abl. of separation.

sed fore quī gravidam *imperiīs bellōque* frementem
230   *Ītaliam* rēgeret, *genus altō ā sanguine* Teucrī
    prōderet, *ac tōtum sub lēgēs mitteret* orbem.
    Sī nūlla accendit *tantārum* glōria *rērum*
    nec super ipse suā mōlītur laude *labōrem,*
    Ascaniōne *pater* Rōmānās invidet *arcēs?*
235   *Quid* struit? *Aut quā* spē inimicā *in gente* morātur
    nec prōlem Ausoniam *et* Lāvīnia respicit *arva?*
    Nāviget! *Haec* summa *est, hic nostrī* nuntius *estō."*
       Dīxerat. Ille patris magnī pārēre *parābat*
    imperiō; et prīmum pedibus tālāria nectit
240   aurea, *quae* sublīmem ālīs sīve *aequora* suprā

---

accendō, ere, ī, ēnsus kindle, inflame
āla, ae *f.* wing
Ascanius, (i)ī *m.* son of Aeneas
aureus, a, um gold(en), of gold
Ausonius, a, um Ausonian, Italian
fremō, ere, uī, itus rage, roar
glōria, ae *f.* renown, glory, fame, pride
gravidus, a, um heavy, burdened,
    pregnant, filled, teeming
inimīcus, a, um hostile, unfriendly
invideō, ēre, vīdī, vīsus begrudge (+ *dat.*)
laus, laudis *f.* glory, praise, merit
Lāvīn(i)us, a, um of Lavinium, an early
    Italian city
lēx, lēgis *f.* law, jurisdiction, term
mōlior, īrī, ītus do, (strive to) accomplish
moror, ārī, ātus delay, tarry, detain
nāvigō (1) (set) sail, navigate

nectō, ere, nex(u)ī, nexus bind, fasten
nuntius, (i)ī *m.* messenger, message
orbis, is *m.* circle, orb(it), earth
pāreō, ēre, uī, itus obey, yield (+ *dat.*)
prōdō, ere, didī, ditus betray, transmit
prōlēs, is *f.* progeny, offspring
regō, ere, rēxī, rēctus rule, direct, guide
respiciō, ere, spexī, spectus look (back)
    at, regard
Rōmānus, a, um Roman, of Rome
sīve, seu whether, or, either if, or if
spēs, eī *f.* hope, expectation
struō, ere, strūxī, strūctus build, plan
sublīmis, e on high, towering, lofty
summa, ae *f.* sum, substance, chief thing
suprā over, above (+ *acc.*)
tālāria, ium *n.* (winged) sandals, anklets
Teucer (crus), crī *m.* early king of Troy

229–30. sed (genetrīx prōmīsit illum) fore (tālem) quī regeret: rel. clause of characteristic; App. 389. **imperiīs:** *with* (future) *empire.*

231. tōtum orbem: Jupiter here anticipates not only the accomplishments of Aeneas, but also those of all his descendants, down to and culminating in Augustus.

232. accendit (illum).

233–34. super ipse laude suā: ipse is emphatic, and has intruded into the prep. phrase. **Pater:** emphatic; could a father do this, and have so little concern for his son? **Ascaniō:** indir. obj. of **invidet. arcēs:** dir. obj. of **invidet.**

235. spē inimīcā: HIATUS separates the two words, which are not in fact to be construed together. **inimīcā gente:** Again Jupiter anticipates later times, when Rome and Carthage will be such bitter foes.

237. Nāviget: volitive or jussive subjunctive; App. 254. **hic nostrī nuntius estō:** *let this be our (my) message.* **nostrī:** gen. pl. of **ego. estō:** imp.

240. ālīs: attached to the **tālāria. (illum) sublīmem. aequora suprā =** **suprā aequora:** ANASTROPHE.

seu *terram* rapidō pariter *cum* flāmine portant.
Tum virgam *capit: hāc animās ille* ēvocat Orcō
pallentēs, *aliās sub* Tartara *trīstia mittit,*
dat somnōs adimit*que, et lūmina morte* resignat.
Illā frētus *agit ventōs et* turbida trānat   245
nūbila. *Iamque* volāns apicem *et* latera ardua *cernit*
Atlantis dūrī *caelum quī* vertice fulcit,
Atlantis, cīnctum adsiduē *cui* nūbibus *ātrīs*
pīniferum *caput et ventō* pulsātur *et* imbrī,
nix umerōs īnfūsa tegit, *tum* flūmina mentō   250

---

adimō, ere, ēmī, ēmptus take away
adsiduē *adv.* constantly, ever, continually
apex, icis *m.* peak, summit, head
arduus, a, um lofty, steep, towering
Atlās, antis *m.* god who supports heaven on his shoulders, grandfather of Mercury; a mountain of Northwest Africa
cingō, ere, cīnxī, cīnctus surround, gird(le)
dūrus, a, um hard(y), harsh, stern
ēvocō (1) call out, summon
flāmen, inis *n.* breeze, blast, wind
flūmen, inis *n.* river, stream, flood
frētus, a, um relying (on) (+ *abl.*)
fulciō, īre, lsī, ltus support, prop
imber, bris *m.* rain, flood, storm, water
īnfundō, ere fūdī, fūsus pour on (in)
latus, eris *n.* side, flank
mentum, ī *n.* chin, beard
nix, nivis *f.* snow

nūbēs, is *f.* cloud, fog, mist
nūbila, ōrum *n.* clouds, cloudiness
Orcus, ī *m.* Hades, (god of) the lower world
pallēns, entis pale, pallid, wan
pariter *adv.* equally, alike
pīnifer, era, erum pine-bearing
portō (1) carry, bear, convey
pulsō (1) beat, strike, lash, batter
rapidus, a, um swift, snatching
resignō (1) (un)seal, open, close
sīve, seu whether, or, either if, or if
Tartara, ōrum *n.* Hades, the lower world
tegō, ere, tēxī, tēctus cover, protect
trānō (1) swim across, float
turbidus, a, um troubled, stormy
umerus, ī *m.* shoulder
vertex, icis *m.* peak, summit, head, top
virga, ae *f.* staff, wand, twig
volō (1) fly, speed

---

242. virgam: the **cādūceus** or magic winged wand carried by Mercury; it is sometimes identified with the staff entwined with serpents associated with the god of healing, Asclepius. **hāc (virgā):** as escort of the souls of the dead, Mercury conducted them in both directions: to Hades after death, and back to the upper world as ghosts. **Orcō:** abl. of separation.

242–44. hāc . . . resignat: the description of Mercury's actions reflects his movement back and forth between the world of the dead and the living.

244. morte: abl. of means or separation.

245. Illā (virgā): abl. with **frētus. Agit ventōs:** *outstrips the winds.*

247. Atlantis: in the following description, Vergil skillfully mingles the conception of Atlas as a god and as a mountain.

248. cīnctum (est). cui: *whose;* dat. of reference.

250. (dē) mentō: abl. of separation.

praecipitant senis, *et* glaciē riget horrida barba.
Hīc prīmum paribus nītēns Cyllēnius ālīs
cōnstitit; *hinc tōtō* praeceps *sē corpore ad undās*
mīsit avī similis, *quae circum lītora, circum*

255 piscōsōs scopulōs humilis volat *aequora* iuxtā.
Haud aliter *terrās inter caelumque* volābat
lītus harēnōsum *ad* Libyae, *ventōsque* secābat
māternō *veniēns ab* avō Cyllēnia *prōlēs.*
Ut prīmum ālātīs tetigit māgālia plantīs,

260 *Aenēān* fundantem *arcēs ac tēcta* novantem
cōnspicit. *Atque illī* stēllātus iaspide fulvā
ēnsis *erat Tyriōque ardēbat* mūrice laena
dēmissa *ex umerīs, dīves quae mūnera Dīdō*

ā́la, ae *f.* wing
ālātus, a, um winged, furnished with wings
aliter *adv.* otherwise, differently
avis, is *f.* bird, fowl
avus, ī *m.* grandfather; ancestor
barba, ae *f.* beard, whiskers
cōnspiciō, ere, spexī, spectus see, look at
cōnstō, āre, stitī, status stand firm, halt
Cyllēnius, (i)ī *m.* the Cyllenean, of Mt.
  Cyllene in Arcadia, birthplace of
  Mercury; *adj.,* Cyllēnius, a, um
  Cyllenean, of Mt. Cyllene in Arcadia,
  birthplace of Mercury
dēmittō, ere, mīsī, missus let down, send
  down, lower, drop
dī(ve)s, dī(vi)tis rich, wealthy
ēnsis, is *m.* sword, knife
fulvus, a, um yellow, tawny, blond
fundō (1) found, build, establish
glaciēs, ēī *f.* ice
harēnōsus, a, um sandy
horridus, a, um bristling, awful, rough
humilis, e low(ly), low-lying, humble

iaspis, idis *f.* jasper, a semi-precious stone
iuxtā *adv.* close (to), next (to) (+ *acc.*)
laena, ae *f.* (woolen) mantle, cloak
Libya, ae *f.* country of Northwest Africa
māgālia, ium *n.* huts, hovels
māternus, a, um maternal, of a mother
mūrex, icis *m.* purple (dye), crimson, scarlet
nītor, ī, sus (nixus) strive, rest on (+ *abl.*)
novō (1) renew, make (new), build
pār, paris equal, balanced, like
piscōsus, a, um fishy, fish-haunted
planta, ae *f.* heel; sole of foot
praeceps, cipitis headlong, headforemost
praecipitō (1) fall headlong, hasten
prōlēs, is *f.* progeny, offspring
rigeō, ēre, uī be stiff, be rigid
scopulus, ī *m.* rock, cliff, crag
secō, āre, uī, ctus cut, cleave, slice
senex, senis *m.* old man
similis, e like, similar (+ *dat.* or *gen.*)
stēllātus, a, um starred, star-spangled
tangō, ere, tetigī, tāctus touch, reach
volō (1) fly, speed

---

252. Hīc: on the summit of Atlas.
ālīs: abl. with **nītēns.**

257. ad lītus: App. 414.

258. māternō avō: Atlas. The mother
of Mercury was Maia, daughter of Atlas.

259. māgālia: the word is not native to
Latin, but is derived from Punic; its use

here succinctly identifies Mercury's exotic
destination (cf. 1.421).

261. iāspide: the initial **i-** is pronounced
separately from **-ā-** (i.e., they do not
combine to form a diphthong).

261–62. stēllātus ēnsis: the hilt was
studded.

fēcerat, et tenuī tēlās discrēverat *aurō.*

Continuō invādit: *"Tū nunc* Karthāginis *altae*   265
fundāmenta locās pulchram*que* uxōrius *urbem*
exstruis? *Heu, rēgnī rērumque* oblīte *tuārum!*
Ipse deum tibi mē clārō dēmittit Olympō
rēgnātor, *caelum et terrās quī nūmine* torquet,
ipse haec ferre iubet celerēs mandāta *per aurās:*   270
Quid struis? *Aut quā* spē Libycīs teris ōtia *terrīs?*
Sī tē nūlla movet tantārum glōria *rērum*
[*nec super ipse tuā* mōlīris laude *labōrem,*]
Ascanium *surgentem et* spēs hērēdis Iūlī
respice, *cui rēgnum Ītaliae* Rōmāna*que tellūs*   275
dēbētur." *Tālī* Cyllēnius *ōre* locūtus

Ascanius, (i)ī *m.* son of Aeneas
celer, eris, ere swift, quick, speedy
clārus, a, um clear, bright, illustrious
continuō *adv.* immediately, at once
Cyllēnius, (i)ī *m.* the Cyllenean; Mercury, born on Mt. Cyllene
dēbeō, ēre, uī, itus owe, be due, be destined
discernō, ere, ere, crēvī, crētus separate
exstruō, ere, strūxī, strūctus build (up), rear
fundāmentum, ī *n.* foundation, base
glōria, ae *f.* glory, renown, fame, pride
hērēs, ēdis *m.* heir, successor
invādō, ere, sī, sus attack, address
Iūlus, ī *m.* Ascanius, son of Aeneas
Karthāgō, inis *f.* Carthage, a city of North Africa
laus, laudis *f.* praise, glory, merit
Libycus, a, um Libyan, of Libya, a country of North Africa
locō (1) place, lay, establish, locate

loquor, ī, locūtus speak, say, tell, talk
mandātum, ī *n.* command, order, behest
mōlior, īrī, ītus undertake, accomplish, do
oblīviscor, ī, ītus (+ *gen.*) forget
Olympus, ī *m.* Greek mountain, home of the gods; heaven
ōtium, (i)ī *n.* leisure, idleness, quiet
pulcher, chra, chrum beautiful, handsome, noble, splendid, illustrious
rēgnātor, ōris *m.* ruler, lord, director
respiciō, ere, spexī, spectus look (back) at, regard
Rōmānus, a, um Roman, of Rome
spēs, eī *f.* hope, expectation
struō, ere, strūxī, strūctus build, contrive
tēla, ae *f.* web, textile
tenuis, e slight, thin, fine, delicate
terō, ere, trīvī, trītus rub, wear, waste
torqueō, ēre, rsī, rtus twist, hurl, sway
uxōrius, a, um wife-ruled, uxorious, hen-pecked

---

264. tenuī aurō: she had interwoven the warp of the fabric with fine gold thread.

266 uxōrius: used as a term of reproach.

267. oblīte: voc. of the participle of **oblīvīscor. rēgnī rērumque:** gen. with a verb of forgetting; App. 288.

273. The line is virtually identical to 233, and was probably reproduced here by an inattentive copyist; brackets are used by editors to indicate that none of the major primary manuscripts contains this line.

274. Iūlī: either possessive genitive (i.e., the hopes that Iulus has) or objective genitive (i.e., the hopes you have for Iulus).

mortālēs vīsūs *mediō* sermōne *relīquit*
et procul in tenuem *ex oculīs* ēvānuit *auram.*
At vērō Aenēās aspectū obmūtuit āmēns,
280   arrēctae*que* horrōre comae *et vōx* faucibus haesit.
Ardet abīre *fugā* dulcēs*que relinquere terrās,*
attonitus *tantō* monitū *imperiōque deōrum.*
Heu quid agat? Quō nunc rēgīnam ambīre *furentem*
audeat adfātū? *Quae prīma* exordia sūmat?
285   *Atque animum nunc hūc* celerem *nunc* dīvidit illūc
in partēsque rapit variās *perque omnia* versat.
Haec alternantī potior sententia *vīsa est:*
Mnēsthea Sergestum*que vocat* fortem*que* Serestum,

---

abeō, īre, iī (īvī), itus depart
adfātus, ūs *m.* address, speech
alternō (1) change, alternate, waver
ambiō, īre, īvī (ii), itus go around;
     conciliate
āmēns, entis mad, frenzied, distraught
arrigō, ere, rēxī, rēctus erect, stand on
     end
a(d)spectus, ūs *m.* sight, appearance
attonitus, a, um thunderstruck,
     astounded
audeō, ēre, ausus sum dare, venture
celer, eris, ere swift, speedy, quick
coma, ae *f.* hair, locks, tresses
dīvidō, ere, vīsī, vīsus divide, distribute
dulcis, e sweet, dear, fond
ēvānēscō, ere, nuī vanish, disappear
exordium, (i)ī *n.* beginning, commence-
     ment
faux, faucis *f.* jaws, throat; gulf
fortis, e brave, strong, valiant, stout

haereō, ēre, haesī, haesus cling (to),
     halt (+ *dat.*)
horror, ōris *m.* shudder(ing), horror,
     alarm
illūc *adv.* there, thither, to that place
Mnēstheus, eī (eos), *acc.* ea *m.* Trojan
     leader
monitus, ūs *m.* advice, warning
mortālis, e mortal, human, earthly
obmūtēscō, ere, tuī be dumb, stand
     speechless
potior, ius preferable, better
rapiō, ere, uī, ptus seize, snatch, rob
sententia, ae *f.* opinion, resolve, view
Serestus, ī *m.* Trojan leader
Sergestus, ī *m.* Trojan leader
sermō, ōnis *m.* conversation, speech
sūmō, ere, mpsī, mptus take, employ
varius, a, um various, different, diverse
versō (1) keep turning, roll, revolve
vīsus, ūs *m.* vision, view, aspect

---

277. mediō (in) sermōne: *in the middle
(of his) speech, abruptly;* App. 246.
     281. fugā: abl. of manner. dulcēs
relinquere terrās (Carthāginis): Vergil
uses the adj. to evoke Aeneas' inner
conflict—even in his eager haste (ardet)
to obey Jupiter, Aeneas cannot help
thinking of how happy he has been in
Carthage.
     283–84. agat, audeat, sūmat: delibera-
tive subjunctives; App. 348. These questions

vividly represent Aeneas' confusion.
furentem (amōre).
     285. animum celerem dīvidit: The
image is Homeric; heroes in doubt are
often described by Homer as "splitting"
their thoughts as they debate alternatives.
     286. rapit (animum), versat
(animum).
     287. (Aenēae) alternantī: whether he
should inform Dido. The participle continues
the imagery of the preceding lines.

classem aptent tacitī *sociōsque ad lītora* cōgant,
arma parent et quae rēbus sit causa novandīs   290
dissimulent; *sēsē* intereā, quandō optima *Dīdō*
nesciat *et tantōs* rumpī *nōn* spēret *amōrēs,*
temptātūrum aditūs *et quae* mollissima *fandī*
tempora, quis rēbus dexter modus. Ōcius *omnēs*
imperiō laetī pārent *et* iussa facessunt.   295

---

aditus, ūs *m.* approach, access
aptō (1) equip, make ready, furnish
causa, ae *f.* cause, reason, occasion
cōgō, ere, coēgī, coāctus muster, compel
dissimulō (1) conceal, dissimulate, pretend otherwise
facessō, ere, (īv)ī, ītus do, make, fulfill
intereā *adv.* meanwhile, (in the) meantime
iussum, ī *n.* command, behest, order
modus, ī *m.* manner, limit, method
mollis, e soft, yielding, easy, mild

nesciō, īre, īvī (iī) not know, be ignorant
novō (1) renew, make new, alter, build
ōcior, ius swifter, quicker; very swift
optimus, a, um best, finest
pāreō, ēre, uī, itus obey, yield (+ *dat.*)
quandō when, since, because
rumpō, ere, rūpī, ruptus break, burst (forth), utter
spērō (1) hope (for, to), expect, suppose
temptō (1) try, attempt, seek, test
tacitus, a, um silent, still, secret
vērō *adv.* truly, indeed, but

289–91. (ut) aptent, cōgant, parent, dissimulent: indir. commands after **vocat,** which implies **et imperat** or something similar; App. 390. **rēbus novandīs:** an expression commonly used for taking a new step, including something as extreme as political revolution. **quae . . . sit causa:** indir. quest.; App. 349.

291–93. sēsē temptātūrum (esse): implied indir. statement, dependent on **vocat,** 288, which implies **et dicit** or something similar; App. 390. **nesciat:**

subjunctive in a dependent clause in indir. statement; App. 390, *b.*

292. rumpī amōrēs: the expression is ambiguous: either Aeneas is counting on the likelihood that Dido will not reveal her true feelings publicly, or he thinks that nothing he can do can damage her love for him.

293–94. quae tempora (sint), quis modus (sit): indir. questions, objects of **temptātūrum (esse);** App. 349.

At rēgīna dolōs (*quis* fallere *possit* amantem?)
praesēnsit, mōtūs*que* excēpit *prīma futūrōs*
omnia tūta timēns. *Eadem* impia *Fāma furentī*
dētulit armārī *classem cursumque parārī.*
300 Saevit inops *animī tōtamque* incēnsa *per urbem*
bacchātur, quālis commōtīs excita *sacrīs*
Thyias, *ubi audītō* stimulant trietērica Bacchō
orgia nocturnus*que vocat clāmōre* Cithaerōn.
Tandem hīs Aenēān compellat *vōcibus* ultrō:

---

amāns, antis *m.* (*f.*) lover
armō (1) arm, equip, furnish
bacchor, ārī, ātus rush wildly, rave
Bacchus, ī *m.* (god of) wine
Cithaerōn, ōnis *m.* Greek mountain near
　Thebes, on which the rites of Bacchus
　were celebrated
commoveō, ēre, mōvī, mōtus move, stir,
　shake, agitate
compellō (1) address, accost, speak to
dēferō, ferre, tulī, lātus carry down,
　report
dolus, ī *m.* deceit, stratagem, fraud
excipiō, ere, cēpī, ceptus catch,
　receive, take (up)
exciō, īre, īvī, itus arouse, excite, stir
fallō, ere, fefellī, falsus deceive,
　cheat, mock

impius, a, um wicked, accursed, disloyal
incendō, ere, ī, ēnsus inflame, burn
inops, opis needy, destitute, bereft (of)
mōtus, ūs *m.* movement, emotion
nocturnus, a, um of the night, nocturnal
orgia, ōrum *n.* mystic rites, rituals
praesentiō, īre, sēnsī, sēnsus perceive
　first, suspect
quālis, e of what sort, (such) as
saeviō, īre, īvī (iī), ītus rage, storm
stimulō (1) spur, goad, prick, incite
Thyias, adis *f.* Bacchant, a woman
　devotee of the worship of Bacchus
timeō, ēre, uī fear, dread
trietēricus, a, um triennial
tūtus, a, um protected, safe, secure
ultrō *adv.* further, voluntarily

296–330. Dido, suspecting the
truth, reproaches Aeneas and, with
tears and prayers, attempts to prevail
on him to remain.

296. possit: deliberative subjunctive;
App. 348.
298. tūta: used concessively, i.e., (no
matter how) *safe,* with **omnia. eadem:**
refers to the first appearance of Fama, at
173. **furentī (Dīdōnī).**
300. animī: gen. with adj. **inops;** App.
287.
302. trietērica: every two years,
counted as three in the ancient system of
inclusive reckoning.

302–3. Thyias: the letters -yi- form a
diphthong (pronounced *we*). The Bacchic
revels celebrated every third year on Mt.
Cithaeron, near Thebes, are depicted in
their most terrifying aspect in Euripides'
tragedy *Bacchae.* When the **sacra** (ritual
objects the precise identity of which
remain unknown) were brought out of
the temple, the female worshippers of
Bacchus ran wild, dressed themselves in
fawn skins, and joined the Bacchic revels,
where they brandished **thyrsī** (*wands*),
and danced to the accompaniment of
clashing cymbals. **audītō Bacchō:** abl.
abs.; *as the cry 'Bacchus' is heard.* The
worshippers shouted '*iō Bacche,*' and
'*Euoe Bacche.*' **stimulant (illam), vocat
(illam).**

"Dissimulāre etiam spērāstī, perfide, *tantum*   305
posse nefās tacitus*que meā* dēcēdere *terrā?*
Nec tē noster amor nec tē data dextera quondam
nec moritūra *tenet* crūdēlī fūnere *Dīdō?*
Quīn etiam hībernō mōlīri *sīdere classem*
et mediīs properās Aquilōnibus *īre per* altum,   310
crūdēlis? *Quid, sī nōn arva* aliēna *domōsque*
ignōtās *peterēs, et Troia antīqua manēret,*
Troia per undōsum *peterētur classibus aequor?*
Mēne fugis? Per ego hās lacrimās dextramque tuam tē
(quandō *aliud mihi iam miserae* nihil *ipsa relīquī*),   315
per cōnūbia *nostra, per* inceptōs hymenaeōs,
sī bene *quid dē tē* meruī, *fuit aut tibi* quicquam

---

aliēnus, a, um belonging to another, other's, alien, foreign
altum, ī *n.* the deep (sea); heaven
Aquilō, ōnis *m.* (north) wind
bene *adv.* well, rightly, securely, fully
cōnūbium, (i)ī *n.* wedlock, marriage
crūdēlis, e, cruel, bloody, bitter
dēcēdō, ere, cessī, cessus depart
dissimulō (1) conceal, dissimulate, pretend otherwise
etiam *adv.* also, even, besides, yet, still
fūnus, eris *n.* funeral, death, disaster
hībernus, a, um wintry, of the winter
hymenaeus, ī *m.* wedding (hymn), so-called after Hymen, god of marriage
ignōtus, a, um unknown, strange

incipiō, ere, cēpī, ceptus begin, undertake
mereō, ēre, uī, itus deserve, earn, merit
mōlior, īrī, ītus prepare, attempt, do
morior, ī, mortuus die, perish
nefās *n. indecl.* impiety, unspeakable thing, crime
nihil, nīl nothing, not at all
perfidus, a, um treacherous, perfidious
properō (1) hasten, hurry, speed
quandō when, since, if ever, because
quīn why not, but that, in fact
quisquam, quicquam anyone, anything
spērō (1) hope (for, to), expect, suppose
tacitus, a, um silent, noiseless, secret
undōsus, a, um billow, wavy

---

305. Dissimulāre: Dido's first word echoes the instructions Aeneas has just given his men (291).

305–6. etiam spērā(vi)stī, perfide, (tē) posse dissimulāre tantum nefās?

307. data dextera: the clasping of right hands was a Roman symbol of marriage, seen frequently in sculpture.

307–8. Note the combination of ANAPHORA and TRICOLON CRESCENS (i.e., the use of three parallel phrases or clauses, balanced so that each is slightly longer than the one preceding it).

309. hībernō sīdere = METONYMY for **tempore.** The ancients regularly suspended

navigation during the winter months.
mōlīri: some manuscripts read **mōlīris** (second person sing.) instead of the inf.

311–13. Quid sī, etc.: you wouldn't sail now, even if you were going back to secure homes in Troy, and were not (as you are) sailing away to strange foreign lands (**arva aliēna**). **Troia peterētur** (**hībernō sīdere**): the conclusion of the pres. contrary-to-fact conditions, **sī peterēs** and **sī manēret;** App. 382.

314–19. Mē: emphatic by position, obj. of **fugis. Per ego** etc: when used in an oath, **per** is best translated *by.* **per lacrimās et per dextram. tē:** obj. of **ōrō.**

dulce *meum*, miserēre *domūs lābentis et* istam,
ōrō, *sī quis* adhūc precibus *locus*, exue *mentem.*

320   *Tē* propter Libycae *gentēs* Nomadum*que* tyrannī
ōdēre, īnfēnsī *Tyriī; tē* propter *eundem*
exstīnctus pudor *et, quā sōlā sīdera* adībam,
fāma prior. *Cui mē* moribundam dēseris hospes
(*hoc solum nōmen* quoniam *dē coniuge* restat)?

325   *Quid* moror? An *mea* Pygmaliōn *dum moenia* frāter
dēstruat *aut captam dūcat* Gaetūlus Iarbās?

---

adeō, īre, iī (īvī), itus approach
adhūc *adv.* to this point, till now
an whether, or
dēserō, ere, uī, rtus desert, forsake
dēstruō, ere, strūxī, strūctus destroy
dulcis, e sweet, dear, pleasant, delightful
exsting(u)ō, ere, īnxī, īnctus extinguish,
   blot out, destroy, ruin
exuō, ere, uī, ūtus bare, doff, discard
frāter, tris *m.* brother
Gaetūlus, a, um of the Gaetuli, an
   African tribe
hospes, itis *m. (f.)* stranger, guest, host
Iarbās, ae *f.* African prince, one of Dido's
   suitors
īnfēnsus, a, um hostile, bitter
iste, ta, tud that (of yours)

Libycus, a, um of Libya, a country of
   North Africa
misereor, ērī, itus pity, commiserate
   (+ *gen.*)
moribundus, a, um dying, about to die
moror, ārī, ātus delay, tarry, hinder
Nomas, adis *m.* tribe of North Africa
ōdī, isse hate, detest, loathe
ōrō (1) to pray (for), entreat, beseech
prex, precis *f.* prayer, entreaty, vow
prior, ius soon, former, first, prior
propter on account of, near (+ *acc.*)
pudor, ōris *m.* shame, modesty, honor
Pygmaliōn, ōnis *m.* brother of Dido
quoniam since, because
restō, āre, stitī remain, be left
tyrannus, ī *m.* ruler, chieftain, tyrant

---

318. miserēre: imperative. domūs:
gen. with misereor; App. 289.

319. sī quis (indef.). locus (sit).

320. Tē propter: ANASTROPHE.

320–21. gentēs et tyrannī ōdēre
(mē). ōdēre = ōdērunt. īnfēnsī (mihi
sunt) Tyriī: the native chieftains, as well
as her own people, resented her kindly
attitude toward Aeneas and the Trojans,
who were foreigners, and her rejection of
their offers of alliance through marriage.

322. et (fāma) quā: abl. of means.
sīdera adībam: *I was approaching the
stars,* i.e., earning immortality through
fame. (exstīncta est) fāma (mea): *(my)
reputation.*

323. moribundam = moritūram.

324. hoc nōmen = hospes. dē coniuge
= dē nōmine coniugis.

325. Quid (= cūr) moror (mortem
meam). An (moror): *am I waiting?* dum
dēstruat, dūcat: anticipatory subjunctives
with dum; App. 374.

Saltem *sī qua mihī dē tē* suscepta *fuisset*
ante fugam subolēs, *sī quis mihi* parvulus aulā
lūderet *Aenēās, quī tē* tamen *ōre referret,*
nōn equidem omnīnō *capta ac* dēserta *vidērer."*   330

---

aula, ae *f.* hall, palace, court
dēserō, ere, uī, rtus desert, forsake
equidem *adv.* indeed, truly, surely
lūdō, ere, sī, sus play, sport, mock
omnīnō *adv.* altogether, completely,
   utterly

parvulus, a, um tiny, very small, little
saltem *adv.* at least, at any rate
subolēs, is *f.* offspring, progeny, child
suscipiō, ere, cēpī, ceptus take up,
   beget, bear
tamen *adv.* however, nevertheless, but

---

327. suscepta: an allusion to the
Roman custom of placing a newborn
child on the ground before the father,
who picked it up if he wished to
acknowledge and rear it as his own.

**327–30. sī fuisset, sī lūderet, . . .
vidērer:** mixed contrary-to-fact
condition; App. 382, d.

328. parvulus: this is the only
appearance of a diminutive adj. in the
Aeneid. The rareness of such an emotional
form of expression probably reflects how
pathetic it is meant to sound coming from
Dido.

329. referret: subjunctive in a rel.
clause of characteristic; App. 389; i.e., *the
sort of child who could remind me of you.*

Dīxerat. *Ille Iovis* monitīs immōta *tenēbat*
lūmina et obnixus *cūram sub* corde premēbat.
Tandem pauca *refert: "Ego tē, quae plūrima fandō*
ēnumerāre valēs, numquam, *rēgīna,* negābō
335   prōmeritam, *nec mē* meminisse pigēbit Elissae
dum memor *ipse meī, dum* spīritus *hōs* rēgit artūs.
Prō *rē* pauca loquar. *Neque ego hanc* abscondere fūrtō
spērāvī (*nē* finge) *fugam, nec coniugis* umquam
praetendī taedās *aut haec in* foedera *vēnī.*
340   *Mē sī fāta meīs* paterentur *dūcere vītam*

---

abscondō, ere, (di)dī, ditus hide
artus, ūs *m.* joint, limb, member, body
cor, rdis *n.* heart, spirit, feelings, soul
Elissa, ae *f.* Dido
ēnumerō (1) recount, enumerate
fingō, ere, fīnxī, fictus fashion, pretend, imagine, form, mold
foedus, eris *n.* treaty, agreement, pact
fūrtum, ī *n.* stealth, theft, trick
immōtus, a, um unmoved, unshaken
loquor, ī, locūtus speak, say, tell, talk
meminī, isse remember, recall (+ *gen.*)
memor, oris mindful, remembering (+ *gen.*)
monitum, ī *n.* advice, warning
negō (1) deny, refuse, say no (not)
numquam *adv.* never, at no time
obnītor, ī, sus (nixus) struggle

patior, ī, passus suffer, endure, allow
paucus, a, um little, few, scanty
piget, ēre, uit it displeases
praetendō, ere, ī, ntus hold before, use as screen
premō, ere, pressī, pressus (re)press, crush
prō instead of, on behalf of, for, before (+ *abl.*)
prōmereor, ērī, itus deserve, render service, merit, earn
regō, ere, rēxī, rēctus rule, direct, guide
spērō (1) hope (for, to), expect, suppose
spīritus, ūs *m.* breath, spirit, life, soul
taeda, ae *f.* (bridal) torch, pinewood torch
umquam *adv.* ever, at any time
valeō, ēre, uī, itus be strong, be able, fare well

331–92. Aeneas replies that he is not following his own desires but the plans of the gods and the stern decrees of fate; Dido responds by cursing him and his descendants, and by fainting into the arms of her slaves.

331. Dīxerat (Dīdō). monitīs: abl. of cause with **tenebāt.**
332. lūmina = oculōs. premēbat = reprimēbat: repressing all outward indications of his feelings.
333–35. Ego, rēgīna, numquam negābō tē prōmeritam (esse dē mē)

plūrima quae: answer to Dido's **sī meruī** of 317. **valēs = potes. Elissae = Dīdōnis;** gen. with **meminī;** App. 288.
336. dum memor (sum) meī.
337. Prō rē: *in defense of my course of action.* The expression is legalistic.
338. nē finge: poetic negative imperative, = **nōlī fingere;** App. 256, *a.*
339. praetendī taedās: the phrase has a double meaning: lit., *I never held the marriage torches before [you],* i.e., in a marriage procession; and *I never held out the prospect (or made a pretense) of marriage.* **haec in foedera:** i.e., of marriage.
340. paterentur: pres. contrary-to-fact condition; App. 382.

auspiciīs *et* sponte *meā* compōnere *cūrās*,
urbem Troiānam *prīmum* dulcēs*que meōrum*
reliquiās colerem, *Priamī tēcta alta manērent*,
et recidīva *manū posuissem* Pergama *victīs*.
Sed nunc Ītaliam magnam Grȳnēus Apollō,   345
Ītaliam Lyciae *iussēre* capessere sortēs;
hic amor, haec patria *est. sī tē* Karthāginis *arcēs*
Phoenissam Libycae*que* aspectus dētinet *urbis*,
quae tandem Ausoniā *Teucrōs* cōnsīdere *terrā*
invidia *est? Et nos* fās extera *quaerere rēgna*.   350
Mē patris Anchīsae, quotiēns ūmentibus *umbrīs*
nox operit *terrās*, quotiēns astra ignea *surgunt*,
admonet *in somnīs et* turbida terret imāgō;

---

admoneō, ēre, uī, itus advise, warn
Apollō, inis *m.* god of light, music, and
    prophecy
a(d)spectus, ūs *m.* sight, appearance
astrum, ī *n.* star, constellation
Ausonius, a, um Ausonian, Italian
auspicium, (i)ī *n.* auspices, authority
capessō, ere, īvī, ītus (try to) seize, reach
colō, ere, uī, cultus cultivate, dwell (in),
    cherish, honor
compōnō, ere, posuī, positus put together,
    settle, calm, quiet
cōnsīdō, ere, sēdī, sessus sit (down),
    settle
dētineō, ēre, uī, tentus hold back, detain
dulcis, e sweet, dear, fond
exterus, a, um outside, foreign
fās *n. indecl.* right, justice, divine law
Grȳnēus, a, um of Grynium, a town in
    Asia Minor, with an oracle of Apollo
igneus, a, um fiery, flaming

imāgō, inis *f.* image, likeness, ghost
invidia, ae *f.* grudge, envy, jealousy
Karthāgō, inis *f.* Carthage, a city of
    North Africa
Libycus, a, um Libyan, of Libya, a
    country of North Africa
Lycia, ae *f.* country of Asia Minor
operiō, īre, uī, rtus cover, hide
patria, ae *f.* homeland, country
Pergama, ōrum *n.* (citadel of) Troy
Phoenissa, ae *f.* Phoenician woman, Dido
quotiēns how often, as often as
recidīvus, a, um revived, renewed
reliquiae, ārum *f.* remnants, relics,
    leavings
sors, rtis *f.* lot, fate, portion, oracle
spōns, spontis *f.* wish, will, desire
terreō, ēre, uī, itus frighten, terrify
Troiānus, a, um Trojan, of Troy
turbidus, a, um troubled, agitated
ūmēns, entis moist, dewy, damp

**343–44. colerem, manērent,
posuissem:** apodoses in the contrary-to-
fact condition; App. 382. **victīs**
(Teucrīs): dat. of reference.

**346. Lyciae sortēs = sortēs Lyciī
Apollinis.**

347. hic: pronounce **hicc** (the full form
was originally **hicce**), making a long
syllable; App. 107, 3, *c.* **hic (est) amor,**

haec patria est: both refer to Italy, each
pronoun being attracted into the gender
of its predicate noun; App. 240, *a.*

349–50. quae invidia est (tibi)
Teucrōs cōnsīdere is the subject and
invidia the predicate of **est.**

350. Et: also, too (as well as you). **fās**
(est).

351–53. patris Anchīsae: with **imāgō.**

mē puer Ascanius *capitisque* iniūria cārī,
355 *quem rēgnō* Hesperiae fraudō *et* fātālibus *arvīs.*
Nunc etiam interpres *dīvum Iove missus ab ipsō*
(testor utrumque *caput*) celerēs mandāta *per aurās*
dētulit: *ipse deum* manifestō *in lūmine vīdī*
intrantem mūrōs *vōcemque hīs* auribus hausī.
360 Dēsine *mēque tuīs* incendere *tēque* querēlis;
Ītaliam nōn sponte *sequor.*"
Tālia dīcentem iamdūdum āversa tuētur
hūc illūc *volvēns oculōs tōtumque* pererrat
lūminibus tacitīs *et sīc* accēnsa profātur:
365 "*Nec tibi dīva parēns generis nec* Dardanus auctor,

---

accendō, ere, ēnsus inflame, kindle, burn
Ascanius, (i)ī *m.* son of Aeneas
auctor, ōris *m. (f.)* author, founder, sponsor
auris, is *f.* ear
āvertor, ī, rsus turn away, avert
cārus, a, um dear, beloved, fond
celer, eris, ere swift, quick, speedy
Dardanus, ī *m.* early king of Troy
dēferō, ferre, tulī, lātus carry down, report
dēsinō, ere, sīvī (iī), situs cease, desist
etiam *adv.* also, even, besides, furthermore
fātālis, e fated, fatal, destined
fraudō (1) defraud, deprive, cheat
hauriō, īre, hausī, haustus drink (in), drain
Hesperia, ae *f.* Hesperia, Italy; lit., the western place

iamdūdum *adv.* long since, for a long time
illūc *adv.* thither, to that place
incendō, ere, ī, ēnsus inflame, kindle, burn
iniūria, ae *f.* wrong, injury, injustice
interpres, etis *m. (f.)* interpreter, agent
intrō (1) enter, penetrate
mandātum, ī *n.* command, mandate
manifestus, a, um clear, manifest
mūrus, ī *m.* (city) wall, battlement
pererrō (1) wander over, survey
profor, ārī, ātus speak (out), say
querēla, ae *f.* complaint, lament
spōns, spontis *f.* wish, will, desire
tacitus, a, um silent, quiet, still, secret
testor, ārī, ātus call to witness, swear by, testify
tueor, ērī, itus (tūtus) watch, protect, eye
uterque, utraque, utrumque each (of two), both

---

354. mē puer Ascanius (movet):
(the thought of) *my son Ascanius urges me on.* **capitis cārī** = Ascanī; obj. gen., *the wrong* (I am doing) *to Ascanius;* App. 284.
   355. rēgnō, arvis: abl. of separation.
   356. interpres dīv(ōr)um: Mercury.
   357. utrumque= et meum et tuum.
   361. sponte (meā).
   362. āversa: describes Dido's

emotional response as much as her physical behavior. **tuētur:** with **iamdūdum,** of past action continued into the present, *has long been watching and is still watching;* App. 351, 1, *b.*
   363. tōtum (Aenēān) pererrat.
   364. tacitīs: an odd epithet for sight **(lūminibus),** used here perhaps to suggest Dido's increasing lack of emotional control.
   365. tibi (est).

perfide, *sed* dūrīs genuit *tē* cautibus horrēns
Caucasus Hyrcānae*que* admōrunt ūbera tigrēs.
Nam quid dissimulō *aut quae mē ad maiōra* reservō?
Num flētū ingemuit *nostrō?* Num *lūmina* flexit?
Num *lacrimās victus dedit aut* miserātus amantem *est?*   370
Quae quibus anteferam? *Iam iam nec maxima Iūnō*
nec Sāturnius *haec oculīs pater* aspicit aequīs.
Nūsquam tūta fidēs. Ēiectum *lītore,* egentem
excēpī *et rēgnī* dēmēns *in parte* locāvī.
Āmissam *classem, sociōs ā morte* redūxī   375

---

admoveō, ēre, mōvī, mōtus move to
aequus, a, um equal, propitious,
   favorable, just
amāns, antis *m. (f.)* lover
āmittō, ere, mīsī, missus lose, let go
anteferō, ferre, tulī, lātus set before,
   prefer, choose first
a(d)spiciō, ere, spexī, spectus see,
   behold, look (at)
Caucasus, ī *m.* rugged mountain range
   between Europe and Asia
cautēs, is *f.* rock, cliff, crag
dēmēns, entis crazy, mad, frenzied
dissimulō (1) pretend otherwise, conceal,
   dissimulate
dūrus, a, um hard(y), harsh, rough
egēns, entis needy, in want, destitute
ēiciō, ere, ēiēcī, ēiectus cast out, eject
excipiō, ere, cēpī, ceptus receive, take
fidēs, eī *f.* faith, trust, confidence
flectō, ere, flexī, flexus bend, move
flētus, ūs *m.* weeping, tears, lament

gignō, ere, genuī, genitus bear,
   produce, beget
horreō, ēre, uī shudder, be rough
Hyrcānus, a, um Hyrcanian, of Hyrcania,
   a wild district on the Caspian Sea
ingemō, ere, uī groan, roar, lament
locō (1) place, locate, establish
miseror, ārī, ātus pity, commiserate
num *interrog.,* expects a negative
   response
nūsquam *adv.* nowhere, never
perfidus, a, um treacherous. perfidious
redūcō, ere, dūxī, ductus lead back,
   restore
reservō (1) reserve, keep back, save
Sāturnius, a, um (born) of Saturn, father
   of Jupiter and Juno
tigris, (id)is *m. (f.)* tiger, tigress
tūtus, a, um protected, safe, secure
ūber, eris *n.* udder, breast; (symbol of)
   fertility

366–67. dūrīs cautibus: abl. of cause
or of description with **horrēns,** or of
place where. **admō(vē)runt ūbera (tibi):**
suckled you.
   368. maiōra (mala): *greater wrongs.*
   369. flētū: abl. of cause. **ingemuit:** the
third person, since she contemptuously
talks about rather than to Aeneas. **lūmina**
= oculōs.

   370. miserātus: from **miseror** with
the acc.; **misereor** takes the gen. **(mē)**
amantem.
   371. Quae quibus anteferam: *what
shall I say (do) first?* Lit., *What shall I
prefer to what?*
   372. Sāturnius pater = Jupiter.
   373. (in) lītore. (eum or **tē) egentem:**
Aeneas had said of himself and his
followers that they were **omnium egēnōs** at
1.599.

(*heu* furiīs incēnsa *feror!*): *nunc* augur Apollō,
nunc Lyciae sortēs, *nunc et Iove missus ab ipsō*
interpres *dīvum fert* horrida iussa *per aurās.*
Scīlicet *is superīs labor est, ea cūra* quiētōs
380   sollicitat. *Neque tē teneō neque dicta* refellō:
ī, sequere Ītaliam ventīs, pete rēgna per undās.
Spērō equidem *mediīs, sī quid pia nūmina possunt,*
supplicia hausūrum scopulīs *et nōmine Dīdō*
saepe *vocātūrum. Sequar ātrīs ignibus* absēns
385   *et, cum* frīgida *mors animā* sēdūxerit artūs,
omnibus umbra locīs aderō. Dabis, improbe, *poenās.*
Audiam et haec Mānēs *veniet mihi fāma sub īmōs.*"

---

absēns, entis absent, separated
Apollō, inis *m.* god of light, music, and
    prophecy
artus, ūs *m.* joint, limb, body
augur, uris *m.* (*f.*) augur, prophet
equidem *adv.* indeed, truly, surely
frīgidus, a, um cold, chill, frigid
furiae, ārum *f.* furies, madness, frenzy
hauriō, īre, hausī, haustus drink (in),
    drain
horridus, a, um rough, horrible
improbus, a, um wicked, cruel
incendō, ere, ī, ēnsus inflame, kindle,
    burn
interpres, etis *m.* (*f.*) interpreter, agent
iussum, ī *n.* command, order, behest

Lycius, a, um Lycian, of Lycia, a
    country of Asia Minor
Mānēs, ium *m.* (souls of) the dead, Hades
quiētus, a, um quiet, serene, calm
refellō, ere, ī contradict, refute
saepe *adv.* often, frequently, again and
    again
scīlicet *adv.* of course, to be sure,
    doubtless
scopulus, ī *m.* rock, cliff, crag
sēdūcō, ere, dūxī, ductus withdraw,
    separate
sollicitō (1) agitate, disquiet, disturb
sors, rtis *f.* lot, destiny, portion, oracle
spērō (1) hope (for, to), expect, suppose
supplicium, (i)ī *n.* punishment, torture

376–77. nunc, nunc, nunc: a
scornful rejoinder to the **nunc, nunc** of
Aeneas, 345, 356; App. 413.
    378–80. Scornfully sarcastic. **is:**
subject, attracted into the gender of the
predicate, App. 240, *a.* **(superōs) quiētōs.**
    381. ī, sequere: imperatives. **sequere
Ītaliam:** a contemptuous rejoinder to the
Ītaliam sequor of 361.
    382–84. mediīs (in) scopulīs: Dido
hopes that the ships of Aeneas may be
wrecked on reefs in the midst of the sea;
App. 246. **quid:** indef., *anything* (=
aliquid) after **sī. (tē) hausūrum (esse).**

Dīdō: acc., a Greek form; dir. obj. of
vocātūrum. ātrīs ignibus: his remorseful
thoughts about Dido will pursue Aeneas
like furies with their *smoking torches.*
Although far away (**absēns**), Dido will
pursue him with the pangs of a guilty
conscience, and after death her ghost will
haunt him wherever he may be.
    385. animā: the ancients often thought
of death as the separation of the body
from the soul.
    386. umbra: (*as*) *a ghost.* **Dabis
poenās:** *you shall pay the penalty, suffer
punishment.*

Hīs medium dictīs sermōnem abrumpit *et aurās*
aegra *fugit sēque ex oculīs* āvertit *et* aufert,
linquēns *multa* metū cūnctantem *et multa parantem*   390
dīcere. Suscipiunt famulae conlāpsa*que* membra
marmoreō *referunt* thalamō strātīs*que* repōnunt.

---

abrumpō, ere, rūpī, ruptus break off
aeger, gra, grum sick, weary, wretched
auferō, auferre, abstulī, ablātus carry
  away, remove
āvertō, ere, ī, rsus turn away, avert
conlābor, ī, lāpsus collapse, faint
cūnctor, ārī, ātus delay, hesitate, linger
famula, ae *f.* female household slave
linquō, ere, līquī, lictus leave, desert

marmoreus, a, um (of) marble, white
membrum, ī *n.* member, limb, body
metus, ūs *m.* fear, dread, anxiety
repōnō, ere, posuī, pos(i)tus replace, lay
  away, store (up), deposit
sermō, ōnis *m.* conversation, speech
strātum, ī *n.* bed, couch; pavement
suscipiō, ere, cēpī, ceptus take up, rear
thalamus, ī *m.* bridal chamber, bedroom

**388. hīs medium dictīs sermōnem
abrumpit:** the combination of interlocked
word order (SYNCHYSIS) and concluding
verb reflects the meaning of the words.

388–89. aurās (= lūcem) fugit: i.e.,
she rushes indoors.

390. metū: abl. of cause; *for fear* (of
making matters worse).

391–92. Suscipiunt: *catch her* (as she
faints and falls). **thalamō:** dat. of
direction; equivalent to **in thalamum. (in)
strātis.**

> *At pius Aenēās*, quamquam lēnīre dolentem
> sōlandō cupit *et dictīs* āvertere *cūrās*,
395 *multa* gemēns *magnōque animum* labefactus *amōre*
> iussa tamen *dīvum* exsequitur *classemque* revīsit.
> *Tum vērō Teucrī* incumbunt *et lītore* celsās
> dēdūcunt *tōtō nāvēs*. Natat ūncta carīna,
> frondentēs*que ferunt rēmōs et* rōbora *silvīs*
400 īnfabricāta *fugae* studiō.
> Migrantēs *cernās tōtāque ex urbe ruentēs:*
> *ac* velut *ingentem* formīcae farris acervum

---

acervus, ī *m.* heap, pile, mass
āvertō, ere, ī, rsus turn away, avert, divert
carīna, ae *f.* keel; ship, boat
celsus, a, um high, lofty, towering
cupiō, ere, īvī (iī), ītus desire, wish
dēdūcō, ere, dūxī, ductus lead down, launch
doleō, ēre, uī, itus grieve, suffer, resent
exsequor, ī, secutus follow out, perform
far, farris *n.* spelt, a kind of grain
formīca, ae *f.* ant
frondēns, entis leafy, fronded
gemō, ere, uī, itus groan, lament, roar
incumbō, ere, cubuī, cubitus recline upon, urge on

īnfabricātus, a, um unfashioned, rough
iussum, ī *n.* command, order, behest
labefaciō, ere, fēcī, factus shake, stagger
lēniō, īre, īvī (iī), ītus soothe, calm
migrō (1) migrate, depart
natō (1) swim, float, overflow
quamquam although, and yet, however
revīsō, ere revisit, see again, return to
rōbur, oris *n.* oak, strength
sōlor, ārī, ātus console, comfort
studium, (i)ī *n.* eagerness, desire, zeal
tamen *adv.* nevertheless, however, but
ung(u)ō, ere, ūnxī, ūnctus anoint, smear, caulk
velut(ī) as, just as
vērō *adv.* truly, indeed, but

393–449. After her own efforts fail, Dido sends her sister Anna to Aeneas, hoping that she may persuade him; but he resists all entreaties.

393. pius: the use of this epithet at this point in the story is striking—to whom or what should we understand that Aeneas' **pietās** is directed? **dolentem (Dīdōnem).**

395. animum: acc. of respect with **labefactus**; App. 311.

397. incumbunt (labōrī).

398. ūncta: the prows of ships were coated with pine pitch to make them impermeable.

398–99. carīna, rēmōs, rōbora: a rather elaborate HYSTERON PROTERON: Vergil first mentions the ships in the water, then their still branch-like oars, and then the trees in the forests from which the wood for both ships and oars was taken. The logical sequence of events is just the opposite.

399. frondentēs: in their eagerness, **studiō**, they do not take time to strip off the leaves. **rēmōs et rōbora:** can be construed as HENDIADYS, i.e., **rēmōs rōboris.**

401. cernās: potential subjunctive; App. 252. Vergil's inclusion of his reader in the "viewing audience," so to speak, creates the illusion that we are watching from the same point of view as Dido.

cum populant hiemis memorēs *tēctōque* repōnunt,
it nigrum *campīs agmen* praedam*que per* herbās
convectant calle angustō: *pars* grandia trūdunt　　　　405
obnixae frūmenta *umerīs, pars agmina* cōgunt
castīgant*que* morās, opere *omnis* sēmita fervet.
Quis tibi tum, Dīdō, cernentī tālia sēnsus,
quōsve dabās gemitūs, *cum lītora* fervere lātē
prōspicerēs *arce ex summā, tōtumque vidērēs*　　　　410
miscērī *ante oculōs tantīs clāmōribus aequor!*
Improbe *Amor, quid nōn* mortālia *pectora* cōgis!
Īre iterum *in lacrimās,* iterum temptāre precandō
cōgitur *et* supplex *animōs* summittere *amōrī,*

---

angustus, a, um　narrow
callis, is *m.* path, track
castīgō (1) reprove, chastise, punish
cōgō, ere, coēgī, coāctus　bring
　together, force
convectō (1) convey, carry along
ferv(e)ō, ēre, (bu)ī　boil, be busy
frūmentum, ī *n.* grain
gemitus, ūs *m.* groan, roar, lament
grandis, e　large, great, tall, huge
herba, ae *f.* herb(age), grass, plant
hiems, emis *f.* winter, storm
improbus, a, um　wicked, cruel, bad
iterum *adv.* again, anew, a second time
lātē *adv.* widely, far and wide
memor, oris　mindful, remembering
　(+ *gen.*)
misceō, ēre, uī, mixtus　mix, mingle
mora, ae *f.* delay, hesitation, loitering

mortālis, e　mortal, human, earthly
niger, gra, grum　black, dark, dusky
obnītor, ī, sus (nixus)　push against,
　strive
opus, eris *n.* work, toil, task, deed
populō (1) devastate, plunder, ravage
praeda, ae *f.* booty, spoils, prey
precor, ārī, ātus　pray, entreat, invoke
prōspiciō, ere, spexī, spectus　see,
　behold
repōnō, ere, posuī, pos(i)tus　lay away,
　store (up)
sēmita, ae *f.* path
sēnsus, ūs *m.* feeling, perception, sense
summittō (sub), ere, mīsī, missus
　lower, submit
supplex, icis　suppliant, humble
temptō (1) try, seek, attempt, test
trūdō, ere, sī, sus　push, shove

**403–5. populant, it . . . campīs
agmen, praedam:** the language is
commonly used of an army.

404–5. it, convectant: the collective
noun, **agmen,** may take its verb either in
the sing. or pl.; App. 236, *a.*

406. agmina cōgunt: *close up the
ranks,* to keep the others from straggling;
another military term.

408. cernentī: echoes **cernās** at 401.
sēnsus (erat).

409. fervere: treated metrically here as
a third conj. verb, although **fervet,** a

second conj. pres. form, has just occurred
(407).

410. prōspicerēs, vidērēs: potential
subjunctive; App. 252. **arce:** probably
some sort of tall watch tower of Dido's
palace.

411. aequor: here, probably the flat
area adjacent to the shore where the men
are busy at their tasks.

412. Improbe Amor: this APOSTROPHE
again suggests that we share Dido's
feelings. **quid cōgis (facere). nōn:**
construe with **cōgis.**

413. temptāre (Aenēān).

415 *nē quid* inexpertum frūstrā moritūra *relinquat.*
"Anna, *vidēs tōtō* properārī *lītore circum:*
undique convēnēre; *vocat iam* carbasus *aurās,*
puppibus et laetī nautae imposuēre corōnās.
Hunc ego sī potuī tantum spērāre dolōrem,
420 *et* perferre, soror, *poterō. Miserae hoc* tamen *ūnum*
exsequere, Anna, *mihī; sōlam nam* perfidus *ille*
tē colere, arcānōs etiam *tibi* crēdere sēnsūs;
sōla virī mollēs aditūs *et tempora* nōrās.
Ī, soror, *atque* hostem supplex adfāre superbum:
425 *nōn ego cum Danaīs* Troiānam exscindere *gentem*

---

adfor, ārī, ātus address, speak to
aditus, ūs *m.* approach, access
Anna, ae *f.* sister of Dido
arcānus, a, um secret, hidden
carbasus, ī *f.* linen; sail
colō, ere, uī, cultus cultivate, honor
conveniō, īre, vēnī, ventus come
  together, convene
corōna, ae *f.* wreath, garland, crown
crēdō, ere, didī, ditus believe, (en)trust
  (+ *dat.*)
dolor, ōris *m.* grief, pain, passion, anger
etiam *adv.* also, even, besides, yet, still
exscindō, ere, scidī, scissus destroy, root
  out
exsequor, ī, secūtus follow out, perform
frūstrā *adv.* in vain, uselessly, ineffectually
hostis, is *m. (f.)* enemy, foe, stranger

impōnō, ere, posuī, positus place
  upon, set to (+ *dat.*)
inexpertus, a, um untried
mollis, e soft, yielding, gentle, delicate
morior, ī, mortuus die, perish
nauta, ae *m.* sailor, seaman, mariner
nōscō, ere, nōvī, nōtus learn; *perf.* know
perferō, ferre, tulī, lātus bear, endure
perfidus, a, um treacherous, perfidious
properō (1) hasten, hurry, speed
sēnsus, ūs *m.* feeling, perception, sense
soror, ōris *f.* sister
spērō (1) hope (for), expect, suppose
superbus, a, um proud, haughty
supplex, icis suppliant, humble
tamen *adv.* however, nevertheless, but
Troiānus, a, um Trojan, of Troy
undique *adv.* on (from) all sides

---

415. nē quid (indef., = **aliquid**)
inexpertum relinquat (et sīc moriātur)
frūstrā: there would be no object in her
dying so long as there was any possibility
of winning back Aeneas.

416. properārī: used impersonally, i.e.,
with no explicit subject. *There is hurrying.*

417. convēnēre: = **convēnērunt.**

418. corōnās: as a sign of joy at the
prospect of immediate departure. On
entering or leaving port, sailors often
decked their ships with garlands.

419. sī potuī: Dido's statement is
ambiguous: either she is affirming that
she was in fact able to endure this sorrow,

or she is using a contrary-to-fact
condition—*if I were able* (i.e., but I am
not).

420. perferre poterō: Dido is
deceiving Anna if she has already
determined on suicide in case she loses
Aeneas.

421–23. According to Vergil's fourth-
century A.D. commentator, Servius, Vergil
here alludes to a different tradition about
Aeneas' stay in Carthage, in which
Aeneas and Anna (not Dido) were lovers.

422. colere, crēdere: historical
infinitives; App. 257.

423. tempora: *(suitable) time* (for
approach). **nō(ve)rās.**

Aulide iūrāvī *classemve ad* Pergama *mīsī,*
nec patris Anchīsae cinerēm mānēs*ve* revellī:
cūr *mea dicta* negat dūrās dēmittere *in* aurēs?
Quō ruit? Extrēmum *hoc miserae det mūnus* amantī:
exspectet facilem*que fugam* ventōs*que ferentēs.*   430
Nōn iam coniugium *antīquum, quod* prōdidit, ōrō,
nec pulchrō *ut* Latiō careat *rēgnumque relinquat:*
tempus ināne *petō,* requiem spatium*que* furōrī,
dum mea mē victam doceat *fortūna* dolēre.
Extrēmam *hanc* ōrō veniam (miserēre sorōris),   435
quam mihi cum dederit cumulātam *morte* remittam."
      Tālibus ōrābat, *tālēsque miserrima* flētūs
fertque refertque soror. *Sed nūllīs ille movētur*

---

amāns, antis *m.* *(f.)* lover
Aulis, idis *f.* port in eastern Greece from
   which the Greek fleet set sail to attack
   Troy
auris, is *f.* ear
careō, ēre, uī be without, lack (+ *abl.*)
cinis, eris *m.* ashes (of the dead), embers
coniugium, (i)ī *n.* wedlock, marriage
cumulō (1) heap (up), pile (high)
cūr why?
dēmittō, ere, mīsī, missus send down, let
   down, let fall; receive
doceō, ēre, uī, itus teach, tell, inform
doleō, ēre, uī, itus grieve, suffer, resent
dūrus, a, um hard(y), harsh, stern
ex(s)pectō (1) (a)wait, expect, hope (for)
extrēmus, a, um last, final, extreme
facilis, e easy, favorable, ready
flētus, ūs *m.* weeping, tears, tearful
   appeal, lament

furor, ōris *m.* madness, frenzy, passion
inānis, e empty, idle, useless, vain
iūrō (1) take oath, swear, conspire
Latium, (i)ī *n.* district in central Italy
mānēs, ium *m.* (souls of) the dead, Hades
misereor, ērī, itus pity, commiserate
   (+ *gen.*)
negō (1) deny, refuse, say no (not)
ōrō (1) pray (to, for), entreat, beseech
Pergama, ōrum *n.* (citadel of) Troy
prōdō, ere, didī, ditus betray, hand
   down
pulcher, chra, chrum beautiful, noble,
   splendid, handsome, illustrious
remittō, ere, mīsī, missus return, repay
requiēs, ētis (ēi) *f.* rest, respite, repose
revellō, ere, ī, vulsus tear off (up, away)
soror, ōris *f.* sister
spatium, (i)ī *n.* space, time, period
venia, ae *f.* favor, pardon, grace

429-30. det, exspectet: jussive
subjunctive; App. 254. **ventōs ferentēs:**
favorable winds, since the participle
suggests that the winds will "bear" them
along.
   **431-32. ōrō . . . ut careat, (ut)
relinquat:** subst. volitive clauses (also
known as indir. command); App. 360.

   432. pulchrō Latiō: contemptuously;
abl. with **careat.**
   435. miserēre: imperative.
   436. cumulātam: participle with
quam, referring to the favor (**veniam**)
which she asks for. **morte:** abl. of time or
means. The meaning of Dido's statement
is obscure, perhaps intentionally so.
   438. fertque refertque (ad Aenēān).

flētibus *aut vōcēs ūllās* tractābilis *audit;*
440 *fāta* obstant placidās*que virī deus* obstruit aurēs.
Ac velut annōsō validam *cum* rōbore quercum
Alpīnī Boreae *nunc hinc nunc* flātibus illinc
ēruere *inter sē* certant; *it* strīdor, *et altae*
cōnsternunt *terram* concussō stīpite frondēs;
445 *ipsa* haeret scopulīs *et* quantum vertice *ad aurās*
aetheriās, *tantum* rādīce *in* Tartara *tendit:*
haud secus adsiduīs *hinc atque hinc* vōcibus hērōs
tunditur, *et magnō* persentit *pectore cūrās;*
mēns immōta *manet, lacrimae volvuntur* inānēs.

---

adsiduus, a, um constant, unceasing
aetherius, a, um high in the air, airy
Alpīnus, a, um Alpine, of the Alps
annōsus, a, um aged, old, full of years
auris, is *f.* ear
Boreās, ae *m.* (north) wind
certō (1) strive, rival, fight, vie
concutiō, ere, ussī, ussus shake, shatter
cōnsternō, ere, strāvī, strātus lay low, strew
ēruō, ere, uī, utus uproot, overthrow
flētus, ūs *m.* weeping, tears, tearful appeal, lament
flātus, ūs *m.* blast, wind, blowing
frōns, ondis *f.* leaf, foliage, frond
haereō, ēre, haesī, haesus cling (to) (+ *dat.*)
hērōs, ōis *m.* hero, mighty warrior
illinc *adv.* from that side, thence
immōtus, a, um unmoved, unshaken
inānis, e empty, idle, useless, vain

obstō, āre, stitī, status hinder, oppose
obstruō, ere, strūxī, strūctus block, stop
persentiō, īre, sēnsī, sēnsus perceive, feel
placidus, a, um calm, kind(ly), peaceful
quantum how much, how greatly, (as much) as
quercus, ūs *f.* oak
rādīx, īcis *f.* root
rōbur, oris *n.* oak, strength
scopulus, ī *m.* rock, cliff, crag
secus *adv.* otherwise, differently
stīpes, itis *m.* stock, trunk, stem
strīdor, ōris *m.* noise, creaking, roar
Tartara, ōrum *n.* the underworld, Hades
tractābilis, e manageable, gentle
tundō, ere, tutūdī, tū(n)sus beat, assail
validus, a, um strong, mighty, sturdy
velut(ī) as, just as
vertex, icis *m.* top, peak, head, summit

---

441. rōbore: abl. of quality; App. 330.
444. concussō stīpite: abl. abs.
445. ipsa (quercus).

446. in: *toward.*
447. hērōs (Aenēās).

BOOK 4.642–705

At trepida *et* coeptīs *immānibus* effera *Dīdō*
sanguineam *volvēns* aciem, maculīs*que* trementēs
interfūsa genās *et* pallida *morte futūrā,*
interiōra *domūs* inrumpit *līmina et altōs*   645
cōnscendit furibunda rogōs ēnsem*que* reclūdit
Dardanium, *nōn hōs quaesītum mūnus in ūsūs.*
Hīc, postquam Īliacās vestēs nōtum*que* cubīle
cōnspexit, paulum *lacrimīs et mente* morāta
incubuit*que* torō *dīxitque novissima* verba: 650

---

aciēs, ēī *f.* edge, line, eye(sight)
coeptum, ī *n.* undertaking, beginning
cōnscendō, ere, ī, ēnsus mount, climb
cōnspiciō, ere, spexī, spectus see, behold
cubīle, is *n.* couch, bed
Dardan(i)us, a, um Trojan, Dardanian
efferus, a, um wild, savage, mad
ēnsis, is *m.* sword, knife
furibundus, a, um wild, frenzied
gena, ae *f.* cheek
Iliacus, a, um Trojan, Ilian
incumbō, ere, cubuī, cubitus recline on (+
    dat.)
inrumpō, ere, rūpī, ruptus break into
interfundō, ere, fūdī, fūsus pour
    among, suffuse
interior, ius inner, interior

macula, ae *f.* spot, splotch, stain
moror, ārī, ātus delay, hesitate, hinder
nōtus, a, um (well) known, familiar
pallidus, a, um pale, wan, pallid
paulus (a) little, slightly, somewhat
postquam after (that), when
reclūdō, ere, sī, sus open, unsheathe
rogus, ī *m.* funeral pyre
sanguineus, a, um bloody, bloodshot
torus, ī *m.* (banqueting) couch, bed
tremō, ere, uī tremble, quiver, shake
trepidus, a, um trembling, excited
ūsus, ūs *m.* use, service, employment
verbum, ī *n.* word, speech, talk
vestis, is *f.* cloth(ing), garment, robe

642–705. Dido's passion reaches
its inevitable conclusion, and her
tormented soul departs from her body.

642. coeptīs: abl. of cause.

643. aciem (oculōrum).

644. genās: acc. of respect with
participle **interfūsa**; App. 311. **morte
futūrā:** abl. of cause with **pallida.**

645. interiōra līmina: of the inner
court, where the pyre had been erected.

647. quaesītum: Dido had apparently
asked Aeneas for the sword, and he had
given it to her as a keepsake.

648. Īliacās vestēs: more presents
from Aeneas; cf. 1.648 ff.

649. lacrimīs et mente: a virtual
HENDIADYS, *in tearful recollection;* abl. of
manner.

650. novissima: *last.*

"Dulcēs exuviae, *dum fāta deusque* sinēbat,
accipite hanc animam mēque hīs exsolvite *cūrīs.*
Vīxī *et quem dederat cursum Fortūna* perēgī,
et nunc magna meī sub terrās ībit imāgō.

655　　Urbem *praeclāram statuī, mea moenia vīdī,*
ulta virum poenās inimīcō *ā* frātre recēpī,
fēlīx, *heu* nimium fēlīx, *sī lītora* tantum
numquam Dardaniae tetigissent *nostra* carīnae."
Dīxit, et *ōs* impressa torō "Moriēmur inultae,

660　　*sed* moriāmur" ait. "*Sīc, sīc* iuvat *īre sub umbrās.*
Hauriat *hunc oculīs ignem* crūdēlis *ab altō*
Dardanus, *et nostrae sēcum ferat* ōmina *mortis.*"
Dīxerat, atque illam media inter tālia ferrō

---

altum, ī *n.* the deep (sea); heaven
carīna, ae *f.* keel; ship, boat
crūdēlis, e cruel, harsh, bloody
Dardan(i)us, a, um Trojan, Dardanian
dulcis, e sweet, dear, fond
exsolvō, ere, ī, solūtus loose(n), free
exuviae, ārum *f.* spoils, relics, mementos
fēlīx, īcis happy, fortunate, blessed
frāter, tris *m.* brother
gradus, ūs *m.* step, gait, pace, stride
hauriō, īre, hausī, haustus drain, drink (in)
imāgō, inis *f.* likeness, image, ghost, soul, form
imprimō, ere, pressī, pressus press (upon), imprint
inimīcus, a, um hostile, enemy, unfriendly

inultus, a, um unavenged, unpunished
iuvō, āre, iūvī, iūtus help, please
morior, ī, mortuus die, perish
nimium *adv.* too (much), excessively
numquam *adv.* never, at no time
ōmen, inis *n.* portent, omen, sign
peragō, ere, ēgī, āctus accomplish, finish
praeclārus, a, um very renowned
recipiō, ere, cēpī, ceptus receive, take
sinō, ere, sīvī, situs permit, allow
statuō, ere, uī, ūtus set (up), found
tangō, ere, tetigī, tāctus touch, reach
tantum *adv.* so much, only, merely
torus, ī *m.* (banqueting) couch, bed
ulcīscor, i, ultus avenge, punish
vīvō, ere, vīxī, vīctus live, be alive

---

651. dum fāta deusque sinēbat: Dido's thoughts momentarily wander, as she thinks of the happier times so recently experienced.
652. exsolvite (per mortem).
657. fēlīx (fuissem): implied conclusion of a past contrary-to-fact condition; App. 382.
659. ōs: obj. of the middle participle **impressa**; a farewell kiss.

660. Sīc, sīc: the repetition has been thought by some to suggest Dido's repeated stabs, though it need not be taken quite so literally.
661–62. Hauriat, ferat: jussive or volitive subjunctive; App. 254. **Dardanus** = Aeneas. **ōmina:** i.e., her death will bring him continual sorrow and misfortune.
663. ferrō: abl. of means or place where (*upon the sword*).

conlāpsam aspiciunt *comitēs*, ēnsem*que* cruōre
spūmantem sparsās*que manūs. It clāmor ad alta*   665
ātria: concussam bacchātur *Fāma per urbem.*
Lāmentīs gemitū*que et* fēmineō ululātū
tēcta fremunt, resonat *magnīs* plangōribus aethēr,
nōn aliter quam *sī* immissīs *ruat* hostibus *omnis*
Karthāgō *aut antīqua* Tyros, *flammaeque furentēs*   670
culmina *perque* hominum *volvantur perque deōrum.*
Audiit exanimis trepidō*que* exterrita *cursū*
unguibus *ōra* soror foedāns *et pectora* pugnīs
per mediōs ruit, ac morientem *nōmine* clāmat:
"*Hoc illud,* germāna, *fuit? Mē* fraude *petēbās?*   675
Hoc rogus iste *mihi, hoc ignēs āraeque parābant?*

---

aethēr, eris *m.* upper air, sky, ether
aliter *adv.* otherwise, differently
a(d)spiciō, ere, spexī, spectus see, behold
ātrium, ī *n.* hall, court, atrium
bacchor, ārī, ātus rave, rush wildly
clāmō (1) shriek, cry (out), call (on)
concutiō, ere, cussī, cussus shake, shatter
conlābor, ī, lāpsus fall in a heap, faint
cruor, ōris *m.* blood, gore
culmen, inis *n.* roof, peak, summit, top
ēnsis, is *m.* sword, knife
exanimis, e breathless, lifeless
exterreō, ēre, uī, itus terrify, frighten
fēmineus, a, um feminine, of women
foedō (1) pollute, defile, disfigure
fraus, fraudis *f.* deceit, guile, fraud
fremō, ere, uī, itus shout, roar, groan
gemitus, ūs *m.* groan, roar, lament
germāna, ae *f.* sister
homō, inis *m. (f.)* man, human, mortal

hostis, is *m. (f.)* enemy, foe, stranger
immittō, ere, mīsī, missus let in, send in
iste, ta, tud that (of yours)
Karthāgō, inis *f.* city of North Africa
lāmenta, ōrum *n.* lamentation, shriek
morior, ī, mortuus die, perish
plangor, ōris *m.* wailing, beating (of
  breast)
pugnus, ī *m.* fist
quam *adv.* how, than, as
resonō (1) (re)sound, roar
rogus, ī *m.* funeral pyre
soror, ōris *f.* sister
spargō, ere, rsī, rsus scatter, sprinkle
spūmō (1) foam, froth, spray
trepidus, a, um trembling, excited
Tyrus (os), ī *f.* city of Phoenicia,
  birthplace of Dido
ululātus, ūs *m.* wail, shriek, howl, shout
unguis, is *m.* nail, claw

---

667. fēmineō ulutātū: the HIATUS between
the two words emphasizes the eerie sound
made by the women.
  669. quam sī ruat: the protasis of a
potential (future less vivid) condition
used as a clause of comparison; App. 383.
  669–71. The SIMILE recalls the fall of Troy
depicted in Book 2.
  670. Tyros: nom. sing., a Greek form;
App. 67.

671: culmina: obj. (twice) of **per**.
hominum, deōrum: i.e., homes of the
residents and temples of the gods.
  672. cursū: abl. of manner.
  673. ōra foedāns et pectora: as an
expression of grief.
  675–76. Hoc, hoc: pronounce **hocc**
(from the original form, **hocce**), making a
long syllable. **Hoc (fuit) illud (quod
parābās):** *was this* (your own death) *that
which you were planning?*

Quid prīmum dēserta querar? Comitemne sorōrem
sprēvistī moriēns? Eadem mē ad fāta vocāssēs:
īdem ambās ferrō dolor atque eadem hōra tulisset.

680　　Hīs etiam strūxī manibus patriōsque vocāvī
vōce deōs, sīc tē ut positā, crūdēlis, abessem?
Exstīnxtī tē mēque, soror, populumque patrēsque
Sīdoniōs urbemque tuam. Date, vulnera lymphīs
abluam et, extrēmus sī quis super hālitus errat,

685　　ōre legam." Sīc fāta gradūs ēvāserat altōs,
sēmianimemque sinū germānam amplexa fovēbat
cum gemitū atque ātrōs siccābat veste cruōrēs.
Illa gravēs oculōs cōnāta attollere rūrsus

---

abluō, ere, uī, ūtus wash (off)
absum, esse, āfuī be away, be distant
ambō, ae, ō both
amplector, ī, plexus embrace, enfold
attollō, ere lift, rear, raise
cōnor, ārī, ātus attempt, try, endeavor
crūdēlis, e cruel, bloody, hardhearted
cruor, ōris m. blood, gore
dēserō, ere, uī, rtus desert, forsake
dolor, ōris m. grief, pain, passion, anger
etiam adv. also, even
ēvādō, ere, sī, sus go forth (from), pass over
exstinguō, ere, īnxī, īnctus blot out, destroy, extinguish
extrēmus, a, um final, last, extreme
foveō, ēre, fōvī, fōtus fondle, cherish
gemitus, ūs m. groan, roar, lament
germāna, ae f. sister
gradus, ūs m. step, gait, pace, stride

gravis, e heavy, grievous, serious
hālitus, ūs m. breath, exhalation
hōra, ae f. hour, season, time
legō, ere, lēgī, lēctus choose, gather, catch
lympha, ae f. water
morior, ī, mortuus die, perish
populus, ī m. people, nation
queror, ī, questus complain, (be)wail
rūrsus, um adv. again, anew, back(ward)
sēmianimis, e half-dead, dying
siccō (1) dry, stanch
Sīdonius, a, um Sidonian, of Sidon, a city of Phoenicia
sinus, ūs m. fold; bosom; bay; hollow
soror, ōris f. sister
spernō, ere, sprēvī, sprētus scorn, reject
struō, ere, strūxī, strūctus build, plan
vestis, is f. cloth(ing), garment, robe
vulnus, eris n. wound, deadly blow

---

677. Quid querar: deliberative question; App. 348.

678–79. vocā(vi)ssēs, tulisset: optative subjunctive, expressing a wish; App. 253.

680. strūxī (tuum rogum).

681. tē positā: abl. abs. ut abessem: purpose; App. 359.

682. Exstīnx(is)tī.

683. Dāte: Anna turns to Dido's attendants to request help in preparing the corpse.

684. (ut) abluam: purpose clause. super: adv.

685. ōre legam: it was a Roman custom to catch with a kiss the last breath of a dying relative or friend. fāta: perf. participle of deponent verb for, fārī; modifies the subject of the sentence, Anna. gradūs: of the funeral pyre.

686. sēmianimem: treat the first -i- as a consonant, and pronounce sēmyanimēmque here.

dēficit; īnfixum strīdit *sub pectore* vulnus.
Ter *sēsē* attollēns cubitō*que* adnixa levāvit,   690
ter revolūta torō *est oculīsque errantibus altō*
quaesīvit caelō lūcem ingemuit*que* repertā.
  Tum Iūnō omnipotēns *longum* miserāta dolōrem
difficilēs*que* obitūs Īrim dēmīsit Olympō
quae luctantem *animam* nexōs*que* resolveret artūs.   695
Nam quia *nec fātō* meritā *nec morte* perībat,
sed misera ante diem subitō*que* accēnsa furōre,
nōndum *illī* flāvum Prōserpina vertice crīnem
abstulerat Stygiō*que caput* damnāverat Orco.

---

accendō, ere, ī, ēnsus inflame, burn
adnītor, ī, sus (nixus) lean on, struggle
artus, ūs *m.* joint, limb, member
attollō, ere lift, rear, raise
auferō, ferre, abstulī, ablātus take away
crīnis, is *m.* hair, locks, tresses
cubitum, ī *n.* elbow, arm
damnō (1) condemn, sentence, doom, devote
dēficiō, ere, fēcī, fectus fail, faint
dēmittō, ere, mīsī, missus send down, let go, drop, lower
difficilis, e difficult, hard, painful
dolor, ōris *m.* grief, pain, passion, anger
flāvus, a, um yellow, tawny, blond
furor, ōris *m.* madness, frenzy, passion
īnfīgō, ere, xī, xus fix, pierce, fasten
ingemō, ere, uī groan, roar, lament
Īris, (id)is *f.* goddess of the rainbow, messenger of Juno
levō (1) lift, lighten, raise, relieve
luctor, ārī, ātus struggle, wrestle
mereō, ēre, uī, itus deserve, earn, merit
miseror, ārī, ātus pity, commiserate

nectō, ere, nexuī, nexus weave, fasten, bind
nōndum *adv.* not yet
obitus, ūs *m.* death, downfall, ruin
Olympus, ī *m.* high Greek mountain, home of the gods; heaven
omnipotēns, entis almighty, omnipotent
Orcus, ī *m.* (god of) the lower world, Hades
pereō, īre, iī (īvī), itus perish, die
Prōserpina, ae *f.* Pluto's queen, goddess of the lower world
quia because
reperiō, īre, repperī, repertus find
resolvō, ere, ī, solūtus loose(n), free, pay
revolvō, ere, ī, volūtus roll over, revolve
strīd(e)ō, ēre, ī hiss, gurgle, rustle
Stygius, a, um Stygian, of the Styx, a river in Hades
subitus, a, um sudden, unexpected
ter three times
torus, ī *m.* (banqueting, funeral) couch, bed
vertex, icis *m.* top, peak, head, summit
vulnus, eris *n.* wound, deadly blow

---

689. strīdit: from the gurgling blood.
  690. cubitō: abl. of means with **adnītor.**
    691. (in) torō.
    692. repertā (lūce): abl. abs.
    695. nexōs (animae). quae resolveret: rel. clause of purpose; App. 388. For the thought see the note on 385.

  696. fātō: natural death was supposed to be occasioned by a decree of the gods.
  meritā nec morte: note the postponement of the conjunction.
    698. illī: dat. of reference. **Prōserpina:** she was supposed to cut a lock from the head of the dying, as a sort of offering to the gods of the lower world.

700   Ergō Īris croceīs *per caelum* rōscida pennīs
        mīlle *trahēns* variōs adversō sōle colōrēs
        dēvolat *et* suprā *caput* astitit. *"Hunc ego* Dītī
        sacrum iussa ferō tēque istō *corpore* solvō":
        Sīc ait et dextrā crīnem secat, *omnis et* ūnā
705   dīlāpsus calor *atque in ventōs vīta* recessit.

---

adversus, a, um opposite, facing
a(d)stō, āre, stitī stand (ready, by)
calor, ōris *m.* heat, warmth, glow
crīnis, is *m.* hair, locks, tresses
croceus, a, um yellow, saffron, ruddy
dēvolō (1) fly down
dīlābor, ī, lāpsus glide away, depart
Dīs, Dītis *m.* Pluto, god of the lower world
ergō *adv.* therefore, then, consequently
Īris, (id)is *f.* goddess of the rainbow,
    messenger of Juno
iste, ta, tud that (of yours)

mīlle; *pl.* **mīlia, ium** *n.* thousand
penna, ae *f.* wing, feather
recēdō, ere, cessī, cessus depart,
    withdraw
rōscidus, a, um dewy
secō, āre, uī, ctus cut, cleave, slice
sōl, sōlis *m.* sun; day
solvō, ere, ī, solūtus loose(n), free, pay
suprā above, over (+ *acc.*)
ūnā *adv.* together, at the same time
varius, a, um varied, different, diverse

---

701. The rainbow. **adversō sōle:** abl.
abls. denoting cause.
702-3. Hunc (crīnem). ego iussa (ā
Iūnōne). istō = tuō, as often.

705. in ventōs: the soul was identified
with the breath, **anima, spīritus** (cf. the
English word *spirit*) and at death vanished
into the air.

SELECTIONS FROM
BOOK 6

Funeris heu tibi causa fui? (6.458)

Illustration for Book 6
"Was I the cause?" by Thom Kapheim

BOOK 6.1–211

Sīc fātur lacrimāns, *classīque* immittit habēnās
et tandem Euboīcīs Cūmārum adlābitur *ōrīs.*
Obvertunt *pelagō* prōrās; *tum* dente tenācī
ancora fundābat *nāvēs et lītora* curvae
praetexunt *puppēs.* Iuvenum *manus* ēmicat *ardēns*   5
lītus in Hesperium; *quaerit pars* sēmina *flammae*
abstrūsa *in* vēnīs silicis, *pars* dēnsa ferārum
tēcta rapit *silvās* inventa*que* flūmina mōnstrat.

ābstrūdō, ere, sī, sus hide (away)
adlābor, ī, lāpsus glide to, approach
(+ *dat.*)
ancora, ae *f.* anchor
Cūmae, ārum *f.* city on the bay of
Naples, founded by settlers from
Chalcis, a city of Euboea
curvus, a, um winding, rounded, bent
dēns, dentis *m.* tooth; fluke (technical
term for triangular point of an anchor)
dēnsus, a, um thick, crowded, dense
ēmicō, āre, uī, ātus flash forth, dart out
Euboīcus, a, um Euboean, of Euboea, a
large island off the eastern coast of
Greece
fera, ae *f.* wild beast
flūmen, inis *n.* river, stream, flood
fundō (1) found, establish, make fast

habēna, ae *f.* rein, curb, check
Hesperius, a, um western, Italian
immittō, ere, mīsī, missus send in (to),
loose(n), give freely
inveniō, īre, vēnī, ventus find, come
upon
iuvenis, is *m.* (*f.*) youth, young person
lacrimō (1) weep, shed tears, lament
mōnstrō (1) point out, show, teach,
guide
obvertō, ere, ī, rsus turn to (+ *dat.*)
praetexō, ere, uī, xtus fringe, cloak
prōra, ae *f.* prow
rapiō, ere, uī, ptus snatch (up), take
sēmen, inis *n.* seed, germ, element
silex, icis *m.* (*f.*) flint, rock, crag
tenāx, ācis gripping, tenacious
vēna, ae *f.* vein

1–41. Aeneas lands at Cumae and
visits the temple of Apollo founded
by Daedalus, the doors of which are
decorated with scenes of great
mythical significance.

1. Sīc fātur (Aenēās): refers to the
lament of Aeneas over Palinurus, who fell
overboard and was drowned, as told in

the latter part of Book 5. **habēnās:** *reins,*
as though the ships were so many fiery
horses surging at the bit.

3. prōrās: ships were anchored with
their prows turned seaward.

6. sēmina: *sparks,* i.e., the "seeds"
from which fires grow, which seemed to
be hidden in the flint till struck out by the
steel.

8. silvās: in apposition with **tēcta.**

At pius Aenēās arcēs quibus altus Apollō
10   praesidet horrendae*que procul* sēcrēta Sibyllae,
    antrum *immāne, petit, magnam cui mentem animumque*
    Dēlius īnspīrat *vātēs* aperit*que* futūra.
    Iam subeunt Triviae lūcōs *atque* aurea *tēcta.*
    Daedalus, *ut fāma est, fugiēns* Mīnōia *rēgna*
15   praepetibus pennīs ausus *sē* crēdere *caelō*

---

antrum, ī *n.* cave, cavern, grotto
aperiō, īre, uī, ertus open, disclose,
    reveal
Apollō, inis *m.* god of light, music, and
    prophecy
audeō, ēre, ausus sum dare, venture
aureus, a, um gold(en), of gold
crēdō, ere, didī, ditus believe, trust
    (+ *dat.*)
Daedalus, ī *m.* famous Greek artisan,
    father of Icarus and builder of the
    labyrinth for King Minos in Crete;
    inventor of the first wings by means of
    which he and Icarus escaped from Crete
Dēlius, a, um Delian, of Delos, birth-
    place of Apollo

futūrum, ī *n.* the future, what is to be
horrendus, a, um dreadful, dire; revered
īnspīrō (1) breathe into, inspire, blow
    into
lūcus, ī *m.* (sacred) grove, wood
Mīnōius, a, um Minoan, of Minos, king
    of Crete
penna, ae *f.* wing, feather
praepes, etis swift, flying
praesideō, ēre, sēdī, sessus rule, protect
    (+ *dat.*)
sēcrētum, ī *n.* secret (place, sanctuary)
Sibylla, ae *f.* the Sibyl, an ancient Italian
    prophetess
Trivia, ae *f.* Hecate, goddess of the lower
    world

---

9. altus: referring to the lofty situation of the temple, which stood on the top of a high hill and was connected in some way with the cave of the Sibyl.

10. procul (ā portū).

12. Dēlius vātēs: Apollo, born on the island of Delos, and giver of oracles. **īnspīrat:** take both metaphorically (*inspires*) and literally (*breathes into*); it was believed that Apollo delived oracles through his priestesses by entering and taking control of their bodies and minds.

13. subeunt (Aenēās et sociī). **Triviae lūcōs:** the grove was sacred to Hecate (Trivia), since it stood near the entrance to the lower world.

14. Daedalus: the most famous mythical artisan of antiquity. With his son, Icarus, he had emigrated to Crete, where Pasiphaē, queen and wife of Minos, had been driven by Neptune to desire a beautiful bull. Daedalus assisted her to gratify her strange passion, and from this union was born the Minotaur, a savage monster, half-man and half-bull. Daedalus was then compelled by Minos to build the labyrinth, a maze within whose winding passages the Minotaur might be confined. Finally Daedalus contrived wings for himself and his son Icarus and thus escaped from Crete. During their flight, Icarus flew too close to the sun, which melted the waxen fastenings of his wings and so caused him to fall into the sea and drown. After the death of Icarus, Daedalus continued his flight to Cumae, where he erected a temple to Apollo, to whom he dedicated his wings, and where he made some beautiful carved doors for the temple. On these doors he engraved the scenes described in 20–30. **ut fāma est:** with this phrase Vergil informs his readers that he is familiar with earlier versions of this tale, and he expects his readers to know it, too.

15. pennīs: abl. of means.

īnsuētum *per* iter gelidās ēnāvit *ad* Arctōs,
Chalcidicā*que* levis *tandem super* astitit *arce.*
Redditus *hīs prīmum terrīs tibi,* Phoebe, sacrāvit
rēmigium ālārum *posuitque immānia* templa.
In foribus lētum Androgeō; *tum* pendere *poenās*   20
Cecropidae *iussī* (*miserum!*) septēna quotannīs
corpora nātōrum; stat ductīs sortibus urna.

āla, ae *f.* wing

Androgeōs (ūs), eō (eī) *m.* son of Minos, king of Crete, for whose murder the Athenians were compelled annually to choose by lot seven youths and seven maidens, who were sent to Crete and fed to the Minotaur

Arctos (us), ī *f.* the Bear, a northern constellation

a(d)stō, āre, stitī stand (by, near)

Cecropidēs, ae *m.* descendant of Cecrops, Athenian; *nom. pl.* **Cecropidae**

Chalcidicus, a, um Chalcidian, of Chalcis, a city of Euboea, from which Cumae was founded

ēnō (1) swim out, fly forth, float

foris, is *f.* door, gate, entrance

gelidus, a, um cold, chilly, icy

īnsuētus, a, um unaccustomed, unused

iter, itineris *n.* way, road, journey

lētum, ī *n.* death, destruction, ruin

levis, e light, swift, nimble, unsubstantial

pendō, ere, pependī, pēnsus weigh out, pay

Phoebus, ī *m.* Apollo, god of light, music, and prophecy

quotannīs *adv.* annually, yearly

reddō, ere, didī, ditus return, restore

rēmigium, (i)ī *n.* oarage, rowing equipment

sacrō (1) consecrate, dedicate, hallow

septēnus, a, um seven (each), by sevens

sors, rtis *f.* lot, destiny, portion, oracle

templum, ī *n.* temple, shrine, sanctuary

urna, ae *f.* urn, jar (used in drawing lots)

---

16. īnsuētum iter: the air, *unused* or *unusual* because Daedalus was the first human to fly.

19. rēmigium ālārum: an unusual mixing of metaphors for an unusual journey—Daedalus' wings are compared to oars, since the movement of oars and wings is similar; hitherto, however, humans had employed only oars.

20-30. An extended description (ECPHRASIS) of the scenes engraved by Daedalus on the temple doors at Cumae. On one side, Aeneas and his men see the: (1) death of Androgeos; and (2) drawing of lots to see who will be sent as victims of the Minotaur. On the other side are depicted: (3) Pasiphae and the Minotaur; (4) the labyrinth (perhaps with Ariadne and Theseus: see below). **lētum (est).**

20. Androgeō: gen., a Greek form; App. 67. The Athenians had murdered

him and as a punishment had been compelled by Minos to send annually seven youths and seven maidens as tribute to Crete, where they were sent into the labyrinth as offerings to the Minotaur. The Minotaur was finally killed by Theseus, an Athenian prince, who had been sent as one of the annual victims. He was assisted by Ariadne, daughter of Minos, who had fallen in love with him and had given him a thread with which to guide his steps and thus to find his way out of the labyrinth with its countless winding passages.

21. Cecropidae (sunt). miserum: acc. of exclamation; App. 318.

22. ductīs sortibus: abl. abs. **stat urna:** the scene represents the moment when the lots have just been drawn from the urn at Athens, to see who should be sent as victims to the Minotaur.

Contrā ēlāta *marī* respondet Cnōsia *tellūs:*
hīc crūdēlis *amor* taurī supposta*que* fūrtō
25   Pāsiphaē mixtum*que genus* prōlēs*que* biformis
Mīnōtaurus inest, Veneris monimenta nefandae,
hīc labor ille domūs et inextrīcābilis error;
magnum rēgīnae sed enim miserātus *amōrem*
Daedalus *ipse* dolōs *tēctī* ambāgēs*que* resolvit,

---

ambāgēs, is *f.* winding (passage)
biformis, e two-formed, double-shaped
Cnōs(s)ius, a, um Cnossian, of Cnossos, a city in Crete
contrā *adv.* opposite, facing
crūdēlis, e cruel, pitiless, bloody
Daedalus, ī *m.* famous Greek artisan, father of Icarus and builder of the labyrinth for King Minos in Crete; inventor of the first wings by means of which he and Icarus escaped from Crete
dolus, ī *m.* deceit, fraud, trick, scheme
effero, ferre, extulī, ēlātus lift (up), raise
enim *adv.* for, indeed, truly
error, errōris *m.* wandering, error
fūrtum, ī *n.* theft, stealth, fraud
inextrīcābilis, e inextricable, insoluble
īnsum, esse, fuī be in, be present

Mīnōtaurus, ī *m.* Cretan monster, half bull and half man, the result of queen Pasiphaë's love for the bull of Minos
misceō, ēre, uī, mixtus mix, mingle
miseror, ārī, ātus pity, commiserate
monimentum (monumentum), ī *n.* reminder, memorial
nefandus, a, um unspeakable, unutterable
Pāsiphaē, ēs *f.* wife of Minos, king of Crete, who fell in love with a beautiful bull and was assisted by Daedalus to gratify her passion
prōlēs, is *f.* progeny, offspring
resolvō, ere, ī, solūtus loose(n), unravel
respondeō, ēre, ī, ōnsus answer, correspond
suppōnō, ere, posuī, pos(i)tus place under, subject to
taurus, ī *m.* bull, ox, bullock
Venus, eris *f.* (goddess of) love

---

23. contrā: *on the opposite side,* i.e., the other door. **marī:** abl. of separation or place where.

24. hīc: i.e., on the door just mentioned. **amor taurī:** the love (i.e., of Pasiphaë) for the bull; **taurī** is obj. gen.; App. 284.

24–26. It is unclear whether we are to imagine one scene here, or several; all the phrases are ultimately linked by the collective **monimenta.**

27. hīc: i.e., again on the door just mentioned. **labor ille domūs:** we would more likely say, "that (famous) house, product of great labor"; but by putting **labor** in the nom., Vergil emphasizes the effort and achievement of Daedalus in building the dreadful dwelling. The word

labor also suggests the struggle of those trapped within. **domūs:** gen. of apposition; App. 281. **error:** the word is ambiguous, describing both the *wandering* involved in the attempt to escape from the labyrinth and the *mistake* of Pasiphaë in fulfilling her desire.

28. rēgīnae: again, ambiguous. At first the word would appear to refer to Pasiphaë, especially in combination with the reference to **amor** in the line; but the title could also be applied to Ariadne, daughter of Minos and Pasiphaë (and so, half-sister of the Minotaur), whose love for the Athenian Theseus caused her to betray her family and help Theseus to escape from the labyrinth.

caeca regēns fīlō vestīgia. *Tū* quoque *magnam*   30
partem opere *in tantō*, sineret dolor, Īcare, *habērēs*.
Bis cōnātus *erat cāsūs* effingere *in aurō*,
bis *patriae* cecidēre *manūs*. Quīn prōtinus *omnia*
perlegerent *oculīs*, nī *iam* praemissus Achātēs
adforet atque ūnā Phoebī Triviae*que* sacerdōs,   35
Dēiphobē Glaucī, *fātur quae tālia rēgī*:
"*Nōn hoc* ista *sibī tempus* spectācula poscit;

Achātēs, is *m.* faithful comrade of Aeneas
bis twice
cadō, ere, cecidī, cāsus fall, fail, sink, die
caecus, a, um blind, dark, hidden
cōnor, ārī, ātus attempt, try, endeavor
Dēiphobē, ēs *f.* prophetess and priestess of Apollo and Hecate
dolor, ōris *m.* grief, pain, passion, anger
fīlum, ī *n.* thread, cord, clue
Glaucus, ī *m.* sea-god possessing prophetic powers, father of Deiphobe, the Cumaean Sibyl
Īcarus, ī *m.* son of Daedalus, who in his flight with his father from Crete flew too near the sun, melted his wings, and fell into the sea, where he was drowned
iste, ta, tud that (of yours)
nisi, nī if not, unless
opus, eris *n.* work (of art); toil, labor

perlegō, ere, lēgī, lēctus survey, examine
Phoebus, ī *m.* Apollo, god of light, music, and prophecy
poscō, ere, poposcī demand, seek, ask
praemittō, ere, mīsī, missus send forward
prōtinus *adv.* continuously, at once
quīn but that, in fact, why not
quoque *adv.* also, even, too, likewise
regō, ere, rēxī, rēctus rule, direct, guide
sacerdōs, ōtis *m. (f.)* priest(ess)
sinō, ere, sīvī, situs permit, allow
spectāculum, i *n.* sight, spectacle
Trivia, ae *f.* Hecate, goddess of the lower world
ūnā *adv.* together, at the same time
vestīgium, (i)ī *n.* step, footstep, track, trace

---

30. caeca vestīgia: Theseus' footsteps, *blind* insofar as, without Ariadne's help, Theseus would not have been able to see the way out of the labyrinth.

31. sineret: verb in the protasis of a contrary-to-fact condition, although *if* (**sī**) has been omitted. **habērēs:** verb in the apodosis of a contrary-to-fact condition. **Īcare:** the voc. is unexpected and strongly emotional—Vergil encourages his readers to address Icarus in their imaginations just as Daedalus must have done in lamenting his son's death.

32. cāsūs: many meanings of the noun are relevant here: *misfortune, falling, loss, death*.

33. cecidēre: Daedalus' hands follow through their movement the fate of Icarus.

34. perlegerent: verb in the apodosis of a contrary-to-fact condition. Aeneas and his companions are "reading" (and interpreting) the images on the door much as Vergil's readers do. **nī:** introduces the protasis of a contrary-to-fact condition.

35. adforet = adesset.

35–36. sacerdōs, Dēiphobē Glaucī: the Sibyl, priestess of Apollo. Understand **fīlia** with **Glaucī**. Glaucus was a sea-god with prophetic powers. **rēgī (Aenēae).**

36. fātur quae: note the postponement of the rel. pronoun.

37. hoc: pronounce **hocc**, making a long syllable. **ista spectācula:** *those sights on which you are gazing.*

nunc grege *dē* intāctō septem mactāre iuvencōs
praestiterit, totidem lēctās *ex* mōre bidentēs."
40   *Tālibus* adfāta *Aenēān* (*nec sacra* morantur
iussa virī) *Teucrōs vocat alta in* templa sacerdōs.

---

adfor, ārī, ātus address, speak to
bidēns, entis *f.* sheep (with two front
  teeth)
grex, gregis *m.* herd, flock
intāctus, a, um untouched, unbroken
iuvencus, ī *m.* bullock, ox
legō, ere, lēgī, lēctus choose, gather
mactō (1) sacrifice, slaughter, kill; honor
  through sacrifice

moror, ārī, ātus delay, tarry, hinder
mōs, mōris *m.* custom, ritual, manner
praestō, āre, stitī, status (stitus) excel,
  be better
sacerdōs, ōtis *m.* (*f.*) priest(ess)
septem seven
templum, ī *n.* temple, sanctuary, sacred
  space
totidem as many, so many

---

38. intāctō: not yet broken and tamed
to the yoke.

39. praestiterit: potential subjunctive
(*it would be better*); App. 252, or fut. perf.
ind. (*it will have been better*, i.e., once it
has been done).

40–41. sacra: used as a substantive,
sacrifices or *rituals*, modified by **iussa**,
and dir. obj. of **morantur**; the subject is **virī**.

41. templa: the English word *temple* is
much narrower in meaning than the Latin

word **templum.** Originally, a **templum**
was simply a sacred space, located
virtually anywhere (on the ground, in the
sky); over time the word came to
designate as well any buildings or other
artificial structures that might be built on
or enclosing a sacred space. Here, as the
next line shows, the **templa** entered by
the Sibyl and the Trojans is an artificial
cave cut into the side of a hill.

The cave of the Sibyl at Cumae.
Photograph by Barbara Weiden Boyd.

Excīsum Euboīcae latus *ingēns* rūpis *in* antrum,
quō lātī dūcunt aditūs centum, ōstia centum,
unde *ruunt* totidem *vōcēs,* respōnsa Sibyllae.
Ventum erat ad līmen, cum virgō "Poscere *fāta*　　　45
tempus" ait; "deus ecce *deus!" Cui tālia fantī*
ante forēs subitō *nōn* vultus, *nōn* color *ūnus,*
nōn cōmptae *mānsēre* comae; *sed pectus* anhēlum,
et rabiē fera corda tument, *maiorque vidērī*
nec mortāle sonāns, adflāta *est nūmine* quandō　　　50

---

adflō (1) breathe upon, blow upon, inspire
aditus, ūs *m.* approach, entrance
anhēlus, a, um panting, gasping
antrum, ī *n.* cave, cavern, grotto
centum hundred
color, ōris *m.* color, hue, tint
cōma, ae *f.* hair, locks, tresses
cōmō, ere, mpsī, mptus arrange
　(properly)
cor, rdis *n.* heart, spirit, feelings, soul
ecce see! look! behold!
Euboīcus, a, um Euboean, of Euboea, a
　large island off the eastern coast of
　Greece from which Cumae was settled
excīdō, ere, ī, sus cut, hew (out)
ferus, a, um wild, fierce, untamed
foris, is *f.* door, gate, entrance

lātus, a, um broad, wide, spacious
latus, eris *n.* side, flank
mortālis, e mortal, human, earthly
ōstium, (i)ī *n.* mouth, entrance; harbor
poscō, ere, poposcī demand, seek, ask
quandō when, since, because
rabiēs, ēī *f.* rage, fury, frenzy
respōnsum, ī *n.* answer, reply, response
rūpēs, is *f.* rock, cliff, crag
Sibylla, ae *f.* ancient Italian prophetess
sonō, āre, uī, itus (re)sound, roar
subitō *adv.* suddenly, unexpectedly
totidem as many, so many
tumeō, ēre, uī swell, be swollen
unde from where, from which source
virgō, inis *f.* unmarried girl, maiden
vultus, ūs *m.* countenance, face, aspect

42–97. Aeneas prays to Apollo,
and promises the god a new temple
in return for his help. Inspired by
Apollo, the Sibyl responds that the
sufferings of Aeneas and his men are
not yet quite over.

42. Euboīcae: see 6.2 and vocabulary.

45. Ventum erat (ā Teucrīs et Sibyllā):
i.e., "they had come." With the impersonal
passive, Vergil emphasizes the action itself
rather than the actors. **līmen (antrī).**

45–46. "Poscere fāta tempus (est)": *it
is time to ask for the oracles.* **"deus ecce
deus!":** the Sibyl apparently enters an
altered state under Apollo's influence and
sees a vision of the god approaching.

47–50. The series of changes in the
Sibyl's appearance communicates the
divine presence to her observers. They
cannot see Apollo, but they can see his
influence on the Sibyl.

47. nōn vultus (mānsit): *her countenance changed.* **ūnus = īdem,** as often.

48. comae: under the influence of the
god, her hair streams forth in wild
disorder. **pectus (est) anhēlum.**

49. maior (est) vidērī: *she is larger to
look upon* = **maior vīsa est.** One of the
effects of her inspiration is to make her
appear larger—it is almost as if she is
swollen from within by Apollo.

50. mortāle: cognate acc.; App. 313.
nec mortāle sonāns (est): *her voice does
not sound human.* **quandō:** note the
postposition of the conjunction.

iam propiōre *deī.* "Cessās *in* vōta precēs*que,*
Trōs" *ait "Aenēā?* Cessās? *Neque* enim *ante* dehīscent
attonitae *magna ōra domūs." Et tālia fāta*
conticuit. Gelidus *Teucrīs per* dūra cucurrit

55   ossa tremor, *funditque* precēs *rēx pectore ab īmō:*
"Phoebe, gravēs *Troiae* semper miserāte *labōrēs,*
Dardana *quī* Paridis dērēxtī *tēla manūsque*
corpus in Aeacidae, *magnās* obeuntia *terrās*
tot *maria* intrāvī duce *tē* penitus*que* repostās

60   Massȳlum *gentēs* praetenta*que* Syrtibus *arva:*
iam tandem Ītaliae fugientis prendimus *ōrās.*

Aeacidēs, ae *m.* descendant of Aeacus,
   Achilles
attonitus, a, um thunderstruck, amazed
cessō (1) cease, pause, delay, hesitate
conticēsco, ere, ticuī become silent, hush
currō, ere, cucurrī, cursus run
Dardanus, a, um Trojan, Dardanian
dehīscō, ere, hīvī yawn, gape, open (up)
dīrigō, ere, rēxi, rēctus direct, guide
dūrus, a, um hard(y), harsh, stern
dux, ducis *m.* leader, guide, chief
enim *adv.* for, indeed, truly
gelidus, a, um cold, chilly, icy
gravis, e heavy, grievous, serious
intrō (1) enter, penetrate
Massȳlī, (ōr)um *m.* tribe of North Africa
miseror, ārī, ātus pity, commiserate
obeō, īre, iī (īvī), itus approach,
   traverse, skirt

os, ossis *n.* bone
Paris, idis (os) *m.* Trojan prince, took
   Helen from Menelaus and thus
   provoked the Trojan war
penitus *adv.* deep(ly), (from) within
Phoebus, ī *m.* Apollo, god of light,
   music, and prophecy
praetendō, ere, ī stretch before, extend
pre(he)ndō, ere, ī, nsus seize, grasp
prex, precis *f.* prayer, entreaty
propior, ius nearer, closer
repos(i)tus, a, um secluded, remote
semper *adv.* always, (for)ever
Syrtis, is *f.* quicksands off the northern
   coast of Africa
tot so many
tremor, ōris *m.* trembling, shudder
Trōs, Trōis *m.* Trojan
vōtum, ī *n.* vow, prayer, votive offering

51–52. Cessās (īre)? Cessās? The
repetition of the verb is a direct challenge
to Aeneas.
   52. Neque ante (quam in vōta eās).
   53. attonitae domūs: i.e., the cave
itself is awestruck by the presence of the
god; the resulting PATHETIC FALLACY
attributes emotion to the inanimate but
eerie dwelling of the Sibyl. **fāta:** from **fōr.**
   55. rēx (Aeneas).
   56. Phoebe miserāte: voc.
   57. dērēx(is)tī: Apollo as god of
archery had directed the fatal arrow of

Paris, which struck Achilles in his heel,
his only vulnerable spot, and killed him.
   60. Syrtibus: dat. with compound
praetenta.
   61. Ītaliae fugientis ōrās: it is unclear
whether the pres. act. participle in fact is
gen. sing. and modifies **Ītaliae** (*the shores
of fleeing Italy*), or is acc. pl. (i.e., =
fugientēs) modifying **ōrās** (*the fleeing
shores of Italy*). The former would be an
interesting example of ENALLAGE (transferred epithet); the latter, while almost as
vivid, is less exceptional.

Hāc Troiāna tenus *fuerit fortūna secūta;*
vōs quoque Pergameae *iam* fās *est* parcere *gentī,*
dīque deaeque omnēs, quibus obstitit Īlium *et ingēns*
glōria Dardaniae. *Tūque, ō* sānctissima *vātēs,*   65
praescia ventūrī, *dā (nōn* indēbita poscō
rēgna meīs fātīs) Latiō cōnsīdere *Teucrōs*
errantēsque deōs agitāta*que nūmina Troiae.*
Tum Phoebō *et* Triviae solidō *dē* marmore templum
īnstituam fēstōs*que diēs dē nōmine* Phoebī.   70
Tē quoque *magna manent rēgnīs* penetrālia *nostrīs:*

---

agitō (1) drive, harass, toss, agitate
cōnsīdō, ere, sēdī, sessus sit (down);
   settle
Dardania, ae *f.* Troy, citadel of Dardanus
fās *n. indecl.* right, justice, divine will
fēstus, a, um festal, festival, pertaining to
   a holiday
glōria, ae *f.* glory, fame, reputation
hāc . . . tenus = hāctenus thus far, up
   until now
Īlium, (i)ī *n.* Troy, Ilium
indēbitus, a, um not due, not owed, undue
īnstituō, ere, uī, ūtus set up, ordain
Latium, (i)ī *n.* Latium, district of central
   Italy
marmor, oris *n.* marble
obstō, āre, stitī, status stand in the way,
   oppose (+ *dat.*)

parcō, ere, pepercī (parsī), parsus
   spare (+ *dat.*)
penetrālia, ium *n.* inner part, sanctuary
Pergameus, a, um Trojan
Phoebus, ī *m.* Apollo, god of light,
   music, and prophecy
poscō, ere, poposcī demand, seek, ask
praescius, a, um foreknowing, prescient
quoque *adv.* also, furthermore, too,
   likewise
sānctus, a, um holy, sacred, sainted
solidus, a, um solid, whole, firm
templum, ī *n.* temple, shrine, sanctuary
tenus *see* **hāc . . . tenus**
Trivia, ae *f.* Hecate, goddess of the lower
   world
Troiānus, a, um Trojan, of Troy
ventūrum, ī *n.* the future, what is to come

**62. hāctenus Troiāna fortūna (mē)
fuerit secūta:** *thus far, and thus far only
let Trojan misfortune have followed* (i.e.,
follow) *me.* **hāc . . . tenus:** TMESIS. **fuerit:**
volitive (jussive) subjunctive; App. 254.

66–67. ventūrī: more picturesque than
futūrī; gen. with **praescia. dā cōnsīdere:**
grant that the Trojans may settle; the inf.
with a verb of granting; App. 260. **(in)
Latiō.**

68. deōs: especially the Trojan penates.

69–70. Vergil here refers to the
magnificent temple to Apollo built by
Augustus on the Palatine, and to the **Lūdī
Apollinārēs,** a great Roman festival in
honor of Apollo. These games, established
during the 2d Punic War, had fallen by

the wayside in Vergil's time but were
revived by Augustus in 17 B.C.. **solidō dē
marmore:** i.e., of extraordinary expense,
since many temples of great importance
culturally but of less personal significance
to Augustus were faced with sheets of
marble, behind which less valuable
material was used.

71. Tē: addressed to the Sibyl; Aeneas
refers to the keeping of the famous
Sibylline books beneath the temple of
Jupiter Optimus Maximus on the
Capitoline at Rome, though this is an
anachronism—traditionally one of the last
kings is said to have brought the Sibylline
books to Rome. Augustus made a point of
moving the Sibylline books from their

hīc ego namque tuās sortēs arcāna*que fāta*
dicta meae gentī pōnam, lēctōs*que* sacrābō,
alma, *virōs*. Foliīs tantum *nē* carmina mandā,
75 *nē* turbāta volent rapidīs lūdibria *ventīs*;
ipsa canās ōrō." *Fīnem dedit ōre* loquendī.
     At Phoebī nōndum patiēns *immānis in* antrō
bacchātur *vātēs, magnum sī pectore possit*
excussisse *deum; tantō* magis *ille* fatīgat
80 *ōs* rabidum, fera corda domāns, fingit*que* premendō.
     Ōstia *iamque domūs* patuēre *ingentia* centum
sponte *suā vātisque ferunt* respōnsa *per aurās*:

---

almus, a, um nourishing, kind(ly)
antrum, ī *n.* cave, cavern, grotto
arcānus, a, um secret, hidden
bacchor, ārī, ātus rave, rage
canō, ere, cecinī, cantus sing (of), chant,
    prophesy, proclaim
carmen, inis *n.* song, verse, oracle
centum hundred
cor, rdis *n.* heart, spirit, feelings, soul
domō, āre, uī, itus tame, subdue
excutiō, ere, cussī, cussus shake off
fatīgō (1) weary, tire (out), harass
ferus, a, um wild, fierce, untamed
fingō, ere, fīnxī, fictus mold, train,
    shape
folium, (i)ī *n.* leaf, foliage
legō, ere, lēgī, lēctus select, gather
loquor, ī, locūtus speak, say, tell, talk
lūdibrium, (i)ī *n.* sport, mockery
magis *adv.* more, rather

mandō (1) order, entrust, commend
nōndum *adv.* not yet
ōrō (1) pray (for), entreat, beseech
ōstium, (i)ī *n.* mouth, entrance; harbor
pateō, ēre, uī lie open, extend
patiēns, entis enduring, tolerating
    (+ *gen.*)
Phoebus, ī *m.* Apollo, god of light,
    music, and prophecy
premō, ere, pressī, pressus (re)press,
    control
rabidus, a, um raving, mad, frenzied
rapidus, a, um swift, snatching, whirling
respōnsum, ī *n.* answer, reply, response
sacrō (1) consecrate, dedicate, hallow
sors, rtis *f.* lot, destiny, portion, oracle
spōns, ntis *f.* free will, choice
tantum *adv.* only, just, so much, so far
turbō (1) confuse, disarrange, disturb
volō (1) fly, speed, flutter

---

earlier home to the new temple of Apollo,
immediately adjacent to his own home on
the Palatine.

73. lēctōs virōs: at first two, then ten,
and finally fifteen men (the **quīndecem-
virī**) were entrusted with the care of the
Sibylline books, which were believed to
contain prophecies dealing with the fate
of Rome and which were consulted in
times of great crisis.

74. nē mandā: nē with the imp. is
chiefly poetic (= **nōlī mandāre**); App.
256, *a.*

75. ventīs: dat. of reference or abl. of
means.

76. (ut tū) ipsa canās: indirect
command with **ōrō**.

77. nōndum Phoebī patiēns: *not yet
submissive to Phoebus*, i.e., she still
struggles against the inspiration of the
god.

78. sī possit: a conditional clause, used
virtually as an indir. quest.

80. fingit (eam): a picture from
breaking a spirited horse, as is the
imagery of the preceding verse.

"Ō tandem magnīs pelagī dēfūncte perīclīs
(sed terrae graviōra manent), in rēgna Lavīnī
Dardanidae venient (mitte hanc dē pectore cūram),   85
sed nōn et vēnisse volent. Bella, horrida bella,
et Thybrim multō spūmantem sanguine cernō.
Nōn Simoīs tibi nec Xanthus nec Dōrica castra
dēfuerint; alius Latiō iam partus Achillēs,
nātus et ipse deā; nec Teucrīs addita Iūnō   90
ūsquam aberit, cum tū supplex in rēbus egēnīs
quās gentēs Italum aut quās nōn ōrāveris urbēs!
Causa malī tantī coniūnx iterum hospita Teucrīs
externīque iterum thalamī.

---

absum, esse, fuī be absent, be lacking
Achillēs, is (eī, ī) *m.* central character of
  Homer's *Iliad,* first among the Greek
  chieftains in the Trojan war
addō, ere, didī, ditus add
castra, ōrum *n.* camp, encampment
causa, ae *f.* reason, cause, occasion
Dardanidēs, ae *m.* Trojan, Dardanian
dēfungor, ī, fūnctus perform, finish
  (+ *abl.*)
dēsum, esse, fuī be lacking, be absent
Dōricus, a, um Doric, Greek
egēnus, a, um needy, poor
externus, a, um outer, foreign
gravis, e heavy, grievous, serious
horridus, a, um bristling, terrible,
  fearsome
hospitus, a, um strange, alien, foreign
Italus, a, um Italian, of Italy

iterum *adv.* anew, a second time, again
Latium, (i)ī *n.* Latium, district of central
  Italy
Lavīnium, (i)ī *n.* city near Rome
malum, ī *n.* evil thing, misfortune,
  disaster
nāscor, ī, nātus be born, rise
ōrō (1) pray (for), entreat, beseech
pariō, ere, peperī, partus (re)produce,
  gain, give birth to
perīc(u)lum, ī *n.* danger, peril, risk
Simoīs, entis *m.* river near Troy
spūmō (1) foam, froth, spray
supplex, icis suppliant, humble
thalamus, ī *m.* bridal chamber, wedlock
Thybris, (id)is, *acc.* **brim,** *m.* the Tiber,
  river of Italy running through Rome
ūsquam *adv.* anywhere, ever
Xanthus, ī *m.* river near Troy

---

83. Ō (tū) dēfūncte: voc. **perīc(u)līs:**
abl. with **dēfungor;** App. 342.
  84. terrae: loc., or gen. with implied
perīcula. graviōra (perīcula).
  86. sed et volent nōn vēnisse. et =
etiam: *even, also.*
  88–91. I.e., the Trojans will face
another "Trojan" war, in Italy.
  89. dēfuerint: fut. perf.; translate as
fut. **alius Achillēs:** i.e., Turnus, who is
central to the action of the last six books
of the *Aeneid.*

90. nātus et ipse deā: Turnus was the
son of the nymph Venilia. **et:** *also, too.*
  91. supplex: Aeneas will be compelled
to go as a suppliant to Evander, who lives
on the Palatine, the later site of Rome; this
episode occurs in Book 8.
  92. Ital(ōr)um.
  93. Causa (erit). coniūnx hospita:
Lavinia, daughter of King Latinus. She
had been betrothed to Turnus, but on the
arrival of Aeneas she was pledged by her
father to him, and like a second Helen
(**iterum**) she was the cause of war.

95   *Tū nē* cēde malīs, *sed* contrā audentior *ītō,*
        quā *tua tē Fortūna* sinet. *Via prīma* salūtis
        (*quod* minimē rēris) Graiā pandētur *ab urbe.*"

---

audeō, ēre, ausus sum dare, venture
cēdō, ere, cessī, cessus yield, go
contrā *adv.* opposite, facing
Graius, a, um Greek
malum, ī *n.* evil thing, misfortune,
    disaster
minimē *adv.* least, not at all

pando, ere, ī, passus spread, open
quā where(by), wherever, in any (some)
    way
reor, rērī, ratus think, suppose, reckon
salūs, ūtis *f.* safety, salvation, health
sinō, ere, sīvī, situs permit, allow

---

95. nē cēde: polite imperative (instead
of **nolī** + inf.). **audentior:** comp. adj.
from **audēns, ntis,** pres. act. part. of
audeō, audēre. ītō: *continue to go.*
    96. quā (viā).

97. (id) quod. Graiā urbe: *from a
Greek city.* The Sibyl refers to Pallanteum
on the Tiber, settled by Evander and his
people, exiles from Arcadia in Greece.
This will be the future site of Rome.

Tālibus ex adytō *dictīs* Cūmaea Sibylla
horrendās canit ambāgēs antrō*que* remūgit,
obscūrīs vēra involvēns: *ea* frēna *furentī*　　　　100
concutit *et* stimulōs *sub pectore* vertit Apollō.
Ut prīmum cessit furor *et* rabida ōra quiērunt,
incipit Aenēās hērōs: *"Nōn ūlla labōrum,*
ō virgō, *nova mī* faciēs inopīna*ve surgit*;
omnia praecēpī *atque animō mēcum ante* perēgī.　　　　105
Ūnum ōrō: quandō *hīc* īnfernī iānua *rēgis*
dīcitur et tenebrōsa palūs Acheronte refūsō,

Acherōn, ontis *m.* river of Hades
adytum, ī *n.* inner sanctuary, shrine
ambāgēs, is *f.* winding, mystery
antrum, ī *n.* cave, cavern, grotto
Apollō, inis *m.* god of light, music, and
　prophecy
canō, ere, cecinī, cantus sing (of), chant,
　prophesy, proclaim
cēdō, ere, cessī, cessus yield, depart
concutiō, ere, cussī, cussus shake, shatter
Cūmaeus, a, um of Cumae, a city near
　Naples
faciēs, ēī *f.* appearance, face, aspect
frēnum, ī *n.* rein, curb, check
furor, ōris *m.* madness, frenzy, fury
hērōs, ōis *m.* hero, mighty warrior
horrendus, a, um horrifying, dire,
　awesome
iānua, ae *f.* door, entrance
incipiō, ere, cēpī, ceptus begin,
　undertake
īnfernus, a, um infernal, pertaining to

the underworld
inopīnus, a, um unexpected, sudden
involvō, ere, ī, volūtus wrap, enfold
obscūrus, a, um dark, dim, obscure
ōrō (1) pray (for), entreat, beseech
palūs, ūdis *f.* swamp, marsh
peragō, ere, ēgī, āctus traverse, finish
praecipiō, ere, cēpī, ceptus anticipate;
　teach
quandō when, since, because
quiēscō, ere, ēvī, ētus rest, calm, cease
rabidus, a, um raving, mad, frenzied
refundō, ere, fūdī, fūsus pour (back,
　out)
remūgiō, īre bellow, roar
Sibylla, ae *f.* ancient Italian prophetess
stimulus, ī *m.* goad, spur
tenebrōsus, a, um dark, gloomy
vertō, ere, ī, rsus turn, change
vērum, ī *n.* truth, reality, right
virgō, inis *f.* unmarried girl, maiden

98–155. Aeneas begs the Sibyl to
guide him on his journey to the
lower world, so that he may meet the
shade of his father Anchises. She
responds by telling him that he must
first find the golden bough.

99. ambāgēs: note the repetition of
this unusual word, seen above (29) in the
description of Daedalus' labyrinth. (**ex** *or*
in) **antrō.**

100. ea (= **tālia**) **frēna:** the figure of
horsemanship is continued from 77–80.
102. quiē(vē)runt.
103. hērōs: anticipates the mention of
other heroes in Aeneas' speech.
104. mī = mihi.
107. dīcitur (esse). Acheronte refūsō:
abl. abs.; **refūsō** describes the movement
of Acheron's waters back and forth. The
overflow of the Acheron was supposed to
form Lake Avernus.

īre ad cōnspectum carī *genitōris et ōra*
contingat; doceās iter *et* sacra ōstia pandās.

110   *Illum ego per flammās et* mīlle *sequentia tēla*
ēripuī hīs umerīs mediōque ex hoste recēpī;
ille meum comitatus iter *maria omnia mēcum*
atque omnēs pelagīque minās *caelīque* ferēbat,
invalidus, *vīrēs* ultrā sortem*que* senectae.

115   Quīn, *ut tē* supplex *peterem et tua līmina* adīrem,
īdem ōrāns mandāta *dabat. Gnātīque patrisque,*
alma, precor, miserēre (*potes namque omnia, nec tē*
nēquīquam lūcīs Hecatē praefēcit Avernīs),
sī potuit mānēs accersere *coniugis* Orpheus

---

accersō, ere, sīvī, sītus summon, invite
adeō, īre, iī (īvī), itus approach
almus, a, um nourishing, kind(ly)
Avernus, a, um of lake Avernus in
    Campania, near Cumae, where there
    was an entrance to the underworld
carus, a, um dear, beloved, fond
comitor, ārī, ātus accompany, attend,
    escort, follow
cōnspectus, ūs *m.* sight, (inter)view
contingō, ere, tigī, tāctus touch, befall
doceō, ēre, uī, ctus teach, tell, inform
Hecatē, ēs *f.* goddess of the lower world
hostis, is *m.* (*f.*) enemy, foe, stranger
invalidus, a, um weak, feeble, infirm
iter, itineris *n.* way, road, journey, route
lūcus, ī *m.* (sacred) grove
mandātum, ī *n.* command, charge, behest
mānēs, ium *m.* (souls of) the dead, Hades
mīlle; *pl.* **mīlia, ium** *n.* thousand

minae, ārum *f.* threat, menace; pinnacle
misereor, ērī, itus pity, commiserate
    (+ *gen.*)
nēquīquam *adv.* in vain, uselessly
ōrō (1) pray (for), entreat, beseech
Orpheus, ī *m.* mythical poet and musician
    of Thrace who descended to Hades to
    bring back his wife Eurydice, but failed
ōstium, (i)ī *n.* mouth, entrance; harbor
pandō, ere, ī, passus spread, open
praeficiō, ere, fēcī, fectus set over
    (+ *acc., dat.*)
recipiō, ere, cēpī, ceptus recover, rescue
precor, ārī, ātus pray, entreat
quīn but that, in fact, why not
senecta, ae *f.* old age
sors, rtis *f.* lot, destiny, portion, oracle
supplex, icis suppliant, humble
ultrā *adv.* beyond; *prep.* + *acc.* more
    than

---

109. contingat (mihi): volitive clause
in apposition with **ūnum** in 106. **doceās,
pandās:** volitive subjunctive used to
make a polite command; App. 254.

    **110–12. Illum ego . . . ille meum
(iter):** double ANAPHORA combined with
ASYNDETON and POLYPTOTON (the repetition
of the same word in different cases) makes for
a vivid image indeed of Aeneas' inseparability
from Anchises before the latter's death.

    112. iter: obj. of the participle
comitātus, deponent and therefore
capable of taking a dir. obj.

    115. ut peterem: indirect command in
apposition with **mandāta.**

    116. Gnātī, patris: genitives with
miserēre (imperative); App. 289. **Gnātī**
is archaic spelling for **nātī.**

    117. potes omnia: *you can (do) all
things.*

    119–20. The story of the poet Orpheus'
descent to the underworld to bring back
to life his beloved wife Eurydice was well
known to Vergil's readers, first and
foremost from his own version of the
story in Book 4 of the *Georgics.*

Thrēiciā frētus citharā fidibus*que* canōrīs,   120
sī frātrem Pollūx alternā *morte* redēmit
itque redit*que viam* totiēns. *Quid* Thēsea, *magnum*
quid memorem Alcīdēn? *Et mī genus ab Iove summō.*"

Alcīdēs, ae *m.* Hercules, son of Jupiter
    and Alcmena, who as one of his labors
    descended to Hades and carried off
    Cerberus, the watchdog of Pluto
alternus, a, um alternate, alternating
canōrus, a, um tuneful, musical
cithara, ae *f.* lyre, harp
fidēs, ium *f.* lyre, strings, cords; chords
frāter, tris *m.* brother
frētus, a, um relying on (+ *abl.*)
memorō (1) (re)call, recount, relate
Pollūx, ūcis *m.* son of Jupiter and Leda;
    after the death of his twin brother

Castor, Pollux shared his immortality
    with him on alternate days
redeō, īre, iī (īvī) itus return
redimō, ere, ēmī, ēmptus redeem
Thēseus, eī (eos), *acc.* **ea** *m.* mythical
    king of Athens, who, among his other
    exploits, descended to Hades with his
    friend Pirithoüs to carry off Proserpina
Thrēicius, a, um Thracian, of Thrace, a
    wild region northeast of Greece
totiēns *adv.* so many times, so often

---

120. Thrēiciā: Orpheus' lamentation
for his dead wife was usually located in
Thrace, a wild region just north of
mainland Greece and associated frequently in myth with irrational behavior
and supernatural events. **citharā, fidibus:**
abl. with **frētus.**

121. frātrem Pollūx: Pollux and his
brother Castor (also known as **Geminī,**
the twins) were sons of Leda, who also
gave birth to twin daughters, Helen and
Clytemnestra. Tradition held that one child
from each of these pairs was the offspring
of Jupiter (who seduced Leda in the form
of a swan), while the other child in each
pair was descended from Tyndareus,
Leda's mortal husband. Thus, one child in
each pair was destined to die, the other, to
be immortal.

122. viam: cognate acc. with **itque
reditque,** i.e., "he journeys the journey";
App. 313. **Thēsea:** acc., a Greek form;
App. 69. Theseus went to the underworld
together with his friend Pirithoüs, hoping
to carry off Proserpina; instead, he was
caught and trapped there by Hades, who
imprisoned him in a stone seat. In some
versions of this tale, when Hercules came

to the underworld (see below, **123**) he
rescued Theseus and brought him back to
the surface of the earth. **magnum:** editors
have disagreed since antiquity over the
punctuation of this line—should a comma
(i.e., a pause) occur after **Thēsea,** or after
magnum? In the former case, **magnum**
would then describe Hercules, mentioned
in the next line (**Alcīdēn**); in the latter,
magnum should be taken to modify
Thēsea. Most editors nowadays prefer the
text as it is printed here, but room for
disagreement remains.

122–23. quid . . . quid: note the
combination of ANAPHORA, ASYNDETON, and
ELLIPSIS so frequent in Vergil.

123. Alcīdēn = Hercules, a name which
cannot be used in dactylic hexameter (‒ ∪ ‒).
As one of Hercules' celebrated twelve
labors, he descended to Hades and carried
off Cerberus, the three-headed dog of
Pluto, which guarded the entrance to the
infernal regions. **et:** Aeneas' point is that
he, too, is a hero, and therefore deserves
to be permitted to test his mettle by a
journey to the underworld. **mī genus
(est). mī** = **mihi:** dat. of possession. **ab
Iove:** through Venus, daughter of Jupiter.

Tālibus ōrābat *dictīs ārāsque tenēbat,*
125   *cum sīc* orsa loquī *vātēs:* "Sate *sanguine dīvum,*
Trōs Anchīsiadē, facilis dēscēnsus Avernō:
noctēs atque diēs patet *ātrī* iānua Dītis;
sed revocāre gradum *superāsque* ēvādere *ad aurās,*
hoc opus, *hic labor est.* Paucī, *quōs* aequus amāvit
130   *Iuppiter aut ardēns* ēvēxit *ad* aethera virtūs,
dīs genitī *potuēre. Tenent* media *omnia silvae,*
Cōcȳtus*que* sinū *lābēns* circumvenit *ātrō.*

---

aequus, a, um equal, level, impartial
aethēr, eris, *acc.* **era** *m.* upper air, sky
amō (1) love, cherish, like
Anchīsiadēs, ae *m.* Aeneas, descendant of Anchises
Avernus, ī *m.* lake of central Italy, where there was an entrance to Hades; Hades
circumveniō, īre, vēnī, ventus encircle
Cōcȳtus, ī *m.* river of Hades
dēscēnsus, ūs *m.* descent
Dīs, Dītis *m.* Pluto, god of Hades
ēvādō, ere, sī, sus escape, come out
ēvehō, ere, vēxī, vectus bear (aloft)
facilis, e easy, favorable, ready
gignō, ere, genuī, genitus bear, beget

gradus, ūs *m.* step, gait, pace, stride
loquor, ī, locūtus speak, say, talk, tell
medium, (i)ī *n.* middle, midst, center
opus, eris *n.* work, task, toil, deed
ordior, īrī, orsus begin, undertake
ōrō (1) pray (for), entreat, beseech
pateō, ēre, uī lie open, extend
paucus, a, um small, few, scanty
revocō (1) recall, call back, retrace
serō, ere, sēvī, satus sow, beget
sinus, ūs *m.* fold, bosom, bay, hollow
Trōs, Trōis *m.* Trojan
virtūs, ūtis *f.* manhood, excellence, (military) valor

---

124. ārāsque tenēbat: i.e., as a suppliant.

125. orsa (est). Sate: voc. **sanguine:** abl. of origin or separation; App. 323, 340. **dīv(ōr)um.**

126. Anchīsiadē: voc. This unusual five-syllable patronymic adds to the weightiness of the Sibyl's speech. **facilis (est) dēscēnsus:** *the descent is easy,* ironic, since the usual (and all too easy) way to do so is by dying. **Avernō:** dat. of direction = **ad Avernum,** or read with some manuscripts **Avernī,** *the descent of Avernus.* Vergil uses the name of the lake as an equivalent to the underworld itself here.

128. revocāre, ēvādere: infinitives used as substantives (i.e., gerunds in the nom.).

129. hoc: pronounce **hocc,** making a long syllable. **hoc, hic;** agree in gender

with their predicate nouns, **opus, labor;** App. 240, *a.* **aequus:** used concessively, since even Jupiter, normally even-handed, has made a few exceptions (as in the case of Ganymede, brought to heaven by Jupiter and ever since a source of deep annoyance to Juno, cf. 1.28).

130. ardēns virtūs: a reference in particular to Hercules, who, though destined to die as the son of a mortal woman, was elevated to divine status by Jupiter as a reward for the hero's exceptional accomplishments and great suffering. The epithet **ardēns** alludes to the moment at which Hercules, still alive but in great torment on his funeral pyre, was instead carried off to heaven.

131. dīs: abl. of origin or separation with **genitī;** App. 323, 340. **potuēre (hoc):** *could do this.*

Quod *sī tantus amor mentī, sī tanta* cupīdō *est,*
bis Stygiōs innāre lacūs, bis nigra *vidēre*
Tartara, *et* īnsānō iuvat indulgēre *labōrī*,   135
accipe quae peragenda prius. Latet arbore opācā
aureus *et* foliīs *et* lentō vīmine rāmus,
Iūnōnī īnfernae *dictus sacer; hunc* tegit *omnis*
lūcus *et* obscūrīs claudunt convallibus *umbrae*.
Sed nōn ante datur tellūris operta subīre   140
auricomōs quam quis dēcerpserit arbore fētūs.
Hoc sibi pulchra *suum ferrī* Prōserpina *mūnus*
īnstituit. *Prīmō* āvulsō *nōn* dēficit alter

---

alter, era, erum (an)other (of two),
  second
arbōs (or), oris *f.* tree; wood(s)
aureus, a, um gold(en), of gold
auricomus, a, um golden-haired, g
  olden-leaved
āvellō, ere, (vuls)ī, vulsus tear (off)
bis twice
claudō, ere, sī, sus (en)close, shut (in)
convallis, is *f.* valley, vale, dale
cupīdō, inis *f.* desire, love, passion
dēcerpō, ere, psī, ptus pluck (off)
dēficiō, ere, fēcī, fectus lack, fail
fētus, ūs *m.* young, offspring, growth
folium, (i)ī *n.* leaf, foliage
indulgeō, ēre, lsī, ltus indulge (in)
  (+ *dat.*)
īnfernus, a, um infernal, pertaining to
  the underworld
innō (1) swim, float (in), navigate
īnsānus, a, um mad, insane, frenzied
īnstituō, ere, uī, ūtus establish, ordain
iuvō, āre, iūvī, iūtus help, please

lacus, ūs *m.* lake, marsh
lateō, ēre, uī lie hidden, hide, lurk
lentus, a, um pliant, flexible; not brittle
lūcus, ī *m.* (sacred) grove
niger, gra, grum black, gloomy, dusky
obscūrus, a, um dark, shadowy, gloomy
opācus, a, um dark, shady, gloomy
opertum, ī *n.* mystery, hidden thing
peragō, ere, ēgī, āctus accomplish
prius *adv.* first, sooner
Prōserpina, ae *f.* wife of Pluto and
  queen of the underworld
pulcher, chra, chrum beautiful,
  handsome, noble, splendid
quam *adv.* how, than, as
quod because, but
rāmus, ī *m.* branch, bough, limb
Stygius, a, um Stygian, of the Styx, a
  river of Hades
Tartara, ōrum *n.* abode of the criminal
  and impious in Hades
tegō, ere, tēxī, tēctus cover, protect
vīmen, inis *n.* twig, shoot

---

133. sī tantus . . . sī tanta: ANAPHORA
and ASYNDETON, combined as often with
ELLIPSIS; take **est** with both subjects, and
mentī (dat. of possession or reference)
with both clauses.
    134. innāre: inf. with **mentī (tuō)**
cupīdō est, which is equivalent to **cupīs,**
you wish. **bis:** the Sibyl reminds Aeneas
that he is indeed mortal, and will make
the journey to the underworld again at the
time of his death.

    136. peragenda (sint). (in) arbore.
    137. foliīs, vīmine: ablatives of
respect.
    138. Iūnōnī infernae: by *infernal
Juno* the Sibyl means "the queen of the
underworld," i.e., Proserpina. **dictus (esse).**
    140-41. ante...quam: *until.*
auricomōs fētūs: the speech of the Sibyl,
like the content of her oracles, is opaque:
"the golden-tressed offspring" is an

aureus, *et* similī frondēscit virga metallō.

145　Ergō altē vestīgā *oculīs et* rīte repertum
carpe *manū; namque ipse volēns* facilis*que sequētur,*
sī tē fāta vocant; aliter *nōn vīribus ūllīs*
vincere, *nec* dūrō *poteris* convellere *ferrō.*
Praetereā iacet exanimum *tibi corpus* amīcī

150　(*heu* nescis) *tōtamque* incestat fūnere *classem,*
dum cōnsulta *petis nostrōque in līmine* pendēs.
Sēdibus hunc refer ante suīs et conde sepulcrō.
Dūc nigrās pecudēs; *ea prīma* piācula *suntō.*

---

aliter *adv.* otherwise
altē　*adv.* on high, loftily
amīcus, ī *m.* friend, lover, comrade
aureus, a, um　gold(en), of gold
carpō, ere, psī, ptus　pluck, pursue
condō, ere, didī, ditus　found, hide, bury
cōnsultum, ī *n.* resolve, decree, oracle
convellō, ere, ī, vulsus　tear (off)
dūrus, a, um　hard(y), harsh, stern
ergō *adv.* therefore, then, consequently
exanimus, a, um　breathless, lifeless
facilis, e　easy, favorable, ready
frondēscō, ere　leaf, sprout
fūnus, eris *n.* funeral, death, disaster
iaceō, ēre, uī, itus　lie (low, outspread)

incestō (1)　defile, pollute
metallum, ī *n.* metal, ore, mine
nesciō, īre, īvī (iī)　not know, be
　ignorant
niger, gra, grum　black, dusky, gloomy
pecus, udis *f.* animal (of the flock)
pendeō, ēre, pependī　hang, depend
piāculum, ī *n.* expiation, crime
praetereā *adv.* besides, also, furthermore
reperiō, īre, repperī, repertus　find
rīte *adv.* properly, ritually
sepulcrum, ī *n.* tomb, grave
similis, e　similar, like
vestīgō (1)　trace, search (for), track (out)
virga, ae *f.* branch, rod, twig

---

almost impenetrable circumlocution for
golden leaves. **quis:** indefinite, = **aliquis.**
dēcerpserit: fut. perf.

　145–46. vestīgā et rīte carpe: the
Sibyl's instructions are simple and clear,
in contrast to the oracle she has delivered.

　149. iacet: *lies* (i.e., unburied). **tibi:** a
very broad use of the dat. of reference,
which may almost remain untranslated
here; we might imagine that the Sibyl
points or looks directly at Aeneas as she
says these words.

　150. tōtam classem: i.e., including
Aeneas, and so making it impossible for
him to sacrifice until he has been properly
purified.

　151. nostrōque in līmine pendēs:
near the end of her speech the Sibyl
reminds us of how this scene began, with
the Trojans' arrival at the threshold of
the Sibyl's cave (45).

　152. Sēdibus = ad sēdēs: dat. of
direction. **hunc:** i.e., the as-yet unnamed
companion of Aeneas. **refer:** imp.; App.
202. **suīs:** *his proper,* unusually referring
to **hunc** instead of to the subject. **(in)
sepulcrō.**

　153. Dūc: imp. **nigrās:** animals with
dark-colored hides were thought to be
appropriate offerings to the gods of the
underworld. **ea:** attracted into the gender
of the predicate; App. 240, a. **suntō:**
archaic 3d pl. imp. of **sum**; App. 120.

Sīc dēmum lūcōs Stygis *et rēgna* invia vīvīs
aspiciēs." *Dīxit*, pressō*que* obmūtuit ōre.   155

---

a(d)spiciō, ere, spexī, spectus see,
    behold
dēmum *adv.* finally, at last
invius, a, um pathless, trackless
lūcus, ī *m.* sacred grove, wood

obmūtēscō, ere, tuī become silent, hush
premō, ere, pressī, pressus (re)press,
    control
Styx, Stygis *f.* river of the underworld
vīvus, a, um alive, living

---

154. vīvīs: dat. with **invia.**

Aenēās maestō dēfīxus *lūmina* vultū
ingreditur linquēns antrum, caecōs*que* volūtat
ēventūs *animō sēcum. Cui* fidus Achātēs
it comes et paribus *cūrīs* vestīgia fīgit.
160   *Multa inter sēsē* variō sermōne serēbant,
quem socium exanimum *vātēs, quod corpus* humandum
dīceret. Atque illī Mīsēnum *in lītore* siccō,
ut vēnēre, vident indignā *morte* perēmptum,
Mīsēnum Aeolidēn, *quō nōn* praestantior alter
165   aere ciēre *virōs* Mārtem*que* accendere cantū.
Hectoris *hic magnī fuerat comes,* Hectora *circum*

---

accendō, ere, ī, ēnsus kindle, stir up,
   arouse
Achātēs, ae *m.* faithful comrade of Aeneas
Aeolidēs, ae *m.* descendant of Aeolus,
   Misenus
aes, aeris *n.* bronze (implement), trumpet
alter, era, erum (an)other (of two), second
antrum, ī *n.* cave, cavern, grotto
caecus, a, um blind, dark, hidden
cantus, ūs *m.* song, music, chant, tune
cieō, ēre, cīvī, citus (a)rouse, stir (up)
dēfīgō, ere, xī, xus fix (down), cast down
ēventus, ūs *m.* outcome, result, event
exanimus, a, um breathless, lifeless
fīdus, a, um faithful, trusty, safe
fīgō, ere, xī, xus fix, plant, pierce
Hector, oris, *acc.* **ora** *m.* Trojan leader
humō (1) bury, inter, cover with earth

indignus, a, um unworthy, undeserved
ingredior, ī, gressus advance, enter
linquō, ere, liquī, lictus leave, desert
maestus, a, um sad, mournful, gloomy
Mārs, rtis *m.* god of war, war
Mīsēnus, ī *m.* Trojan trumpeter
pār, paris equal, like, matched
perimō, ere, ēmī, ēmptus destroy
praestāns, antis excellent, superior
sermō, ōnis *m.* conversation, speech
serō, ere, uī, rtus join, discuss
siccus, a, um dry, thirsty
varius, a, um various, different, diverse
vestīgium, (i)ī *n.* track, footprint, step,
   trace
volūtō (1) revolve, turn (over), roll
vultus, ūs *m.* countenance, face, aspect

> 156–211. After seeing to the
> appropriate funeral rites for his
> comrade Misenus, Aeneas seeks and
> finds the golden bough; but its
> acquisition is difficult.

156. lūmina = **oculōs**; acc. with
dēfīxus, perf. pass. participle used as a
Greek middle.
159. cūrīs: abl. of manner.
**161–62. quem socium . . . , quod
corpus . . . dīceret**: indir. quest. after
Multa sermōne serēbant (160).

162–64. Mīsēnum, Mīsēnum: the
repetition (EPANALEPSIS) of Misenus' name
adds to the pathos of their discovery: we
can almost hear the men exclaiming in
sorrow over their dead companion's
body.
163. vēnēre = **vēnērunt**.
164. quō: abl. of comparison. **nōn
alter (erat) praestantior.**
165. ciēre, accendere: infinitives used
to specify in what ways Misenus was
superior (**praestantior**); also known as
the epexegetic inf.; App. 265.
166. Hectora: acc. (a Greek form)
with **circum**. The postposition of the

et lituō pugnās īnsignis obībat *et* hastā.
Postquam *illum vītā victor* spoliāvit Achillēs,
Dardaniō *Aenēae sēsē* fortissimus hērōs
addiderat *socium, nōn inferiōra secūtus.*   170
Sed tum, forte cavā *dum* personat *aequora* conchā,
dēmēns, *et* cantū *vocat in* certāmina *dīvōs,*
aemulus exceptum Trītōn, *sī* crēdere dignum *est,*
inter saxa virum spūmōsā inmerserat *undā.*
Ergō *omnēs magnō circum clāmōre* fremēbant,   175
praecipuē *pius Aenēās. Tum* iussa Sibyllae,
haud mora, fēstīnant flentēs, *aramque* sepulcrī

Achillēs, is (eī, ī) *m.* central character
of Homer's *Iliad,* and first among the
Greek chieftains in the Trojan war
addō, ere, didī, ditus add
aemulus, a, um emulous, imitative (of),
jealous
cantus, ūs *m.* song, music, chant, tune
cavus, a, um hollow, vaulted
certāmen, inis *n.* rivalry, contest
concha, ae *f.* (sea) shell, conch
crēdō, ere, didī, ditus believe, trust
Dardanius, a, um Trojan, Dardanian
dēmēns, entis mad, crazy, foolish
dignus, a, um worthy, deserving
ergō *adv.* therefore, then, consequently
excipiō, ere, cēpī, ceptus catch, receive
fēstīnō (1) hasten, hurry, speed
fleō, ēre, ēvī, ētus weep, lament, mourn
fortis, e brave, strong, valiant
fremō, ere, uī, itus murmur, lament

hasta, ae *f.* spear, lance, dart
hērōs, ōis *m.* hero, mighty warrior
immergō, ere, rsī, rsus plunge, drown
īnsignis, e distinguished, marked
iussum, ī *n.* order, command, behest
lituus, ī *m.* (curved) trumpet
mora, ae *f.* delay, hesitation, hindrance
obeō, īre, iī (īvī) itus enter, approach
personō, āre, uī, itus sound through,
make (re)sound
postquam after (that), when
praecipuē *adv.* especially, particularly
pugna, ae *f.* battle, fight, combat
sepulcrum, ī *n.* tomb, grave
spoliō (1) despoil, plunder, rob (+ *abl.*)
Sibylla, ae *f.* ancient Italian prophetess
spūmōsus, a, um foamy, frothy
Trītōn, ōnis *m.* sea-god famous for his
skill in blowing a conch (sea shell) as a
trumpet

---

prep. creates an opportunity for ANAPHORA
and ASYNDETON, here also combined with
POLYPTOTON (the repetition of the same
word in different cases).
    167. et lituō . . . et hastā: abl. of
specification with **īnsignis.**
    168. illum: i.e., Hector. **vītā:** abl. of
separation with **spoliāvit.**
    170. nōn īnferiōra secūtus: LITOTES.
    171. conchā: abl. of means. Misenus'
use of the conch shell is interpreted by
Triton as a direct challenge, since the
conch was normally the sea-god's
instrument.

    173. aemulus: modifies **Trītōn,** and so
inverts the natural relationship between
men and gods—i.e., now Triton senses
that he has been surpassed on the conch
by a mere mortal. **crēdere:** inf. with adj.
dignum for specification (= epexegetic
inf.); App. 265.
    173–74. exceptum . . . virum: the
unusual separation of epithet from noun
is HYPERBATON, the effect of which here is to
place special emphasis on **virum. (in)
spūmōsā undā.**
    177. haud mora (est). āram sepulcrī:
= **pyram.**

congerere arboribus *caelōque* ēdūcere certant.
Ītur in antīquam silvam, stabula *alta* ferārum;
180   prōcumbunt piceae, sonat icta secūribus īlex
fraxineae*que* trabēs cuneīs *et* fissile rōbur
scinditur, advolvunt *ingentēs montibus* ornōs.
Nec nōn Aenēās opera *inter tālia prīmus*
hortātur *sociōs* paribus*que* accingitur *armīs.*
185   *Atque haec ipse suō trīstī cum* corde volūtat
aspectāns *silvam* immēnsam, *et sīc forte* precātur:
"*Sī nunc sē nōbīs ille* aureus arbore rāmus
ostendat nemore *in tantō*! Quandō *omnia* vērē

---

accingō, ere, cīnxī, cīnctus gird
advolvō, ere, ī, volūtus roll
arbōs (or), oris *f.* tree; wood(s)
a(d)spectō (1) look at, behold
aureus, a um gold(en), of gold
certō (1) strive, fight, vie, contend
congerō, ere, gessī, gestus heap up
cor, rdis *n.* heart, spirit, feelings, soul
cuneus, ī *m.* wedge; block (of seats)
ēdūcō, ere, dūxī, ductus lead out, raise
fera, ae *f.* wild beast
fissilis, e easily split, cleavable
fraxineus, a, um ashen, of ash(wood)
hortor, ārī, ātus urge, encourage, incite
icō, ere, īcī, ictus strike, smite
īlex, icis *f.* holm-oak
immēnsus, a, um boundless, measureless
nemus, oris *n.* (sacred) grove, wood

opus, eris *n.* work, task, deed, labor
ornus, ī *f.* ash-tree
ostendō, ere, ī, ntus show, display
pār, paris equal, like, matched
picea, ae *f.* pitch-pine
precor, ārī, ātus pray, entreat, invoke
prōcumbō, ere, cubuī, cubitus fall
quandō when, since, because
rāmus, ī *m.* branch, bough, limb
rōbur, oris *n.* oak; strength
scindō, ere, scidī, scissus split, cleave
secūris, is *f.* axe
sonō, āre, uī, itus (re)sound, roar
stabulum, ī *n.* stable, stall, lair, den
trabs (trabēs), trabis *f.* beam, timber, tree
vērē *adv.* truly, correctly
volūtō (1) revolve, roll (over)

---

178. arboribus: abl. of means. caelō =
ad caelum: dat. of direction.

179–82. These lines are perhaps the most
famous example in the entire *Aeneid* of the
influence of the poet Ennius on Vergil.
Quintus Ennius (239–169 B.C.) was the first
great hexameter epic poet in Latin, author of
the fifteen-book *Annales*, covering the
history of Rome from the fall of Troy to his
own day. Only fragments of the *Annales*
now survive; Macrobius, a Vergilian scholar
of the 5th century A.D., preserves this
fragment (*Ann.* 6.175–79 Skutsch) as part of
a discussion of how Vergil adapts the work
of his great predecessors:

  incedunt arbusta per alta, securibus
    caedunt,

percellunt magnas quercus, exciditur
    ilex,
fraxinus frangitur atque abies
    consternitur alta,
pinus proceras pervortunt: omne
    sonabat
arbustum fremitu silvai frondosai.

179. Ītur: like the impersonal ventum
erat above (45), this emphasizes the action
rather than the actors.

182. scinditur: both trabēs and rōbur
are subjects, but the verb agrees with the
one closer to it.

183. prīmus: i.e., Aeneas sets a hard-
working example for his men.

184. accingitur: *girds himself;* a
passive form used as a Greek middle.

heu nimium *dē tē vātēs*, Mīsēne, locūta *est.*"
Vix ea fātus erat, geminae cum forte columbae   190
ipsa sub ōra virī caelo vēnēre volantēs,
et viridī sēdēre solō. *Tum maximus* hērōs
māternās agnōscit avēs *laetusque* precātur:
"*Este* ducēs, *ō, sī qua via est, cursumque per aurās*
dērigite *in* lūcōs *ubi* pinguem dīves opācat   195
rāmus humum. *Tūque, ō,* dubiīs *nē* dēfice rēbus,
dīva parēns." *Sīc* effātus vestīgia pressit
observāns *quae* signa *ferant, quō tendere* pergant.
Pascentēs *illae tantum* prōdīre volandō
quantum aciē *possent oculī servāre sequentum.*   200

---

aciēs, ēī *f.* edge; eye(sight); battle line
agnōscō, ere, nōvī, nitus recognize
avis, is *f.* bird, fowl
columba, ae *f.* dove, a bird sacred to
   Venus
dēficiō, ere, fēcī, fectus fail, faint
dērigō (dīrigō), ere, rēxī, rēctus direct,
   guide
dī(ve)s, dī(vi)tis rich, wealthy
dubius, a, um doubtful, wavering
dux, ducis *m. (f.)* leader, guide, chief
effor, ārī, ātus speak (out), say
hērōs, ōis *m.* hero, mighty warrior
humus, ī *f.* ground, soil, earth
loquor, ī, locūtus speak, say, talk, tell
lūcus, ī *m.* (sacred) grove, wood
māternus, a, um of a mother, maternal
Mīsēnus, ī *m.* Trojan trumpeter

nimium *adv.* too (much), excessively
observō (1) watch, guard, observe
opācō (1) darken, shade, shadow
pascō, ere, pāvī, pāstus feed, pasture
pergō, ere, perrēxī, perrēctus proceed
pinguis, e fat, fertile, rich
precor, ārī, ātus pray, entreat, invoke
premō, ere, pressī, pressus (re)press
prōdeō, īre, iī (īvī), itus advance
quantum (as much) as, as far as
rāmus, ī *m.* branch, limb, bough
sedeō, ēre, sēdī, sessus sit, settle
signum, ī *n.* sign, signal, token, mark
solum, ī *n.* ground, soil, earth
vestīgium, (i)ī *n.* step, track, trace
viridis, e green, fresh, vigorous
volō (1) fly, speed, flutter

187–88. Sī: with pres. subjunctive
ostendat, expressing a wish, "o (I wish)
that"; App. 253. **(in) arbore.**
   188–89. omnia vērē . . . locūta est:
the discovery of Misenus' corpse has
served to prove the reliability of the
Sibyl's prophecies.
   191. ōra virī = oculōs Aenēae.
   **192. sēdēre = sēdērunt. (in) viridī
solō.**
   193. māternās avēs: doves were
traditionally associated with Venus.
   194. qua = aliqua. cursum (vestrum).

   196. dubiīs rēbus: *wavering fortunes;*
dat. with **dēfice. nē dēfice: = nōlī
dēficere;** App. 256, *a.*
   197. (re)pressit.
   198. quae . . . ferant, quō pergant:
indir. questions dependent on **observāns.**
   199. tantum: *only so far.* **prōdīre:**
hist. inf.; App. 257. **volandō:** abl. of the
gerund, expressing means.
   200. aciē servāre: *keep them in sight.*
possent: relative clause of purpose
introduced by **quantum. equent(i)um:**
subst., *of those following (them).*

Inde *ubi vēnēre ad* faucēs grave olentis Avernī,
tollunt sē celerēs liquidum*que per* āera *lapsae*
sēdibus optātīs *geminā super* arbore sīdunt,
discolor unde *aurī per* rāmōs *aura* refulsit.
205 Quāle solet *silvīs* brūmālī frīgore vīscum
fronde virēre *novā, quod nōn sua* sēminat arbōs,
et croceō fētū teretēs circumdare truncōs,
tālis erat speciēs *aurī* frondentis opācā
īlice, *sīc* lēnī crepitābat brattea *ventō*.

āēr, āeris, *acc.* **āera,** *m.* air, mist, fog
arbōs (or), oris *f.* tree; wood(s)
Avernus, ī *m.* lake in central Italy where there was an entrance to Hades
brattea, ae *f.* thin sheet, plate, foil
brūmālis, e wintry, of winter
celer, eris, ere swift, quick, fleet
circumdō, dare, dedī, datus surround
crepitō (1) rattle, rustle, crash
croceus, a, um yellow, saffron
discolor, ōris of different color(s)
faucēs, ium *f.* throat, jaws; pass(age)
fētus, ūs *m.* offspring, shoot
frigus, oris *n.* cold, frost, chill
frondēns, entis leafy, fronded
frōns, frondis *f.* leaf, foliage, frond
gravis, e heavy, foul, serious
īlex, icis *f.* holm-oak

inde *adv.* thence, next, thereupon
lēnis, e light, gentle, soft, moderate
liquidus, a, um clear, liquid, fluid
quālis, e (of) what sort, (such) as
oleō, ēre, uī smell, stink
opācus, a, um dark, shady, gloomy
optō (1) choose, desire, hope (for)
rāmus, ī *m.* branch, limb, bough
refulgeō, ēre, lsī gleam, shine, glitter
sēminō (1) sow, produce, bear
sīdō, ere, (sēd)ī sit, settle
soleō, ēre, itus sum be accustomed
speciēs, ēi *f.* appearance, sight, aspect
teres, etis smooth, rounded, polished
truncus, ī *m.* trunk, stem, body
unde whence, from what source
vireō, ēre be green, grow, flourish
vīscum, ī *n.* mistletoe

---

201. grave: translate as an adv. with **olentis;** App. 310.

203. (in) sēdibus optātīs. geminā: some manuscripts read **geminae,** modifying **columbae;** but this is likely to be a mistake made by a scribe recalling its appearance in 190. **geminā** modifying **arbore** is to be preferred because of the striking image it creates: the tree in which the doves settle is "double," i.e., double (both green and gold) in nature. **super arbore:** *on top of the tree.*

204. discolor: i.e., the bough is of a contrasting color. **aurī . . . aura:** the precise meaning of this phrase has been a

topic of scholarly debate since antiquity. It is likely in any case that Vergil is describing something virtually ineffable—the reflection of the golden bough (but not the bough itself) shining through the dark branches, perhaps.

205. brūmālī frīgore: abl. of time when.

206. fronde novā: abl. of manner. **quod:** rel. pronoun, referring to **vīscum. quod nōn sua sēminat arbōs:** the mistletoe is a parasite, and its leaves and berries therefore are different from those of the tree on which it grows (**arbōs sua**).

Corripit *Aenēās* extemplō avidus*que* refringit   210
cūnctantem, *et vātis* portat *sub tecta* Sibyllae.

---

avidus, a, um eager, greedy, ardent
corripiō, ere, uī, reptus snatch (up)
cūnctor, ārī, ātus delay, cling, linger
extemplō *adv.* immediately, at once

portō (1) carry, bear, take, convey
refringō, ere, frēgī, frāctus break off
Sibylla, ae *f.* ancient Italian prophetess

---

211. cūnctantem: the ENJAMBMENT of this participle makes it all the more striking—why does the bough hesitate?

This was not one of the possibilities mentioned by the Sibyl in 146–48.

Cape of Misenum, named for Aeneas' lost comrade.
Photograph by Barbara Weiden Boyd.

BOOK 6.450–476

450   *Inter quās* Phoenissa recēns *ā* vulnere *Dīdō*
errābat silvā in magnā; quam Trōius hērōs
ut prīmum iuxtā *stetit* agnōvit*que per umbrās*
obscūram, quālem *prīmō quī surgere* mēnse
aut videt aut vīdisse putat *per* nūbila lūnam,
455   dēmīsit *lacrimās* dulcī*que* adfātus *amōre est:*
"*Īnfēlīx* Dīdō, vērus *mihi* nuntius ergō

---

adfor, ārī, ātus address, accost
agnōscō, ere, nōvī, nitus recognize
dēmittō, mittere, mīsī, missus send down, let fall, drop, lower
dulcis, e sweet, dear, fond
ergō *adv.* therefore, then, consequently
hērōs, ōis *m.* hero, mighty warrior
iuxtā near, next, close to (+ *acc.*)
lūna, ae *f.* moon, moonlight
mēnsis, is *m.* month
nūbilum, ī *n.* cloud, cloudiness

nuntius, (i)ī *m.* messenger, message
obscūrus, a, um dark, obscure, dim
Phoenissa, ae *f.* Phoenician (woman), Dido
putō (1) think, suppose, consider
quālis, e (such) as, of what sort
recēns, entis recent, fresh
Trōius, a, um Trojan, of Troy
vērus, a, um true, real, genuine
vulnus, eris *n.* wound, deadly blow

450–76. Among those who have died for love Aeneas sees the shade of Dido. He attempts to defend his sudden departure from Carthage, but she scornfully turns away and returns to Sychaeus, her first husband.

450. Inter quās: Dido is the last in a list of mythical females about whose sad deaths we are reminded as Aeneas observes them in the underworld. Translate **quās** as a demonstrative, *these women.* **recēns ā vulnere: recentī vulnere** (*with a fresh wound*) would be more natural in English; but Vergil wants to emphasize not only the freshness of

Dido's wound, but also her very recent arrival in the underworld.

451. quam: with **iuxtā** and understood with **agnōvit** in 452.

453–54. This SIMILE comparing Dido to the elusive new (crescent) moon merits comparison to that with which we (and Aeneas) were introduced to her at 1.498–502.

455. amōre: abl. of manner.

456. nuntius: we may well wonder how this message was delivered to Aeneas; it has not been mentioned before. At the beginning of Book 5, Vergil tells us only that the Trojans see flames in Carthage as they sail off, and that thoughts of what a woman scorned may do lead them to ominous suspicions.

vēnerat exstinctam *ferrōque* extrēma *secūtam?*
Fūneris *heu tibi* causa *fuī? Per sīdera* iūrō,
per superōs et sī qua fidēs *tellūre sub īmā est,*
invītus, *rēgīna, tuō dē lītore* cessī.   460
Sed mē iussa *deum, quae nunc hās īre per umbrās,*
per loca senta sitū cōgunt *noctemque* profundam,
imperiīs ēgēre suīs; nec crēdere quīvī
hunc tantum tibi mē discessū *ferre* dolōrem.
Siste gradum *tēque* aspectū *nē* subtrahe *nostrō.*   465
Quem fugis? Extrēmum *fātō quod tē* adloquor *hoc est."*
Tālibus Aenēās ardentem et torva tuentem
lēnībat *dictīs animum lacrimāsque* ciēbat.
Illa solō fīxōs *oculōs* āversa *tenēbat*

---

adloquor, ī, locūtus address, accost
a(d)spectus, ūs *m.* sight, vision, aspect
āvertō, ere, ī, rsus turn away, avert
causa, ae *f.* cause, reason, occasion
cēdō, ere, cessī, cessus yield, depart
cieō, ēre, cīvī, citus stir (up), (a)rouse
cōgō, ere, coēgī, coāctus force (together)
crēdō, ere, didī, ditus believe, trust (+ *dat.*)
discessus, ūs *m.* departure, separation
dolor, ōris *m.* grief, pain, passion, anger
exstinguō, ere, īnxī, īnctus quench, destroy, extinguish
extrēma, ōrum *n.* end, death, funeral
extrēmus, a, um final, last, utmost
fidēs, eī *f.* faith, honor, pledge

fīgō, ere, xī, xus fasten, fix, pierce
fūnus, eris *n.* funeral, death, disaster
gradus, ūs *m.* step, gait, pace, stride
invītus, a, um unwilling, reluctant
iūrō (1) swear (by), take oath
iussum, ī *n.* command, order, behest
lēniō, īre, īvī, ītus soften, soothe, calm
profundus, a, um deep, profound, vast
queō, quīre, īvī (iī), ītus be able, can
sentus, a, um rough, thorny
sistō, ere, stetī, status stay, stop
situs, ūs *m.* position; neglect; decay
solum, ī *n.* ground, earth, soil
subtrahō, ere, trāxī, tractus withdraw
torvus, a, um fierce, grim, lowering
tueor, ērī, itus (tūtus) look (at), watch

---

457. (tē) exstīnctam (esse). extrēma (= mortem) secutam (esse).

461. iussa de(ōr)um: see 4.237 and 270.

466. Extrēmum: *this is the last (word, or speech) I shall address to you.* **quod:** cognate acc. **hoc:** pronounce **hocc**, making a long syllable. **hoc est:** it is unusual, to say the least, to conclude a line with two monosyllables; their appearance here, though perhaps inelegant, is certainly emphatic.

467. torva: neut. acc. pl. used adverbially, probably in imitation of the similar Greek construction.

467–68. tuentem . . . animum: the expression is unusually contorted—how can one's *mind* or *anger* be imagined as *watching?* Vergil implies that Dido is effectively consumed by her anger—it is all that remains of her.

468. lēnībat = lēniēbat, which could not be used in hexameter (– ∪ – ∪). It has a conative meaning here, *he tried to soothe,* App. 351, 2, *a.*

470　*nec* magis inceptō vultum sermōne *movētur*
　　quam *sī* dūra silex *aut stet* Marpēsia cautēs.
　　Tandem corripuit *sēsē atque* inimīca refūgit
　　in nemus umbriferum, *coniūnx ubi* prīstinus *illī*
　　respondet *cūrīs* aequat*que* Sychaeus *amōrem.*
475　*Nec* minus *Aenēās* cāsū concussus inīquō
　　prōsequitur *lacrimīs* longē *et* miserātur *euntem.*

---

aequō (1) equal(ize), match, level
cāsus, ūs *m.* chance, (mis)fortune
cautēs, is *f.* rock, cliff, crag
concutiō, ere, cussī, cussus shake,
　shatter, agitate
corripiō, ere, uī, reptus snatch (up, away)
dūrus, a, um hard(y), harsh, stern
incipiō, ere, cēpī, ceptus begin, undertake
inimīcus, a, um hostile, unfriendly
inīquus, a, um unjust, harsh, uneven
longē *adv.* (from) afar, at a distance
magis *adv.* more, rather
Marpēs(s)ius, a, um of Marpe(s)sus, a
　mountain on the island of Paros
　famous for its white marble

minus *adv.* less
miseror, ārī, ātus pity, commiserate
nemus, oris *n.* (sacred) grove, forest
prīstinus, a, um ancient, former
prōsequor, ī, secūtus follow, attend
quam *adv.* how, than, as
refugiō, ere, fūgī flee (away), shun
respondeō, ēre, ī, ōnsus answer;
　sympathize with
sermō, ōnis *m.* conversation, speech
silex, icis *m. (f.)* flint, rock, crag
Sychaeus, ī *m.* deceased husband of Dido
umbrifer, era, erum shady
vultus, ūs *m.* countenance, face, aspect

---

470. vultum: acc. of respect.; App.
311. **sermōne:** the word is ironic, since it
suggests conversation; yet Dido does not
respond.
　471. Marpēsia cautēs: Marpessus on
the Greek island of Paros was renowned
as a source of fine marble for sculpture.

　473. umbriferum: the double meaning
is active here: the underworld is filled
with both gloom and the shades of the
dead. **ubi:** the conjunction has been
postponed. **illī:** dat. of reference.
　475. cāsū (Dīdōnis).
　476. prōsequitur et miserātur (eam).

BOOK 6.847–901

"Excūdent *aliī* spīrantia mollius aera
(crēdō equidem), vīvōs *dūcent dē* marmore vultūs,
ōrābunt causās melius, *caelīque* meātūs
dēscrībent radiō *et surgentia sīdera dīcent:*   850
tū regere *imperiō* populōs, Rōmāne, mementō

---

aes, aeris *n.* bronze
causa, ae *f.* cause, case (at law)
crēdō, ere, didī, ditus believe, suppose
dēscrībō, ere, psī, ptus mark out, map
equidem *adv.* indeed, truly, surely
excūdō, ere, ī, sus hammer out, fashion
marmor, oris *n.* marble
meātus, ūs *m.* course, path, motion
melior, ius better, superior, finer

molliter *adv.* softly, gently, gracefully
ōrō (1) pray (for), entreat, plead, argue
populus, ī *m.* people, nation
radius, (i)ī *m.* rod, spoke, compass
regō, ere, rēxī, rēctus rule, guide, direct
Rōmānus, a, um Roman, of Rome
spīrō (1) breathe, blow, live, quiver
vīvus, a, um living, alive, natural
vultus, ūs *m.* countenance, face, aspect

847–901. Anchises, displaying to Aeneas a parade of Roman heroes in the underworld, pauses to reflect on Rome's destiny as a military and political power. The two culminating figures in the parade are the elder Marcellus and the younger Marcellus, to the latter of whom Anchises devotes a lengthy and emotional description. Their tour of the underworld concludes with a review of the tasks still awaiting Aeneas. Aeneas and the Sibyl then depart; Aeneas and his companions set sail once more, and head up the Italian coast towards Latium.

847. **Excūdent:** Anchises uses the future tense repeatedly in this passage, to describe the great moments in the history of a people which does not yet exist. The

entire passage is proleptic—that is, it looks forward in time and outside the frame of the rest of the tale told in the *Aeneid* as a whole. This instance of PROLEPSIS is worth considering from several perspectives: from the point of view of both Anchises and Aeneas, the events and characters foretold do not yet exist except as a promise of the fates; from the point of view of Vergil and his readers, these events and characters are already reflections of the past. **aliī:** the implied reference here is to the Greeks, whose accomplishments in sculpture, rhetoric, and the sciences are guaranteed by Anchises' prescience. **spīrantia aera:** bronze statues so lifelike that they seem to breathe.

847–48. sculptors, orators.

849–50. astronomers. **dīcent = vocābunt.**

851. **Rōmāne:** addressed to the Roman people in general, and to Aeneas in particular—he represents the people whose nation and identity do not yet exist, but are assured by the fates.

(*hae tibi erunt* artēs), pāc*que* impōnere mōrem,
parcere subiectīs *et* dēbellāre superbōs."
    Sīc pater Anchīsēs, atque haec mīrantibus addit:
855 "Aspice, *ut* īnsignis spoliīs Mārcellus opīmīs
ingreditur *victorque virōs* superēminet *omnēs.*
Hic *rem* Rōmānam *magnō* turbante tumultū
sistet eques, sternet Poenōs Gallum*que* rebellem,

---

addō, ere, didī, ditus add
a(d)spiciō, ere, spexī see, look at
dēbellō (1) exhaust through war, crush
eques, itis *m.* cavalryman, knight, man of
    equestrian rank
Gallus, a, um Gallic, Gaul
impōnō, ere, posuī, positus place on,
    impose, establish
ingredior, ī, gressus step, stride, enter
īnsignis, e distinguished, marked,
    noteworthy
Mārcellus, ī *m.* 1. Marcus Claudius
    Marcellus, d. 208 B.C.; famous Roman
    consul, served in both 1st and 2d Punic
    Wars; 2. Marcus Claudius Marcellus,
    42–23 B.C.; son of Octavia, sister of
    Augustus, and first husband of
    Augustus' daughter Julia
mīror, ārī, ātus wonder (at), admire

mōs, mōris *m.* custom, usage, rule, law
opīmus, a, um rich, splendid, sumptuous;
    spolia opīma "spoils of honor," won
    when a Roman general with his own
    hand slew the general of the enemy
parcō, ere, pepercī (parsī), parsus spare
    (+ *dat.*)
pāx, pācis *f.* peace, quiet, repose
Poenus, a, um Phoenician, Carthaginian
rebellis, e rebellious, insurgent
Rōmānus, a, um Roman, of Rome
sistō, ere, stetī, status stop, stand
spolium, (i)ī *m.* spoil, booty, plunder
sternō, ere, strāvī, strātus lay low, strew
subiciō, ere, iēcī, iectus vanquish
superbus, a, um proud, haughty
superēmineō, ēre tower above
tumultus, ūs *m.* tumult, uprising, clamor
turbō (1) confuse, shake, disturb

---

852. **hae:** attracted into the gender of
the predicate; App. 240, *a.* **pācī:** some
editors prefer **pācis,** gen., instead of the
dat. printed here; but **pācī** makes much
better sense with **impōnere,** while **pācis** is
not supported by the manuscripts.
    854. **(Aenēae et Sibyllae) mīrantibus.**
    855. **spoliīs opīmīs:** the technical term
in Latin for arms and other booty taken
on the field of battle by the victorious
from the vanquished general, whom he
has slain with his own hand. These were
won before by Romulus early in his
kingship and by Cossus in 428 B.C. (the
latter of these is mentioned at 841), and
finally by the elder Marcellus in 222 B.C.
When Augustus came to power, he
decreed that, since he had **imperium** and

was effectively commander-in-chief, only
he and his successors could claim the
honor henceforth. **Mārcellus:** M.
Claudius Marcellus, who served in the
First Punic War, was an outstanding
general in the Second Punic War, and was
an ancestor of the younger Marcellus
described below.
    857. **tumultū:** the war with the Gauls
in Italy, in which the elder Marcellus had
killed Viridomarus, leader of the Gauls, at
Clastidium (222 B.C.), and stripping him
of his armor had obtained the third and
last **spolia opīma** (the **tertia arma capta**
of 859).
    858. **eques:** *(though but) a man of
equestrian rank,* though the term also
serves as a reminder that the battle of
Clastidium was waged by cavalry.

tertia*que arma patrī* suspendet *capta* Quirīnō."

Atque hīc Aenēās (ūnā *namque īre vidēbat*   860
ēgrēgium formā iuvenem *et* fulgentibus *armīs*,
sed frōns *laeta* parum *et* dēiectō *lūmina* vultū)
"*Quis, pater, ille, virum quī sīc* comitātur *euntem?*
Fīlius, anne aliquis *magnā dē* stirpe nepōtum?
Quī strepitus circā *comitum!* Quantum īnstar *in ipsō!*   865
Sed nox ātra caput trīstī circumvolat *umbrā.*"
Tum pater Anchīsēs lacrimīs ingressus obortīs:
"*Ō gnāte, ingentem* lūctum *nē quaere tuōrum;*

---

aliquis, quid some(one), any(one)
an(ne) *interrog.* whether, or
circā *adv.* around, about
circumvolō (1) fly around, fly about
comitor, ārī, ātus accompany, attend, escort, follow
dēiciō, ere, iēcī, iectus cast down
ēgregius, a, um extraordinary, distinguished
fīlius, (i)ī *m.* son
forma, ae *f.* form, beauty, shape
frōns, frontis *f.* front, forehead, brow
fulg(e)ō, ēre, lsī shine, gleam, glitter
ingredior, ī, gressus stride, begin, enter
īnstar *n. indecl.* likeness, weight, dignity

iuvenis, is *m. (f.)* youth, young (man, woman)
lūctus, ūs *m.* grief, mourning, sorrow
nepōs, ōtis *m.* grandson; descendant
oborior, īrī, ortus arise, spring up
parum *adv.* slightly, too little, not
quantus, a, um so (much, great, many), as
Quirīnus, ī *m.* the deified Romulus as god of war
stirps, pis *f.* stock, lineage, race
strepitus, ūs *m.* uproar, noise
suspendō, ere, ī, ēnsus hang up
tertius, a, um third
ūnā *adv.* together, at the same time
vultus, ūs *m.* countenance, face, aspect

---

859. suspendet: Vergil introduces another technical term, here part of the vocabulary for making a dedication of spoils to a god by hanging them in (or on) the temple. **Quirīnō:** the name comes as something of a surprise, since the **spolia opīma** were traditionally dedicated not to Quirinus but to Jupiter Feretrius. It is not wise to suppose, however, as some editors have done, that Vergil was confused; it is far more likely that this alteration serves a purpose here—perhaps to bring special honor to Romulus, who as the first winner of **spolia opīma** began the tradition of dedication of Jupiter Feretrius; since upon his death Romulus was deified as Quirinus, Vergil may well intend to remind us here of both divinities associated with the ritual.

860. Aenēās (dīcit). ūnā (cum Mārcellō).

862. frōns (erat). et lūmina (erant) dēiectō vultū: abl. of description, = **et lūmina (erant) dēiecta. lūmina = oculī,** as often.

863. virum: i.e., the elder Marcellus. **ille:** the younger M. Claudius Marcellus, i.e., the son of Augustus' sister Octavia and husband of Augustus' daughter Julia; born in 42 B.C. Augustus had chosen him to be his successor, but he died in 23 B.C.

864. nepōtum (nostrōrum).

865. strepitus: indicating the future fame and popularity of the younger Marcellus.

867. ingressus (est).

868–86. Ancient tradition reports that these lines were recited by Vergil to Augustus and Octavia, the mother of Marcellus. Octavia is said to have fainted upon hearing the poet's tribute to her son.

868. gnāte: archaic spelling of **nāte.**

870

875

ostendent *terrīs hunc* tantum *fāta neque* ultrā
esse sinent. Nimium *vōbīs* Rōmāna propāgō
vīsa potēns, *superī*, propria *haec sī dōna fuissent.*
Quantōs *ille virum magnam* Māvortis *ad urbem
campus aget* gemitūs! *Vel quae*, Tiberīne, *vidēbis*
fūnera, *cum* tumulum praeterlābēre recentem!
Nec puer Īliacā quisquam *dē gente* Latīnōs
in tantum spē *tollet* avōs, *nec* Rōmula *quondam
ūllō sē tantum tellūs* iactābit alumnō.
Heu pietās, *heu* prīsca fidēs invicta*que bellō
dextera! Nōn illī sē* quisquam impūne *tulisset*

---

alumnus, ī *m.* nursling, (foster) child
avus, ī *m.* grandfather; ancestor
fidēs, eī *f.* trust, fidelity, pledge
fūnus, eris *n.* funeral, death, disaster
gemitus, ūs *m.* groan(ing), wail(ing)
iactō (1) toss, vaunt, boast
Īliacus, a, um Ilian, Trojan
impūne *adv.* unpunished, with impunity
invictus, a, um unconquered, invincible
Latīnus, a, um Latin, of Latium
Māvors, rtis *m.* Mars, god of war
nimium *adv.* too (much), too great(ly)
ostendō, ere, ī, ntus show, display
pietās, ātis *f.* loyalty, devotion, sense of
    duty, righteousness, nobility
potēns, entis powerful, mighty
praeterlābor, ī, lāpsus glide by

prīscus, a, um ancient, primitive
propāgō, inis *f.* offshoot, offspring, race
proprius, a, um one's own, special, secure
quantus, a, um how (great, much,
    many), as
quisquam, quaequam, quidquam
    any(one, thing)
recēns, entis recent, fresh, new
Rōmānus, a, um Roman, of Rome
Rōmulus, a, um of Romulus, Roman
sinō, ere, sīvī, situs permit, allow
spēs, eī *f.* hope, expectation
tantum *adv.* so much, so great(ly), only
Tiberīnus, ī *m.* (god of) the Tiber, river
    on which Rome is situated
tumulus, ī *m.* mound, tomb
ultrā *adv.* beyond, farther

---

869. neque ultrā: Marcellus was only
nineteen at the time of his death.

871. vīsa (esset): apodosis in a past
contrary-to-fact condition; App. 382. **sī
fuissent:** protasis in a past contrary-to-fact
condition. **haec dōna:** Marcellus.

872. vir(ōr)um. Māvortis: modifies
both **urbem**, since Rome was founded by
Romulus, a son of Mars, and **campus**
(873), since the part of the city through
which the funeral procession would have
gone was the flat, open land just north of
the ancient city center, known as the
campus Martius (*"field of Mars"*). It is
on this plain that the populace of Rome
would have gathered to witness the
funeral.

873. Tiberīne: Anchises addresses the
divinity inhabiting the Tiber, anticipating
the sympathy that he, in anthropomorphic
form, can offer.

874. tumulum: the magnificent
mausoleum of Augustus, begun by the
emperor in 28 B.C. (and probably barely
finished at the time of Marcellus' death).
Marcellus was the first of what would
eventually be many members of the Julio-
Claudian clan to be buried here.
praeterlābēre = praeterlābēris.

876. spē: *by the hope* (of his future
greatness).

879. illī = Mārcellō: dat. with **obvius
(880). tulisset:** apodosis of a contrary-to-
fact condition, with the condition itself

obvius armātō, seu *cum* pedes *īret in* hostem   880
seu spūmantis *equī* foderet calcāribus armōs.
Heu, miserande *puer, sī* quā *fāta* aspera rumpās—
tū Mārcellus *eris. Manibus date* līlia plēnīs
purpureōs spargam flōrēs *animamque* nepōtis
hīs saltem accumulem *dōnīs, et* fungar inānī   885
mūnere." Sīc tōtā passim rēgiōne vagantur
āeris *in campīs* lātīs *atque omnia* lūstrant.
Quae postquam *Anchīsēs nātum per* singula *dūxit*

---

accumulō (1) heap up; pile up; honor
āēr, āeris *m.* air, mist, fog
armō (1) arm, equip, furnish
armus, ī *m.* shoulder, flank, side
asper, era, erum rough, harsh, fierce
calcar, āris *n.* spur, goad
flōs, ōris *m.* flower, blossom, bloom
fodiō, ere, fōdī, fossus dig, pierce, spur
fungor, ī, fūnctus perform, fulfil (+ *abl.*)
hostis, is *m.* enemy, foe, stranger
inānis, e empty, useless, unavailing
lātus, a, um wide, broad, spacious
līlium, (i)ī *n.* lily
lūstrō (1) purify; survey; traverse
Mārcellus, ī *m.* 1. Marcus Claudius
    Marcellus, d. 208 B.C.; famous Roman
    consul, served in both 1st and 2d Punic
    Wars; 2. Marcus Claudius Marcellus,
    42–23 B.C.; son of Octavia, sister of
    Augustus, and first husband of

Augustus' daughter Julia
miseror, ārī, ātus pity, commiserate
nepōs, ōtis *m.* grandson; descendant
obvius, a, um before, meeting (+ *dat.*)
passim *adv.* everywhere, all about
pedes, itis *m.* footsoldier, infantry
plēnus, a, um full, filled, complete
postquam after (that), when
purpureus, a, um purple, crimson, bright
quā *adv.* where(by), wherever, in any
    (some) way
regiō, ōnis *f.* district, region, quarter
rumpō, ere, rūpī, ruptus break, burst
    (forth)
saltem *adv.* at least, at any rate
singulī, ae, a each, one by one
sīve, seu or if, whether, or
spargō, ere, rsī, rsus scatter, sprinkle
spūmō (1) foam, froth, spray
vagor, ārī, ātus wander, roam, rove

(the **sī**-clause) implied. If expressed, it
would be something like *if he had lived
long enough.*

882. sī rumpās: protasis of a fut. less vivid
condition, the apodosis of which is not
expressed; App. 381. The exact interpretation of this and the following verse has
been long debated. What exactly is
Anchises saying? Some have understood
him to mean that the young man before
him will come to merit the name
Marcellus, or will be a "real" Marcellus,
only if he manages to overcome his sad
fate; but many now think it more likely
that we are to imagine here an outburst on
Anchises' part, breaking off with an
APOSIOPESIS as he is overcome by emotion

at the sight of the youth. Anchises is then
saying, "You will (i.e., must) be Marcellus;
oh, if only you were to break your harsh
fate somehow!" **quā (viā).**

883. date: Anchises addresses Aeneas and
the Sibyl; but we may also imagine that
through Anchises Vergil himself is
addressing his readers.

884–85. purpureōs: a color indicative
of both distinguished rank and deserved
honor. **spargam, accumulem, fungar:**
understand either as volitive subjunctive;
App. 254, or as subjunctive in a sequence
of ind. commands after **date**, with **ut**
implied.

**886. vagantur (Anchīsēs et Aenēās et
Sibylla).**

incendit*que animum fāmae venientis amōre,*
890   exim *bella virō* memorat *quae* deinde gerenda,
Laurentēs*que* docet populōs urbem*que* Latīnī,
et quō quemque modō *fugiatque feratque labōrem.*
  Sunt geminae Somnī portae, *quārum* altera *fertur*
cornea, *quā* vērīs facilis *datur* exitus *umbrīs,*
895   altera candentī perfecta nitēns elephantō,
sed falsa *ad caelum mittunt* īnsomnia Mānēs.
Hīs ibi tum *nātum* Anchīsēs ūnā*que* Sibyllam
prōsequitur *dictīs* portā*que* ēmittit eburnā;
ille viam secat *ad nāvēs sociōsque* revīsit.

---

alter, era, erum one (of two), other (of two), second
candēns, entis shining, white, gleaming
corneus, a, um of horn
deinde *adv.* thence, next, thereupon
doceō, ēre, uī, ctus teach (about), tell
eburnus, a, um (of) ivory
elephantus, ī *m.* elephant, ivory
ēmittō, ere, mīsī, missus send forth
exim, exin(de) *adv.* from there, next, thereupon
exitus, ūs *m.* exit, outlet, egress
facilis, e easy, favorable, ready
falsus, a, um false, deceitful, mock
gerō, ere, gessī, gestus bear, wage
ibi *adv.* there, then
incendō, ere, ī, ēnsus inflame, kindle
īnsomnium, (i)ī *n.* dream, vision
Latīnus, ī *m.* early king of Italy, whose daughter, Lavinia, married Aeneas

Laurēns, entis of Laurentum, a city near Rome
Mānēs, ium *m.* (souls of) the dead, Hades
memorō (1) recount, (re)call, relate
modus, ī *m.* manner, measure, limit
nitēns, entis gleaming, bright, shining
perficiō, ere, fēcī, fectus finish, make
populus, ī *m.* people, nation
porta, ae *f.* door, gate, entrance, exit
prōsequor, ī, secūtus follow, escort
quisque, quaeque, quidque (quodque) each, every(one)
revīsō, ere revisit, see again
secō, āre, uī, ctus cut, cleave; pass through
Sibylla, ae *f.* ancient Italian prophetess
Somnus, ī *m.* Sleep, Slumber personified as a divinity
ūnā *adv.* together, at the same time
vērus, a, um true, real, genuine, honest

---

890. virō: dat. of agent with passive periphrastic construction; App. 302. **gerenda (sint).**

892. fugiat, ferat: subjunctives in indirect question, introduced by **docet . . . quōmodō. quō . . . modō:** normally written as either one or two words; the intrusion of **quemque** here creates a true TMESIS.

893. fertur (esse) = dīcitur (esse). Again Vergil implies that the two gates from the underworld are part of a

tradition already known to his readers: in this case, first and foremost from Homer, who describes the two Gates of Dreams in *Odyssey* 19.562-67.

895. candentī elephantō: abl. of material; App. 324. The association of ivory with deception is based in part on a play on words: the Greek verb *elepha*iresthai means "to deceive."

896. sed: i.e., through this gate.
899. ille: Aeneas.

Tum sē ad Caiētae rēctō *fert līmite portum.*   900
Ancora *dē* prōrā iacitur; *stant lītore puppēs.*

---

ancora, ae *f.* anchor
Caiēta, ae *f.* Italian coast city near Rome (modern Gaeta)
iaciō, ere, iēcī, iactus throw, cast, hurl

līmes, it is m. limit, boundary; route, course
prōra, ae *f.* prow (of a ship)
rēctus, a, um right, straight, direct

---

900. Caiētae: modern Gaeta, on the coast of Italy about halfway between the bay of Naples and the mouth of the Tiber. **rēctō līmite:** (sailing) *straight along the coastline;* abl. of route. All of the earliest manuscripts of the *Aeneid,* as well as Servius, read **lītore** rather than **līmite** here; but later manuscripts have **līmite.**

Both words can be made to fit the meaning; but since Vergil uses **lītore** in the same position in the next line, I think it preferable to suppose that Vergil would have avoided unnecessary repetition here.

901. This line, which repeats 3.277, serves to bring this powerful book to a calm close.

Mausoleum of Augustus (Marcellus was the first to be buried here).

Photograph by
Barbara Weiden Boyd.

Theater of Marcellus (built in his memory by Augustus).

Photograph by
Barbara Weiden Boyd.

SELECTIONS FROM
BOOK 10

Stat sua cuique dies (10.467)

Illustration for Book 10
" Every man's last day is fixed" by Thom Kapheim

BOOK 10.420–509

Quem sic Pallas *petit ante precatus:*   420
"*Da nunc,* Thybri *pater, ferro, quod* missile libro,
fortunam atque viam duri per pectus Halaesi.
Haec arma exuvias*que viri tua* quercus *habebit.*"
Audiit illa deus; dum texit Imaona Halaesus,
Arcadio *infelix telo dat pectus* inermum.   425

Arcadius, a, um Arcadian, of Arcadia
exuviae, arum, *f.* spoils, armor
Halaesus, i, *m.* Halaesus, an exiled Greek
    warrior now settled in Italy and enemy
    of the Trojans
Imaon, Imaonos, *m.* Imaon, an Italian
    comrade of Halaesus, mentioned only
    here
inermus, a, um (also **inermis, e**)
    unarmed, defenseless

libro (1) balance, weigh
missilis, e able or ready to be thrown,
    hurled, sent
Pallas, Pallantis, *m.* Pallas, son of the
    Arcadian king Evander and ally of
    Aeneas
quercus, us, *f.* oak tree
tego, ere, texi, tectus cover, protect
Thybris, Thybridis, *m.* Tiber (both the
    river and the god dwelling in it)

10.420–38. As Pallas, son of
Evander, approaches the end of his
aristeia, or "display of glory on the
battlefield," Vergil describes another
victory by the youth. After killing
Halaesus, he and his men confront
Lausus and his renegade Etruscans,
fighting on behalf of the Rutulians.

quod missile libro: Pallas is holding a
javelin and preparing to hurl it as soon as
his prayer is finished.

422. fortunam atque viam: the direct
object of **da** (421); HENDIADYS, = **fortunam
viae.**

423. tua quercus habebit: spoils will
be hung on the tree as an offering to the
god. The oak tree is usually associated
with Jupiter, rather than with Tiber.

424. dum texit: = **dum tegebat.**
Imaona: Greek accusative; note the
elision with the next name. Imaon, an
Italian fighting with Halaesus against the
Trojans, is mentioned only here.

420. Quem: Halaesus, one of the
leaders of the Italian troops. As Vergil
tells us at 7.723–4, he is an enemy of the
very name of Troy (in some versions of
the myths surrounding Halaesus, this is
because he is himself Greek in origin).
sic: adv. with **precatus.**

421. Thybri: voc. Pallas addresses
Tiber as father not only because he is
divine, but also because Tiber is the
divinity who protects Pallas' homeland.

425. infelix: describes Halaesus. **telo
dat pectus:** the wound must be fatal, but
Vergil does not tell us this (except
indirectly, with the word **caede** in the
next line). The action of battle is meant to
move quickly here.

At non caede *viri tanta* perterrita Lausus,
pars ingens belli, sinit *agmina: primus* Abantem
oppositum interimit, *pugnae* nodum*que moramque.*
Sternitur Arcadiae *proles, sternuntur* Etrusci
430   *et vos, O* Grais imperdita *corpora, Teucri.*
Agmina concurrunt *ducibusque et viribus* aequis;
extremi addensent acies *nec* turba *moveri*
tela manusque sinit. *Hinc* Pallas instat *et* urget,

Abas, Abantis, *m.* Abas, an Etruscan
    warrior
acies, ei, *f.* line of battle
addenseo, ere, — thicken, pack densely
aequus, a, um equal
caedes, is, *f.* killing, slaughter
concurro, ere, concurri, concursus join
    battle, come together in battle
Etruscus, a, um Etruscan, of or having
    to do with Etruria (a region in Italy
    north of Latium)
Graius, a, um Greek, of the Greeks or of
    Greece
imperditus, a, um not destroyed

insto, are, institi, instaturus approach,
    press upon, pursue
**interimo (or interemo), ere, interemi,
    interemptus** destroy, kill
Lausus, i, *m.* son of Mezentius, the
    renegade Etruscan ally of Turnus
nodus, i, *m.* knot, node
oppono, ere, opposui, oppositus oppose,
    set against
perterreo, ere, perterrui, perterritus
    frighten thoroughly
sino, ere, sivi, situs allow, permit; here,
    desert
turba, ae, *f.* mob, crowd, tumult
urgeo, ere, ursi, — drive, urge, press hard

---

426. At: emphasizes the change in
focus: we now hear of Lausus' accomplishments in battle. **tanta:** TRANSFERRED
EPITHET modifying **caede** (= **tanti** [or **talis**]
viri caede). **perterrita:** modifies **agmina.**
The word order suggests that Lausus stays
right in the middle of his troops.
    427. pars ingens belli: in apposition
with **Lausus.**
    428. pugnae nodumque moramque: in
apposition with **Abantem.** The image is
unusual: Abas is like a knot, i.e., an
obstacle or impediment. The ancient
commentator Servius noted this unusual
expression, and observed that its linking
with **moram** helps to clarify the meaning
of **nodum.** Abas holds his ground,
impeding the progress of the battle. (Some
modern commentators think the image is
even stronger—Abas is like knot in a
piece of wood, which cannot therefore be
cut.)

429. Sternitur . . . sternuntur:
ANAPHORA and ASYNDETON, a frequent
combination in Vergil.
    430. et vos, . . . , Teucri: voc., to mark
the emotional highpoint of the scene, as
well as its irony: these Trojans survived
the Greeks only to be killed in Italy. **Grais:**
dat. of agent. **imperdita corpora:** in
apposition with **Teucri. corpora:**
SYNECDOCHE for the persons addressed.
    431. ducibusque et viribus aequis:
Pallas and Lausus are well matched.
    432. extremi addensent acies: *the
troops in the rear pack the ranks together.*
The verb is very rare, appearing only one
other time in Latin. **moveri:** complementary inf. with **sinit.** Note the reflexive
function of the passive voice.
    433. sinit: the last syllable is long
before the caesura. **hinc. . . hinc:** ANAPHORA
and ASYNDETON, here emphasizing the
equality of this match.

hinc contra Lausus, *nec multum* discrepat aetas,
egregii *forma, sed quis Fortuna* negarat   435
in patriam reditus. *Ipsos* concurrere *passus*
haud tamen inter se magni regnator Olympi;
mox *illos sua fata manent maiore sub hoste.*

---

aetas, atis, *f.* age, time of life
concurro, ere, concurri, concursus join
  battle, come together in battle
discrepo, are, discrepui (or **discrepavi**),
  — disagree, be different
egregius, a, um distinguished, excellent
mox *adv.* soon, presently

nego (1) deny, refuse
Olympus, i, *m.* Mt. Olympus, according
  to Greek myth the home of the gods
patria, ae, *f.* native country, homeland
reditus, us, *m.* return, return trip
regnator, oris, *m.* ruler

**434. nec multum discrepat aetas
(eorum):** the emphasis on their similarities
continues. **multum:** adv.

435. egregii: modifies both Pallas and
Lausus. **forma:** abl. of specification (with
egregii). **quis:** = **quibus;** here, equivalent
to **eis. negarat:** = **negaverat.**

436–7. Ipsos . . . haud tamen: the
emphasis is on **ipsos**—Jupiter permits the
followers of the two young leaders to
clash, but not the young leaders themselves.

438. manent: here, transitive. **maiore
sub hoste:** Pallas will be killed by Turnus,
Lausus by Aeneas.

Interea soror alma monet succedere Lauso
440   Turnum, *qui volucri curru medium secat agmen.*
Ut vidit socios: "Tempus desistere *pugnae;*
solus ego in Pallanta *feror, soli mihi* Pallas
debetur; cuperem *ipse parens* spectator *adesset."*
Haec ait, et socii cesserunt *aequore iusso.*
445   *At* Rutulum abscessu iuvenis *tum iussa superba*
miratus stupet *in* Turno *corpusque per ingens*

---

abscessus, us, *m.* departure, absence
almus, a, um loving, kind, nurturing
cedo, ere, cessi, cessus yield, withdraw
cupio, ere, cupivi (or **cupii**), **cupitus**
  desire
debeo, ere, debui, debitus owe, be
  obliged
desisto, ere, destiti, destitus cease from,
  stop (+ dat.)
iuvenis, is, *m.* youth
miror (1) to marvel at

moneo, ere, monui, monitus warn,
  advise
Rutulus, a, um of or concerning the
  Rutulians, an Italian tribe
spectator, oris, *m.* viewer, spectator
stupeo, ere, stupui gaze at in awe, be
  stupefied at
succedo, ere, successi, successus
  approach, come from beneath (+ dat.)
Turnus, i, *m.* Turnus, leader of the
  Rutulians and opponent of Aeneas

10.439–73. Turnus and Pallas
confront each other on the battlefield.
As the tension mounts before their
duel, Hercules briefly considers
intervening to save Pallas; Jupiter
reminds Hercules that everyone's life
must end at a time allotted by fate.

439. soror alma: the nymph Juturna,
sister of Turnus; her momentary
appearance here ironically foreshadows
her reappearance in Book 12, when she is
unable to save her brother. **monet
succedere:** inf. with **monere** is poetic, in
place of the prosaic indirect command
monet ut succedat; App. 360, a. **Lauso:**
dat. with **succedere.**
  440. volucri curru: abl. of means.
  441. Ut vidit socios (ait). tempus (est).
pugnae: either gen. or dat. of separation
(the former is a construction borrowed
from Greek).
  442. Pallanta: Greek acc. Note the
powerful effect of repetition and word
order in this line.

  443. cuperem (ut): impf. subjunctive
used independently to express an
unaccomplished wish (in the present): I
wish that he were present, **adesset** (but he
is not); App. 253. The tense of **adesset** is
determined by the sequence of tenses.
ipse parens: Evander. **spectator:** in
apposition with **ipse parens.**
  444. aequore iusso: abl. of separation,
and a good example of the compactness
of the Latin participle. The transference
of the participle from **socii** to **aequore** is
also a good example of ENALLAGE (i.e., a
TRANSFERRED EPITHET). (Some editors prefer
to read **socii . . . iussi** on the grounds that
this would be a more natural Latin
construction; but it is also the more
prosaic alternative.) Note also the
meaning of **aequor** here (and again
below, at 10.451): *"level plain,"* as
opposed to the meaning *"sea"* (i.e., its
flat surface) found so often elsewhere in
the *Aeneid.*
  445. Rutulum: = **Rutulorum.**
abscessu: abl. of circumstance; App. 329.
  446. in Turno: at the sight of Turnus.

lumina volvit obitque truci *procul omnia* visu,
talibus et dictis it contra dicta tyranni:
"*Aut* spoliis *ego iam raptis* laudabor opimis
aut leto insigni: sorti pater aequus utrique *est.*   450
Tolle minas." *Fatus medium* procedit *in aequor;*
frigidus Arcadibus coit *in* praecordia *sanguis.*
Desiluit Turnus biiugis, pedes apparat *ire*
comminus; *utque* leo, specula *cum vidit ab alta*
stare procul campis meditantem *in* proelia taurum,   455
advolat, *haud alia est* Turni *venientis imago.*

---

adiuvo, are, adiuvi, adiutus help
advolo (1) fly to
aequus, a, um fair, even, equal
apparo (1) prepare
biiugus, a, um yoked two together; *m.pl.*
  as a substantive, chariot (i.e., **equi**
  biiugi = **currus**)
coeo, -ire, coii (or **coivi**), **coitus** go
  together, come together
comminus *adv.* hand-to-hand, at close
  quarters
desilio, ire, desilui, desultus jump down
frigidus, a, um cold, chilled, frozen
laudo (1) praise
leo, leonis, *m.* lion
meditor (1) consider, think over,
  practice
minae, arum, *f. pl.* threats
obeo, ire, obivi (or **obii**), **obitus** go over,
  go around; (here) survey

opimus, a, um rich, abundant (of spoils,
  arms taken from a defeated general by
  a victorious general)
pedes, itis, *m.* foot-traveller; (person) on
  foot
praecordia, orum, *n. pl.* heart, breast
procedo, ere, processi, processus
  proceed, go forth
proelium, i, *n.* battle
specula, ae, *f.* lookout, high place
spolium, i, *n.* hide (of an animal);
  commonly, in the n. pl., spoils, arms
  stripped from an enemy
taurus, i, *m.* bull
trux, trucis fierce, wild
tyrannus, i, *m.* tyrant
uterque, utraque, utrumque each (of
  two)
visus, us, *m.* sight

---

447. obit: i.e., he "goes over" Turnus
with his eyes.

448. talibus et dictis: = **et talibus
dictis.**

449. spoliis . . . raptis . . . opimis: take
either as abl. abs. or abl. of cause (see
below, 450). The phrase **spolia opima** is a
technical term for the spoils won and
dedicated by Roman generals who had
killed leaders of the enemy force in single
combat; see notes on 6.855–59.

450. leto insigni: abl. of cause.

452. Arcadibus: dat. of reference. **in
praecordia:** acc. because the blood
rushes *into* their breasts.

453. biiugis: abl. of separation. **pedes:**
in apposition with Turnus, the (implied)
subject of **apparat.**

454. utque: introduces a SIMILE. **vidit:**
the perfect tense here imitates the Greek
use of the gnomic aorist in similar
contexts—in both cases, the effect is a
timeless description.

455. stare: inf. in indirect statement;
the subject of the indirect statement is
taurum. meditantem in proelia:
practicing for a battle. The use of **in** here
indicates purpose.

Hunc ubi contiguum *missae fore credidit* hastae,
ire prior Pallas, *si qua fors* adiuvet *ausum*
viribus imparibus, *magnumque ita ad aethera fatur*:

460   *"Per patris* hospitium *et mensas, quas* advena *adisti,*
te precor, Alcide, coeptis *ingentibus adsis.*
Cernat semineci *sibi me rapere arma* cruenta
victoremque ferant morientia lumina Turni."
Audiit Alcides iuvenem *magnumque sub imo*

465   corde premit *gemitum lacrimasque* effundit *inanes.*
Tum genitor natum dictis adfatur amicis:
"Stat sua cuique *dies,* breve *et* inreparabile *tempus*

---

adfor, adfari, adfatus address
advena, ae, *m./f.* stranger, immigrant,
  newcomer
Alcides, ae, *m.* Alcides, patronymic for
  Hercules
amicus, a, um friendly, kind
brevis, e brief, short
cerno, ere, crevi, certus see, discern,
  perceive
coeptum, i, *n.* undertaking
contiguus, a, um next to, near, close;
  able to be touched
cor, cordis, *n.* heart
cruentus, a, um bloody

effundo, ere, effudi, effusus pour
  forth
hasta, ae, *f.* spear
hospitium, ii, *n.* hospitality
impar, is uneven, unequal, ill-matched
inreparabilis, e irreparable, irretrievable
iuvenis, is, *m.* youth
premo, ere, pressi, pressus press, repress,
  suppress
quisque, quaeque, quidque (or **quodque**)
  indefinite pronoun whoever, whichever
  (it may be), each one
seminex, necis *m./f./n. adj.* half-dead,
  dying

---

457. ubi hunc (i.e., **Turnum**)
contiguum missae hastae fore (*Pallas*)
credidit. fore: = **futurum esse**; future inf.
in indirect statement.

458. ire: historical infinitive. **si qua:** =
si (ali)qua, abl. of means or respect. (Be
sure to scan this line to ascertain the case
of **qua**—it does *not* modify **fors**.)
adiuvet: the use of the pres. subjunctive
reflects Pallas' own optimistic thoughts.
ausum (Pallantem).

459. viribus imparibus: abl. of means
or specification.

460. hospitium et mensas: HENDIADYS, =
hospitium mensae. advena: nom. in
apposition with an implied **tu,** subject of
adisti.

461. Alcide: Greek vocative. **coeptis
ingentibus:** dat. with **adsis.**

462-3. Cernat . . . ferant: jussive
subjunctives.

462. semineci sibi: reflexive, describing
the person who is subject of **cernat;** dat.
of separation with **rapere;** App. 305.
rapere: inf. in indirect statement; **me** is its
subject.

463. victorem: in apposition with
(me), implied direct object of **ferant.**
morientia lumina: nom.

464-73. In the *Iliad* (16.431–61), Zeus
had briefly debated whether or not to save
the life of his beloved son Sarpedon by
removing him from battle; Zeus does not
do so, and Sarpedon dies. Here, Vergil has
Hercules consider saving Pallas; Jupiter
uses his own experience to convince
Hercules not to intervene.

466. natum: Hercules is the son of
Jupiter and Alcmene. **dictis . . . amicis:**
abl. of means or manner (i.e., *with
friendly words* or *in a friendly manner*).

467. sua cuique: the reflexive adjective
and a form of **quisque** (case and number

omnibus est vitae; sed famam extendere *factis,*
hoc virtutis opus. *Troiae sub moenibus altis*
tot gnati cecidere deum, quin occidit *una*   470
Sarpedon, *mea* progenies; *etiam sua* Turnum
fata vocant metas*que dati* pervenit *ad* aevi."
Sic ait, atque oculos Rutulorum reicit *arvis.*

---

aevum, i, *n.* age, life-span
extendo, ere, extendi, extensus/extentus
    extend, increase
meta, ae, *f.* turning point
occido, ere, occidi, occasus fall, die
opus, operis, *n.* work, achievement
pervenio, ire, perveni, perventus reach

progenies, ei, *f.* offspring, posterity
reicio, ere, reieci, reiectus throw back,
    reject, turn away
Sarpedon, onis, *m.* Sarpedon, Lycian son
    of Jupiter and ally of the Trojans
virtus, utis, *f.* courage, excellence in
    battle

---

of both to be determined by the syntax of the sentence in which they appear) are used together to form expressions like the English "to/for each, his/her/one's own"; here, *one's day (i.e., of destiny) is fixed for each person.* **dies:** fem. form is used for a fixed day. **cuique:** dat. of reference.

468. omnibus: dat. of possession. **factis:** abl. of means.

469. hoc (est) virtutis opus.

470. gnati: archaic spelling of **nati. cecidere:** = **ceciderunt. deum:** = **deorum. quin:** with the indicative, creates strong emphasis (*in fact*). **una:** adv.; together (i.e., with so many other sons of gods).

471. Sarpedon: son of Jupiter (Zeus) and Europa, killed by Achilles' companion Patroclus in the Trojan War. **mea progenies:** nom. in apposition with **Sarpedon.**

472. metas . . . dati . . . aevi: the image is of a race nearing its completion. Racers would go a certain number of times around the turning-post (**meta**) in the arena before reaching the completion of the competition. **dati (sibi). (Turnus) pervenit.**

473. Rutulorum: take with **arvis** (not **oculos). arvis:** abl. of separation.

At Pallas *magnis* emittit *viribus* hastam
475   vaginaque *cava* fulgentem deripit ensem.
Illa volans *umeri surgunt qua* tegmina *summa*
incidit, *atque viam* clipei molita *per oras*
tandem etiam magno strinxit *de corpore* Turni.
Hic Turnus *ferro* praefixum *robur* acuto
480   *in* Pallanta diu librans iacit *atque ita fatur*:
"Aspice num mage *sit nostrum* penetrabile *telum*."
Dixerat; at clipeum, *tot ferri terga, tot* aeris,

---

acutus, a, um sharp
aes, aeris, *n.* bronze
aspicio, ere, aspexi, aspectus watch,
  look at, consider
clipeus, i, *m.* (or **clipeum, i,** *n.*) round
  shield
deripio, ere, deripui, dereptus snatch
  away, pull
diu *adv.* for a long time
emitto, ere, emisi, emissus send forth,
  shoot, hurl
ensis, is, *m.* sword
fulgeo, ere, fulsi shine, gleam
hasta, ae, *f.* spear
iacio, ere, ieci, iactus throw

incido, ere, incidi fall, strike
libro (1) balance, weigh
mage = **magis** (comparative adv.)
molior, iri, molitus set in motion, push,
  force
num whether (introducing an indirect
  question)
penetrabilis, e able to be penetrated, able
  to penetrate
praefigo, ere, praefixi, praefixus tip,
  point (i.e., put a point on something)
stringo, ere, strinxi, strictus graze
tegmen, inis, *n.* covering, protection
vagina, ae, *f.* scabbard, sheath for a sword
volo (1) to fly

10.474–89. Pallas and Turnus cast
spears in turn. Pallas only grazes
Turnus' shield; but Turnus' missile
hits home, and Pallas falls to the
ground dying.

474. magnis . . . viribus: abl. of
means.

475. vagina cava: abl. of separation.

476–7. Read as **Illa volans incidit qua
tegmina summa umeri surgunt. umeri . . .
tegmina summa:** i.e., the upper edge of
the breastplate protecting his shoulders.
This line describes in general terms where
the spear strikes Turnus; the description
that follows in 477–8 (see below) gives
more specific details.

477–8. Read as **atque (hasta) viam
per clipei oras molita tandem etiam de
magno corpore Turni strinxit. magno**

strinxit de corpore: stringo is usually
transitive and takes an acc. direct object.
Here, however, Vergil emphasizes the fact
that Pallas is able to strike only a small
part of Turnus' huge body; understand
something like **aliquid** (i.e., **de magno
corpore**) as the implied direct object.

479. Hic: adv. **ferro . . . acuto:** abl. of
means. **robur:** the material is used in
METONYMY for the tool made from it.

481. num . . . sit: indirect question
after **aspice**; App. 349.

482. tot ferri terga, tot aeris: in
apposition with **clipeum. ferri terga:**
terga literally means "backs" or "hides,"
but here is extended to include types of
metal in layers.

482–5. Read as **at vibranti ictu cuspis
medium clipeum transverberat, tot ferri
terga, tot aeris, quem pellis tauri
circumdata totiens obeat, loricaeque
moras.** The shield is made from equal

quem pellis totiens obeat circumdata tauri,
vibranti cuspis *medium* transverberat ictu
loricae*que moras et pectus* perforat *ingens.*   485
Ille rapit calidum frustra *de vulnere telum:*
una eademque via sanguis animusque sequuntur.
Corruit *in vulnus* (sonitum *super arma dedere)*
et terram hostilem *moriens petit ore* cruento.

---

calidus, a, um hot
circumdo, dare, circumdedi,
    circumdatus surround, put around
corruo, ere, corrui rush down, fall
cruentus, a, um bloody
cuspis, idis, *f.* spear, spear-point
frustra *adv.* in vain
hostilis, e of the enemy, pertaining to the
    enemy
ictus, us, *m.* blow, strike (NB: do not
    confuse this fourth-declension noun
    with the verb from which it is derived;

cf. the perf. pass. participle **ictus** at
    12.926)
lorica, ae, *f.* leather cuirass
obeo, ire, obivi, obitus surround, go
    around
pellis, is, *f.* skin, hide
perforo (1) pierce, perforate, puncture
sonitus, us, *m.* sound
taurus, i, *m.* bull
totiens so many times, as many times
transverbero, are pierce through,
    transfix
vibro (1) vibrate, shake

---

numbers of layers of iron and bronze,
and a bull's-hide covering goes around it
an equal number of times.

483. obeat: subjunctive in a concessive
clause. The point is that Pallas' shield is
pierced *in spite of* its dense fabric.

484. vibranti . . . ictu: abl. of means.
Note how the word order of the line plays
upon the meaning of the central word,
medium.

485. loricae . . . moras: Pallas' cuirass
is meant to slow down the course of an
attacker's weapon and so dull its effect; in
this case, however, it is no match for
Turnus' spear.

486. Ille: Pallas. **frustra:** take with
rapit.

487. una eademque via: abl. of
route; App. 298. **eadem:** the first two

vowels, normally a short and a long
respectively, are here combined in
SYNEZESIS to create one long vowel. The
resulting long syllable is elided with the
long vowel at the end of the preceding
word. **sanguis:** note the lengthening of
the last syllable.

488. super: understand either as an
adv., or = **super (***eum***).**

489. terram hostilem: the earth upon
which Pallas falls is not in fact alien soil,
but is the territory of the Italians. The adj.
thus reflects an emotional perception
rather than a fact; it is also proleptic
(PROLEPSIS), in the sense that Pallas'
homeland will eventually fall into the
hands of the Trojan enemy. **petit ore**
cruento: abl. of means; the image of
"biting the dust" comes from Homer.

490　　　　　*Quem* Turnus *super* adsistens:
　　　　　"Arcades, *haec*" *inquit* "memores *mea dicta referte*
　　　　　Evandro: *qualem meruit,* Pallanta remitto.
　　　　　Quisquis *honos tumuli,* quidquid solamen humandi *est,*
　　　　　largior. *Haud illi stabunt* Aeneia parvo
495　　　　hospitia." *Et laevo pressit pede talia fatus*
　　　　　exanimem *rapiens immania* pondera baltei
　　　　　impressum*que* nefas: *una sub nocte* iugali
　　　　　caesa *manus* iuvenum foede thalami*que* cruenti,

---

adsisto, ere, adstiti (or **astiti**) stand next
　to, stand by
Aeneius, a, um of Aeneas
balteus, i, *m.* baldric
Evander, dri, *m.* Evander, exile from
　Arcadia now living in Latium, and
　father of Pallas
exanimis, e lifeless
hospitium, ii, *n.* hospitality
humo (1) bury
imprimo, ere, impressi, impressus press
　upon

iugalis, e having to do with marriage,
　matrimonial
largior, iri, largitus bestow, grant
memor, oris remembering, mindful (of)
　(+ gen.)
nefas, *n. indecl.* (lit., unspeakable thing)
　crime
parvus, a, um small, little
pondus, eris, *n.* weight
quisquis, quidquid (or **quicquid**)
　indefinite adj. whoever, whatever
remitto, ere, remisi, remissus send back
solamen, inis, *n.* consolation

> 10.490–509. Turnus gloats over
> Pallas' body, and tears the baldric
> from the youth.

490. See note on 2.233 for half-lines in
the *Aeneid.* **Quem** = **eum** (i.e., **Pallanta**).
super: either adv., or prep. with **quem.**
　491. Arcades: voc.; in this pl. Greek
form, the final syllable is long. **memores
. . . referte:** *"remember and carry back."*
The use of the verbal adjective **memores**
is analogous to the use of a present
participle—it describes an action
contemporaneous with the time of the
finite verb with which it is construed.
　492. Evandro: although this spelling is
conventional in Latin, scan the first
syllable of Evander's name as the Greek
diphthong **Eu-.** **qualem:** i.e., dead.
meruit: the subject is Evander.

　493. Quisquis honos tumuli (*est*).
tumuli and **humandi** are both gen.
　494. illi: to Evander. **stabunt . . . parvo:**
"will cost little." **parvo:** abl. of price.
　495. laevo . . . pede: abl. of means.
The use of the left foot is ominous for
Turnus himself.
　496. baltei: the baldric is a swordbelt
worn over one shoulder and reaching the
hip on the other side of the body. The last
two vowels of this word are here scanned
as a diphthong (i.e., in SYNEZESIS: see
above, on 10.487) for metrical purposes.
　497. impressum . . . nefas: a scene
depicting a famous crime (to be described
and identified in the second half of this
verse and the following verse) is
engraved on the baldric. Vergil emphasizes the scene by imagining the crime
itself rather than a picture of it. **una sub
nocte iugali:** the placement of **una** at the
beginning of the phrase emphasizes the

quae Clonus Eurytides *multo* caelaverat *auro*;
quo nunc Turnus ovat spolio gaudet*que* potitus.   500
Nescia *mens hominum fati sortisque futurae*
et servare modum rebus sublata secundis!
Turno *tempus erit magno cum optaverit* emptum
intactum Pallanta, *et cum* spolia ista *diemque*
oderit. *At socii multo gemitu lacrimisque*   505
impositum scuto *referunt* Pallanta frequentes.

---

caedo, ere, cecidi, caesus cut down,
  kill, slaughter
caelo (1) engrave, emboss
Clonus, i, *m.* Clonus, name of a
  craftsman mentioned only in the *Aeneid*
cruentus, a, um bloody
emo, ere, emi, emptus buy, purchase
Eurytides, is, *m.* patronymic, meaning
  "son of Eurytus"
foedus, a, um foul, horrible
frequens, entis (pl.) in great numbers
gaudeo, ere, —, gavisus (semideponent)
  rejoice, take pleasure (in)

intactus, a, um untouched
iuvenis, is, *m.* youth
iste, a, ud this (of yours), that (of yours)
nescius, a, um unknowing, ignorant (of)
odi, isse, osus (defective vb.) hate
ovo, are exult, rejoice
potior, iri, potitus win power over, get
  possession of (+ *abl.*)
scutum, i, *n.* shield
spolium, i, *n.* hide (of an animal);
  commonly, in the pl., spoils
thalamus, i, *m.* wedding chamber,
  bedroom

---

fact that the events described took place
during the course of one night. The word
iugali is the first clue Vergil gives to the
identification of this scene.

498. caesa manus . . . cruenti: only
with both halves of this line is the picture
complete: the scene depicted is the
slaughter of the fifty sons of Aegyptus by
their fifty cousin-wives the Danaids
(daughters of king Danaus). In more
extensive versions of the story, we learn
that only one of the sisters, Hypermestra,
refrained from the murder. Vergil's
omission of all proper names from this
description suggests that the story was
very well known to his readers in
antiquity and would have been easily
recognized.

499. quae: n. pl., referring back to the
scenes on the baldric. **Clonus Eurytides:**
this craftsman is heard of only here. **multo
. . . auro:** abl. of material.

500. quo . . . spolio: i.e., the **balteus;**
both **gaudeo** and **potior** take the abl. **quo**
= **eo.**

501. Nescia . . . futurae: hominum is
subjective gen. with **mens; fati sortisque
futurae** is objective gen. with **nescia;**
App. 284.

502. servare: inf. with **nescia;** verbs of
knowing and their derivatives are
followed by the inf. to express what we
know/do not know how to do (note that
there is no separate word for "how" in
Latin for expressions of this sort). **rebus
. . . secundis:** abl. of means.

503. magno: abl. of price with
emptum (esse).

503–5. optaverit . . . oderit: fut. perf.
indicative in two parallel temporal *cum*-
clauses; App. 370.

505. multo gemitu lacrimisque: abl. of
manner.

506. scuto: dat. with compound
participle **impositum;** App.298.

O dolor atque decus *magnum* rediture *parenti,*
haec te prima dies bello dedit, haec eadem aufert,
cum tamen ingentes Rutulorum *linquis* acervos!

---

acervus, -i, *m.* heap, pile
aufero, -ferre, abstuli, ablatus carry
  away

decus, -oris, *n.* honor, glory
redeo, -ire, redii, reditus return, go back

---

507. O dolor . . . parenti: pathetic
APOSTROPHE to Pallas, now dead.
  509. cum tamen: concessive; the use of
the indicative with concessive **cum** is
unusual, but is probably intended to make
this APOSTROPHE to Pallas as vivid as
possible.

SELECTIONS FROM
BOOK 12

...di me terrent (12.895)

Illustration for Book 12
" It is the gods I fear" by Thom Kapheim

BOOK 12.791-842

Iunonem interea rex omnipotentis Olympi
adloquitur fulva *pugnas de nube* tuentem:
"*Quae iam finis erit, coniunx? Quid* denique restat?
Indigetem Aenean scis *ipsa et* scire fateris
795 deberi *caelo fatisque ad sidera tolli.*
Quid struis? *Aut qua spe* gelidis *in nubibus* haeres?
Mortalin decuit violari *vulnere divum?*

---

adloquor, loqui, adlocutus address
debeo, ere, debui, debitus owe
decet, ere, decuit (only 3d pers.) be
  fitting, be suitable, be proper
denique *adv.* finally, at last, (esp. at the
  end of a list) in short, in a word
fateor, eri, fassus admit, acknowledge
fulvus, a, um golden yellow, tawny
gelidus, a, um icy, cold
haereo, ere, haesi, haesus cling, stick, sit
  fast
Indiges, Indigetis, *m.* deified hero,

patron deity
mortalis, e mortal, having to do with a
  mortal, of a mortal
Olympus, i, *m.* Mt. Olympus, home of
  the gods
omnipotens, entis all-powerful
resto, are, restiti be left, remain
scio, ire, scivi (or scii), **scitus** know
struo, ere, struxi, structus arrange,
  build, prepare, contrive
tueor, eri, tutus behold, watch, gaze upon
violo (1) injure, dishonor, violate

12.791–806. The gods watch from
Mt. Olympus as Aeneas and Turnus
confront each other in a duel. Jupiter
addresses Juno, telling her it is time at
last to give up her enmity towards the
Trojans.

792. omnipotentis: a TRANSFERRED
EPITHET, since it more appropriately describes
Jupiter **rex** than it does Mt. Olympus.
794. Indigetem: in apposition with
Aenean. Here Jupiter refers to the
worship of Aeneas as Indiges after his
death. Archaeological remains of what
may have been a fifth-century B.C.
sanctuary of Sol Indiges have been
located outside of Rome, near the site of

ancient Lavinium; but precise identification
of this sanctuary with Aeneas Indiges
awaits furthur archaeological support.
Aenean: Greek acc. **scire (te) fateris.**
795. deberi . . . tolli: indirect statement
after **scis . . . et scire fateris;** the subject of
the indirect statement is **Indigetem . . .
Aenean.** At Book 1.259–60, Jupiter had
promised Venus that Aeneas would be
deified. He refers to the same destiny here.
796. qua spe: abl. of manner or cause.
796–9. Jupiter's use of RHETORICAL
QUESTIONS betrays his frustration with
Juno's continuing wrath.
797. mortalin: = **mortali + ne. violari:**
inf. with **decuit.** Earlier in Book 12 (319–
22), Aeneas had been wounded in the leg
by an arrow; there it was unclear whether
the origin of the shot was human or divine.

Aut ensem (quid enim sine te Iuturna *valeret?)*
ereptum reddi Turno *et vim* crescere *victis?*
Desine *iam tandem* precibus*que* inflectere *nostris,*   800
ne te tantus edit tacitam *dolor et mihi curae*
saepe tuo dulci tristes *ex ore* recursent.
Ventum ad supremum est. Terris agitare *vel undis*
Troianos *potuisti,* infandum accendere *bellum,*
deformare *domum et* luctu miscere hymenaeos: 805

---

accendo, ere, accendi, accensus inflame,
  ignite, kindle
agito (1) drive, stir, agitate
cresco, ere, crevi, cretus spring up,
  grow, increase
deformo (1) disfigure, mar, spoil
desino, ere, desinii (or **desii,** or **desinivi**),
  desitus cease, stop
edo, esse (or **edere**), **edi, esus** consume,
  eat, eat up
hymenaeus, i, *m.* wedding song; the
  wedding ceremony itself
infandus, a, um unspeakable, abomi-
  nable

inflecto, ere, inflexi, inflexus bend,
  change, influence
Iuturna, ae, *f.* sister of Turnus; Jupiter
  had made her an immortal river nymph
luctus, us, *m.* grief, mourning
misceo, ere, miscui, mixtus mix,
  intermingle, confound
prex, precis, *f.* prayer, request, entreaty
recurso, are return persistently, keep
  recurring
tacitus, a, um silent
tristis, e sad
Troianus, a, um Trojan, of Troy
valeo, ere, valui, valiturus be strong, be
  able, be well

---

798. valeret: impf. subjunctive used to
express potential in the past: *"for what
would/could Juturna have been able [to
accomplish] without you?"*
**798–9. ensem . . . ereptum reddi
Turno:** in fact, at 12.731-3, the sword with
which Turnus was fighting had broken; he
had actually picked up a comrade's sword
by mistake (733–41). At 12.784-5, Juturna
restores Turnus' sword to him. **reddi . . . et
. . . crescere:** infinitives with **decuit. victis:**
dat. of reference.
800. precibus: abl. of means; the abl.
of **prex** is used only in the pl. **inflectere:**
2d sing. pres. pass. imperative.
801–2. ne . . . edit . . . et . . . recursent:
indirect commands after **precibus** (i.e., as
if Jupiter had said, **"precor ne edit . . . et
recursent"**). **edit** is an alternative archaic
form of the pres. subjunctive, usually (and
in some manuscripts of Vergil) written
edat. recursent: like **edit,** subjunctive in
indirect command after **precibus.**

803. Ventum . . . est: the impersonal
perf. pass. is used instead of the perf. act.
to emphasize the action involved; here, =
venimus. ad supremum: in the n. sing.,
supremum can be used as a substantive:
"to the last moment," "to the end." **terris
. . . vel undis:** abl. of place where.
**803–5. agitare . . . accendere . . .
deformare . . . miscere:** complementary
infs. with **potuisti.**
805. deformare domum: Juno and her
agent Allecto have caused turmoil in the
household of Lavinia, Latinus her father,
and Amata her mother, in order to
maintain their relentless harassment of
Aeneas. **luctu miscere hymenaeos:** earlier
in Book 12 (593–611), Amata is driven
to commit suicide by her own fear that
Turnus has been killed in battle.
Ironically, her death removes a major
obstacle to the marriage planned between
Aeneas and Lavinia.

ulterius *temptare* veto."

---

ulterior, ius *comp. adj.* farther, further,
beyond

veto, are, vetui, vetitus forbid

---

806. ulterius: adv.

Column of Jupiter, Mainz, Romano-Germanic Museum.
Photograph by Raymond V. Schoder, S.J.

        Sic Iuppiter orsus;
sic dea summisso *contra* Saturnia *vultu:*
"Ista quidem quia *nota mihi tua, magne,* voluntas,
Iuppiter, et Turnum *et terras* invita *reliqui;*

810   *nec tu me* aëria *solam nunc sede videres*
digna indigna *pati, sed flammis* cincta *sub ipsa*
starem acie *traheremque* inimica *in* proelia *Teucros.*
Iuturnam *misero* (fateor) succurrere fratri
suasi *et pro vita maiora audere* probavi,

815   *non ut tela tamen, non ut* contenderet arcum;

---

acies, ei, *f.* line of battle, battle array
aërius, a, um of the air, airy, heavenly
arcus, us, *m.* bow (for an arrow)
cingo, ere, cinxi, cinctus encircle, gird
contendo, ere, contendi, contentus
    bend, draw tight; shoot, aim
dignus, a, um worthy
fateor, eri, fassus admit, confess
frater, tris, *m.* brother
indignus, a, um unworthy
inimicus, a, um unfriendly
invitus, a, um unwilling
iste, ista, istud this, that (of yours)
ordior, iri, orsus begin, undertake

probo (1) approve, commend, recommend
proelium, i, *n.* battle, skirmish
quia *conj.* since
quidem *adv.* (adding emphasis) in fact,
    indeed
Saturnius, a, um Saturnian, descended
    from Saturn; the Olympian gods are
    the children of Saturn
suadeo, ere, suasi, suasus persuade,
    advise, urge
succurro, ere, succurri, succursus run to
    aid, help
summitto, ere, summisi, summissus let
    down, lower
voluntas, tatis, *f.* will, desire

12.806–28. Juno responds that she
has already submitted to Jupiter's will;
he will have the peace he desires. She
asks in return that the newly-formed
Italian nation not be called "Trojan,"
and not have any of the hallmarks of
Trojan culture, especially language
and clothing.

806. orsus (est).
807. sic (locuta est). summisso . . .
vultu: abl. abs. **contra:** adv. **Saturnia:** a
common epithet for Juno in the *Aeneid.*
808. Ista . . . tua . . . voluntas: the two
adjectives, along with the emphatic
placement of **i**sta, emphasize that Juno is
describing Jupiter's will, not her own. **nota
(est). magne:** voc. with **Iuppiter** (809).
809. invita: this adj. is often used, as

here, concessively: "though unwilling."
810. me . . . solam: subject of *pati*
(811). **aëria . . . sede:** abl. of place. **videres:**
"[otherwise], you would not see me . . ."
Juno is using the impf. subjunctive to
express the apodosis of a present
contrary-to-fact condition; the protasis,
here not made explicit, would be
something like **nisi haec fieri velles.**
811. (et) digna (et) indigna. flammis:
abl. of means.
812. starem . . . traheremque: the
apodosis continues.
813–4. succurrere . . . suasi: = ut
succurreret suasi (indirect command).
The alternative construction with inf. + acc.
occurs frequently in poetry; App. 360, a.
814. pro vita: i.e., on behalf of
Turnus' life. **(eam) audere.**
815. non ut . . . tamen, non ut
contenderet: a double result clause,

adiuro Stygii *caput* implacabile fontis,
una superstitio *superis quae reddita divis.*
Et nunc cedo equidem pugnasque exosa *relinquo.*
Illud te, nulla fati quod lege *tenetur,*
pro Latio obtestor, *pro* maiestate *tuorum:*   820
cum iam conubiis pacem felicibus (esto)
component, *cum iam leges et* foedera *iungent,*
ne vetus indigenas *nomen mutare* Latinos
neu Troas fieri *iubeas Teucrosque vocari*
aut vocem mutare viros aut vertere vestem.   825

---

adiuro (1) call to witness, swear by
compono, ere, composui, compositus
    bring together, compose, construct
conubium, ii, *n.* right of intermarriage
exosus, a, um hating, detesting
felix, icis happy, fortunate
fio, fieri become, be made
foedus, eris, *n.* pact
fons, fontis, *m.* spring, source
implacabilis, -e implacable, irreconcilable
indigena, ae, *m.* native, sprung from the
    land

Latinus, a, um of or from Latium, Latin
lex, legis, *f.* law
maiestas, tatis, *f.* greatness, dignity
neu = neve (ne + ve)
obtestor (1) make appeal to, beseech
pax, pacis, *f.* peace
Stygius, a, um Stygian, having to do
    with the river Styx
superstitio, onis, *f.* superstition, (here)
    object of dread
Tros, Trois, *m.* a Trojan, a person from
    Troy

---

with the verb in the impf. subjunctive;
the presence of **tamen** indicates that the
clause is restrictive, i.e., *"but not so that . . ."*

816. Stygii . . . fontis: the river Styx is
one of the great rivers of the underworld.
An oath sworn in its name is the most
solemn oath a god can make.

817. una superstitio: nom. in
apposition with the oath described in the
preceding line. **superis . . . divis:** dat.

818. exosa is ambiguous here; Juno is
saying either that she hates the battles, and
so is abandoning them, or that she is
abandoning the battles although she hates
to do so.

819. Illud: looks ahead to Juno's entire
request, contained in lines 821-8. **nulla . . .
lege:** abl. of means. **quod:** antecedent is
illud.

820. tuorum: Juno refers to the Italians
as Jupiter's people because their posterity
is to descend from Latinus, son of
Faunus, grandson of Picus, and great-
grandson of Saturnus, father also of the
Olympians.

821. conubiis . . . felicibus: abl. of
means. **esto:** 3d sing. fut. imp., used
concessively: *"and so be it"*; App. 255.

822. component . . . iungent: Juno
never identifies the subject explicitly, but
she refers here to the Trojans and Latins
joined and at peace.

823-4. ne . . . neu . . . iubeas:
hortatory subjunctive, used to express a
command that is also a plea.

**823-5. mutare . . . fieri . . . vocari . . .
mutare . . . vertere:** all inf. with **ne . . .
iubeas.**

Sit Latium, *sint* Albani *per* saecula *reges,*
sit Romana potens Itala *virtute* propago:
occidit, occiderit*que* sinas *cum nomine Troia.*"

Albanus, a, um of or from Alba Longa
  (the settlement founded by Ascanius 300
  years before Romulus was to found Rome)
Italus, a, um Italian, having to do with
  Italy
occido, ere, occidi, occasus fall, perish, end
Latium, ii, *n.* Latium (the area surrounding
  Rome)

potens, potentis powerful, mighty
propago, ginis, *f.* offspring, descendant,
  posterity
Romanus, a, um Roman, having to do
  with Rome
saeculum, i, *n.* century, age
sino, ere, sivi, situs permit, allow

---

826. Albani . . . reges: the Alban kings,
a legendary list of the many kings who
ruled for the three hundred years between
Ascanius' founding of Alba Longa and
Romulus' new foundation, Rome.

**826–8. sit . . . sint . . . sit . . . occidit,
occiderit:** the combination of ANAPHORA and
ASYNDETON here is emphatic as usual; Juno
uses it to express almost simultaneously her
desire for the Italians to survive and for
Troy, if not the Trojans themselves, to
disappear from the face of the earth.

827. Itala virtute: abl. of specification
(denoting the reason for Roman ascen-
dancy) or source (because ethnic origins
are the topic).

828. occiderit . . . sinas: both
subjunctives continue Juno's plea. Their
juxtaposition without a clear indication of
the syntactical relationship between the
two (**occidisse sinas** would be the usual
construction) suggests the emotional nature
of Juno's speech. **Troia:** the placement of
the name at the end of the line (and speech)
captures Juno's single-mindedness.

Aeneas performing a sacrifice upon his arrival in Italy. Ara Pacis.
Photograph by Barbara Weiden Boyd.

Olli subridens *hominum rerumque* repertor:
"*Es* germana *Iovis Saturnique altera proles,*   830
irarum tantos volvis sub pectore fluctus.
Verum *age et inceptum* frustra summitte *furorem:*
do quod vis, et me victusque volensque remitto.
Sermonem Ausonii *patrium moresque tenebunt,*
utque est nomen erit; commixti *corpore tantum*   835
subsident *Teucri. Morem* ritus*que sacrorum*
adiciam *faciamque omnes uno ore* Latinos.
Hinc genus Ausonio *mixtum quod sanguine surget,*
supra *homines,* supra *ire deos pietate videbis,*
nec gens ulla tuos aeque celebrabit *honores.*"   840

---

adicio, ere, adieci, adiectus add, confer
in addition
aequus, a, um equal
Ausonius, a, um of or having to do with
Ausonia, i.e., Italy; **Ausonii, orum,** *m.*
pl., the people of Italy
celebro (1) celebrate, observe solemnly
commisceo, ere, commiscui, commixtus
mingle together, unite
frustra *adv.* in vain
germanus, a, um sibling

remitto, ere, remisi, remissus concede,
yield, grant
repertor, oris, *m.* inventor, creator
sermo, onis, *m.* speech, language
subrideo, ere, subrisi, subrisus smile
subsido, ere, subsedi sink, fall, give way
summitto, ere, summisi, summissus let
down, lower
supra *prep.* + *acc.* above, over
verum *adv.* but

12.829–42. Jupiter agrees to
Juno's terms, and promises in
addition that the new Italian nation
will honor her more than does any
other people.

829. Olli: = **illi;** dat. with **subridens.**
repertor (respondit).

830. In acknowledging that he and Juno
are siblings and both children of Saturn,
Jupiter indicates that the reconciliation of
a family squabble is at hand.

832. frustra: take with **inceptum . . .**
furorem, not **summitte.**

833. do (id) quod vis. victusque
volensque: Jupiter recognizes Juno's
power over him while emphasizing their

like-mindedness; he will go along gladly,
if she will yield.

834. Ausonii: the name of this tribe
comes from one of the ancestral names
for Italy, Ausonia.

835. corpore: abl. of specification.
tantum: Jupiter wants to emphasize that
the mixture of the two peoples will occur
only on the physical level; in other
characteristics, the Italian influence will
be dominant.

837. uno ore: abl. of description.

838. Hinc: i.e., from the Trojans now
in Italy. **Ausonio . . . sanguine:** treat as
either abl. of material or means.

839. pietate: abl. of specification.

840. nec gens ulla . . . aeque: i.e., no
other nation will equal the devotion of
this one.

Adnuit *his Iuno et mentem* laetata retorsit;
interea excedit *caelo nubemque relinquit.*

---

adnuo, ere, adnui, adnutus nod, give
  assent
excedo, ere, excessi, excessus go out,
  withdraw

laetor (1) feel joy, be glad
retorqueo, ere, retorsi, retortus turn
  back, (here) change (i.e., direction)

---

841. mentem retorsit: the metaphor is
strong—it is as if Juno is physically
moving the orientation of her mind as she
changes her feelings regarding the
Trojans.
  842. caelo: abl. of separation.

Ceres (or Venus?) Promoting the Peaceful Fertility of Italy.
Ara Pacis.
Photograph by Barbara Weiden Boyd.

BOOK 12.887–952

Aeneas instat *contra telumque* coruscat
ingens arboreum, *et saevo sic pectore fatur:*
"Quae nunc deinde mora est? Aut quid iam, Turne, retractas?
Non cursu, saevis certandum *est* comminus *armis.*   890
Verte omnes tete in facies et contrahe quidquid
sive *animis* sive *arte vales; opta ardua* pennis

---

arboreus, a, um of a tree, (made) from a
    tree, treelike
certo (1) strive, struggle, do battle
comminus *adv.* hand-to-hand
contraho, ere, contraxi, contractus
    collect, draw together
corusco (1) brandish, shake
insto, are, institi, instaturus press upon,

threaten, pursue
penna, ae, *f.* feather, (in pl.) wing
quisquis, quidquid *indefinite pronoun*
    whoever, whatever
retracto (1) draw back
ive = **si + ve, aut si**
valeo, ere, valui, valiturus be able, be
    strong, have power

12.887–902. Aeneas pursues
Turnus across the battlefield, and
challenges him to hand-to-hand
combat. Turnus responds that he does
not fear Aeneas; his only source of fear
is the gods, especially Jupiter. He then
attempts to hurl a huge stone at Aeneas.

887. instat contra: the adv. reinforces
the verb—Aeneas' pursuit of Turnus will
soon bring the two heroes face to face.

888. ingens arboreum: *"huge, tree-like."*
The combination of two adjectives in
ASYNDETON reinforces the meaning of each,
and implies that these impressions are moving
in quick succession through Turnus' thoughts.

889. Quae . . . ? Aut quid . . . ?:
Aeneas does not wait for an answer to his
RHETORICAL QUESTIONS. **nunc deinde . . .
iam:** with three temporal adverbs, Aeneas
indicates that their final confrontation has
begun at last.

890. Read as **Non cursu (certandum
est), saevis certandum est comminus
armis.** The contrast here is not only
between the two ablatives of means, **cursu**
and **saevis . . . armis**, but also between
comminus and its implied opposite. Were
they to fight while running, the distance
between them would, presumably, help
Turnus and hinder Aeneas; fighting in
close combat is more likely to bring this
confrontation to a swift conclusion.
certandum est: the impersonal n. sing.
form of the passive periphrastic is used
when the verb in question is intransitive.

891. Verte . . . in facies: Aeneas
suggests that Turnus try to become like
Proteus, the sea-divinity who is able to
transform himself into countless shapes and
appearances. (The English adj. "protean"
is derived from this creature's name.) **tete:**
emphatic form of the acc. pronoun **te.**

891–2. contrahe quidquid . . . vales:
"bring together whatever" (i.e., strength
or resources) *"you can"* (i.e., to help

astra sequi clausum*que cava te condere terra.*"
Ille caput quassans: "*Non me tua* fervida terrent
895   dicta, ferox; di me terrent *et Iuppiter hostis.*"
Nec plura effatus *saxum* circumspicit *ingens,*
saxum antiquum ingens, campo quod forte iacebat,
limes agro *positus* litem *ut* discerneret *arvis.*
Vix illum lecti bis sex cervice subirent,

---

ager, agri, *m.* field, plowed land
cervix, icis, *f.* neck
circumspicio, ere, circumspexi,
    circumspectus look around (for), get
    sight of
claudo, ere, clausi, clausus shut, close
discerno, ere, discrevi, discretus divide,
    separate; dissolve (a dispute)
effor, effari, effatus (defective vb.)
    speak out, utter

ferox, ocis wild, fierce
fervidus, a, um fiery, impetuous, violent
limes, itis, *m.* boundary, boundary stone
lis, litis, *f.* dispute, lawsuit
quasso (1) shake
sex *indecl. adj.* six
subeo, ire, subii, subitus undergo, go
    under
terreo, ere, terrui, territus terrify, make
    fearful

---

yourself). **sive animis sive arte:** abl. of
means.
892-3. opta ardua . . . condere terra:
Aeneas suggests two contrasting ways in
which Turnus can hope to escape him: by
flying up to the heavens (**ardua pennis
astra sequi**), or by burying himself deep in
the earth (**clausum . . . cava te condere
terra**). Of course, neither is possible.
pennis: abl. of means. **ardua . . . astra:**
direct object of **sequi. sequi . . . condere:**
complementary infs. with **opta. cava . . .
terra:** abl. of place where. **te:** direct
object of **condere.**
894. Ille: Turnus (*dixit*). **Non me tua:**
note the emphatic placement of **Non me,**
and its juxtaposition to **tua.** The
confrontation between the two enemies is
reflected in the patterns of language used
by Vergil.
894-5. fervida . . . ferox: Turnus
emphasizes both epithets with this play on
words.
895. di me: ASYNDETON between this
clause and what precedes is emphatic.
Once again Turnus juxtaposes the two
entities at odds with each other, here
himself and the gods. **Iuppiter hostis:**
again, the placement is emphatic.

896-900. The image of a hero lifting a
stone of such massiveness that not even
several of today's best men could do so
goes back to Homer (*Iliad* 12.445-9).
**896-7. saxum . . . ingens, saxum . . .
ingens:** this example of EPANALEPSIS is
varied by the addition of **antiquum** to the
phrase on its second appearance. The
repetition focuses our attention on the
stone as Turnus' best and last hope.
897. saxum antiquum ingens: the
combination of elision and spondaic
rhythm captures the weight and mass of
the stone. **campo:** abl. of place where.
898. agro: abl. of place where. **litem:**
direct object of **discerneret. discerneret:**
an unusual ZEUGMA occurs in the use of this
verb with both **litem** and **arvis:** the
boundary stone *settles* disagreements by
dividing the fields. **arvis:** dat. of advantage
or reference.
899. Vix: take with the number **bis
sex:** "*not even twelve men . . .*" **illum:**
refers syntactically to **limes** (898),
although in meaning it actually looks
back to **saxum** (896-7). **bis sex:** Vergil
uses this poetic periphrasis for **duodecim,**
a word which cannot be used in dactylic
verse. **cervice:** abl. of means. **subirent:**

qualia *nunc hominum* producit *corpora tellus;*   900
ille manu raptum trepida *torquebat in hostem*
altior insurgens *et cursu* concitus *heros.*

---

concio (or **concieo**), **ire** (or **ere**), **concivi,**
  concitus stir up, rouse
insurgo, ere, insurrexi, insurrectus rise
  up

produco, ere, produxi, productus bring
  forth, produce
qualis, e such (as)
trepidus, a, um agitated

---

impf. subjunctive in the apodosis of an
incomplete present contrary-to-fact
condition (i.e., even if twelve of today's
best men tried to do so, they could not lift
it on their necks).

    900. qualia . . . hominum . . .
corpora: in apposition with **lecti** (i.e.,
homines); the case of **qualia** can be
understood as an instance of relative
attraction: i.e., **qualia (sunt) corpora
hominum (quos) nunc producit tellus.** In
this construction, the correlative adj.
qualia has been "attracted," i.e., drawn
into, the case and number of the implied
relative **quos;** App. 242, a.

    901. manu . . . trepida: abl. of means.
raptum: i.e., **saxum. manu raptum . . .**

torquebat: two actions are described, one
completed (**raptum**) and one not
(**torquebat**). The perfect participle
suggests that the first of these was
accomplished quickly, while the
imperfect **torquebat** hints at the difficulty
Turnus is having in hurling the stone (see
below, 903–8).

    902. altior: the comparative adj. is
more vivid than an adv. **heros:** the
emphatic final word of the line is in
apposition with **ille,** which began the
preceding line. This picture of Turnus in
his final display of heroics will almost
immediately be destroyed by the
description that follows.

> *Sed neque* currentem *se nec* cognoscit *euntem*
> *tollentemve manu saxumve immane moventem;*
905 genua labant, gelidus concrevit frigore *sanguis.*
> *Tum* lapis *ipse viri* vacuum *per inane volutus*
> *nec* spatium evasit *totum neque* pertulit ictum.
> *Ac velut in somnis, oculos ubi* languida *pressit*
> *nocte* quies, nequiquam avidos extendere *cursus*
910 *velle videmur et in mediis* conatibus aegri

---

aeger, aegra, aegrum sick, unwell
avidus, a, um eager
cognosco, ere, cognovi, cognitus know, recognize
conatus, us, *m.* attempt, effort
concresco, ere, concrevi, concretus stiffen, congeal
curro, ere, cucurri, cursus run
evado, ere, evasi, evasus traverse, pass beyond
extendo, ere, extendi, extensus (or extentus) stretch out, extend
frigus, oris, *n.* coldness, chill
gelidus, a, um icy, cold
genu, us, *n.* knee

ictus, us, *m.* blow, hit (NB: do not confuse this fourth-declension noun with the verb from which it is derived; cf. the perf. pass. participle **ictus** at 12.926)
labo (1) sink, give way
languidus, a, um weak, sluggish
lapis, idis, *m.* stone
nequiquam *adv.* in vain
perfero, ferre, pertuli, perlatus convey, accomplish, complete
quies, etis, *f.* quiet, rest
spatium, i, *n.* space
vacuus, a, um empty

12.903–27. All physical strength seems to leave Turnus, and the stone he has thrown falls weakly before hitting its intended mark. Recognizing that he is now in mortal peril, Turnus is overcome by fear and indecision. Aeneas takes advantage of this opportunity to hurl his spear, and Turnus is brought to his knees.

903–4. currentem . . . euntem . . . tollentem . . . moventem: the four present participles modifying **se**, placed in pairs in these two lines, draw out the picture of Turnus' dream-like stupor: it is as if he repeatedly performs these actions, but to no avail.

904. saxum: direct object of both **tollentem** and **moventem.**

905. genua: scan -**nu**- as a double consonant, i.e., -**nv**-. **frigore:** abl. of cause.

906. viri: subjective gen., referring to Turnus. **vacuum per inane:** the n. adj. **inane** is used here as a substantive, "the void."

908. Ac velut: introduces a SIMILE. **languida:** modifies **quies** (909).

909. nocte: abl. of means. **extendere:** complementary inf. with **velle videmur** (910).

910. videmur: the passive (or Greek middle) forms of this vb. are often used in descriptions of what *appears* or *seems* to be happening in a dream. Note that Latin prefers to use such forms of this verb personally, i.e., *"we seem to want to . . .,"* whereas in English we usually say, *"it seems that we want to . . ."* (i.e., we use the verb impersonally). **aegri:** modifies the subject of **succidimus** (911).

succidimus; *non* lingua valet, *non corpore notae*
sufficiunt *vires nec vox aut* verba *sequuntur*:
sic Turno, *quacumque viam virtute petivit,*
successum *dea dira* negat. *Tum pectore* sensus
vertuntur varii; Rutulos aspectat *et urbem*   915
cunctatur*que metu letumque* instare tremescit,
nec quo se eripiat, nec qua vi tendat in hostem,
nec currus usquam *videt* aurigam*ve sororem.*
    Cunctanti *telum Aeneas* fatale coruscat,
sortitus *fortunam oculis, et corpore toto*   920

---

aspecto (1) gaze upon, look at attentively
auriga, ae, *m./f.* charioteer, chariot-driver
corusco (1) brandish, shake
cunctor, ari, cunctatus delay, hesitate
fatalis, e fatal, bearing death
insto, are, institi, instaturus press upon,
    threaten
lingua, ae, *f.* tongue
nego (1) deny, refuse
sensus, us, *m.* thought, feeling

sortior, iri, sortitus obtain by lot, select
successus, us, *m.* approach, success
succido, ere, succidi sink down, fall
sufficio, ere, suffeci, suffectus be
    sufficient, be adequate
tremesco, ere begin to shake, dread
usquam *adv.* anywhere
verbum, i, *n.* word
valeo, ere, valui, valiturus be strong, be
    powerful

---

911. corpore: abl. of place where.

911–2. notae . . . vires: i.e., Turnus
knew his own strength before; now, what
he once knew has disappeared.

913. sic: marks the end of the SIMILE and
return to the main narrative. **Turno:** dat.
with **negat** (914). **quacumque:** either
adverbial abl. of place where, i.e.,
"wherever he sought . . .," or abl. adj.
modifying the abl. of means **virtute,** i.e.,
"with whaever bravery he sought . . ."
The first of these is preferable.

914. dea dira: one of the Furies,
perhaps Allecto, who had begun to
torment Turnus in Book 7. The Furies
are sometimes called the **Dirae** in Latin.
pectore: abl. of place where.

915. Rutulos . . . et urbem: direct
objects of **aspectat.**

915–8. aspectat . . . cunctatur . . .
tremescit . . . videt: all these actions
effectively explain why Turnus' feelings
are in a state of flux (**sensus vertuntur**
varii, 914–5).

916. metu: abl. of means. **letum . . .**
instare: acc. and inf. in indirect statement
with **tremescit:** *"he dreads* (the fact) *that*
death is close . . ."

917–8. nec quo . . . nec qua vi . . . nec
currus . . . aurigamve sororem: all the
objects of **videt.** The first two are indirect
questions with vbs. in the subjunctive, the
last two are simple direct objects.

919. Cunctanti: echoes **cunctatur** from
916; dat. (indirect object) with **coruscat.**

920. sortitus . . . oculis: *"having*
selected with his eyes," i.e., having looked
and found. **fortunam:** here not *"fate,"*
but *"chance,"* *"opportunity."* **corpore**
toto: abl. of means.

eminus intorquet. Murali concita numquam
tormento *sic saxa* fremunt *nec* fulmine *tanti*
dissultant crepitus. Volat *atri* turbinis instar
exitium *dirum* hasta *ferens orasque* recludit
925   loricae *et* clipei *extremos* septemplicis *orbes;*
per medium stridens transit femur. Incidit ictus
ingens ad terram duplicato poplite Turnus.

---

clipeus, i, *m.* (or clipeum, i, *n.*) round
    shield
concio (or concieo), ire (or ere), concivi,
    concitus bring together; move
    violently
crepitus, us, *m.* (the sound of) rattling,
    clashing
dissulto (1) leap apart, burst asunder
duplicatus, a, um doubled (from duplico
    [1] double up, fold)
eminus *adv.* at a distance
exitium, ii, *n.* destruction
femur, oris (or inis), *n.* thigh
fremo, ere, fremui, fremitus resound,
    whiz
fulmen, inis, *n.* lightning flash, thunder-
    bolt
hasta, ae, *f.* spear
(ico), ere, ici, ictus strike, hit, smite
    (commonly used only in the perfect
    system)

incido, ere, incidi fall, sink
instar *n. indecl.* image, likeness; (+ *gen.*)
    like, equal to
intorqueo, ere, intorsi, intortus hurl,
    aim
lorica, ae, *f.* leather cuirass
muralis, e of a wall
numquam *adv.* never
poples, itis, *m.* knee, back of the knee
recludo, ere, reclusi, reclusus reveal,
    expose
septemplex, icis of seven layers
strido, ere, stridi make a harsh noise,
    hiss
tormentum, i, *n.* machine for hurling
transeo, ire, transii (or transivi),
    transitus go through, pierce
turbo, inis, *m.* something which whirls,
    whirlwind
volo (1) to fly

921-2. Murali . . . tormento: a war-
machine that catapults stones against the
enemy's walls; abl. of means.

**921-3. numquam . . . sic . . . nec . . .
tanti:** a negative SIMILE, emphasizing not
similarity but difference. The sound
produced by Aeneas' throw is far greater
than that generated by massive machines
of war or by thunder.

922. fulmine: abl. of separation or
source. **tanti:** modifies **crepitus** (923).

923. Volat: its subject is **hasta** (924).
atri turbinis instar: another SIMILE, this
time a short one paralleling the swiftness
with which the spear flies.

924-5. orasque . . . orbis: Aeneas'
spear makes an opening in the edge of
Turnus' cuirass and the outermost layer
of his shield, and so wounds him.

926. stridens: modifies **hasta** (924).

Consurgunt gemitu Rutuli *totusque* remugit
mons circum et vocem late nemora alta remittunt.
Ille humilis *supplex oculos dextramque precantem*   930
protendens *"Equidem merui nec* deprecor*" inquit:*
*"*utere *sorte tua. Miseri te si qua parentis*
tangere *cura potest,* oro *(fuit et tibi talis*
Anchises *genitor)* Dauni *miserere* senectae
et me, seu corpus spoliatum *lumine* mavis,   935
redde meis. Vicisti et victum tendere palmas

---

consurgo, ere, consurrexi, consurrectus
  rise, stand up
Daunus, i, *m.* Turnus' father
deprecor (1) plead against, seek to avoid
humilis, e humble, low, on the ground
malo, malle, malui prefer
misereor, eri, miseritus feel pity (+ *gen.*)
protendo, ere, protendi, protentus
  stretch forth, extend

remugio, ire resound, bellow back
remitto, ere, remisi, remissus send back,
  return
senecta, ae, *f.* old age
spolio (1) strip, deprive
tango, ere, tetigi, tactus touch
utor, uti, usus use, take advantage of
  (+ *abl.*)

12.928–52. Turnus pleads for
mercy; but Aeneas notices that Turnus is
wearing the baldric of the dead Pallas,
and resolves to take Turnus' life in turn.

928. gemitu: abl. of attendant
circumstance. **remugit:** an ONOMATOPOETIC
word.
928–9. Note how Vergil focuses our
attention on Turnus' fall by allowing us
to see, and hear, the reaction not only of
the Rutulians but of nature itself.
929. circum: adv.
930. humilis: nom., with **Ille. humilis
supplex:** pairing of adjs. in ASYNDETON (see
also above, 12.888) places emphasis on
both. Note that both adjs. have both a
literal, physical meaning and are indicative
of Turnus' mental condition: **humilis**
means both *"on the ground"* and *"humble,"*
(< *"brought low"*), while **supplex** means
both *"bent"* or *"folded,"* and *"begging"*
(< *"supplicating on his knees"*).
**930–1. oculos dextramque precantem
protendens:** a virtual ZEUGMA, since the

participle **protendens** is to be taken both
figuratively with **oculos** (*"extending his
eyes,"* i.e., *"looking at,"* *"gazing"*) and
literally with **dextram** (*"extending his
hand"*).
932. Miseri . . . parentis: Turnus tries
to evoke Aeneas' sense of mercy by
alluding to the famous scene at the close
of the *Iliad* (especially Book 24.485–506),
when Achilles, reminded by Priam of his
own father, shows mercy and restores to
Priam the body of his dead son Hector.
qua: = **aliqua** (the prefix ali- disappears
after si/nisi); nom. with **cura** (933).
933. talis: Turnus' point is that his
father is old and unfortunate, as Anchises
was before his death.
934. Dauni . . . senectae: the first is
subjective gen. with **senectae;** the second
is the object of **miserere. miserere:** imp.
935. me (vivum). me, seu corpus: both
are dir. objs. of **redde** (936). **lumine:** abl.
of separation (with **spoliatum**).
936. meis: i.e., Turnus' family and the
Rutulians as a whole. **Vicisti et victum:**
the repetition is emphatic. **victum (me).
victum tendere palmas:** **victum** is subject

Ausonii *videre; tua est* Lavinia *coniunx,*
ulterius *ne tende* odiis." *Stetit acer in armis*
Aeneas volvens oculos dextramque repressit;
940   *et iam iamque magis* cunctantem flectere sermo
coeperat, *infelix umero cum* apparuit *alto*
balteus *et notis* fulserunt cingula bullis
Pallantis *pueri, victum quem vulnere* Turnus
straverat atque umeris inimicum *insigne gerebat.*
945   *Ille, oculis* postquam *saevi* monimenta *doloris*

---

appareo, ere, apparui, apparitus appear
Ausonii, orum, *m.* the people of Italy
balteus, i, *m.* baldric
bulla, ae, *f.* stud, knob
cingula, orum, *n. pl.* swordbelt
coepi, ere, coeptus begin
cunctor (1) delay, hesitate
flecto, ere, flexi, flexus bend, turn
fulgeo, ere, fulsi flash, gleam

inimicus, a, um hostile, belonging to the
enemy
monimentum, i, *n.* reminder, memorial
odium, i, *n.* hatred
postquam *conj.* after
reprimo, ere, repressi, repressus press
back, restrain
sermo, onis, *m.* speech, conversation
ulterior, ius, *comp. adj.* farther, beyond

---

acc. and **palmas** is object acc. in indirect
statement (introduced by **Ausonii videre,**
937).

937. **videre:** alternative form of 3d pl.
perf. act. indicative.

938. **ne tende:** negative imp., poetic
alternative for the prosaic **noli tendere.**
odiis: abl. of specification or respect.
Stetit: the verb both emphasizes the
physical relationship between the two
heroes (Aeneas stands while Turnus
kneels) and creates a static pause as we
await Aeneas' decision.

940–1. **iam iamque magis . . .**
coeperat: the repetition of **iam** enhances
the picture of Aeneas as he pauses and
hesitates, on the brink of yielding to
Turnus' wishes.

941. **infelix:** this adj.'s placement at the
beginning of its clause, before the
subordinating conjunction **cum,** underlines
the thematic importance of the word in its
last appearance in the poem. Note how its
physical distance (HYPERBATON) from the
noun it actually modifies, **balteus** (942), adds
to the suspense of the scene: momentarily
we wonder whether it describes Aeneas,

or Turnus, or someone or something else.
umero . . . alto: abl. of place where.

942. **balteus:** emphatic first position—
the baldric stands out in this line as it does
in Aeneas' eyes. **notis:** familiar to Aeneas.
notis . . . bullis: abl. of means.

943. **Pallantis:** emphatic first position
again; note how the gen. **Pallantis** is
located in the text immediately beneath the
word it modifies, **balteus. pueri:** this detail
evokes the pathos of Pallas' death at an
early age; it also suggests that Aeneas is
thinking of another son besides himself
and Turnus (see above, 932–4) whose
father has been shown no mercy, i.e.,
Evander. **victum:** echoes Turnus'
description of himself moments earlier,
936. **vulnere:** abl. of means, with either
victum or (preferably) **straverat** (944).

944. **atque umeris inimicum insigne**
gerebat: only loosely linked to the clause
preceding it—the syntax would normally
demand repetition of the rel. pronoun in
the gen., **cuius.** Aeneas' rapid thinking,
however, is reflected in Vergil's
description of what the hero sees.

945. **Ille:** Aeneas. **oculis:** abl. of means.

exuvias*que* hausit, furiis accensus *et ira*
terribilis: *"Tune hinc* spoliis indute *meorum*
eripiare mihi? Pallas *te hoc vulnere,* Pallas
immolat *et poenam* scelerato *ex sanguine* sumit."
Hoc dicens ferrum adverso *sub pectore condit*   950
fervidus; ast *illi solvuntur* frigore *membra*
vitaque cum gemitu fugit indignata *sub umbras.*

---

accendo, ere, accendi, accensus set on
    fire, inflame
adversus, a, um facing, in front
ast *conj.* = **at**
exuviae, arum, *f.* spoils
fervidus, a, um burning, fiery, hot
frigus, oris, *n.* coldness, chill
furia, ae, *f.* (in pl.) fury, madness
haurio, ire, hausi, haustus drink in
immolo (1) sacrifice, offer

indignor (1) deem unworthy, despise
induo, ere, indui, indutus clothe, dress in
scelero (1) pollute, defile
spolium, ii, *n.* hide (of an animal);
    commonly, in the n. pl., spoils, arms
    stripped from an enemy
sumo, ere, sumpsi, sumptus take up,
    assume; exact (a penalty)
terribilis, e dreadful, terrible, terrifying

**945–6. saevi monimenta doloris
exuviasque:** a virtual HENDIADYS—Aeneas
sees not two different things but the
baldric alone, which is both a
monimentum in his eyes and **exuviae** to
Turnus.

946–7. furiis . . . terribilis: take **furiis**
as abl. of means with **accensus, ira** as abl.
of specification with **terribilis.**

947. terribilis (dixit). Tune: = **tu + ne.
spoliis:** abl. of means. **indute:** voc.
meorum: Turnus actually wears only the
spoils of Pallas; but Aeneas indicates that
they are the symbolic property, at least, of
all his followers.

948. eripiare: deliberative subjunctive;
alternative 2d sing. pres. pass. ending for
eripiaris. mihi: dat. of separation. **Pallas
. . . Pallas:** the repetition of the name
indicates how completely the memory of
Pallas now fills Aeneas' mind. **hoc**

vulnere: abl. of means.

949. immolat: this verb comes as a
surprise, given its subject; after all, the
dead Pallas cannot literally perform a
sacrifice. Aeneas suggests that in acting
on Pallas' behalf he acts as Pallas, doing
to Turnus what Pallas would do were he
still alive.

950. adverso sub pectore: though
Turnus kneels and Aeneas stands, they are
effectively face to face.

951. fervidus: emphatic first position
again; for the adj. applied to Aeneas, see
above, 12.894. **illi:** = **Turno;** dat. of
reference. **frigore:** abl. of means.

952. indignata: modifies **vita.** (Be
careful not to translate this participle as its
false cognate, "indignant"—the point is
rather that, as it descends to the underworld,
Turnus' soul angrily laments its fate.)

A SELECTED BIBLIOGRAPHY

No bibliography of Vergil's *Aeneid* can hope to be complete or even comprehensive. I have simply focused, therefore, on recent work available in English and of particular relevance to the selections contained in this textbook. Most of the works cited are from the late 80s and 90s; exceptions are works of particular relevance and/or lasting impact. And of course, most are in English; but I have been unable to exclude a small number of works in Italian whose influence continues to be profound. While these are likely to be above and beyond the ability and interest of even the most avid Vergilian student, teachers with modest everyday Italian should be able to use these books and articles to their profit. Finally, I remind my readers to avail themselves of the wonderful Vergilian bibliography that appears in *Vergilius*, the annual publication of the Vergilian Society.

Texts and Commentaries

In composing this textbook, I have relied on four important predecessors:

Harrison, S. J., ed. *Vergil, Aeneid 10: With Introduction, Translation, and Commentary*. Oxford, 1991.

Pharr, Clyde, ed. *Vergil's Aeneid, With a Selective Bibliography by Alexander G. McKay*. Wauconda, IL, 1998.

Traina, A., ed. *Virgilio: L'utopia e la storia (Il libro xii dell'Eneide e antologia delle opere)*. Turin, 1997.

Williams, R. D., ed. *The Aeneid of Virgil: Books 7–12*. Basingstoke and London, 1973; repr. 1984.

General Studies of and Collections of Essays on the *Aeneid*

Harrison, S. J., ed. *Oxford Readings in Vergil's Aeneid*. Oxford and New York, 1990.

Heinze, R. *Vergil's Epic Technique*, trans. H. and D. Harvey and F. Robertson. Bristol, 1993. (A valuable translation of the time-honored classic.)

Horsfall, N. *A Companion to the Study of Virgil*. Mnemosyne Supplement 151. Leiden and New York, 1995.

Martindale, C., ed. *The Cambridge Companion to Virgil*. Cambridge, 1997.

Quinn, S. ed. *Why Vergil? A Collection of Interpretations*. Wauconda, IL, 2000.

(Harrison, Martindale, and Quinn are available in paperback, and should be on every Vergil teacher's shelf; Heinze and Horsfall should be within easy reach in the closest college or university library.)

Works Focusing on the Passages in this Textbook

Feeney, D. C. "The Reconciliations of Juno." *CQ* 34 (1984) 179–94. (Reprinted with corrections in Harrison [1990], 339–62.)

Galinsky, G. K. "The Anger of Aeneas." *AJP* 109 (1988) 321–48.

———. "How to Be Philosophical about the End of the *Aeneid*." *ICS* 19 (1994) 191–201.

O'Higgins, D. "The Emperor's New Clothes: Unseen Images on Pallas' Baldric." *Hermathena* 158 (1995) 61–72.

Petter, G. "Desecration and Expiation as a Theme in the *Aeneid*." *Vergilius* 40 (1994) 76–84.

Putnam, M. C. J. "Virgil's Danaid Ekphrasis." *ICS* 19 (1994) 171–89.

Schork, R. J. "The Final Simile in the *Aeneid*: Roman and Rutulian Ramparts." *AJP* 107 (1986) 260–70.

Spence, S. "Clinching the Text: The Danaids and the End of the *Aeneid*." *Vergilius* 37 (1991) 11–19.

Stahl, H.-P. "The Death of Turnus: Augustan Vergil and the Political Rival." In *Between Republic and Empire: Interpretations of Augustus and His Principate*, edited by K. Raaflaub and M. Toher, 174–211. Berkeley and Los Angeles, 1990.

Thomas, R. F. "The Isolation of Turnus: *Aeneid* Book 12." In *Vergil's Aeneid: Augustan Epic and Political Context*, edited by H.-P. Stahl. London, 1997.

Works for Further Reading and Research

a. on the *Aeneid*

Barchiesi, A. *La traccia del modello: effetti omerici nella narrazione virgiliana.* Pisa, 1984.

Boyle, A. "The Canonic Text: Virgil's *Aeneid.*" In *Roman Epic*, edited by A. Boyle, 79–107. London and New York, 1993.

Cairns, F. *Virgil's Augustan Epic.* Cambridge, 1989.

Clausen, W. *Virgil's Aeneid and the Tradition of Hellenistic Poetry.* Berkeley and Los Angeles, 1987.

Conte, G. B. *The Rhetoric of Imitation: Genre and Poetic Memory in Virgil and Other Latin Poets*, edited by C. P. Segal. Ithaca, NY and London, 1986.

Corte, F. della, et al., eds. *Enciclopedia Virgiliana.* Six volumes. Rome, 1984–91.

Feeney, D. C. *The Gods in Epic.* Oxford, 1991.

Gillis, D. *Eros and Death in the Aeneid.* Rome, 1983.

Hardie, P. R. *Virgil's Aeneid: Cosmos and Imperium.* Oxford, 1986.

Horsfall, N. M. "The Aeneas Legend from Homer to Virgil." In *Roman Myth and Mythography*, by J. N. Bremmer and N. M. Horsfall, 12–24. BICS Suppl. 52. London, 1987.

Lyne, R. O. A. M. *Further Voices in Vergil's Aeneid.* Oxford, 1987.

———. *Words and the Poet: Characteristic Techniques of Style in Vergil's Aeneid.* Oxford, 1989.

Mackie, C. J. *The Characterisation of Aeneas.* Edinburgh, 1988.

Nagle, B. R. "Open-ended Closure in the *Aeneid.*" *CW* 76 (1983) 257–63.

O'Hara, J. J. *Death and the Optimistic Prophecy in Vergil's Aeneid.* Princeton, 1990.

———. *True Names: Vergil and the Alexandrian Tradition of Etymological Wordplay.* Ann Arbor, 1996.

Petrini, M. *The Child and the Hero: Coming of Age in Catullus and Vergil.* Ann Arbor, 1997.

Putnam, M. C. J. *Virgil's Aeneid: Interpretation and Influence.* Chapel Hill and London, 1995.

Stahl, H.-P., ed. *Vergil's Aeneid: Augustan Epic and Political Context.* London, 1997.

b. on the Augustan context

Galinsky, G. K. *Augustan Culture: An Interpretive Introduction.* Princeton, 1996.

Gurval, R. *Actium and Augustus: The Politics and Emotions of Civil War.* Ann Arbor, 1995.

White, P. *Promised Verse: Poets in the Society of Augustan Rome.* Cambridge, MA and London, 1993.

Zanker, P. *The Power of Images in the Age of Augustus.* Ann Arbor, 1988.

c. on the survival of Vergil

Martindale, C., ed. *Virgil and His Influence.* Bristol, 1984.

Wright, D. H. *The Vatican Vergil: A Masterpiece of Late Antique Art.* Princeton, 1993.

GRAMMATICAL APPENDIX

GRAMMATICAL APPENDIX

ALPHABET; PRONUNCIATION; QUANTITY; ACCENT

1. With the exception that it has no **w** the Latin alphabet is the same as the English, which has been borrowed from it.

2. The vowels, as in English, are **a, e, i, o, u,** and sometimes **y.** The other letters are consonants.

SOUNDS OF THE LETTERS

3. Vowels. All Latin vowels are either long or short. All long vowels are indicated in this text by having the mark (–) placed over them, as **nōn,** *not.* All unmarked vowels in this book are to be considered short.

4. Latin vowels have the following sounds:

LONG	SHORT
ā as in father: **āra,** *altar*	a as in ask: **anima,** *soul*
ē as in they: **mēns,** *mind*	e as in red: **bellum,** *war*
ī as in machine: **dīvus,** *divine*	i as in hit: **mittō,** *send*
ō as in bone: **mōns,** *mountain*	o as in obey: **aequor,** *sea*
ū as in prune: **lūx,** *light*	u as in full: **fuga,** *flight*

5. Diphthongs. A diphthong is the union of two vowels in a single syllable. The sounds of the Latin diphthongs are:

ae as *ai* in *ai*sle: **caelum,** *heaven*
au as *ou* in h*ou*se: **aurum,** *gold*
ei as *ei* in fr*ei*ght: **ei,** *alas!*
oe as *oi* in b*oi*l: **poena,** *punishment*
eu as *eh-oo* (*oo* as in sp*oo*n, but fused with the *eh* sound into a single syllable): **heu,** *alas!*
ui somewhat as *we,* but with a more vocalic sound of the **u: cui,** *to whom*

6. Consonants. In general the consonants have the same sounds as in English, but there are the following exceptions:

c as *k,* always hard, as in *c*ome: **faciō,** *do, make*
g always hard, as in *g*et: **fugiō,** *flee*
j (consonantal **i**) as *y* in *y*et: **jubeō,** *order*
s as in *s*it, never as in ri*s*e: **cāsus,** *chance*
t as in *t*ie, never as in na*t*ion: **tālis,** *such*
v (consonantal **u**) as *w* in *w*ill: **videō,** see
x as in e*x*tra, always hard: **rēx,** *king*
bs, bt, as *ps, pt:* **urbs,** *city;* **obtineō,** *gain, obtain*
ch as *k* in *k*ite: **pulcher,** *beautiful*
gu (usually), **qu,** and sometimes **su** before a vowel, as *gw, kw,* and *sw,* respectively: **sanguis,** *blood;* **qui,** *who;* **suādeō,** *persuade*
ph as *p-h* (as *p-h* in sa*ph*ead, but without the break): **philosophia,** philosophy
th as *t-h* (as *t-h* in fa*th*ead, but without the break): **Corinthus,** Corinth

a. Modern printed texts often use the same character (**i**) for both vocalic and consonantal **i** (**i, j**), as well as only one character for vocalic and consonantal **u** (**u, v**). The Romans did not employ separate characters to distinguish between the vocalic and consonantal uses of these letters.

b. When coming between vowels within a word, **j** is regularly doubled in pronunciation, although written but once, as **major,** *greater;* **pejor,** *worse;* **ejus,** *of him;* **hujus,** *of this;* **cujus,** *of whom;* **ajō,** *say.* These are to be pronounced as though spelled **majjor, pejjor, ejjus, hujjus, cujjus, ajjō.** This rule does not apply to **j**, which was originally initial, but which comes between vowels as a result of composition, as **praejūdicō,** *prejudge;* **bijugī,** *chariot.*

c. When followed by the letter **i**, as in compounds of **jaciō,** *throw,* **j,** although pronounced, is not ordinarily written in the classical period, as **coniciō,** *throw together;* **dēiciō,** *cast down;* **ēiciō,** *throw out;* **reiciō,** *throw back.* These are to be pronounced as though spelled **conjiciō, dējiciō, ējiciō, rejiciō,** and in this text they are so written.

7. Doubled Consonants. All doubled consonants are to be sounded separately, not as one consonant as is customary in English. Thus **puella,** *girl,* must be pronounced **pu-el-la,** and not **pu-ell-a** as in English; so also **er-rō,** *wander, stray;* **oc-cu-pō,** *occupy.*

8. Double Consonants. The double consonants are **x** and **z; x** is equivalent to **ks** or **cs; z,** a Greek letter, originally **zd,** may be pronounced as **z** in *lazy.*

SYLLABLES

9. A Latin word has as many syllables as it has vowels and diphthongs; as **so-ci-us,** *comrade;* **vo-cā-re,** *to call;* **moe-ni-a,** *walls;* **ac-ci-pi-ō,** *receive.*

10. In dividing a Latin word into syllables, a single consonant is pronounced with the following vowel, as **ca-put,** *head.*

11. A consonant followed by **l** or **r** (except **ll** or **rr**) is usually pronounced with the **l** or **r**, as **pa-trēs,** *fathers;* **pū-bli-cus,** *public.*

12. In all other combinations of two or more consonants between vowels, the first consonant is pronounced with the preceding vowel, and the others with the vowel following, as **her-ba,** *herb;* **mōn-strō,** *show;* **ar-ma,** *arms.*

13. Exceptions. Compound words are divided in accordance with their original elements, as **ab-est,** *he is absent;* **trāns-eō,** *I pass across.*

QUANTITY

14. The quantity of a syllable is the term used to denote the relative amount of time employed in pronouncing it. About twice as much time should be used in pronouncing a long syllable as a short one.

15. A syllable is said to be long by *nature* when it contains a long vowel or a diphthong. It is said to be long by *position* when its vowel is followed by two or more consonants which are separated in pronunciation (10–12), or by either of the double consonants **x** or **z** (8), or by **j**, which was regularly doubled in pronunciation (6 *b*). **H** never helps to make a syllable long, and **qu** counts as a single consonant. Thus the first syllable of **adhūc**, *thus far,* and of **aqua**, *water,* is short.

16. Except under the metrical accent (394), a final syllable ending in a short vowel regularly remains short before a word beginning with two consonants or a double consonant.

17. If a consonant followed by **l** or **r** comes after a short vowel, the syllable containing the short vowel is said to be *common*, i.e, it may be either long or short, according to the pleasure of the one using it.

18. NOTE: This is due to the fact that the **l** and **r** blend so easily with the preceding consonant that the combination takes scarcely more time than a single consonant. When the **l** or **r** is separated in pronunciation from the preceding consonant, as may be done in all cases, more time is required in pronunciation and the preceding syllable is treated as long.

19. Observe that the *vowel* in a long syllable may be either long or short, and is to be pronounced accordingly. Thus in **errō**, *wander;* **captō**, *seize;* **vertō**, *turn;* **nox**, *night;* the first *vowel* in each case is short, and must be so pronounced, according to 4, but the syllable is long, and must occupy more time in pronunciation, according to 14, 15.

20. A vowel is regularly short before another vowel, or **h**, as **aes-tu-ō**, *boil;* **de-us**, *god;* **tra-hō**, *draw.*

a. This rule does not apply to Greek words in Latin, such as **ā-ēr**, *air;* **I-xi-ōn**, *Ixion* (a proper name).

21. A vowel is regularly short before **nt** or **nd**. Observe that the *syllable* in this case is long.

22. A vowel is regularly short before any final consonant except **s**.

a. Some monosyllables ending in **l, r, n**, and **c**, have a long vowel as **sōl**, *sun;* **pār**, *equal;* **nōn**, *not;* **sīc**, *so.*

23. A vowel is regularly long before **ns, nf, nx**, and **nct**.

24. Diphthongs and vowels derived from diphthongs or contracted from other vowels are regularly long.

ACCENT

25. Words of two syllables have the accent or stress on the first (penult), as **a′-mō,** *love.*

a. The last syllable of a word is called the ultima (**ultimus,** *last*); the next to the last syllable is called the penult (**paene,** *almost;* **ultimus,** *last*); and the syllable before the penult is called the antepenult (**ante,** *before;* **paene,** *almost;* **ultimus,** *last*).

26. Words of more than two syllables (polysyllabic words) have the accent on the penult when the penult is long, on the antepenult when the penult is short or common (17), as **aes-tu-ā′-re,** *boil;* **a′-ni-mus,** *mind.*

27. Enclitics. Certain words are not ordinarily written separately but are regularly appended to the word they introduce. The most common of these are **-que,** *and;* **-ve,** *or;* and **-ne** (sign of a question). They are called enclitics and, when appended to words accented on the antepenult, add an accent to the ultima, as **fo′ribus′que,** *and from the doorway.* When an enclitic is appended to a word of two syllables having a long ultima, the accent is shifted to the ultima; as **amō′que,** *and I love;* but **be′llaque,** *and wars;* **i′taque,** *and so.*

PRONUNCIATION OF LATIN WORDS IN ENGLISH

28. Latin words and phrases commonly used in English are to be pronounced according to the ordinary English system of pronunciation; for example, in **alumnī,** the final **ī** is to be pronounced as *i* in **five,** and the **u** as *u* in b*u*m; and in the phrase **via** Chicago, **v** is to be pronounced as in *v*ine, and **i** as in *v*ine; in the phrase **vōx populī,** *the voice of the people,* **v** as in *v*oice, **ō** as in *o*x, **u** as in d*u*e, **ī** as in d*i*e.

NUMBER

29. In Latin there are two numbers: the singular, denoting one; the plural, denoting more than one. For the poetic plural see 243.

CASES

30. In Latin there are seven cases:

1. **The nominative** is the case of the subject.
2. **The genitive** is usually equivalent to the English possessive or to the objective with the preposition *of.*
3. **The dative** is the case of the indirect object or of personal interest.
4. **The accusative** is usually the case of the direct object.
5. **The vocative** is the case of direct address.
6. **The ablative** is the case of adverbial relation.
7. **The locative** is the case of the place where.

DECLENSIONS

31. There are five declensions in Latin, which are characterized by the final letter of their respective stems *(stem characteristic)*. For practical purposes and regularly in lexicons they are also distinguished by the ending of the genitive singular.

DECLENSION	STEM CHARACTERISTIC	GENITIVE SINGULAR
I.	ā (a)	ae
II.	o	ī
III.	a consonant or i	is
IV.	u	ūs
V.	ē	eī

a. The first, second, and fifth declensions are called vowel declensions; the third and fourth, which really form but one, the consonant declension, **i** and **u** being considered semiconsonants.

32. The case endings in combination with the stem characteristics give rise to the following systems of terminations for the five declensions:

SINGULAR

	I.	II.	III.	IV.	V.
NOM.	a	us; wanting; **um**	s; wanting	us; ū	ēs
GEN.	ae	ī	is	ūs	eī, ē
DAT.	ae	ō	ī	uī; ū	eī, ē
ACC.	am	um	em, im	um, ū	em
VOC.	a	e; wanting; **um**	s; **wanting**	us, u	ēs
ABL.	ā	ō	e, ī	ū	ē

PLURAL

	I.	II.	III.	IV.	V.
NOM. VOC.	ae	ī, a	ēs; a, ia	ūs, ua	ēs
GEN.	ārum	ōrum	um, ium	uum	ērum
DAT. ABL.	īs	īs	ibus	ubus, ibus	ēbus
ACC.	ās	ōs, a	ēs, īs; a, ia	ūs, ua	ēs

33. General Rules of Declension.

a. The vocative is like the nominative, except in the singular of the second declension, when the nominative ends in **us**.

b. In the third, fourth, and fifth declensions the nominative, accusative, and vocative cases are alike in the plural.

c. Neuter substantives have the nominative, accusative, and vocative alike; in the plural these cases always end in **a**.

d. The dative and ablative plural are alike in all declensions.

FIRST DECLENSION

34. The stem ends in **ā**. The nominative-vocative singular is the simple stem with shortened stem vowel and no case ending.

Sg.			Pl.	
Nom.	**terra,** f; (*a, the*) *land*		**terrae,** (*the*) *lands*	
Gen.	**terrae,** *of* (*a, the*) *land,* (*a, the*) *land's*		**terrārum,** *of* (*the*) *lands,* (*the*) *lands'*	
Dat.	**terrae,** *to, for* (*a, the*) *land*		**terrīs,** *to, for* (*the*) *lands*	
Acc.	**terram,** (*a, the*) *land*		**terrās,** *to, for* (*the*) *lands*	
Voc.	**terra,** O *land! land!*		**terrae,** O *lands! lands!*	
Abl.	**terrā,** *from, with, by, in, on, at* (*a, the*) *land*		**terrīs,** *from, with, by, in, on, at* (*the*) *lands*	

a. The locative singular of the first declension is like the genitive: **Rōmae,** *at Rome;* **mīlitiae,** *abroad* (i. e., engaged *in warfare*).

b. The genitive singular sometimes ends in **āī** in poetry; the genitive plural sometimes takes the form **um** instead of **ārum.**

c. The ending **ābus** is found (along with the regular ending) in the dative and ablative plural of **dea,** *goddess,* and **fīlia,** *daughter.*

35. Rule of Gender. Nouns of the first declension are feminine, except when they refer to males.

SECOND DECLENSION

36. The stem ends in **o,** which in the classical period usually becomes **u.** In combination with the case endings it frequently disappears altogether. In the vocative singular (except in neuters) it becomes **e.**

a. The nominative ends in **s** (m., f.) and **m** (n.). But many masculine stems in which the original final vowel, **o,** was preceded by **r** have dropped the **us** of the nominative and the **e** of the vocative, and inserted **e** before the **r,** if it was preceded by a consonant; thus original **pueros** became **puer,** *boy,* and **libros** became **liber,** *book.*

b. The final **o** was often retained after **u** or **v** until the first century A.D.; as **servos,** *slave.*

37. Animus, *spirit;* **puer,** *boy;* **vir,** *man;* **bellum,** *war,* are declined as follows:

Sg.				
Nom.	**animus,** m.	**puer,** m.	**vir,** m.	**bellum,** n.
Gen.	**animī**	**puerī**	**virī**	**bellī**
Dat.	**animō**	**puerō**	**virō**	**bellō**
Acc.	**animum**	**puerum**	**virum**	**bellum**
Voc.	**anime**	**puer**	**vir**	**bellum**
Abl.	**animō**	**puerō**	**virō**	**bellō**
Pl. Nom.	**animī**	**puerī**	**virī**	**bella**
Gen.	**animōrum**	**puerōrum**	**virōrum**	**bellōrum**
Dat.	**animīs**	**puerīs**	**virīs**	**bellīs**
Acc.	**animōs**	**puerōs**	**virōs**	**bella**
Voc.	**animī**	**puerī**	**virī**	**bella**
Abl.	**animīs**	**puerīs**	**virīs**	**bellīs**

a. Words in **ius** (**ium**) have the genitive singular for the most part in ī until the first century A.D.; without change of accent: **inge′nī** (nom., **ingenium**), *of genius;* **Vergi′lī,** *of Vergil.*

b. Proper names in **ius** have the vocative in ī, without change of accent: **Antō′nī, Tu′llī, Gā′ī, Vergi′lī. Fīlius,** *son,* and **genius,** *genius,* form their vocative in like manner: **fīlī, genī.** In solemn discourse **us** of the nominative is employed also for the vocative. So regularly **deus,** *O god!*

c. The locative singular ends in ī like the genitive, as **Rhodī,** *at Rhodes;* **Tarentī,** *at Tarentum.*

d. In the genitive plural **um** instead of **ōrum** is often found.

e. The locative plural is identical with the ablative: **Delphīs,** *at Delphi.*

f. The declension of **deus,** m., *god,* is irregular:

Sg.	Nom.	deus	Pl.	dī, deī, diī
	Gen.	deī		deōrum, deum
	Dat.	deō		dīs, deīs, diīs
	Acc.	deum		deōs
	Voc.	deus		dī, deī, diī
	Abl.	deō		dīs, deīs, diīs

38. Rule of Gender. Nouns of the second declension ending in **us** or **r** are masculine; in **um** neuter.

a. **Exceptions.** Feminine are: (1) cities and islands, as **Corinthus, Samus;** (2) most trees, as **fāgus,** *beech;* **pirus,** *pear tree;* (3) **alvus,** *belly;* **colus,** *distaff;* **humus,** *ground;* **vannus,** *wheat fan;* (4) many Greek nouns, as **atomus,** *atom.*

Neuters are: **pelagus,** *sea;* **vīrus,** *venom;* **vulgus,** the *rabble.*

Third Declension

39. The stem ends in a consonant or in the close vowels (or semivowels) **i** and **ū.** The stems are divided according to their last letter, called the stem characteristic:

I. Consonant Stems

1. *Liquid stems,* ending in **l, m, n, r.**
2. *Sibilant stems,* ending in **s.**
3. *Mute stems* { *a.* Ending in **b, p.** *b.* Ending in **g, c.** *c.* Ending in **d, t.**

II. *i*-Stems

40. 1. The nominative singular, masculine and feminine, case ending is **s,** which, however, is dropped after **l, n, r, s,** and combines with **c** or **g** to form **x.** In the other cases, the endings are added to the unchanged stem. The vocative of the third declension is always like the nominative.

2. Neuters always form the nominative without the addition of a case ending and the accusative and vocative cases in both numbers are like the nominative. The nominative plural ends in **a**.

I. Consonant Stems

41. 1. Liquid Stems in *l*

Form the nominative without the case ending **s**. These comprise:

a. Those in which the stem characteristic is preceded by a vowel; thus:

Sg.			Pl.	
	Nom.	cōnsul, m., *consul*		cōnsulēs, *consuls*
	Gen.	cōnsulis		cōnsulum
	Dat.	cōnsulī		cōnsulibus
	Acc.	cōnsulem		cōnsulēs
	Voc.	cōnsul		cōnsulēs
	Abl.	cōnsule		cōnsulibus

b. Two neuter substantives with stems in **ll**, one of which is lost in the nominative: **mel, mellis,** *honey;* **fel, fellis,** *gall.*

42. Rules of Gender. Third declension nouns having their stems in **l** are regularly masculine; those having stems in **ll** are neuter.

43. 2. Liquid Stems in *n*

Most masculine and feminine stems form the nominative singular by dropping the stem characteristic and changing a preceding vowel to **o**. Some masculine and most neuter stems retain the stem characteristic in the nominative and change a preceding **i** to **e**.

		MASCULINE		NEUTER
Sg.	Nom.	sermō, m., *conversation*	homō, m., *man*	nōmen, n., *name*
	Gen.	sermōnis	hominis	nōminis
	Dat.	sermōnī	hominī	nōminī
	Acc.	sermōnem	hominem	nōmen
	Voc.	sermō	homō	nōmen
	Abl.	sermōne	homine	nōmine
Pl.	Nom.	sermōnēs	hominēs	nōmina
	Gen.	sermōnum	hominum	nōminum
	Dat.	sermōnibus	hominibus	nōminibus
	Acc.	sermōnēs	hominēs	nōmina
	Voc.	sermōnēs	hominēs	nōmina
	Abl.	sermōnibus	hominibus	nōminibus

44. Rules of Gender. 1. Third declension nouns ending in **ō** are masculine, except those ending in **dō, gō,** and **iō,** which are mostly feminine.

2. Third declension nouns in **en (men)** are regularly neuter.

45. 3. LIQUID STEMS IN *r*

Form nominative without **s.**

Sg.			
	NOM.	**soror,** f., *sister*	**pater,** m., *father*
	GEN.	**sorōris**	**patris**
	DAT.	**sorōrī**	**patrī**
	ACC.	**sorōrem**	**patrem**
	VOC.	**soror**	**pater**
	ABL.	**sorōre**	**patre**
Pl.	NOM.	**sorōrēs**	**patrēs**
	GEN.	**sorōrum**	**patrum**
	DAT.	**sorōribus**	**patribus**
	ACC.	**sorōrēs**	**patrēs**
	VOC.	**sorōrēs**	**patrēs**
	ABL.	**sorōribus**	**patribus**

a. **Imber,** *shower;* **linter,** *skiff;* **ūter,** *bag;* **venter,** *belly,* have the genitive plural in **ium. Imber** has also sometimes the ablative singular in **ī.**

46. Rules of Gender. 1. Third declension nouns in **er** and **or** are usually masculine. 2. Third declension nouns in **ar** and **ur** are neuter.

47. 4. SIBILANT STEMS

The nominative has no additional **s,** and in masculines changes **e** to **i,** and in neuters **e** or **o** to **u** before **s.**

In the oblique cases, the **s** of the stem usually passes over, between two vowels, into **r.**

Sg.			
	NOM. ACC. VOC.	**genus,** n., *kind*	**corpus,** n., *body*
	GEN.	**generis**	**corporis**
	DAT.	**generī**	**corporī**
	ABL.	**genere**	**corpore**
Pl.	NOM. ACC. VOC.	**genera**	**corpora**
	GEN.	**generum**	**corporum**
	DAT. ABL.	**generibus**	**corporibus**

48. Rules of Gender. 1. Masculine are third declension nouns in **is (eris),** and **ōs (ōris).**

2. Neuter are third declension nouns in **us (eris, oris)** and in **ūs (ūris).**

49. 5. MUTE STEMS

All masculines and feminines of mute stems have **s** in the nominative. Before **s** a **p** or **b** is retained, a **c** or **g** combines with it to form **x,** a **t** or **d** is dropped.

a. Most polysyllabic mute stems change their stem vowel **i** to **e** in the nominative.

50. Stems in *p* or *b*

Sg.			Pl.	
Nom.	princeps, m., *leader*		Pl.	principēs
Gen.	principis			principum
Dat.	principī			principibus
Acc.	principem			principēs
Voc.	princeps			principēs
Abl.	principe			principibus

51. Stems in *c* or *g*

Sg.		Pl.	
Nom.	dux, m., *leader*	Pl.	ducēs
Gen.	ducis		ducum
Dat.	ducī		ducibus
Acc.	ducem		ducēs
Voc.	dux		ducēs
Abl.	duce		ducibus

52. Stems in *t* or *d*

Sg.		Pl.	
Nom.	comes, m., f., *companion*	Pl.	comitēs
Gen.	comitis		comitum
Dat.	comitī		comitibus
Acc.	comitem		comitēs
Voc.	comes		comitēs
Abl.	comite		comitibus

Sg.		Pl.	
Nom.	pes, m., *foot*	Pl.	pedēs
Gen.	pedis		pedum
Dat.	pedī		pedibus
Acc.	pedem		pedēs
Voc.	pes		pedēs
Abl.	pede		pedibus

Sg.		Pl.	
Nom.	caput, n., *head*	Pl.	capita
Gen.	capitis		capitum
Dat.	capitī		capitibus
Acc.	caput		capita
Voc.	caput		capita
Abl.	capite		capitibus

a. The following mute stems have certain irregular forms: **cor** (gen. **cordis**), *heart;* **nox** (gen. **noctis**), *night;* **lac** (gen. **lactis**), *milk.*

53. Monosyllabic mute stems, with the characteristic preceded by a consonant, have the genitive plural in **ium: urbium,** *of cities;* **arcium,** *of citadels;* **montium,** *of mountains;* **noctium,** *of nights.*

a. Monosyllabic mute stems, with characteristic preceded by a long vowel or diphthong, vary: **dōtium,** *of dowries;* **lītium,** *of lawsuits;* **faucium,** *of throats;* **fraudum (ium),** *of frauds;* **laudum (ium),** *of praises;* but **vōcum,** *of voices.*

b. Most monosyllabic stems with characteristic preceded by a short vowel, have **um: opum,** *of resources;* but **fac-ium,** *of torches;* **nuc-um (ium),** *of nuts;* **niv-ium (um),** *of snows.*

c. Polysyllabic stems in **nt** and **rt** have more frequently **ium**, as **clientium** (**um**), *of clients;* **cohortium** (**um**), *of companies.*

d. Polysyllabic feminine stems in **āt** have either **um** or **ium**, as **aetātum** or **aetātium**, *of ages;* **civitātum** or **civitātium**, *of states;* the rest have usually **um**. **Palūs**, *marsh,* has usually **palūdium**.

54. Rule of Gender. Mute stems, with nominative in **s**, are usually feminine.

II. *i*-STEMS

55. Masculines and feminines form their nominative in **s**.

a. Some feminines change the stem vowel **i** to **ē** in the nominative.

b. Neuters change the stem vowel **i** to **e** in the nominative. This **e** is generally dropped after **l** and **r** in polysyllabic neuters.

c. Stems in **i** have genitive plural in **ium**.

d. Neuter stems in **i** have the ablative singular in **ī** and nominative plural in **ia**.

56.	Sg.	Nom.	hostis, m., *enemy*	mare, n., *sea*	animal, n., *living being*
		Gen.	hostis	maris	animālis
		Dat.	hostī	marī	animālī
		Acc.	hostem	mare	animal
		Voc.	hostis	mare	animal
		Abl.	hostī	marī	animālī
	Pl.	Nom.	hostēs	maria	animālia
		Gen.	hostium	marium	animālium
		Dat.	hostibus	maribus	animālibus
		Acc.	hostēs	maria	animālia
		Voc.	hostēs	maria	animālia
		Abl.	hostibus	maribus	animālibus

a. The accusative singular ending **im** is found always in **sitis**, *thirst;* **tussis**, *cough;* **vīs**, *strength;* and in names of towns and rivers in **is**, as **Neāpolis**, *Naples;* **Tiberis**, *Tiber;* usually in **febris**, *fever;* **puppis**, *stern of ship;* **restis**, *cable;* **secūris**, *ax;* **turris**, *tower;* occasionally in **clāvis**, *key;* **crātis**, *hurdle;* **cutis**, *skin;* **messis**, *harvest;* **navis**, *ship.*

b. The ablative in **ī** is found in i-stem nouns that regularly have **im** in the accusative (except perhaps **restis**, *rope, cable);* also not infrequently in **amnis**, *river;* **avis**, *bird;* **canālis**, *canal;* **cīvis**, *citizen;* **classis**, *fleet;* **fīnis**, *end;* **fūstis**, *club;* **ignis**, *fire;* **orbis**, *circle;* **unguis**, *claw;* occasionally in **anguis**, *snake;* **bīlis**, *bile;* **clāvis**, *key;* **collis**, *hill;* **corbis**, *basket;* **messis**, *harvest;* regularly in neuters in **e**, **al**, and **ar**, except in **rēte**, *net;* and in the proper nouns **Caere**, **Praeneste**.

c. In the genitive plural instead of the ending **ium, um** is found always in **canis,** *dog;* **juvenis,** *young man;* **pānis,** *bread;* **sēnex,** *old man;* **struēs,** *heap;* **volucris,** *bird;* usually in **apis,** *bee;* **sēdēs,** *seat;* **vātēs,** *bard;* frequently in **mēnsis,** *month.*

d. The accusative plural ending **īs** is found frequently in the classical period along with **ēs.**

57. Rule of Gender. *a.* i-stems, with nominative in **ēs,** are feminine, unless they refer to males; those with nominative in **is** are partly masculine, partly feminine.

b. i-stems, with nominative in **e, al, ar,** are neuter.

c. The rest are feminine.

FOURTH DECLENSION

58. The fourth declension embraces only dissyllabic and polysyllabic stems in **u.**

a. The endings are the same as those of **i**-stems of the third declension.

b. In the genitive and ablative singular, and in the nominative, accusative, and vocative plural (sometimes, too, in the dative singular), the **u** of the stem absorbs the vowel of the ending, and becomes long.

c. In the dative and ablative plural **u** generally becomes **i** before the ending **bus.**

59.		MASCULINE	NEUTER
Sg.	NOM.	cāsus, m., *chance*	cornū, n., *horn*
	GEN.	cāsūs	cornūs
	DAT.	cāsuī (cāsū)	cornū
	ACC.	cāsum	cornū
	VOC.	cāsūs	cornū
	ABL.	cāsū	cornū
Pl.	NOM.	cāsūs	cornua
	GEN.	cāsuum	cornuum
	DAT.	cāsibus	cornibus
	ACC.	cāsūs	cornua
	VOC.	cāsūs	cornua
	ABL.	cāsibus	cornibus

60. Domus, f., *house,* is declined: **sg.** gen. **domūs;** dat. **domuī;** acc. **domum;** voc. **domus;** abl. **domō;** loc. **domī (domuī); pl.** nom. **domūs;** gen. **domōrum;** dat.–abl. **domibus;** acc. **domōs, domūs.**

61. Rule of Gender. Fourth declension nouns in **us** are generally masculine; those in **ū** are neuter.

a. But feminine are **acus,** *needle;* **domus,** *house;* **īdūs** (pl.), *the ides;* **manus,** *hand;* **penus,** *victuals;* **porticus,** *piazza;* **tribus,** *tribe.*

Fifth Declension

62. The stem ends in ē; the nominative in ēs.

a. In the genitive and dative singular the stem vowel **e** is shortened after a consonant.

b. The accusative singular always ends in **em;** 22.

c. The ending in the genitive singular is that of the second declension, **ī;** the other endings are those of the third declension.

63.

		Masculine	Feminine
Sg.	Nom.	**diēs**, m., f., *day*	**rēs**, f., *thing*
	Gen.	**diēī (diē)**	**reī**
	Dat.	**diēī (diē)**	**reī**
	Acc.	**diem**	**rem**
	Voc.	**diēs**	**rēs**
	Abl.	**diē**	**rē**
Pl.	Nom.	**diēs**	**rēs**
	Gen.	**diērum**	**rērum**
	Dat.	**diēbus**	**rēbus**
	Acc.	**diēs**	**rēs**
	Voc.	**diēs**	**rēs**
	Abl.	**diēbus**	**rēbus**

a. The genitive, dative, and ablative plural are rarely found except in **diēs** and **rēs.**

b. Many words of the fifth declension have a parallel form, which follows the first declension, as **mollitiēs** or **mollitia,** *softness.* Where this is the case, forms of the fifth declension are usually found only in the nominative, accusative, and ablative singular.

64. Rule of Gender. Fifth declension nouns are feminine except **diēs** which in the singular is either masculine or feminine, and in the plural masculine, and **merīdiēs,** *midday,* which is always masculine.

Declension of Greek Nouns

65. Greek nouns, especially proper names, are commonly Latinized and declined regularly according to their stem characteristic. Some Greek nouns, however, either retain their Greek form exclusively or have the Greek and Latin forms side by side. These variations occur principally in the singular.

a. In the plural the declension is usually regular, but the third declension often shows **ĕs** in the nominative and **ăs** in the accusative. In the genitive plural the endings **ōn** and **eōn** are found in the titles of books, as **Georgicōn,** *of the Georgics;* **Metamorphōseōn,** *of the Metamorphoses.*

66. FIRST DECLENSION

Sg.				
Nom.	Pēnelopē	Aenēās	Anchīsēs
Gen.	Pēnelopēs	Aenēae	Anchīsae
Dat.	Pēnelopae	Aenēae	Anchīsae
Acc.	Pēnelopēn	Aenēam (ān)	Anchīsēn (am)
Voc.	Pēnelopē	Aenēā	Anchīsē (ā, a)
Abl.	Pēnelopā	Aenēā	Anchīsā

67. SECOND DECLENSION

Sg.				
Nom.	Dēlos (us)	Īlion (um)	Panthūs	Androgeōs (us)
Gen.	Dēlī	Īliī	Panthī	Androgeī (eō)
Dat.	Dēlō	Īliō	Panthō	Androgeō
Acc.	Dēlon (um)	Īlion (um)	Panthūn	Androgeōn (ō, ōna)
Voc.	Dēle	Īlion (um)	Panthū	Androgeōs
Abl.	Dēlō	Īliō	Panthō	Androgeō

68. THIRD DECLENSION

Sg.				
Nom.	Solōn (Solō)	āēr, *air*	Xenophōn	Atlās
Gen.	Solōnis	āeris	Xenophōntis	Atlantis
Dat.	Solōnī	āerī	Xenophōntī	Atlantī
Acc.	Solōna (em)	āera (em)	Xenophōnta (em)	Atlanta
Voc.	Solōn	āēr	Xenophōn	Atlā
Abl.	Solōne	āere	Xenophōnte	Atlante

Sg.			
Nom.	Thalēs	Paris	hērōs
Gen.	Thal-ētis (is)	Paridis (os)	hērōis
Dat.	Thal-ētī (ī)	Paridī (ī)	hērōī
Acc.	Thal-ēta (ēn, em)	Par-ida (im, in)	hērōa (em)
Voc.	Thalē	Pari (Paris)	hērōs
Abl.	Thalē	Paride	hērōe

69. MIXED DECLENSIONS

	II AND III	II AND III	II AND III
Sg. Nom.	Orpheus	Athōs	Oedipūs
Gen.	Orpheī (eī)	Athō (ōnis)	Oedip-odis (ī)
Dat.	Orpheō (eī)	Athō	Oedipidī
Acc.	Orpheum (ea)	Athō (ōn, ōnem)	Oedip-um (oda)
Voc.	Orpheu	Athōs	Oedipe
Abl.	Orpheō	Athōne	Oedip-ide (ō)

	II AND III	II AND III	II AND III
Sg. Nom.	Achillēs (eus)	Sōcrates	Dīdō
Gen.	Achillis (e)ī, eos	Sōcratis (ī)	Dīdūs (ōnis)
Dat.	Achillī	Sōcratī	Dīdō (ōnī)
Acc.	Achillem (ea, ēn)	Sōcratēn (em)	Dīdō (ōnem)
Voc.	Achillēs (ē, eu, e)	Sōcratē (es)	Dīdō
Abl.	Achille, (ī)	Sōcrate	Dīdō (ōne)

ADJECTIVES

70. The Adjective adds a quality to its noun or pronoun. Adjectives have the same declension as nouns, and according to the stem characteristics are of the first and second or third declension.

ADJECTIVES OF THE FIRST AND SECOND DECLENSION

71. Stems end in **o** for masculine and neuter, **ā** for feminine; nominative in **us (er), a, um.** The same variations in termination occur as in nouns, except that adjectives in **ius** form the genitive and vocative singular regularly. See 37, *a*.

		M.	F.	N.
Sg.	Nom.	bonus, *good*	bona	bonum
	Gen.	bonī	bonae	bonī
	Dat.	bonō	bonae	bonō
	Acc.	bonum	bonam	bonum
	Voc.	bone	bona	bonum
	Abl.	bonō	bonā	bonō
Pl.	Nom.	bonī	bonae	bona
	Gen.	bonōrum	bonārum	bonōrum
	Dat.	bonīs	bonīs	bonīs
	Acc.	bonōs	bonās	bona
	Voc.	bonī	bonae	bona
	Abl.	bonīs	bonīs	bonīs
Sg.	Nom.	miser, *wretched*	misera	miserum
	Gen.	miserī	miserae	miserī
	Dat.	miserō	miserae	miserō
	Acc.	miserum	miseram	miserum
	Voc.	miser	misera	miserum
	Abl.	miserō	miserā	miserō
Pl.	Nom.	miserī	miserae	misera
	Gen.	miserōrum	miserārum	miserōrum
	Dat.	miserīs	miserīs	miserīs
	Acc.	miserōs	miserās	misera
	Voc.	miserī	miserae	misera
	Abl.	miserīs	miserīs	miserīs
Sg.	Nom.	pulcher, *beautiful*	pulchra	pulchrum
	Gen.	pulchrī	pulchrae	pulchrī
	Dat.	pulchrō	pulchrae	pulchrō
	Acc.	pulchrum	pulchram	pulchrum
	Voc.	pulcher	pulchra	pulchrum
	Abl.	pulchrō	pulchrā	pulchrō
Pl.	Nom.	pulchrī	pulchrae	pulchra
	Gen.	pulchrōrum	pulchrārum	pulchrōrum
	Dat.	pulchrīs	pulchrīs	pulchrīs
	Acc.	pulchrōs	pulchrās	pulchra
	Voc.	pulchrī	pulchrae	pulchra
	Abl.	pulchrīs	pulchrīs	pulchrīs

a. All participles ending in **us, a, um,** are inflected like **bonus.**

72. In poetry we find **um** alongside of **ōrum** and **ārum** in the genitive plural.

a. In the dative and ablative plural **iīs** from adjectives in **ius** is often contracted to is especially in names of months and in adjectives formed from proper names.

73. The so-called **Pronominal Adjectives** show certain peculiarities in the genitive and dative singular. These adjectives are: **alter,** *one of the two;* **alteruter** (a combination of **alter** and **uter**), *either of the two;* **alius,** *other;* **neuter,** *neither;* **nullūs,** *none;* **sōlus,** *sole;* **tōtus,** *whole;* **ūllus,** *any;* **ūnus,** *one;* **uter,** *which of the two.*

74.		M.	F.	N.
Sg.	Nom.	alter, *one of two*	altera	alterum
	Gen.	alterīus	alterīus	alterīus
	Dat.	alterī	alterī	alterī
	Acc.	alterum	alteram	alterum
	Abl.	alterō	alterā	alterō
Sg.	Nom.	alius	alia	aliud
	Gen.	alīus	alīus	alīus
	Dat.	aliī	aliī	aliī
	Acc.	alium	aliam	aliud
	Abl.	aliō	aliā	aliō
Sg.	Nom.	ūllus, *any*	ūlla	ūllum
	Gen.	ūllīus	ūllīus	ūllīus
	Dat.	ūllī	ūllī	ūllī
	Acc.	ūllum	ūllam	ūllum
	Abl.	ūllō	ūllā	ūllō
Sg.	Nom.	uter	utra	utrum
	Gen.	utrīus	utrīus	utrīus
	Dat.	utrī	utrī	utrī
	Acc.	utrum	utram	utrum
	Abl.	utrō	utrā	utrō

Like **uter** is declined **neuter;** like **ūllus** are declined **nūllus, sōlus, tōtus, ūnus.** The plural is regular.

a. The genitive **alīus** is very rare, and its place is usually taken by **alterīus** or **aliēnus.**

b. The **i** of the ending **īus** (except in **alīus**) is often shortened in poetry. This is usually the case with **alter,** and regularly in the compounds of **uter;** as **utriusque.**

c. In the compound **alteruter** we usually find both parts declined; sometimes the second only.

d. **Alius** has its nominative and accusative singular neuter irregularly **aliud.**

ADJECTIVES OF THE THIRD DECLENSION

75. The declension of the adjectives of the third declension follows the rules given for nouns. Most adjectives of the third declension are vowel stems in **i**, with two (rarely three) endings in the nominative. The remaining adjectives of the third declension are consonant stems and have one ending only in the nominative.

ADJECTIVES OF TWO OR THREE ENDINGS

76. These have (except stems in **ri**) one ending in the nominative for masculine and feminine, one for neuter. Most stems in **i** form the masculine and feminine alike, with nominative in **s**; but the nominative neuter weakens the characteristic **i** into **e**. Compare **mare**, *sea*.

a. Several stems in **i**, preceded by **r** (**cr, tr, br**), form the nominative masculine, not by affixing **s**, but by dropping the **i** and inserting short **e** before the **r**, as, stem, **ācri**, *sharp;* nom., **ācer** (m.), **ācris** (f.), **ācre** (n.).

77.

		M., F.	N.
Sg.	Nom.	omnis, *all*	omne
	Gen.	omnis	omnis
	Dat.	omnī	omnī
	Acc.	omnem	omne
	Voc.	omnis	omne
	Abl.	omnī	omnī
Pl.	Nom.	omnēs	omnia
	Gen.	omnium	omnium
	Dat.	omnibus	omnibus
	Acc.	omnēs (īs)	omnia
	Voc.	omnēs	omnia
	Abl.	omnibus	omnibus

		M.	F.	N.
Sg.	Nom.	ācer, *sharp*	ācris	ācre
	Gen.	ācris	ācris	ācris
	Dat.	ācrī	ācrī	ācrī
	Acc.	ācrem	ācrem	ācre
	Voc.	ācer	ācris	ācre
	Abl.	ācrī	ācrī	ācrī
Pl.	Nom.	ācrēs	ācrēs	ācria
	Gen.	ācrium	ācrium	ācrium
	Dat.	ācribus	ācribus	ācribus
	Acc.	ācrēs (īs)	ācrēs (īs)	ācria
	Voc.	ācrēs	ācrēs	ācria
	Abl.	ācribus	ācribus	ācribus

ADJECTIVES OF ONE ENDING

78. Adjective stems of one ending (consonant stems) end with **l, r, s; p, b; t, d; c, g.**

79. Present active participles are also consonant stems and follow the same declension.

80. The consonant stem adjectives have the same forms in all the genders, except that in the accusative singular and in the nominative, accusative, and vocative plural, the neuter is distinguished from the masculine and feminine.

81. Consonant stem adjectives follow in part the declension of **i**-stem nouns; thus:

1. In the ablative singular they have **ī** or **e**; when used as nouns, commonly **e**.

a. The participles, as such, have **e**; but used as nouns or adjectives either **e** or **ī**, with a tendency to **ī**.

2. In the neuter plural they have **ia**; except all comparatives (91), **vetus,** *old,* and **ūber,** *fertile,* which have **vetera** and **ūbera**. Many have no neuter.

3. In the genitive plural they have **ium,** when the stem characteristic is preceded by a long vowel or a consonant; **um,** when the characteristic is preceded by a short vowel. The participles regularly have **ium**.

82.

		M., F.	N.		M., F.	N.
Sg.	Nom.	fēlīx, *lucky*	fēlīx	Sg.	recēns, *recent*	recēns
	Gen.	fēlīcis	fēlīcis		recentis	recentis
	Dat.	fēlīcī	fēlīcī		recentī	recentī
	Acc.	fēlīcem	fēlīx		recentem	recēns
	Voc.	fēlīx	fēlīx		recēns	recēns
	Abl.	fēlīcī (e)	fēlīcī (e)		recentī (e)	recentī (e)
Pl.	Nom.	fēlīcēs	fēlīcia	Pl.	recentēs	recentia
	Gen.	fēlīcium	fēlīcium		recentium	recentium
	Dat.	fēlīcibus	fēlīcibus		recentibus	recentibus
	Acc.	fēlīcēs (īs)	fēlīcia		recentēs (īs)	recentia
	Voc.	fēlīcēs	fēlīcia		recentēs	recentia
	Abl.	fēlīcibus	fēlīcibus		recentibus	recentibus

		M., F.	N.		M., F.	N.
Sg.	Nom.	vetus, *old*	vetus	Sg.	amāns, *loving*	amāns
	Gen.	veteris	veteris		amantis	amantis
	Dat.	veterī	veterī		amantī	amantī
	Acc.	veterem	vetus		amantem	amāns
	Voc.	vetus	vetus		amāns	amāns
	Abl.	vetere (ī)	vetere (ī)		amante (ī)	amante (ī)
Pl.	Nom.	veterēs	vetera	Pl.	amantēs	amantia
	Gen.	veterum	veterum		amantium	amantium
	Dat.	veteribus	veteribus		amantibus	amantibus
	Acc.	veterēs (īs)	vetera		amantēs (īs)	amantia
	Voc.	veterēs	vetera		amantēs	amantia
	Abl.	veteribus	veteribus		amantibus	amantibus

a. In the poets, **e** is often found for ī in the ablative singular. Also in classical prose we find regularly **paupere**, *poor;* **vetere**, *old;* and frequently **dīvite**, *rich;* **sapiente**, *wise.*

b. In the nominative and accusative plural **īs** for **ēs** belongs to early Latin and the poets, but a few cases of this accusative are found in Cicero. In the case of participles **īs** is very common, and is the rule in Vergil and Horace.

c. In the genitive plural **cicur**, *tame;* **vetus**, *old;* **dīves**, *rich,* have **um** instead of **ium;** so also many compound adjectives.

d. In the poets and in later writers, **um** is not infrequently found where classical prose uses **ium.**

COMPARISON OF ADJECTIVES

83. **The Degrees of Comparison** are: positive, comparative, and superlative.

84. **The Comparative** is formed by adding to the consonant stems the endings **ior** for the masculine and feminine, and **ius** for the neuter.

85. **The Superlative** is formed by adding to the consonant stems the endings **issimus, a, um** (earlier **issumus**).

86. Vowel stems, before forming the comparative and superlative, drop their characteristic vowel.

87.

POSITIVE	COMPARATIVE	SUPERLATIVE
altus, a, um, *high*	**altior, ius**, *higher*	**altissimus, a, um**, *highest*
fortis, e, *brave*	**fortior, ius**, *braver*	**fortissimus**, *bravest*
fēlīx, *happy*	**fēlīcior, ius**, *happier*	**fēlīcissimus**, *happiest*
recēns, *recent*	**recentior, ius**, *more recent*	**recentissimus**, *most recent*

88. Peculiarities of Comparison. Adjectives in **er** add the superlative ending **rimus** directly to the nominative masculine. The comparative has the regular formation. See 84.

89.

POSITIVE	COMPARATIVE	SUPERLATIVE
miser, era, erum, *wretched*	**miserior, miserius**	**miserrimus**
celer, eris, ere, *swift*	**celerior, celerius**	**celerrimus**
ācer, ācris, ācre, *sharp*	**ācrior, ācrius**	**ācerrimus**

a. Six adjectives in **ilis** add **limus** (earlier **lumus**) to the stem, after dropping **i**, to form the superlative: **facilis**, *easy;* **difficilis**, *hard;* **similis**, *like;* **dissimilis**, *unlike;* **gracilis**, *slender;* and **humilis**, *low.*

Pos. **facilis** COMP. **facilior, ius** SUP. **facillimus, a, um**

90. Participles used as adjectives are subject also to the same laws of comparison: as **amāns**, *loving;* **amantior**, *more loving;* **amantissimus**, *most loving;* **apertus**, *open;* **apertior, apertissimus.**

91. The superlative follows the declension of adjectives of three endings of the first and second declensions; 71. The comparative is declined according to the third declension, thus:

	M., F.	N.		M., F.	N.
Sg. Nom.	altior, *higher*	altius	Pl.	altiōrēs	altiōra
Gen.	altiōris	altiōris		altiōrum	altiōrum
Dat.	altiōrī	altiōrī		altiōribus	altiōribus
Acc.	altiōrem	altius		altiōrēs (īs)	altiōra
Voc.	altior	altius		altiōrēs	altiōra
Abl.	altiōre (ī)	altiōre (ī)		altiōribus	altiōribus

92. Irregular Comparison. Certain adjectives are irregular in their comparison:

Positive	Comparative	Superlative
bonus, *good*	melior, melius	optimus
malus, *bad*	pejor, pejus	pessimus
magnus, *great*	major, majus	maximus
parvus, *small*	minor, minus	minimus
multus, *much*	Sg. plūs (no dat. nor abl.)	plūrimus
	Pl. plūres, plūra	
	complūres, complūra (ia)	
nequam, *worthless*	nequior, nequius	nequissimus
frūgī (indecl.), *frugal*	frūgālior	frūgālissimus

a. For the pronunciation of **major** and **pejor** = **majjor, pejjor**, see 6, *b.*

b. The older form of the superlative ended in **umus.**

ADVERBS

93. Most adverbs are either oblique cases or mutilated forms of oblique cases of adjectival, nominal or pronominal stems.

94. The cases from which they are derived are principally the accusative and the ablative.

ADVERBS FORMED FROM ADJECTIVES

95. Many adverbs are formed from the ablative case of adjectives in **us**: **tūtō**, *safely;* **prīmō**, *at first.*

a. Many adverbs are formed from an old ablative form (ē) of adjectives in **us** and **er**: **altē**, *loftily;* **pulchrē**, *beautifully.*

b. Many adverbs are formed from accusative singular neuter adjectival and pronominal stems: **multum**, *much;* **facile**, *easily.* This is true of all comparatives: **facilius**, *more easily.* To the comparatives belong also **magis**, *more;* **nimis**, *too.*

c. Adverbs are regularly formed from adjectives and participles of the third declension by the addition of **ter (iter)** to the stem; stems in **nt** dropping the **t**, and stems in **c** or **g** inserting the connecting vowel **i** before the ending: **fortiter**, *bravely;* **ferōciter**, *wildly;* **prūdenter**, *prudently.*

COMPARISON OF ADVERBS

96. The comparative of the adverb is the accusative neuter of the comparative of the adjective. See 95, *b*. The superlative ends in **issimē, errimē, illimē** (earlier **issumē, errumē, illumē**), or irregularly, according to the superlative of the adjective. See 87, 88, 89, 92.

97. POSITIVE	COMPARATIVE	SUPERLATIVE
altē, *loftily*	altius	altissimē
pulchrē, *beautifully*	pulchrius	pulcherrimē
miserē, *poorly*	miserius	miserrimē
fortiter, *bravely*	fortius	fortissimē
audācter, *boldly*	audācius	audācissimē
tūtō, *safely*	tūtius	tūtissimē
facile, *easily*	facilius	facillimē
bene, *well*	melius	optimē
male, *ill*	pejus	pessimē
[parvus], *small*	minus, *less*	minimē, *least*
[magnus], *great*	magis, *more*	maximē, *most*
multum, *much*	plūs, *more*	plūrimum
citō, *quickly*	citius	citissimē
diū, *long*	diūtius	diūtissimē
saepe, *often*	saepius	saepissimē
nūper, *recently*	——	nūperrimē
satis, *enough*	satius, *better*	

NUMERALS

NUMERAL ADJECTIVES

98. The **Cardinal Numerals**, as **ūnus**, *one;* **duo**, *two;* **decem**, *ten,* answer the question **quot**, *how many?* and are the numbers used in counting.

a. The Ordinal Numerals, as **prīmus (ūnus)**, *first;* **secundus (alter)**, *second;* **decimus**, *tenth,* answer the question **quotus**, *which one in the series?*

99. The cardinal numerals are indeclinable, except: **ūnus**, *one;* **duo**, *two;* **trēs**, *three;* the hundreds beginning with **ducentī**, *two hundred;* and the plural **mīlia**, *thousands,* which forms **mīlium** and **mīlibus**.

	M.	F.	N.	M., F.	N.
Nom.	duo, *two*	duae	duo	trēs, *three*	tria
Gen.	duōrum	duārum	duōrum	trium	trium
Dat.	duōbus	duābus	duōbus	tribus	tribus
Acc.	duōs, duo	duās	duo	trēs (trīs)	tria
Abl.	duōbus	duābus	duōbus	tribus	tribus

a. For the declension of **ūnus** see **73–74**.

100. The **Distributive Numerals**, as **singulī**, *one each;* **bīnī**, *two each;* **dēnī**, *ten each,* answer the question **quotēnī**, *how many each?*

101. Numeral Adverbs, as **semel,** *once;* **bis,** *twice;* **ter,** *thrice,* answer the question **quotiēns,** *how often?*

PRONOUNS

102. A Pronoun is a word that may be substituted for a noun. Latin pronouns may be divided into six classes: personal (including reflexive), demonstrative, intensive, relative, interrogative, and indefinite.

a. All but the personal pronouns may be used as pronominal adjectives.

b. The possessive adjectives are often classified as possessive pronouns.

A. PERSONAL PRONOUNS

103. The Personal Pronoun of the First Person.

Sg.	NOM.	**ego,** *I*	Pl.	**nōs,** *we*
	GEN.	**meī,** *of me*		**nostrī, nostrum,** *of us*
	DAT.	**mihǐ (mī),** *to, for me*		**nōbīs,** *to, for us*
	ACC.	**mē,** *me*		**nōs,** *us*
	ABL.	**mē,** *from, with, by me*		**nōbīs,** *from, with, by us*

a. Compare the corresponding possessive adjectives:

Sg.	**meus, a, um,** (VOC. m., **mī**),	Pl.	**noster, nostra, nostrum,**
	mine, my own		*our(s), our own*

b. The oblique cases of **ego** may also be used with reflexive force: **meī,** *of myself,* etc.

104. The Personal Pronoun of the Second Person.

Sg.	NOM.	**tū,** *you*	Pl.	**vōs,** *you*
	GEN.	**tuī,** *of you*		**vestrī, vestrum,** *of you*
	DAT.	**tibǐ,** *to, for you*		**vōbīs,** *to, for you*
	ACC.	**tē,** *you*		**vōs,** *you*
	ABL.	**tē,** *from, with, by you*		**vōbīs,** *from, with, by you*

a. Compare the corresponding possessive adjectives:

Sg.	**tuus, a, um,** *your(s), your own*	Pl.	**vester, vestra, vestrum,**
			your(s), your own

b. The oblique cases of **tū** may also be used with reflexive force: **tuī,** *of yourself,* etc.

105. The Personal Pronouns of the Third Person.

a. **Is, ea, id,** *he, she, it,* 107, used also as a demonstrative, *this, that,* is the ordinary form of the third personal pronoun. It lacks the possessive adjective.

b. The original personal pronoun of the third person, together with its possessive, is used only as a reflexive in Latin, and therefore lacks a nominative. See 106.

106. The Personal (Reflexive) Pronoun of the Third Person.

	Sg.		Pl.
NOM.	——		——
GEN.	**suī,** *of him(self), her(self), it(self)*		**suī,** *of them(selves)*
DAT.	**sibĭ,** *to, for him(self), her(self), it(self)*		**sibĭ,** *to, for them(selves)*
ACC.	**sē, sēsē,** *him(self), her(self), it(self)*		**sē, sēsē,** *them(selves)*
ABL.	**sē, sēsē,** *from, with, by him(self), her(self), it(self)*		**sē, sēsē,** *from, with, by them(selves)*

a. Compare the corresponding possessive adjective, **suus, a, um,** *his (own), her (own), its (own); their (own), theirs.*

b. The enclitic **–met** is sometimes added to certain forms of the personal pronouns; as **egomet,** *I myself.*

c. The enclitic **–pte** is sometimes added to the ablative singular of the possessive adjective; as **suōpte ingeniō,** *by his own genius.*

107.   *B.* DEMONSTRATIVE PRONOUNS

1. **is,** *this, that; he, she, it*

		M.	F.	N.
Sg.	NOM.	**is**	**ea**	**id**
	GEN.	**ejus**	**ejus**	**ejus**
	DAT.	**eī**	**eī**	**eī**
	ACC.	**eum**	**eam**	**id**
	ABL.	**eō**	**eā**	**eō**
Pl.	NOM.	**iī, eī, ī**	**eae**	**ea**
	GEN.	**eōrum**	**eārum**	**eōrum**
	DAT.	**iīs, eīs, īs**	**iīs, eīs, īs**	**iīs, eīs, īs**
	ACC.	**eōs**	**eās**	**ea**
	ABL.	**iīs, eīs, īs**	**iīs, eīs, īs**	**iīs, eīs, īs**

a. For the pronunciation of **ejus** (= **ejjus**) see 6, *b.*

b. This pronoun is often used as a third personal pronoun, *he, she, it;* 105, *a.*

2. **īdem, (is + dem),** *the same*

		M.	F.	N.
Sg.	NOM.	**īdem**	**eadem**	**idem**
	GEN.	**ejusdem**	**ejusdem**	**ejusdem**
	DAT.	**eīdem**	**eīdem**	**eīdem**
	ACC.	**eundem**	**eandem**	**idem**
	ABL.	**eōdem**	**eādem**	**eōdem**
Pl.	NOM.	**īdem, eīdem, iīdem**	**eaedem**	**eadem**
	GEN.	**eōrundem**	**eārundem**	**eōrundem**
	DAT.	**īsdem, eīsdem, iīsdem**	**īsdem, eīsdem, iīsdem**	**īsdem, eīsdem, iīsdem**
	ACC.	**eōsdem**	**eāsdem**	**eadem**
	ABL.	**īsdem, eīsdem, iīsdem**	**īsdem, eīsdem, iīsdem**	**īsdem, eīsdem, iīsdem**

a. For the pronunciation of **ejusdem** = **ejjusdem,** see 6, *b.*

3. hic, *this*

		M.	F.	N.
Sg.	NOM.	hic	haec	hoc
	GEN.	hujus	hujus	hujus
	DAT.	huic	huic	huic
	ACC.	hunc	hanc	hoc
	ABL.	hōc	hāc	hōc
Pl.	NOM.	hī	hae	haec
	GEN.	hōrum	hārum	hōrum
	DAT.	hīs	hīs	hīs
	ACC.	hōs	hās	haec
	ABL.	hīs	hīs	hīs

a. For the pronunciation of **hujus** = **hujjus**, see 6, *b.*

b. The full forms with −ce are rare in classical Latin, except in the phrase **hujusce modī**, *of this kind.*

c. When followed by a word which begins with a vowel or **h**, the nominative singular of the masculine, **hic**, and the nominative and accusative singular of the neuter, **hoc**, are usually pronounced as though spelled **hicc**, **hocc**, making these syllables long by position; 15.

4. iste, *that (of yours)*

		M.	F.	N.
Sg.	NOM.	iste	ista	istud
	GEN.	istĭus	istĭus	istĭus
	DAT.	istī	istī	istī
	ACC.	istum	istam	istud
	ABL.	istō	istā	istō
Pl.	NOM.	istī	istae	ista
	GEN.	istōrum	istārum	istōrum
	DAT.	istīs	istīs	istīs
	ACC.	istōs	istās	ista
	ABL.	istīs	istīs	istīs

a. Iste combines with −ce, but in classical Latin the only common forms are **istuc** (for **istud**) and **istaec** (for **ista**).

5. ille, *that*

		M.	F.	N.
Sg.	NOM.	ille	illa	illud
	GEN.	illĭus	illĭus	illĭus
	DAT.	illī	illī	illī
	ACC.	illum	illam	illud
	ABL.	illō	illā	illō
Pl.	NOM.	illī	illae	illa
	GEN.	illōrum	illārum	illōrum
	DAT.	illīs	illīs	illīs
	ACC.	illōs	illās	illa
	ABL.	illīs	illīs	illīs

108. C. THE INTENSIVE PRONOUN

ipse, *self*

		M.	F.	N.
Sg.	Nom.	ipse	ipsa	ipsum
	Gen.	ipsĭus	ipsĭus	ipsĭus
	Dat.	ipsī	ipsī	ipsī
	Acc.	ipsum	ipsam	ipsum
	Abl.	ipsō	ipsā	ipsō
Pl.	Nom.	ipsī	ipsae	ipsa
	Gen.	ipsōrum	ipsārum	ipsōrum
	Dat.	ipsīs	ipsīs	ipsīs
	Acc.	ipsōs	ipsās	ipsa
	Abl.	ipsīs	ipsīs	ipsīs

109. D. THE RELATIVE PRONOUN

quī, *who*

		M.	F.	N.
Sg.	NOM.	quī	quae	quod
	GEN.	cujus	cujus	cujus
	DAT.	cui	cui	cui
	ACC.	quem	quam	quod
	ABL.	quō	quā	quō
Pl.	NOM.	quī	quae	quae
	GEN.	quōrum	quārum	quōrum
	DAT.	quibus	quibus	quibus
	ACC.	quōs	quās	quae
	ABL.	quibus	quibus	quibus

a. For the pronunciation of **cujus** = **cujjus,** see 6, *b.*

b. **Quī** may also be used as a relative adjective.

c. The dative-ablative plural **quīs** is common in the poets at all periods and occurs also occasionally in prose writers.

d. The ablative singular **quī** for all genders is the prevalent form in early times; and in combination with **cum,** as **quīcum,** *with whom,* is preferred to **quō, quā,** by Cicero.

110. General Relatives are:

PRONOUN	**quisquis,** *whoever*
	quidquid, quicquid, *whatever*
ADJECTIVE	**quīquī, quaequae, quodquod,** *whatsoever*
	quīcumque, quaecumque, quodcumque, *whichever*

111. E. THE INTERROGATIVE PRONOUN

PRONOUN	**quis?** *who?*		**quid?** *what?*
ADJECTIVE	**quī?**	**quae?**	**quod?** *which?*
PRON. AND ADJ.	**uter?**	**utra?**	**utrum?** *who? which of two?*

		M., F.	N.
Sg.	Nom.	quis?	quid?
	Gen.	cujus?	cujus?
	Dat.	cui?	cui?
	Acc.	quem?	quid?
	Abl.	quō?	quō?

a. The plural of the interrogative pronoun and both numbers of the interrogative adjective coincide with the forms of the relative **quī, quae, quod.**

112.   *F.* Strengthened Interrogatives

Pronoun	**quisnam?** *who, pray*		**quidnam?** *what, pray?*
	ecquis? *(is there) anyone*		**ecquid?** *(is there) anything?*
Adjective	**quīnam?**	**quaenam?**	**quondam?** *which, pray?*
	ecquī?	**ecqua? (ecquae?)**	**ecquod?** *is there any?*

113.   *G.* The Indefinite Pronoun

aliquis	aliqua (rare)	**aliquid,** *somebody, someone or other, anybody*
quis	qua	**quid,** *someone, anyone*

a. The adjective forms are **aliquī, aliqua, aliquod,** *some, any;* **quī, quae (qua), quod,** *some, any.*

114. The declension of the pronominal adjectives has been given, 73–74. They are: **ūllus, a, um,** *any;* **nūllus, a, um,** *no one, not one;* **alius, a, ud,** *another;* **alter, era, erum,** *the other, one (of two);* **neuter, tra, trum,** *neither of two;* **ambō, ae, ō,** *both.* The corresponding substantives for **nūllus** and **nūllum** are **nēmō** and **nihil,** the latter of which forms only **nihilī** (gen.) and **nihilō** (abl.) and those only in certain combinations.

a. Some of the more important compounds of these adjectives are:

nōnnūllus, a, um, *some, many a,* declined like **nūllus.**
alteruter, alterutra, alterutrum, *the one or the other of the two*
uterque, utraque, utrumque, *each of two, either*
utervis, utravis, utrumvis *whichever you please of the two*
uterlibet, utralibet, utrumlibet, *whichever you please of the two*

THE VERB

115. The inflection given to the verbal stem is called conjugation and expresses:

1. **Person: First, Second, Third.**
2. **Voice: Active, Passive, Middle.**

a. The active voice denotes that the action proceeds from the subject: **parō,** *I prepare.* The passive voice denotes that the subject receives the action of the verb: **paror,** *I am prepared.* The middle voice has passive form and denotes the subject as acting either for itself or upon itself (reflexive) as: **paror,** *I prepare (for) myself.* This is chiefly a poetic usage.

3. **Tense: Present, Imperfect, Future, Perfect, Pluperfect, Future Perfect.**

4. **Mood: Indicative, Subjunctive, Imperative.**

a. The indicative is the mood of the fact: **parō,** *I prepare.* The subjunctive is the mood of the wish, command, or qualified statement: **parem,** *may I prepare, I may prepare;* **paret,** *may he prepare, let him prepare;* **sī paret,** *if he should prepare.* The imperative is the mood of command: **parā,** *prepare!*

CONJUGATION

116. The stem of a verb is variously modified, either by change of vowel or by addition of suffixes, and appears in the following forms:

1. **The Present Stem:** being the stem of the present, imperfect, and future tenses. These forms are called the present system.

2. **The Perfect Stem:** being the stem of the perfect, pluperfect, and future perfect tenses of the active. These forms are called the perfect system.

3. **The Perfect Passive Participial Stem:** which is used to form the perfect, pluperfect and future perfect tenses of the passive and also the future active and perfect passive participles, infinitives, and the supine. These forms are called the participial system.

117. 1. The perfect, pluperfect, and future perfect tenses in the passive voice are formed by the combination of the perfect passive participle with forms of the verb **sum,** *be, exist.*

2. The future passive infinitive is formed by the combination of the supine with the present passive infinitive of **eō,** *go.*

3. The infinite parts of the verb are formed by the addition of the following endings to the present, perfect, or participial stem:

		ACTIVE	*PASSIVE*
INFINITIVE	*Pres.*	re	rī, ī
	Perf.	isse	us (a, um) esse
	Fut.	ūrus (a, um) esse	um īrī
PARTICIPLES	*Pres.*	ns (*Gen.* ntis)	——
	Perf.	——	us (a, um)
	Fut.	ūrus (a, um)	——

GERUND	GERUNDIVE	SUPINE
ndī, (dō, dum, dō)	ndus (a, um)	um, ū

THE VERB sum, *be, exist*

PRINCIPAL PARTS: sum, esse, fuī

118. INDICATIVE   **119.** SUBJUNCTIVE

PRESENT

		INDICATIVE	SUBJUNCTIVE
Sg.	1.	**sum,** *I am*	**sim**[1]
	2.	**es,** *you are*	**sīs**
	3.	**est,** *he, she, it, is*	**sit**
Pl.	1.	**sumus,** *we are*	**sīmus**
	2.	**estis,** *you are*	**sītis**
	3.	**sunt,** *they are*	**sint**

IMPERFECT

Sg.	1.	**eram,** *I was*	**essem (forem)**
	2.	**erās,** *you were*	**essēs (forēs)**
	3.	**erat,** *he was*	**esset (foret)**
Pl.	1.	**erāmus,** *we were*	**essēmus (forēmus)**
	2.	**erātis,** *you were*	**essētis (forētis)**
	3.	**erant,** *they were*	**essent (forent)**

FUTURE

Sg.	1.	**erō,** *I shall be*	
	2.	**eris,** *you will be*	
	3.	**erit,** *he will be*	
			(lacking)
Pl.	1.	**erimus,** *we shall be*	
	2.	**eritis,** *you will be*	
	3.	**erunt,** *they will be*	

PERFECT

Sg.	1.	**fuī,** *I have been, I was*	**fuerim**
	2.	**fuistī,** *you have been, you were*	**fuerīs**
	3.	**fuit,** *he has been, he was*	**fuerit**
Pl.	1.	**fuimus,** *we have been, we were*	**fuerīmus**
	2.	**fuistis,** *you have been, you were*	**fuerītis**
	3.	**fuērunt, fuēre,** *they have been, they were*	**fuerint**

PLUPERFECT

Sg.	1	**fueram,** *I had been*	**fuissem**
	2.	**fuerās,** *you had been*	**fuissēs**
	3.	**fuerat,** *he had been*	**fuisset**
Pl.	1.	**fuerāmus,** *we had been*	**fuissēmus**
	2.	**fuerātis,** *you had been*	**fuissētis**
	3.	**fuerant,** *they had been*	**fuissent**

---

[1] The meaning of the subjunctive varies greatly, according to its use, and is best learned from the sections on syntax.

FUTURE PERFECT

Sg. 1. **fuerō,** *I shall have been*
2. **fueris,** *you will have been*
3. **fuerit,** *he will have been*

(lacking)

Pl. 1. **fuerimus,** *we shall have been*
2. **fueritis,** *you will have been*
3. **fuerint,** *they will have been*

120. IMPERATIVE

	PRESENT			FUTURE	
Sg. 1. ——	Pl. ——		Sg. 1. ——	Pl. ——	
2. **es,** *be*	**este,** *be*		**estō,** *you shall be*	**estōte,** *you shall be*	
3. ——	——		**estō,** *he shall be*	**suntō,** *they shall be*	

121. INFINITIVE

PRES. **esse,** *to be*
PERF. **fuisse,** *to have been*
FUT. **futūrus (a, um) esse, fore,** *to be about to be*

122. PARTICIPLES

PRES. only in the compounds **absens,** *absent,* **praesens,** *present* (79)
FUT. **futūrus, a, um,** *to be about to be* (71, *a*)

123. COMPOUNDS OF **sum**

absum, *be away, absent.* PERF. **(abfuī) āfuī,** PRES. PART. **absens,** *absent.*
adsum, *be present.* PERF. **affuī (adfuī)**
dēsum, *be wanting*
insum, *be in*
intersum, *be between*
obsum, *be against, hurt.* PERF. **obfuī (offuī)**
possum, *be able*
praesum, *be over, superintend.* PRES. PART. **praesens,** *present*
prōsum, *be for, profit*
subsum, *be under.* No PERF.
supersum, *be or remain, over.*

These are all inflected like sum, but **prōsum** and **possum** require special treatment by reason of their composition.

124. **Prōsum,** *profit*

In the forms of **prōsum, prōd–** is used before vowels, thus:

	INDICATIVE	SUBJUNCTIVE
PRES.	**prōsum, prōdes, prōdest;**	**prōsim**
	prōsumus, prōdestis, prōsunt	
IMPERF.	**prōderam**	**prōdessem**
FUT.	**prōderō**	——
PERF.	**prōfuī**	**prōfuerim**
PLUPERF.	**prōfueram**	**prōfuissem**
FUT. PERF.	**prōfuerō**	——

INFINITIVE

PRES. prōdesse;   FUT. prōfutūrum esse (prōfore);   PERF. prōfuisse.

125.   **Possum,** *be able, can*

Possum is compounded of **pot** (**potis, pote**) and **sum; t** becomes **s** before **s**. The perfect forms and the present participle are from an old form **poteō, potēre.**

	INDICATIVE	SUBJUNCTIVE
	PRESENT	
Sg. 1.	**possum,** *I am able, can*	**possim**
2.	**potes**	**possīs**
3.	**potest**	**possit**
Pl. 1.	**possumus**	**possīmus**
2.	**potestis**	**possītis**
3.	**possunt**	**possint**
	IMPERFECT	
Sg. 1.	**poteram,** *I was able, could*	**possem**
2.	**poterās**	**possēs**
3.	**poterat**	**posset**
Pl. 1.	**poterāmus**	**possēmus**
2.	**poterātis**	**possētis**
3.	**poterant**	**possent**
	FUTURE	
Sg. 1.	**poterō,** *I shall be able*	
2.	**poteris**	
3.	**poterit**	
		(lacking)
Pl. 1.	**poterimus**	
2.	**poteritis**	
3.	**poterunt**	
	PERFECT	
Sg. 1.	**potuī,** *I have been able*	**potuerim**
2.	**potuistī**	**potuerīs**
3.	**potuit**	**potuerit**
Pl. 1.	**potuimus**	**potuerīmus**
2.	**potuistis**	**potuerītis**
3.	**potuērunt, ēre**	**potuerint**
	PLUPERFECT	
Sg. 1.	**potueram,** *I had been able*	**potuissem**
2.	**potuerās**	**potuissēs**
3.	**potuerat**	**potuisset**
Pl. 1.	**potuerāmus**	**potuissēmus**
2.	**potuerātis**	**potuissētis**
3.	**potuerant**	**potuissent**

FUTURE PERFECT

Sg. 1. **potuerō,** *I shall have been able*
   2. **potueris**
   3. **potuerit**

                              (lacking)

Pl. 1. **potuerimus**
   2. **potueritis**
   3. **potuerint**

INFINITIVE	PARTICIPLE
PRES. **posse**	PRES. **potēns** (79)
PERF. **potuisse**	

REGULAR VERBS

SYSTEMS OF CONJUGATION

126. 1. There are two systems of conjugation, the vowel and the consonant. The consonant system is confined to a small class. The vowel system comprises four conjugations, distinguished by the vowel characteristics of the present stem, **ā, ē, e, ī,** which may be found by dropping **re** from the present infinitive active. The consonant preceding the short vowel stem characteristic is called the consonant stem characteristic.

2. From the present stem, as seen in the present indicative and present infinitive active; from the perfect stem, as seen in the perfect indicative active; and from the perfect passive participial stem, can be derived all forms of the verb. These forms are accordingly called the principal parts; and in the regular verbs appear in the four conjugations as follows:

	PRES. IND.	PRES. INF.	PERF. IND.	PERF. PART.
I.	**parō**	**parāre**	**parāvī**	**parātus,** *prepare*
II.	**habeō**	**habēre**	**habuī**	**habitus,** *have*
III.	**dīcō**	**dīcere**	**dīxī**	**dīctus,** *say*
	capiō	**capere**	**cēpī**	**captus,** *take*
IV.	**audiō**	**audīre**	**audīvī**	**audītus,** *hear*

FORMATION OF THE TENSES

127. The tenses are formed by the addition of the personal endings to the various stems, either directly or by means of certain tense signs, as shown in the paradigms.

128. While no practical rules for the formation of the tenses can be given, it is well to observe that:

1. The second person singular imperative active is the same as the present stem.

2. The imperfect subjunctive may be formed from the present infinitive active by adding **m,** etc. for active and **r,** etc. for passive.

3. The second person singular imperative passive and second person singular present passive in **re** are the same as the present infinitive active. Hence **ris** is preferred in the present indicative passive in order to avoid confusion.

4. The present subjunctive active and future indicative active in the third and fourth conjugations are alike in the first person singular.

5. The future perfect indicative active and the perfect subjunctive active differ only in the first person singular, except for the quantity of the i.

6. **Euphonic changes** sometimes occur in the consonant stem characteristic in the perfect and participial stem. Characteristic **b** before **s** and **t** becomes **p**; **g** and **qu** before **t** become **c**; **c, g, qu**, with **s**, become **x**; **t** and **d** before **s** are assimilated, and then sometimes dropped; thus: **scrībō, scrīpsī (scrībsī), scrīptus; legō, lēctus (lēgtus); coquō, coctus (coqtus); dīcō, dīxī (dīcsī); jungō, jūnxī (jūngsī); coquō, coxī (coqsī); edō, ēsus (edsus); cēdō, cessī (cedsī); mittō, mīsī (mitsī), missus (mitsus).**

First Conjugation

Conjugation of *parō*, *prepare*

Principal Parts: **parō, parāre, parāvī, parātus**

ACTIVE

129. INDICATIVE		**130.** SUBJUNCTIVE
	PRESENT	

I prepare, am preparing, do prepare

Sg.	1. **paro**		**parem**
	2. **parās**		**parēs**
	3. **parat**		**paret**
Pl.	1. **parāmus**		**parēmus**
	2. **parātis**		**parētis**
	3. **parant**		**parent**

IMPERFECT

I prepared, was preparing, did prepare

Sg.	1. **parābam**		**parārem**
	2. **parābās**		**parārēs**
	3. **parābat**		**parāret**
Pl.	1. **parābāmus**		**parārēmus**
	2. **parābātis**		**parārētis**
	3. **parābant**		**parārent**

FUTURE

I shall prepare, shall be
  preparing

Sg. 1. **parābo**
    2. **parābis**
    3. **parābit**

                                        (lacking)

Pl. 1. **parābimus**
    2. **parābitis**
    3. **parābunt**

PERFECT

I prepared, have prepared, did
  prepare

Sg. 1. **parāvī**   **parāverim**
    2. **parāvistī**   **parāverīs**
    3. **parāvit**   **parāverit**

Pl. 1. **parāvimus**   **parāverīmus**
    2. **parāvistis**   **parāverītis**
    3. **parāvērunt, ēre**   **parāverint**

PLUPERFECT

I had prepared

Sg. 1. **parāveram**   **parāvissem**
    2. **parāverās**   **parāvissēs**
    3. **parāverat**   **parāvisset**

Pl. 1. **parāverāmus**   **parāvissēmus**
    2. **parāverātis**   **parāvissētis**
    3. **parāverant**   **parāvissent**

FUTURE PERFECT

I shall have prepared

Sg. 1. **parāverō**
    2. **parāveris**
    3. **parāverit**

                                        (lacking)

Pl. 1. **parāverimus**
    2. **parāveritis**
    3. **parāverint**

131.   IMPERATIVE

	PRESENT	FUTURE
Sg. 1.	——	——
2.	**parā,** *prepare*	**parātō,** *you shall prepare*
3.	——	**parātō,** *he shall prepare*
Pl. 1.	——	——
2.	**parāte,** *prepare*	**parātōte,** *you shall prepare*
3.	——	**parantō,** *they shall prepare*

132.   INFINITIVE

PRES.   **parāre,** *to prepare*
PERF.   **parāvisse,** *to have prepared*
FUT.   **parātūrus, a, um esse,** *to be about to prepare*

133.   GERUND   **134.**   SUPINE
GEN.   **parandī,** *of preparing*
DAT.   **parandō,** *to, for preparing*
ACC.   **parandum,** *preparing, to prepare*   **parātum,** *to prepare*
ABL.   **parandō,** *with, from, by preparing*   **parātū,** *to prepare, in the preparing*

135.   PARTICIPLES

PRES. *Nom.*   **parāns** *(Gen.* **parantis**), *preparing* (79)
FUT.   **parātūrus, a, um,** *(being) about to prepare* (71, *a*)

FIRST CONJUGATION

PASSIVE

136. INDICATIVE   **137.** SUBJUNCTIVE

PRESENT

I am (being) prepared
Sg. 1. **paror**   **parer**
    2. **parāris, re**   **parēris, re**
    3. **parātur**   **parētur**

Pl. 1. **parāmur**   **parēmur**
    2. **parāminī**   **parēminī**
    3. **parantur**   **parentur**

IMPERFECT

1 was (being) prepared
Sg. 1. **parābar**   **parārer**
    2. **parābāris, re**   **parārēris, re**
    3. **parābātur**   **parārētur**

Pl. 1. **parābāmur**   **parārēmur**
    2. **parābāminī**   **parārēminī**
    3. **parābantur**   **parārentur**

FUTURE

I shall be prepared
Sg. 1. **parābor**
    2. **parāberis, re**
    3. **parābitur**
                                           (lacking)
Pl. 1. **parābimur**
    2. **parābiminī**
    3. **parābuntur**

PERFECT

I have been prepared, was prepared

Sg.	1. parātus, a, um	sum	parātus, a, um	sim
	2.	es		sīs
	3.	est		sit

Pl.	1. parātī, ae, a	sumus	parātī, ae, a	sīmus
	2.	estis		sītis
	3.	sunt		sint

PLUPERFECT

I had been prepared

Sg.	1. parātus, a, um	eram	parātus, a, um	essem
	2.	erās		essēs
	3.	erat		esset

Pl.	1. parātī, ae, a	erāmus	parātī, ae, a	essēmus
	2.	erātis		essētis
	3.	erant		essent

FUTURE PERFECT

I shall have been prepared

Sg.	1. parātus, a, um	erō
	2.	eris
	3.	erit

Pl.	1. parātī, ae, a	erimus
	2.	eritis
	3.	erunt

138.   IMPERATIVE

	PRESENT	FUTURE
Sg. 1.	——	——
2.	parāre, *be prepared*	
3.	——	parātor, *you shall be prepared*
		parātor, *he shall be prepared*
Pl. 1.	——	——
2.	parāminī, *be prepared*	——
3.	——	parantor, *they shall be prepared*

139.   INFINITIVE

PRES.	parārī, *to be prepared*
PERF.	parātus, a, um esse, *to have been prepared*
FUT.	parātum īrī, *to be about to be prepared*

140. PARTICIPLE

PERF.   parātus, a, um, *having been prepared* (71, *a*)

141. GERUNDIVE

parandus, a, um, *(about) to be prepared; must be, ought to be prepared* (71, *a*)

SECOND CONJUGATION
Conjugation of *habeō*, have
PRINCIPAL PARTS: habeō, habēre, habuī, habitus

	ACTIVE		*PASSIVE*	
	142. INDICATIVE	**143.** SUBJUNCTIVE	**144.** INDICATIVE	**145.** SUBJUNCTIVE

PRESENT

Sg. 1.	habeō	habeam	habeor	habear
2.	habēs	habeās	habēris, re	habeāris, re
3.	habet	habeat	habētur	habeātur
Pl. 1.	habēmus	habeāmus	habēmur	habeāmur
2.	habētis	habeātis	habēminī	habeāminī
3.	habent	habeant	habentur	habeantur

IMPERFECT

Sg. 1.	habēbam	habērem	habēbar	habērer
2.	habēbās	habērēs	habēbāris, re	habērēris, re
3.	habēbat	habēret	habēbātur	habērētur
Pl. 1.	habēbāmus	habērēmus	habēbāmur	habērēmur
2.	habēbātis	habērētis	habēbāminī	habērēminī
3.	habēbant	habērent	habēbantur	habērentur

FUTURE

Sg. 1.	habēbō		habēbor
2.	habēbis		habēberis, re
3.	habēbit		habēbitur
Pl. 1.	habēbimus		habēbimur
2.	habēbitis		habēbiminī
3.	habēbunt		habēbuntur

PERFECT

Sg. 1.	habuī	habuerim	habitus, a, um {sum, es, est}	habitus, a, um {sim, sīs, sit}
2.	habuistī	habuerīs		
3.	habuit	habuerit		
Pl. 1.	habuimus	habuerīmus	habitī, ae, a {sumus, estis, sunt}	habitī, ae, a {sīmus, sītis, sint}
2.	habuistis	habuerītis		
3.	habuērunt, ēre	habuerint		

PLUPERFECT

Sg. 1.	habueram	habuissem	habitus, a, um {eram, erās, erat}	habitus, a, um {essem, essēs, esset}
2.	habuerās	habuissēs		
3.	habuerat	habuisset		
Pl. 1.	habuerāmus	habuissēmus	habitī, ae, a {eramus, eratis, erant}	habitī, ae, a {essēmus, essētis, essent}
2.	habuerātis	habuissētis		
3.	habuerant	habuissent		

FUTURE PERFECT

Sg.				
	1.	habuerō	habitus, a, um	erō
	2.	habueris		eris
	3.	habuerit		erit

Pl.				
	1.	habuerimus	habitī, ae, a	erimus
	2.	habueritis		eritis
	3.	habuerint		erint

146. IMPERATIVE

		PRESENT	FUTURE	PRESENT	FUTURE
Sg.	1.	——	——	——	——
	2.	habē	habētō	habēre	habētor
	3.	——	habētō	——	habētor
Pl.	1.	——	——	——	——
	2.	habēte	habētōte	habēminī	——
	3.	——	habentō	——	habentor

147. INFINITIVE

PRES.	habēre	habērī
PERF.	habuisse	habitus, a, um esse
FUT.	habitūrus, a, um esse	habitum īrī

148. GERUND **149.** SUPINE **150.** PARTICIPLES

GERUND		SUPINE		PARTICIPLES	
GEN.	habendī			PRES. *Nom.* habēns; *Gen.* habentis (79)	
DAT.	habendō			FUT.	habitūrus, a, um (71, *a*)
ACC.	habendum	ACC.	habītum	PERF.	habitus, a, um (71, *a*)
ABL.	habendō	ABL.	habitū		

GERUNDIVE

habendus, a, um (71, *a*)

THIRD CONJUGATION

Conjugation of *dīcō*, say

PRINCIPAL PARTS: **dīcō, dīcere, dīxī, dictus**

	ACTIVE		*PASSIVE*	
151. INDICATIVE	**152.** SUBJUNCTIVE	**153.** INDICATIVE	**154.** SUBJUNCTIVE
		PRESENT		
Sg. 1. dīcō	dīcam	dīcor	dīcar
2. dīcis	dīcās	dīceris, re	dīcāris, re
3. dīcit	dīcat	dīcitur	dīcātur
Pl. 1. dīcimus	dīcāmus	dīcimur	dīcāmur
2. dīcitis	dīcātis	dīciminī	dīcāminī
3. dīcunt	dīcant	dīcuntur	dīcantur

INDICATIVE	SUBJUNCTIVE	INDICATIVE	SUBJUNCTIVE
		IMPERFECT	
Sg. 1. dīcēbam	dīcerem	dīcēbar	dīcerer
2. dīcēbās	dīcerēs	dīcēbāris, re	dīcerēris, re
3. dīcēbat	dīceret	dīcēbātur	dīcerētur
Pl. 1. dīcēbāmus	dīcerēmus	dīcēbāmur	dīcerēmur
2. dīcēbātis	dīcerētis	dīcēbāminī	dīcerēminī
3. dīcēbant	dīcerent	dīcēbantur	dīcerentur

		FUTURE	
Sg. 1. dīcam		dīcar	
2. dīcēs		dīcēris, re	
3. dīcet		dīcētur	
Pl. 1. dīcēmus		dīcēmur	
2. dīcētis		dīcēminī	
3. dīcent		dīcentur	

		PERFECT			
Sg. 1. dīxī	dīxerim	dictus, a, um	sum / es / est	dictus, a, um	sim / sīs / sit
2. dīxistī	dīxerīs				
3. dīxit	dīxerit				
Pl. 1. dīximus	dīxerīmus	dictī, ae, a	sumus / estis / sunt	dictī, ae, a	sīmus / sītis / sint
2. dīxistis	dīxerītis				
3. dīxērunt, ēre	dīxerint				

		PLUPERFECT			
Sg. 1. dīxeram	dīxissem	dictus, a, um	eram / erās / erat	dictus, a, um	essem / essēs / esset
2. dīxerās	dīxissēs				
3. dīxerat	dīxisset				
Pl. 1. dīxerāmus	dīxissēmus	dictī, ae, a	eramus / eratis / erant	dictī, ae, a	essēmus / essētis / essent
2. dīxerātis	dīxissētis				
3. dīxerant	dīxissent				

		FUTURE PERFECT	
Sg. 1. dīxerō		dictus, a, um	erō / eris / erit
2. dīxeris			
3. dīxerit			
Pl. 1. dīxerimus		dictī, ae, a	erimus / eritis / erint
2. dīxeritis			
3. dīxerint			

155.   IMPERATIVE

	PRESENT	FUTURE	PRESENT	FUTURE
Sg. 1. ——	——	——	——
2. dīc[1]	dīcitō	dīcere	dīcitor
3. ——	dīcitō	——	dīcitor
Pl. 1. ——			
2. dīcite	dīcitōte	dīciminī	——
3. ——	dīcuntō	——	dīcuntor

[1]See 202.

156. INFINITIVE

Pres.	dīcere		dīcī
Perf.	dīxisse		dictus, a, um esse
Fut.	dictūrus, a, um esse		dictum īrī

157. GERUND   **158.** SUPINE   **159.** PARTICIPLES

Gen. dīcendī
Dat. dīcendō
Acc. dīcendum   Acc. dictum
Abl. dīcendō   Abl. dictū

Pres. *Nom.* dīcēns; *Gen.* dīcentis (79)
Fut.   dictūrus, a, um (71, *a*)
Perf.   dictus, a, um (71, *a*)

160. GERUNDIVE

dīcendus, a, um (71, *a*)

Verbs in iō of the Third Conjugation

161. Many verbs of the third conjugation with present indicative in **iō,** change **i** to **e** before **r** and drop it when it would come before **e** or **i** in all tenses of the present system except the future, participle, and gerund. Otherwise they follow the inflection of **dīcere.**

162. These verbs are **capiō,** *take;* **cupiō,** *desire;* **faciō,** *do, make;* **fodiō,** *dig;* **fugiō,** *flee;* **jaciō,** *throw;* **pariō,** *produce, bear;* **quatiō,** *shake;* **rapiō,** *snatch;* **sapiō,** *be wise,* and their compounds; also compounds of **-liciō, -spiciō;** and the deponents **gradior,** *go,* and its compounds; **morior,** *die,* and its compounds; **patior,** *endure, suffer,* and its compounds.

Synopsis of Present System of *capiō, take*

Principal Parts: **capiō, capere, cēpī, captus**

		ACTIVE		*PASSIVE*	
		163. Indicative	**164.** Subjunctive	**165.** Indicative	**166.** Subjunctive
			PRESENT		
Sg.	1.	capiō	capiam	capior	capiar
	2.	capis	capiās	capieris, re	capiāris, re
	3.	capit	capiat	capitur	capiātur
Pl.	1.	capimus	capiāmus	capimur	capiāmur
	2.	capitis	capiātis	capiminī	capiāminī
	3.	capiunt	capiant	capiuntur	capiantur
			IMPERFECT		
Sg.	1.	capiēbam	caperem	capiēbar	caperer
		etc.	etc.	etc.	etc.
			FUTURE		
Sg.	1.	capiam		capiar	
	2.	capiēs		capiēris, re	
		etc.		etc.	

167.   IMPERATIVE

	PRESENT	FUTURE	PRESENT	FUTURE
Sg. 1.	——	——		——
2.	cape	capitō	capere	capitor
3.	——	capitō	——	capitor
Pl. 1.	——	——	——	——
2.	capite	capitōte	capiminī	——
3.	——	capiuntō	——	capiuntor

168.   INFINITIVE

PRES.   capere   capī

169. PARTICIPLE   **170.** GERUND   **171.** GERUNDIVE
PRES. capiēns (79)   *Gen.* capiendī   capiendus, a, um (71, *a*)

FOURTH CONJUGATION

Conjugation of *audiō*, hear

PRINCIPAL PARTS: **audiō, audīre, audīvī, audītus**

	ACTIVE		*PASSIVE*	
	172. INDICATIVE	**173.** SUBJUNCTIVE	**174.** INDICATIVE	**175.** SUBJUNCTIVE

PRESENT

	INDICATIVE	SUBJUNCTIVE	INDICATIVE	SUBJUNCTIVE
Sg. 1.	audiō	audiam	audior	audiar
2.	audīs	audiās	audīris, re	audiāris, re
3.	audit	audiat	audītur	audiātur
Pl. 1.	audīmus	audiāmus	audīmur	audiāmur
2.	audītis	audiātis	audīminī	audiāminī
3.	audiunt	audiant	audiuntur	audiantur

IMPERFECT

	INDICATIVE	SUBJUNCTIVE	INDICATIVE	SUBJUNCTIVE
Sg. 1.	audiēbam	audīrem	audiēbar	audīrer
2.	audiēbās	audīrēs	audiēbāris, re	audīrēris, re
3.	audiēbat	audīret	audiēbātur	audīrētur
Pl. 1.	audiēbāmus	audīrēmus	audiēbāmur	audīrēmur
2.	audiēbātis	audīrētis	audiēbāminī	audīrēminī
3.	audiēbant	audīrent	audiēbantur	audīrentur

FUTURE

	INDICATIVE	INDICATIVE
Sg. 1.	audiam	audiar
2.	audiēs	audiēris, re
3.	audiet	audiētur
Pl. 1.	audiēmus	audiēmur
2.	audiētis	audiēminī
3.	audient	audientur

PERFECT

Sg.	1.	audīvī	audīverim	audītus, a, um	sum es est	audītus, a, um	sim sīs sit
	2.	audīvistī	audīverīs				
	3.	audīvit	audīverit				

Pl	1.	audīvimus	audīverīmus	audītī, ae, a	sumus estis sunt	audītī, ae, a	sīmus sītis sint
	2.	audīvistis	audīverītis				
	3.	audīvērunt, ēre	audīverint				

PLUPERFECT

Sg.	1.	audīveram	audīvissem	audītus, a, um	eram erās erat	audītus, a, um	essem essēs esset
	2.	audīverās	audīvissēs				
	3.	audīverat	audīvisset				

Pl	1.	audīverāmus	audīvissēmus	audītī, ae, a	erāmus erātis erant	audītī, ae, a	essēmus essētis essent
	2.	audīverātis	audīvissētis				
	3.	audīverant	audīvissent				

FUTURE PERFECT

Sg.	1.	audīverō	audītus, a, um	erō eris erit
	2.	audīveris		
	3.	audīverit		

Pl	1.	audīverimus	audītī, ae, a	erimus eritis erunt
	2.	audīveritis		
	3.	audīverint		

176.   IMPERATIVE

		PRESENT	FUTURE	PRESENT	FUTURE
Sg.	1.	——	——	——	——
	2.	audī	audītō	audīre	audītor
	3.	——	audītō	——	audītor
Pl.	1.	——	——	——	——
	2.	audīte	audītōte	audīminī	——
	3.	——	audiuntō	——	audiuntor

177.   INFINITIVE

PRES.	audīre	audīrī
PERF.	audīvisse	audītus, a, um esse
FUT.	audītūrus, a, um esse	audītum īrī

178. GERUND   179. SUPINE   180. PARTICIPLES

178. GERUND	179. SUPINE	180. PARTICIPLES
GEN. audiendī		PRES. *Nom.* audiēns; *Gen.* audientis (79)
DAT. audiendō		FUT. audītūrus, a, um (71, *a*)
ACC. audiendum	ACC. audītum	PERF. audītus, a, um (71, *a*)
ABL. audiendō	ABL. audītū	

181.   GERUNDIVE

audiendus, a, um

DEPONENT VERBS

182. Deponent verbs have the passive form, but are active in meaning. They have also the present and future active participles, and the future active infinitive. Thus a deponent verb alone can have a present, future, and perfect participle, all with active meaning. The gerundive, however, is passive in meaning as well as in form. The conjugation differs in no particular from that of the regular conjugation.

I. First Conjugation

Conjugation of *moror*, delay

Principal Parts: **moror, morārī, morātus**

183. INDICATIVE	**184.** SUBJUNCTIVE

PRESENT

I delay, am delaying, do delay

Sg.	1. **moror**	**morer**
	2. **morāris, re**	**morēris, re**
	3. **morātur**	**morētur**
Pl.	1. **morāmur**	**morēmur**
	2. **morāminī**	**morēminī**
	3. **morantur**	**morentur**

IMPERFECT

I was delaying, delayed, did delay

Sg.	1. **morābar**	**morārer**
	2. **morābāris, re**	**morārēris, re**
	3. **morābātur**	**morārētur**
Pl.	1. **morābāmur**	**morārēmur**
	2. **morābāminī**	**morārēminī**
	3. **morābantur**	**morārentur**

FUTURE

I shall delay, will delay

Sg.	1. **morābor**	
	2. **morāberis, re**	
	3. **morābitur**	
Pl.	1. **morābimur**	
	2. **morābiminī**	
	3. **morābuntur**	

PERFECT

I have delayed, delayed, did delay

Sg.	1. **morātus, a, um sum**	**morātus, a, um sim**
	2. **es**	**sīs**
	3. **est**	**sit**

Pl.	1.	morātī, ae, a	sumus	morātī, ae, a	sīmus
	2.		estis		sītis
	3.		sunt		sint

PLUPERFECT

I had delayed

Sg.	1.	morātus, a, um	eram	morātus, a, um	essem
	2.		erās		essēs
	3.		erat		esset

Pl.	1.	morātī, ae, a	erāmus	moriti, ae, a	essēmus
	2.		erātis		essētis
	3.		errant		essent

FUTURE PERFECT

I shall (will) have delayed

Sg.	1.	morātus, a, um	erō
	2.		eris
	3.		erit

Pl.	1.	morātī, ae, a	erimus
	2.		eritis
	3.		erunt

185. IMPERATIVE

		PRESENT	FUTURE
Sg.	1.	——	——
	2.	morāre, *delay*	morātor, *you shall delay*
	3.	——	morātor, *he shall delay*
Pl.	1.	——	——
	2.	morāminī, *delay*	——
	3.	——	morantur, *they shall delay*

186. INFINITIVE

PRES.	morāri, *to delay*
FUT.	morātūrus, a, um esse, *to be about to delay*
PERF.	morātus, a, um esse, *to have delayed*

187. SUPINE

ACC.	morātum, *to delay, for delaying*
ABL.	morātū, *to delay, in the delaying*

188. PARTICIPLES

PRES.	morāns, antis, *delaying* (79)
FUT.	morātūrus, a, um, *about to delay* (71, *a*)
PERF.	morātus, a, um, *having delayed* (71, *a*)

189. GERUNDIVE

morandus, a, um, *(one) to be delayed, about to be delayed* (71, *a*)

190. GERUND

GEN. **morandī,** *of delaying*

II. Second, Third, Fourth Conjugations

Synopsis of *fateor, confess; **sequor,** follow; **patior,** endure; **experior,** try*

191. INDICATIVE

Pres.	fateor	sequor	patior	experior
	fatēris, etc.	sequeris	pateris	experīris
Imperf.	fatēbar	sequēbar	patiēbar	experiēbar
Fut.	fatēbor	sequar	patiar	experiar
Perf.	fassus sum	secūtus sum	passus sum	expertus sum
Pluperf.	fassus eram	secūtus eram	passus eram	expertus eram
Fut. Perf.	fassus erō	secūtus erō	passus erō	expertus erō

192. SUBJUNCTIVE

Pres.	fatear	sequar	patiar	experiar
	fateāris, etc.	sequāris	patiāris	experiāris
Imperf.	fatērer	sequerer	paterer	experīrer
Perf.	fassus sim	secūtus sim	passus sim	expertus sim
Pluperf.	fassus essem	secūtus essem	passus essem	expertus essem

193. IMPERATIVE

Pres.	fatēre	sequere	patere	experīre
Fut.	fatētor	sequitor	patitor	experītor

194. INFINITIVE

Pres.	fatērī	sequī	patī	experīrī
Fut.	fassūrus esse	secūtūrus esse	passūrus esse	expertūrus esse
Perf.	fassus esse	secūtus esse	passus esse	expertus esse

195. PARTICIPLES

Pres.	fatēns	sequēns	patiēns	experiēns
Fut.	fassūrus	secūtūrus	passūrus	expertūrus
Perf.	fassus	secūtus	passus	expertus

196. GERUND

	fatendī	sequendī	patiendī	experiendī

197. GERUNDIVE

	fatendus	sequendus	patiendus	experiendus

198. SUPINE

	fassum	secūtum	passum	expertum
	fassū	secūtū	passū	expertū

PERIPHRASTIC CONJUGATION

199. The periphrastic conjugation arises from the combination of the future participle active and passive (the gerundive) with forms of the verb **sum.**

a. The active periphrastic denotes something about to take place.

b. The passive periphrastic denotes necessity or duty.

200.   *ACTIVE*

	INDICATIVE	SUBJUNCTIVE
PRES.	**parātūrus (a, um) sum,** *am about to prepare*	**parātūrus (a, um) sim**
IMPERF.	**parātūrus eram,** *was about to prepare*	**parātūrus essem**
FUT.	**parātūrus erō,** *shall be about to prepare*	
PERF.	**parātūrus fuī,** *have been, was, about to prepare*	**parātūrus fuerim**
PLUPERF.	**parātūrus fueram,** *had been about to prepare*	**parātūrus fuissem**
FUT. PERF.	**parātūrus fuerō,** *shall have been about to prepare*	

INFINITIVE

PRES.	**parātūrus (a, um) esse,** *to be about to prepare*
PERF.	**parātūrus (a, um) fuisse,** *to have been about to prepare*

201.   *PASSIVE*

PRES.	**parandus (a, um) sum,** *have to be prepared;* *ought to be, must be prepared*	**parandus (a, um) sim**
IMPERF.	**parandus eram,** *had to be prepared; ought to be, must be prepared*	**parandus essem, forem**
FUT.	**parandus erō,** *shall have to be prepared*	
PERF.	**parandus fuī,** *have had to be prepared*	**parandus fuerim**
PLUPERF.	**parandus fueram,** *had had to be prepared*	**parandus fuissem**
FUT. PERF.	**parandus fuerō,** *shall have had to be prepared*	

INFINITIVE

PRES.	**parandus (a, um) esse,** *to have to be prepared*
PERF.	**parandus fuisse,** *to have had to be prepared*

202. Irregular Imperatives: Four verbs, **dīcō,** *say,* **dūcō,** *lead,* **faciō,** *do, make,* **ferō,** *bear,* form the present imperative active **dīc, dūc, fac, fer.** But in early Latin **dīce, dūce, face** are common. The compounds follow the usage of the simple verbs, except prepositional compounds of **faciō. Sciō,** *know,* lacks the present imperative **scī.**

203. Gerunds and Gerundives. The older ending of the gerund and gerundive in the third and fourth conjugations was **undus;** and **endus** was found only after **u.** In classical times **undus** is frequent, especially in verbs of the third and fourth conjugations; later, **endus** is the regular form.

204. 1. Syncopated and Shorter Forms. The perfects in **āvī, ēvī, īvī** often drop the **v** before **s** or **r** and contract the vowels throughout, except those in **īvī,** which admit the contraction only before **s.** These forms are called syncopated. They are found in all periods, and in the poets are used to suit the meter.

				PERFECT	
INDIC.	Sg.	1.	——		——
		2.	**parāvistī, parāstī**		**audīvistī, audīstī**
		3.	——		——
	Pl.	1.	——		——
		2.	**parāvistis, parāstis**		**audīvistis, audīstis**
		3.	**parāvērunt, parārunt**		**audīvērunt, audiērunt**
SUBJ.			**parāverim, parārim**		**audīverim, audierim**
			etc.		etc.
				PLUPERFECT	
INDIC.			**parāveram, parāram**		**audīveram, audieram**
			etc.		etc.
SUBJ.			**parāvissem, parāssem**		**audīvissem, audīssem**
			etc.		etc.
				FUTURE PERFECT	
INDIC.			**parāverō, parārō**		**audīverō, audierō**
			etc.		etc.
				INFINITIVE	
PERF.			**parāvisse, parāsse**		**audīvisse, audīsse**

2. In the first and third persons singular and in the first person plural of the perfect, syncope occurs regularly only in perfects in **īvī,** and there is no contraction. It is most common in the perfects of **eō,** *go,* and **petō,** *seek.* The unsyncopated forms are always common except those of **eō,** which are very rare in good prose, but occur more often in the poets for metrical reasons.

3. **nōvī,** *I know,* and **mōvī,** *I have moved,* are also contracted, especially in their compounds.

Sg. 2. nōstī. Pl. 2. nōstis. 3. nōrunt. *Subj.* **nōrim,** etc. *Pluperf.* **nōram,** etc. *Subj.* **nōssem,** etc. *Inf.* **nōsse.**

But the future perfect **nōrō** is found only in compounds.

a. Similar contractions are seen in **mōvī,** but not so often.

4. The shorter form of the ending of the perfect active indicative third plural, **ēre** instead of **ērunt,** and of the second singular, **re** instead of **ris,** is often found. Thus **amāvēre** = **amāvērunt,** *they have loved,* and **amābāre** = **amābāris,** *you were loved.*

SEMIDEPONENTS

205. 1. A few verbs form the perfect forms only as deponents:

audeō, audēre, ausus sum, *dare*
fīdō, fīdere, fīsus sum, *trust*
gaudeō, gaudēre, gāvīsus sum, *rejoice*
soleō, solēre, solitus sum, *be accustomed*

IRREGULAR VERBS

206. Irregular in the conjugation of the present stem are:

1. **orior, orīrī, ortus,** *arise*

The present indicative is usually formed according to the third conjugation; the imperfect subjunctive is always **orerer;** but the future participle is **oritūrus.** The compounds follow the same usage except **adorīrī,** *rise up at, attack,* which follows the fourth conjugation.

2. **eō,** *go.*

The stem is **ī,** which, before **a, o, u,** becomes **e.**

PRINCIPAL PARTS: **eō, īre, īvī (iī), itus**

207. INDICATIVE				**208.** SUBJUNCTIVE
PRES.	Sg.	1.	**eō,** *I go*	**eam**
		2.	**īs**	**eās**
		3.	**it**	**eat**
	Pl.	1.	**īmus**	**eāmus**
		2.	**ītis**	**eātis**
		3.	**eunt**	**eant**
IMPERF.			**ībam,** *I went*	**īrem**
FUT.			**ībō,** *I shall go*	—
PERF.			**īvī (iī),** *I have gone*	**īverim (ierim)**
PLUPERF.			**īveram (ieram),** *I had gone*	**īvissem (īssem)**

209. IMPERATIVE

	Sg.	1.	—	—
		2.	**ī,** *go*	**ītō,** *you shall go*
		3.	—	**ītō,** *he shall go*
	Pl.	1.	—	—
		2.	**īte,** *go*	**ītōte,** *you shall go*
		3.	—	**euntō,** *they shall go*

210. INFINITIVE
PRES. **īre**
FUT. **itūrus esse**
PERF. **īvisse (īsse)**

211. PARTICIPLES
PRES. **iēns** (*Gen.* **euntis**)
FUT. **itūrus**

212. GERUND
eundī, etc.

213. SUPINE
itum, *to go*

a. Like the simple verb are inflected most of the compounds, except in the perfect system, where **iī** is the regular form. **Vēneō,** *be for sale,* and **pereō,** *perish,* serve as passives to **vendō,** *sell,* and **perdō,** *destroy.* **Ambiō,** *solicit,* follows the fourth conjugation throughout.

b. The passive of the simple verb **eō** is found only in the impersonal forms **ītur, ībātur, itum est, īrī** (in combination with the supine). But compounds with transitive force are conjugated regularly: so, **praetereō** forms **praetereor, īris, ītur, īmur, īminī, euntur, ībar,** etc.; **itus sum, eram, erō, euntor, ītor, īrī, eundus.**

3. **ferō,** *bear.*

The endings beginning with **t, s,** and **r** are added directly to the root, **fer.**

a. Some forms of **ferō** are lacking and are supplied by **tul** and **(t)lā.**

PRINCIPAL PARTS: **ferō, ferre, tulī, lātus**

ACTIVE

214. INDICATIVE				**215.** SUBJUNCTIVE
PRES.	Sg.	1.	**ferō,** *I bear*	**feram**
		2.	**fers**	**ferās**
		3.	**fert**	**ferat**
	Pl.	1.	**ferimus**	**ferāmus**
		2.	**fertis**	**ferātis**
		3.	**ferunt**	**ferant**
IMPERF.			**ferēbam,** *I was bearing*	**ferem**
FUT.			**feram,** *I shall bear*	——
PERF.			**tulī,** *I have borne*	**tulerim**
PLUPERF.			**tuleram,** *I had borne*	**tulissem**
FUT. PERF.			**tulerō,** *I shall have borne*	——

216.			IMPERATIVE	
	Sg.	1.	——	——
		2.	**fer,** *bear*	**fertō,** *you shall bear*
		3.	——	**fertō,** *he shall bear*
	Pl.	1.	——	——
		2.	**ferte,** *bear*	**fertōte,** *you shall bear*
		3.	——	**feruntō,** *they shall bear*

217. INFINITIVE		**218.** PARTICIPLES
PRES.	**ferre**	**ferēns, ferentis,** *bearing*
FUT.	**lātūrus esse**	
PERF.	**tulisse**	**lātūrus**

219. GERUND	**220.** SUPINE
ferendī, etc.	**lātum, lātū**

PASSIVE

221. INDICATIVE | **222.** SUBJUNCTIVE

PRES. Sg. 1. **feror,** *I am borne* — **ferar**
2. **ferris** — **ferāris**
3. **fertur** — **ferātur**

Pl. 1. **ferimur** — **ferāmur**
2. **feriminī** — **ferāminī**
3. **feruntur** — **ferantur**

IMPERF. **ferēbar** — **ferer**
FUT. **ferar** — ——
PERF. **lātus sum** — **lātus sim**
PLUPERF. **lātus eram** — **lātus essem**
FUT. PERF. **lātus erō** — ——

223. IMPERATIVE

Sg. 1. —— — ——
2. **ferre,** *be borne* — **fertor,** *you shall be borne*
3. —— — **fertor,** *he shall be borne*

Pl. 1. —— — ——
2. **feriminī,** *be borne* — ——
3. —— — **feruntor,** *they shall be borne*

224. INFINITIVE | **225.** PARTICIPLES

PRES. **ferrī,** *to be borne* — PERF. **latus, a, um,** *borne*
FUT. **lātum īrī,** *to be about to be borne*
PERF. **lātus esse,** *to have been borne*

226. GERUNDIVE **ferendus, a, um,** *ought to be borne*

4. fīō, *become*

227. Fīō is conjugated in the present, imperfect, and future, according to the fourth conjugation, but in the subjunctive imperfect and in the infinitive the stem is increased by **e**; thus, **fierem, fierī,** *to become.* In these forms the **i** is short, but elsewhere it is long except before final **t.** The infinitive ends in **rī,** and the whole verb in the present system is treated as the passive of **faciō,** *do, make* (161–171). The rest of the verb is formed as a regular passive of **faciō.**

228. PRINCIPAL PARTS: **fīō, fierī, factus sum**

PRES. INDIC. **fīō,** *I am made, I become* — SUBJ. **fīam, fīas, fīat,** etc.
fīs, fit, fīmus, fītis, fīunt
IMPERF. **fīēbam,** *I was made, I became* — **fierem, fierēs,** etc.
FUT. **fīam,** *I shall be made (become)*
PERF. **factus sum** — **factus sim,** etc.
PLUPERF. **factus eram** — **factus essem,** etc.
FUT. PERF. **factus erō**

IMPERATIVE | INFINITIVE

(**fī**) (**fītō**) — PRES. **fierī,** *to become*
(**fītō**) — PERF. **factus esse,** *to have become*
FUT. **factum īrī,** *to be about to become*

229. When compounded with prepositions, **faciō** changes the **a** of the stem into **i**, and forms the passive in classical Latin regularly from the same stem: **perficiō,** *achieve;* passive, **perficior; interficiō,** *destroy;* passive, **interficior.** When compounded with words other than prepositions, **faciō** retains its **a,** and uses **fīō** as its passive: **patefaciō,** *lay open;* passive, **patefīō; calefaciō,** *warm;* passive, **calefīō.**

230. volō, *wish;* **nōlō,** *be unwilling;* **mālō,** *prefer.*

PRINCIPAL PARTS: **volō, velle, voluī**
nōlō, nōlle, noluī
mālō, mālle, māluī

231. INDICATIVE

PRES.	volō	nōlō	mālō
	vīs	nōn vīs	māvīs
	vult	nōn vult	māvult
	volumus	nōlumus	mālumus
	vultis	nōn vultis	māvultis
	volunt	nōlunt	mālunt
IMPERF.	volēbam	nōlēbam	mālēbam
FUT.	volam	nōlam	mālam
	volēs, etc.	nōlēs, etc.	mālēs, etc.
PERF.	voluī	nōluī	māluī, etc.
PLUPERF.	volueram	nōlueram	mālueram, etc.
FUT. PERF.	voluerō	nōluerō	māluerō, etc.

232. SUBJUNCTIVE

PRES.	velim	nōlim	mālim
	velīs	nōlis	mālīs
	velit	nōlit	mālit
	velīmus	nōlimus	mālīmus
	velītis	nōlitis	mālītis
	velint	nōlint	mālint
IMPERF.	vellem	nōllem	māllem
PERF.	voluerim	nōluerim	māluerim, etc.
PLUPERF.	voluissem	nōluissem	māluissem, etc.

233. IMPERATIVE

Sg. **nōlī, nōlītō**
Pl. **nōlīte, nōlītōte, nōluntō**

234. INFINITIVE

PRES.	velle	nōlle	mālle
PERF.	voluisse	nōluisse	māluisse

235. PARTICIPLES

PRES.	volēns	nōlēns	——

PRINCIPAL RULES OF SYNTAX

AGREEMENT

236. A verb agrees with its subject in number and person, as **ego vocō,** *I call;* **tū vocās,** *you call.*

a. A collective noun may take its predicate in the plural, as **pars veniunt,** *part come.*

b. The nearer subject is preferred to the more remote, as **mīlitēs et dux vēnit,** *the leader and his troops came.*

c. The copula may agree in number with the predicate noun, as **amantium īrae amōris integrātiō est,** *lovers' quarrels are love's renewal.* Compare "the wages of sin is death."

237. The adjective agrees with its noun in gender, number, and case, as **tālis vir,** *such a man;* **tālēs virī,** *such men;* **tālia dōna,** *such gifts.*

238. The common attribute of two or more substantives generally agrees with the nearest, rather than with the most important, as **cūncta maria terraeque patēbant,** *all seas and lands lay open.*

239. The common predicate attribute of two or more subjects is usually in the plural, as **pater et māter mortuī sunt,** *father and mother are dead;* but may agree with the nearest or most important, as **Caesar mortuus est et Jūlia,** *Caesar is dead, and Julia also.*

a. When the persons of the subjects are different, the predicate takes the first in preference to the second; the second in preference to the third.

b. When the genders of the subjects are different, the predicate attribute takes the nearest gender or the strongest (the masculine being the strongest of things with life, the neuter of those without), as **pater et māter mortuī sunt,** *father and mother are dead;* **mūrus et porta dē caelō tācta erant,** *wall and gate had been struck by lightning.*

240. The predicate substantive agrees with its subject in case, as **ille vir erat dux,** *that man was leader.*

a. The pronoun used as subject is commonly attracted into the gender of the predicate as **negat Epicūrus; hoc enim vestrum lūmen est,** *Epicurus says No; for he is your great light!*

241. The appositive agrees with its subject in case; if possible, also in number and person, as **Aenēās, pius dux,** *Aeneas, the devoted leader;* **Aenēās et Dīdō, superbī ducēs,** *Aeneas and Dido, proud leaders.*

291

242. The relative pronoun agrees with its antecedent in gender, number, and person, as **vir quī adest,** *the man who is present;* **dōna quae adsunt,** *the gifts which are here;* **ego quī hoc dīcō,** *I who say this.*

a. Occasionally the antecedent is attracted into the case of the relative, as **urbem quam statuō vestra est,** *the city which I am founding is yours.*

243. Poetic Plural. The plural is often used instead of the singular, especially in poetry, to generalize a statement, for metrical reasons, or for rhetorical effect, as **īrae,** *wrath, wrathful passions;* **fortitūdinēs,** *gallant actions;* **ōra,** *face, features;* **scēptra,** *scepter;* **silentia,** *silence.*

a. **Plural of Modesty.** The plural of the first person is sometimes used instead of the singular, as **dīximus multa,** *we (I) have spoken much.* Similarly **nōs** in all its cases for **ego,** etc., and **noster** in all its forms for **meus,** etc. This usage in English is sometimes called the "editorial we."

244. Disproportion is indicated by the comparative with **quam prō,** *than for;* **quam ut,** *than that;* **quam quī,** *than who;* as **minor caedēs quam prō tantā victōriā fuit,** *the loss was (too) small for so great a victory;* **major sum quam cui fortūna nocēre possit,** *I am too great for fortune possibly to hurt me.*

245. In comparing two qualities, use either **magis quam** with the positive, as **dīsertus magis est quam sapiēns,** *he is eloquent rather than wise (more eloquent than wise);* or a double comparative, **acūtiōrem sē quam ornātiōrem vult,** *he wishes to be acute rather than ornate.*

246. Superlatives denoting order and sequence are often used partitively and then usually precede their substantives, as **summa aqua,** *the surface* (of the) *water;* **summus mōns,** *the top* (of the) *mountain;* **prīmō vēre,** *in the beginning* (of) *spring.* Similarly in **mediā urbe,** *in the midst of the city;* **reliqua, cētera Graecia,** *the rest of Greece,* and the like.

PRONOUNS

247. Since the form of the verb indicates its person, the nominative of the personal pronouns is used only for emphasis or contrast, as **ego rēgēs ējēcī, vōs tyrannōs intrōdūxistis,** *I drove out kings; you bring in tyrants.*

a. The forms **meī, tuī, nostrī, vestrī** are used as objective genitives; **nostrum** and **vestrum** as partitive genitives (284, 286).

248. The reflexive is used regularly when reference is made to the grammatical subject, as **ipse sē quisque dīligit, quod sibi quisque cārus est,** *everyone loves himself, because everyone is dear to himself.*

a. The reflexive is sometimes used when reference is made to the logical subject, as **ferunt sua flāmina classem,** *their own (favorable) breezes wait the fleet.*

b. The reflexive is used of the principal subject when reference is made to the thought or will of that subject, especially in indirect discourse or in substantive volitive clauses (clauses of desire), as **sentit animus sē vī suā movērī,** *the mind feels that it moves by its own force;* **ā mē petīvit ut sēcum essem,** *he asked me to be with him;* **librōs quōs frāter suus relīquisset mihi dōnāvit,** *he gave me the books* (as he said) *that his brother had left.*

249. The possessive adjective is used instead of the genitive of the first and second person pronouns, as **socius meus,** *a comrade of mine;* **tēlum tuum,** *a weapon of yours;* **amor meus,** *my love (which I feel);* **spēs tua,** *your hope (which you have).*

a. The appositive to a possessive adjective is in the genitive, as **urbs meā ūnīus operā fuit salva,** *the city was saved by my exertions alone.*

ADJECTIVES FOR ADVERBS

250. With words of inclination and disinclination, knowledge and ignorance, order and position, time and season, the adjective is commonly employed for the adverb, as **id faciō volēns,** *I do this willing(ly).*

SPECIAL USE OF MOODS

251. The Indicative, not the subjunctive, is commonly used to express possibility, power, obligation, and necessity, as **possum persequī permulta oblēctāmenta rērum rūsticārum,** *I might rehearse very many delights of country life;* **ad mortem tē dūcī oportēbat,** *you ought to have been led to execution.*

252. The Potential Subjunctive. The present or perfect subjunctive may be used to express possibility in the present or future, as **tē superesse velim,** *I should like for you to survive;* **Platōnem nōn nimis valdē laudāverīs,** *you can't praise Plato too much;* the imperfect subjunctive to express possibility in the past, **crēderēs victōs,** *you would (might) have thought them beaten.*

253. The Optative Subjunctive. The subjunctive, sometimes with **utinam,** *would that,* is often used in expressions of wishing. The negative is **nē. Valeās,** *farewell!* **nē veniant,** *may they not come!* **utinam nē nātus essem,** *would that I had not been born!* **utinam vīveret frāter,** *would that my brother were alive!*

254. The Volitive Subjunctive. The subjunctive may be used in expressions of will, asseveration, command, or concession, as **stet haec urbs,** *may this city continue to stand;* **moriar sī magis gaudērem,** *may I die if I could be more glad:* **amēmus patriam,** *let us love our country;* **sit deus,** *granted that he is a god.* This subjunctive is often called jussive, hortatory, or concessive, according as it expresses a command, an exhortation, or a concession, respectively.

255. The present imperative looks forward to immediate, the future imperative to contingent, fulfilment, as **haec dīcite vestrō rēgī,** *tell this to your king;* **cōnsulēs nēminī pārentō,** *the consuls shall obey no one.*

256. The negative of the imperative is regularly **nōlī** with the infinitive; as **nōlī fugere,** *don't flee!* sometimes **nē** or **cavē (nē)** with the present or perfect subjunctive is also used, as **cavē (nē) faciās,** *don't do it!* **nē mortem timeās** (or **timuerītis**), *don't fear death!*

a. In poetry **nē** is often found with the imperative, as **nē timē,** *fear not!* **nē fuge,** *don't run!*

INFINITIVES

257. The Historical Infinitive. The present infinitive, with the subject in the nominative, is sometimes used to give a rapid sequence of events, as **hinc Ulixēs terrēre,** *henceforth Ulysses began to frighten (me).* This is called the historical infinitive.

258. The Infinitive as Neuter Subject. The infinitive with or without a subject may be treated as a neuter subject, object, or predicate, as **dulce et decōrum est prō patriā mori,** *it is sweet and glorious to die for one's fatherland;* **turpe est vincī,** *it is shameful to be conquered;* **scit vincere,** *he knows (how) to conquer;* **vīvere est cogitāre,** *to live is to think, living is thinking.*

259. The Complementary Infinitive. The infinitive is used with verbs of will, desire, power, duty, habit, inclination, resolve, continuance, purpose, etc., as **cupit mori,** *he wishes to die;* **dēbet haec vulnera patī,** *he ought to suffer these wounds.* This is called the complementary infinitive.

260. The Infinitive as Object. The accusative with infinitive is used as the object of verbs of emotion, will, and desire; as **tē vēnisse gaudeō,** *I rejoice that you have come;* **mē dīcere vult,** *he wishes me to speak.*

261. The Infinitive of Purpose. In poetry the infinitive is often used to express purpose, as **nōn populāre vēnimus,** *we have not come to pillage.*

262. The Infinitive of Exclamation. The infinitive with accusative subject is used in exclamation or exclamatory questions, as **mē dēsistere,** *what! I desist?*

263. The Infinitive of Indirect Statement (Indirect Discourse). The infinitive is used after verbs of saying, showing, believing, and perceiving, to express an indirect statement; the present infinitive expresses action contemporary with that of the governing verb, the perfect infinitive action prior to it, the future infinitive action future to it, as **dīcit tē errāre,** *he says that you are wrong;* **dīcēbat tē errāre,** *he was saying that you were wrong;* **dīcēbat tē errāsse,** *he was saying that you had been wrong.*

a. The future infinitive of **sum** followed by **ut** and the subjunctive is used in indirect statement of future action when the verb has no future participle, as **dīcit fore (futūrum esse) ut metuās,** *he says that you will fear.*

264. The Infinitive with Nouns. The poets and later prose writers use the infinitive with nouns denoting attention or opportunity, as **amor cāsūs cognōscere nostrōs,** *desire to know our misfortunes;* **adfectāre potestās,** *opportunity to seize.*

265. The Infinitive with Adjectives. The infinitive is used with many adjectives and with participles of adjectival force, as **nescia vincī pectora,** *hearts not knowing (how) to yield;* **certa morī,** *determined to die.*

GERUNDS AND GERUNDIVES

266. The genitive of the gerund or gerundive is used chiefly after substantives and adjectives that require a complement, as **sapientia ars vīvendī putanda est,** *philosophy is to be considered the art of living;* **nūlla spēs plācandī deī,** *no hope of appeasing god;* **cupidus maledīcendī,** *eager to abuse.*

267. The dative of the gerund or gerundive is used mainly in postclassical Latin after words of fitness and function; also after words of capacity and adaptation, and to express purpose, as **tēla apta mittendō,** *weapons suitable for hurling;* **comitia cōnsulibus creandīs,** *elections for nominating consuls.*

268. The accusative of the gerund or gerundive is used with **ad** to express purpose, as **ad bellandum venimus,** *we come to make war.*
a. The accusative of the gerundive is used in agreement with the direct object of verbs of giving, sending, and leaving, etc., to indicate purpose, as **id mihi servandum dedit,** *he gave it to me to keep;* **Conōn mūrōs reficiendōs cūrat,** *Conōn has the walls rebuilt;* **patriam dīripiendam relīquimus,** *we have left our country to be plundered.*

269. The ablative of the gerund or gerundive is used to denote means and cause, rarely manner, as **ūnus homō nōbīs cūnctandō restituit rem,** *one man by delaying raised our cause again.*

SUPINES

270. The supine in **um** (accusative) is used chiefly after verbs of motion to express purpose, as **veniunt spectātum,** *they come to see.*

271. The supine in **ū** (ablative) is used chiefly with adjectives to indicate respect, as **mīrābile dictū,** *wonderful to relate (in the relating);* **mīrābile vīsū,** *wonderful to see (in the seeing).*

PARTICIPLES

272. The Present Participle denotes continuance, the perfect participle denotes completion at the time of the principal verb.

273. The participle is used after verbs of perception and representation to express the actual condition of the object at the time, as **Catōnem vīdī in bibliothēcā sedentem multīs circumfūsum librīs,** *I saw Cato sitting in the library with an ocean of books about him;* **illam audīvī fūrtīvā vōce loquentem,** *I heard her talking in a stealthy tone.*

274. The Future Participle is used in poetry and occasionally in prose to express desire or purpose, as **fabricāta est māchina īnspectūra domōs ventūraque dēsuper urbī,** *it has been built as an engine of war, to spy into our homes and come down upon the city from above.*

275. The Perfect Participle passive is used after verbs of causation and desire, to denote that entire fulfilment is demanded or desired, as **sī quī voluptātibus dūcuntur, missōs faciant honōrēs,** *if any are led captive by sensual pleasures, let them give up honors* (at once and forever).

CASES

NOMINATIVE

276. The subject of a finite verb is in the nominative, as **urbs stat,** *the city is standing.*

277. The subject of a historical infinitive is in the nominative, as **Ulixēs terrēre,** *Ulysses began to terrorize (me).*

278. The predicate of a finite form of the verb *to be,* **sum,** or of a verb of seeming or becoming, or of the passive of a verb of making, choosing, showing, thinking, or calling, is in the nominative, as **pater est rēx,** *his father is king;* **pater fit rēx,** *his father becomes king;* **pater vocātur rēx,** *his father is called king.*

279. When an active verb of saying, showing, believing, or perceiving, is changed to the passive, the accusative subject of the infinitive may become the nominative subject of the leading verb, as **urbs dīcitur magna fuisse,** *the city is said to have been great.* Compare **dīcunt urbem fuisse magnam,** *they say that the city was great.*

GENITIVE

280. Genitive of Material. The genitive may be used to denote the material or substance of which a thing consists, as **flūmina lactis,** *rivers of milk.* See 324 for the ablative of material.

281. The Appositional Genitive is used with **vōx, nōmen, verbum, rēs, urbs,** etc., as **nōmen amīcitiae,** *the name of friendship;* **urbem Patavī,** *the city of Patavium.*

282. The Epexegetical Genitive (or genitive of explanation) is used after **genus, vitium, culpa,** etc., as **virtūtēs continentiae, gravitātis, jūstitiae, fideī,** *the virtues of self-control, earnestness, justice, honor.*

283. The Possessive Genitive is used to denote possession, as **domus rēgis,** *the palace of the king, the king's palace.*

284. The Subjective Genitive is used of the subject of the action indicated by the substantive; **the Objective Genitive,** of the object of that action, as **metus hostium,** *the fear of the enemy,* which may mean: (1) the fear which the enemy feel (subjective genitive) or (2) the fear felt toward the enemy (objective genitive). The objective genitive is used with nouns, adjectives, and participles used as adjectives, as **cupīdō glōriae,** *desire for glory;* **tempestātum potentem,** *ruling the storms;* **memorem vestrī, oblītum suī,** *mindful of you, forgetful of himself.*

285. Genitive of Quality. The genitive with an adjective may be used to describe a person or thing, as **homō maximī corporis,** *a man of gigantic size.* This is called the genitive of quality (characteristic, description). Compare the ablative of quality or characteristic (330).

a. The genitive of quality (or description) or the possessive genitive may be used as a predicate, as **id virtūtis est,** *that is a mark of virtue;* **hujus erō vīvus, mortuus hujus erō,** *hers I shall be living; dead, hers shall I be;* **haec domus est patris meī,** *this house is my father's.*

286. The Partitive Genitive stands for the whole to which a part belongs, as **pars hominum,** *part of the men;* **maximus omnium,** *greatest of all.* This is sometimes called the genitive of the whole.

287. Genitive with Special Adjectives and Verbs. Adjectives and verbs of fullness and want, of knowledge and ignorance, of desire and disgust, of participation and power, may take the genitive. Also some present participles used as adjectives, and in later Latin some verbals in **āx,** as **plēnus labōris,** *full of toil;* **egēnus omnium,** *in need of everything;* **cōnscius rēctī,** *conscious of right;* **ignārus malī,** *ignorant of misfortune;* **cupidus aurī,** *desirous of gold;* **dīligēns vērī,** *careful (a lover of) the truth;* **capāx imperī,** *capable of empire;* **implentur veteris Bacchī,** *they fill themselves with old wine.*

288. Genitive with Verbs. Verbs of reminding, remembering, and forgetting usually take the genitive, as **meminit malōrum, oblītus est bonōrum,** *he remembers the evil, forgets the good.*

a. Sometimes these verbs take the accusative, especially of things, as **haec ōlim meminisse juvābit,** *to remember these things will one day be a pleasure.*

289. Verbs of Emotion take the genitive, as **miserēre animī nōn digna ferentis,** *pity a soul enduring what it does not deserve.*

290. Impersonal verbs of emotion take the accusative of the person who feels, and the genitive of the exciting cause, as **tuī mē miseret, meī piget,** *I pity you, I loathe myself.*

291. Verbs of accusing, convicting, condemning, and acquitting take the genitive of the charge, as **accūsātus est prōditiōnis,** *he was accused of treason;* **damnātus est caedis,** *he was convicted of murder;* **absolūtus est crīminis,** *he was acquitted of the charge.*

292. Genitive of Value. Verbs of rating and buying take the genitive of the general value, as **parvī exīstimāre,** *to consider of small account;* **ēmit equōs tantī quantī Caesar voluit,** *he bought the horses at the price Caesar wanted.*

293. Interest and **rēfert** take the genitive of the person, rarely of the thing concerned, as **interest omnium rēctē facere,** *it is to the interest of all to do right;* **rēfert omnium,** *it concerns everybody.*

a. Sometimes the ablative singular feminine of the possessive adjective is used, as **meā interest, meā rēfert,** *I am concerned.*

294. Genitive of Respect. The genitive is used with various adjectives to denote the respect to which a thing is true, as **aeger animī,** *sick at heart.* This is sometimes called the genitive of specification.

DATIVE

295. The Indirect Object is put in the dative, as **aurum hominī dat,** *he gives gold to the man.*

296. Some verbs of giving take either the dative and the accusative, or the accusative and the ablative, as **hominī aurum dōnat,** *he presents the gold to the man;* **hominem aurō dōnat,** *he presents the man with gold.*

297. Dative with Special Verbs. Many verbs meaning favor, help, trust, bid and forbid, believe, persuade, obey, serve, threaten, pardon, spare, join, and contend, take the dative, as **invideō nēminī,** *I envy no one;* **cēdit fortūnae,** *he yields to fortune;* **id mihi placet,** *that pleases me;* **pārēmus ducī,** *we obey our leader;* **crēdit hominī,** *he trusts the man.*

298. Dative with Compounds. Many intransitive verbs compounded with **ad, ante, con, in, inter, ob, post, prae, sub,** and **super,** may take a dative, as **accēdō equō,** *I approach the horse;* **antecellit omnibus,** *he excels all;* **nox incubat marī,** *night broods over the sea;* **piger ipse sibi obstat,** *this lazy man stands in his own way.*

a. Transitive verbs so compounded also take an accusative, as **mē vestrīs ōrīs deus appulit,** *god drove me to your shores.*

299. Dative of Possession. The dative is used with **esse** to denote possession, as **est ager nōbīs,** *we have a field.*

300. The Ethical Dative is used of the personal pronouns only, as **ecce tibi homō,** *here's your man!* **tibi bellum geret,** *he shall wage war (for you, let me tell you).*

301. The Dative of Reference is used of the person interested or concerned in the action or of the person to whom a statement is referred, as **deō altāria fūmant,** *the altars smoke in honor of the god;* **pulchra est multīs,** *she is beautiful to many* (in the eyes of many); **est urbe ēgressīs tumulus,** *as you go out of town (to those who have gone out of town) there is a mound.* This is also called the dative of interest, and at times is called the dative of advantage and of disadvantage.

302. The Dative of Agent is used with a passive verb, especially with the gerundive, as **id faciendum mihi,** *this must be done by me, I must do this;* **vetor fātīs,** *I am forbidden by the fates;* **urbs capta est mihi,** *the city was captured by me.*

303. Dative of Purpose. The dative may denote the object for which (purpose), as **pars optāre locum tēctō,** *part were choosing a site for a home.*

a. The Dative of Purpose is often used in combination with the dative of reference (301), as **auxiliō iīs fuit,** *he was a help to them;* **id erit cūrae mihi,** *that shall be my care.*

304. Dative with Adjectives. Adjectives of friendliness, fullness, likeness, nearness, with their opposites, take the dative, as **similis est hominī,** *he is like a man;* **homō amīcus est mihi,** *the man is friendly to me;* **id erit ūtile omnibus,** *this will be useful to all;* **proximus sum egomet mihi,** *myself am nearest to me.*

305. Dative of Separation. Many verbs of warding off, robbing, and ridding, depriving, and separation take a dative, especially in poetry, as **ēripiēs mihi hunc errōrem,** *you will rid me of this mistake;* **silicī scintillam excūdit,** *he strikes a spark from the flint.* This is called the dative of separation.

306. Dative of Direction. In poetry the place to which, or limit of motion, is often expressed by the dative, as **it clāmor caelō,** *a shout goes to heaven;* **multōs dēmittimus Orcō,** *we send many to Hades.*

ACCUSATIVE

307. The **Direct Object** of active transitive verbs is in the accusative case and may denote either the object effected or the object affected, as **bellum gerunt,** *they wage war* (object *effected* or result produced); **condidit urbem,** *he founds the city* (object *effected*); **capit urbem,** *he captures the city* (object *affected*); **rēx dūcit hominēs,** *the king leads the men* (object *affected*).

308. Accusative with Compounds. Many intransitive verbs, mostly those of motion, compounded with **ad, ante, circum, con, in, inter, ob, per, praeter, sub, subter, super,** and **trāns,** take the accusative, as **adit urbem,** *he approaches the city;* **poenam subit,** *he submits to punishment.*

a. Transitive verbs thus compounded may have two accusatives, as **exercitum flūmen trājēcit,** *he threw his army across the river.*

309. In poetry the passive is often used in a reflexive or middle sense, as **fertur in hostīs,** *he charges upon the enemy.*

a. When thus used the verb may take an accusative as a direct object, as **ferrum cingitur,** *he girds on (girds himself with) the steel;* **sinūs collēcta,** *having gathered her robes;* **tūnsae pectora,** *beating their breasts;* **īnsternor umerōs,** *I spread over my shoulders.*

310. The accusative and ablative of certain adjectives are used adverbially, as **multum jactātus,** *much tossed;* **prīmō,** *at first.* See 93–94.

311. Accusative of Respect. In poetry the accusative is often used with an adjective or verb to denote the part concerned, as **nūda genū,** *with knee bare (bare as to her knee);* **ōs umerōsque deō similis,** *like a god in (as to) face and shoulders.* This is called the accusative of respect or specification.

312. Accusative with Prepositions. The accusative is used with many prepositions, the most important being

> ante, apud, ad, adversum
> circum, cis, ob, trāns, secundum
> penes, pōne, prope, per,
> post, and all in –ā, and –ter.[1]

313. Cognate Accusative. Intransitive verbs may take an accusative of similar form or meaning, as **dum vītam vīvās,** *as long as you live;* **somnium somniāvī,** *I dreamed a dream.* This is called a cognate accusative.

314. Accusative of Extent. The accusative may express extent in space, time, or degree, as **tumulum centum pedēs altum,** *a mound one hundred feet high;* **fuit rēx decem annōs,** *he was king ten years;* **sī mē amās tantum quantum tē amō,** *if you love me as I love you.* This is called the accusative of extent. With expressions of time this is often called the accusative of duration of time.

---

[1] Observe the metrical form of these four lines.

315. Place Whither (place to which) is regularly denoted by the accusative with the preposition **ad** or **in,** as **vēnit ad Ītaliam,** *he came to Italy.* This is sometimes called the accusative of limit of motion.

a. The names of towns, small islands, **domus,** and **rūs,** do not ordinarily take the preposition, as **vēnit Rōmam,** *he came to Rome;* **pater, venī domum,** *father, come home!* **fugiunt rūs,** *they flee to the country.*

b. In poetry also the preposition is often omitted, as **Ītaliam Lāvīnaque vēnit lītora,** *he came to Italy and the Lavinian shores.*

316. Two Accusatives. Verbs meaning to inquire, require, teach, and conceal take two accusatives, one of the person, one of the thing, as **quis tē illud docuit,** *who taught you that?* **Mīlēsiōs nāvem poposcit,** *he demanded a ship of the Milesians;* **quid mē istud rogās,** *why do you ask me that?*

a. Verbs of naming, making, taking, choosing, and showing, take two accusatives of the same person or thing, as **vocant urbem Rōmam,** *they call the city Rome;* **illum rēgem faciunt,** *they make him king.*

317. The Subject of the Infinitive is regularly in the accusative, as **vult mē dīcere,** *he wishes me to speak.*

a. A predicate noun in such an infinitive phrase agrees with the subject, as **volunt eum rēgem esse,** *they wish him to be king.*

318. Accusative of Exclamation. The accusative may be used in exclamations, as **mē miserum,** *poor me!* **prō deum fidem,** *for heaven's sake!*

ABLATIVE

319. Place Where is denoted by the ablative, usually with **in,** as **in altō et in terrīs,** *on sea and on land.*

a. With names of towns and small islands the locative is used to express place where, as **Rōmae,** *at Rome.* See 345.

b. In poetry the preposition is often omitted, as **terrā marīque,** *on land and sea;* **Ītaliā,** *in Italy;* **lītore,** *on the shore;* **pectore,** *in his heart.*

320. Place Whence is denoted by the ablative, usually with **ex, dē,** or **ab,** as **ex marī,** *out of the sea.*

a. With names of towns, small islands, **domō,** *from home,* and with **rūre,** *from the country,* the preposition is regularly omitted, as **Karthāgine,** *from Carthage.*

b. In poetry the preposition is often omitted, as **venit (ex) Ītaliā,** *he comes from Italy.*

321. Ablative of Accompaniment. Accompaniment (attendance) is denoted by the ablative with **cum,** as **venit cum sociīs,** *he comes with his comrades.*

a. With **mē, tē, sē, nōbīs, vōbīs, quō, quā, quibus,** the preposition **cum** is regularly appended, as **mēcum,** *with me;* **tēcum,** *with you;* **sēcum,** *with him(self), with them(selves).*

322. Time When or Within Which is denoted by the ablative, as **urbem cēpit nocte,** *he captured the city at night;* **nocte pluit tōtā,** *it rains all night.*

323. Origin (source or descent) is denoted by the ablative with or without **ex** or **dē,** as **nātus deā,** *born of a goddess (goddess-born);* **ex mē atque ex hōc nātus es,** *you are his son and mine.*

324. Ablative of Material. Material is denoted by the ablative, usually with **ex,** as **domus facta ex saxā, ex ferrō,** *a house made of stone, of iron;* **aere clipeus,** *a shield of bronze.* See 280 for the genitive of material.

325. Ablative of Respect. The respect in which a verb, adjective, or noun is to be taken is denoted by the ablative, as **sunt quīdam hominēs nōn rē sed nōmine,** *some people are human beings not in fact (reality), but in name (only).* This is sometimes called the ablative of specification.

326. Ablative of Accordance. The ablative, usually with **dē** or **ex,** is used to express that in accordance with which a thing is done or judged, as **ex senātūs cōnsultō,** *in accordance with the decree of the senate.*

a. With certain words accordance is usually expressed by the ablative without a preposition, as **cōnsuētūdine suā,** *according to his custom;* **tuō cōnsiliō,** *in accordance with your plan;* **meā sententiā,** *in my opinion.*

327. Ablative with Comparatives. Comparatives without **quam** are followed by the ablative, as **exēgī monumentum aere perennius,** *I have erected a monument more enduring than bronze;* **Ō mātre pulchrā fīlia pulchrior,** *O daughter fairer than a mother fair!*

328. Ablative of Manner. Manner is denoted by the ablative regularly with an adjective or with **cum,** as **cum virtūte vīvere,** *to live virtuously;* **id fēcit magnā cum cūrā,** *he did it very carefully.*

a. The simple ablative of certain nouns may be used to denote manner, as **cāsū,** *by chance;* **vī,** *by force.*

329. Ablative of Attendant Circumstance. Attendant circumstance, situation, or result may be expressed by the ablative, usually with a modifier, and without a preposition, but sometimes with **cum,** as **magnō intervallō,** *at a great distance;* **frequentissimō senātū,** *at a crowded meeting of the senate;* **imperiō suō,** *under his full power;* **clāmōre,** *with shouting;* **cum tuā perniciē,** *with (to) your destruction;* **magnō (cum) dolōre omnium,** *to the great grief of all.*

330. Ablative of Quality. Quality or description is denoted by the ablative regularly with an adjective, as **stātūra fuit humilī,** *he was of low stature.* This is sometimes called the ablative of characteristic or description. See 285 for the genitive of quality.

331. Ablative of Means. Means or instrument is denoted by the ablative, without a preposition, as **clārē videō oculīs,** *I see clearly with my eyes;* **pugnābant armīs,** *they fought with arms.*

332. Ablative of Cause. Cause may also be expressed by the ablative without a preposition, as **ōdērunt peccāre bonī virtūtis amōre,** *the good hate to sin from love of virtue.*

333. Ablative of Agent. The agent is denoted by the ablative with **ā (ab),** as **urbs capta est ab illō duce,** *the city was captured by that leader.*

334. The Standard of Measurement is denoted by the ablative, as **magnōs hominēs virtūte mētimur, nōn fortūnā,** *we measure great men by worth, not by fortune.*

335. Measure of Difference is put in the ablative, as **sōl multīs partibus est major quam terra ūniversa,** *the sun is many parts (a great deal) larger than the whole earth.* This is also sometimes called the degree of difference.

336. Ablative of Price. Definite price is put in the ablative, as **ēmit morte immortālitātem,** *he purchased deathlessness with death.*

a. General value is expressed by the genitive. See 292.

337. Ablative with Adjectives. The ablative is used with **dignus, indignus, frētus, contentus,** and **laetus,** and with adjectives of fullness and abundance, as **contentus hōc equō,** *content with this horse;* **dignus poenā,** *worthy of punishment;* **indignus poenā,** *unworthy of punishment.*

a. Also the verb **dignor,** *deem worthy,* takes the ablative in poetry and later prose, as **haud tālī mē dignor honōre,** *I do not deem myself worthy of such honor.*

338. The Ablative of Route is used to denote the way by which, as **prōvehimur pelagō,** *we sail forth over the sea.*

339. Ablative with Prepositions. The ablative is used with many prepositions, the most important being

> abs (ab, ā), cum, cōram, dē
> prae, prō, sine, ex (or ē).

340. Ablative of Separation. Separation is expressed by the ablative case, with or without a preposition. This ablative is used especially with verbs of depriving, of freedom, and of want, as **sē prīvāvit oculīs,** *he deprived himself of his eyes;* **omnibus egēre rēbus,** *to be in need of everything;* **tē ab eō līberō,** *I free you from him.* This is called the ablative of separation.

a. The ablative of separation is also used with **aliēnus** and with adjectives of freedom and want, as **aliēnum mājestāte deōrum**, *inconsistent with the dignity of the gods;* **līber cūrā**, *free from care.*

341. The ablative is used with **opus** and **ūsus**, as **opus est mihi aurō**, *I need gold;* **ūsus est dictīs bonīs**, *there is need of kind words.*

342. Ablative with Special Verbs. **Ūtor, fruor, fungor, potior, vēscor**, and their compounds take the ablative, as **hīs vōcibus ūsa est**, *she spoke (used) these words;* **abūsus est nostrā patientiā**, *he used up our patience;* **fruimur lūce vītae**, *we enjoy the light of life;* **fungor officiō**, *I am performing my duty;* **potītur victōriā**, *he gains the victory;* **lacte vēscuntur**, *they live on milk.*

343. Ablative Absolute. The ablative, combined with a participle, adjective, or noun, may serve to express the circumstances in which an act takes place, as **duce victō, abeunt**, *the leader having been conquered, they depart;* **urbe captā, hominēs redeunt**, *the city having been captured, the men return.* This phrase is called the ablative absolute.

a. The ablative absolute phrase may have an accessory idea of time, cause, or condition, as **Caesare cōnsule haec lēx lāta est**, *this law was passsed in Caesar's consulship.*

VOCATIVE

344. Vocative. The vocative, with or without **Ō**, *O*, is used in addressing a person or thing, as **Mūsa**, *O Muse!* **Aeole**, *O Aeolus!* **Ō rēgīna**, *O queen!*

LOCATIVE

345. Names of towns and small islands of the first and second declensions, **humus, domus**, and **rūs**, are put in the locative of the place where, as **Rōmae**, *at Rome;* **Crētae**, *in Crete;* **humī**, *on the ground;* **domī**, *at home.*

a. In poetry the names of countries and large islands also are sometimes found in the locative, as **Libyae**, *in Libya.*

ADVERBS

346. Adverbs qualify verbs, adjectives, and other adverbs, as **male vīvit**, *he lives badly;* **bene labōrat**, *he works well;* **ferē omnēs**, *almost all;* **nimis saepe**, *too often.*

QUESTIONS

347. *a.* A question for information merely is generally introduced by **–ne**, as **videtne patrem**, *does he see his father?*

b. A question that expects the answer *yes* is generally introduced by **nōnne**, as **nōnne vidēs**, *don't you see?*

c. A question that expects the answer no is generally introduced by **num**, as **num vidēs patrem**, *you don't see your father (do you)?*

MOODS IN INTERROGATIVE SENTENCES

348. The Deliberative Question has its verb in the subjunctive, as **dīcam an taceam,** *shall I speak or hold my tongue?* **quid facerem,** *what was I to do?*

a. Occasionally the present indicative is used in deliberative questions, as **quem sequimur,** *whom are we to follow?*

349. The Indirect Question has its verb in the subjunctive, as **quaerēmus** (1) **quid fēcerit,** (2) **quid faciat,** (3) **quid factūrus sit,** *we shall ask what he has done, what he is doing, what he is going to do (will do).*

350. The direct form of these three questions would be: (1) **quid fēcit?** (2) **quid facit?** (3) **quid faciet** (or **factūrus est**)?

TENSES

351. There are six tenses in Latin: the present, imperfect, future, perfect, pluperfect, and future perfect.

1. **The Present** denotes continuance in the present; it is used: (1) of that which is going on now (specific present), as **auribus teneō lupum,** *I am holding a wolf by the ears;* (2) of statements that apply to all time (universal present), as **probitās laudātur et alget,** *honesty is praised and freezes.*

a. **The Historical Present.** The present is used far more frequently than in English as a lively representation of the past, as **cohortīs incēdere jubet,** *he orders the cohorts to advance.* This is called the historical present.

b. The present is used in Latin of actions that continue into the present, especially with **jam,** now, **jam diū,** *now for a long time,* **jam prīdem,** *now long since,* as **Mithridātēs annum jam tertium et vīcēsimum rēgnat,** *Mithridates has been reigning now going on twenty-three years.*

c. The present is sometimes used for the future, or to denote attempted action (conative present), as **quam prendimus arcem,** *what citadel are we to seize?* **uxōrem dūcis,** *are you to be married?* **quid mē terrēs,** *why do you try to frighten me?*

2. **The Imperfect Tense** denotes continued or repeated action in the past, as **pugnābam,** *I was fighting, I kept fighting, I used to fight.* The imperfect is employed to represent manners, customs, situations; to describe and to particularize.

a. **The Imperfect of Endeavor.** The imperfect is used of attempted and interrupted, intended and expected actions (imperfect of endeavor, conative imperfect), as **urbem relinquēbat,** *he was trying to leave the city;* **lēx abrogābātur,** *the law was to be abrogated.*

b. The imperfect and the historical perfect serve to supplement each other. The imperfect dwells on the process; the historical perfect states the result. The imperfect counts out the items; the historical perfect gives the sum. The two tenses are often so combined that the general statement is given by the historical perfect, the particulars of the action by the imperfect, as **Verrēs in forum vēnit; ardēbant oculī; tōtō ex ōre crūdēlitās ēminēbat,** *Verres came into the forum; his eyes were blazing; cruelty was standing out from his whole countenance.*

3. **The Future Tense** denotes continuance in the future, as **scrībam,** *I shall be writing.* It is also used to express indefinite action in the future, as **scrībam,** *I shall write.*

a. The future is sometimes used in an imperative sense, as in English, as **cum volet, accēdēs; cum tē vītābit, abībis,** *when she wants you, approach; when she avoids you, begone sir.* Compare such English expressions as "Thou shalt not kill."

b. A similar use is that of the future in asseverations, as **ita mē amābit Juppiter,** *so help me, Jove!*

4. **The Perfect Tense** has two distinct uses: the pure perfect and the historical perfect.

a. **The Pure Perfect** expresses completion in the present and hence is sometimes called the present perfect. It is used of an action that is now over and gone, as **vīximus,** *we have lived* (life for us has been); **Troja fuit,** *Troy has been* (but is no longer). It is more frequently used to denote the present result of a more remote action (resulting condition), as **āctum est, perīstī,** *it is all over, you are ruined;* **equum et mūlum Brundisiī tibi relīquī,** *I have left a horse and mule for you at Brundisium* (they are still there).

b. **The Historical or Indefinite Perfect** states a past action, without reference to its duration, simply as a thing attained, an occurrence, as **vēnī, vīdī, vīcī,** *I came, I saw, I conquered;* **Milō domum vēnit, calceōs et vestīmenta mūtāvit, paulisper commorātus est,** *Milo came home, changed shoes and clothes, tarried a little while.*

5. **The Pluperfect** denotes completion in the past and is used of an action that was completed before another was begun, as **fuerat inimīcus,** *he had been my enemy.*

6. **The Future Perfect** denotes both completion and attainment, as **fēcerō,** *I shall have done it,* or *I shall do it* (once and for all).

352. The Latin tenses are divided into primary (principal) and secondary (historical).

a. **The Primary Tenses** have to do with the present and future; they are the present, pure perfect, future, and future perfect.

b. **The Secondary Tenses** have to do with the past; they are the historical present, imperfect, historical perfect, and pluperfect.

MOODS IN SUBORDINATE SENTENCES

SEQUENCE OF TENSES

353. Primary (principal) tenses are ordinarily followed by primary tenses, secondary (historical) by secondary tenses, as follows:

(1) All forms that relate to the present and future (primary tenses)	are regularly followed by	the present subjunctive (for continued action); the perfect subjunctive (for completed action).
(2) All forms that relate to the past (secondary tenses)	are regularly followed by	the imperfect subjunctive (for continued action); the pluperfect subjunctive (for completed action).

a. The action which is completed with regard to the leading verb may be in itself a continued action. So in English: *I do not know what he has been doing, I did not know what he had been doing.* The Latin is unable to make this distinction, and so the imperfect indicative *(he was doing)* is represented in the dependent form by the perfect or pluperfect, thus: **nesciō quid fēcerit, nescīvī quid fēcisset.**

b. The above rule is subject to several modifications:

1. Tense refers to time, not merely to tense form, so that

(a). The historical present may be felt according to its sense as *past* or according to its tense as *present.*

(b). The pure perfect may be felt according to its starting-point as *past,* or according to its completion as *present.*

2. The effect of a past action may be continued into the present or the future.

3. The dependent clause may depend on two or more clauses with their verbs in different tenses, and so follow a varying sequence.

4. An original imperfect or pluperfect subjunctive does not change its tense even when made to depend on a primary leading verb, for example, in unreal conditions (382, *a*).

354. The future relation of a verb in a dependent subjunctive clause may be made clearer by the use of an active periphrastic, as **cognōscam, quid factūrus sīs,** *I shall (try to) find out what you are going to do;* **cognōvī quid factūrus essēs,** *I have found out (know) what you were going to do.*

355. In Indirect Discourse (indirect statement) all verbs in subordinate clauses are in the subjunctive and follow the general rule of sequence of tenses. See 390.

QUOD CLAUSES

356. Quod, *the fact that, in that,* is used with the indicative to introduce explanatory clauses after verbs of adding and dropping, doing and happening, and after demonstrative expressions, as **adde quod vīcimus,** *add the fact that we have won;* **praetereō quod nōn mānsit,** *I pass over the fact that he did not remain;* **bene facis quod tacēs,** *you do well in that you keep silent;* **hāc rē est īnfēlīx, quod victus est,** *in this he is unfortunate, in that he was conquered.*

CAUSAL CLAUSES

357. Quod, quia, quoniam and **quandō** take the indicative in direct discourse, the subjunctive in implied indirect discourse, to express cause, as **fūgit quod timēbat,** *he fled because he was afraid;* **fūgit quod timēret,** *he fled because (as he said) he was afraid.*

358. Quod is used after verbs of emotion with the indicative in direct discourse, the subjunctive in implied indirect discourse, to give the reason (ground), as **gaudet quod vēnērunt,** *he rejoices that they have come;* **gaudet quod vēnerint,** *he rejoices that (as he says) they have come.*

PURPOSE CLAUSES

359. Purpose is expressed by the present or imperfect subjunctive with **ut** or **nē,** as **vēnit ut dūceret hominēs,** *he came to lead (that he might lead) the men;* **fugit nē capiātur,** *he flees lest he be (that he may not be) captured.* For the relative clauses of purpose see 388.

360. Substantive Volitive Clauses. The present or imperfect subjunctive with **ut** or **nē** is used in a substantive clause after verbs of will and desire, as **ōrō ut veniās,** *I beg that you come;* **volō ut veniat,** *I wish him to come;* **voluī nē venīret,** *I wished him not to come.* Such a clause is called a substantive volitive clause.

a. The infinitive may also be used with such verbs, especially in poetry.

b. **Jubeō** regularly takes the accusative and infinitive.

VERBS OF HINDERING

361. A verb of preventing, refusing, and the like may take **nē** or **quōminus** with the subjunctive, as **obstat nē veniat,** *he hinders him from coming.*

362. A negatived verb of preventing, refusing, and the like may take **quīn** or **quōminus** with the subjunctive, as **nihil obstat quīn** (or **quōminus**) **sīs beātus,** *nothing hinders you from being happy.*

VERBS OF FEARING

363. A verb of fear may be followed by **nē** or **ut** (= **nē** + **nōn**) with any tense of the subjunctive, as **timeō nē hostis veniat,** *I fear lest the enemy come, that* *he is coming, that he will come;* **timeō nē hostis vēnerit.** *I lear lest the enemy have come, that (it will turn out that) he has come;* **timeō ut amīcus veniat,** *I fear lest my friend come not, that he is not coming, will not come.*

RESULT CLAUSES

364. The subjunctive with **ut** or **ut nōn** is used to denote result, as **tanta vīs deōrum est ut eīs nōn possīmus obstāre,** *so great is the power of the gods that we cannot oppose them;* **nēmō est tam fortis ut nōn possit cadere,** *no one is so strong but he can (that he cannot) fall.*

a. A relative pronoun is sometimes used instead of **ut,** as **nēmō est tam fortis quī nōn possit cadere.**

365. A verb of effecting has the subjunctive with **ut, nē,** or **ut nōn,** as **faciam ut veniat,** *I shall make (have) him come;* **faciam nē veniat,** *I shall bring it about that he does not come.*

366. Negatived or questioned verbs of doubt and uncertainty may be followed by the subjunctive with **quīn,** as **nōn dubium est quīn urbs capiātur,** *there is no doubt (but) that the city is being captured.*

367. Substantive Clauses of Result. The subjunctive with **ut** is often used in a substantive clause to give the contents or character of a prceding substantive, adjective, or pronoun, as **tōtum in eō est, ut tibi imperēs,** *all depends on this, your self-command (that you rule yourself);* **id est proprium cīvitātis, ut sit lībera,** *this is the peculiar privilege of a state, to be free (that it be free).* This is called the substantive clause of result.

TEMPORAL CLAUSES

368. Ut, ut prīmum, cum, cum prīmum, ubi, ubi prīmum, simul ac, simul atque, in the sense of *as soon as,* and **postquam** take the perfect indicative, as **postquam vēnit dux, urbs capta est,** *after the leader came, the city was captured;* **ut vīdit urbem captam, fūgit,** *as (soon as) he saw the city captured, he fled.*

a. The imperfect indicative is used of overlapping action, and the pluperfect indicative when a definite interval is given, as **ut vidēbat hostēs vincentēs, rediit domum,** *as he saw the enemy were conquering, he returned home;* **postquam cēperat urbem, mīlitēs dūcit domum,** *after he had captured the city, he led his soldiers home.*

369. When two repeated actions are contemporaneous, both are put in the indicative in tenses of continuance, as **rēx bellum gerēbat cum volēbat,** *the king waged war whenever he wished.*

370. When one repeated action comes before another, the antecedent action is put in the perfect, pluperfect, or future perfect indicative, the subsequent in the present, imperfect, or future indicative, according to the relation, as **quotiēns cecidit, surgit,** *as often as he falls (has fallen), he rises;* **quotiēns ceciderat, surgēbat,** *as often as he fell (had fallen), he rose;* **quotiēns ceciderit, surget,** *as often as he falls (shall have fallen), he will rise.*

371. Dum, dōnec, quoad, and **quamdiū,** *so long as, while,* take the indicative of all tenses, as **vīta dum superest, bene est,** *while (as long as) there is life, it is well;* **dōnec grātus eram tibī, fēlīx fuī,** *while I was pleasing to you, I was fortunate;* **quoad potuit restitit,** *he resisted as long as he could.*

372. Dum, *while, while yet,* usually takes the present indicative when the verb of the main clause is in the past tense, as **dum hae rēs aguntur, urbs ardēbat;** *while these things were going on, the city was burning.*

373. Dum, dōnec, and **quoad,** *until,* take the present, historical present, historical perfect, or future perfect indicative, when suspense or anticipation are not involved, as **manēbō dum venit,** *I shall remain until he comes;* **mānsī dum (quoad, dōnec) vēnit,** *I remained until he came.* See 374.

374. Dum, dōnec, and **quoad,** *until,* take the subjunctive when suspense, anticipation, or design is involved, as **mānsī dum venīret,** *I remained until he could come;* **exspectō dum veniat,** *I am waiting for him to come.* See 373.

375. Dum, modo, and **dummodo,** *if only, provided only,* take the present or imperfect subjunctive in a proviso clause, as **ōderint dum metuant,** *let them hate so long as they fear (provided that, if they will only fear);* **veniat, dum maneat,** *let him come, provided that he remains.*

376. Antequam and **priusquam** take the indicative present, perfect, or future perfect when the time limit is stated as a fact, as **antequam abeō, dīcam pauca,** *before I go, I shall say a few words;* **antequam abiit, dīxerat pauca,** *before he went, he had said a few words.*

a. **Antequam** and **priusquam** take the subjunctive when the action is anticipated, contingent, or designed, as **urbem capit priusquam rēx veniat,** *he captures the city before the king may arrive (too soon for the king to arrive);* **ante vidēmus fulgōrem quam sonum audiāmus,** *we see the flash of lightning before we hear the sound (of thunder).*

CUM CLAUSES

377. Temporal *cum*, *when,* is used with all tenses of the indicative to designate merely temporal relations, as **animus nec cum adest nec cum discēdit appāret,** *the soul is not visible, either when it is present or when it departs;* **pāruit cum necesse erat,** *he obeyed when it was necessary.*

378. Descriptive *cum, when,* is used with the imperfect and pluperfect subjunctive to give the circumstances under which an action took place, as **cum dīmicāret, occīsus est,** *when he engaged in battle, he was slain;* **Caesar cum id nuntiātum esset, mātūrat ab urbe proficīscī,** *when this was (had been) announced to Caesar, he hastened to set out from the city.* This **cum** is sometimes called **cum** circumstantial.

379. Causal or **Concessive** *cum, when, whereas, although,* is used with any tense of the subjunctive, as **quae cum ita sint, dēbet fugere,** *since these things are so, we must flee;* **cum pār esset armīs, tamen dēbuerat fugere,** *although he was equal in arms, nevertheless he had to flee.*

CONDITIONAL SENTENCES

380. The Logical (More Vivid or **Simple) Conditional Sentence** regularly has the same tense of the indicative in both the subordinate clause (the condition or protasis) and the principal clause (the conclusion or apodosis) as follows:

CONDITION	CONCLUSION
Sī id crēdis,	errās.
If you believe that,	*you are wrong.*
Sī id crēdēbās,	errābās.
If you believed that,	*you were wrong.*
Sī id crēdidistī,	errāvistī.
If you (have) believed that,	*you were (have been) wrong.*
Sī id crēdēs,	errābis.
If you (shall) believe that,	*you will be wrong.*
Sī id crēdideris,	errāveris.
If you shall have believed that,	*you will have been wrong.*

381. The Ideal (Less Vivid) Conditional Sentence regularly has the present or perfect subjunctive, in both clauses, as follows:

CONDITION	CONCLUSION
Sī id crēdās,	errēs.
If you should (were to) believe that,	*you would be wrong.*
Sī id crēdideris,	errāveris (rare)
If you should (prove to) have believed that,	*you would have been wrong.*

a. In indirect discourse, or indirect statement, the verb of the conditional clause of a logical or less vivid conditional sentence is in the subjunctive and follows the general rule of sequence of tenses, as **dīcō tē, sī id crēdās, errāre; dīxī tē, sī id crēderēs, errāre.**

382. The Unreal (Contrary to Fact) Conditional Sentence regularly has the imperfect subjunctive in both clauses if contrary to present fact, and the pluperfect subjunctive in both clauses if contrary to past fact, as follows:

CONDITION	CONCLUSION
Sī id crēderēs,	errārēs.
If you believed that (but you do not),	*you would be wrong.*
Sī id crēdidissēs,	errāvissēs.
If you had believed that (but you did not),	*you would have been wrong.*

a. In indirect discourse the verb of an unreal condition is in the same mood and tense as it would be in direct discourse, and the verb of an unreal conclusion takes one of four special periphrastic forms, as follows:

Dīcō (dīxī) tē, tē errātūrum esse.	{ (active, contrary to present fact)
Dīcō (dīxī) sī id crēdidissēs, tē errātūrum fuisse.	{ (active, contrary to past fact)
Dīcō (dīxī) sī id crēderēs, fore ut dēciperēris.	{ (passive, contrary to present fact)
Dīcō (dīxī) sī id crēdidissēs, futūrum fuisse ut dēciperēris.	{ (passive, contrary to past fact)

b. Similarly in substantive clauses, as follows:

Nōn dubitum est quīn, sī id crēderēs, errārēs.
Nōn dubitum erat quīn, sī id crēdidissēs, errātūrus fuerīs.

c. In poetry the present subjunctive is often used in both clauses of an unreal conditional sentence.

d. All conceivable combinations of types of mixed conditions and conclusions may be used; as the conclusion may have the form of a wish, command, statement of obligation, necessity, etc. These mixed forms are especially common with verbs which convey a future idea, as **dēbeō,** *ought;* **possum,** *be able, can;* **studeō,** *desire;* **volō,** *will, wish,* as **sī Pompēius prīvātus esset, tamen is mittendus erat,** *if Pompey were a private citizen, nevertheless he ought to be sent;* **vincite sī vultis,** *have your way if you will.*

383. Ut sī, ac sī, quasi, quam sī, tamquam, tamquam sī, velut, or **velut sī,** and the subjunctive are used in a clause of comparison, as **tantus metus patrēs cēpit, velut sī jam ad portās hostis esset,** *a great fear took hold of the senators, as if the enemy were already at the gates.*

a. The subjunctive verb in such a clause follows the rule of sequence of tenses.

CONCESSIVE CLAUSES

384. A Concessive Clause may be introduced by **etsī, etiamsī,** or **tametsī,** with the indicative or subjunctive; by **quamquam,** with the indicative only; by **quamvīs,** with the subjunctive only.

RELATIVE CLAUSES

385. The Relative Clause as such, that is, a clause used as an adjective to modify a noun, regularly has its verb in the indicative, as **amō virum quī fortis est,** *I like a man who is brave, I like a brave man.*

386. An indefinite or general relative clause usually has its verb in the indicative; so explanatory **quī,** when equivalent to **quod,** as **errāverim fortasse, quī mē aliquid putāvī,** *I may have erred in thinking myself to be something.*

387. A relative clause that depends on an infinitive or a subjunctive, and forms an integral part of the thought, has its verb in the subjunctive by attraction, as **pigrī est ingeniī contentum esse iīs quae sint ab aliīs inventa,** *it is the mark of a lazy mind to be content with what has been found out by others.*

388. A relative clause has its verb in the subjunctive when **quī** is equivalent to **ut is** in an expression of purpose, as **ēripiunt aliīs quod aliīs dent,** *they snatch from some to give to others.* This is called the relative clause of purpose.

389. A relative clause has its verb in the subjunctive when **quī** is equivalent to **ut is** in a clause of description or characteristic; so after an indefinite antecedent, after **dignus, indignus, idōneus, aptus,** etc., as **multī sunt quī ēripiant,** *there are many to snatch away;* **sunt (eī) quī dīcant,** *there are those who say (some say);* **dignus est quī cōnsul fīat,** *he is worthy of being made consul.* This is called the subjunctive of characteristic.

INDIRECT DISCOURSE

390. Indirect discourse (indirect statement), as opposed to direct discourse, gives the main drift of a speech and not the exact words.

a. Indirect discourse depends on some verb of saying, showing, believing, perceiving, or thinking, expressed or implied.

b. In indirect discourse a principal statement has its verb in the infinitive, as **dīcit eōs vēnisse,** *he says that they have come;* **dīcit eōs venīre,** *he says that they are coming;* a question or a command has its verb in the subjunctive, as **quaerit quid velint,** *he asks what they want;* **quaesīvit quid vellent,** *he asked what they wanted;* **dīcit hominibus ut veniant,** *he tells the men to come;* **dīxit hominibus ut fugerent,** *he told the men to flee.*

c. A subordinate clause in indirect discourse has its verb in the subjunctive. See 355.

VERGIL'S METER

THE DACTYLIC HEXAMETER
(sections 391–410)

Vergil used dactylic hexameter, the meter of epic poetry, to compose the *Aeneid*. Homer (8th century B.C.) established the epic character of dactylic hexameter by using it to compose the *Iliad* and the *Odyssey*; many other early Greek epic poems, now lost, were composed in the same meter. Beginning in the 3rd century B.C., Latin poets began to experiment with adapting dactylic hexameter to their language. This was no easy task— Greek has a much larger vocabulary, including many more words with multiple short syllables, than does Latin, and is therefore better suited than Latin to dactylic hexameter. Vergil is generally considered by scholars and other admirers to have been the first to bring dactylic hexameter to perfection in Latin; in fact, many believe that he was the first *and* last Latin poet to do so. Whether this is true or not, there is no better introduction to Latin meter than through Vergil; and, strained and odd-sounding though the results may be at first, it is in fact possible with practice to get a reasonable idea of how Latin poetry might have sounded 2000 years ago. It is important to make this attempt both for its own sake and because much ancient poetry, including the *Aeneid*, was intended to be heard; and a well-read excerpt can be quite powerful.

The term **dactylic hexameter** is derived from Greek. **Hexameter** means "six measures" (**hex**, "six"; **metron**, "measure"). A **dactyl** is a measure consisting of one long and two short syllables; the name **dactyl** comes from the Greek word for "finger" (**daktylos**), since with its two joints a finger can be imagined as consisting of one longer and two shorter sections. A line of dactylic hexameter consists of five dactylic measures (or, as they are commonly called, "feet") followed by a final measure of two syllables, the first of which is always long. Any of the five dactyls can be replaced by a **spondee** (a measure consisting of two long syllables). The pattern of long and short syllables in dactylic hexameter looks like this (*Aen.* 1.1–11):

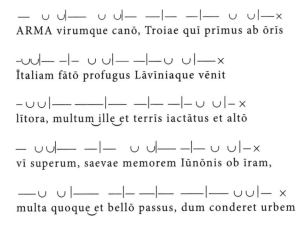

ARMA virumque canō, Troiae quī prīmus ab ōrīs

Ītaliam fātō profugus Lāvīniaque vēnit

lītora, multum ille et terrīs iactātus et altō

vī superum, saevae memorem Iūnōnis ob īram,

multa quoque et bellō passus, dum conderet urbem   5

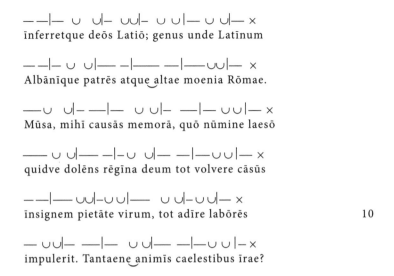

— —|— ∪ ∪|— ∪∪|— ∪ ∪ ∪|— ∪ ∪|— ×
īnferretque deōs Latiō; genus unde Latīnum

— —|— ∪ ∪|— — —|— — —|— —∪∪|— ×
Albānīque patrēs atque altae moenia Rōmae.

— ∪ ∪|— —|— ∪ ∪|— —|— ∪∪|— ×
Mūsa, mihī causās memorā, quō nūmine laesō

— — ∪ ∪|— — —|— ∪ ∪|— —|— ∪∪|— ×
quidve dolēns rēgīna deum tot volvere cāsūs

— —|— ∪∪|— ∪ ∪|— ∪ ∪|— ∪ ∪|— ×
īnsignem pietāte virum, tot adīre labōrēs   10

— ∪∪|— —|— ∪ ∪|— —|— ∪ ∪|— ×
impulerit. Tantaene animīs caelestibus īrae?

Note that the final syllable in a line is always indicated by ×. It can be either long or short; its Latin name, **syllaba anceps**, means "ambiguous" or "undecided syllable."

Most lines of hexameter consist of a combination of dactyls and spondees. The variety of combinations available would have kept the spoken verse from sounding monotonous. Note, however, that lines consisting entirely of spondees are very rare, and that Vergil uses a spondee in the fifth foot only on rare occasions. Such lines (i.e., those with a fifth-foot spondee) are called "spondaic lines," or **spondeiazontes** (singular, **spondeiazon**). Lines consisting entirely of dactyls are relatively unusual as well, although they are not as rare as spondaic lines.

Latin meter is **quantitative**. Every syllable in a Latin word has a quantity, either "long" or "short." Syllable length is determined (a) by nature or (b) by position. See items 14–24 above for general guidelines on how to determine the length of a syllable.

Some special features of the Latin hexameter should be noted:

Elision – when one word ends with a vowel, diphthong, or –m, and the following word begins with a vowel or h-, the first vowel or diphthong is elided, i.e., blended, with the second. The length of the resulting combination syllable will generally be whatever the length of the second syllable originally was. There are examples of elision above in lines 3, 5, 7, and 11.

Hiatus – see the list of rhetorical and stylistic devices below.

Consonantal vowels – when used in combination with other vowels (e.g., *Iuppiter*, *coniunx, genua*), the vowels -i- and -u- can sometimes serve as consonants, pronounced as -j- and -w-, respectively. As such, they do not create diphthongs with the vowels next to them, and they can lengthen a preceding short syllable if combined with another consonant. There is an example above in line 2, *Laviniaque*, where the second -i- is treated as a consonant.

Synizesis – see the list of rhetorical and stylistic devices below.

Hypermetric lines – occasionally a hexameter ends with a syllable that can elide with the first syllable of the next line. This final syllable is not needed to complete the metrical pattern of the line in which it appears.

GLOSSARY OF RHETORICAL TERMS,
FIGURES OF SPEECH, AND METRICAL DEVICES
MENTIONED IN THE NOTES
(sections 411–447)

The following definitions are for the most part based on those found in Pharr's edition of *Aeneid* 1–6. Note, however, that several terms are new to the list, and in one case a term has been redefined.

Alliteration is the repetition of the same letter or sound, usually at the beginning of a series of words, as at *Aen.* 1.124, *Interea* **m**agno **m**isceri **m**urmure pontum. **Alliteration** is often used in combination with **Onomatopoiea** (see below), as in this example.

Anaphora is the repetition of a word or words at the beginning of successive clauses. E.g., *Aen.* 10.429, **Sternitur** *Arcadiae proles,* **sternuntur** *Etrusci.* In Vergil, **Anaphora** is often used in combination with **Asyndeton** (see below), as in this example.

Anastrophe is the inversion of the normal order of words, as at *Aen.* 4.320, **te propter.**

Aposiopesis ("a falling silent") is a breaking off in the middle of a sentence, the syntax of which is never resumed. E.g., *Aen.* 1.135, **Quos ego—sed motos praestat componere fluctus,** when Neptune decides to suppress his wrath, at least temporarily.

Apostrophe is a sudden break from the previous narrative for an address, in the second person, of some person or object, absent or present. E.g., *Aen.* 10.507, **O dolor atque decus magnum rediture parenti,** addressed to the dead Pallas.

Asyndeton is the omission of conjunctions, as at *Aen.* 12.888, **ingens arboreum.**

Chiasmus is an arrangement of words in a mirroring, or ABBA, pattern, found most often with pairs of nouns and adjectives. E.g., *Aen.* 1.184, **Navem** *in conspectu* **nullam,** **tres** *litore* **cervos;** see *Aen.* 1.209 for an example involving nouns and verbs.

Ecphrasis is an extended and elaborate description of a work of art, a building, or a natural setting. E.g., *Aen.* 6.20–33, describing the scenes on the doors of the temple of Apollo at Cumae.

Ellipsis is the omission of one or more words which must be logically supplied in order to create a grammatically complete expression. E.g., *Aen.* 6.122–23, *Quid Thesea, magnum / quid* **memorem** *Alciden?*, where the verb **memorem** must be employed twice, once in each clause.

Enallage is the transference of an epithet from the word to which it strictly belongs to another word connected with it in thought. E.g., *Aen.* 10.444, **socii** *cesserunt* **aequore iusso** = **socii** *cesserunt* **aequore iussi**, where the participle **iusso** takes the place of the more prosaic **iussi**.
(N.B.: this definition is sometimes mistakenly given in textbooks and notes for a related but not identical figure of speech, **Hypallage**. The figure of speech sometimes called **Hypallage** is identical to **Metonymy** [see below].)

Enjambment is the continuation of a unit of thought beyond the end of one verse and into the first few feet of the next. E.g., *Aen.* 2.12–13, *quamquam animus meminisse horret luctuque refugit /* **incipiam**, where *incipiam* completes the meaning of the preceding line; a strong pause follows immediately thereafter.

Epanalepsis is the repetition of a word (often a proper name) in successive clauses or lines of verse for dramatic and/or emotional effect. (It can sometimes appear in combination with **Anaphora** and **Asyndeton** [see above for both terms].) E.g., *Aen.* 12.896–97, *Nec plura effatus* **saxum** *circumspicit ingēns, /* **saxum** *antiquum ingēns, ...*

Euphemism is the avoidance of a direct, sometimes blunt manner of speaking in favor of a more subtle and sometimes diluted form of expression. E.g., *Aen.* 1.219, the circumlocution **extrema pati** instead of the explicit **mori**.

Hendiadys is the expression of an idea by means of two nouns connected by a conjunction instead of by a noun and a modifying adjective, or by one noun modified by another. E.g., *Aen.* 10.422, **fortunam atque viam** = **fortunam viae**.

Hiatus is the avoidance in meter of elision between one word ending in a vowel and another beginning with a vowel (or h). E.g., *Aen.* 4.667, **femineo ululatu**. Here as often the metrical device enhances **Onomatopoiea** (see below).

Hyperbaton is the distanced placement of two words which are logically meant to be understood together. E.g., *Aen.* 12.941–42, **infelix** *umero cum apparuit alto /* **balteus**, where the epithet-noun combination **infelix balteus** is dislocated, and added emphasis is thus given to each word.

Hyperbole is exaggeration for rhetorical effect. E.g., *Aen.* 1.103, *fluctusque ad sidera tollit*.

Hysteron proteron is the reversal of the natural or logical order of ideas. E.g., *Aen.* 2.258–59, *inclusos utero* **Danaos et** *pinea furtim* / **laxat claustra** *Sinon*, where, contrary to logic, the Greeks are said to be released from the horse *before* it is opened.

Litotes is understatement, often enhanced by the use of the negative. E.g., *Aen.* 6.170, **non inferiora** *secutus*.

Metonymy is the substitution of one word for another which it suggests. E.g., *Aen.* 10.479, **robur = hasta**.

Onomatopoeia is the use of words of which the sound suggests the sense. E.g., *Aen.* 12.928–29, *totusque* **remugit** *mons circum*.

Pathetic fallacy is the attribution of human emotion to inanimate objects. E.g., *Aen.* 6.53, **attonitae** *magna ora domus*, where the dwelling of the Sibyl is described as "awestruck," when in fact awe is felt by those who observe it. When used with adjectives, **Pathetic fallacy** is a special type of **Transferred epithet** (see below).

Pleonasm is exceptional (and usually unnecessary) fullness of expression, typical of archaic Latin style. E.g., *Aen.* 2.524, **ore effata**.

Polyptoton is the repetition of a noun or pronoun in different cases at the beginning of successive phrases or clauses. E.g., *Aen.* 6.166, **Hectoris** *hic magni fuerat comes,* **Hectora** *circum* ... **Polyptoton** is a form of **Anaphora**, and often is found with **Asyndeton** (see above).

Polysyndeton is an overabundance of conjunctions, as at *Aen.* 1.85–86, *una Eurus***que** *Notus***que** *ruunt creber***que** *procellis* / *Africus* ...

Rhetorical question is a question that anticipates no real answer. E.g., *Aen.* 10.793 (Jupiter to Juno): **"Quae iam finis erit, coniunx?"**

Prolepsis is the inclusion in the main story of references to events which in fact will occur after the dramatic time of the poem, and to the people and circumstances involved in these later events. E.g., *Aen.* 6.847–50, **Excudent ... ducent ... orabunt ... describent ... dicent**, all used to describe the Romans who will be descended from Aeneas and who are not themselves characters in the *Aeneid.*

Simile is a figure of speech which likens or asserts an explicit comparison between two different things. E.g., *Aen.* 10.454–56, **utque leo, specula cum vidit ab alta ... haud alia est Turni venientis imago.**

Synchysis is interlocking word order; many variations on the pattern abAB exist. E.g., *Aen.* 4.388, **His medium dictis sermonem.**

Synecdoche is the use of a part for the whole, or the reverse. E.g., *Aen.* 10.430, *et vos, O Grais* **imperdita corpora,** *Teucri,* where **corpora** is used of persons.

Synizesis is a metrical effect whereby two contiguous vowels within the same word and normally pronounced separately are slurred into one syllable. E.g., *Aen.* 1.120, **Ilionei**, where the last two vowels, normally pronounced as a short vowel followed by a long, become one long vowel.

Tmesis ("splitting") is the separation into two parts of a word normally written as one, often for a (quasi-)visual effect. E.g., *Aen.* 2.218–19, *bis collo squamea* **circum** / **terga dati**, where **circum** + **dati** = **circumdati**; the word **terga** is literally "surrounded" by the two parts of **circumdati**.

Transferred Epithet is an epithet which has been transferred from the word to which it strictly belongs to another word connected with it in thought. E.g., *Aen.* 10.426, **tanta caede = tanti viri caede.**
(see also **Enallage** [above], an ancient name for the same stylistic feature.)

Tricolon crescens is the accumulation of three parallel phrases or clauses, each of which is at least one syllable longer than that preceding it. E.g., *Aen.* 4.307–8, **Nec te noster amor** [6 syllables] **nec te data dextera quondam** [9 syllables] / **nec moritura tenet crudeli funere Dido?** [15 syllables]. **Tricolon crescens** is often found in combination with **Anaphora** and **Asyndeton** (see above).

Zeugma is the joining of two words by a modifying or governing word which strictly applies to only one of them. E.g., *Aen.* 12.898, *limes agro positus* **litem** *ut* **discerneret arvis**, where zeugma occurs in the use of the verb **discerneret** with both **litem** and **arvis:** the boundary stone *settles* disagreements by *dividing* the fields.

Please note:

Sections 391–410 and 411–447 of the "Grammatical Appendix" are revised in the current edition. Some of the items attributed to these sections in the "Index to the Grammatical Appendix" have been omitted, and others, not listed in the Index, have been added. The Index was compiled for the Pharr edition (i.e., before the revisions) and is otherwise accurate. It is included here because of its usefulness in locating items in the rest of the Appendix.

INDEX TO THE GRAMMATICAL APPENDIX

(The references are to sections.)

ă, ending of acc. sing. of Greek nouns, 68; nom., acc. and voc. pl. ending of neuters, 33, *c*

ā, prepositions ending in, 312

ā or ab with abl., 320, 333, 339

Ability, verbs of with inf., 259

Ablative, defined, 30; in **ābus,** 34, *c;* in **ī,** 55, *d,* 56, *b,* 77, 81, 82, *a;* prepositions with, 339; adv. forms of, 310; of supine, 271; pl. like the dat., 33, d; **quīs** and **quī** as abl. and dat., 109, *c, d*

Ablative, Syntax: abs., 343; accompaniment, 321; accordance, 326; as adv., 95, 310, 328, *a;* agent, 333; with adjectives (**dignus, aliēnus,** etc.), 337, 340, *a;* cause, 332; gerund(ive), 269; with comparatives, 327; degree of difference, 335; with dep. verbs (**ūtor,** etc.), 342; with **dignor,** 337, *a;* with **dōnō,** 296; manner, 328; material, 324; means, 331; with gerund(ive), 269; measurement, 334; with **opus est** and **ūsus est,** 341; origin, 323; place where, 319; place whence, 320; with prepositions, 339; price, 336; respect, 325; route, 338; separation, 340; time, 322

Abounding, words of with gen., 287

Absolute, abl. abs., 343

absum, conj., 123

ābus, dat. and abl. ending, 34, *c*

Accent, 25–27; metrical, 394; of nouns in **ius, ium,** 37, *a, b*

Accompaniment, abl. of with **cum,** 321

Accomplishing, verbs of, 365

Accordance, abl. of, 326

Accusative, defined, 30; in neuters like nom., 33, *c;* sing. in **a,** 68; sing. in **im,** 56, *a;* pl. in **īs,** 56, *d,* 83, *b;* of supine, 270; names of towns, **domus** and **rūs,** 315, *a*

Accusative, Syntax: adv., 309–311, 95, *b;* cognate, 313; direct obj., 307; exclamation, 318; extent, 314; Greek, 309–311; subj. of inf., 317; with middle voice, 309; with prepositions, 312; respect, 311; of gerund(ive) with **ad,** 268; two accusatives: verbs of asking, making, etc., 316; remembering and forgetting, 288, *a;* compound verbs, 308

Accusing and acquitting, gen. with verbs of, 291

ācer, decl., 77; compar., 89

ac sī, in clauses of compar., 383

Action, see tenses, moods, etc.

Active voice, 115, *a;* changed to pass., 279; act. periphrastic, 199, *a*

ad, with acc., 312; dat. with compounds of, 298; acc. with compounds of, 308; with gerund(ive), 268

adde quod, with indic., 356

Adjectives, definition, 70; **a** and **o** stems, 71; **i** stems, 76; consonant stems, 80–82; three termination, 77; compar., 83–92; decl. of compar., 91; num. adjectives, 98–100; pronom. adjectives, 73, 102, *a,* 113, *a,* 114; poss. adjectives, 103, *a,* 104, *a,* 106, *a*

Adjectives, Syntax: agreement, 237–239; as adverbs, 95, 250, 310; with inf., 265; with gen., 287; with dat., 304; with abl., 337; pred., 239; double compar., 245

Advantage, dat. of, 301

Adverbial accusative, 310; adv. abl., 328

Adverbs, 93–97; formation, 95; compar., 96–97; adjectives used adverbially, 250, 310, 328, *a;* use, 346; double compar., 245; num. adverbs, 101

Adversative clauses, 379, 384

adversum, with acc., 312

ae, diphthong, 5

aeger, decl. like **pulcher,** 71

Aenēās, decl., 66
āēr, decl., 68
aethēr, decl. like **āēr,** 68
Affecting, acc. of, 307
Affirmative, expressed by two negatives, 431; **nōnne** for affirmative answer, 347, *b*
Agent, dat. of, 302; abl. of, 333
ager, decl. like masc. of **pulcher,** 71
Agreement, nouns: appos., 241; pred., 240, 278, 317, *a;* adjectives: 237–238; pred., 239; poss., 249; pronouns: rel., 242; dem., 240, *a;* verbs: 236; according to sense, 236, *a,* 444
āī, ending of gen. sing., 34, *b*
ajō, pronounced **aj-jō,** 6, *b*
al, decl. of nouns in, 56
aliēnus, for gen. of **alius,** 74, *a;* abl. with 340, *a*
aliquis (aliquī), decl., 113
alius, decl., 74
Alliteration, 411
Alphabet, 1–6
alter, decl., 74; **alterīus** in gen. for **alīus,** 74, *a;* ordinal num., 98
alterīus for **alīus,** 73, *a*
Although, how expressed, 379, 384
an, in double questions, 348
Anacolouthon, 412
Anaphora, 413
Anastrophe, 414
anceps, syllaba, 393
Anchīsēs, decl., 66
Androgeōs, decl., 67
Andromachē, decl. like **Pēnelopē,** 66
animal, decl., 56
Answer to questions, 347
ante, prep. with acc., 312; dat. with compounds of, 298; acc. with compounds of, 308
Antecedent, agreement of rel. pron. with, 242; attracted to case of rel., 242, *a;* undefined in char. clauses, 389
Antepenult, 25, *a*
antequam, with indic., 376; with subj., 376, *a*
Anticipation, clauses of, 440; attraction of antecedent to case of rel., 242, *a*
Antithesis, 415
apis, gen. pl. in **ium,** 56, *c*
Apodosis, defined, 380

Aposiopesis, 416
Apostrophe, 417
Appointing, verbs of with two accusatives, 316, *a*
Apposition, 241; pronouns and poss. adjectives, 249; expressed by gen., 281; **quod** and **ut** clauses with nouns and pronouns, 356, 367; inf. with nouns, 264
aptus, with dat. of gerund(ive), 267; with rel. clause of char., 389
apud, prep. with acc., 312
āre, inf. ending, 132
ăs, acc. pl. of Greek nouns in, 65, *a*
Asking, verbs of with two accusatives, 316; questions, 347–349
Asseverations, with fut. indic., 351, 3, *b;* subj., 254
Asyndeton, 418
At, translated by prep. with abl., 319; by loc., 345
āter, decl. like **pulcher,** 71
Athōs, decl. like **Androgeōs,** 67
Atlās, decl., 68
atque, simul atque, 368; **ac sī,** 383
Attendant circumstance, abl. of, 329
Attraction, antecedent to case of rel., 242, *a;* dem. to gender of pred., 240, *a;* of verb in rel. clauses to subjunctive, 387
au, diphthong, 5
audeō, semi-deponent, 205
audiō, conj., 172; with dat., 297
avis, decl., 65, b
ăx, gen. with verbal adjectives in, 287

b, stems in, 50; becomes **p** before **s** and **t,** 128, 6
Becoming, verbs of, constr. with, 278
Believing, verbs of, with dat., 297; pers. constr. with pass., 279
bene, compar., 97
Beseeching, verbs of, with **ut (nē),** 360
bis, num. adv., 101
bonus, compar., 92; decl., 71
Brachylogy, 419
Buying, abl. with verbs of, 336

c, stems ending in, 51; represents changed **g** before **t,** 128, 6
Caere, decl., 56, *b*

Caesura, 409–410
canālis, decl., 56, *b*
canis, decl., 56, *c*
capiō, conj., 163–171
caput, decl., 52
Cardinal numerals, 98–99
careō, abl. with, 340
Cases, 30; endings, 32; of pred. substantive, 240, 278; for uses see nom.,
gen., etc.
cāsus, decl., 59
Cause, abl. of, 332; gerund(ive), 269;
expressed by abl. abs., 343, *a*; clauses
with **quod, quia, quoniam, quandō,**
357–358; **cum** with subj., 379; rel.
clause, 386
Causing, verbs of, with perf. part., 275;
with gerundive, 268, *a*
Caution, constr. with verbs of, 363
cavē, in prohibitions, 256
–ce, enclitic, 107, 3, *b,* 4, *a*
Ceasing, complementary inf. with verbs
of, 259
cētera, partitive use, 246
Characteristic, rel. clause of, 389; abl. of,
330; gen. of, 285
Chiasmus, 420
Choosing, two accusatives with verbs
of, 316, *a*
circum, prep. with acc., 312; dat. with
compounds of, 298; acc. with compounds of, 308
Circumstances, part., 273; abl. abs., 343;
cum descriptive, 378; abl., 329
cis, prep. with acc., 312
Cities and islands, names of, fem., 38, *a*;
in acc., 315, *a*; abl., 320, *a*; loc., 345
Clauses, see substantive, temporal, conditional, etc.
Cognate accusative, 313
Collective nouns, with pl. verbs, 236, *a*
comes, decl., 52
Command, imp., 255; subj., 254; fut.
indic., 351, 3, *a*; in ind. disc., 390, *b*
Commanding, verbs of, with dat., 297;
with inf., 360, *a, b*; with subj., 360
Common syllables, 17
Comparative, 84; decl., 91; of adverbs,
96; double compar., 245; conjunc-
tions, 383

Comparison, of adjectives, 83; of adverbs, 96; disproportion, 244; abl. of,
327; degree of difference, 335; clauses
of with **ut sī, quasi,** etc., 383; metaphor, 432; simile, 441
Complement, subj., 278–279; obj.,
316, *a,* 317, *a*; agreement with subj.,
238–240
Complementary infinitive, 259
Complex sentences, see clauses
Compounds, of **sum,** 123; of **faciō** and
fīō, 229; dat. with, 298
Compound verbs, with dat., 298; with
dat. and acc., 298, *a*; with acc., 308;
with two accusatives, 308, *a*
con-, in composition with dat., 298; in
composition with acc., 308
Conative, pres., 351, 1, *c*; impf., 351, 2, *a*
Concessive clauses, with **cum,** 379; with
etsī, quamquam, quamvīs, etc., 384;
concessive subj., 254; see participles
and abl. abs.
Conclusion, see conditions
Condemning and convicting, gen. with
verbs of, 291
Condition, of an object, expressed by
part., 273
Conditions, simple, 380; more vivid, 380;
ideal (less vivid), 381; contrary to fact
(unreal), 382, *c*; mixed, 382, *d*; in ind.
disc., 381, *a,* 382, *a*; in substantive
clauses, 382, *c*; abl. abs., 343, *a*
Conjugation, 116, 126–128; see verbs and
first, second, etc.
Conjunctions, see **ut, cum,** etc.; omission
of, 418; asyndeton, 418; polysyndeton,
349; compar. conjunctions, 383
cōnor, conj., 183; inf. with, 259
cōnscius, with gen., 287
Consecutive clauses, 364–367
Consonantal, **i** and **u,** 6, *a, b, c,* 401
Consonants, 6–8; quantity, 15, 17
cōnstrūctiō ad sēnsum, 236, *a,* 444;
reflex. refers to logical subj., 248, *a*
Construction, see cases, moods, etc.
cōnsul, decl., 41, *a*
contentus, abl. with, 337
Continued action, pres., 351, 1; impf.,
351, 2; hist. inf., 257; sequence of
tenses, 353

Continuing, verbs of, with complementary inf., 259
Contracted perfects, 204
Contracted verb forms, 204; contracted vowels long, 24
Contracting, undertaking, verbs of, with gerund(ive), 268, *a*
Contradiction, oxymoron, 435
Contrary to fact conditions, 382
cōram, with abl., 339
cornū, decl., 59
corpus, decl., 47
Crasis, 204, vowels resulting from long, 24
cujus, see **quī;** pronunciation, 6, *b*
cum (preposition), 339; enclitic, 321, *a;* abl. of accompaniment, 321
cum clauses, temporal, 377; descriptive, 378; causal, 379; concessive, 379; **cum** (*whenever*), 370, 377
cum prīmum, 368
cupidus, with gen., 287

d, stems ending in, 52; before **s,** 128, 6, 124
Dactyl, 392; fifth foot usually a dactyl, 395
Date, **cum** with indic., 377
Dative, defined, 30; sing. in **āī** (first decl.), 34, *b;* sing. in **ī** (second decl.), 74; pl. in **īs** for **iīs** (**deus**), 37, *f;* pl. in **ubus** (fourth decl.), 58, *c*
Dative, Syntax: with adjectives, 267, 304; agent, 302; compounds, 298; direction, 306; double dat., 303, *a;* ethical, 300; ind. obj., 295; poss., 299; purpose, 303; reference, 301, 303, *a;* separation, 305; with special verbs, 297
dē, with abl., 329; place whence, 320; origin, 323; accordance, 326
dea, decl., 34, *c*
dēbeō, with complementary inf., 259; indic. for obligation, 251; in conditions, 382, *d*
Declensions, 31–33; first, 34–35; second, 36–38; third, 39–57; fourth, 58–61; fifth, 62–64; of Greek nouns, 65–69; of adjectives, 71–82, 91; of numerals, 99; of pronouns, 103–114
Defective verbs, 205

Degree of difference, abl. of, 335
Deliberative questions (subjunctive), 348
Dēlos, decl., 67
Demonstrative pronouns, decl., 107; as subj. attracted to gender of pred., 240, *a;* as adjectives, 102, *a*
Deponent verbs, 182; first conj., 163, 190; second, third, fourth conj., 191–198; participles of, 182; abl. with, 342; semi-deponents, 205
Depriving, verbs of, with abl., 340; with dat., 305
Descriptive genitive, 285; abl., 330; impf., 351, *a, b;* **cum** descriptive, 378
Desire, expressions of with gen., 287; clauses of, 360; in ind. disc., 248, *b;* verbs of with inf., 260; expressed by fut. part., 274; volitive subj., 253
dēsum, conj., 123; dat. with, 301
deum = **deōrum,** 37, *d, f*
deus, decl., 37, *f*
dexter, decl. like **miser,** 71
dīcō, ind. disc., 263, 390; imp. **dīc,** 202
diēs, decl., 63; gender, 64
dignor, with abl., 337, *a*
dignus, with abl., 337; with rel. clause, 389
Diphthongs, 5; always long, 24
Direct, obj., 307; question, 347; reflex., 106, 248
Direction, dat. of, 306
Disproportion, **quam (prō, ut), quī,** 244
Distance, acc., 314
Distributive, numerals, 100; pronouns, see **quisque** and **uterque**
diū, compar., 97
domus, abl. of, 320, *a;* loc., 345; acc., 315, *a;* decl., 60; gender, 61, *a*
dōnec, with indic., 371; with subj., 374
dōnō, with dat. or abl., 269
Double consonants, 7; **s** and **z,** 8; double questions, 348; double accusatives, 308, 316; double datives, 303, *a;* double comparatives, 245
Doubting, verbs of; potential subj., 252; deliberative question, 348; subst. clause with **quīn,** 366; *cf.* 382, *b*
dūc, imperative, 202

dum, 371; with indic., 371–373; with subj., 374; in proviso clauses, 375
duo, decl., 99
Duration, acc., 314; abl., 322
Duty, expressed by indic., 251; by periphrastic, 199, *b,* 382, *d*
dux, decl., 51

ē, prep.; see **ex;** adv. ending, 95, *a*
ecquis, 112
Editorial "we," 243, *a*
Effecting, acc. of, 307; verbs of: with perf. part., 275; with result clause, 365
egeō, abl. with, 340
ego, decl., 103; omission, 247; for emphasis and contrast, 247
ei, diphthong, 5
Elision, 398, 402
Ellipsis, 421
Emotion, verbs of with gen., 289; with inf., 260; with **quod** and indic. or subj., 358; see exclamation
Emphasis, see figures of speech, 106, *b, c,* and 247
Enallage, 422
Enclitics, 27; **–que,** 27; **–met,** 106, *b;* **–pte,** 106, *c;* **–ce,** 107, 3, *b,* 4, *a;* **–nam,** 112; **–cum,** 321, *a;* **–ve,** 27; **–ne,** 27, 347, *a*
Endings (regular), of nouns, 32; of infinitives and participles, 117, 3; see declensions and conjugations
Endings (irregular), gen. sing. in **āī,** 34, *b;* gen., dat. sing. **ē** for **eī** in fifth decl., 63; gen. pl. **um,** 34, *b,* 37, *d;* acc. pl. **īs,** 56, *d,* 83, *b;* gen. sing. **īus,** 74; gen. pl. **ium,** 77, 81, 3, 55, *c;* abl. sing. **ī,** 55, *d,* 77, 81, 1; nom. and acc. pl. **ia,** 55, *d,* 81, 2; dat., abl. pl. **ābus,** 34, *c;* acc. **im,** 56, *a;* gen. pl. **ōn,** 65, *a;* acc. sing. in, 68; **āsti, ārunt, ēre,** etc., 204
English pronunciation of Latin words, 28
Envy, verbs of with dat., 297
eō, see **is, ea, id**
eō, conj., 207–213; compounds of, 213, *a;* **īrī** in fut. pass. inf., 117, 2, 213, *b*
er, nom. ending, 37, 74, 77
ēre for **ērunt,** 204, 4; **ere** for **eris,** 204, 4
esse, see **sum**

Esteeming, verbs of, double acc., 316; abl. with **dignor,** 337, *a*
Ethical dative, 300
etsī, etiamsī, in concessive clauses, 384
eu, diphthong, 5
Euphemism, 423
Euphony, 424; in verb stems, 128, 6
ex (ē), prep. with abl., 339; place whence, 320; origin, 323; accordance, 326; material, 324
Exchanging, verbs of with abl., 336
Exclamations, subj., 253; imp., 255, 256; inf., 262; acc., 318; voc., 344; fut. ind. in asseverations, 351, 3, *b;* apostrophe, 417
Exhortations, subj., 254; imp., 255; **ut** clause, 360
Extent of space and time, acc., 314

fac, imp. of **faciō,** 202
facilis, decl. like **omnis,** 77; compar., 89, *e*
faciō, conj. like **capiō,** 163; imp. **fac,** 202; two accusatives, 316, *a;* **faciō ut** (**nē**), 365; pass. of, 227; compounds of, 229
fāgus, gender, 38, *a*
fateor, conj., 191–198
Favor, verbs of with dat., 297
Fearing, clauses with **nē** or **ut,** 363
Feeling, verbs of with gen., 289–290; with **quod** and indic. or subj., 358
Feet, in verse, 392; fifth foot, 395
fel, decl., 41, *b*
fēlīx, decl., 82; compar., 87
Feminine, first decl. (mostly), 35; second decl.: cities, islands, trees, and a few others, 38, *a;* third decl., nouns in **dō, gō, iō,** 44; i stems in **ēs,** 57; some i stems in **is,** 57; all other i stems, 57; mutes in **s,** 54; fourth decl., a few in **us,** 61, *a;* fifth decl., all but **diēs** and **meridiēs,** 64
fer, imp. of **ferō,** 202
ferō, conj., 214–225; imp., 202
fīdō, semi-deponent, 205; with dat., 297
Fifth declension, 62–64
Figures of Speech, 411–447
fīlia, decl., 34, *c*
fīlius, decl., 37, *a, b*

Final clauses, 359–360

fīō, conj., 228; compounds, 229; pass. of **faciō,** 227

First conjugation, 129–141; deponents, 183–190

First declension, 34–35

Fitness, adjectives of, with dat., 304; of gerund(ive), 267

fore (futūrus esse), 121; **fore ut** in ind. disc., 263, *a; cf.* 382, *a*

Forgetting, verbs of, with gen., 288; acc., 288, *a;* complementary inf., 259

Forms, 29–275; see nouns, verbs, etc.

Fourth conjugation, 172–181; deponents, 191–198

Fourth declension, 58–61

Freedom, adjectives and verbs with abl., 340; adjectives and verbs with gen., 287

frētus, with abl., 337

frūgī, compar., 92

fruor, with abl., 342

fuī, see **sum**

Fullness, expressions of, with gen., 287; with abl., 337

fungor, with abl., 342

Future perfect tense, 351, 6; in conditions, 380; in temporal clauses, 370; like perf. subj., 128, 5

Future tense, 251, 3; specific and universal, 351, 3; as imperative, 351, 3, *a;* asseverative, 351, 3, *b;* part. expressing purpose, 274; conditions, 380–381; formation of pass. inf., 117, 2, 213, *b;* expressed by **fore ut,** 263, *a;* use of periphrastic, 199, *a;* in subj., 354

g, stems in, 51; changes to **c** before **t,** 128, 6

Gender, rules of, 35, 38, 42, 48, 54, 57, 61, 64; attraction of pronouns, 240, *a;* and see masculine, feminine and neuter; of pred. complement, 239, *b*

Genitive, defined, 30; **āī** for **ae,** 34, *b;* **um** for **ōrum,** 37, *d;* **um** and **ium,** 53, 55, *c,* 56, *c,* 77, 81, 3; **ē** for **eī,** 63; **īus,** 73–74; poss. adj. as gen., 249; two forms for pers. pronouns, 247, *a*

Genitive, Syntax: material, 280; appos., 261; explanatory, 282; poss., 283; subj.,

284; obj., 284; quality, 285; part., 286; pred., 285, *a;* with adjectives, 287; with verbs, 287–291; value, 292; with interest and **rēfert,** 293; respect, 294; genitive of gerund(ive), 266

genius, decl., 37, *b*

genū, decl., 59

genus, decl., 47

Gerund(ive), 117, 3, 203; for formation see verbs, conj. of, uses of, 266–269; with dat. of agent, 302; in **undus,** 203; see periphrastic; of dep. verbs, 182

Giving, verbs of, with gerundive, 268, *a*

gracilis, decl., 77; compar., 89, *a*

Greek accusative, 309, 311

Greek nouns, decl., 65–69

Guilt, expressions of, with gen., 287, 291

h, never makes position, 15; vowels short before, 20; elision before, 398; hiatus before, 399

habeō, conjug., 142–150

Having, verbs of with gerundive, 268, *a;* verbs of with perf. part., 275

Helping, verbs of with dat., 297

Hendiadys, 425

hērōs, decl., 68

Hesitation, clauses of, 363, 366

Hexameter, 391–397

Hiatus, 399; semi-hiatus, 400

hic, decl., 107; pronounced **hicc,** 107, 3, *c*

Himself, **ipse,** 108; **sē,** 106, 248

Hindering, clauses with **nē, quīn** or **quōminus,** 361–362

Historical inf., 257; with subj. nom., 277; pres., 351, 1, *a;* with secondary sequence, 353, *b,* 1 (*a*)

homō, decl., 43

Hortatory subjunctive, 254

humus, loc. of, 345; gender, 38, *a*

Hypallage, 426

Hyperbaton, 427

Hyperbole, 428

Hypermeter, 402

Hysteron Proteron, 429

i, vowel, 4; semi-vowel (consonantal), 6, *a,* 401; after **j,** 6, *b, c;* **i** stems, 55, 76;

changed to **e** in **iō** verbs, 161, 206, 1; **i** and **u** in dat., abl. pl., 58, *c*

ī, imperative of **eō,** 209; voc. ending, 37, *b;* abl. ending, 55, *d,* 77, 81, 1; loc. ending, 37, *c;* pres. pass. inf. ending, 117, 3; nom. pl. of **is, ea, id,** 107

ia, nom. and acc. pl. ending, 55, *d,* 81, 2

Ictus, in verse, 392, 394, 404

Ideal conditions, 361

īdem, decl., 107

idōneus, with dat. of purpose, 303; gerund, 267; with rel. clause, 389

īdūs, decl., 59; gender, 61, *a*

ignis, decl., 56, *b*

iī, or **ī** in gen., 37, *a;* **iī** for **eī,** 107; **iī** perfect of **eō,** 207; in compounds, 213, *a*

iīs, for **eīs,** 107

ille, decl., 107

im, acc. ending, 56, *a*

Imperative, 115, 4; for formation see under verbs, conjugation of; irregular imperatives, 202; pres. and fut. 255; neg. 256; fut. ind. as imp., 351, 3, *a;* in ind. disc., 390, *b*

Imperfect tense, 351, a; of **possum,** etc., for pluperf., 251, 382, *d;* conative, 351, 2, *a;* descriptive, 351, 2, *b;* in temp. clauses, 368, *a,* 371; in conditions, 380, 382, *d;* sequence of tenses, 353; formation of impf. subj., 128, 2

imperō, with dat., 297; with subst. vol. clause, 360

Impersonal verbs, forms of **eō,** 213, *b;* with gen., 290; impers. constructions, 258, 366

Implied indirect discourse, 357–358; *cf.* 248, *b,* 390.

in, acc. ending, 68

in, prep. with acc., 315; prep. with abl., 319; verbs compounded with, 298

Inclination, adjectives of, with dat., 304; expressions of, 251–254; adjectives of, for adverbs, 250

Indefinite antecedent, 389; pronouns, 113

Indicative, 115, 4; to denote possibility, 251, 382, *d;* in deliberative questions, 348, *a;* with **quod** in explanatory clauses, 356; in causal clauses, 357–

358; in temporal clauses, 368–373, 377; present with **dum,** 372; simple (more vivid) conditions, 380; in unreal conditions, 382, *d;* in concessive clauses, 384

Indirect command, 390

Indirect discourse, 263, 390; subordinate clauses in, 355; conditions in, 382, *a;* implied, 357–358; *cf.* 248, *b;* commands in, 390, *b;* tense of inf. in, 263

Indirect object, 295

Indirect questions, 349; *cf.* 353, *a;* use of periphrastic in, 354

Infinitive, formation, 117, 2–3; of deponents, 182; contraction of perf., 204; see also conjugations

Infinitive, Syntax: with adjectives, 265; *cf.* 258; pred. nom. with, 317, *a;* complementary, 259; purpose, 261; exclamatory, 262; as subject, 258; hist., 257, 277; subj. acc., 317; in ind. disc., 263, 390, *b;* for **ut**-clause, 360, *a;* with **jubeō,** 360, *b;* with nouns, 264; as obj., 260

Inflection, 29–235; see declension, conjugation, etc.

Informal indirect discourse, 367, 358; *cf.* 248, *b*

Instrumental ablative, 531; of gerund(ive), 269

Intensive suffixes, 106, *b, c;* pronoun, 108; *cf.* 248

inter, prep. with acc., 312; verbs compounded with, 298

interest with gen. of person, 293; with abl. of poss. adj., 293, *a*

Interjections, 318, 344

Interrogative pronouns and adjectives, 111–112; sentences, 347

Intransitive verbs with dat., 297; with cognate acc., 313

iō, gender of nouns in, 44; verbs in, 162

ipse, decl., 108; for use *cf.* 248

īrī, in fut. pass. inf., 213, *b*

Irony, 430

Irregular verbs, conj., 206–235

īs, acc. pl. ending, 56, *d*

is, ea, id, decl., 107; as pers. pron. of third person, 105, *b*

Islands, names of, gender, 38, *a;* acc., 315, *a;* abl., 320, *a;* loc., 345
īsse, syncopated form, 204
iste, decl., 107, 4
Iterative imperfect, 351, 2
ium, gen. pl. ending, 55, *c,* 77, 81, 3; decl. of words in, 37, *b*
ius ending, declension of words in, 37, *b;* gen. sing. ending, 74; see also declension of pronouns

j, the letter, 6, *a, b, c*
jaciō, conj., 161, 227–229; compounds, 6, *c,* 229; pass. of, 227–229
jam, with pres. indic., 351, *b*
jubeō, with inf., 360, *b*
Jussive subjunctive, 254

Knowing, verbs of, see indirect discourse
Knowledge, adjectives of with gen., 287; adjectives of as adverbs, 250

l, nouns in, 56; stems in, 41, *b;* in common syllables, 17–18
lac, decl., 52, *a*
laetus, with abl., 337
Leaving, verbs of with gerundive, 268, *a*
Length, of vowels, 20–23; of syllables, 14–19, 396, 407
Less vivid, conditions, 381
Letters, of alphabet, 1–8
liber, noun, 36, *a*
līber, adjective, decl. like miser, 71; with abl. of separation, 340, *a*
Likeness, adjectives of with dat., 304
Liquids, in common syllables, 17; stems in, 41–46
Litotes, 431
Locative, defined, 30; first decl., 34, *a;* second decl., 37, *c;* of domus, 60; use, 345; loc. gen., 294
Logical, constructions, sing. coll. subj. with pl. verb, 236, *a,* 444; copula agrees with pred. noun, 236, *c;* pron. attracted to gender of pred., 240, *a;* reflex. referring to logical subj., 248, *a;* logical conditions, 280

m, final syllable in, 398
magis, compar., 97; in double comparisons, 245
magnus, compar. of, 92
Making, verbs of, two accusatives, 316, *a;* gerundive, 268, *a;* perfect part., 275
male, compar., 97
mālō, conj., 230; see comparison malus, compar., 92
Manner, abl. of, 328; gerund(ive), 269; implied in part., 273
manus, decl., 59; gender, 61, *a*
mare, decl., 56
Masculine, first decl., referring to males, 35; second decl. in us or r (mostly), 38; third decl. stems in 1, 42; nouns in ō, except dō, gō, and iō, 44; nouns in is (eris) and ōs (oris), 48; some i stems in is, 57; nouns in er and or, 46; fourth decl. in us (mostly), 61; fifth decl. only diēs and meridiēs, 64
Material, expressed by gen., 280; by abl., 324
Means, abl. of, 331; with gerund(ive), 269
Measure, abl. of, 334
medius, used partitively, 246
mel, decl., 41
melior, see bonus
meminī, with gen., 288; with acc., 288, *a*
memor, with gen., 287
–men, suffix, 44, 2
–met, enclitic, 106, *b*
Metaphor, 432
Meter, 391–410
Metonymy, 433
Metrical scheme, of the hexameter, 394
meus, form, 103, *a;* as gen. of ego, 249
mī, voc. of meus, 103, *a;* short for mihi
Middle voice, 115, *a;* with obj. acc., 309, *a*
mihi, see ego
mīles, decl. like comes, 52
mīlle, numeral, 99
minus, compar., 97; in double comparisons, 245
miser, decl., 71
misereor, with gen., 289
miseret, with gen. and acc., 290

Modesty, pl. of, 243, *a;* subjunctive of, 252

modo, in proviso clauses, 375

Monosyllabic, nouns of third decl., 53

Mood, 115, 4: for forms see verbs; for uses see indic., subj., etc.

More vivid conditions, 380

moror, conj., 183–190

Motion, end of, with dat., 306; with acc., 315

mōvī, contracted forms of, 204, 3

multus, compar., 92

mūnus, decl. like **genus,** 47

Mute stems, decl., 49–54

n, stems in, 43

-nam, enclitic, 27, 112

Names of towns and islands, abl., 320, *a;* loc., 345; acc., 315, *a*

Naming, verbs of, with two accusatives, 316, *a*

nātus, with abl. of origin, 323

nāvis, decl., 56, *a*

-ne, enclitic, 27; in questions, 347, *a*

nē, in prohibitions, 253, 256, *a;* in purpose clauses, 359; with verbs of hindering, refusing, etc., 361; with verbs of fearing, 363; result, 365; omitted after **cavē,** 256

Nearness, adjectives of with dat., 304

Necessity, indic., 251, 382, *d;* pass. periphrastic, 199, *b;* 382, *d;* see command

Negative, answer expected, 347, *c;* double neg., 431; purpose clause, 359; clause of fearing, 363; result clause, 364; see prohibitions

nēmō, missing forms supplied by **nūllus,** 114; **nēmō est quī,** 364, *a*

nēquam, comparison of, 92

Neuter, adjectives with inf., 258; complement with subjects of different genders, 239, *b*

Neuter, pronom. adj., 114; decl., 74

Neuter, second decl. in **um** and a few in **us,** 38; third decl. stems in **ll,** 42; nouns in **en,** 44, 2; nouns in **ar, ur,** 46, 2; **i** stems in **e, al, ar,** 57, *b;* nouns in **us** (eris), **ūs** (ūris), 48, 2; fourth decl. in **ū,** 61

nf, vowels long before, 23

nihil, forms of, 114

nimis, compar., 95, *b*

No, questions expecting answer, 347, *c*

nōlī(te), in prohibitions, 256

nōlō, conj., 230

Nominative, defined, 30; like acc. and voc. pl. in third, fourth, and fifth declensions, 33, *b;* like acc., and voc. in all neuters; in **a,** 34; in **us (os), um, er** and **ir,** 36; in **l,** 41; in **ō** and **en,** 43; in **or** and **er,** 45; in **us,** 47; in **s,** 50–51; in **ēs,** 52; in **is, e, al,** 56; in **us, ū,** 59; in **ēs,** 62

Nominative case, 30; as subj., 276; with hist. inf., 277; as subjective complement, 278, 279; of gerund supplied by inf., 258; agreement of verb with, 236; double nom., 239, 241

nōnne, for affirmative answer, 347, *b*

nōs, see **ego;** pl. for sing., 243; nom. emphatic, 247

nostrī, nostrum, 247, *a*

Nouns: decl., 31–69; appos., 241; pred., 240, 278–279, 317, *a;* with infinitives, 264; and see gender

nōvī, contracted forms of, 204, 3; perf. with pres. meaning, 204, 3, 354

nox, decl., 53; quantity of vowel, 19

ns, vowels long before, 23

nt, vowels short before, 21

nūllus and **nēmō,** 114; decl., 74

num, for negative answer, 347, *c;* in questions, 347, *c*

Number, 29; pl. for sing., 243, 236, *a,* 444; and see agreement of pred. attribute, 239

Numerals, 98–101

ō, nouns in, 43; gender of nouns in, 44

Ō, interj. with voc., 344

ob, prep. with acc., 312; verbs compounded with, 298

Obeying, verbs of, with dat., 297

Object, direct, 307; ind., 295; clauses, 360–363, 365; inf. as obj., 260

Objective genitive, 284; of pers. pronouns, 247, *a;* objective complement, 317, *a*

Obligation, indic., 251, 382, *d;* periphrastic, 199, *b,* 382, *d;* subj., 253; see command

oblīvīscor, gen., 288; acc., 288, *a*

obsum, 123; dat. with, 298
Occasion, expressed by part., 273
ōdisse, see 204, 3
oe, diphthong, 5
Oedipūs, decl., 69
Omission, of pers. pron., 247
omnis, decl., 77
on, ōn, Greek endings, 65, *a,* 67, 68, 69
Onomatopoeia, 434
oportet, 251, 382, *d*
Optative, subjunctive, 253
opus est, with abl., 341
ōrātiō oblīqua, see indirect discourse
Ordinal numerals, 98, *a*
Origin, abl. of, 323
orior, conj., 206
ōrō, constr. of verbs depending on, 360
Orpheus, decl., 69
os, nom. sing. of second decl., 36, *a, b;*
   Greek nominatives in 67, 69
Oxymoron, 435

p, represents changed **b** before **s** and **t,**
   128, 6; stems in, 50
paenitet, with gen. and acc., 290
Panthūs, decl., 67
pār, with gen., 287; with dat., 304; with
   dat. of gerund(ive), 267
Paraleipsis, 436
Participles, formation, 117, 3; compar.,
   90; of deponents, 182, 205; tenses of,
   272–275; gerundive, 266, 269; periphrastic, 199; decl. of pres., 82
Partitive genitive, 286; of pers. pronouns,
   247, *a*
parvī, gen. of value, 292
parvus, compar., 92
Passive voice, 115, *a;* formation of perf.
   system, 116, 3; constr. with verbs of
   saying, 279; pass. periphrastic, 199,
   b, cf. 382, *d;* gerundive constructions,
   267, 268; middle and reflex. use, 309;
   perf. pass. system, 116, 3; fut. pass. inf.,
   117, 2, 213, *b;* with dat. of agent, 302
Past perfect, see pluperfect
patior, conj., 191–198
pelagus, gender of, 38, *a*
Penalty, gender of, 38, *a*
penes, prep. with acc., 312
Penult, 25, *a*

per, prep. with acc., 312
Perception, verbs of, with part., 273; see
   indirect discourse
Perfect tense, 351, 4; pres. state, 351, 4, *a;*
   past act, 351, 4, *b;* temp. clauses, 368,
   370, 376; perf. subj. both primary and
   secondary inf. in ind. disc., 263; participle, 275; in conditions, 381, 353, *b,*
   1, *b;* in ind. disc., 382, *a, b;* contracted
   perfects, 204
Periphrastic conjugation, 199–201; as
   fut. subj., 354; conditions in ind. disc.,
   382, *a;* in contrary to fact apodosis,
   382, *d;* in ind. questions, 354; with
   dat. of agent, 302
Person, agreement of verb, 236; agreement of rel. pron., 242; for forms see
   conjugations
Personal construction, of pass. with
   inf., 279
Personal pronouns, forms, 103; omission, 247; as part. gen., 247, *a;* in appos.
   to poss. adjectives, 249
Personification, 437
Persuading, verbs of with dat., 297
pēs, decl., 52
piget, with acc. and gen., 290
Pity, verbs of, with gen. and acc., 290
Place whither, 315, 306; where, 319;
   whence, 320; extent, 314
Pleasing, verbs of, with dat., 297
Plenty, expressions of, with gen., 287
plēnus, gen. with, 287; abl. with, 337
Pleonasm, 438
Pluperfect, 351, 5; indic. in time clauses,
   370; subj. in unreal conditions, 362; secondary sequence in ind. disc. 353, 382,
   a, b; in cum descriptive clauses, 378
Plural, see number, agreement, etc.; poetic, 243, 444; editorial, 243, *a*
plūs, compar., 92, 97
Polysyndeton, 439
Possession, gen., 283; dat., 299
Possessive adjectives (pronouns), forms,
   103–106; used as gen. of pron., 249
Possibility, indic., 251, 382, *d;* subj., 252,
   cf. 386; periphrastic, 382, *d;* in causal
   clauses, 357–358; with **antequam** and
   priusquam, 376, *a;* in conditions, 381;
   in relative clauses, 389

possum, conj., 125; to express possibility, 251, 382, *d;* in apodosis, 382, *d*

post, prep. with acc., 312; verbs compounded with, 298, 308

postquam, with indic., 368

Potential, indic., 251; subj., 252; see possibility

potior, with abl., 342

Power, adjectives of, with gen., 287; nouns of, with inf., 264

prae, prep. with abl., 339

Predicate adjective, 239, 279; pred. noun, 236, *c,* 240, 317, *a,* 278; pred. acc., 317, *a,* 279; pred. acc. becomes pred. noun in pass., 279; pred. noun with inf., 317, *a;* pred. use of participles, 273, 275; pred. gen., 285, *a;* of gerund(ive), 266; pred. adj. with inf., 258; pred. with pass. verbs of saying, etc., 279; pred. dat., 303, *a;* see agreement

Prepositions, with acc., 312; with abl., 339; omitted, 315, *a, b;* 319, *b,* 320, *a, b,* 340; **cum** appended to certain words, 321, *a;* assimilation, *cf.* 123, compounds of with dat., 298; with acc., 308

Present tense, 351; specific and universal, 351, 1; hist., 351, 1, *a;* with **jam** as perf., 351,1, *b;* conative (as fut.), 351, 1, *c;* part., 272; decl., 82; indic. with **dum,** 372; inf. in ind. disc., 263

Preterition, 436

Preventing, verbs of, with **nē, quōminus, quīn,** 361–362; with abl. of separation, 340

Price, abl. of, 336; gen. of, 292

Primary tenses, 352, *a;* sequence of tenses, 353

prīmus, *beginning of,* 246

princeps, decl., 50

Principal parts, 126

priusquam, with indic., 376; with subj., 376, *a*

prō, prep. with abl., 329; **prō ut, quam prō,** 244, cf. 383; interj., 318

Prohibitions, subj., 253; imp., 256; obj. clauses (volitive), 360; hindering, 361–362; in ind. disc., 390, *b*

Prolepsis, 440

Pronouns, 102–114; pers., 103–106; omitted, 247; reflex., 106; use of, 248; dem.,

107; attraction of, 240, *a;* intensive, 108; rel., 109–110; general relatives, 110; agreement of relatives. 242; relative clauses, 385–389; interrog., 111–112; adj., 111, *a;* pronom. adjectives, 73–74, 114; see poss.; indef., 113; distributive, see **quisque** and **uterque** as part. gen., 247, *a;* in appos. to poss. adj., 249

Pronunciation, Latin, 4–8; of Latin words in English, 28; of **i** and **u** as consonants, 401

Prosody, 391–410

prōsum, conj., 124

Protasis, 380; see conditions

Proviso clauses, vol. subj., 254; with **dum (modo),** 375

proximus, with dat., 304

-pte, enclitic, 106, c

pudet, with gen. and acc., 290

puer, decl., 37

pulcher, decl., 71; compar., 88

pulchrē, compar., 97

Purpose, inf., 261; gerund(ive), 268; fut. part., 274; **ut** and **nē** with subj., 359; rel. clause of, 388; supine in **um,** 270; dat. of, 303

qu, pronunciation, 6; counts as single consonant, 15; becomes **x** with **s,** 128, 6

Quality, gen., 285; abl., 330; two qualities compared, 245

quam, omission of in compar., 327; **quam prō, quam ut, quam quī,** 244; **quam sī,** 383; with two positives, 245; with two comparatives, 245; **antequam** and **priusquam** separated, 376, *a*

quamquam, with indic. in concessive clauses, 384

quamvīs, with subj. in concessive clauses, 384

quandō, in causal clauses, 357

quantī, gen. of value, 292

Quantity, of vowels, 20–24; of syllables, 14–19; in verse, 392–397, 404, 407; numerals, 99–101

quasi, in clauses of comparison, 383

-que, enclitic, 27

Questions, 347; deliberative, 348; ind., 349, 354; exclamatory, 262

quī, decl., 109; abl. form **quī,** 109, *d;* = **ut is,** 389; see relative

quia, in causal clauses, 357

quīcumque, general relative, 110

quīn, after verbs of hindering, refusing, etc., 362; after neg. expressions of doubt, 366

quis, interrog., decl., 111; indef., 113

quīs, dat., abl. pl. of **quī,** 109, *c*

quisque, use with reflex., 248

quisquis, general rel., 110

quoad, with indic., 371; with subj., 374

quod, rel. pron., 109; with indic. in explanatory clauses, 356; with indic. and subj. in causal clauses, 357–358; in ind. disc. 355

quōminus, after verbs of hindering, refusing, etc., 361–362

quoniam, in causal clauses, 357

quot, numeral adv., 98

quotiēns, numeral adv., 101; in temp. clauses, 320

quum = cum

r, for **s** between two vowels, 47; stems in **r,** 45; nouns in **r,** 36, *a,* 37; adjectives in **r,** 71, 74, 76, 77, 91; see liquids

re, for **ris,** 204, 4

Reading of verse, 405–408

Reference, dat. of, 301, 303, *a;* gen., 294; acc., 311; abl., 325

rēfert, with gen. of person, 293; with abl. of poss. adj., 293, *a*

Reflexive pronouns, forms, 103–106; use, 248

Refusing, verbs of, 361–362

Regarding, two accusatives with verbs of, 316, *a;* constr. with pass. verbs of, 279

Relative clauses, 385; explanatory, 386; dependent, 387; purpose, 388; result, 364, *a;* char., 389

Relative pronouns, decl. 109; agreement, 242; in comparison, 244

reliquus, partitive use = *rest of,* 246

Remembering, verbs of, with gen., 288; acc., 288, *a*

Removing, verbs of, with abl., 340

Repeated action, impf., indic., 351, 2; in temp. clauses, 369–370; sequence of tenses, 353

rēs, decl., 63

Resisting, verbs of, with dat., 297; with **nē, quīn, quōminus,** 361, 362

Resolving, verbs of, complementary inf., 259; subst. vol. clause with, 360

Respect, abl. of, 325; acc. of, 311

Restricted, rel. clause, 387

Result clauses, 364; rel. clause of, 364, *a;* sequence of tenses, 353; explanatory clause of, 367

rēte, decl., 56, *b*

Rhotacism, 47

Rhythm of Latin verse, 407

ri, adjective stems in, 76, *a*

rogō, two accusatives, 316; inf. with, 360; **ut** (volitive) clause, 360

Route, abl. of, 338

rūs, decl. and gender, 48, 2; acc., 315, *a;* abl., 320, *a;* loc., 345

s, changed to **r** between vowels, 47; change of mutes before **s** in verb stems, 128, 6; stems in **s,** 47; nom. ending, 32

saepe, compar., 97

satis, with gen., 286; compar., 97

Saying, verbs of, ind. disc., 263, 390; constr. with pass., 279

Scansion, 404

scītō, fut. used as pres. imperative, 202

sē, reflex. pron., 106, 248

Second conjugation, principal parts, 126; forms, 142–150; deponents, 191–198

Second declension, 36–38

Secondary object, 308, 316; tenses, 352, *b,* 353

secundum, prep. with acc., 312

Selling, verbs of with gen., 292; with abl., 336

Semi-hiatus, 400; semi-deponents, 205; semi-vowels, 6, *a, b, c;* 401

senex, decl., 56, *c*

Separation, dat. of, 305; abl. of, 340

Sequence of Tenses, 353; conditions in ind. disc., 381, *a;* suppositions in ind. disc., 383, *a;* for examples see 358, 360, 363, 374, 390, *b*

sequor, conj., 191–198

Service, dat. of, 303; dat. with adjectives of, 304

Serving, dat. with verbs of, 297

Sharing, adjectives of with gen., 287

sī, conditions, 380–382; suppositions, 383; **ut sī, ac sī, quam sī,** 383

Simile, 441

similis, with gen., 287; with dat., 304

simul ac (atque), with indic., 368

Singular, with pl. verb, 236, 444; see number, agreement, etc.

singulus, distributive num., 100

Situation, participle, 273; **cum** descriptive, 378; **dum** with pres. ind., 372; rel. clause, 385; abl., 329

soleō, semi-deponent, 305; complementary inf. with, 259

sōlus, with rel. clause, 389

Source, abl. of., 323

Space, extent of with acc., 314

Specification, with gen., 294; abl., 325; abl. of supine, 271; acc., 311

Spelling, **j** and **v,** 6, *a, b, c*

Spondee, 392; spondaic verse, 395

Stem of nouns, 31, 34, 36, 39–40, 58, 62; of adjectives, 71, 75–76, 78–81; stems in **i,** 55, 76; of verbs, 116, 126–128

sub, prep. with acc., 312; compounds of with dat., 298; with acc., 308

Subject, 276; agreement of verb with, 236; coll., 236, *a,* 444; two subjects, 236, *b;* subject of different persons, 239, *a;* omitted pers. pronouns, 247; impers. verbs, *cf.* 240; indef. second person, *cf.* 252; imp., 255; of hist. inf., 257; subj. acc., 260, 317; exclamatory inf., 262; ind. disc., 263, 390; inf. as subj., 258

Subjective genitive, 284; poss. adj. as, 249

Subjunctive, 115, 4; potential, 252; opt., 253; vol., 254, 360; in causal clauses, 357–358, 379; in purpose clauses, 359; with verbs of hindering, refusing, etc., 361–362; in ideal and unreal conditions, 381–382; comparisons with **ut sī, quasi,** etc., 383; double comparisons with **quam sī, quam ut,** 244; **cum** descriptive, 378; concessive clauses with **cum,** 379; with **etsī** and **quamvīs,** 384; rel. clauses of attraction, 387; purpose, 388; char., 389; result, 364, *a;* deliberative questions, 348; ind. questions, 349, 354; temp. clauses of anticipation, 374,

376, *a;* result clauses, 364–367; with verbs of fearing, 363; prohibitions; 256; of modesty, *cf.* 252; proviso, 375; subordinate clauses in ind. disc., 357, 358, *cf.* 248, *b;* tenses of, 353

Subordinate clauses, sequence of tenses, 353; in ind. disc., 390 *b, c;* see temporal, result, conditional, etc.

Substantive (volitive) clauses of desire, 360; hindering, 361–362; fearing, 363; result, 365–367; conditions in, 382, *b;* **quod** with indic., 356

Suffixes, see enclitics, endings

suī, decl., 106; use, 248

sum, conj., 118; compounds of, 123; fut. inf. with **ut** in ind. disc., 263, *a;* agreement with pred. noun, 236, *c;* with dat. of poss., 299; **sunt quī,** 389; simple sentence with, 278

summus, *top of,* partitive, 246

super, prep. with acc., 312; in composition with dat., 298; with acc., 308

Superlative, 85, 88, 89, *a;* used partitively as noun, 246

Supine, for forms see conjugations; uses, 270–271

Suppositions with **ut sī, quasi, velut,** etc., 383

suus, forms, 106, *a;* uses, 248

syllaba anceps, 393

Syllables, division of, 9–13, 18; named, 25, *a;* final syllable of hexameter line, 393; long syllable shortened, 400; short syllable lengthened, 394, *a;* first syllable of each foot long, 394; long and short syllables, 14–19, 396; two syllables united, 403

Synapheia, 402

Synchysis, 442

Synecdoche, 443

Synesis, 444

Synizesis, 403

Syntax, 236–390

t, assimilated before **s,** 128, 6, 125; stems ending in, 52

taedet, with gen. and acc., 290

tametsī, in concessive clauses, 384

tamquam (sī), in clauses of comparison, 383; simile, 441

tantī, gen. of value, 292

Teaching, verbs of, two accusatives, 316

Temporal clauses, 368–377; of action prior to the main verb, 368, 370; of action contemporaneous with the main verb, 369, 371–373, 377; of action later than the main verb, 374–376; abl. abs., 343, *a*

Tenses, 115, 3; formation of, 127; pres., impf., etc. and verbs of imp., 255; of inf., 263, 390; of part., 272; uses of, 351; primary and secondary, 352; sequence of, 353

–ter, adv. suffix, 95, *c*

ter, num. adv., 101

Terminations, of nouns, 32; of verbs, 127–128; of infinitives and participles, 117; see endings, enclitics, declension, conjugation, etc.

Than, compar. of adjectives, 83–92; compar. of adverbs, 93–97; omission of **quam,** 327; *than if,* 383; *than that,* 244

Thinking, see indirect discourse, constr. with pass., 279; with acc. and inf., *cf.* 317, *a*

Third conjugation, principal parts, 126; forms **dīcō,** 151–160; **capiō,** 163–171; deponents: **sequor, patior,** 191–198

Third declension, stems in **l,** 41–42; **n,** 43–44; **r,** 45–46; **s,** 47–48; **p** or **b,** 50; **c** or **g,** 51; **t** or **d,** 52; **i,** 55–57

Time, from which, 320; when, within which, 322; till which, 315; extent, 314; expressed by abl. abs., 343, *a;* see temp. clauses; time in pronouncing syllables, 14, 408

timeō, with subj., 363

Tmesis, 445

too . . . to, two clauses compared, 244

tōtus, decl., 73; all of, partitive use, 246

Towns, names of; see cities

Trajection, 427

trāns, prep. with acc., 312; acc. with compounds of, 308

Transferred epithet, 446

Trees, names of, gender, 38, *a*

trēs, decl., 99

tū, decl., 104; omission, emphatic, 247

tuī, obj. gen., 247, *a*

Two accusatives, 308, *a,* 316; two datives, 303, *a*

u, sometimes pronounced like **v,** 6, *a;* after **g, q,** 6, 15; for **i** in superlatives, 85, 89, *a;* for **e** in gerund(ive), 203; noun stems in **u,** 58; **i** and **u** in dat., abl. pl., 58, *c*

ubi, with indic., 368

ubus, for **ibus** in dat., abl. pl., 58, *c*

ui, diphthong, 5

ūllus, decl., 74

Ultima, 25, *a*

um, gen. pl. ending, first decl., 34, *b,* second decl., 37. *d;* third decl., 53, *a, b, c, d,* 56, *c,* 81, 3, 82, *c, d*

Understatement, 431, see potential subj., 252

Undertaking, verbs of, with acc. of gerund(ive), 268, *a*

Unreal conditions, 382

ūnus, decl., 74; **ūnus est quī,** 389

urbs, decl., 53

ūsus est, with abl., 341

ut clauses: fearing, 363; **fore ut,** 263; indic., 368; indirect commands, 390, *b;* omitted, 256; purpose, 359; result, 364; sequence of tenses, 353; **ut sī,** 383; substantive, 360, 367; temporal, 368

uter and **uterque,** decl., 74, *b;* compounds of **uter,** 114, *a*

utinam, in unfulfilled wishes, 253

ūtor, with abl., 342

v, omitted in perf. forms, 204; use of, 6, *a;* as a consonant in poetry, 401

Value, gen. of, 292

vannus, gender, 38, *a*

–ve, enclitic, 27

velim, vellem, subj. of modesty, 252; opt., 253

velut (sī), in clauses of comparison, 383; simile, 441

vēneō, compound of **eō,** 213, *a;* see selling

Verbal adjectives, in **āx** with gen., 287

Verbs, inflection of, 115; stems, 116, 128, 6; conj., 116; principal parts,

126; first conj., 12–141; second conj., 142–150; third conj., 151–160, **dīcō;** 161–171, **capiō;** fourth conj., 172–181; dep., 182–198; semi-dep., 205; periphrastic. 199–203, 263, *a;* syncopated forms, 204; irregular, 206–235; **sum,** 118–122; principal parts, 126; general rules, 128

Verbs, uses of, agreement, 236; with gen., 287–291; **interest** and **rēfert,** 293; with dat., 297–298; with abl., 342; see names of moods and tenses, ind. disc., etc.

Versification, 391–404

vēscor, with abl., 342

vester, 104

vestrī, vestrum, 247, *a*

vetō, acc. and inf. with, 260, 360, *a*

vetus, decl., 82; rhotacism, 47

videor, dat. of reference, 301; pred. nom., 279; complementary inf., 259: ind. disc., 263–390

vir, decl., 37

vīs, decl., 56, *a*

Vocative, defined, 30; second decl., sing., 36; of words in **ius, ium,** 37, *b;* **deus,** 37, *f;* **meus,** 103, *a;* Greek nouns, 66–69; use, 344

Voices, 115, 2, *a;* middle with obj. acc., 309, *a;* see active, middle, passive

Volitive, subj., 254; substantive with **ut** (**nē**) after verbs of will, desire, etc., 360; in ind. disc., 390, b

volō, conj., 230; with inf., 260, 317; with subj., 360; with part., 275

vōs, see **tū**

voster, see **vester**

Vowels, long and short, 3–4, 20–24; long vowels marked, 3, 397; elision of final vowels in verse, 398; syncopation, 204; synizesis, 403; long vowel shortened, 400

vulgus, gender, 38, *a*

Want, words of with gen., 287; with abl., 340

Way, by which, abl., 328, 331, 338

Whole, gen. of, 286

Wishes, inf., 260, 317; subj., 253, 254; ind. disc., 390, b; **ut** (volitive) clause, 360

x, nom. ending, 51, 82; in verb stems (**c, g, qu** and **s**), 128, 6; double consonant, 8; makes position, 15

Yes, questions expecting, 347, *b*

z, double consonant, 8; makes position, 15

Zeugma, 447

FREQUENCY LISTS FOR VOCABULARY DRILL

There are three of these lists: (1) Words found 12–23 times in the first six books of the *Aeneid* (pp. 97–100); (2) Words found 6–11 times in the first six books (pp. 101–106); (3) General Word List: Words found twenty-four times or more in the first six books (pp. 108–111 and pull-out, inside of back cover).

WORDS FOUND 12–23 TIMES IN *AENEID* 1-6

abeō go away, depart
ācer sharp, piercing
addō give to, ADD
aequō (make) level, EQUALIZE
aether upper air, ETHER
affor speak to, address
agnōscō RECOGNIZE, understand
āla wing
aliquis some(one), any(one)
alter other (of two), second
amīcus friend(ly), AMICABLE
amittō lose, send away
amō love, cherish
an whether
annus year
antrum cave, cavern
aperiō uncover, open
arbor tree
arduus Steep, ARDUOUS
ars ART, skill
artus (*noun*) joint, limb
asper rough, harsh
aspiciō look (at), behold
astō stand (by, near)
astrum star, constellation
attollō lift (up), arouse
audeō be eager, dare

aureus of gold, gold(en)
auris EAR
auster south(wind)
autem moreover, however
auxilium support, assistance
āvertō turn from, AVERT

bis twice

cadō fall, die
caecus blind, unseeing
canō sing (of), CHANT
carīna keel, ship
cārus dear
causa CAUSE, reason
cavus hollow
cēdō yield, CEDE
celer swift
celsus high, lofty
centum one hundred
certamen contest
certus settled, CERTAIN
cingō encircle, gird
cinis ashes, CINDERS
clārus CLEAR, famous
colō CULTIVATE, worship
coma hair, foliage (of a tree)

condō put together, found
cōnsīdō settle, SUBSIDE
cōnsistō take position
contrā against, opposite
cor heart
corripiō snatch (up)
crēdō believe, trust, CREDIT
crīnis hair (of the head)
crūdēlis CRUEL, pitiless
currus chariot
custōs guard, CUSTODIAN

deinde then, thereupon
dēmittō let down
dēserō abandon, DESERT
dīrus fearful, DIRE
doceō teach
dolor pain, grief
dolus trick(ery), artifice
dulcis sweet
dūrus hard, harsh
dux leader, guide

ecce lo! behold!
efferō bear out, extol
effundō pour out
enim for, truly
ēnsis sword, steel
equidem indeed, certainly
ergō therefore, ERGO
etiam also, even
exerceō train, EXERCISE
extrēmus farthest, EXTREME

faciēs figure, FACE
fallō deceive
fās divine right (law)
fax torch
ferus wild, FIERCE
fidēs (good) faith, reliability, FIDELITY
fīdus faithful, trustworthy
fīgō (trans)FIX, fasten
flūmen stream, river
forma shape, beauty

fortis brave, strong
fūnus FUNERAL, death
furor madness, FURY

gemitus groan(ing), lamentation
gerō bear, accomplish
gravis heavy, GRAVE
gurges whirlpool, sea

haereō stick (to), ADHERE
harēna sand
hērōs HERO
homō man, person
horreō shudder, bristle (at)
hortor urge, EXHORT
hospes guest, host
hostis (public) enemy, HOSTILE

ignārus IGNORANT
imāgō IMAGE, form
impellō drive, IMPEL
impleō fill (up)
impōnō place on, IMPOSE
inānis empty, vacant
incendō set on fire, excite
incipiō begin
inde thence, thereupon
inquam quoth, say
īnsignis marked, distinguished, SIG-
    NIFICANT
intereā meanwhile
iter road, journey
iterum again, a second time

jaceō lie
jactō toss, boast
jugum yoke, ridge
jungō JOIN
juvenis young, youth, JUVENILE
juvō help, please
juxtā near, next to

laevus left (hand), awkward
lateō lie hid, be hidden

lātus broad, wide
latus side, flank
laus praise, glory
legō gather, COLLECT
lētum death, ruin
licet it is permitted (LICIT)
linquō leave, RELINQUISH
loquor speak, talk
lūcus (sacred) grove
lūstrō cleanse, illumine

maestus sad, dejected
malus bad, evil
mānēs soul(s), spirit(s), MANES
membrum MEMBER, limb
memorō recall, recount
mēnsa table
mereō deserve, MERIT
metus fear, dread
misceō mix, mingle
miseror pity, COMMISERATE
modus measure, manner
mōlēs mass(ive structure)
mōnstrō DEMONSTRATE, show, teach
mōnstrum omen, MONSTER
mora delay, hindrance
morior die
moror delay, hinder
mōs manner, custom
mūrus wall
mūtō change

nemus glade, grove
nepōs grandson, descendant
nimbus rainstorm, cloud
nisi if not, unless
nōscō learn, know
nūbēs (storm) cloud
numerus NUMBER, amount

obscūrus dark, OBSCURE
ōmen OMEN, portent
(ops), opis assistance, resources
optō choose, desire, OPT

opus work; necessity
orbis circle, ORBIT
ordō succession, ORDER
ōrō pray, plead
os bone

palma PALM, blade of oar
pandō spread out, EXPAND
pār equal
pariō bear
patior permit, suffer
pietās loyalty, devotion, PIETY
placidus gentle, PLACID
pontus sea, the deep
populus PEOPLE, nation
porta gate, PORTAL
poscō demand, claim
post after, behind
praeceps headlong, PRECIPITOUS
praemium reward, PREMIUM
precor PRAY, invoke
premō PRESS, pursue
prior earlier, PRIOR
prō before, for
prōlēs offspring, descendants
prope near(by)
pugna fight, battle
pulcher beautiful, handsome

quālis of what kind?
quam how, as, than
quīcumque whoever, whichever, whatever
quiēscō rest, sleep
quīn (but) that
quoque also, too

rāmus branch, bough
rapiō seize, snatch
ratis raft, ship
reddō give back, RENDER
repōnō restore, bury
respiciō regard, consider
rōbur oak (tree), strength

rumpō break, burst
rūrsus back, again

sacerdōs priest(ess)
sacrō devote, CONSECRATE
saepe often
saevus fierce, raging
scelus wicked deed, crime
scopulus crag, cliff
secō cut
secundus second, favorable
sedeō sit, be settled
senex old, aged
signum mark, SIGN(AL)
similis like, SIMILAR
sine without (*abl.*)
sōl sun
solum bottom, ground
solvō loosen, release
sonitus BOUND, noise
sonō SOUND, RESOUND
soror sister
sors lot, fate
spargō scatter, DISPERSE
spērō hope
spēs hope
spūmō foam, SPUME
sternō STREW, overthrow
subitus sudden
superbus proud, haughty
superō overcome, surpass
supplex kneeling, SUPPLIANT

taceō be silent (TACIT)
tam so

tamen nevertheless
templum TEMPLE, shrine
temptō try, ATTEMPT
ter thrice
tergum back, rear
thalamus bridal chamber
torqueō twist, wind
tot so many
tremō tremble, quake
tumulus mound
turbō confuse, DISTURB

unde whence
undique from (on) all sides

varius VARIED, VARIOUS
vel or
velut just as, even as
vertex whirl, VORTEX, VERTEX
vertō turn
vester your(s)
vestīgium track, trace, VESTIGE
vestis clothing, garment, VESTURE
vetus old, ancient
virgō maiden, girl
viridis VERDANT, green
virtūs manliness, valor, VIRTUE
vitta fillet, band
volucer flying, winged; bird
voveō solemnly promise, vow
vulnus wound
vultus countenance, face

WORDS FOUND 6–11 TIMES IN *AENEID* 1–6

absum be away, be ABSENT
accēdō go to, ACCEDE
accendō kindle
accingō gird (on)
aciēs sharp edge; battle line
acuō sharpen
adeō (*adv.*) to such a degree
adeō (*vb.*) go to, visit
aditus approach, access
adytum shrine, inner sanctuary
aeger sick, weak
aēneus of bronze, brazen
aequus level, EQUAL
āēr AIR, fog
aes copper, bronze
aestās summer
aestus boiling, tide
aeternus ETERNAL, everlasting
aetherius airy, ETHEREAL
aevum age, eternity
agger mound, dike
aggredior approach, attack
agitō AGITATE, drive
albus white
alloquor speak to, address
almus fostering, kindly
ambō both
āmēns mad, frantic, DEMENTED
amnis river, stream
amplector embrace, surround
amplus AMPLE, spacious
animus spirit, mind
appāreō APPEAR
aptō fit on, equip, ADAPT
aqua water
arceō confine, restrain
arcus bow, ARCH
argentum silver; money
armō ARM, equip
arrigō raise (up), ERECT

auctor originator, founder, AUTHOR
auferō bear away, remove
auspicium omen, AUSPICES
āvellō tear away, pluck off
avus grandfather, ancestor
axis AXLE, AXIS, chariot

bōs bull, cow, ox; *pl.* cattle
bracchium (fore)arm
brevis short, BRIEF

caedēs killing, slaughter
caedō fell, kill
caeruleus dark blue, CERULEAN
caestus CESTUS, boxing glove
cardō pivot, hinge
carmen song, poem
carpō pluck
castrum fortress; *pl.*, camp
cautēs crag, pointed rock
certō contend, fight
cervīx neck
cēterus the other(s)
ceu just as, as if
chorus choral dance, band
cieō move, agitate
citus stirred up, swift
claudō CLOSE, shut
clipeus (round) shield
coepī have begun
cognōmen (sur)name, COGNOMEN
cōgō collect, compel
colligō COLLECT, gather
collum neck
comitor ACCOMPANY, attend
committō join, entrust, perform
compellō hail, greet
complector embrace
compleō fill COMPLETELY
compōnō put together, arrange

concutiō shake, shatter
conjugium union, marriage
cōnscius CONSCIOUS
cōnsilium plan, COUNSEL, council
cōnspiciō catch sight of, behold
contendō struggle, CONTEND
contingō touch, happen (to)
continuus unbroken, CONTINUOUS
cōnūbium wedlock, marriage
convellō tear to pieces, destroy
conveniō come together, CONVENE
convertō turn about, change
cornū horn
corōna CROWN, wreath
crēber thick, frequent
cruentus bloody
cruor blood
culmen top, summit
cupīdō desire, eagerness
currō run
curvus bent, CURVED

daps banquet, feast
decōrus becoming, adorned
decus beauty, glory
dēferō bear away, report
dē(j)iciō throw, cast (down)
dēligō choose, SELECT
dēmēns distracted, DEMENTED
dēmum finally, at last
dēnsus thick, DENSE
dēscendō climb down, DESCEND
dignus worthy (abl.)
dīgredior step away, depart
discō learn
discrīmen crisis, risk
dīversus different, DIVERSE
dīvīnus DIVINE, godlike
dominus master, lord
dōnec until
ductor leader, guide
dūdum already, now for a long time
duo two

ēdūcō lead forth
effor speak (out)
effugiō flee (away), escape
ēgregius distinguished, uncommon
ēlābor slip (out), escape
ēn lo! behold!
epulae banquet, feast
error ERROR, mistake
ēruō cast out, overthrow
ēvādō go forth, EVADE
exanimus lifeless, breathless
excēdō go forth, withdraw
excipiō take out, EXCEPT
excutiō shake (out, off)
exigō drive out, EXACT
exorior rise (up), appear
expediō extricate, disentangle
exspectō watch for, await, EXPECT
exstinguō EXTINGUISH, destroy
extemplō immediately, suddenly
exterreō TERRIFY, frighten
exuō put off, strip
exuviae spoils, armor

facilis easy (to do), FACILE
famēs hunger, FAMINE
famulus servant, house slave
fastīgium slope, summit
fātālis FATED, FATAL
fateor admit, confess
fatīgō weary, tire
faucēs jaws, gullet
fēlīx lucky, FELICITOUS
fēmina FEMALE, woman
feriō smite, strike
fingō shape, invent
fīō become
flectō bend, turn
fleō weep, (be)wail
flētus weeping, tears
fluō FLOW
fluvius stream, river
foedō defile, pollute
foedus treaty, league

folium leaf, FOLIAGE
foris door
formīdō dread, apprehension
foveō foster, protect
frangō break, shatter
frāter brother
fremō murmur, roar
fretum strait of water, sea
frōns leaf, foliage, FROND
frōns forehead, FRONT
frūstrā in vain, vainly
fulgeō gleam, flash
fulmen lightning, thunderbolt
fulvus yellow, tawny
fūnis rope, cable
furiae rage, FURY

galea helmet
gaudeō rejoice
gelidus frosty, ice-cold, GELID
gemō groan, lament
genū knee
germānus own brother (sister)
gignō beget, bear
glomerō collect, assemble
glōria GLORY, fame
gradior step, walk
gradus step, pace, GRADE
gremium lap, bosom
gressus step, walk

habitō occupy, INHABIT
hasta spear
hauriō draw, drain
herba HERB, grass
hibernus wintry
hiems winter; storm
horridus rough, fearful, HORRID
hospitium HOSPITALITY, welcome
humus ground
hymenaeus HYMEN, god of marriage

ictus blow, stroke
ignōtus unknown

imber rain(storm)
immēnsus boundless, IMMENSE
immittō send in, let go
immōtus UNMOVED, IMMOVABLE
impius impious, disloyal
incēdō PROCEED, go in(to)
incertus UNCERTAIN
inclūdō shut in, confine, INCLUDE
incumbō lie on, lean on
induō put on, don
īnfandus unspeakable
īnferō bear in (against)
īnfundō pour (rush) in
ingeminō redouble, repeat
ingredior step in, enter
inimīcus (personal) ENEMY, hostile
inīquus UNEQUAL, unjust
īnsequor follow, pursue
īnsidiae ambush, treachery
īnsōns innocent
īnstaurō renew, refresh, RESTORE
īnstruō arrange, plan
īnsula island
intendō strain, stretch
interior inner, INTERIOR
intrō go within, ENTER
intus within
invādō attack, INVADE
inveniō come upon, find
invideō look on, ENVY, hate
iste that (of yours, contemptible)
ita so, thus

jaciō hurl, throw
jūs right, JUSTICE, law
juvencus bullock, heifer
juventa youth
juventūs youth

lacrimō shed tears, weep
lacus LAKE
latex fluid, liquid
laurus LAUREL
levis light, slight

levō lift, remove
lēx law, rule
lībō sip, pour a LIBATION
locō place, LOCATE
longaevus aged
lūctus grief, mourning
lūdus game; school
lūna moon

mactō sacrifice, offer
magister MASTER, chief
magnanimus great-souled, MAGNANI-
    MOUS
mandō hand over, commission
meminī REMEMBER
memor mindful
mergō IMMERSE, plunge
mēta boundary, goal
metuō fear, dread
mīlle one thousand
mīrābilis MARVELOUS, wonderful
mīror wonder at, MARVEL at
misereō pity, COMMISERATE
mōlior heap up, build
mollis soft, gentle
moneō advise, ADMONISH
monumentum reminder, MONUMENT
mortālis MORTAL
murmur MURMUR(ING)

nauta sailor
nefandus unspeakable, wicked
nefās impiety, wickedness
negō deny, refuse
nēquīquam in vain, vainly
niger black
nihil nothing
nimius excessive, too much
nōdus knot, NODE
nūbilus cloudy, misty
nuntius messenger, message
nympha NYMPH

ob on account of (acc.)

ob(j)iciō oppose, throw in the way
oblīvīscor forget
obsideō besiege, occupy
obstipēscō be amazed, stand agape
occurrō run to meet, OCCUR
offerō present, offer
ōlim once, at that time
omnipotēns OMNIPOTENT, all powerful,
    almighty
onerō load, burden
opācus dark, obscure, OPAQUE
orior arise, begin
ostendō show, stretch toward
ostentō show, display
ōstium mouth, entrance
ovō rejoice

parcō spare (dat.)
pāreō obey (dal.)
pascō feed (on), PASTURE
passim generally, everywhere
pateō lie open, extend
patera bowl, (libation) cup
paucī few
pāx PEACE
pecus cattle, flock
pellō strike, drive
pendeō hang, be SUSPENDED
penetrālis inner, interior; n.pl., shrine
penitus thoroughly, utterly
peragō finish, accomplish
pereō PERISH, be lost
perferō bear (to the end), endure
perficiō accomplish, PERFECT
perīculum danger, PERIL
pestis plague, PESTILENCE
pharetra quiver for arrows
pingō PAINT, DEPICT, embroider
pinguis fat, rich
pinna feather, wing
plausus APPLAUSE
plēnus full
polus POLE, heavens
pondus weight

portō carry
postis (door)POST, portal
postquam after
potior obtain (*abl.; gen.*)
praecipitō throw headlong, PRECIPI-
TATE
praeda booty, PREY
praestō furnish, excel
praesum be in charge (at the head of)
praetereā besides, moreover
prex PRAYER, entreaty
principium beginning
prōcēdō go forward, PROCEED
prōcumbō lie forward, sink (to the ground)
proelium battle, fight
prohibeō forbid, PROHIBIT
prō(j)iciō hurl, PROJECT
prōmittō send forth, PROMISE
propinquō approach (*dat.*)
proprius one's own, peculiar
prōra PROW
prōspiciō look forward, provide
prōtinus at once, immediately
pūbēs youth, men
pulsō beat, lash
purpureus crimson

quamquam although, however
quandō when? at some time
quantus how great? as great as
quatiō shake
quattuor four
quiēs rest, QUIET
quisquam anyone
quisque each, everyone
quisquis whoever, whichever, whatever
quod because; (as for) the fact that

rapidus swift, RAPID
recēdō RECEDE, withdraw
recēns fresh, new, RECENT
recipiō take back, RECEIVE
recūsō refuse

redeō go back, return
redūcō lead back
regiō REGION, district
rēgius ROYAL, REGAL
rēgnō REIGN, rule
regō rule, DIRECT
reliquiae remnant, remains
reor reckon, suppose
repente suddenly
reperiō find (out)
repetō demand, reseek, REPEAT
requīrō demand, REQUIRE
resīdō settle (down), sink
resolvō untie, loose(n)
respondeō answer, RESPOND
retrō back(ward)
revellō tear off
revīsō REVISIT, come back to
revocō call back, REVOKE
rīpa bank, shore
rīte duly, fittingly
ruīna downfall, RUIN
rūpēs crag, rock

saeviō rage
sagitta arrow
sal SALT, brine
salsus SALTY, SALTED
salūs health, safety
satis enough, sufficient
scēptrum SCEPTER; rule
sciō know (how)
sēcernō separate
semper always, ever
sententia feeling, opinion
sentiō feel, perceive
sepeliō perform rites of burial
septem SEVEN
sepulcrum tomb, SEPULCHER
serēnus clear, SERENE
sermō conversation, discourse
serō SOW
signō designate, mark
sileō be SILENT

simulācrum image, likeness
simulō pretend, SIMULATE
sinister left
sinō allow, permit
sistō set, stand
spatium SPACE
spēlunca cave
spīrō breathe, blow
spolium trophy, SPOILS
statuō STATION, ESTABLISH
stirps trunk, stock, race
strīdeō hiss, whiz
stringō draw (tight), graze
struō pile up, CONSTRUCT
studium zeal, eagerness
sub(j)iciō drive in, expose, SUBJECT
sublīmis lofty, SUBLIME
succēdō approach (closely), SUCCEED
sūmō take (up), ASSUME
supersum remain, survive
suscipiō take up, undertake
suspendō SUSPEND, hang up

tangō TOUCH
tardus slow, late, TARDY
taurus bull
tempestās TEMPEST, storm
tenebrae darkness
tenuis thin, TENUOUS
terreō frighten, TERRIFY
tertius third
testor call to witness, TESTIFY
timeō fear, dread
torus bed, couch
trabs beam, trunk of tree
trepidus agitated, excited

trēs three
tumidus swollen, swelling
turba mob, crowd, tumult
turbō tornado, whirlwind

ūber udder, fertility
ulterior beyond, farther, ULTERIOR
ultor avenging, avenger
ultrō beyond, furthermore
ūmidus moist, HUMID
umquam ever, at any time
urgeō drive, URGE
uterque each of two, both
uterus womb, belly

vacuus empty, VACANT
vādō go, advance
vadum ford, shallow
valeō be strong, be able
validus strong, VALID
vallēs VALLEY
vānus empty, VAIN
vehō go, CONVEY, carry
vēlō VEIL, cover
veneror VENERATE, worship
verbum word
verrō sweep, scour
versō turn (often), keep turning
vīnum WINE, VINE
vīscus vitals, entrails, VISCERA
vīsus sight, VISION
vīvō live, subsist
vīvus alive, living
volūtō roll, REVOLVE
vulgus the common people

GENERAL WORD LIST

WORDS FOUND 24 TIMES OR MORE IN *AENEID* 1–6

ā, ab, abs (away) from, by (*abl.*)

ac, atque and, also; as, than

accipiō, ere, cēpī, ceptus receive, AC-CEPT; learn, hear, conceive

Acestēs, ae *m.* king in Sicily

āctus, a, um *see* **agō**

ad to, toward, at, near, about (*acc.*)

adfore; adforem, ēs, et *see* **adsum**

adsum, esse, fuī be present, assist (*dat.*)

Aenēās, ae, *acc.* **ān,** *m.* Trojan prince, son of Venus and Anchises, hero of the *Aeneid*

aequor, oris *n.* sea, waves; (level) plain

age, agite (agō) up! come! lead on!

agmen, inis *n.* army, line, troop; course

agō, ere, ēgī, āctus lead, drive, do, treat, pass, conduct

ajō, ais, ait; ajunt say, speak, assert

alius, a, ud other, another, else

altus, a, um (on) high, lofty, deep

amor, ōris *m.* love, desire, passion

Anchīsēs, ae, *acc.* **ēn,** *m.* Trojan prince, father of Aeneas

anima, ae *f.* air, breath, life, soul, shade

animus, ī *m.* soul, spirit, breath, courage; anger, pride; purpose, thought

ante before (*acc.*); sooner, previously

antīquus, a, um ANCIENT, old, aged, former, of olden times, time-honored

āra, ae *f.* altar

ardeō, ēre, arsī, arsus burn, be eager

arma, ōrum *n.* ARMS, equipment, tools

arvum, ī *n.* plowed land, field, region

arx, arcis *f.* citadel, fort; height, hill

at, ast but, yet, however, at least

āter, tra, trum black, gloomy, deadly

atque, ac and, also; as, than

audiō, īre, īvī (iī), ītus hear (of), hearken

aura, ae *f.* breeze, air; favor; light

aurum, ī *n.* gold (object, equipment)

aut or, either; **aut ... aut** either ... or

bellum, ī *n.* war(fare), combat, fight

caelum, ī *n.* sky, heaven; weather

campus, ī *m.* plain, field, level surface

capiō, ere, cēpī, captus take, seize, catch; CAPTIVATE; deceive; occupy

caput, itis *n.* head; summit; life, person

cāsus, ūs *m.* chance, (mis)fortune; fall

cernō, ere, crēvī, crētus DISCERN, perceive, understand, decide; fight

circum around, about, at, near (*acc.*)

clāmor, ōris *m.* shout, roar, applause

classis, is *f.* fleet, army, ship

comes, itis m. (*f.*) comrade, follower

conjūnx, jugis *m.* (*f.*) husband, wife

corpus, oris *n.* body, CORPSE, form

cum (*conj.*) when, while, since, although

cum (*prep.*) with (*abl.*)

cūnctus, a, um all, whole, entire

cūra, ae *f.* care, anxiety, grief; love

cursus, ūs *m.* COURSE, running; haste

Danaus, a, um Danaan, Greek

dē (down, away) from, of, concerning, according to (*abl.*)

dea, ae *f.* goddess

deus, ī *m.* god, divinity, DEITY

dexter, (e)ra, (e)rum right (hand); favorable; *f. subst.* right hand

dīcō, ere, dīxī, dictus say, speak, tell, call, name, describe, chant

dictum, ī *n.* word, speech, command

Dīdō, ōnis *f.* legendary founder and queen of Carthage

diēs, diēī *m.* (*f.*) DAY, time, season

dīvus, a, um DIVINE, heavenly, deified; *subst.* DIVINITY, god, goddess

dō, dare, dedī, datus give (forth), grant, allow, bestow; put, place, make

domus, ūs *f.* house(hold), home, abode; family, race, line

dōnum, ī *n.* gift, offering, prize, reward

dūcō, ere, dūxī, ductus lead, draw (out), protract; PRODUCE; think

dum while, as long as, until, provided

ē, ex out of, from, according to (*abl.*)

ēgī *see* **agō**

ego, meī (*pl.* **nōs, nostrum**) I

eō, īre, īvī (iī), itus go, proceed, come

equus, ī *m.* horse, steed, charger

ēripiō, ere, uī, reptus snatch (from), tear away; rescue; hasten

errō (1) stray, wander, ERR; linger

et and, also, even, too; **et ... et** both ... and

euntis, ī, em, e, ēs, ium, ibus *see* **eō**

ex, ē out of, from, according to (*abl.*)

faciō, ere, fēcī, factus do, make, perform; grant, offer; suppose

fāma, ae *f.* FAME, report, reputation

fāre, fārī; fātur; fātus, a, um *see* **for**

fātum, ī *n.* FATE, destiny, doom; oracle

ferō, ferre, tulī, lātus bear, endure; wear; report, say; carry (off), plunder; extol; tend; grant, offer

ferrum, ī *n.* iron; sword, weapon, tool

fessus, a, um tired, weary, feeble, worn

fīnis, is *m.* (*f.*) end, limit, border; country; goal; starting-place

flamma, ae *f.* FLAME, fire, torch; love

flūctus, ūs *m.* wave, tide, flood, sea

for, fārī, fātus speak, say, tell, utter

fore; forem, ēs, et *see* **sum**

fors, fortis *f.* chance, FORTUNE, hap

fortūna ae *f.* FORTUNE, chance, luck

fuga, ae *f.* flight, haste, exile, speed

fugiō, ere, fūgī flee (from), escape, shun

fundō, ere, fūdī, fūsus pour (out), shed; lay low, slay, rout; extend

furō, ere, uī rage, rave, be frantic

futūrus, a, um FUTURE, destined (to be), impending, about to be; *see* **sum**

geminus, a, um twin, double, two

genitor, ōris *m.* begetter, father, sire

gēns, gentis *f.* clan, race, nation, herd

genus, eris *n.* birth, origin, race; descendant; kind, family

habeō, ēre, uī, itus have, hold; consider

haud not, by no means, not at all

heu alas! ah! ah me!

hīc (*adv.*) here, there, hereupon

hic, haec, hoc this, that; he, she, it

hinc from this place, hence, thence

honōs (or), ōris *m.* HONOR, glory, reward; offering, sacrifice; charm, grace

hūc to this place, hither, here

ī, ībam, ībo, īre, it, īte *see* **eo**

īdem, eadem, idem same, the same

ignis, is *m.* fire, flame, light, lightning, star; passion, love, fury, wrath

ille, la, lud that (famous); he, she, it

immānis, e huge, monstrous, enormous, mighty, dreadful, cruel, atrocious

imperium, (i)ī *n.* command, power, dominion, rule, sway, mastery, realm(s)

īmus, a, um *superl. of* **īnferus**

in in, on, in the case of, among (*abl.*); into, against, until, toward (*acc.*)

īnfēlīx, īcis unfortunate, accursed, unhappy, ill-omened, unlucky, wretched

īnferus, a, um low, below, underneath

ingēns, entis enormous, mighty, huge

inter between, among, during (*acc.*)

ipse, sa, sum (him, her, it)self; very

īra, ae *f.* wrath, rage, anger, passion

īre *see* **eō**

is, ea, id this, that; he, she, it

it, īte *see* **eō**

Ītalia, ae *f.* Italy

jam now, already, finally, at once

Jovis, ī, em, e *see* **Juppiter**

jubeō, ēre, jussī, jussus command, order, bid, enjoin (upon), urge

Jūnō, ōnis *f.* queen of the gods

Juppiter, Jovis *m.* king of the gods

jussī; jussus, a, um *see* **jubeō**

lābor, ī, psus slip (by), slide, glide (by), descend; fail; faint, fall, perish; flow

labōs (or), ōris *m.* LABOR, hardship, task

lacrima, ae *f.* tear, compassion

laetus, a, um happy; fertile; fat, sleek

līmen, inis *n.* threshold, doorway, entrance; abode; shrine; palace

lītus, oris *n.* shore, strand, coast, beach

locus, ī *m.* (*pl.* **locī, loca**) place, region; condition, situation; opportunity

longus, a, um long, wide, distant

lūmen, inis *n.* light, lamp; eye; life

lūx, lūcis *f.* light, sun, day; life; glory

magnus, a, um great, large, huge, vast; noble, illustrious, mighty, important

major, majus *compar. of* **magnus**

maneō, ēre, mānsī, mānsus remain, abide, linger, stay, (a)wait

manus, ūs *f.* hand; band, troop; deed

mare, is *n.* sea

māter, tris *f.* mother, dam; MATRON

maximus *superl. of* magnus

medius, a, um mid(dle), INTERMEDIATE

mēns, mentis *f.* mind, feeling, intention

meus, a, um my (own), mine

miser, era, erum MISERABLE, unhappy, wretched, unfortunate, pitiable

mittō, ere, mīsī, missus send, hurl, DISMISS, let go; end, finish; offer, pay

moenia, ium *n.* walls; city; structures

mōns, montis *m.* MOUNTAIN, height

mors, rtis *f.* death, destruction, ruin

moveō, ēre, mōvī, mōtus move; ponder

multus, a, um much, many, abundant

mūnus, eris *n.* function, duty; gift

nam, namque for; indeed, truly

nātus, ī *m.* son, child, young

nāvis, is *f.* ship, boat, vessel, galley

–ne *sign of a question;* whether, or

nē lest, that not, no, not

neque, nec nor, neither, and not; **neque … neque** neither … nor

nōmen, inis *n.* NAME, fame, renown

nōn not, no

noster, tra, trum our (own), ours

novus, a, um new, young, strange, late

nox, noctis *f.* night, darkness; sleep

nūllus, a, um none, no, no one

nūmen, inis *n.* divinity, divine power (will, favor, purpose, presence)

nunc (but) now, soon, as it is

Ō O! oh! ah!

oculus, ī m. eye

olle *etc., old forms of* **ille**

omnis, e all, every, whole, universal

ōra, ae *f.* shore, coast, region, border

ōs, ōris *n.* mouth, face; speech

parēns, entis *m.* (*f.*) PARENT, ancestor, father, mother

parō (1) PREPARE, make (ready)

pars, rtis *f.* PART, portion, share, side

pater, tris *m.* father, ancestor, sire

patrius, a, um PATERNAL, ancestral, native

pectus, oris *n.* breast, heart, soul

pelagus, ī *n.* sea, flood, waves

per through, by (means of), over, among, because of, during (*acc.*)

pēs, pedis *m.* foot; sheet-rope, sheet

petō, ere, īvī (iī), ītus seek, attack, aim (at), ask; scan

pius, a, um devoted, loyal, righteous

plūrēs *compar. of* **multus**

plūrimus *superl. of* **multus**

plūs *compar. of* **multus**

poena, ae *f.* PUNISHMENT, PENALTY, satisfaction, revenge, vengeance

pōnō, ere, posuī, pos(i)tus put, place (aside); found, establish; bury

portus, ūs *m.* PORT, harbor, haven

possum, posse, potuī be able, can, avail

Priamus, ī m. Priam, king of Troy

prīmus, a, um first, foremost, chief

procul far, at a distance, (from) afar

puer, ī *m.* boy, child ; slave

puppis, is *f.* stern; ship, vessel, galley

quaerō, ere, quaesīvī, quaesītus seek (in vain), miss, inquire, ask, try

–que and, also, even; **–que ... –que** both ... and

quī, quae, quod who, which, what, that

quis (qua), quid, (quī, quae, quod) who? which? what? why? any, some(one)

quō whither, where(fore), whereby

quondam (at) some time, formerly, ever

referō, ferre, tulī, lātus bear back, restore, carry off; reproduce, renew, recall; RELATE, say; (re)pay

rēgīna, ae *f.* queen; *adj.* ROYAL

rēgnum, ī *n.* royal power, kingdom, REALM, rule, sway, sovereignty

relinquō, ere, līquī, lictus leave, desert, surrender, abandon, RELINQUISH

rēmus, ī *m.* oar

rēs, reī *f.* thing, affair, matter, deed, fact, fortune; state, commonwealth

rēx, rēgis *m.* king; *adj.* ruling, ROYAL

ruō, ere, ī, ru(i)tus fall; rush; sink; plow

sacer, era, erum SACRED, holy, consecrated; accursed; *n. subst.* SACRIFICE, holy implement (object); mystery

sanguis, inis *m.* blood; race, descendant

saxum, ī *n.* stone, rock, reef, cliff, crag

sed but, moreover, however

sēdēs, is *f.* seat; abode, habitation; bottom; tomb; shrine; place, region

sequor, ī, secūtus follow, attend, pursue, accompany, seek

servō (1) OBSERVE, watch; PRESERVE, save, guard, keep, rescue; nurse

sī whether, if (only), in case that

sīc thus, so, in this manner

sīdus, eris *n.* star, constellation, meteor; season, weather; heaven

silva, ae *f.* forest, wood(s), tree(s)

simul at the same time, together; **simul (ac, atque)** as soon as

socius, (i)ī *m.* ally, comrade, follower

sōlus, a, um alone, only, lonely, SOLE

somnus, ī *m.* sleep, slumber, dream

stō, āre, stetī, status stand (fast, up); halt; endure; stick (to), remain

sub (from) under, close (to), beneath, (deep) in, after (*acc., abl.*)

subeō, īre, īvī (iī), itus go under, bear; approach, enter; arise (*dat.*)

sublātus, a, um *see* **tollō**

suī (of) himself, herself, itself, themselves; him, her, it, them

sum, esse, fuī, futūrus be, exist

summus *superl. of* **superus**

super above, beyond, left, in addition, upon, concerning, about (*acc., abl.*)

superus, a, um upper, higher, above; *subst.* god, divinity

suprēmus, a, um *superl. of* **superus**
surgō, ere, surrēxī, surrēctus raise, (a) rise, spring up, SURGE
sustulī *see* **tollō**
suus, a, um his, her, its, their (own)

tālis, e such, of such sort, the following
tandem at length, finally; pray
tantus, a, um so great, so much, so far
tēctum, ī *n.* roof; house, home, abode
tellūs, ūris *f.* earth, land, country
tēlum, ī *n.* weapon; wound, blow
tempus, oris *n.* time; occasion, crisis
tendō, ere, tetendī, tentus stretch; hasten, strive, (EX)TEND, aim; tent
teneō, ēre, uī, tus have, hold, restrain
terra, ae *f.* earth, land, country, soil
Teucrus, a, um Teucrian, Trojan
tollō, ere, sustulī, sublātus lift, raise, upheave, stir up; remove, destroy
tōtus, a, um all, every, whole, full
trahō, ere, trāxī, tractus drag (out), draw (in), lead, PROTRACT, spend
trīstis, e sad, unhappy, dreary, fatal
Troja, ae *f.* Troy, a city of Asia Minor
tū, tuī (*pl.* **vōs, vestrum**) you
tulī *see* **ferō**
tum, tunc then, at that time; further
tuus, a, um your(s), your own
Tyrius, a, um Tyrian, Carthaginian

ubi where, when, as soon as
ūllus, a, um any, anyone

umbra, ae *f.* shade, shadow, ghost
umerus, ī *m.* shoulder
unda, ae *f.* wave, billow, water, sea
ūnus, a, um one, only, alone, single
urbs, urbis *f.* city, town
ut(ī) as, when; that, so that; how

vastus, a, um desolate, VAST, enormous
vātēs, is *m.* (*f.*) prophet, seer, bard
–ve, vel or, either, even; **vel … vel** either … or
velim, velle, vellem *see* **volō**
vēlum, ī *n.* cloth, canvas, sail
veniō, īre, vēnī, ventus come, go
ventus, ī *m.* wind, breeze, blast, air
via, ae *f.* WAY, road, journey, street
victor, ōris *m.* VICTOR; *adj.* VICTORIOUS
videō, ēre, vīdī, vīsus see, perceive; *pass.* be seen, appear, seem (best)
vincō, ere, vīcī, victus conquer, surpass
vir, ī *m.* (real) man; hero; husband
vīrēs *pl. of* **vīs**
vīs, vīs *f.* force, VIOLENCE, energy
vīta, ae *f.* life, soul, spirit
vix scarcely, feebly, with difficulty
vocō (1) call, name, address, CONVOKE, INVOKE, invite, challenge
volō, velle, voluī will, wish, be willing
volvō, ere, ī, volūtus REVOLVE, (un)roll, roll (round, through); undergo
vōx, cis *f.* VOICE, word, speech, sound

VOCABULARY

A

a(d)spectō (1) look at, see, face, behold

a(d)spectus, ūs *m.* sight, appearance, vision, aspect

a(d)spiciō, ere, spexī, spectus see, behold, look (at)

a(d)stō, āre, stitī stand (on, at, near, by) (+ *dat.*)

Abās, antis *m.* Trojan leader (1.121); Etruscan warrior (10.427)

abdō, ere, didī, ditus hide, put away, bury

abeō, īre, iī (īvī), itus depart

abiēs, etis *f.* fir, pine

abigō, ere, ēgī, āctus drive (away), force

abluō, ere, uī, ūtus wash (off)

abnuō, ere, uī, ūtus nod, dissent, refuse

abripiō, ere, uī, reptus carry off, snatch away

abrumpō, ere, rūpī, ruptus break off

abscessus, ūs, *m.* departure, absence

abscondō, ere, (di)dī, ditus hide

absēns, entis absent, separated, distant

absistō, ere, stitī cease, stop

abstineō, ēre, uī, tentus refrain, restrain

ābstrūdō, ere, sī, sus hide (away)

absum, esse, āfuī be away, be distant, be lacking

Acamās, antis *m.* Greek leader

accēdō, ere, cessī, cessus approach, reach

accendō, ere, ī, ēnsus inflame, kindle, enrage

accersō, ere, sīvī, sītus summon, invite

accingō, ere, cīnxī, cīnctus gird (on), equip

accumbō, ere, cubuī, cubitus recline (at) (+ *dat.*)

āccumulō (1) heap up; pile up; honor

ācer, cris, cre sharp, fierce, spirited

acervus, ī *m.* heap, pile, mass

Achātēs, ae *m.* faithful comrade of Aeneas

Acherōn, ontis *m.* river of Hades

Achillēs, is (eī, ī) *m.* central character of Homer's *Iliad*, first among the Greek chieftains in the Trojan war

Achīvus, a, um Achaean, Greek

aciēs, ēī *f.* edge; eye(sight); battle line, army

acūtus, a, um sharp, pointed, keen

addenseō, ēre, — thicken, pack densely

addō, ere, didī, ditus add

adeō *adv.* to such an extent, so (much)

adeō, īre, iī (īvī), itus approach, encounter

adfātus, ūs *m.* address, speech

adflīgō, ere, xī, ctus strike down, shatter

adflō (1) breathe upon, blow upon, inspire

adfluō, ere, flūxī, flūxus flow together

adfor, fārī, fātus address, accost, speak to

adgredior, ī, gressus attack, address, approach

adhūc *adv.* to this point, till now

adiciō, ere, adiēcī, adiectus add, confer in addition

adimō, ere, ēmī, ēmptus take away

aditus, ūs *m.* approach, entrance, access

adiūrō (1) call to witness, swear by

adiuvō, āre, adiūvī, adiūtus help

adlābor, ī, lāpsus glide to, approach (+ *dat.*)

adloquor, ī, locūtus address, accost

admīror, ārī, ātus wonder (at), admire

admoneō, ēre, uī, itus advise, warn

admoveō, ēre, mōvī, mōtus move to

adnītor, ī, sus (nixus) lean (against, on), struggle

adnuō, ere, uī, ūtus nod assent, promise

adōrō (1) worship, adore, honor

adquīrō, ere, quīsīvī, sītus acquire, gain

adservō (1) guard, watch

adsiduē *adv.* constantly, ever, continually

adsiduus, a, um constant, unceasing

adsistō, ere, adstitī (or astitī), — stand next to, stand by

adsurgō, ere, surrēxī, surrēctus rise

adultus, a, um grown, adult

advena, ae, m./f. stranger, immigrant, newcomer

adveniō, īre, vēnī, ventus arrive, reach

adversor, ārī, ātus oppose, resist (+ *dat.*)

adversus, a, um opposite, facing

advertō, ere, ī, rsus turn to, heed

advolō (1) fly to

advolvō, ere, ī, volūtus roll

adytum, ī *n.* inner shrine, sanctuary

Aeacidēs, ae *m.* descendant of Aeacus, Achilles, Greek chieftain

aedēs, ium *f.* house, home

aedificō (1) build, construct, erect

aeger, gra, grum sick, weary, wretched

aemulus, a, um emulous, imitative (of), jealous

Aeneadae, (ār)um *m.* descendants (followers) of Aeneas

Aenēius, a, um of Aeneas

aēnum, ī *n.* bronze (vessel, kettle)

aēnus, a, um (of) bronze, brazen

Aeolia, ae *f.* one of the Liparian Islands near Sicily

Aeolidēs, ae *m.* descendant of Aeolus, Misenus

Aeolus, ī *m.* god of the winds

aequaevus, a, um of equal age

aequō (1) (make) equal, match, level, even

aequus, a, um equal, level, propitious, favorable, just, impartial

āēr, āeris, *acc.* āera, *m.* air, mist, fog

aerātus, a, um bronze, brazen

aereus, a, um (of) bronze, brazen

āērius, a, um of the air, airy, heavenly

aes, aeris *n.* bronze (implement), trumpet

aestās, ātis *f.* summer

aestus, ūs *m.* flood, tide, boiling, surge; heat

aetās, ātis *f.* age, time

aeternus, a, um eternal, everlasting

aethēr, eris, *acc.* era *m.* upper air, sky, ether, heaven

aetherius, a, um of the upper air, high in the air, airy, ethereal

aevum, ī *n.* age, life, time, eternity

Āfricus, a, um African, of Africa

Āfricus, ī *m.* (southwest) wind

Agathyrsī, ōrum *m.* people of Scythia in southeastern Europe

Agēnor, oris *m.* king of Phoenicia

ager, grī *m.* field, territory, land

agger, eris *m.* mound, heap, dike, dam, bank

aggerō (1) heap up, pile up, increase

agitātor, ōris *m.* driver, charioteer

agitō (1) drive, harass, toss, agitate

agnōscō, ere, nōvī, nitus recognize

Aiāx, ācis *m.* Greek leader, who in the sack of Troy had taken Priam's daughter, Cassandra, by force from the sanctuary of Minerva

āla, ae *f.* wing, (group of) hunters

ālātus, a, um winged, furnished with wings

Alba, ae *f.* Alba Longa, city of central Italy founded by Ascanius 300 years before Romulus was to found Rome

Albānus, a, um Alban, of Alba Longa in central Italy, mother city of Rome

Alcīdēs, ae *m.* patronymic (meaning "descendant of Alceus") for Hercules, son of Jupiter and Alcmena

āles, itis *m.* (*f.*) bird, fowl

Alētēs, ae *m.* Trojan leader

aliēnus, a, um belonging to another, other's, alien, foreign

aliquī, qua, quod some, any

aliquis (quī), qua, quid (quod) some(one), any(one)

aliquis, quid some(one), any(one)

aliter *adv.* otherwise, differently

alligō (1) bind, hold (to)

almus, a, um nourishing, kind(ly)

alō, ere, uī, (i)tus nourish, rear, cherish

Alpīnus, a, um Alpine, of the Alps

altāria, ium *n.* altar

altē *adv.* on high, loftily

alter, era, erum one (of two), other (of two), second

alternō (1) change, alternate, waver

alternus, a, um alternate, alternating

altum, ī *n.* the deep (sea); heaven

alumnus, ī *m.* nursling, (foster) child

alvus, ī *f.* belly, body

amāns, antis *m.* *(f.)* lover

amārus, a, um bitter, unpleasant

Amāzonis, idis *f.* Amazon, female warrior

ambāgēs, is *f.* winding (passage), mystery, devious tale

ambiō, īre, īvī (iī), itus go around; conciliate

ambō, ae, ō both

ambrosius, a, um ambrosial, immortal

āmēns, entis mad, crazy, frenzied, insane, distracted

amiciō, īre, uī (ixī), ictus infold, wrap

amictus, ūs *m.* wrap, robe

amicus, a, um friendly, kind(ly)

amīcus, ī *m.* friend, lover, comrade

āmittō, ere, mīsī, missus let go, lose

amnis, is *m.* river, stream, torrent

amō (1) love, cherish, like

amplector, ī, plexus embrace, encompass

amplus, a, um large, grand, ample, full, spacious, wide

Amycus, ī *m.* a Trojan

an *interrog.* or, whether

an(ne) *interrog.* whether, or

Anchīsiadēs, ae *m.* Aeneas, descendant of Anchises

ancora, ae *f.* anchor

Androgeōs (ūs), eō (eī) *m.* son of Minos, king of Crete, for whose murder the Athenians were compelled annually to choose by lot seven youths and seven maidens, who were sent to Crete and fed to the Minotaur

anguis, is *m.* *(f.)* snake, serpent

angustus, a, um narrow

anhēlus, a, um panting, gasping

Anna, ae *f.* sister of Dido

annālis, is *m.* story, record, annals

annōsus, a, um aged, old, full of years

annus, ī *m.* year, season

anteferō, ferre, tulī, lātus set before, prefer, choose first

Antēnor, ōris *m.* Trojan leader, fled after the fall of Troy and settled in northern Italy at Patavium, modern Padua

Antheus, eī, *acc.* **ea,** *m.* Trojan leader, comrade of Aeneas

antrum, ī *n.* cave, cavern, grotto

aper, prī *m.* wild boar

aperiō, īre, uī, ertus open, disclose, reveal

apertus, a, um open(ed), clear

apex, icis *m.* peak, summit, head

apis, is *f.* bee

Apollō, inis *m.* god of light, music, and prophecy

appāreō, ēre, uī, itus appear

apparō (1) prepare

appellō, ere, pulī, pulsus drive to (+ *dat.*)

aptō (1) equip, make ready, furnish

aqua, ae *f.* water

Aquilō, ōnis *m.* (north) wind

aquōsus, a, um watery, rainy

Ārae, ārum *f.* the Altars, a ledge of rocks between Sicily and Africa

arboreus, a, um branching, tree-like

arbōs (or), oris *f.* tree; wood

Arcadius, a, um Arcadian, of Arcadia

arcānum, ī *n.* secret, mystery

arcānus, a, um secret, hidden

arceō, ēre, uī keep off, defend, restrain

Arctos (us), ī *f.* the Bear, a northern constellation

arcus, ūs *m.* bow

arduus, a, um lofty, steep, towering

argentum, ī *n.* silver

Argī, ōrum *m.* Argos, city of southern Greece, home of Diomedes, a Greek chieftain against Troy

Argīvus, a, um Argive, Greek

Argolicus, a, um Argive, Greek

arguō, ere, uī, ūtus prove, make clear

āridus, a, um dry

ariēs, etis *m.* (battering) ram

armentum, ī *n.* heard, flock, drove, cattle

armiger, erī *m.* armorbearer, squire

armō (1) arm, equip, furnish

armus, ī *m.* shoulder, flank, side

arō (1) plow, till, furrow

arrigō, ere, rēxī, rēctus erect, raise, prick up, stand on end

ars, artis *f.* art(istry), skill, artifice

artifex, icis *m.* artist, artisan

artus, a, um close (fitting)

artus, ūs *m.* joint, limb, member, body

Ascanius, (i)ī *m.* son of Aeneas

ascendō, ere, ī, ēnsus ascend, mount

Asia, ae *f.* Asia (Minor)

asper, era, erum rough, harsh, fierce

Assaracus, ī *m.* early king of Troy

ast conj. = at

astrum, ī *n.* star, constellation

asy-lum, ī *n.* refuge, sanctuary

Atlās, antis *m.* god who supports heaven on his shoulders, grandfather of Mercury; a mountain of Northwest Africa

Atrīdēs, ae *m.* son of Atreus, (1) Agamemnon, (2) Menelaus; leaders of the Greeks against Troy

ātrium, ī *n.* hall, court, atrium

attollō, ere lift, rear, raise

attonitus, a, um thunderstruck, astounded

auctor, ōris *m.* (*f.*) author, founder, sponsor

audeō, ēre, ausus sum dare, venture

auferō, auferre, abstulī, ablātus carry away, remove, take off

augur, uris *m.* (*f.*) augur, prophet

augurium, (i)ī *n.* augury, prophecy

aula, ae *f.* hall, palace, court

Aulis, idis *f.* port in eastern Greece from which the Greek fleet set sail to attack Troy

aureus, a, um gold(en), of gold

auricomus, a, um golden-haired, golden-leaved

aurīga, ae, *m./f.* charioteer, chariot-driver

auris, is *f.* ear
Aurōra, ae *f.* (goddess of) dawn
Ausonius, a, um Ausonian, Italian
auspex, icis *m.* protector, guide; seer
auspicium, (i)ī *n.* auspices, authority
Auster, trī *m.* (south) wind
ausus, ī *n.* daring deed, daring
autem *adv.* but, however, moreover
Automedōn, ontis *m.* Greek leader
auxilium, (i)ī *n.* aid, help, assistance
avārus, a, um covetous, greedy
āvehō, ere, vēxī, vectus carry, convey (away)
āvellō, ere, āvellī or **āvulsī, āvulsus** tear (off, from)
Avernus, a, um of lake Avernus in Campania, near Cumae, where there was an entrance to the underworld
āvertō, ere, ī, rsus keep off, turn aside, turn away, avert
āvertor, ī, rsus turn away, avert
avidus, a, um eager, greedy, ardent
avis, is *f.* bird, fowl
āvius, a, um pathless, remote
avus, ī *m.* grandfather; ancestor
axis, is *m.* axle, axis; height

B

bacchor, ārī, ātus rush wildly, rave, rage
Bacchus, ī *m.* (god of) wine
balteus, ī, *m.* baldric
barba, ae *f.* beard, whiskers
barbaricus, a, um barbaric, foreign

Barcaeī, ōrum *m.* tribe of North Africa
beātus, a, um happy, blessed, fortunate
bellātrīx, īcis *f.* warrior
bellō (1) wage war, battle
bene *adv.* well, rightly, securely, fully
benignus, a, um kind(ly), benign
bibō, ere, ī drink (of, in)
bidēns, entis *f.* with two teeth, two-year-old (sheep)
biformis, e two-formed, double-shaped
bīgae, ārum *f.* two-horse chariot
biiugus, a, um yoked two together; *m.pl.* as a substantive, chariot (i.e., **equi biiugi = currus**)
bīnī, ae, a two (each), by twos
bipennis, is *f.* double ax
birēmis, is *f.* bireme, galley (with two banks of oars)
bis twice
bonus, a, um good, kind(ly), useful
Boreās, ae *m.* (north) wind
bracchium, (i)ī *n.* (fore)arm
brattea, ae *f.* thin sheet, plate, foil
brevis, e short, shallow
breviter *adv.* shortly, briefly, concisely
brūma, ae *f.* midwinter
brūmālis, e wintry, of winter
bulla, ae, *f.* stud, knob
Byrsa, ae *f.* citadel of Carthage

C

cadō, ere, cecidī, cāsus fall, fail, sink, die
cadus, ī *m.* jar, urn

caecus, a, um blind, dark, hidden

caedēs, is *f.* slaughter, murder, massacre

caedō, ere, cecīdī, caesus cut (down), kill

caelestēs, ium (um) *m. (f.)* divinities, gods

caelestis, e divine, heavenly

caelō (1) engrave, emboss

Caesar, aris *m.* (1) Julius Caesar; (2) Augustus Caesar

Caīcus, ī *m.* comrade of Aeneas

Caiēta, ae *f.* Italian coast city near Rome (modern Gaeta in Italy)

calcar, āris *n.* spur, goad

caleō, ēre, uī be hot, burn

calidus, a, um hot

callis, is *m.* path, track

calor, ōris *m.* heat, warmth, glow

candēns, entis shining, white, gleaming

canis, is *m. (f.)* dog, hound

canō, ere, cecinī, cantus sing (of), chant, prophesy, proclaim

canōrus, a, um tuneful, musical

cantus, ūs *m.* song, music, chant, tune

cānus, a, um white, gray, hoary

capessō, ere, īvī, ītus (under)take, perform, (try to) seize, reach

capra, ae *f.* she-goat

captīvus, a, um captive, captured

capulus, ī *m.* hilt, handle, head

Capys, yos, *acc.* yn *m.* comrade of Aeneas

carbasus, ī *f.* linen; sail

carcer, eris *m.* prison, enclosure

cardō, inis *m.* hinge, pivot, socket

careō, ēre, uī, itus be free from, lack (+ *abl.*)

carīna, ae *f.* keel; ship, boat

carmen, inis *n.* song, verse, oracle

carpō, ere, psī, ptus pluck, consume, waste

carus, a, um dear, beloved, fond

Cassandra, ae *f.* Trojan prophetess, punished by Apollo and so never believed

castīgō (1) reprove, chastise, punish

castra, ōrum *n.* camp, encampment

cāsus, ūs *m.* chance, (mis)fortune

caterva, ae *f.* band, troop, crowd

Caucasus, ī *m.* rugged mountain range between Europe and Asia

causa, ae *f.* cause, reason, occasion, case (at law)

cautēs, is *f.* rock, cliff, crag

caverna, ae *f.* hollow, cavity, cave

cavō (1) hollow out

cavus, a, um hollow, vaulted

Cecropidēs, ae *m.* descendant of Cecrops, Athenian; *nom. pl.* Cecropidae

cēdō, ere, cessī, cessus yield, depart

celebrō (1) celebrate, observe solemnly

celer, eris, ere swift, speedy, quick

celerō (1) hasten, hurry, speed

cella, ae *f.* cell, storeroom

cēlō (1) hide, conceal

celsus, a, um high, lofty, towering

centum hundred

Cereālis, e of Ceres, (goddess of) grain

Cerēs, eris *f.* (goddess of) grain

cernō, ere, crēvī, cretus (or rarely, certus) see, discern, perceive

certāmen, inis *n.* contest, rivalry, strife

certē *adv.* certainly, surely

certō (1) strive, fight, vie, contend

certus, a, um fixed, sure, certain, reliable

cerva, ae *f.* deer, doe

cervīx, īcis *f.* neck

cervus, ī *m.* stag, deer

cessō (1) cease, pause, delay, hesitate

cēterus, a, um rest, remaining, other

ceu (just) as, as if

Chalcidicus, a, um Chalcidian, of Chalcis, a city of Euboea, from which Cumae was founded

chlamys, ydis *f.* cloak, mantle, cape

chorus, ī *m.* chorus, dance, band

cieō, ēre, cīvī, citus (a)rouse, stir (up)

cingō, ere, cīnxī, cīnctus encircle, surround, gird(le)

cingulum, ī *n.* belt, girdle; cingula, ōrum, *n. pl.* swordbelt

cinis, eris *m.* ashes (of the dead), embers

circā *adv.* around, about

circumdō, dāre, dedī, datus surround, place around (+ *dat.*)

circumspiciō, ere, circumspexī, circumspectus look around (for), get sight of

circumstō, āre, stetī surround, stand around

circumveniō, īre, vēnī, ventus encircle

circumvolō (1) fly around, fly about

Cithaerōn, ōnis *m.* Greek mountain near Thebes, on which the rites of Bacchus were celebrated

cithara, ae *f.* lyre, harp

citō *adv.* quickly, soon

citus, a, um quick, swift

cīvis, is *m.* (*f.*) citizen, compatriot

clam *adv.* secretly

clāmō (1) shriek, cry (out), call (on)

clārus, a, um clear, bright, illustrious

claudō, ere, sī, sus (en)close, shut (in)

claustra, ōrum *n.* barrier, bar, bolt

claustrum, ī *n.* bolt, fastening, barrier

clipeus, ī *m.* (or clipeum, ī, *n.*) round shield, buckler

Cloanthus, ī *m.* Trojan leader

Clonus, ī, *m.* Clonus, name of a craftsman (mentioned only in the *Aeneid*)

Cnōs(s)ius, a, um Cnossian, of Cnossos, a city in Crete

Cōcy-tus, ī *m.* river of Hades

coeō, īre, coiī (or coīvī), coitus go together, come together

coepī, isse, ptus begin, commence

coeptum, ī *n.* undertaking, beginning

coetus, ūs *m.* company, band, flock

Coeus, ī *m.* one of the Titans, a giant, son of Earth

cognōmen, inis *n.* (sur)name, cognomen, nickname

cognōscō, ere, nōvī, nitus learn; know

cōgō, ere, coēgī, coāctus bring together, force, muster, compel

colligō, ere, lēgī, lēctus collect, gather

collis, is *m.* hill

collum, ī *n.* neck
colō, ere, uī, cultus cultivate,
  dwell (in), cherish, honor
colōnus, ī *m.* colonist, settler
color, ōris *m.* color, hue, tint
coluber, brī *m.* snake, serpent
columba, ae *f.* dove, a bird sacred
  to Venus
columna, ae *f.* column, pillar
cōma, ae *f.* hair, locks, tresses
comitātus, ūs *m.* retinue, train,
  company
comitō (1) accompany, attend,
  escort, follow
comitor, ārī, ātus accompany,
  attend, escort, follow
commendō (1) entrust, commit
comminus *adv.* hand to-hand, at
  close quarters
commisceō, ēre, uī, mixtus mix,
  mingle
commissum, ī *n.* fault, crime
committō, ere, mīsī, missus
  commit
commoveō, ēre, mōvī, mōtus
  move, stir, shake, agitate
commūnis, e (in) common, joint,
  mutual
cōmō, ere, mpsī, mptus arrange
  (properly)
compāgēs, is *f.* joint, seam,
  fastening
compellō (1) address, accost,
  speak to
complector, ī, plexus embrace,
  enfold
compleō, ēre, ēvī, ētus fill,
  complete
compōnō, ere, posuī, pos(i)tus
  compose, construct, calm, quiet
compre(he)ndō, ere, ī, ēnsus
  grasp

cōnātus, ūs, *m.* attempt, effort
concēdō, ere, cessī, cessus yield,
  come
concha, ae *f.* (sea) shell, conch
concidō, ere, ī fall (in a heap)
conciliō (1) win over, unite
conciō (or concieō), īre (or ēre),
  concīvī, concitus bring
  together; move violently, stir
  up, rouse
conclāmō (1) cry, shout, exclaim
conclūdō, ere, sī, sus (en)close
concrescō, ere, concrēvī,
  concrētus stiffen, congeal
concrētus, a, um grown together,
  hardened, matted
concurrō, ere, (cu)currī, cursus
  run together, join battle, fight
  with (+ *dat.*)
concursus, ūs *m.* throng, crowd
concutiō, ere, cussī, cussus shake,
  shatter, agitate
condēnsus, a, um crowded, thick,
  dense
condō, ere, didī, ditus found,
  establish; hide, bury
cōnfīdō, ere, sus sum trust (in)
  (+ *dat.*)
cōnfīō, fierī, fectus be done, be
  finished
cōnfundō, ere, fūdī, fūsus
  confuse
congerō, ere, gessī, gestus heap up
congredior, ī, gressus meet, fight
  with (+ *dat.*)
coniciō, ere, iēcī, iectus hurl,
  shoot
coniugium, (i)ī *n.* wedlock;
  husband, wife
coniungō, ere, iūnxī, iūnctus join
conlābor, ī, lāpsus fall in a heap,
  faint, collapse

cōnor, ārī, ātus attempt, try, endeavor

cōnscendō, ere, ī, ēnsus mount, climb, ascend, embark

cōnscius, a, um conscious; confederate

cōnsīdō, ere, sēdī, sessus sit (down), settle

cōnsilium, (i)ī n. plan, advice

cōnsistō, ere, stitī, stitus stand (fast), rest, stop, settle

cōnspectus, ūs m. sight, (inter) view

cōnspiciō, ere, spexī, spectus see, look at, behold

cōnsternō, ere, strāvī, strātus lay low, strew

cōnstituō, ere, uī, ūtus establish, resolve

cōnstō, āre, stitī, status stand firm, halt

cōnsulō, ere, uī, ltus consult, consider

cōnsultum, ī n. resolve, decree, oracle

cōnsūmō, ere, mpsī, mptus consume, waste

consurgō, ere, consurrexī, consurrectus rise, stand up

contendō, ere, ī, ntus strive, contend; bend, draw tight; shoot, aim

conticēscō, ere, ticuī become silent, hush

contiguus, a, um next to, near, close; able to be touched

contingō, ere, tigī, tāctus touch, befall

continuō adv. immediately, at once

contorqueō, ēre, rsī, rtus hurl, twirl

contra opposite, facing, against, in reply (+ acc.); adv. opposite, facing, in reply

contrahō, ere, contraxī, contractus collect, draw together

contrārius, a, um opposite, opposing

contundō, ere, tudī, tū(n)sus bruise, crush

cōnūbium, (i)ī n. right of intermarriage, marriage

convallis, is f. valley, vale, dale

convectō (1) convey, carry along

convellō, ere, ī, vulsus tear (off, up), shatter

conveniō, īre, vēnī, ventus come together, assemble

convertō, ere, ī, rsus turn (around), reverse

convexum, ī n. hollow, vault, dome, sky

convīvium, (i)ī n. feast, banquet

convolvō, ere, ī, volūtus roll, coil

coōrior, īrī, ortus (a)rise

cōpia, ae f. abundance, plenty, forces

cor, cordis n. heart, spirit, feelings

cōram adv. before the face, face to face, openly

corneus, a, um of horn

cornū, ūs n. horn, tip, end

corōna, ae f. wreath, garland, crown

corripiō, ere, uī, reptus seize, snatch up

corrumpō, ere, rūpī, ruptus spoil, ruin

corruō, ere, corruī, — rush down, fall

coruscō (1) brandish, shake

coruscus, a, um waving, quivering, flashing

costa, ae *f.* rib, side

cot(h)urnus, ī *m.* high boot, buskin

crāstinus, a, um tomorrow's, of tomorrow

crātēr, ēris *m.* mixing bowl

crēber, bra, brum frequent, repeated, crowded

crēdō, ere, didī, ditus believe, (en)trust (+ *dat.*)

crepitō (1) rattle, rustle, crash

crepitus, ūs, *m.* (the sound of) rattling, clashing

crescō, ere, crēvī, crētus spring up, grow, increase

Crēsius, a, um of Crete, Cretan

Crētes, ium *m.* Cretans, inhabitants of Crete

crētus, a, um grown, sprung

Creūsa, ae *f.* wife of Aeneas, lost during the sack of Troy

crīnis, is *m.* hair, locks, tresses

crispō, āre, ātus brandish, wave

cristātus, a, um plumed, crested

croceus, a, um yellow, saffron, ruddy

crūdēlis, e, cruel, bloody, bitter

cruentus, a, um bloody, cruel

cruor, ōris *m.* blood, gore

cubīle, is *n.* couch, bed

cubitum, ī *n.* elbow, arm

culmen, inis *n.* roof, peak, summit, top

culpa, ae *f.* fault, blame, weakness, sin, guilt

Cūmae, ārum *f.* city on the bay of Naples, founded by settlers from Chalcis, a city of Euboea

Cūmaeus, a, um of Cumae, a city near Naples

cumulō (1) heap (up), pile (high)

cumulus, ī *m.* heap, mass, pile

cūnctor, ārī, ātus delay, cling, linger, hesitate

cuneus, ī *m.* wedge; block (of seats)

cupīdō, inis *f.* love, desire, longing

cupiō, ere, īvī (iī), ītus desire, wish

cūr why? for what reason?

cūrō (1) care (for, to), heed, regard

currō, ere, cucurrī, cursus run

currus, ūs *m.* chariot, car

curvus, a, um curved, winding, bent

cuspis, pidis *f.* point, spear, lance

custōs, ōdis *m.* (*f.*) guard(ian), keeper

Cyclōpius, a, um Cyclopean, of the Cyclopes, huge one-eyed giants of Sicily

Cyllēnius, (i)ī *m.* the Cyllenean, of Mt. Cyllene in Arcadia, birthplace of Mercury; *adj.*, Cyllēnius, a, um Cyllenean, of Mt. Cyllene in Arcadia, birthplace of Mercury

Cy-mothoē, ēs *f.* a sea nymph

Cynthus, ī *m.* mountain in Delos, birthplace of Apollo and Diana

Cytherēa, ae *f.* Venus, goddess of Cythera, a Greek island where Venus was born from the foam of the sea

D

Daedalus, ī *m.* famous Greek artisan, father of Icarus and builder of the labyrinth for King Minos in Crete; inventor of the first wings by means of which he and Icarus escaped from Crete

damnō (1) condemn, sentence, doom, devote

daps, dapis *f.* feast, banquet

Dardan(i)us, (i)ī *m.* Trojan, Dardanian

Dardan(i)us, a, um Trojan, Dardanian

Dardania, ae *f.* Troy, citadel of Dardanus

Dardanidēs, ae *m.* Dardanian, Trojan

Dardanis, idis *f.* Trojan woman

Dardanius, a, um Dardanian, Trojan

Dardanus, ī *m.* early king of Troy

Daunus, ī, *m.* Turnus' father

dēbellō (1) exhaust through war, crush

dēbeō, ēre, uī, itus owe, be due, be destined

dēbitus, a, um due, owed, destined

dēcēdō, ere, cessī, cessus depart

dēcerpō, ere, psī, ptus pluck (off)

decet, ēre, decuit, — (only 3d pers.) be fitting, be suitable, be proper

dēcipiō, ere, cēpī, ceptus deceive

dēclīnō (1) turn aside, bend down, droop

dēcurrō, ere, (cu)currī, cursus run (down), hasten

decus, oris *n.* ornament, glory, dignity

dēdūcō, ere, dūxī, ductus lead forth, lead down, launch

dēfendō, ere, ī, fēnsus ward off, protect

dēferō, ferre, tulī, lātus carry (down), report

dēfessus, a, um weary, tired, worn

dēficiō, ere, fēcī, fectus fail, faint, be lacking

dēfīgō, ere, fīxī, fīxus fix (down), fasten

dēfluō, ere, flūxī, flūxus flow down

dēformō (1) disfigure, mar, spoil

dēfungor, ī, fūnctus perform, finish (+ *abl.*)

dēgener, eris degenerate, base, ignoble

dehinc *adv.* then, thereupon

dehīscō, ere, hīvī yawn, gape, open (up)

dēiciō, ere, iēcī, iectus throw (down), cast down, dislodge

deinde *adv.* thence, next, thereupon

Dēiopēa, ae *f.* a nymph

Dēiphobē, ēs *f.* prophetess and priestess of Apollo and Hecate

dēligō, ere, lēgī, lēctus choose, select

Dēlius, a, um Delian, of Delos, birthplace of Apollo

Dēlos, ī *f.* island of the Aegean, birthplace of Apollo

dēlūbrum, ī *n.* shrine, temple, sanctuary

dēmēns, entis crazy, mad, distracted

dēmittō, ere, mīsī, missus send down, let down, drop, lower, derive

dēmō, ere, mpsī, mptus remove, take away

dēmum *adv.* at length, finally

dēnī, ae, a ten (each), by tens

dēnique *adv.* finally, at last (esp. at the end of a list), in short, in a word

dēns, dentis *m.* tooth; fluke
(technical term for triangular
point of an anchor)

dēnsus, a, um thick, crowded,
dense

dēpascor, ī, pāstus feed on,
devour

dēprecor (1) plead against, seek to
avoid

dērigō (dīrigō), ere, rēxī, rēctus
direct, guide

dēripiō, ere, dēripuī, dēreptus
snatch away, pull

dēsaeviō, īre, īvī (iī), ītus rage
(furiously)

dēscendō, ere, ī, ēnsus descend

dēscēnsus, ūs *m.* descent

dēscrībō, ere, psī, ptus mark out,
map

dēserō, ere, uī, rtus desert,
forsake

dēsiliō, īre, dēsiluī, — jump down

dēsinō, ere, sīvī (iī), situs cease,
desist (+ *dat.*)

dēsistō, ere, stitī, stitus cease
(from), desist

dēspectō (1) look down (on)

dēspiciō, ere, spexī, spectus look
down on, scorn, despise,
disdain

dēstruō, ere, strūxī, strūctus
destroy

dēsuētus, a, um unaccustomed,
unused

dēsum, esse, fuī be absent, lack

dēsuper *adv.* from above

dētineō, ēre, uī, tentus detain,
hold back

dētorqueō, ēre, rsī, rtus turn
(away)

dētrūdō, ere, sī, sus push off,
dislodge

dēveniō, īre, vēnī, ventus come
(down), arrive (at)

dēvolō (1) fly down

dī(ve)s, dī(vi)tis rich, wealthy
(+ *gen.*)

Diāna, ae *f.* goddess of the hunt
and of the mountains

diciō, ōnis *f.* power, rule, sway

dicō (1) consecrate, assign,
proclaim

Dictaeus, a, um of Dicte, a
mountain in Crete; Cretan

difficilis, e difficult, hard,
painful

diffugiō, ere, fūgī flee apart,
scatter

diffundō, ere, fūdī, fūsus scatter,
spread

dignor, ārī, ātus deem worthy,
deign (+ *abl.*)

dignus, a, um worthy, suitable,
fit(ting)

dīgredior, ī, gressus (de)part,
separate

dīlābor, ī, lāpsus glide away,
depart

dīligō, ere, lēxī, lēctus love,
cherish

dīmoveō, ēre, ōvī, ōtus divide,
remove

dīrigō, ere, rēxi, rēctus direct,
guide

dīripiō, ere, uī, reptus plunder,
ravage, tear from

dīrus, a, um dire, awful, dreadful

dis(s)iciō, ere, iēcī, iectus scatter,
disperse

Dīs, Dītis *m.* Pluto, god of Hades

discernō, ere, ere, crēvī, crētus
divide, separate; dissolve (a
dispute)

discolor, ōris of different color(s)

discrepō, āre, discrepuī (or **discrepāvī**), — disagree, be different

discrīmen, inis *n.* crisis, danger

discussus, ūs *m.* departure, separation

disiciō, ere, iēcī, iectus scatter, disperse

disiungō, ere, iūnxī, iūnctus separate, disconnect

dispellō, ere, pulī, pulsus drive apart, disperse, scatter

dissultō (1) leap apart, burst asunder

dissimulō (1) conceal, dissimulate, pretend otherwise, hide, disguise

distendō, ere, ī, ntus distend, stretch

diū *adv.* a long time, long

dīvellō, ere, ī (or vulsī), vulsus tear apart

dīversus, a, um scattered, various, separated, different

dīvidō, ere, vīsī, vīsus divide, separate, distribute

dīvīnus, a, um divine, celestial, holy

doceō, ēre, uī, ctus teach (about), tell, inform

doleō, ēre, uī, itus suffer, grieve (at), be angry (at, with), resent

Dolopes, um *m.* Greeks of Thessaly

dolor, ōris *m.* grief, pain, passion, anger

dolus, ī *m.* deceit, wiles, trick, fraud, scheme

dominor, ārī, ātus rule (over) (+ *dat.*)

dominus, ī *m.* master, lord, ruler

domō, āre, uī, itus tame, subdue

dōnec until, while, as long as

Dōricus, a, um Doric, Spartan, Greek

dorsum, ī *n.* back, ridge, reef

dōtālis, e of a dowry, as a dowry

dracō, ōnis *m.* dragon, serpent

Dryopes, um *m.* a people of northern Greece

dubius, a, um doubtful, wavering

ductor, ōris *m.* leader, chieftain, guide

dulcis, e sweet, dear, fond

duo, ae, o two

duplex, icis double, both

duplicātus, a, um doubled (from **duplicō** [1] double up, fold over)

dūrō (1) harden, endure

dūrus, a, um hard(y), harsh, rough, stern

E

eburnus, a, um (of) ivory

ecce see! look! behold!

edāx, ācis devouring, eating, consuming

edō, ere (ēsse), ēdī, ēsus eat, consume

ēdūcō, ere, dūxī, ductus lead out, raise

efferō, ferre, extulī, ēlātus carry (out), raise

efficiō, ere, fēcī, fectus make, form

effodiō, ere, fōdī, fossus dig out, excavate

effor, ārī, ātus speak (out), say

effugiō, ere, fūgī flee (from), escape

effundō, ere, fūdī, fūsus pour out

egēns, entis needy, in want,
   destitute

egēnus, a, um needy, poor

egeō, ēre, uī need, lack, require (+
   abl.)

ēgredior, ī, gressus go out,
   disembark

ēgregius, a, um extraordinary,
   distinguished

ei alas! ah!

ēiciō, ere, iēcī, iectus cast out,
   eject

ēlābor, ī, lāpsus slip out, escape

elephantus, ī *m.* elephant, ivory

Elissa, ae *f.* Dido

ēmicō, āre, uī, ātus flash forth,
   dart out

ēminus adv. at a distance

ēmittō, ere, mīsī, missus send
   forth, shoot, hurl

emō, ere, ēmī, emptus buy,
   purchase

ēmoveō, ēre, mōvī, mōtus move
   from

ēn see! look! behold!

Enceladus, ī *m.* one of the Titans, a
   giant, son of Earth

enim *adv.* for, indeed, truly

ēniteō, ēre, uī shine forth, gleam,
   glitter

ēnō (1) swim out, fly forth, float

ēnsis, is *m.* sword, knife

ēnumerō (1) recount, enumerate

Ēous, a, um of the dawn, eastern

Epēos, ī *m.* Greek leader, maker of
   the wooden horse

epulae, ārum *f.* banquet, feast

epulor, ārī, ātus feast, banquet
   (+ *abl.*)

eques, itis *m.* cavalryman, knight,
   man of equestrian rank

equidem *adv.* indeed, truly, surely

Erebus, ī *m.* underworld, Hades

ergō *adv.* therefore, then,
   consequently

error, ōris *m.* error, wandering,
   deceit, trick

ērubēscō, ere, ērubuī reverence,
   blush (before)

ēruō, ere, uī, utus overthrow, tear
   up

etiam *adv.* also, even, besides, yet,
   still

Etruscus, a, um Etruscan, of or
   having to do with Etruria
   (a region in Italy north of
   Latium)

Euboïcus, a, um Euboean, of
   Euboea, a large island off the
   eastern coast of Greece from
   which Cumae was settled

Eurōpa, ae *f.* Europe

Eurōtās, ae *m.* river of Sparta,
   center of the worship of Diana

Eurus, ī *m.* (east) wind

Eurytidēs, is, *m.* patronymic,
   meaning "son of Eurytus"

ēvādō, ere, sī, sus go forth (from),
   escape, pass over, traverse

ēvānēscō, ere, nuī vanish,
   disappear

ēvehō, ere, vēxī, vectus bear
   (aloft)

ēveniō, īre, vēnī, ventus come out,
   happen

ēventus, ūs *m.* outcome, result,
   event

ēvertō, ere, ī, rsus overturn,
   destroy

ēvincō, ere, vīcī, victus overcome,
   surmount

ēvocō (1) call out, summon

ex(s)pectō (1) (a)wait, expect, hope
   (for), linger

exanimis, e lifeless; also,
exanimus, a, um breathless,
lifeless

exaudiō, īre, īvī (iī), ītus hear,
hearken

excēdō, ere, cessī, cessus
withdraw, depart

excidium, (i)ī n. destruction,
overthrow

excīdō, ere, ī, sus cut out, destroy;
fall from, perish

exciō, īre, īvī, itus arouse, excite,
stir

excipiō, ere, cēpī, ceptus catch,
receive, take (up)

exclāmō (1) cry (out), shout,
exclaim

excubiae, ārum f. watch(fire),
sentinel

excūdō, ere, ī, sus hammer out,
fashion

excutiō, ere, cussī, cussus cast
out, shake off

exeō, īre, iī (īvī), itus go forth,
depart

exerceō, ēre, uī, itus drive,
exercise, perform, be busy,
train

exhālō (1) breathe out, exhale

exhauriō, īre, hausī, haustus
drain, exhaust; bear

exigō, ere, ēgī, āctus drive out,
complete, pass; determine,
discover

exiguus, a, um small, scanty,
petty

exim, exin(de) adv. from there,
next, thereupon

eximō, ere, ēmī, ēmptus take
away, remove

exitiālis, e fatal, destructive,
deadly

exitium, iī, n. destruction

exitus, ūs m. exit, issue, end

exordium, (i)ī n. beginning,
commencement

exorior, īrī, ortus (a)rise, spring
up

exōsus, a, um hating, detesting

expediō, īre, īvī (iī), ītus bring
out, prepare

expendō, ere, ī, pēnsus expiate,
pay (for)

experior, īrī, pertus try,
experience

expleō, ēre, ēvī, ētus fill (out),
fulfil

explōrō (1) explore, search (out)

exposcō, ere, poposcī demand,
entreat

exprōmō, ere, mpsī, mptus
express, bring forth

exquīrō, ere, quīsīvī, quīsītus
seek (out)

exsanguis, e bloodless, lifeless,
pale

exscindō, ere, scidī, scissus
destroy, root out

exsequor, ī, secutus follow out,
perform

exserō, ere, uī, rtus thrust out,
expose

exsilium, (i)ī n. exile, place of exile

exsolvō, ere, ī, solūtus loose(n),
free

exspectō (1) await (eagerly), expect

exspīrō (1) breathe out, exhale

exsting(u)ō, ere, īnxī, īnctus
extinguish, blot out, destroy,
ruin

exstruō, ere, strūxī, strūctus
build (up), rear

exsultō (1) leap forth, dance,
surge, exult

exsuperō (1) surmount, mount
(high)

exta, ōrum *n.* entrails, vitals

extemplō *adv.* immediately, at
once, suddenly

extendō, ere, extendī, extensus (or
extentus) stretch out, extend,
increase

externus, a, um outer, foreign

exterreō, ēre, uī, itus terrify,
frighten

exterus, a, um outside, foreign

extrēma, ōrum *n.* end, death,
funeral

extrēmus, a, um final, last,
furthest

exuō, ere, uī, ūtus bare, doff,
discard

exūrō, ere, ussī, ustus burn (up)

exuviae, ārum *f.* spoils, booty,
relics, mementos; slough

F

fabricātor, ōris *m.* constructor,
maker

fabricō (1) fashion, make

facessō, ere, (īv)ī, ītus do, make,
fulfill

faciēs, ēī *f.* appearance, face,
aspect

facilis, e easy, favorable, ready

factum, ī *n.* deed, act, exploit

fallō, ere, fefellī, falsus deceive,
cheat, mock, beguile, escape
the notice (of)

falsus, a, um false, deceitful, mock

famēs, is *f.* hunger

famula, ae *f.* female household
slave

far, farris *n.* spelt, a kind of grain

fās *n. indecl.* right, justice, divine
will

fastīgium, (i)ī *n.* top, roof, summit

fātālis, e fatal, deadly, fated,
fateful

fateor, ērī, fassus confess, agree

fatīgō (1) weary, tire (out), harass

fatīscō, ere split, open, gape

faucēs, ium *f.* jaws, throat; pass,
entrance

faux, faucis *f.* jaws, throat; gulf

fax, facis *f.* firebrand, torch

fēlix, īcis happy, fortunate, blessed

fēmina, ae *f.* woman, female

fēmineus, a, um feminine, of
women

femur, oris (or **inis**), *n.* thigh

fenestra, ae *f.* window, opening,
breach

fera, ae *f.* wild beast

ferīna, ae *f.* game, venison

feriō, īre strike, smite, beat, kill

ferōx, ōcis fierce, spirited, fiery,
wild, savage

ferus, a, um wild, savage, fierce,
cruel

ferus, ī *m.* beast, monster, horse

ferv(e)ō, ēre, (ferbu)ī glow, boil;
be busy

fervidus, a, um burning, fiery,
hot, impetuous, violent

fēstīnō (1) hasten, hurry, speed

fēstus, a, um festal, festival,
pertaining to a holiday

fētus, a, um teeming, pregnant,
filled

fētus, ūs *m.* offspring, brood,
shoot, swarm

fībula, ae *f.* brooch, buckle, clasp

fictum, ī *n.* falsehood, fiction

fidēs, ēī *f.* faith, belief,
trust(worthiness), honor,
pledge **Fidēs, eī** *f.* Faith,
Honor (personified)

fidēs, ium *f.* lyre, strings, cords; chords

fīdūcia, ae, *f.* confidence, trust

fīdus, a, um faithful, trustworthy, safe

fīgō, ere, fīxī, fīxus fix, fasten, pierce

fīlius, (i)ī *m.* son

fīlum, ī *n.* thread, cord, clue

fingō, ere, fīnxī, fictus fashion, pretend, imagine, form, mold, shape

fīō, fierī, factus become, be made, arise

firmus, a, um firm, strong, solid

fissilis, e easily split, cleavable

flāmen, inis *n.* breeze, blast, wind

flammō (1) inflame, burn, fire, kindle

flātus, ūs *m.* blast, wind, blowing

flāvus, a, um yellow, tawny, blond

flectō, ere, flexī, flexus bend, move, turn, guide

fleō, ēre, ēvī, ētus weep, lament, mourn

flētus, ūs *m.* weeping, tears, tearful appeal, lament

flōreō, ēre, uī bloom, flourish, blossom

flōreus, a, um flowery

flōs, ōris *m.* flower, blossom, bloom

fluentum, ī *n.* stream, flood

flūmen, inis *n.* river, stream, flood

fluō, ere, flūxī, flūxus flow, stream, ebb

fodiō, ere, fōdī, fossus dig, pierce, spur

foedō (1) befoul, defile, pollute; mar, mangle, disfigure

foedus, a, um foul, loathsome, filthy

foedus, eris *n.* treaty, agreement, pact

folium, (i)ī *n.* leaf, foliage

fōmes, itis *m.* tinder, fuel, shaving

fōns, fontis *m.* fountain, source

foris, is *f.* door, gate, entrance

forma, ae *f.* form, beauty, shape

formīca, ae *f.* ant

fors(it)an *adv.* perhaps, possibly, perchance

fortis, e strong, brave, valiant

fortūnātus, a, um fortunate, blessed

foveō, ēre, fōvī, fōtus cherish, fondle

fraglāns, antis fragrant, sweet-smelling

fragor, ōris *m.* crash, uproar

frangō, ere, frēgī, frāctus break, crush, shatter

frāter, tris *m.* brother

frāternus, a, um fraternal, of a brother

fraudō (1) defraud, deprive, cheat

fraus, fraudis *f.* deceit, guile, fraud

fraxineus, a, um ashen, of ash(wood)

fremō, ere, uī, itus murmur, lament, groan, roar, rage

frēnō (1) curb, check, restrain

frēnum, ī *n.* rein, curb, check, bridle

frequens, entis (in pl.) in great numbers

frētus, a, um relying on (+ *abl.*)

frīgidus, a, um cold, chill, frigid

frigus, oris *n.* cold, frost, chill

frondēns, entis leafy, fronded

frondēscō, ere leaf, sprout

frondeus, a, um leafy

frōns, frondis *f.* leaf, foliage, frond

frōns, frontis *f.* front, forehead, brow

frūmentum, ī *n.* grain

frūstrā *adv.* in vain, uselessly, ineffectually

frustum, ī *n.* piece, part

frūx, frūgis *f.* fruit, grain

fūcus, ī *n.* drone

fugō (1) put to flight, rout

fulciō, īre, lsī, ltus support, prop

fulg(e)ō, ēre (or ere), lsī shine, flash, gleam

fulmen, inis *n.* thunderbolt, lightning

fulvus, a, um tawny, yellow, blond

fundāmentum, ī *n.* foundation, base

fundō (1) found, establish, make fast

fungor, ī, fūnctus perform, fulfil (+ *abl.*)

fūnis, is *m.* rope, cable

fūnus, eris *n.* funeral, death, disaster

furiae, ārum *f.* furies, madness, frenzy

furibundus, a, um wild, frenzied

furor, ōris *m.* madness, frenzy, fury **Furor, ōris** *m.* Madness, Rage, Frenzy (personified)

fūrtim *adv.* stealthily, furtively, secretly

fūrtīvus, a, um secret, stolen

fūrtum, ī *n.* stealth, theft, trick, fraud

futūrum, ī *n.* the future, what is to be

G

Gaetūlus, a, um of the Gaetuli, a tribe of North Africa

galea, ae *f.* helmet

Gallus, a, um Gallic, Gaul

Ganymēdēs, is *m.* son of Laōmedon, king of Troy; carried off by Jupiter's eagle and made cupbearer to the gods

Garamantis, idis of the Garamantes, an African tribe

gaudeō, ēre, gāvisus sum (semideponent) rejoice, exult

gaudium, (i)ī *n.* joy, rejoicing

gaza, ae *f.* wealth, treasure

gelidus, a, um cold, chilly, icy

gemitus, ūs *m.* groan(ing), wail(ing), lament

gemō, ere, uī, itus groan (for), lament

gena, ae *f.* cheek

genetrīx, trīcis *f.* mother

genū, ūs *n.* knee

germāna, ae *f.* sister

germānus, ī *m.* brother

germānus, a, um sibling

gerō, ere, gessī, gestus bear, carry (on), wage

gestō (1) bear, wear, carry

gignō, ere, genuī, genitus bear, produce, beget

glaciēs, ēī *f.* ice

Glaucus, ī *m.* sea-god possessing prophetic powers, father of Deiphobe, the Cumaean Sibyl

glomerō (1) roll together, gather, collect

glōria, ae *f.* renown, glory, fame, pride

gradior, ī, gressus walk, stride, march, go, proceed

gradus, ūs *m.* step, gait, pace, stride
Graius, a, um Greek
grāmen, inis *n.* grass, herb, plant
grandaevus, a, um aged, old
grandis, e large, great, tall, huge
grandō, inis *f.* hail(storm, stones)
grātēs, ium *f.* thanks, requital, reward
grātus, a, um welcome, pleasing, grateful
gravidus, a, um heavy, burdened, pregnant, filled, teeming
gravis, e heavy, weighty, serious; venerable; pregnant
graviter *adv.* heavily, violently, greatly
gremium, (i)ī *n.* bosom, lap, embrace
gressus, ūs *m.* step, walk, course, gait
grex, gregis *m.* herd, flock
Gry-nēus, a, um of Grynium, a town in Asia Minor, with an oracle of Apollo
gurges, itis *m.* whirlpool, abyss, gulf
gustō (1) taste, eat
Gyās, ae, *acc.* **ān** *m.* a Trojan

H

habēna, ae *f.* rein, curb, check
habilis, e easily handled, handy
habitus, ūs *m.* appearance, garb
hāc . . . tenus = hāctenus thus far, up until now
hāc *adv.* here, there
haereō, ēre, haesī, haesus stick (to), cling (to) (+ *dat.*), halt
Halaesus, ī, *m.* Halaesus, an Italian warrior and enemy of the Trojans

hālitus, ūs *m.* breath, exhalation
hālō (1) breathe (forth), be fragrant
Hammōn, ōnis *m.* Hammon (or Ammon), god of North Africa, famous for his oracle and identified by the Romans with Jupiter
harēna, ae *f.* sand, beach
harēnōsus, a, um sandy
Harpalycē, ēs *f.* Thracian princess and huntress, renowned for her speed
harundō, inis *f.* reed, arrow
hasta, ae *f.* spear, lance, dart
hastīle, is *n.* spear(-shaft), lance
hauriō, īre, hausī, haustus drain, drink (in)
Hebrus, ī *m.* Thracian river
Hecatē, ēs *f.* goddess of the lower world
Hector, oris, *acc.* **ora** *m.* Trojan leader, son of Priam and Hecuba
Hectoreus, a, um Hectorean, of Hector, leader of the Trojans
Hecuba, ae *f.* wife of Priam
herba, ae *f.* herb(age), grass, plant
hērēs, ēdis *m.* heir, successor
hērōs, ōis *m.* hero, mighty warrior
Hesperia, ae *f.* Hesperia, Italy; lit., the western place
Hesperius, a, um Hesperian, western, Italian
heus ho! hello!
hīberna, ōrum *n.* winter (quarters)
hībernus, a, um wintry, of the winter, stormy
hiems, emis *f.* winter, storm
homō, inis *m.* (*f.*) man, mortal, human

hōra, ae *f.* hour, season, time

horrendus, a, um horrifying, dire, awesome

horreō, ēre, uī bristle, shudder, tremble

horrēscō, ere, horruī shudder, tremble

horridus, a, um bristling, awful, rough

horror, ōris *m.* horror, terror, shudder(ing)

hortor, ārī, ātus urge, encourage, incite

hospes, itis *m. (f.)* guest, host, stranger

hospitium, (i)ī *n.* hospitality, welcome

hospitus, a, um strange, alien, foreign

hostia, ae *f.* victim, sacrifice

hostīlis, e of the enemy, pertaining to the enemy

hostis, is *m. (f.)* enemy, foe, stranger

humilis, e low(ly), low-lying, humble

humō (1) bury, inter, cover with earth

humus, ī *f.* ground, soil, earth

hymenaeus, ī *m.* wedding (hymn), so-called after Hymen, god of marriage

Hyrcānus, a, um Hyrcanian, of Hyrcania, a wild district on the Caspian Sea

I

iaceō, ēre, uī, itus lie (low, outspread)

iaciō, ere, iēcī, iactus thrown, cast, hurl

iactō (1) toss, buffet, vaunt, utter

iaculor, ārī, ātus hurl, throw, fling

iamdūdum *adv.* long since, for a long time

iānua, ae *f.* door, gate, entrance

Iarbās, ae *m.* African chieftain, one of Dido's suitors

iaspis, idis *f.* jasper, a semi-precious stone

ibi *adv.* there, then

ibīdem in the same place

Īcarus, ī *m.* son of Daedalus, who in his flight with his father from Crete flew too near the sun, melted his wings, and fell into the sea, where he was drowned

(īcō), ere, īcī, ictus strike, smite (commonly used only in the perfect system)

ictus, ūs *m.* stroke, blow, wound

Īda, ae *f.* mountain near Troy

ideō *adv.* therefore, for this reason

ignārus, a, um ignorant, unaware, inexperienced; unknown, strange

ignāvus, a, um lazy, idle

igneus, a, um fiery, flaming

ignōbilis, e inglorious, common, lowly

ignōtus, a, um unknown, strange

īlex, icis *f.* holm-oak

Īliacus, a um Trojan, Ilian

Īlias, adis *f.* Trojan woman

īlicet *adv.* immediately, at once

Īlioneus, eī *m.* Trojan leader

Īlium, (i)ī *n.* Troy, Ilium

Īlius, a, um Ilian, Trojan

illīc *adv.* there, at that place

illinc *adv.* from that side, thence

illūc *adv.* there, thither, to that place

Illyricus, a, um Illyrian, Dalmatian, of Illyria, a region east of the Adriatic

Īlus, ī *m.* Ascanius, son of Aeneas

imāgō, inis *f.* likeness, image, ghost, soul, form

Imāon, Imāonos, *m.* Imaon, an Italian comrade of Halaesus, mentioned only in the *Aeneid*

imbellis, e unwarlike, harmless

imber, bris *m.* rain, flood, storm, water

immemor, oris unmindful, heedless, forgetful

immēnsus, a, um boundless, measureless, immense

immergō, ere, rsī, rsus plunge, drown

immineō, ēre overhang, menace (+ *dat.*)

immītis, e fierce, cruel

immittō, ere, mīsī, missus let in, send in (to), loose(n), give freely

immolō (1) sacrifice, offer

immōtus, a, um unmoved, immovable, unshaken

impār, aris unequal, ill-matched

impellō, ere, pulī, pulsus strike (against), drive, force

impēnsus, a, um vast, vehement

imperditus, a, um not destroyed

impius, a, um unholy, impious, disloyal

implācābilis, e implacable, irreconcilable

impleō, ēre, ēvī, ētus fill (with) (+ *gen.*)

implicō, āre, āvī (uī), ātus (itus) entwine

impōnō, ere, posuī, positus place upon, set to, impose (+ *dat.*)

imprimō, ere, pressī, pressus press (upon), imprint

improbus, a, um wicked, cruel, bad

imprōvidus, a, um unforeseeing, heedless

impūne *adv.* unpunished, with impunity

inānis, e empty, idle, useless, vain

incautus, a, um unaware, unsuspecting

incēdo, ere, cessī, cessus march, go (majestically)

incendō, ere, ī, ēnsus inflame, kindle, burn

inceptum, ī *n.* beginning, undertaking, purpose

incertus, a, um uncertain, doubtful, wavering

incessus, ūs *m.* walk, gait, stride

incestō (1) defile, pollute

incidō, ere, incidī, — fall, sink; strike

incipiō, ere, cēpī, ceptus begin, undertake

inclūdō, ere, sī, sus (en)close, confine

inclutus, a, um famous, renowned

incognitus, a, um unknown

incubō, āre, uī (āvī), itus (ātus) recline, lie upon, brood over (+ *dat.*)

incultus, a, um untilled, wild

incumbō, ere, cubuī, cubitus lean upon, overhang, urge on, brood over, lower (over) (+ *dat.*)

incūsō (1) accuse, blame, chide

incutiō, ere, cussī, cussus strike (into) (+ *dat.*)

indāgō, inis *f.* (circle of) nets, snares

inde *adv.* thence, afterward, thereupon

indēbitus, a, um not due, not owed, undue

indigena, ae, *m.* native, sprung from the land

Indiges, Indigetis, *m.* deified hero, patron deity

indignor, ārī, ātus be angry, chafe; deem unworthy, despise

indignus, a, um undeserved, unworthy

indulgeō, ēre, lsī, ltus indulge in, yield to (+ *dat.*)

induō, ere, uī, ūtus don, clothe, put on

inermis, e unarmed; also, **inermus, a, um**

iners, rtis lazy, spiritless, tame, idle

inexpertus, a, um untried

inextrīcābilis, e inextricable, insoluble

īnfabricātus, a, um unfashioned, rough

īnfandus, a, um unspeakable, accursed

īnfectus, a, um not done, false

īnfēnsus, a, um hostile, bitter

īnfernus, a, um infernal, pertaining to the underworld

īnferō, ferre, tulī, lātus bear in, bring (to), present

īnfēstus, a, um hostile, threatening

īnfīgō, ere, xī, xus fix, pierce, fasten

īnflectō, ere, flexī, flexus bend, turn

īnfrēnus, a, um unbridled, without bridles

īnfundō, ere, fūdī, fūsus pour (into, upon)

ingeminō (1) redouble, repeat, increase

ingemō, ere, uī groan, roar, lament

ingredior, ī, gressus advance, enter

inhiō (1) yawn, gape

inhospitus, a, um inhospitable, wild

inhumātus, a, um unburied

inimīcus, a, um hostile, enemy, unfriendly

inīquus, a, um unfair, unjust, hostile

iniūria, ae *f.* wrong, insult, injustice

inlābor, ī, lāpsus glide in(to) (+ *dat.*)

inlīdō, ere, sī, sus dash against (into) (+ *dat.*)

innectō, ere, x(u)ī, xus weave, connect

innō (1) swim, float (in), navigate

innūptus, a, um unmarried, virgin

inopīnus, a, um unexpected, sudden

inops, opis needy, destitute, bereft (of)

inquam, is, it say

inreparābilis, e irreparable, irretrievable

inrītō (1) vex, enrage, provoke

inrumpō, ere, rūpī, ruptus break into

inruō, ere, uī rush in

īnsānia, ae *f.* madness, frenzy, folly

īnsānus, a, um mad, insane, frenzied

īnscrībō, ere, psī, ptus mark

īnsequor, ī, secūtus follow, pursue

īnsidiae, ārum *f.* snare, ambush, treachery

īnsignis, e distinguished, marked, splendid

īnsinuō (1) wind, creep, coil

īnsomnium, (i)ī *n.* dream, vision in sleep

īnsonō, āre, uī (re)sound, roar, echo

īnspiciō, ere, spexī, spectus look into

īnspīrō (1) breathe into, inspire, blow into

īnstar *n. indecl.* likeness, dignity, image (+ *gen.*)

īnstaurō (1) renew, refresh, repeat

īnstituō, ere, uī, ūtus establish, ordain

īnstō, āre, stitī urge on, press on (+ *dat.*)

īnstruō, ere, strūxī, strūctus equip, array, build; instruct

īnsuētus, a, um unaccustomed, unused

īnsula, ae *f.* island

īnsum, esse, fuī be in, be present

īnsuper *adv.* above, besides

īnsuperābilis, e unconquerable

īnsurgō, ere, īnsurrexī, īnsurrectus rise up

intāctus, a, um untouched, virgin

intendō, ere, ī, ntus stretch, extend

intentō (1) threaten, aim

intentus, a, um intent, eager, strained

intereā *adv.* meanwhile, (in the) meantime

interfor, fārī, fātus interrupt

interfundō, ere, fūdī, fūsus pour among, suffuse

interimō (or **interemō**), **ere, interēmī, interemptus** destroy, kill

interior, ius inner, interior

interpres, etis *m. (f.)* interpreter, agent

interrumpō, ere, rūpī, ruptus interrupt

intexō, ere, xuī, xtus weave (in), cover

intimus, a, um inmost

intonō, āre, uī thunder, roar

intorqueō, ēre, rsī, rtus hurl (against) (+ *dat.*)

intrā within, inside, in(to) (+ *acc.*)

intractābilis, e unmanageable, intractable

intrō (1) enter, penetrate

intus *adv.* within, inside

inultus, a, um unavenged, unpunished

inūtilis, e useless, futile, valueless

invādō, ere, sī, sus attack, address

invalidus, a, um weak, feeble, infirm

invehō, ere, ēxī, ectus carry in, convey

inveniō, īre, vēnī, ventus find, come upon

invictus, a, um unconquered, invincible

invideō, ēre, vīdī, vīsus begrudge (+ *dat.*)

invidia, ae *f.* grudge, envy, jealousy

invīsō, ere, ī, sus visit, look on, view

invīsus, a, um hateful, hated, odious

invītus, a, um unwilling, reluctant

invius, a, um pathless, trackless

involvō, ere, ī, volūtus wrap, envelop

Īris, (id)is *f.* goddess of the rainbow, messenger of Juno

iste, ta, tud that (of yours)

Italus, a, um Italian, of Italy

iter, itineris *n.* way, road, journey, route

iterum *adv.* anew, a second time, again

iuba, ae *f.* mane, crest

iubar, aris *n.* ray of light, sunshine

iūdicium, (i)ī *n.* decision, judgment

iugālis, e of wedlock, matrimonial

iugum, ī *n.* yoke, (mountain) ridge

Iūlius, (i)ī *m.* (1) Julius Caesar; (2) Augustus Caesar

Iūlus, ī *m.* Ascanius, son of Aeneas

iungō (1) join, unite, yoke together

iungō, ere, iūnxī, iūnctus join, unite

iūrō (1) take oath, swear, conspire

iūs, iūris *n.* right, law, decree, justice

iussum, ī *n.* order, command, behest

iussus, ūs *m.* command, order, behest

iūstus, a, um just, fair, right(eous)

Iūturna, ae, *f.* sister of Turnus; Jupiter had made her an immortal river nymph

iuvenālis, e youthful, of a young man

iuvencus, ī *m.* bullock, ox

iuvenis, is *m. (f.)* youth, young (man or woman)

iuventa, ae *f.* youth, young manhood, young womanhood

iuventūs, ūtis *f.* youth, (group of) young men

iuvō, āre, iūvī, iūtus help, please

iuxtā *adv.* close (to), next (to) (+ *acc.*)

K

Karthāgō, inis *f.* Carthage, great commercial city in North Africa, rival of Rome

L

labefaciō, ere, fēcī, factus shake, stagger

labō (1) totter, waver, sink, vacillate

lacrimō (1) weep, shed tears, lament

lacus, ūs *m.* lake, marsh

laedō, ere, sī, sus strike, hurt, offend, thwart

laena, ae *f.* (woolen) mantle, cloak

laetitia, eae *f.* joy, gladness, delight

laetor, ārī, ātus rejoice, exult

laeva, ae *f.* left hand

laevus, a, um left, foolish, unlucky

lambō, ere lick, lap

lāmenta, ōrum *n.* lamentation, shriek

lāmentābilis, e lamentable, pitiable, sad

lampas, adis *f.* torch, lamp, light

languidus, a, um weak, sluggish

Lāocoōn, ontis *m.* Trojan priest of Neptune

lapis, idis, *m.* stone

lāpsō, āre slip, stumble, totter, fall

lāpsus, ūs *m.* gliding, rolling, sinking

largior, īrī, largītus bestow, grant

largus, a, um abundant, copious

lassus, a, um tired, weary, worn (out)

lātē *adv.* widely, far and wide

latebra, ae *f.* hiding place, cavern, lair

lateō, ēre, uī lie hid, hide, lurk, escape the notice (of)

latex, icis *m.* liquid, water, wine

Latīnus, a, um Latin, of Latium

Latīnus, ī *m.* early king of Italy, whose daughter, Lavinia, married Aeneas

Latium, (i)ī *n.* Latium, district of central Italy

Lātōna, ae *f.* mother of Apollo and Diana

lātus, a, um broad, wide, spacious

latus, eris *n.* side, flank

laudō (1) praise

Laurēns, entis of Laurentum, a city near Rome

laurus, ī (ūs) *f.* laurel (tree)

laus, laudis *f.* glory, praise, merit

Lausus, ī, m. son of Mezentius, the renegade Etruscan ally of Turnus

Lāvīn(i)us, a, um Lavinian, of Lavinium, an early Italian city

Lavīnium, (i)ī *n.* city near Rome

laxō (1) loosen, free, open, release

laxus, a, um loose, open, lax

lēgifer, era, erum law-bringing

legō, ere, lēgī, lēctus choose, collect, select

Lēnaeus, a, um Lenaean, Bacchic, of Bacchus, god of wine

lēniō, īre, īvī (iī), ītus soothe, calm, soften

lēnis, e light, gentle, soft, moderate

lentus, a, um pliant, flexible; not brittle

leō, ōnis *m.* lion

lētālis, e deadly, mortal, lethal, fatal

lētum, ī *n.* death, destruction, ruin

levis, e light, unsubstantial, slight, swift

levō (1) lift, lighten, raise, relieve

lēx, lēgis *f.* law, jurisdiction, regulation, decree

lībō (1) pour (as a libation), offer

lībrō (1) balance, weigh

Liburni, orum *m.* Liburnians, Illyrians

Libya, ae *f.* country of North Africa

Libycus, a, um Libyan, of Libya, a country of North Africa

licet, ēre, uit, itum it is permitted

lignum, ī *n.* wood, timber

ligō (1) bind, tie, fasten

līlium, (i)ī *n.* lily

limbus, ī *m.* border, fringe, hem

līmes, it is m. limit, boundary; route, course

lingua, ae *f.* tongue, language

linquō, ere, līquī, lictus leave, desert

līquēns, entis liquid, flowing

liquidus, a, um clear, liquid, fluid

līs, lītis, *f.* dispute, lawsuit

litō (1) sacrifice (favorably), appease

lituus, ī *m.* (curved) trumpet

locō (1) place, locate, establish

Longa, ae *f.* Alba Longa, a city in central Italy, mother city of Rome

longaevus, a, um aged, very old

longē *adv.* far (off, from), at a distance

loquor, ī, locūtus speak, say, tell, talk

lōrīca, ae, *f.* leather cuirass

lōrum, ī *n.* thong, leather strap, rein

lūbricus, a, um slippery, slimy

Lūcifer, erī *m.* morning star, light-bringer

luctor, ārī, ātus struggle, wrestle

lūctus, ūs *m.* grief, mourning, sorrow

lūcus, ī *m.* (sacred) grove, wood

lūdibrium, (i)ī *n.* sport, mockery

lūdō, ere, sī, sus play with, deceive, mock

lūna, ae *f.* moon, moonlight

lūnātus, a, um crescent, moon-shaped

luō, ere, ī atone for

lupa, ae *f.* she-wolf

lūstrō (1) purify, survey, traverse

lūstrum, ī *n.* space of five years, sacred season; marsh, bog, lair

luxus, ūs *m.* luxury, splendor, excess

Lyaeus, ī *m.* Bacchus, (god of) wine

Lycia, ae *f.* country of Asia Minor

Lycius, a, um Lycian, of Lycia, a country of Asia Minor

Lycus, ī *m.* a Trojan

Lȳdius, a, um Lydian, of Lydia, a country of Asia Minor, said to be the original home of the Etruscans who settled in Italy

lympha, ae *f.* water

lȳnx, lȳncis *m.* *(f.)* lynx, wild cat

M

Machāōn, onis *m.* Greek leader and surgeon

māchina, ae *f.* machine, engine, device

mactō (1) sacrifice, slaughter, kill; honor through sacrifice

macula, ae *f.* spot, splotch, stain

maculōsus, a, um spotted

madeō, ēre, uī drip, be wet, reek

Maeonius, a, um Maeonian, Lydian, Asiatic

maereō, ēre mourn, grieve, pine (for)

maestus, a, um sad, mournful, gloomy

māgālia, ium *n.* huts, hovels

mage = magis (comparative adv.)

magis *adv.* more, rather

magister, trī *m.* master, pilot

magistrātus, ūs *m.* magistrate, officer

magnanimus, a, um great-souled

Maia, ae *f.* daughter of Atlas and mother of Mercury, messenger of the gods

māiestās, tātis, *f.* greatness, dignity

male *adv.* badly, ill, scarcely, not

mālō, mālle, māluī prefer, wish (in preference)

malum, ī *n.* evil thing, misfortune, disaster

malus, a, um bad, evil, wicked, baneful

mamma, ae *f.* breast

mandātum, ī *n.* command, mandate, charge, behest

mandō (1) command, entrust,
  enjoin
mandō, ere, ī, mānsus champ,
  chew
Mānēs (or mānēs), ium *m.* (souls
  of) the dead, Hades
manifestus, a, um clear, manifest
Mārcellus, ī *m.* 1. Marcus
  Claudius Marcellus, d. 208
  BC; famous Roman consul,
  served in both 1st and 2d
  Punic Wars; 2. Marcus
  Claudius Marcellus, 42-23
  BC; son of Octavia, sister of
  Augustus, and first husband
  of Augustus' daughter Julia
marītus, ī *m.* (prospective)
  husband, suitor
marmor, oris *n.* marble
marmoreus, a, um (of) marble,
  white
Marpēs(s)ius, a, um of Marpe(s)
  sus, a mountain on the island
  of Paros famous for its white
  marble
Mārs, Mārtis *m.* god of war
Massy̱-lī, (ōr)um *m.* tribe of North
  Africa
Massy̱-lus, a, um of the Massyli, a
  people of North Africa
māternus, a, um of a mother,
  maternal
mātūrō (1) hasten, speed; ripen
Maurūsius, a, um Moorish
Māvors, rtis *m.* Mars, god of war
Māvortius, a, um Martian, of
  Mars, god of war
meātus, ūs *m.* course, path,
  motion
meditor, ārī, ātus meditate,
  design, consider, think over,
  practice

medium, (i)ī *n.* middle, midst,
  center
medulla, ae *f.* marrow
mel, mellis *n.* honey
melior, ius better, superior,
  preferable
membrum, ī *n.* member, limb,
  (part of) body
meminī, isse remember, recall
  (+ *gen.*)
Memnōn, onis *m.* Ethiopian king,
  son of Aurora and ally of the
  Trojans, slain by Achilles
memor, oris remembering,
  mindful, unforgetting (+ *gen.*)
memorābilis, e memorable,
  glorious
memorō (1) (re)call, recount,
  relate
Menelāus, ī *m.* Greek leader,
  Helen's husband
mēnsa, ae *f.* table
mēnsis, is *m.* month
mentior, īrī, ītus lie, deceive,
  pretend
mentum, ī *n.* chin, beard
mercor, ārī, ātus buy, purchase
Mercurius, (i)ī *m.* messenger of
  the gods, god of commerce,
  and escort of departed souls to
  Hades
mereō, ēre, uī, itus deserve, earn,
  merit
meritum, ī *n.* desert, service, merit
mēta, ae *f.* goal, limit, bound,
  turning-point
metallum, ī *n.* metal, ore, mine
metuō, ere, uī fear, dread
metus, ūs *m.* fear, anxiety, dread
micō, āre, uī quiver, flash, dart
migrō (1) migrate, depart
mīles, itis *m.* soldier(y), warrior(s)

mīlle; *pl.* **mīlia, ium** *n.* thousand

minae, ārum *f.* threat, menace; pinnacle

Minerva, ae *f.* goddess of wisdom and the arts

minimē *adv.* least, not at all

ministrō (1) tend, serve, supply

Minōius, a, um Minoan, of Minos, king of Crete

minor, ārī, ātus tower (over); threaten (+ *dat.*)

Minōtaurus, ī *m.* Cretan monster, half bull and half man, the result of queen Pasiphaë's love for the bull of Minos

minus *adv.* less

mīrābilis, e wonderful, marvelous

mīrandus, a, um wonderful, marvelous

mīror, ārī, ātus wonder (at), admire

mīrus, a, um wonderful, marvelous

misceō, ēre, uī, mixtus confuse, mix, mingle, stir (up)

Mīsēnus, ī *m.* Trojan trumpeter

miserābilis, e miserable, wretched

misereor, ērī, itus pity, commiserate (+ *gen.*)

missilis, e able or ready to be thrown, hurled, sent

mītēscō, ere become mild

mitra, ae *f.* mitre, cap, turban

Mnēstheus, eī (eos), *acc.* **ea** *m.* Trojan leader

mōbilitās, ātis *f.* activity, motion, speed

modo *adv.* only, (just) now

modus, ī *m.* manner, measure, limit, method

mōlēs, is *f.* mass, burden, heap, structure; difficulty

mōlior, īrī, ītus undertake, (strive to) accomplish, do

molliō, īre, īvī (iī), ītus soothe, tame

mollis, e soft, yielding, easy, mild, tender

molliter *adv.* softly, gently, gracefully

moneō, ēre, monuī, monitus warn, advise

monimentum (monumentum), ī *n.* reminder, memorial

monitum, ī *n.* advice, warning

monitus, ūs *m.* advice, warning

mōnstrō (1) point out, show, teach, guide

mōnstrum, ī *n.* prodigy, portent, monster

mora, ae *f.* delay, hesitation, hindrance

moribundus, a, um dying, about to die

morior, ī, mortuus die, perish

moror, ārī, ātus delay, tarry, hinder, hesitate

morsus, ūs *m.* bite, biting, jaws, fangs

mortālis, is *m.* mortal, man, human, earthly

mōs, mōris *m.* custom, ritual, manner

mōtus, ūs *m.* movement, emotion

mox *adv.* soon, presently

mūgītus, ūs *m.* bellow(ing), roar

mulceō, ēre, lsī, lsus calm, soothe

multiplex, icis manifold, multiple

mūniō, īre, īvī (iī), ītus fortify

mūrālis, e of a wall

mūrex, icis *m.* purple (dye), crimson, scarlet

murmur, uris *n.* murmur, roar, rumble

mūrus, ī *m.* (city) wall, battlement, rampart

Mūsa, ae *f.* Muse, patron goddess of the liberal arts

mūtō (1) (ex)change, transform, alter

Mycēnae, ārum *f.* city of central Greece, home of Agamemnon, learder of the Greek expedition against Troy

Myrmidones, um *m.* Greeks of Thessaly, subjects of Achilles

N

nārrō (1) relate, recount, report, narrate

nāscor, ī, nātus be born, rise

nāta, ae *f.* daughter

natō (1) swim, float, overflow

nauta, ae *m.* sailor, seaman, mariner

nāvigō (1) (set) sail, navigate

nebula, ae *f.* cloud, mist, fog

necdum *adv.* not yet, nor yet

nectar, aris *n.* nectar

nectō, ere, nex(u)ī, nexus bind, fasten

nefandus, a, um unspeakable, unutterable

nefās *n. indecl.* impiety, unspeakable thing, crime

negō (1) deny, refuse, say no (not)

nemus, oris *n.* (sacred) grove, wood

Neoptolemus, ī *m.* Pyrrhus, son of Achilles

nepōs, ōtis *m.* grandson; descendant

Neptūnus, ī *m.* Neptune, god of the sea

nēquīquam *adv.* in vain, uselessly, idly

nesciō, īre, īvī (iī) not know, know not, be ignorant

nescius, a, um ignorant, unaware

neu, nēve and (that) not, and lest

nī, nisi if not, unless, except

niger, gra, grum black, gloomy, dusky

nigrāns, antis black, dusky, dark

nigrēscō, ere, gruī turn black, darken

nihil, nīl nothing, not at all

nimbus, ī *m.* rainstorm, (storm) cloud

nimium *adv.* too (much), too great(ly), excessively

nisi, nī if not, unless

nitēns, entis gleaming, bright, shining

nitidus, a, um shining, bright, sleek

nītor, ī, sus (nixus) strive, rest on (+ *abl.*)

niveus, a, um snowy, white

nix, nivis *f.* snow

nō (1) swim, float

nocturnus, a, um of the night, nocturnal

nōdō (1) (tie in a) knot, bind, fasten

nōdus, ī *m.* knot, node; fold, coil

Nomas, adis *m.* tribe of North Africa

nōndum *adv.* not yet

nōscō, ere, nōvī, nōtus learn; *perf.* know

nōtus, a, um (well) known, familiar

Notus, ī *m.* (south) wind

novem nine

novō (1) renew, make (new), build

noxa, ae *f.* crime, fault, hurt, harm

nūbēs, is *f.* cloud, fog, mist
nūbila, ōrum *n.* clouds, cloudiness
nūbilum, ī *n.* cloud, cloudiness
nūdō (1) (lay) bare, strip, expose
nūdus, a, um naked, bare, nude, open
num *interrog.,* expects a negative response
numerus, ī *m.* number, multitude
Numidae, ārum *m.* tribe of North Africa
numquam *adv.* never, at no time
nuntia, ae *f.* messenger
nuntiō (1) announce
nuntius, (i)ī *m.* messenger, message
nurus, ūs *f.* daughter(-in-law)
nūsquam *adv.* nowhere, never
nūtrīmentum, ī *n.* food, fuel, nourishment
nūtrīx, īcis *f.* nurse
Nympha (or **nympha**), **ae** *f.* numph, a minor divinity of the forests, waters, etc., appearing to humans as a beautiful maiden

O

ob on account of (+ *acc.*)
obeō, īre, iī (īvī), itus enter, approach, traverse, skirt
obiciō, ere, iēcī, iectus present, place before
obiectō (1) throw to, expose
obiectus, ūs *m.* projection, hang
obitus, ūs *m.* death, downfall, ruin
oblīviscor, ī, lītus forget (+ *gen.*)
obmūtēscō, ere, tuī be dumb, stand speechless
obnītor, ī, sus (nixus) push against, strive

oborior, īrī, ortus (a)rise, spring up
obruō, ere, uī, utus overwhelm, crush
obscēnus, a, um foul, filthy, disgusting
obscūrus, a, um dark, shadowy, gloomy, dim
observō (1) observe, watch, note
obsideō, ēre, sēdī, sessus besiege, beset
obstipēscō, ere, stipuī be dazed, stand agape
obstō, āre, stitī, status stand in the way, oppose (+ *dat.*)
obstruō, ere, strūxī, strūctus block, stop
obtestor (1) make appeal to, beseech
obtūtus, ūs *m.* gaze, view
obvertō, ere, ī, rsus turn to (+ *dat.*)
obvius, a, um in the way, meeting, to meet (+ *dat.*)
occāsus, ūs *m.* fall, destruction
occidō, ere, occidī, occāsus fall, perish, end, die
occulō, ere, uī, ltus hide, conceal
occultō (1) hide, conceal, secrete
occumbō, ere, cubuī, cubitus fall (in death)
Ōceanus, ī *m.* ocean
ōcior, ius swifter, quicker; very swift
ōdī, isse hate, detest, loathe
odium, (i)ī *n.* hate, hatred, enmity
odor, ōris *m.* odor, fragrance
odōrus, a, um smelling, keen-scented
offerō, ferre, obtulī, oblātus present
Oīleus, eī *m.* Greek king, father of Ajax

oleō, ēre, uī smell, stink

ōlim *adv.* (at) some time, once

Olympus, ī *m.* high Greek mountain, home of the gods; heaven

ōmen, inis *n.* portent, omen, sign

omnīnō *adv.* altogether, completely, utterly

omnipotēns, entis almighty, all-powerful

onerō (1) load, burden

onus, eris *n.* burden, load

onustus, a, um laden, burdened

opācō (1) darken, shade, shadow

opācus, a, um dark, gloomy, dusky

operiō, īre, uī, rtus cover, hide

opertum, ī *n.* mystery, hidden thing

opīmus, a, um rich, splendid, sumptuous; **spolia opīma** "spoils of honor," won when a Roman general with his own hand slew the general of the enemy

opperior, īrī, per(i)tus await, wait for

oppetō, ere, īvī (iī), ītus encounter, meet (death)

oppōnō, ere, posuī, positus oppose, place against

opprimō, ere, pressī, pressus overwhelm, crush

ops, opis *f.* help, resources, power, wealth

optimus, a, um best, finest

optō (1) choose, desire, hope (for)

opulentus, a, um rich, wealthy

opus, eris *n.* work, task, toil, deed

orbis, is *m.* circle, fold, coil, orb, revolution

Orcus, ī *m.* Hades, (god of) the lower world

ordior, īrī, orsus begin, undertake

ordō, inis *m.* order, line, array

Orēas, adis *f.* Oread, a mountain nymph

orgia, ōrum *n.* mystic rites, rituals

Oriēns, entis *m.* Orient, the East

orīgō, inis *f.* origin, beginning, source

Ōrīōn, ōnis *m.* the storm-bringing constellation, named for a famous hunter transported to heaven

ornus, ī *f.* ash-tree

ōrō (1) beseech, pray (for), entreat

Orontēs, is (ī) *m.* comrade of Aeneas

Orpheus, ī *m.* mythical poet and musician of Thrace who descended to Hades to bring back his wife Eurydice, but failed

ortus, ūs *m.* rising, source

os, ossis *n.* bone

ōsculum, ī *n.* dainty lips; kiss

ostendō, ere, ī, ntus show, display

ostentō (1) show (off), display, exhibit, parade

ōstium, (i)ī *n.* mouth, entrance; harbor

ostrum, ī *n.* purple, scarlet, crimson

ōtium, (i)ī *n.* leisure, idleness, quiet

ovō, āre, — exult, rejoice

P

pābulus, ī *n.* fodder, pasture

pacīscor, ī, pactus stipulate, bargain, fix

Pallas, adis *f.* Minerva, goddess of wisdom and the arts

Pallās, Pallantis, *m.* Pallas, son of the Arcadian king Evander and ally of Aeneas

pallēns, entis pale, pallid, wan

pallidus, a, um pale, wan, pallid

palma, ae *f.* palm, hand

palūs, ūdis *f.* swamp, marsh

pandō, ere, ī, passus spread, open, loosen

Paphus (os), ī *f.* city of Cyprus, famous center of the worship of Venus

pār, paris equal, like, similar (+ *dat.*)

Parcae, ārum *f.* the Fates

parcō, ere, pepercī (parsī), parsus spare (+ *dat.*)

pāreō, ēre, uī, itus obey, yield (+ *dat.*)

pariō, ere, peperī, partus (re) produce, gain, acquire, give birth to

Paris, idis *m.* Trojan prince, son of Priam, took Helen from her husband Menelaus and thus caused the Trojan War

pariter *adv.* equally, side by side

partior, īrī, ītus distribute, divide

partus, ūs m. birth, offspring

parum *adv.* slightly, too little, not

parvulus, a, um tiny, very small, little

parvus, a, um small, little

pascō, ere, pāvī, pāstus feed (on), graze, eat

pascor, ī, pāstus feed, graze

Pāsiphaē, ēs *f.* wife of Minos, king of Crete, who fell in love with a beutiful bull and was assisted by Daedalus to gratify her passion

passim *adv.* everywhere, all about

pāstor, ōris *m.* shepherd, herdsman

Patavium, (i)ī *n.* city of northern Italy, modern Padua, about twenty miles west of Venice

patefaciō, ere, fēcī, factus lay open

pateō, ēre, uī lie open, be evident, extend

patera, ae *f.* (libation) bowl

patēscō, ere, uī open up, be revealed

patiēns, entis enduring, tolerating (+ *gen.*)

patior, ī, passus suffer, endure, allow

patria, ae *f.* homeland, country

paucus, a, um little, few, light, scanty

paulus (a) little, slightly, somewhat

pavidus, a, um fearful, frightened

pavor, ōris *m.* terror, shuddering, alarm

pāx, pācis *f.* peace, favor, grace, repose

pecus, oris *n.* flock, herd, swarm

pecus, udis *f.* animal (of the flock)

pedes, itis *m.* footsoldier, infantry; foot-traveller; on foot

Pēlīdēs, ae *m.* descendant of Peleus, Achilles

pellis, is, *f.* skin, hide

pellō, ere, pepulī, pulsus drive (away), dismiss

pelta, ae *f.* light shield

penātēs, ium *m.* household gods

pendeō, ēre, pependī hang, depend

pendō, ere, pependī, pēnsus weigh out, pay

penetrābilis, e able to be penetrated, able to penetrate

penetrālia, ium *n.* chamber, sanctuary, inner room

penetrālis, e inmost, interior

penetrō (1) enter, penetrate

penitus *adv.* deep within, deeply, wholly

penna, ae *f.* wing, feather

Penthesilēa, ae *f.* queen of the Amazons, ally of the Trojans, slain by Achilles

peplus (um), ī *m. (n.)* robe, gown

peragō, ere, ēgī, āctus accomplish, finish, traverse

peragrō (1) wander through, scour

percutiō, ere, cussī, cussus strike, astound

pereō, īre, iī (īvī), itus perish, die

pererrō (1) wander through, traverse

perferō, ferre, tulī, lātus bear, endure; convey, accomplish, complete

perficiō, ere, fēcī, fectus finish, make

perfidus, a, um treacherous, perfidious

perflō (1) blow (over, through

perforō (1) pierce, perforate, puncture

perfundō, ere, fūdī, fūsus soak, drench

Pergama, ōrum *n.* (citadel of) Troy

Pergameus, a, um Trojan

pergō, ere, perrēxī, perrēctus proceed

perhibeō, ēre, uī, itus present, say

perīc(u)lum, ī *n.* danger, peril, risk

perimō, ere, ēmī, ēmptus destroy

Periphās, antis *m.* Greek leader

perlābor, ī, lāpsus glide over

perlegō, ere, lēgī, lēctus survey, examine

permisceō, ēre, uī, mixtus mix, mingle

permittō, ere, mīsī, missus entrust, allow

pernīx, īcis active, nimble, swift

perpetuus, a, um continual, lasting

perrumpō, ere, rūpī, ruptus break through

persentiō, īre, sēnsī, sēnsus feel deeply, perceive (thoroughly)

persolvō, ere, ī, solūtus pay fully

personō, āre, uī, itus sound through, make (re)sound

pertaedet, ēre, taesum it wearies (+ *gen.*)

pertemptō (1) try; master, possess

perterreō, ēre, perterruī, perterritus frighten thoroughly

perveniō, īre, pervēnī, perventus reach

pestis, is *f.* plague, destruction. scourge

phalānx, angis *f.* phalanx, troop

pharetra, ae *f.* quiver

Phoebēus, a, um of Phoebus (Apollo), god of light, music, and prophecy

Phoebus, ī *m.* Apollo, god of light, music, and prophecy, brother of Diana, goddess of the chase

Phoenissa, ae *f.* Phoenician (woman), Dido

Phoenīx, īcis *m.* the name of a Greek leader; Phoenician

Phrygius, a, um Phrygian, Trojan

Phryx, Phrygis Phrygian, Trojan
Phthīa, ae *f.* city and district of
northern Greece, home of
Achilles, a Greek chieftain
against Troy
piāculum, ī *n.* expiation, crime
picea, ae *f.* pitch-pine
pictūra, ae *f.* picture, painting
pietās, ātis *f.* loyalty, devotion,
(sense of) duty
piget, ēre, uit it displeases
pīneus, a, um of pine
pingō, ere, pīnxī, pictus paint,
embroider, tattoo
pinguis, e fat, fertile, rich
pīnifer, era, erum pine-bearing
piscōsus, a, um fishy, fish-
haunted
placeō, ēre, uī, itus please (+ *dat.*)
placidus, a, um peaceful, calm,
quiet
plācō (1) calm, quiet
plaga, ae *f.* net, snare, toils; region,
tract
plangor, ōris *m.* clamor, wailing,
beating (of the breast), shriek
planta, ae *f.* heel; sole of foot
plēnus, a, um full, complete,
swelling
plūma, ae *f.* feather, plume
Poenus, a, um Phoenician,
Carthaginian
Poenus, ī *m.* Carthaginian,
Phoenician
Polītēs, ae *m.* son of Priam, slain
by Neoptolemus (Pyrrhus)
polliceor, ērī, itus promise, offer
Pollūx, ūcis *m.* son of Jupiter and
Leda; after the death of his
twin brother Castor, Pollux
shared his immortality with
him on alternate days

polus, ī *m.* pole, sky, heaven
pondus, eris *n.* weight, burden
pōne *adv.* behind, after
pontus, ī *m.* sea, waves
poples, itis, *m.* knee, back of the
knee
populō (1) devastate, plunder,
ravage
populus, ī *m.* people, nation,
crowd
porta, ae *f.* door, gate, entrance,
exit
porticus, ūs *f.* colonnade, corridor,
portico
portō (1) carry, bear, take, convey
poscō, ere, poposcī demand, seek,
ask
post after, behind (+ *acc.*); *adv.*
afterward
posterus, a, um following, later,
next
posthabeō, ēre, uī, itus place after,
esteem less
postis, is *m.* post, door, gate
postquam after (that), when
potēns, entis powerful, ruling
(+ *gen.*)
potior, īrī, ītus possess, gain
(+ *abl.*)
potior, ius preferable, better
potius *adv.* rather, preferably
praeceps, cipitis headlong,
headforemost
praecipiō, ere, cēpī, ceptus
anticipate; teach
praecipitō (1) fall headlong,throw,
hasten
praecipuē *adv.* especially,
particularly
praeclārus, a, um very renowned
praecordia, ōrum, *n. pl.* heart,
breast

praeda, ae *f.* booty, spoils, prey
praeficiō, ere, fēcī, fectus set over (+ *acc., dat.*)
praefīgō, ere, praefixī, praefixus tip, point (i.e., put a point on something)
praemittō, ere, mīsī, missus send forward
praemium, (i)ī *n.* reward, prize
praepes, etis swift, flying
praeruptus, a, um steep, towering
praescius, a, um foreknowing, prescient
praesēns, entis present, instant
praesentiō, īre, sēnsī, sēnsus perceive first, suspect
praesēpe, is *n.* stall, hive
praesideō, ēre, sēdī, sessus rule, protect (+ *dat.*)
praestāns, antis excellent, superior
praestō, āre, stitī, status (stitus) excel, be better
praetendō, ere, ī, ntus hold before, use as screen;stretch before, extend
praetereā *adv.* besides, also, furthermore
praetereō, īre, iī (īvī), itus surpass, pass (by)
praeterlābor, ī, lāpsus glide by
praetexō, ere, uī, xtus fringe, cloak
praevertor, ī, rsus outstrip, surpass
prāvum, ī *n.* wrong, perverse act
pre(he)ndō, ere, ī, nsus seize, grasp
precor, ārī, ātus pray, entreat, invoke
premō, ere, pressī, pressus (re)press, control, overwhelm

pretium, (i)ī *n.* price, reward, value
prex, precis *f.* (usually in pl.) prayer, entreaty, vow
prīmō *adv.* at first, in the beginning
princeps, cipis *m. (f.)* chief, leader
principiō *adv.* at first, in the first place
prior, ius soon, former, first, prior
prīscus, a, um ancient, primitive
prīstinus, a, um ancient, former
prius *adv.* former(ly), sooner, first
prō instead of, on behalf of, for, before (+ *abl.*)
probō (1) test, prove, approve
prōcēdō, ere, cessī, cessus advance
procella, ae *f.* blast, gale
prōcumbō, ere, cubuī, cubitus fall (forward), sink
prōdeō, īre, iī (īvī), itus advance
prōdūcō, ere, prōduxī, prōductus bring forth, produce
proelium, iī, *n.* battle, skirmish
prōdō, ere, didī, ditus betray, hand down
proficīscor, ī, fectus set out, depart
profor, ārī, ātus speak (out), say
profugus, a, um exiled, fugitive
profundus, a, um deep, profound, vast
prōgeniēs, ēī *f.* offspring, progeny
prōgignō, ere, genuī, genitus bring forth, bear
prōgredior, ī, gressus advance, proceed
prōlābor, ī, lāpsus slide, fall, perish
prōlēs, is *f.* progeny, offspring
prōmereor, ērī, itus deserve, render service, merit, earn

prōmittō, ere, mīsī, missus
promise

prōmō, ere, mpsī, mptus bring
forth

prōnuba, ae *f.* matron of honor,
bride's attendant

prōnus, a, um leaning forward,
headlong

propāgō, inis *f.* offshoot, offspring,
descendant, posterity

properō (1) hasten, hurry, speed

propior, ius nearer, closer

proprius, a, um one's own,
permanent

propter on account of, near (+ *acc.*)

prōpugnāculum, ī *n.* rampart,
battlement

prōra, ae *f.* prow (of a ship)

prōruptus, a, um dashing,
furious

prōsequor, ī, secūtus follow,
attend, escort

Prōserpina, ae *f.* wife of Pluto and
queen of the underworld

prōspectus, ūs *m.* view

prōspiciō, ere, spexī, spectus look
out on, see

prōtendō, ere, prōtendī, prōtentus
stretch forth, extend

prōtinus *adv.* continuously, at
once

prōvehō, ere, vēxī, vectus carry,
convey

proximus, a, um nearest

pūbēs, is *f.* youth, young men

pudor, ōris *m.* shame, modesty,
honor

puella, ae *f.* girl

pugna, ae *f.* battle, fight, combat

pugnō (1) fight, oppose, resist
(+ *dat.*)

pugnus, ī *m.* fist

pulcher, chra, chrum beautiful,
handsome, splendid,
illustrious, noble

pulsō (1) beat, strike, lash, batter

pulverulentus, a, um dusty

pulvis, pulveris *m.* dust

Pūnicus, a, um Phoenician,
Punic, Carthaginian

purpureus, a, um purple,
crimson

putō (1) think, suppose, consider

Pygmaliōn, ōnis *m.* brother of
Dido

Pyrrhus, ī *m.* Neoptolemus, son
of Achilles

Q

quā *adv.* where(by), wherever, in
any (some) way

quālis, e (such) as, of what sort

quam *adv.* how, than, as

quamquam although, and yet,
however

quandō when, since, if ever,
because

quantum how much, how greatly,
(as much) as

quantus, a, um how great, how
much, how many, as much
(as)

quassō (1) shake, shatter, toss

quater four times

queō, quīre, īvī (iī), ītus be able,
can

quercus, ūs *f.* oak

querēla, ae *f.* complaint, lament

queror, ī, questus complain, (be)
wail

quia because, since

quīcumque, quaecumque,
quodcumque whoever,
whatever

quidem (adding emphasis) in fact, indeed

quiēs, ētis *f.* quiet, rest, sleep, peace

quiēscō, ere, ēvī, ētus rest, calm, cease

quiētus, a, um quiet, serene, calm

quīn that not, but that, why not, even in fact

quīnquāgintā fifty

quippe *adv.* to be sure, surely, indeed

Quirīnus, ī *m.* Romulus, legendary founder of Rome

quisquam, quaequam, quicquam any(one), any(thing)

quisquam, quicquam anyone, anything

quisque, quaeque, quidque (quodque) each, every(one)

quisquis, quidquid (quicquid) *indef. pron.;* **quisquis, quodquod** *indef. adj.* whoever, whatever

quod because, but

quoniam since, because

quoque *adv.* also, furthermore, even, too, likewise

quot as many as

quotannīs *adv.* annually, yearly

quotiēns how often, as often as

R

rabidus, a, um raving, mad, frenzied

rabiēs, ēī *f.* rage, fury, frenzy

radius, (i)ī *m.* rod. spoke, ray, compass

rādīx, īcis *f.* root

rāmus, ī *m.* branch, bough, limb

rapidus, a, um swift, snatching, whirling

rapiō, ere, uī, ptus snatch (away), seize, ravish; whirl

raptō (1) snatch, drag, carry off

raptum, ī *n.* plunder, prey, booty

rārus, a, um scattered, wide-meshed

ratiō, ōnis *f.* manner, purpose, reason

ratis, is *f.* raft, ship, boat

raucus, a, um hoarse, sounding, clanging

re(l)liquiae, ārum *f.* rest, remnant(s), leaving(s)

rebellis, e rebellious, insurgent

recēdō, ere, cessī, cessus depart, withdraw

recēns, entis recent, fresh, new

recidīvus, a, um revived, renewed

recipiō, ere, cēpī, ceptus receive, accept, take back, recover

reclūdō, ere, sī, sus disclose, reveal

recondō, ere, didī, ditus establish; hide

rēctus, a, um right, straight, direct

recursō (1) run back, come back, recur

recutiō, ere, cussī, cussus strike (back), shake

reddō, ere, didī, ditus return, give back, render

redeō, īre, iī (īvī) itus return

redimō, ere, ēmī, ēmptus redeem

reditus, ūs *m.* return (trip)

redoleō, ēre, uī be fragrant, smell (of)

redūcō, ere, dūxī, ductus bring back, lead back

redux, ucis led back, restored

refellō, ere, ī contradict, refute

reflectō, ere flexī, flexus turn back

refringō, ere, frēgī, frāctus break off

refugiō, ere, fūgī flee, retreat, recoil

refulgeō, ēre, lsī gleam, shine, glitter

refundō, ere, fūdī, fūsus pour (back, out)

regiō, ōnis *f.* district, region, quarter

rēgius, a, um royal, regal, kingly

rēgnātor, ōris *m.* ruler, lord, director

rēgnō (1) rule, reign

regō, ere, rēxī, rēctus rule, guide, direct

rēiciō, ere, rēiēcī, rēiectus throw back, reject, turn away

reliquiae, ārum *f.* remnants, relics, leavings

rēmigium, (i)ī *n.* oarage, rowing equipment

remittō, ere, mīsī, missus return, repay, send back, concede, yield, grant

remordeō, ēre, dī, rsus gnaw, trouble

removeō, ēre, mōvī, mōtus remove

remūgiō, īre bellow, roar, resound

Remus, ī *m.* twin brother of Romulus

renovō (1) renew, revive

reor, rērī, ratus suppose, think, reckon

repellō, ere, reppulī, repulsus drive back, repel

rependō, ere, ī, ēnsus balance, compensate

reperiō, īre, repperī, repertus find (out)

repertor, ōris, *m.* inventor, creator

repetō, ere, īvī (iī), ītus seek again, repeat, retrace

repleō, ēre, ēvī, ētus fill, stuff

repōnō, ere, posuī, pos(i)tus replace, lay away, store (up), deposit

repos(i)tus, a, um secluded, remote

reprimō, ere, repressī, repressus press back, restrain

requiēs, ētis (ēī) *f.* rest, respite, repose

requīrō, ere, quīsīvī (siī), quīsītus seek again, deplore

reservō (1) reserve, keep back, save

resīdō, ere, sēdī sit down

resignō (1) (un)seal, open, close

resistō, ere, stitī stop, resist (+ *dat.*)

resolvō, ere, ī, solūtus loose(n), free, pay, unravel

resonō (1) (re)sound, roar

respiciō, ere, spexī, spectus look (back) at, regard

respondeō, ēre, ī, ōnsus answer; sympathize with

respōnsum, ī *n.* answer, reply, response

restō, āre, stitī remain, be left

resupīnus, a, um supine, on the back

resurgō, ere, surrēxī, surrēctus rise again

rēte, is *n.* net, snare, toils

retegō, ere, tēxī, tēctus uncover, disclose

retorqueō, ēre, retorsī, retortus turn back, change (i.e., direction)

retractō (1) draw back

retrō *adv.* back(ward), again

revellō, ere, ī, vulsus tear off (up, away)

revertor, ī, rsus return, turn back

revīsō, ere revisit, see again, return to

revocō (1) recall, call back, retrace

revolvō, ere, ī, volūtus roll over, revolve

Rhēsus, ī *m.* Thracian prince, ally of the Trojans, slain on the first night after his arrival at Troy

rīdeō, ēre, rīsī, rīsus smile, laugh (at)

rigeō, ēre, uī be stiff, be rigid

rīma, ae *f.* crack, fissure

rīpa, ae *f.* bank, shore

rīte *adv.* properly, ritually

rōbur, oris *n.* oak; strength

rogus, ī *m.* funeral pyre

Rōma, ae *f.* Rome, a city and empire

Rōmānus, a, um Roman, of Rome

Rōmulus, a, um of Romulus, Roman

Rōmulus, ī *m.* legendary founder of Rome, son of Mars and Rhea Silvia, a Vestal virgin

rōscidus, a, um dewy

roseus, a, um rosy, pink

rota, ae *f.* wheel; chariot

rudēns, entis *m.* rope, cable

ruīna, ae *f.* downfall, ruin

rūmor, ōris *m.* rumor, report, gossip

rumpō, ere, rūpī, ruptus break, burst (forth), utter

rūpēs, is *f.* rock, cliff, crag

rūrsus, um *adv.* again, anew, back(ward)

rūs, rūris *n.* country (district)

Rutulus, a, um Rutulian, of the Rutulians, a tribe of central Italy

S

Sabaeus, a, um Sabaean, of Saba in southern Arabia, famous for its incense

sacerdōs, dōtis *m.* *(f.)* priest(ess)

sacrō (1) hallow, consecrate, dedicate

saeculum, ī *n.* generation, age, century

saepe *adv.* often, frequently, again and again

saepiō, īre, psī, ptus hedge in, inclose

saeviō, īre, īvī (iī), ītus rage, storm

saevus, a, um fierce, harsh, stern

sagitta, ae *f.* arrow

sal, salis *n.* *(m.)* salt (water), sea

saltem *adv.* at least, at any rate

saltus, ūs *m.* forest, glade, pasture; leap, bound, dancing

salum, ī *n.* (lit., salt) sea, brine

salūs, ūtis *f.* safety, salvation, health

Samos, ī *f.* island of the Aegean, center of the worship of Juno

sānctus, a, um sacred, holy, revered

sanguineus, a, um bloody, blood-red

saniēs, ēī *f.* blood, gore

sānus, a, um sane, sound, rational

Sarpēdōn, onis, *m.* Sarpedon, Lycian son of Jupiter and ally of the Trojans

sat(is) *adv.* enough, sufficient(ly)

sator, ōris *m.* sower; begetter, father

Sāturnia, ae *f.* Juno, daughter of Saturn, father of the gods

Sāturnius, a, um (born) of Saturn, father of Jupiter and Juno

saucius, a, um wounded, hurt

scaena, ae *f.* stage, background

scandō, ere, ī, scānsus mount, climb

scelerātus, a, um criminal, wicked

scelerō (1) pollute, defile

scelus, eris *n.* crime, impiety, sin

scēptrum, ī *n.* staff, scepter, power

scīlicet *adv.* of course, to be sure, doubtless

scindō, ere, scidī, scissus split, divide

scintilla, ae *f.* spark

sciō, īre, īvī (iī), ītus know (how), understand

scopulus, ī *m.* rock, cliff, crag

scūtum, ī *n.* shield

Scyllaeus, a, um of Scylla, a ravenous sea-monster, part woman and part sea creature, girdled with fierce dogs and destructive to mariners who attempted to sail past her cave situated on a narrow strait opposite the great whirlpool Charybdis

Scy-rius, a, um Scyrian, of Scyros, an island in the Aegean sea where Neoptolemus (Pyrrhus) was born

sēcessus, ūs *m.* inlet, recess

secō, āre, uī, sectus cut, slice, cleave

sēcrētum, ī *n.* secret (place, sanctuary)

secundus, a, um following, favorable, obedient

secūris, is *f.* axe

secūrus, a, um free from care, careless, heedless (+ *gen.*)

secus *adv.* otherwise, differently

sedeō, ēre, sēdī, sessus sit, settle

sedīle, is *n.* seat, bench

sēditiō, ōnis *f.* riot, strife

sēdūcō, ere, dūxī, ductus withdraw, separate

sēgnis, e slow, slothful, inactive

sēmen, inis *n.* seed, germ, element

sēmianimis, e half-dead, dying

sēminex, necis half-dead, dying

sēminō (1) sow, produce, bear

sēmita, ae *f.* path

sēmivir, virī half-man, effeminate

semper *adv.* always, (for)ever

senātus, ūs *m.* senate, council of elders

senecta, ae *f.* old age

senex, senis *m.* old man

sēnī, ae, a six (each), by sixes

senior, ōris *m.* old (aged) man, sire

sēnsus, ūs *m.* feeling, perception, sense

sententia, ae *f.* opinion, purpose, view

sentiō, īre, sēnsī, sēnsus feel, perceive

sentus, a, um rough, thorny

sepeliō, īre, īvī (iī), pultus bury, inter

septem seven

septemplex, icis of seven layers

septēnus, a, um seven (each), by sevens

sepulcrum, ī *n.* tomb, grave, burial

serēnō (1) calm, clear

serēnus, a, um serene, calm, fair, clear

Serestus, ī *m.* Trojan leader

Sergestus, ī *m.* Trojan leader

sermō, ōnis *m.* conversation, speech

serō, ere, sēvī, satus sow, beget

serō, ere, uī, rtus join, discuss

serpēns, entis *m.* *(f.)* serpent, snake

serpō, ere, psī, pstus creep (on), crawl

sertum, ī *n.* wreath, garland

serviō, īre, īvī (iī), ītus be a slave, serve (+ *dat.*)

servitium, (i)ī *n.* slavery, bondage

seu, sīve whether, or (if)

sex six

sībilus, a, um hissing, whirring

Sibylla, ae *f.* the Sibyl, an ancient Italian prophetess

siccō (1) dry, stanch

siccus, a, um dry, thirsty

Siculus, a, um Sicilian, of Sicily, a large island south of Italy

sīdō, ere, (sēd)ī sit, settle

Sīdonius, a, um of Sidon, a famous city of Phoenicia

signum, ī *n.* sign, signal, token, mark

silentium, (i)ī *n.* silence, quiet, stillness

sileō, ēre, uī be silent, be still

silex, icis *m.* *(f.)* flint, rock, crag

similis, e like, similar (+ *dat.* or *gen.*)

Simoīs, entis *m.* river near Troy

simulācrum, ī *n.* image, phantom, likeness

simulō (1) pretend, imitate, feign

sine without (+ *abl.*)

singulī, ae, a each, one by one

sinō, ere, sīvī, situs permit, allow; desert

Sinōn, ōnis *m.* a lying Greek

sinuō (1) fold, curve, twist, wind

sinus, ūs *m.* fold, bosom, bay, hollow

sistō, ere, stetī, status stand, stop, stay

sitis, is *f.* thirst, drought

situs, ūs *m.* position; neglect; decay

sīve, seu whether, or, either if, or if

sociō (1) unite, ally, share (as partner)

sōl, sōlis *m.* sun; day

sōlāmen, inis, *n.* consolation

soleō, ēre, itus sum be accustomed

solidus, a, um solid, firm, massive

solium, (i)ī *n.* throne, seat

sollemnis, e annual, customary, solemn

sollicitō (1) agitate, disquiet, disturb

sōlor, ārī, ātus console, comfort, solace

solum, ī *n.* ground, soil, earth

solvō, ere, ī, solūtus loose(n), release, break down, free, pay

Somnus, ī *m.* Sleep, Slumber personified as a divinity

sonipēs, pedis *m.* prancing steed (lit., "of resounding hoof")

sonitus, ūs *m.* sound, roar, crash, noise

sonō, āre, uī, itus (re)sound, roar

sonōrus, a, um roaring, howling

sopor, ōris *m.* sleep, slumber

soror, ōris *f.* sister

sors, rtis *f.* lot, destiny, portion, oracle

sortior, īrī, ītus draw (by) lot, allot

spargō, ere, rsī, rsus scatter, sprinkle

Spartānus, a, um Spartan, of Sparta, in southern Greece

spatior, ārī, ātus walk, stride

spatium, (i)ī n. space, time, period

speciēs, ēī f. appearance, sight, aspect

spectāculum, i n. sight, spectacle

spectātor, ōris, m. viewer, spectator

specula, ae, f. lookout, high place

speculor, ārī, ātus spy out, watch

spēlunca, ae f. cave, cavern, grotto

spernō, ere, sprēvī, sprētus scorn, reject

spērō (1) hope (for, to), expect, suppose

spēs, eī f. hope, expectation

spīra, ae f. fold, coil, spire

spīritus, ūs m. breath, spirit, life, soul

spīrō (1) breathe (forth), blow, quiver (i.e., with signs of life)

spoliō (1) despoil, plunder, rob (+ abl.)

spolium, (i)ī n. hide (of an animal); commonly, in the n. pl., spoils, arms stripped from an enemy

spōns, spontis f. wish, will, desire

spūma, ae f. foam, froth, spray

spūmeus, a, um foamy, frothy

spūmō (1) foam, froth, spray

spūmōsus, a, um foamy, frothy

squāleō, ēre, uī be rough, be filthy

squāmeus, a, um scaly

stabilis, e firm, stable, lasting

stabulum, ī n. stable, stall, lair, den

stāgnum, ī n. still waters, depth

statiō, ōnis f. station, anchorage

statuō, ere, uī, ūtus set (up), found

stēllātus, a, um starred, star-spangled

sternō, ere, strāvī, strātus lay low, spread, strew

Sthenelus, ī m. Greek leader

stimulō (1) spur, goad, prick, incite

stimulus, ī m. goad, spur

stīpes, itis m. stock, trunk, stem

stīpō (1) stuff, crowd, throng, stow

stirps, pis f. stock, lineage, race

strātum, ī n. bed, couch; pavement

strepitus, ūs m. uproar, noise

strīd(e)ō, ere (or ēre), dī grate, creak, whir, hiss

strīdor, ōris m. noise, creaking, roar

stringō, ere, strinxī, strictus graze

struō, ere, strūxī, strūctus build, plan

studium, (i)ī n. eagerness, desire, zeal

stupeō, ēre, uī be dazed, stand agape (at)

stuppeus, a, um (of) flax or hemp (used in the production of rope)

Stygius, a, um Stygian, of the Styx, a river in Hades

Styx, Stygis f. river of the underworld

suādeō, ēre, āsī, āsus persuade, advise

subeō, īre, subiī, subitus undergo, go under

subiciō, ere, iēcī, iectus place under (+ dat.)

subigō, ere, ēgī, āctus subdue

subitō *adv.* suddenly

subitus, a, um sudden, unexpected

sublīmis, e on high, aloft, uplifted

subnectō, ere, nex(u)ī, nexus tie (beneath), fasten

subnixus, a, um resting on (+ *abl.*)

subolēs, is *f.* offspring, progeny, child

subrīdeō, ēre, rīsī smile (at)

subrigō, ere, surrēxī, rēctus raise, rise

subsīdō, ere, subsēdī, — sink, fall, give way

subsistō, ere, stitī halt, stop, withstand

subter beneath, below

subtrahō, ere, trāxī, tractus withdraw

subvolvō, ere, ī, volūtus roll up

succēdō, ere, cessī, cessus approach, come from beneath (+ *dat.*)

successus, ūs, *m.* approach, success

succidō, ere, succidī, — sink down, fall

succingō, ere, cīnxī, cīnctus gird (up)

succumbō, ere, cubuī, cubitus yield (to) (+ *dat.*)

succurrō, ere, succurrī, succursus run to aid, help

sufferō, ferre, sustulī, sublātus withstand, endure

sufficiō, ere, fēcī, fectus supply, suffuse; be sufficient

suffundō, ere, fūdī, fūsus full, suffuse

sulcus, ī *m.* furrow, trench, ditch

summa, ae *f.* sum, substance, chief thing

summergō (subm–), ere, rsī, rsus sink, drown

summittō (subm–), ere, mīsī, missus lower, submit

sūmō, ere, mpsī, mptus take, assume; (+ **poenam**) exact (a penalty)

superbus, a, um proud, haughty

superēmineō, ēre tower above

superō (1) surmount, surpass, overcome, survive

supersum, esse, fuī survive, remain

superstitiō, ōnis, *f.* superstition, object of dread

supīnus, a, um flat, upturned

supplex, icis *m.* (*f.*) suppliant; *adj.* suppliant, humble

suppliciter *adv.* beseechingly, humbly

supplicium, (i)ī *n.* punishment, torture

suppōnō, ere, posuī, pos(i)tus place under, subject to

suprā above, over (+ *acc.*)

sūra, ae *f.* (calf of) leg

suscipiō, ere, cēpī, ceptus take up, beget, bear, receive

suspendō, ere, ī, ēnsus suspend, hang (up)

suspēnsus, a, um suspended, agitated

suspiciō, ere, spexī, spectus look from beneath, suspect, look up at

suspīrō (1) draw a deep breath, sigh

Sy-chaeus, ī *m.* deceased husband of Dido

Syrtis (or syrtis), is *f.* region of quicksand on the northern coast of Africa; sand bar, reef

T

tābeō, ēre drip, soak, melt, waste

tabula, ae *f.* plank, board

tacitus, a, um silent, noiseless, secret

taeda, ae *f.* (bridal) torch, pinewood torch

taedet, ēre, uit, taesum *impersonal vb.* it wearies

tālāria, ium *n.* (winged) sandals, anklets

tam *adv.* so (much), such

tamen *adv.* nevertheless, however

tangō, ere, tetigī, tāctus touch, reach

tantum *adv.* so much, so great(ly), only

Tartara, ōrum *n.* abode of the criminal and impious in Hades

taurīnus, a, um of a bull

taurus, ī *m.* bull, ox, bullock

teg(i)men, inis *n.* cover(ing), skin

tegō, ere, tēxī, tēctus cover, hide, protect

tēla, ae *f.* web, textile

temperō (1) control, restrain, refrain

tempestās, ātis *f.* tempest, storm; time

templum, ī *n.* temple, sanctuary, sacred space

temptō (1) try, test, seek, examine

tenāx, ācis tenacious, holding (to)

tenebrōsus, a, um dark, gloomy

Tenedos, ī *f.* small island near Troy

tentōrium, (i)ī *n.* tent

tenuis, e slight, thin, fine, delicate

tenus *see* **hāc . . . tenus**

tenus to up to, as far as (+ *abl.*)

ter three times

terebrō (1) bore into, pierce

teres, etis smooth, rounded, polished

tergum, ī *n.* back, body, rear

tergus, oris *n.* back, hide

terminō (1) bound, limit

ternī, ae, a three (each), by threes

terō, ere, trīvī, trītus rub, wear, waste

terreō, ēre, uī, itus frighten, terrify

terribilis, e dreadful, terrible

terrificō (1) frighten, terrify, alarm

territō (1) frighten, terrify, alarm

tertius, a, um third

testor, ārī, ātus call to withess, swear by, testify

testūdō, inis *f.* tortoise, vault, dome

Teucer (crus), crī *m.* early king of Troy

Teucria, ae *f.* Troy, (the land of Teucer)

thalamus, ī *m.* marriage chamber, bedroom

theātrum, ī *n.* theater

thēsaurus, ī *m.* treasure chest, place for storage

Thēseus, eī (eos), *acc.* **ea** *m.* mythical king of Athens, who, among his other exploits, descended to Hades with his friend Pirithoūs to carry off Proserpina

Thessandrus, ī *m.* Greek leader

Thoās, antis *m.* Greek leader

Thrēicius, a, um Thracian, of Thrace, a wild region northeast of Greece

Thrēissa, ae *f.* Thracian, of Thrace, a district northeast of Greece

Thybris, (id)is, *acc.* **brim,** *m.* the Tiber, river of Italy running through Rome; the god dwelling in the river

Thyias, adis *f.* Bacchant, a woman devotee of the worship of Bacchus

Thymoetēs, ae *m.* Trojan leader

thymum, ī *n.* thyme, a flowering plant

Tiberīnus, a, um of the Tiber, an Italian river on which Rome is situated

Tiberīnus, ī *m.* (god of) the Tiber, river on which Rome is situated

tigris, (id)is *m.* *(f.)* tiger, tigress

Timāvus, ī *m.* river of northern Italy, runs underground about twenty-five miles and emerges near the upper end of the Adriatic Sea into which it flows with a strong current

timeō, ēre, uī fear, dread, be anxious

timor, ōris *m.* fear, anxiety, dread

Tītān, ānis *m.* a divine ancestor of the Olympian gods, identified with the sun

togātus, a, um toga-clad

tonitrus, ūs *m.* thunder

tormentum, ī, n. machine for hurling

torqueō, ēre, rsī, rtus twist, sway, hurl

torreō, ēre, uī, tostus parch, roast

torus, ī *m.* (banqueting, funeral) couch, bed

torvus, a, um fierce, grim, lowering

tot so many, as many

totidem as many, so many

totiēns so often, so many times

trabs (trabēs), trabis *f.* beam, timber, tree

tractābilis, e manageable, favorable

trāiciō, ere, iēcī, iectus throw across, pierce

trānō (1) swim across, float

tranquillus, a, um tranquil, calm

trānseō, īre, iī (īvī), itus pass (by), go through, pierce

trānsferō, ferre, tulī, lātus transfer

trānsfīgō, ere, xī, xus pierce, transfix

trānsmittō, ere, mīsī, missus cross, send across

transverberō, āre, — pierce through, transfix

tremefaciō, ere, fēcī, factus make tremble, appall, alarm

tremendus, a, um terrible, dreadful

tremescō, ere, — begin to shake, dread

tremō, ere, uī tremble, quiver, shake

tremor, ōris *m.* trembling, shudder

trepidō (1) tremble; scurry; quiver

trepidus, a, um trembling, excited

trēs, tria three

tridēns, entis *m.* trident, symbol of Neptune as god of the sea

trietēricus, a, um triennial

trīgintā thirty

Trīnacrius, a, um Trinacrian, Sicilian

trīstis, e sad

trisulcus, a, um threefold, tripartite, forked

Trītōn, ōnis *m.* sea-god famous for his skill in blowing a conch (sea shell) as a trumpet

Trītōnis, idis *f.* Minerva, goddess of wisdom and the arts

triumphus, ī *m.* triumph, victory

Trivia, ae *f.* Hecate, goddess of the lower world

Troiānus, a, um Trojan, of Troy

Trōilus, ī *m.* youngest son of Priam

Trōius, a, um Trojan

Trōs, Trōis *m.* Trojan

trucīdō (1) slay, slaughter, butcher

trūdō, ere, sī, sus push, shove

truncus, ī *m.* trunk, body, torso

trux, trucis fierce, wild

tueor, ērī, itus (tūtus) watch, look at, protect, eye

tumeō, ēre, uī swell, be swollen

tumidus, a, um swollen, sweilling

tumultus, ūs *m.* tumult, uprising, clamor

tumulus, ī *m.* hill, mound

tundō, ere, tutūdī, tū(n)sus beat, assail

turba, ae *f.* mob, crowd

turbidus, a, um troubled, agitated

turbō (1) throw into confusion, agitate

turbō, inis *m.* whirl(wind, pool), storm

tūricremus, a, um incense-burning

Turnus, ī, *m.* Turnus, leader of the Rutulians and opponent of Aeneas

turpis, e shameful, disgraceful

turris, is *f.* tower, turret

tūs, tūris *n.* incense, unguent

tūtus, a, um protected, safe, secure

Ty-dīdēs, ae *m.* son of Tydeus, Diomedes, who fought against Aeneas in single combat before Troy and would have killed him had Venus not spirited her son away

tyrannus, ī *m.* ruler, chieftain, tyrant

Tyrrhēnus, a, um Tyrrhenian, of Etruria, a district of northwestern Italy

Tyrus (os), ī *f.* city of Phoenicia, birthplace of Dido

U

ūber, eris *n.* udder, breast; (symbol of) fertility

ubīque *adv.* everywhere, anywhere

ulcīscor, ūi, ultus avenge, punish

Ulixēs, is (eī, ī) *m.* Odysseus, the wily Greek leader who is the central character in Homer's *Odyssey* (his name in Latin is **Ulixes**, or Ulysses)

ulterior, ius farther, further, beyond

ultimus, a, um last, final, farthest

ultrā more than (+ *acc.*); *adv.* beyond

ultrō *adv.* further, voluntarily

ululātus, ūs *m.* wail, shriek, howl, shout

ululō (1) howl, wail, shout, shriek

umbō, ōnis *m.* boss, knob, shield

umbrifer, era, erum shady

ūmectō (1) wet, moisten

ūmēns, entis moist, dewy, damp

umerus, ī *m.* shoulder

umquam *adv.* ever, at any time

ūnā *adv.* together, at the same time

ūnanimus, a, um one-minded, sympathizing

uncus, a, um curved, bent, hooked

unde from where, from which source

undique *adv.* everywhere, from all sides

undōsus, a, um billow, wavy

ung(u)ō, ere, ūnxī, ūnctus anoint, smear, caulk

unguis, is *m.* nail, claw

urgeō, ēre, ursī drive, force, press

urna, ae *f.* urn, jar (used in drawing lots)

ūrō, ere, ussī, ustus burn, consume

ūsquam *adv.* anywhere, ever

ūsus, ūs *m.* use, service, employment

uterque, utraque, utrumque each (of two), both

uterus, ī *m.* belly, womb

ūtor, ī, ūsus use, employ (+ *abl.*)

uxōrius, a, um wife-ruled, uxorious, hen-pecked

V

vacca, ae *f.* heifer, young cow

vacō (1) be free (from), be at leisure

vacuus, a, um empty, free, vacant

vādō, ere go, proceed, advance

vadum, ī *n.* shallow, shoal, depth(s)

vāgīna, ae, *f.* scabbard, sheath for a sword

vagor, ārī, ātus wander, roam, rove

vagor, ārī, ātus wander, spread abroad

valeō, ēre, uī be strong, avail, be able

validus, a, um strong, mighty, sturdy

vallis, is *f.* valley, vale, dale

vānus, a, um vain, idle, empty, useless, false

varius, a, um varied, different, diverse

vastō (1) ravage, devastate, (lay) waste

vehō, ere, vēxī, vectus carry, convey

vēlivolus, a, um winged with sails

vellō, ere, vulsī, vulsus tear (up)

vēlō (1) veil, cover, deck, clothe

vēlōx, ōcis swift, quick, rapid, fleet

velut(ī) (even) as, just as

vēna, ae *f.* vein

vēnābulum, ī *n.* hunting spear

vēnātrīx, īcis *f.* huntress

vendō, ere, didī, ditus sell

venēnum, ī *n.* poison, venom, drug

venia, ae *f.* favor, pardon, grace

vēnor, ārī, ātus hunt, go hunting

ventūrum, ī *n.* the future, what is to come

Venus, eris *f.* goddess of love and beauty, love

verbum, ī *n.* word, speech, talk

vereor, ērī, itus fear, dread, revere

vērō *adv.* truly, indeed, but

verrō, ere, ī, versus sweep

versō (1) keep turning, roll, revolve

vertex, icis *m.* peak, summit, head, top; whirlpool

vertō, ere, ī, rsus (over)turn, (ex)change

verū, ūs *n.* spit, spike

vērum, ī *n.* truth, right, reality; *adv.* but

vērus, a, um true, real, genuine, honest

Vesper, eris (erī) *m.* (god of the) evening (star)

Vesta, ae *f.* goddess of the hearth

vester, tra, trum your(s), your own

vestibulum, ī *n.* entry, vestibule

vestīgium, (i)ī *n.* track, footprint, step, trace

vestīgō (1) trace, search (for), track (out)

vestis, is *f.* garment, cloth(ing), robe

vetō, āre, uī, itus forbid, prevent

vetus, eris old, aged, ancient, former

vibrō (1) quiver, vibrate, dart

vicissim in turn, by turns

vīctus, ūs *m.* living, food, victuals

vigil, īlis *m.* (*f.*) guard, watchman, sentinel; *adj.* wakeful, watchful, sleepless

vīmen, inis *n.* twig, shoot

vinc(u)lum, ī *n.* chain, bond, cable

vinciō, īre, vīnxī, vīnctus bind, tie

vindicō (1) vindicate, claim (as free), rescue

vīnum, ī *n.* wine

violō (1) outrage, violate, defile

vireō, ēre be green, grow, flourish

virga, ae *f.* staff, wand, twig

virgō, inis *f.* girl, maid(en)

viridis, e green, fresh, vigorous

virtūs, ūtis *f.* manliness, excellence in battle, valor

vīscum, ī *n.* mistletoe

vīscus, eris *n.* vitals, flesh

vīsum, ī *n.* sight, appearance, vision

vīsus, ūs *m.* sight, view, vision, aspect

vītālis, e of life, vital

vitta, ae *f.* fillet, garland, band

vīvō, ere, vīxī, vīctus live, be alive

vīvus, a, um living, natural, alive

volātilis, e flying, winged, swift

volō (1) fly, move with speed

volucer, cris, cre swift, winged

volūmen, inis *n.* fold, coil, roll

voluntās, ātis *f.* will, wish, consent

volūtō (1) revolve, turn (over), roll, ponder

vorō (1) swallow (up)

vōtum, ī *n.* vow, prayer, (votive) offering

voveō, ēre, vōvī, vōtus vow, consecrate

vulgō (1) publish, make known

vulgus, ī *n.* (*m.*) crowd, throng, herd

vulnus, eris *n.* wound, deadly blow

vultus, ūs *m.* countenance, face

X

Xanthus, ī *m.* river near Troy

Z

Zephyrus, ī *m.* (*west*) *wind*

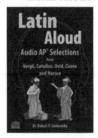